Complete Preparation for the SAT®

Complete Preparation for the SAT®

By Karl Weber

Books for Professionals
Harcourt Brace Jovanovich, Publishers • San Diego New York London

Copyright © 1986 by Books for Professionals, Inc.

All rights reserved. No part of this publication may be reproduced or transmitted in any form or by any means, electronic or mechanical, including photocopy, recording, or any information storage and retrieval system, without permission in writing from the publisher.

Requests for permission to make copies of any part of the work should be mailed to: Permissions, Harcourt Brace Jovanovich, Publishers, Orlando, Florida 32887.

"Scholastic Aptitude Test" and "SAT" are registered trademarks of the College Entrance Examination Board. This publication was prepared by Harcourt Brace Jovanovich, Inc., which is solely responsible for its contents. It is not endorsed by any other organization.

Acknowledgments

The passage about colonial music on page 114 is taken from *American Music* by Irving L. Sablosky, The Chicago History of American Civilization, edited by Daniel J. Boorstin. © 1969 by The University of Chicago. All rights reserved. Reprinted by permission of The University of Chicago Press.

The passage about the fine and lesser arts on page 237 is taken from "The Arts: Fine and Plain" by George A. Kubler, in *Perspectives on American Folk Art*, edited by Ian M. G. Quimby and Scott T. Swank (New York: W. W. Norton & Company, Inc., 1980). Reprinted by permission of the publisher.

The passage about academic freedom on page 239 is taken from *Philosophy of Education* by John Dewey (Totowa, N.J.: Littlefield, Adams & Co., 1975), pages 79–80. Reprinted by permission of Philosophical Library, Inc., New York.

The passage about the boyhood of Angelo Herndon on page 336 is taken from *You Cannot Kill the Working Class* by Angelo Herndon (New York: n.d.), excerpted in *Afro-American History: Primary Sources*, edited by Thomas R. Frazier (New York: Harcourt Brace & World, 1970).

The passage about film on page 392 is taken from *What Is a Film?* by Roger Manvell (London: Macdonald & Co., Ltd., 1965). Reprinted by permission of the publisher.

The synonym study on page 73 is taken from *The American Heritage Dictionary of the English Language*. © 1969 by Houghton Mifflin Company. Reprinted by permission from *The American Heritage Dictionary of the English Language*.

The practice test directions throughout the book are reprinted by permission of Educational Testing Service.

The two SAT questions on page 197 and page 198 are selected from *Taking the SAT*. College Entrance Examination Board, 1981. Reprinted by permission of Educational Testing Service, the copyright owner of the test questions.

Permission to reprint the two SAT questions does not constitute review or endorsement by Educational Testing Service or the College Board of this program as a whole or of any other test questions or testing information it may contain.

Printed in the United States of America

Library of Congress Cataloging-in-Publication Data

Weber, Karl, 1953–
Complete preparation for the SAT.

1. Scholastic aptitude test—Study guides. I. Title.
LB2353.57.W4 1986 378'.1664 85-17674
ISBN 0-15-601224-3

First edition

B C D E

For Matthew, Laura, and Karen

Contents

PART 3 *SAT Study Program: Unit 1* 63

How to Use This Book

Complete Preparation for the SAT is a comprehensive study program and workbook for the Scholastic Aptitude Test. It includes five full-length practice tests carefully modeled on the actual SAT, each with explanatory answers and self-scoring instructions. It also includes sixteen lessons covering every area tested on the SAT. Lesson 0 is a basic introduction to the SAT. The other fifteen lessons are divided into three units, each containing lessons on every test area. As you work your way through the book, you should make steady progress in every SAT area. You can, of course, use the materials in this book in any order you like, but they are arranged so that there is a clear progression from one section of the book to the next.

Since the SAT tests skills that take time to develop, it's best to begin preparing for the exam several weeks before you plan to take it. However, even a short period of study is better than none. Below are three study plans of varying lengths that you can choose from depending on the amount of time that you are able (and willing) to devote to preparing for the SAT. Follow the one that best fits your needs.

Study Plan for Six Weeks or More

Follow the plan below if you have six weeks or more before you are scheduled to take the SAT.

1. Start by studying Lesson 0: SAT Orientation. It will give you a good idea of what the SAT is like and prepare you for the other lessons in the SAT study program in this book.

2. Take Practice Test 1: Pretest. Simulate real test conditions: do the whole test in one uninterrupted session, stick to the allotted times, use the answer sheet provided, don't use reference books or other aids—and don't peek at the answers!

3. Follow the scoring instructions at the end of Practice Test 1 to figure out your raw scores and your scaled scores on the pretest.

4. Study the explanatory answers for Practice Test 1. Read about the questions you got right as well as those you got wrong. You may learn some techniques or tricks you hadn't thought of before, or you may find that you got some answers right for the wrong reasons.

5. Analyze your results on Practice Test 1. Which sections did you do well on? Which sections did you do poorly on? Did certain types of questions give you extra trouble? Did you lose points because of time pressure? The answers to these questions will tell you what skills to emphasize in your later study and practice.

6. Study Lessons 1–5 in Part 3 of this book. They will teach you skills and techniques to improve your performance in every SAT area.

7. Take Practice Test 2. Check and analyze your results just as you did with Practice Test 1.

8. Study Lessons 6–10 in Part 5. They will build on the skills and techniques introduced in Lessons 1–5.

9. Take Practice Test 3. Check and analyze your results. Your SAT study program should be helping to boost your scores by now.

10. Study Lessons 11–15 in Part 7. These will complete your SAT study program.

11. Take Practice Test 4. Check and analyze your results. If you're still unsatisfied with your scores in any area, review the lessons that cover that area.

12. Take Practice Test 5: Final Readiness Test. This is your "dress rehearsal" for the real SAT. Check and analyze your results.

13. The night before the exam, read the Last-Minute Checklist at the end of this book. Get a good night's sleep.

If you follow this study plan, you can take the SAT with confidence. You'll be prepared to earn your highest possible scores.

Study Plan for Two to Five Weeks

Follow the plan below if you have two to five weeks before you are scheduled to take the SAT.

1. Start by studying Lesson 0: SAT Orientation. It will give you a good idea of what the SAT is like and prepare you for the other lessons in the SAT study program in this book.
2. Take Practice Test 1: Pretest. Simulate real test conditions: do the whole test in one uninterrupted session, stick to the allotted times, use the answer sheet provided, don't use reference books or other aids—and don't peek at the answers!
3. Follow the scoring instructions at the end of Practice Test 1 to figure out your raw scores and your scaled scores on the pretest.
4. Study the explanatory answers for Practice Test 1. Read about the questions you got right as well as those you got wrong. You may learn some techniques or tricks you hadn't thought of before, or you may find that you got some answers right for the wrong reasons.
5. Analyze your results on Practice Test 1. Which sections did you do well on? Which sections did you do poorly on? Did certain types of questions give you extra trouble? Did you lose points because of time pressure? The answers to these questions will tell you what skills to emphasize in your later study and practice.
6. Study Lessons 1–5 in Part 3 of this book. They will teach you skills and techniques to improve your performance in every SAT area.
7. Study Lessons 6–10 in Part 5. They will build on the skills and techniques introduced in Lessons 1–5.
8. Study Lessons 11–15 in Part 7. These will complete your SAT study program.
9. Take Practice Test 5: Final Readiness Test. This is your "dress rehearsal" for the real SAT. Check and analyze your results. Try to isolate your single weakest area. Review the lessons that cover the skills for that area.
10. The night before the exam, read the Last-Minute Checklist at the end of this book. Get a good night's sleep.

This study plan is an effective way to prepare for the SAT when your time is somewhat limited.

Study Plan for Two Weeks or Less

Follow the plan below if you have less than two weeks before you are scheduled to take the SAT.

1. Start by studying Lesson 0: SAT Orientation. It will give you a good idea of what the SAT is like and prepare you for the other lessons in the SAT study program in this book.
2. Take Practice Test 1: Pretest. Simulate real test conditions: do the whole test in one uninterrupted session, stick to the allotted times, use the answer sheet provided, don't use reference books or other aids—and don't peek at the answers!
3. Follow the scoring instructions at the end of Practice Test 1 to figure out your raw scores and your scaled scores on the pretest.
4. Study the explanatory answers for Practice Test 1. Read about the questions you got right as well as those you got wrong. You may learn some techniques or tricks you hadn't thought of before, or you may find that you got some answers right for the wrong reasons.
5. Analyze your results on Practice Test 1. Which sections did you do well on? Which sections did you do poorly on? Did certain types of questions give you extra trouble? Did you lose points because of time pressure? The answer to these questions will tell you what skills to focus on in your remaining study sessions.
6. Study Lesson 1 in Part 3 of this book. It covers basic test-taking strategies that will enhance your overall performance on the SAT.

7. Try to isolate the one or two SAT areas in which you are the weakest. Study the lessons that cover the skills for those areas. (Lessons 4 and 11, in particular, are recommended because they provide practical advice on how to tackle quantitative comparisons and verbal analogies, two types of SAT questions that most students have had little or no experience with.)

8. If you have time, take Practice Test 5: Final Readiness Test. Consider it your "dress rehearsal" for the real SAT. Check and analyze your results.

9. The night before the exam, read the Last-Minute Checklist at the end of this book. Get a good night's sleep.

This study plan will help you gain the greatest possible benefit from a very limited amount of study time.

PART

1

You and the SAT

LESSON 0
SAT Orientation

OBJECTIVES

☐ To understand the format, purpose, and importance of the SAT
☐ To explore the three test areas on the SAT: verbal, mathematical, and TSWE
☐ To become familiar with the eight types of questions on the SAT

What Is the SAT?

0.1 Introduction

If you're a high school student planning on college, you'll probably have to take the Scholastic Aptitude Test—the SAT. Most colleges in the United States and Canada require SAT scores before they'll consider you for admission. So it pays to prepare yourself to get your highest possible scores on the exam. To help you do that is the purpose of this book.

The SAT contains five 30-minute sections covering both verbal skills and mathematical skills. You'll also take a separate 30-minute grammar test along with the SAT. This is the Test of Standard Written English, or TSWE. So there are six 30-minute sections altogether.

0.2 How the SAT Is Scored

All the questions on the SAT and TSWE are multiple-choice questions. The test is scored by machine, and scores are curved according to a special formula designed to compensate for tests that are extra hard or extra easy.

You'll receive three main test scores: an SAT-verbal score, an SAT-mathematical score, and a TSWE score. The two SAT scores range from 200 (lowest) to 800 (highest). In recent years, average SAT-verbal scores have been between 420 and 430. A good score would be around 530, an excellent score around 580. The number of students scoring higher than 680 is minuscule. You'll also receive two verbal subscores, one for reading comprehension and one for vocabulary. These scores range from 20 to 80. A score over 53 is good.

Average SAT-mathematical scores are currently around 470. A good score would be around 580, an excellent score around 630. Very few students score higher than 720.

The TSWE is scored on a different scale, running from 20 (lowest) to 60+ (highest). Any score over 53 is a good one.

0.3 How Scores Are Used

The colleges you apply to will receive all of your scores. They will use the SAT scores in deciding whether or not to admit you. Your SAT scores are one of the two most important factors in determining your acceptance or rejection by a good college; your high school grade point average is the other. Less important, usually, are extracurricular or community activities, letters of recommendation from teachers and friends, your application essay, interviews with school officials, and other factors.

Colleges do not use your TSWE score in deciding whether or not to admit you. Instead, they use the score to place you in an English course after they've already admitted you. If you score high on the TSWE, you might be excused from a freshman course in English composition. If you score low, you may have to take a remedial course.

It's possible to get into a competitive college with SAT scores that are only average, or even a little below. A student with strong high school grades, interesting and varied outside activities, enthusiastic letters of recommendation, and a record of personal achievement may be sought after by fine colleges despite low SAT scores. On the other hand, a student with a poor overall record may be rejected by a college even if his or her SAT scores are high. So the SAT is not all-important.

Nevertheless, the higher your SAT scores are, the better your chances of getting into the college of your choice. When two students appear roughly equal in other ways, their SAT scores often determine which student is accepted by a college and which student is rejected. Some colleges will not even consider an applicant whose SAT scores fall below a certain minimum.

Many colleges publish information on the average SAT scores of their students. When applying to a particular college, ask about the SAT scores they look for. The college admissions office can usually provide this information.

0.4 Registering for the SAT

The SAT is written and administered by the Educational Testing Service (ETS). The test is given seven times a year in high schools throughout the United States. Your guidance counselor can tell you this year's dates for the SAT and give you the necessary registration forms.

It's usually best to take the SAT in the spring of your junior year of high school. The SAT is given in March or April and again in May. Either springtime test date is fine. You'll be sure to receive your test scores in plenty of time to apply to colleges in the fall of your senior year. You'll also have enough time to take the exam again if your scores are low.

One word of warning: Don't take the SAT without preparation, "for practice," figuring that you can boost your scores with a second exam. This is bad strategy. Here's why: When the test makers report your scores to the colleges, they always report the scores from earlier tests you took. They advise college admissions officers to use the *average* of all your scores in making admissions decisions. Suppose you took the SAT "for practice" and earned an SAT-verbal score of 380. If you retook the exam and scored 500, your average for the two exams would work out to 440. You'd have been much better off preparing thoroughly before taking the exam the *first* time and earning the 500 then.

Your high school can provide you with the current edition of the *SAT Student Bulletin*, which tells you how to register for the exam. Also ask for *Taking the SAT*, a booklet produced by ETS, which describes the exam and includes a sample test. This is a valuable reference tool. Get a copy soon and study it carefully.

0.5 The SAT and Other Exams

College-bound high school students usually face other exams besides the SAT. It's helpful to know something about how the SAT relates to these other exams.

During their junior year of high school, many students take the Preliminary Scholastic Aptitude Test, or PSAT. This exam, also written and administered by ETS, contains most of the same types of test questions as the SAT. PSAT scores are not used for college admissions, but they are a useful guide in preparing for the SAT. They can help you determine which SAT areas you need to study most. PSAT scores are also used in selecting students for National Merit Scholarships. If you earn a high score on the PSAT and meet certain other qualifications, you may be eligible to receive a college scholarship. Ask your high school guidance counselor for details.

Many college-bound students also take the American College Testing Program Assessment, or ACT. Though ACT scores are used in college admissions decisions just as SAT scores are, the ACT is given by a different test-making company than the SAT, and it is different in its structure and content. The ACT puts less emphasis on general academic skills and more emphasis on factual knowledge in fields such as science, social studies, and English grammar. You may find the ACT harder or easier than the SAT, depending on your own areas of strength and the kinds of high school courses you've taken. Some colleges will accept only SAT scores, others will accept either SAT or ACT scores, and a few will accept only ACT scores. Check with the colleges you plan to apply to. If they accept either SAT or ACT scores, you may want to take both exams. Then you can use the scores only from the exam on which you did better. There are books similar to this one designed to help you prepare for the ACT. The exam is not the same as the SAT, so one book can't serve for both exams.

At the time you take the SAT, you may also take one or more Achievement Tests given by ETS.

These are tests that cover various high school subjects: English composition, math, chemistry, history, foreign languages, and many others. Each test is 1 hour long, includes multiple-choice questions, and is scored on the same 200-to-800 scale as the SAT. Many colleges require that you take one or more Achievement Tests when you apply because your scores on these tests reflect what you have learned in your high school courses. Preparing for an Achievement Test is like preparing for a final exam in a course. You should review your class notes, textbooks, and any other materials you used when taking the course. High scores on Achievement Tests make you a more attractive candidate for college admission.

0.6 Skills Tested on the SAT

Although the *A* in SAT stands for *aptitude*, the SAT is not a true aptitude test. It doesn't measure any inborn or unchanging ability. Instead, it measures skills you've developed throughout your schooling. It measures your knowledge of English, your ability to read and understand, your ability to think clearly, and your knowledge of basic rules of math. These are all skills that you've learned and used in school for years. There is nothing mysterious about them.

These skills can definitely be improved through study and practice. Two purposes of this book are to show you which skills you need to improve for the SAT and to help you improve them before you take the test.

0.7 Test-Wiseness

The SAT favors students who are test-wise. *Test-wiseness* is skill in taking tests. The test-wise student knows how to use time effectively when taking a test, how to tell what a question is getting at, how and when to guess, and how to relax and concentrate while taking a test.

This book can help make you more test-wise. It is designed to increase your skill in taking tests—especially the Scholastic Aptitude Test. Therefore, it will give you the facts you need about the SAT along with the most helpful test-taking strategies. It will also provide the guided practice you need. If you're familiar with what to expect on the SAT before you take it, you'll be more relaxed and confident and more able to concentrate. You'll be ready to earn your highest possible scores.

Now let's look at the overall structure and format of the SAT.

The SAT Format

0.8 Six Sections, Three Test Areas

Each SAT exam is unique. No one can tell you *exactly* what to expect when you take the exam. However, some features of the test remain the same from one SAT to the next. This section will explain the basic format of every SAT.

Every SAT includes six 30-minute test sections. With time spent filling out forms and a short break between sections, the whole test takes between $3\frac{1}{2}$ and 4 hours.

The six sections cover three different test areas:

Verbal sections test your understanding of words and your ability to comprehend what you read.

Mathematical sections test your ability to use basic principles of arithmetic, algebra, and geometry.

Test of Standard Written English (TSWE) sections test your knowledge of the rules of grammar and English usage.

As you learned before, the TSWE is not really part of the SAT. You'll get a separate TSWE score, which colleges don't use—or aren't supposed to use, anyway—in deciding whether or not to admit you. But the TSWE is always given with the SAT, so it is included in this book as if it were part of the SAT.

The six sections of your SAT will include two verbal sections, two mathematical sections, and one TSWE section. The remaining section may cover any of the three areas. It is "experimental"—that is, it contains new questions that are being tried out by the test makers. It *won't count* on your SAT (or TSWE) score. The problem is that you won't be able to tell which of the six sections is the experimental one. It's not marked in any way. So you have to do your best on every section.

0.9 A Typical SAT Format

There is no set order for the six test sections. The following format is a typical one:

Section 1: Verbal
Section 2: Mathematical
Section 3: TSWE
Section 4: Verbal
Section 5: Mathematical
Section 6: Verbal or Mathematical

However, any test area can appear in any position on the exam. So your SAT may start off with a mathematical section or a TSWE section instead of a verbal section.

Now let's take a closer look at each of the three SAT test areas.

The SAT Test Areas

0.10 The Verbal Sections

Verbal sections on the SAT include four different types of questions: antonyms, analogies, sentence completions, and reading comprehension questions. Like every question on the SAT, all four types are multiple-choice.

0.11 Antonyms

Antonym questions test your knowledge of vocabulary—that is, word meanings. In each antonym question, you'll be given a word, followed by five different words labeled A, B, C, D, and E. You must figure out which of the five lettered words is *opposite* in meaning to the original word. Here's an example:

PARSIMONIOUS: (A) forgiving (B) reclusive
(C) lucrative (D) grandiose (E) generous

If you know that *parsimonious* means about the same as *stingy* or *miserly*, you can probably pick the correct antonym: choice E, *generous*. As you can see, the key to doing well on antonym questions is knowing the meanings of many words—especially hard words like those used in college-level reading.

0.12 Analogies

Analogy questions mainly test your skill at logical thinking. In each analogy question, you'll be given a pair of words that are related to one another in some way. Then you'll be given five more pairs of words labeled A, B, C, D, and E. You have to figure out which two words are related to one another in the same way as the original pair. Here's an example:

NAIL:HAND:: (A) talon:eagle (B) tooth:bite
(C) toe:foot (D) claw:paw (E) hoof:horse

The vocabulary in this example is not hard. (*Talon* is the only word you might find unfamiliar; it means "the claw of a bird of prey.") The difficulty of the question is in figuring out its underlying logic. To answer it, you have to understand the relationship between *nail* and *hand*.

You might sum up the relationship in a sentence like this: "A *nail* is the hard, sharp part growing at the end of one finger on a *hand*." You then have to decide which of the five lettered choices consists of a pair of words that are related in the same way. The correct answer in this case is choice D. Almost the same sentence can be used to sum up the relationship between *claw* and *paw*: "A *claw* is the hard, sharp part growing at the end of one finger on a *paw*." (The parts of a paw may not be called "fingers," but you get the idea.) If you try to use the same sentence with answer choices A, B, C, and E, you'll see why they are wrong.

0.13 Sentence Completions

Sentence completions are the third type of question in the verbal sections of the SAT. In a sentence completion question, you'll be given a sentence with one or two blanks, each indicating a word or group of words that has been left out. The sentence is followed by five choices of words that could be put into the blank or blanks. Your job is to figure out which of the five choices best fits the meaning of the sentence. Here's an example:

> Although the democratic principles set forth in the Bill of Rights seem ---- enough, the application of those principles in particular situations has given rise to ---- disputes over the last two centuries.
>
> (A) controversial..numerous
> (B) simple..countless
> (C) noble..fascinating
> (D) extensive..certain
> (E) straightforward..few

As you can see, picking the right answer for a sentence completion question can be tricky. You need to understand the point the sentence is making and how the ideas in the sentence are related. In this case, the word *although* shows that the two ideas in the sentence are being contrasted. The words given in answer choice B fit into such a contrast. When they are plugged into the two blanks in the sentence, they suggest that although the ideas in the Bill of Rights are simple, applying those ideas has led to many disagreements. If you try plugging in the words from the other answer choices, the logic of the sentence doesn't hold up. The contrast is lost. So B is the correct answer for this example.

0.14 Reading Comprehension Questions

Reading comprehension questions will take up most of your time in the verbal sections of the SAT. (You won't have more of these questions to answer, but they take longer.) You'll be given two, three, or four passages to read. These range from about a hundred words long to almost five hundred words long—that is, from one paragraph to about five paragraphs. The passages deal with a wide variety of subjects, including social and political problems, scientific facts, historical events, art, literature, and philosophy. You may even get a passage that tells a story. Each passage is followed by a group of questions designed to test how well you understand what you read. You don't have to know anything about the subject beforehand to answer the questions. You just need to understand the passage.

The types of questions vary. Some ask about the main idea of the passage. Some ask about specific details mentioned in the passage. Some test your understanding of the author's argument in the passage—what the author is trying to prove and what evidence the author gives to prove it. And some questions ask about the mood, style, or tone of the passage.

To answer every reading comprehension question correctly, you need to read carefully and to dig out the subtle points of the passage. But even if you understand only the main ideas or only certain parts of the passage, you can usually answer some of the questions correctly.

0.15 Two Verbal Formats

Every verbal section on the SAT contains a mixture of all four types of verbal questions. Verbal sections usually follow one of these two formats:

Verbal Format A	
15	Antonyms
5	Sentence completions
10	Reading comprehension questions (2 or 3 passages)
5	Sentence completions
10	Analogies
45	Total questions

Verbal Format B	
10	Antonyms
5	Sentence completions
10	Analogies
15	Reading comprehension questions (3 or 4 passages)
40	Total questions

On your SAT, you'll probably get one verbal section that follows Format A and one that follows Format B.

0.16 The Mathematical Sections

Mathematical sections on the SAT contain two different types of questions: math problems and quantitative comparisons. Both are multiple-choice.

0.17 Math Problems

Except that they're multiple-choice, the math problems on the SAT are similar to the math problems you're used to seeing in high school textbooks and on typical classroom exams. You're simply given a problem to solve along with five answer choices labeled A, B, C, D, and E.

The math problems on the SAT cover a wide range of topics. Problems on elementary algebra are very common. For example, you may be given an equation and told to solve for x. Or you may be given a word problem like those that begin "Margaret works three times as fast as Jane and four times as fast as Ellen" or "Joe is three times as old as Bill was when Bill was four years younger than Sam is today." (You know the kind.) With a word problem, you must create your own equation to find the answer.

Another common topic for the math problems is plane geometry. Questions about the size of an angle, the length of the perimeter of a rectangle, or the area of a triangle or circle are typical. Some questions deal with coordinate graphs on which geometric figures may be drawn. A number of the problems include diagrams.

Other math problems may cover many different math topics. There will probably be a handful of problems dealing with basic arithmetic. For example, you may have to multiply or divide some fractions or figure out some percentages or ratios. There will be a few problems involving exponents and roots. There will be a few problems dealing with odd and even numbers, prime numbers, factoring, negative numbers, and other basic characteristics of numbers. There may be one or two problems that call for you to read a graph or a chart. And there will be a few questions that seem unrelated to anything you've studied in a math course—questions testing your logical skills on quantitative problems. Some of these are more like puzzles or brain teasers than traditional math problems.

0.18 Quantitative Comparisons

Quantitative comparisons are the second type of question in the mathematical sections of the SAT. In these questions, you won't be called upon to solve a problem. Instead, you'll simply be given two columns, labeled "Column A" and "Column B." In each column will appear a "quantity." The quantity may be a number—243. It may include both numbers and algebraic unknowns—$2x + 11$. It may even be a verbal description of some quantity—the number of inches in one mile. In each quantitative comparison question, your job is to compare Column A with Column B and decide which quantity is greater. There are four possible answers:

If the quantity in Column A is greater, the answer is A.
If the quantity in Column B is greater, the answer is B.

If the two quantities are equal, the answer is C.

If the relationship between the two quantities cannot be determined from the information given, the answer is D.

You'll usually be given some information about the two quantities to help you compare them. This information is printed in the center, above the two quantities. It may include an equation, a chart or a table, a geometric figure, a diagram, or other information.

Some quantitative comparisons are deliberately set up so that the two quantities *cannot* be compared on the basis of the information given. For example, you may be given the quantity $4x^2$ in Column A and the quantity $3x^2 + 3x$ in Column B but no clue to the value of the unknown, x. In such a case, you can't tell which quantity is greater, so the correct answer is D. As this example shows, some quantitative comparisons test your ability to tell what can and cannot be deduced from a given set of facts.

Quantitative comparisons cover many different math topics, especially elementary algebra and plane geometry. Some are very easy and can be answered in a few seconds. Others are tricky and require careful thought. However, most do *not* require calculations.

0.19 Two Mathematical Formats

There are two typical formats for mathematical sections on the SAT:

Mathematical Format A

7	Math problems
20	Quantitative comparisons
8	Math problems
35	Total questions

Mathematical Format B

25	Math problems only
25	Total questions

On your SAT, you'll probably get one mathematical section that follows Format A and one that follows Format B.

0.20 The TSWE

Two types of questions appear on the Test of Standard Written English: usage questions and error corrections. Both test your knowledge of some basic rules of English grammar and usage.

0.21 Usage Questions

Each usage question consists of a sentence with four words or phrases underlined and labeled A, B, C, and D, and one phrase—"no error"—underlined and labeled E. Some usage sentences are correct; others contain one—but no more than one—error in grammar or usage. You must decide whether or not a sentence contains an error. If it does, the error is the "correct" answer to the question—that is, it's the underlined word or phrase that would have to be changed, deleted, or moved in order to make the sentence grammatically correct. If the sentence does not contain an error, the correct answer is choice E. Here's a sample usage question:

> The reason for the vast increase in (A) the numbers of women entering the work force (B) during the last two decades have (C) never been fully (D) articulated. No error (E)

This sentence is grammatically wrong. The subject of the sentence (*reason*) does not agree with the verb (*have been articulated*) in number. The subject is singular, but the verb is plural. To correct this error, you'd have to change either the subject or the verb. The subject is not underlined, however; only the verb is—or, to be exact, the helping verb *have*. So to correct this sentence, you'd have to change the underlined verb *have* to *has*. Therefore, the correct answer to this question is choice C.

Notice that you just have to be able to *pick out* the error in a usage question. You don't necessarily have to know how to correct it.

0.22 Error Corrections

Error corrections are the second type of question on the TSWE. Each error correction, like a usage question, consists of a sentence that may or may not contain an error. In this type of question, however, only one portion of the sentence is underlined. (Sometimes this "portion" includes the entire sentence.) The sentence is followed by five different ways of writing the underlined portion. You must choose the one that is best—the one that is not only correct but also clear, concise, and graceful. Here's an example:

> An expert in one of the most fascinating fields of modern science, <u>Dr. Henderson's lecture on plasma physics enthralled the students</u>.
>
> (A) Dr. Henderson's lecture on plasma physics enthralled the students
> (B) the students were enthralled by Dr. Henderson's lecture on plasma physics
> (C) Dr. Henderson enthralled the students with his lecture on plasma physics
> (D) plasma physics was the subject of Dr. Henderson's lecture to the students
> (E) Dr. Henderson lectured the students, and enthralled them, on plasma physics

Notice that answer choice A is exactly the same as the original sentence. If you think the original sentence is correct and well written, choose answer A. Otherwise, choose the best of the other four alternatives.

In this example, the original sentence contains a misplaced modifier. The opening phrase, *an expert in one of the most fascinating fields of modern science*, describes (or modifies) Dr. Henderson. However, that phrase does not appear next to *Dr. Henderson*, as it should. Instead, the sentence seems to make the phrase describe Dr. Henderson's lecture, which makes no sense.

Choices C and E both correct this error by putting the words *Dr. Henderson* next to the modifying phrase. However, choice C is the better answer. It is less awkward than choice E, and it doesn't contain the ambiguous clause *Dr. Henderson lectured the students*, which makes it sound as if he scolded them.

As you can see, error corrections are often more challenging than usage questions. You must draw finer distinctions among answers and have a good ear for a well-written sentence.

0.23 The TSWE Format

The usual TSWE format includes both types of questions. It looks like this:

TSWE Format

25	Usage questions
15	Error corrections
10	Usage questions
50	Total questions

PART
2

Practice Test 1: Pretest

PRACTICE TEST 1: ***Directions***

This practice test, closely modeled on the real SAT, is for you to take before you start your study program. The answers and scoring instructions that begin on page 42 will help you analyze your performance, identify your strengths and weaknesses, and determine which SAT skills you need to work on most.

Directions: Set aside $3\frac{1}{2}$ hours without interruption for taking this test. The test is divided into six 30-minute sections. You may wish to use a timer or an alarm to time yourself on each section. Do not work past the 30-minute limit for any section. If you finish a section before time is up, you may check your work on that section, but you are <u>not to work on any other section</u>. You may take a 5-minute break between sections.

Do not worry if you are unable to finish a section or if there are some questions you cannot answer. Do not waste time puzzling over a question that seems too difficult for you. You should work as rapidly as you can without sacrificing accuracy.

Students often ask whether they should guess when they are uncertain about the answer to a question. Your test scores will be based on the number of questions you answer correctly minus a fraction of the number you answer incorrectly. Therefore, it is improbable that random or haphazard guessing will change your scores significantly. If you have some knowledge of a question, you may be able to eliminate one or more of the answer choices as wrong. It is generally to your advantage to guess which of the remaining choices is correct. Remember, however, not to spend too much time on any one question.

Mark all your answers on the answer sheet on the facing page. (For your convenience, you may wish to remove this sheet from the book and keep it in front of you throughout the test.) Mark only one answer for each question. Be sure that each mark is dark and that it completely fills the answer space. In each section of the answer sheet, there are 5 answer spaces for each of 50 questions. When there are fewer than 5 answer choices for a question or fewer than 50 questions in a section of your test, leave the extra answer spaces blank. Do not make stray marks on the answer sheet. If you erase, do so completely.

You may use any available space on the pages of the test for scratchwork. Do not use books, dictionaries, reference materials, calculators, slide rules, or any other aids. Do not look at the answer key or any other parts of this book. It is important to take this practice test in the same way that you will take the actual SAT.

When you have completed all six test sections, turn to the answers and scoring instructions that follow the test.

PRACTICE TEST 1: *Answer Sheet*

Directions: Use a No. 2 pencil only for completing this answer sheet. Be sure each mark is dark and completely fills the intended space. Completely erase any errors or stray marks. Start with number 1 for each new section. If a section has fewer than 50 questions or if a question has fewer than 5 answer choices, leave the extra answer spaces blank.

	SECTION 1	SECTION 2	SECTION 3	SECTION 4
1	(A) (B) (C) (D) (E)	(A) (B) (C) (D) (E)	(A) (B) (C) (D) (E)	(A) (B) (C) (D) (E)
2	(A) (B) (C) (D) (E)	(A) (B) (C) (D) (E)	(A) (B) (C) (D) (E)	(A) (B) (C) (D) (E)
3	(A) (B) (C) (D) (E)	(A) (B) (C) (D) (E)	(A) (B) (C) (D) (E)	(A) (B) (C) (D) (E)
4	(A) (B) (C) (D) (E)	(A) (B) (C) (D) (E)	(A) (B) (C) (D) (E)	(A) (B) (C) (D) (E)
5	(A) (B) (C) (D) (E)	(A) (B) (C) (D) (E)	(A) (B) (C) (D) (E)	(A) (B) (C) (D) (E)
6	(A) (B) (C) (D) (E)	(A) (B) (C) (D) (E)	(A) (B) (C) (D) (E)	(A) (B) (C) (D) (E)
7	(A) (B) (C) (D) (E)	(A) (B) (C) (D) (E)	(A) (B) (C) (D) (E)	(A) (B) (C) (D) (E)
8	(A) (B) (C) (D) (E)	(A) (B) (C) (D) (E)	(A) (B) (C) (D) (E)	(A) (B) (C) (D) (E)
9	(A) (B) (C) (D) (E)	(A) (B) (C) (D) (E)	(A) (B) (C) (D) (E)	(A) (B) (C) (D) (E)
10	(A) (B) (C) (D) (E)	(A) (B) (C) (D) (E)	(A) (B) (C) (D) (E)	(A) (B) (C) (D) (E)
11	(A) (B) (C) (D) (E)	(A) (B) (C) (D) (E)	(A) (B) (C) (D) (E)	(A) (B) (C) (D) (E)
12	(A) (B) (C) (D) (E)	(A) (B) (C) (D) (E)	(A) (B) (C) (D) (E)	(A) (B) (C) (D) (E)
13	(A) (B) (C) (D) (E)	(A) (B) (C) (D) (E)	(A) (B) (C) (D) (E)	(A) (B) (C) (D) (E)
14	(A) (B) (C) (D) (E)	(A) (B) (C) (D) (E)	(A) (B) (C) (D) (E)	(A) (B) (C) (D) (E)
15	(A) (B) (C) (D) (E)	(A) (B) (C) (D) (E)	(A) (B) (C) (D) (E)	(A) (B) (C) (D) (E)
16	(A) (B) (C) (D) (E)	(A) (B) (C) (D) (E)	(A) (B) (C) (D) (E)	(A) (B) (C) (D) (E)
17	(A) (B) (C) (D) (E)	(A) (B) (C) (D) (E)	(A) (B) (C) (D) (E)	(A) (B) (C) (D) (E)
18	(A) (B) (C) (D) (E)	(A) (B) (C) (D) (E)	(A) (B) (C) (D) (E)	(A) (B) (C) (D) (E)
19	(A) (B) (C) (D) (E)	(A) (B) (C) (D) (E)	(A) (B) (C) (D) (E)	(A) (B) (C) (D) (E)
20	(A) (B) (C) (D) (E)	(A) (B) (C) (D) (E)	(A) (B) (C) (D) (E)	(A) (B) (C) (D) (E)
21	(A) (B) (C) (D) (E)	(A) (B) (C) (D) (E)	(A) (B) (C) (D) (E)	(A) (B) (C) (D) (E)
22	(A) (B) (C) (D) (E)	(A) (B) (C) (D) (E)	(A) (B) (C) (D) (E)	(A) (B) (C) (D) (E)
23	(A) (B) (C) (D) (E)	(A) (B) (C) (D) (E)	(A) (B) (C) (D) (E)	(A) (B) (C) (D) (E)
24	(A) (B) (C) (D) (E)	(A) (B) (C) (D) (E)	(A) (B) (C) (D) (E)	(A) (B) (C) (D) (E)
25	(A) (B) (C) (D) (E)	(A) (B) (C) (D) (E)	(A) (B) (C) (D) (E)	(A) (B) (C) (D) (E)
26	(A) (B) (C) (D) (E)	(A) (B) (C) (D) (E)	(A) (B) (C) (D) (E)	(A) (B) (C) (D) (E)
27	(A) (B) (C) (D) (E)	(A) (B) (C) (D) (E)	(A) (B) (C) (D) (E)	(A) (B) (C) (D) (E)
28	(A) (B) (C) (D) (E)	(A) (B) (C) (D) (E)	(A) (B) (C) (D) (E)	(A) (B) (C) (D) (E)
29	(A) (B) (C) (D) (E)	(A) (B) (C) (D) (E)	(A) (B) (C) (D) (E)	(A) (B) (C) (D) (E)
30	(A) (B) (C) (D) (E)	(A) (B) (C) (D) (E)	(A) (B) (C) (D) (E)	(A) (B) (C) (D) (E)
31	(A) (B) (C) (D) (E)	(A) (B) (C) (D) (E)	(A) (B) (C) (D) (E)	(A) (B) (C) (D) (E)
32	(A) (B) (C) (D) (E)	(A) (B) (C) (D) (E)	(A) (B) (C) (D) (E)	(A) (B) (C) (D) (E)
33	(A) (B) (C) (D) (E)	(A) (B) (C) (D) (E)	(A) (B) (C) (D) (E)	(A) (B) (C) (D) (E)
34	(A) (B) (C) (D) (E)	(A) (B) (C) (D) (E)	(A) (B) (C) (D) (E)	(A) (B) (C) (D) (E)
35	(A) (B) (C) (D) (E)	(A) (B) (C) (D) (E)	(A) (B) (C) (D) (E)	(A) (B) (C) (D) (E)
36	(A) (B) (C) (D) (E)	(A) (B) (C) (D) (E)	(A) (B) (C) (D) (E)	(A) (B) (C) (D) (E)
37	(A) (B) (C) (D) (E)	(A) (B) (C) (D) (E)	(A) (B) (C) (D) (E)	(A) (B) (C) (D) (E)
38	(A) (B) (C) (D) (E)	(A) (B) (C) (D) (E)	(A) (B) (C) (D) (E)	(A) (B) (C) (D) (E)
39	(A) (B) (C) (D) (E)	(A) (B) (C) (D) (E)	(A) (B) (C) (D) (E)	(A) (B) (C) (D) (E)
40	(A) (B) (C) (D) (E)	(A) (B) (C) (D) (E)	(A) (B) (C) (D) (E)	(A) (B) (C) (D) (E)
41	(A) (B) (C) (D) (E)	(A) (B) (C) (D) (E)	(A) (B) (C) (D) (E)	(A) (B) (C) (D) (E)
42	(A) (B) (C) (D) (E)	(A) (B) (C) (D) (E)	(A) (B) (C) (D) (E)	(A) (B) (C) (D) (E)
43	(A) (B) (C) (D) (E)	(A) (B) (C) (D) (E)	(A) (B) (C) (D) (E)	(A) (B) (C) (D) (E)
44	(A) (B) (C) (D) (E)	(A) (B) (C) (D) (E)	(A) (B) (C) (D) (E)	(A) (B) (C) (D) (E)
45	(A) (B) (C) (D) (E)	(A) (B) (C) (D) (E)	(A) (B) (C) (D) (E)	(A) (B) (C) (D) (E)
46	(A) (B) (C) (D) (E)	(A) (B) (C) (D) (E)	(A) (B) (C) (D) (E)	(A) (B) (C) (D) (E)
47	(A) (B) (C) (D) (E)	(A) (B) (C) (D) (E)	(A) (B) (C) (D) (E)	(A) (B) (C) (D) (E)
48	(A) (B) (C) (D) (E)	(A) (B) (C) (D) (E)	(A) (B) (C) (D) (E)	(A) (B) (C) (D) (E)
49	(A) (B) (C) (D) (E)	(A) (B) (C) (D) (E)	(A) (B) (C) (D) (E)	(A) (B) (C) (D) (E)
50	(A) (B) (C) (D) (E)	(A) (B) (C) (D) (E)	(A) (B) (C) (D) (E)	(A) (B) (C) (D) (E)

REMOVE ANSWER SHEET BY CUTTING ON DOTTED LINE

SECTION 5

1 Ⓐ Ⓑ Ⓒ Ⓓ Ⓔ
2 Ⓐ Ⓑ Ⓒ Ⓓ Ⓔ
3 Ⓐ Ⓑ Ⓒ Ⓓ Ⓔ
4 Ⓐ Ⓑ Ⓒ Ⓓ Ⓔ
5 Ⓐ Ⓑ Ⓒ Ⓓ Ⓔ
6 Ⓐ Ⓑ Ⓒ Ⓓ Ⓔ
7 Ⓐ Ⓑ Ⓒ Ⓓ Ⓔ
8 Ⓐ Ⓑ Ⓒ Ⓓ Ⓔ
9 Ⓐ Ⓑ Ⓒ Ⓓ Ⓔ
10 Ⓐ Ⓑ Ⓒ Ⓓ Ⓔ
11 Ⓐ Ⓑ Ⓒ Ⓓ Ⓔ
12 Ⓐ Ⓑ Ⓒ Ⓓ Ⓔ
13 Ⓐ Ⓑ Ⓒ Ⓓ Ⓔ
14 Ⓐ Ⓑ Ⓒ Ⓓ Ⓔ
15 Ⓐ Ⓑ Ⓒ Ⓓ Ⓔ
16 Ⓐ Ⓑ Ⓒ Ⓓ Ⓔ
17 Ⓐ Ⓑ Ⓒ Ⓓ Ⓔ
18 Ⓐ Ⓑ Ⓒ Ⓓ Ⓔ
19 Ⓐ Ⓑ Ⓒ Ⓓ Ⓔ
20 Ⓐ Ⓑ Ⓒ Ⓓ Ⓔ
21 Ⓐ Ⓑ Ⓒ Ⓓ Ⓔ
22 Ⓐ Ⓑ Ⓒ Ⓓ Ⓔ
23 Ⓐ Ⓑ Ⓒ Ⓓ Ⓔ
24 Ⓐ Ⓑ Ⓒ Ⓓ Ⓔ
25 Ⓐ Ⓑ Ⓒ Ⓓ Ⓔ
26 Ⓐ Ⓑ Ⓒ Ⓓ Ⓔ
27 Ⓐ Ⓑ Ⓒ Ⓓ Ⓔ
28 Ⓐ Ⓑ Ⓒ Ⓓ Ⓔ
29 Ⓐ Ⓑ Ⓒ Ⓓ Ⓔ
30 Ⓐ Ⓑ Ⓒ Ⓓ Ⓔ
31 Ⓐ Ⓑ Ⓒ Ⓓ Ⓔ
32 Ⓐ Ⓑ Ⓒ Ⓓ Ⓔ
33 Ⓐ Ⓑ Ⓒ Ⓓ Ⓔ
34 Ⓐ Ⓑ Ⓒ Ⓓ Ⓔ
35 Ⓐ Ⓑ Ⓒ Ⓓ Ⓔ
36 Ⓐ Ⓑ Ⓒ Ⓓ Ⓔ
37 Ⓐ Ⓑ Ⓒ Ⓓ Ⓔ
38 Ⓐ Ⓑ Ⓒ Ⓓ Ⓔ
39 Ⓐ Ⓑ Ⓒ Ⓓ Ⓔ
40 Ⓐ Ⓑ Ⓒ Ⓓ Ⓔ
41 Ⓐ Ⓑ Ⓒ Ⓓ Ⓔ
42 Ⓐ Ⓑ Ⓒ Ⓓ Ⓔ
43 Ⓐ Ⓑ Ⓒ Ⓓ Ⓔ
44 Ⓐ Ⓑ Ⓒ Ⓓ Ⓔ
45 Ⓐ Ⓑ Ⓒ Ⓓ Ⓔ
46 Ⓐ Ⓑ Ⓒ Ⓓ Ⓔ
47 Ⓐ Ⓑ Ⓒ Ⓓ Ⓔ
48 Ⓐ Ⓑ Ⓒ Ⓓ Ⓔ
49 Ⓐ Ⓑ Ⓒ Ⓓ Ⓔ
50 Ⓐ Ⓑ Ⓒ Ⓓ Ⓔ

SECTION 6

1 Ⓐ Ⓑ Ⓒ Ⓓ Ⓔ
2 Ⓐ Ⓑ Ⓒ Ⓓ Ⓔ
3 Ⓐ Ⓑ Ⓒ Ⓓ Ⓔ
4 Ⓐ Ⓑ Ⓒ Ⓓ Ⓔ
5 Ⓐ Ⓑ Ⓒ Ⓓ Ⓔ
6 Ⓐ Ⓑ Ⓒ Ⓓ Ⓔ
7 Ⓐ Ⓑ Ⓒ Ⓓ Ⓔ
8 Ⓐ Ⓑ Ⓒ Ⓓ Ⓔ
9 Ⓐ Ⓑ Ⓒ Ⓓ Ⓔ
10 Ⓐ Ⓑ Ⓒ Ⓓ Ⓔ
11 Ⓐ Ⓑ Ⓒ Ⓓ Ⓔ
12 Ⓐ Ⓑ Ⓒ Ⓓ Ⓔ
13 Ⓐ Ⓑ Ⓒ Ⓓ Ⓔ
14 Ⓐ Ⓑ Ⓒ Ⓓ Ⓔ
15 Ⓐ Ⓑ Ⓒ Ⓓ Ⓔ
16 Ⓐ Ⓑ Ⓒ Ⓓ Ⓔ
17 Ⓐ Ⓑ Ⓒ Ⓓ Ⓔ
18 Ⓐ Ⓑ Ⓒ Ⓓ Ⓔ
19 Ⓐ Ⓑ Ⓒ Ⓓ Ⓔ
20 Ⓐ Ⓑ Ⓒ Ⓓ Ⓔ
21 Ⓐ Ⓑ Ⓒ Ⓓ Ⓔ
22 Ⓐ Ⓑ Ⓒ Ⓓ Ⓔ
23 Ⓐ Ⓑ Ⓒ Ⓓ Ⓔ
24 Ⓐ Ⓑ Ⓒ Ⓓ Ⓔ
25 Ⓐ Ⓑ Ⓒ Ⓓ Ⓔ
26 Ⓐ Ⓑ Ⓒ Ⓓ Ⓔ
27 Ⓐ Ⓑ Ⓒ Ⓓ Ⓔ
28 Ⓐ Ⓑ Ⓒ Ⓓ Ⓔ
29 Ⓐ Ⓑ Ⓒ Ⓓ Ⓔ
30 Ⓐ Ⓑ Ⓒ Ⓓ Ⓔ
31 Ⓐ Ⓑ Ⓒ Ⓓ Ⓔ
32 Ⓐ Ⓑ Ⓒ Ⓓ Ⓔ
33 Ⓐ Ⓑ Ⓒ Ⓓ Ⓔ
34 Ⓐ Ⓑ Ⓒ Ⓓ Ⓔ
35 Ⓐ Ⓑ Ⓒ Ⓓ Ⓔ
36 Ⓐ Ⓑ Ⓒ Ⓓ Ⓔ
37 Ⓐ Ⓑ Ⓒ Ⓓ Ⓔ
38 Ⓐ Ⓑ Ⓒ Ⓓ Ⓔ
39 Ⓐ Ⓑ Ⓒ Ⓓ Ⓔ
40 Ⓐ Ⓑ Ⓒ Ⓓ Ⓔ
41 Ⓐ Ⓑ Ⓒ Ⓓ Ⓔ
42 Ⓐ Ⓑ Ⓒ Ⓓ Ⓔ
43 Ⓐ Ⓑ Ⓒ Ⓓ Ⓔ
44 Ⓐ Ⓑ Ⓒ Ⓓ Ⓔ
45 Ⓐ Ⓑ Ⓒ Ⓓ Ⓔ
46 Ⓐ Ⓑ Ⓒ Ⓓ Ⓔ
47 Ⓐ Ⓑ Ⓒ Ⓓ Ⓔ
48 Ⓐ Ⓑ Ⓒ Ⓓ Ⓔ
49 Ⓐ Ⓑ Ⓒ Ⓓ Ⓔ
50 Ⓐ Ⓑ Ⓒ Ⓓ Ⓔ

SECTION 1

Time—30 minutes

40 QUESTIONS

For each question in this section, choose the best answer and blacken the corresponding space on the answer sheet.

Each question below consists of a word in capital letters, followed by five lettered words or phrases. Choose the word or phrase that is most nearly opposite in meaning to the word in capital letters. Since some of the questions require you to distinguish fine shades of meaning, consider all the choices before deciding which is best.

Example:

GOOD: (A) sour (B) bad (C) red
(D) hot (E) ugly

Ⓐ ● Ⓒ Ⓓ Ⓔ

1. WAVER: (A) compel obedience (B) remain impartial (C) act decisively (D) yield consent (E) move rapidly

2. INTANGIBLE: (A) corporeal (B) particular (C) existent (D) noteworthy (E) moral

3. FORGO: (A) deny (B) surrender to (C) insist upon (D) accept (E) reply to

4. PASSÉ: (A) classical (B) predicted (C) present-day (D) topical (E) modish

5. IMPEACH: (A) exonerate (B) elect (C) deny (D) investigate (E) promote

6. SOBRIETY: (A) lassitude (B) inebriation (C) decay (D) altruism (E) conviviality

7. INVALUABLE: (A) costly (B) worthless (C) cheapened (D) fetid (E) monetary

8. SPORADIC: (A) inadvertent (B) level (C) repetitious (D) constant (E) oblique

9. INFRINGE: (A) honor (B) withdraw (C) accept (D) interdict (E) endorse

10. PARIAH: (A) independent person (B) person of wealth (C) eccentric person (D) person of noble status (E) accepted person

Each sentence below has one or two blanks, each blank indicating that something has been omitted. Beneath the sentence are five lettered words or sets of words. Choose the word or set of words that best fits the meaning of the sentence as a whole.

Example:

Although its publicity has been ----, the film itself is intelligent, well-acted, handsomely produced, and altogether ----.

(A) tasteless..respectable (B) extensive..moderate (C) sophisticated..amateur (D) risqué..crude (E) perfect..spectacular

● Ⓑ Ⓒ Ⓓ Ⓔ

11. The Small Business Association opposes the bill because it feels the bill will place an unfair burden on companies with ---- employees.

(A) few (B) female (C) many (D) skilled (E) well-paid

12. Because evidence indicates that the prehistoric plants and animals in Africa and South America were ----, geologists believe that the two continents were once ----.

(A) carnivorous..submerged
(B) various..uninhabited
(C) distinct..unconnected
(D) similar..joined
(E) aquatic..landlocked

13. Every individual has some ----, whether or not he or she knows it; for all of our ---- are guided by some set of values that we consciously or unconsciously hold.

(A) purpose..beliefs
(B) importance..deeds
(C) flaw..mistakes
(D) philosophy..actions
(E) knowledge..behaviors

GO ON TO THE NEXT PAGE

14. The neoclassical critics turned Aristotle's comments about poetry into ---- to be obeyed; they transformed his simple ---- into a set of inflexible dogmas.

(A) rules..decrees
(B) laws..observations
(C) statements..words
(D) notations..doctrines
(E) beliefs..remarks

15. Despite his claim to have only the best interests of public school students at heart, the mayor's ---- motives for the new educational plan were ----.

(A) ulterior..unpublicized
(B) political..obvious
(C) economic..doubtful
(D) practical..well known
(E) pedagogical..apparent

Each question below consists of a related pair of words or phrases, followed by five lettered pairs of words or phrases. Select the lettered pair that best expresses a relationship similar to that expressed in the original pair.

Example:

YAWN:BOREDOM:: (A) dream:sleep
(B) anger:madness (C) smile:amusement
(D) face:expression (E) impatience:rebellion

16. FRAME:HOUSE:: (A) pedestal:statue
(B) skeleton:body (C) mainspring:watch
(D) air:balloon (E) beam:ceiling

17. AUDITORIUM:HEAR::
(A) library:refer
(B) studio:enjoy
(C) gallery:see
(D) museum:buy
(E) classroom:educate

18. PREDESTINED:FATE::
(A) random:destiny
(B) deliberate:logic
(C) foreordained:desert
(D) unplanned:order
(E) deserved:merit

19. PEDANT:LEARNING::
(A) braggart:boasting
(B) martinet:domination
(C) miser:riches
(D) hypocrite:falsity
(E) chauvinist:patriotism

20. ARMISTICE:HOSTILITIES::
(A) reconciliation:enemies
(B) conquest:invasion
(C) settlement:dispute
(D) treaty:negotiation
(E) cease-fire:bullets

21. BRISTLE:BRUSH:: (A) straw:broom
(B) handle:mop (C) ivory:comb
(D) picket:fence (E) wire:grid

22. EARNEST:IMPLORE::
(A) deprived:request
(B) eager:accept
(C) wistful:muse
(D) authoritative:command
(E) anxious:insist

23. STEER:TILLER:: (A) start:ignition
(B) guide:pilot (C) control:navigator
(D) sail:compass (E) turn:axle

24. TYRO:EXPERIENCE::
(A) sage:wisdom
(B) ignoramus:knowledge
(C) novice:enthusiasm
(D) amateur:ability
(E) initiate:veteran

25. CROSS-EXAMINE:WITNESS::
(A) declaim:lecturer
(B) convict:jury
(C) interrogate:suspect
(D) select:judge
(E) consider:evidence

GO ON TO THE NEXT PAGE

Each passage below is followed by questions based on its content. Answer all questions following a passage on the basis of what is stated or implied in that passage.

The Federal Theater Project was, in many respects, the most visible and the most controversial of the Works Progress Administration (WPA) projects. In its array of works it provided something for everyone: circus, vaudeville, classical and contemporary drama, ethnic theater, musical comedy, marionette shows, experimental stage works, social protest drama, modern dance, and traveling troupes of players. Its critics charged that federal theater was radical, immoral, wasteful, nonproductive, and Communist-dominated. Its advocates claimed that the project created aesthetically exciting productions, used the skills of thousands of performers and technicians, and brought to widespread audiences the thrill of live theater that many had never experienced before.

To direct the project, Harry Hopkins chose Hallie Flanagan, the guiding hand behind the Experimental Theater at Vassar. She drew up a plan for dividing the country into regional units, each with its own director, each drawing stimulation from its own locale, and each providing jobs for local theater personnel who were on relief. While they floundered with the paper work and red tape that were always a part of work relief programs, Mrs. Flanagan and her associates dreamed of building a truly national theater that would produce artistically and socially important drama of professional quality and regional identity.

Despite the emphasis on nationwide activity, the New York City project blossomed first, probably because so much of American theatrical activity was already centered there. In its first year, it presented the premier performance of T. S. Eliot's *Murder in the Cathedral.* Another unit worked on developing Living Newspapers, documentary plays on timely topics such as farm problems or the faults of public utilities. With action and dialogue drawn from the daily news, their scripts did not hesitate to step on the toes of businessmen and politicians.

Progress in the rest of the country seemed slower. However, in a determined demonstration of the potential scope of federal theater, joint productions of Sinclair Lewis's *It Can't Happen Here* were undertaken. On October 27, 1936, the play opened simultaneously in twenty-one theaters in seventeen states. There were three productions in New York City: one in Yiddish, one by the Suitcase Theatre on Staten Island, and the "standard" version at the Adelphi Theatre.

Despite its apparent success, the Federal Theater Project was doomed, almost from the beginning, to an early death. Its enemies were powerful and determined. When Congress began deliberations on WPA appropriations for 1939–1940, the sessions of criticism aimed at the Federal Theater Project became particularly vitriolic. Overall, allocations for the WPA were cut. The Federal Theater Project was terminated outright, receiving just a brief extension for finishing up. The lights went out on federal theater on June 30, 1939.

26. It can be inferred that all of the following were goals of the Federal Theater Project EXCEPT to

(A) reduce the number of unemployed people in the nation
(B) organize all theatrical activity in the United States under federal guidance
(C) present theater productions in areas where no theaters had previously existed
(D) create a theatrical forum for new social and political ideas
(E) provide jobs for actors and actresses

27. It can be inferred that both critics and supporters of the Federal Theater Project would consider its program

(A) ambitious
(B) nonpartisan
(C) useful
(D) artistically successful
(E) necessary

28. It can be inferred that those who criticized the Federal Theater Project on political grounds probably objected most strongly to its

(A) production of *Murder in the Cathedral*
(B) emphasis on projects of local and regional interest
(C) mounting of joint productions of certain plays
(D) Living Newspaper dramas
(E) use of Yiddish in certain productions

29. The author describes the productions of *It Can't Happen Here* mainly to illustrate the Federal Theater Project's

(A) emphasis on politically and socially significant dramas
(B) success at providing theater for audiences of every type
(C) interest in the development of ethnic theater
(D) attempt to build a nationwide theater program
(E) eagerness to produce plays by the best contemporary writers

30. The passage implies that the Federal Theater Project came to an end mainly because of

(A) lack of money caused by the Great Depression
(B) hostility on the part of congressional leaders
(C) protests by business interests around the country
(D) lack of interest outside New York City
(E) poor management on the part of the project directors

The very solid mantle rock, which descends to about 1800 miles below the earth's surface, seems to behave, over periods of millions of years, like a very sluggish fluid. Something, perhaps the temperature difference between the white-hot region near the core and the cooler region near the crust, drives slow-moving cycles of rising and descending currents in the mantle rock itself.

Evidently, these currents rise beneath the thin-crusted ocean floor, thrust up the midocean ridges, and generate the stresses that produce transverse cracks and shallow earthquakes. This rising is believed to be the force that causes materials to well up through the crust, replacing and spreading the old sea floor and pushing drifting continents apart.

Where the currents begin their descent at the edges of continents, they produce compressive pressures and massive folding in the form of trenches and mountain ranges. These regions are the sites of deeper earthquakes and of most volcanism.

31. The passage deals mainly with
    (A) cycles of movement within the material forming the mantle rock
    (B) geological activity on the ocean floor
    (C) how the earth's mountain ranges were probably formed
    (D) the similarities between the behavior of the mantle rock and that of certain fluids
    (E) how movements in the mantle rock may produce changes in the earth's surface

32. According to the passage, currents in the mantle rock appear to be the result of
    (A) temperature changes in the mantle rock near the earth's core
    (B) the stresses produced by the emergence of midocean ridges
    (C) variations in temperature at different depths within the mantle rock
    (D) pressures produced by underground earthquakes
    (E) the fact that the crust on the ocean floor is relatively thin

33. It can be inferred from the passage that the continents are
    (A) made from material that once formed part of the ocean floor
    (B) largely the result of earthquakes and volcanic activity
    (C) subject to destruction by the compressive forces at work beneath them
    (D) further apart than they previously were
    (E) relatively recent features of the earth's geological history

Shipwrecks are apropos of nothing. If men could only train for them and have them occur when the men had reached pink condition, there would be less drowning at sea.

Of the four in the boat, none had slept any time worth mentioning for two days and two nights previous to the wreck, and in the excitement of clambering about the deck of a foundering ship they had also forgotten to eat heartily.

For these reasons, and for others, neither the oiler nor the correspondent could row very well at this time. The correspondent wondered how in the name of all that was sane could there be people who thought it amusing to row a boat. It was not an amusement; it was a diabolical punishment. He mentioned this, and the weary-faced oiler smiled in full sympathy.

"Take her easy, now, boys," said the captain. "Don't spend yourselves. If we have to run a surf, you'll need all your strength, because we'll have to swim for it. Take your time."

Slowly the land arose from the sea. From a black line it became a line of black and a line of white—trees and sand. The distant lighthouse reared high.

"None of those other boats could have got ashore to give word of the wreck," said the oiler, in a low voice. "Else the lifeboat would be out hunting us."

34. The men in the boat are probably
    (A) sailors attempting to save their damaged ship from sinking
    (B) coast guard sailors seeking the bodies of shipwreck victims
    (C) the only survivors of some calamity at sea
    (D) members of a ship's crew who have been cast adrift after a mutiny
    (E) sailors whose ship has drifted off course in the ocean

35. The passage implies that the men in the boat are suffering most severely from
    (A) despair
    (B) thirst
    (C) loneliness
    (D) fatigue
    (E) anxiety

36. The tone of the first paragraph of the passage may most accurately be described as
    (A) rueful and ironic
    (B) somber and tragic
    (C) gravely philosophical
    (D) witty and comical
    (E) detached and objective

GO ON TO THE NEXT PAGE

The measurement of specific heats and latent heats, part of the study of thermodynamics, gives us clues both to the nature of the forces between atoms and molecules and to the arrangement and motion of atoms in solids, liquids, and gases.

At very low temperatures, say within 5 or 10 degrees of absolute zero, there is little atomic motion left, and most specific heats appear to approach zero. However, there are quite a few substances whose specific heats rise again when the temperature drops to 1 K or lower. Such bumps or peaks in specific heat curves are often caused by the interactions between the tiny natural magnetic fields associated with the motion and spin of the electrons surrounding some atoms and, at extremely low temperatures, by the still weaker "magnets" associated with some atomic nuclei.

These magnets can be thought of as fields of permanently orbiting or spinning charged particles. Thus, we speak of orbital magnetism and of electronic and nuclear spin magnetism, or "spin" for short. These elementary magnets can interact with their neighbors just as ordinary bar magnets interact with each other, except that the permissible energies of elementary magnets do not vary continuously but in specific units, or quanta. The tiny magnets can interact by pairing with reversed polarity, thus canceling or neutralizing each other's magnetic fields; or they can interact by falling in line, thus reinforcing each other's polarity. Either arrangement represents a higher order than the random magnetic pattern that prevails at higher temperatures. The tiny magnets also respond to an externally applied magnetic field, and this response forms the basis of the magnetic susceptibility thermometer.

Most of the magnets' pairing or ordering interactions are exceedingly weak. Because the energies corresponding to them are so much less than the energies corresponding to thermal motion at ordinary temperatures, they cannot become predominant to form stable assemblies until the very lowest temperatures are reached, when atomic and molecular motion is nearly nonexistent. The peak in the specific heat at or below 1 K corresponds to the gradual ordering as the temperature is lowered (or to disordering as the temperature is raised).

37. The author is primarily concerned with describing

(A) how low temperatures affect the movement of atomic particles
(B) the relationship between energy levels and temperature
(C) the magnetic properties of various types of atomic particles
(D) how low temperatures can be used in the study of magnetism
(E) the effects of the magnetic properties of atoms at very low temperatures

38. According to the passage, the rise in specific heat of some substances when the temperature falls below 1 K is

(A) an example of the effects of measurement error on scientific data
(B) an apparent anomaly requiring a special explanation
(C) one of the irregularities that generally arise toward the extremes of any scale
(D) consistent with the pattern exhibited elsewhere in the specific heat curves of most substances
(E) an example of the inexplicable quality of certain natural phenomena

39. It can be inferred from the passage that the specific heat of a substance

(A) will increase as a result of interaction between magnetic fields at very low temperatures
(B) is mainly determined by the strength of subatomic magnetic forces
(C) varies according to the type of atomic motion present
(D) will generally increase as the temperature approaches 0 K
(E) depends on the type of magnetic pairing exhibited among atoms

40. It can be inferred from the passage that the magnetic susceptibility thermometer

(A) may be used only with substances that are highly magnetic
(B) contains some substance that is highly responsive to external magnetic forces
(C) measures the degree of atomic motion present in a substance
(D) measures the strength of the bonds between atoms and molecules in a substance
(E) is useful only at extremely low temperatures

S T O P

IF YOU FINISH BEFORE TIME IS CALLED, YOU MAY CHECK YOUR WORK ON THIS SECTION ONLY. DO NOT WORK ON ANY OTHER SECTION IN THE TEST.

SECTION 2

Time—30 minutes

35 QUESTIONS

In this section solve each problem, using any available space on the page for scratchwork. Then indicate the one correct answer in the appropriate space on the answer sheet.

The following information is for your reference in solving some of the problems.

Circle of radius r: Area $= \pi r^2$; Circumference $= 2\pi r$
The number of degrees of arc in a circle is 360.
The measure in degrees of a straight angle is 180.

Definitions of symbols:

$=$	is equal to	$\leq$	is less than or equal to
$\neq$	is unequal to	$\geq$	is greater than or equal to
$<$	is less than	$\parallel$	is parallel to
$>$	is greater than	$\perp$	is perpendicular to

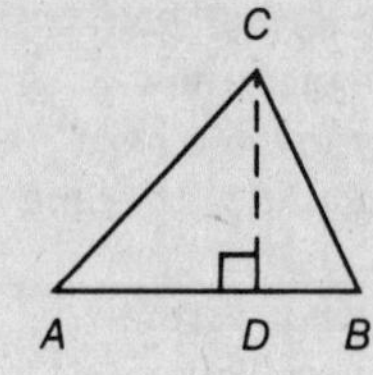

Triangle: The sum of the measures in degrees of the angles of a triangle is 180.

If $\angle CDA$ is a right angle, then

(1) area of $\triangle ABC = \frac{AB \times CD}{2}$

(2) $AC^2 = AD^2 + DC^2$

Note: Figures which accompany problems in this test are intended to provide information useful in solving the problems. They are drawn as accurately as possible EXCEPT when it is stated in a specific problem that its figure is not drawn to scale. All figures lie in a plane unless otherwise indicated. All numbers used are real numbers.

---

1. $x \div \frac{2}{5} =$

(A) 40 percent of x (B) $\frac{2}{5x}$ (C) $\frac{2x}{5}$

(D) $2.5x$ (E) $0.4x$

2. A company's sales for the first three quarters of a year average \$4.2 million per month. How much must the company's sales for the last quarter total to raise the average monthly sales for the entire year to \$4.5 million?

(A) \$5.4 million
(B) \$8.2 million
(C) \$16.2 million
(D) \$18.1 million
(E) \$20.3 million

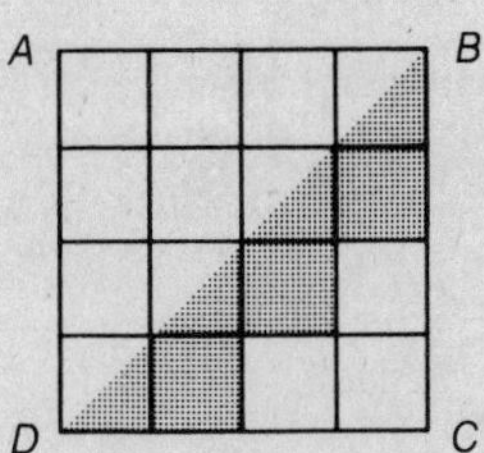

3. Each side of square $ABCD$ above is four units long. What is the area in square units of the shaded portion?

(A) $3\frac{1}{2}$ (B) 5 (C) 6 (D) 7 (E) 8

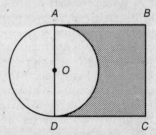

4. In the figure above, side AD of square $ABCD$ passes through the center of circle O. If the length of a side of square $ABCD$ is 2, what is the area of the shaded region?

(A) $\frac{\pi^2}{2}$ (B) $4 - \pi$ (C) $4 - \frac{\pi}{2}$

(D) 2π (E) $2\pi^2$

5. If $\frac{3}{4}$ of a is 18, then $\frac{1}{3}$ of $a =$

(A) 6 (B) 8 (C) 9 (D) 10 (E) 12

GO ON TO THE NEXT PAGE

6. Let $a = bc$, where $a \neq 0$. If b is divided by 3 and c is multiplied by 3, then a is

(A) unchanged
(B) divided by 3
(C) multiplied by 3
(D) divided by 9
(E) multiplied by 9

7. Sixty students try out for a high school baseball team. Of these, exactly 22 can play the infield, exactly 30 can play the outfield, and exactly 9 can play both the infield and the outfield. How many of the 60 students can play neither the infield nor the outfield?

(A) 22 (B) 17 (C) 14 (D) 13 (E) 8

Questions 8-27 each consist of two quantities, one in Column A and one in Column B. You are to compare the two quantities and on the answer sheet blacken space

A if the quantity in Column A is greater;
B if the quantity in Column B is greater;
C if the two quantities are equal;
D if the relationship cannot be determined from the information given.

Notes: 1. In certain questions, information concerning one or both of the quantities to be compared is centered above the two columns.
2. In a given question, a symbol that appears in both columns represents the same thing in Column A as it does in Column B.
3. Letters such as x, n, and k stand for real numbers.

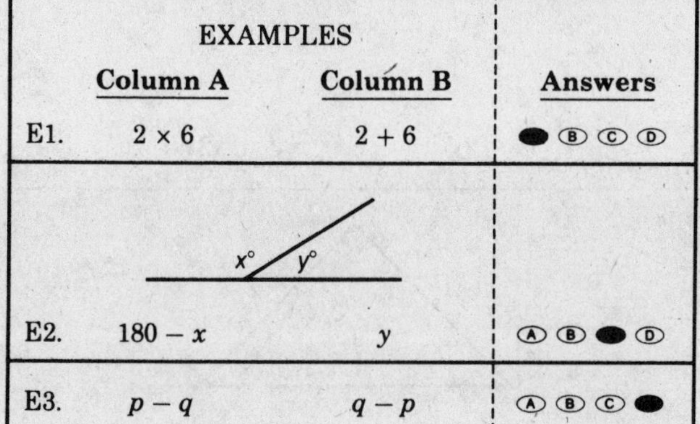

EXAMPLES

	Column A	Column B	Answers
E1.	2×6	$2 + 6$	● Ⓑ Ⓒ Ⓓ
E2.	$180 - x$	y	Ⓐ Ⓑ ● Ⓓ
E3.	$p - q$	$q - p$	Ⓐ Ⓑ Ⓒ ●

	Column A	Column B
8.	$0.02 - 0.002$	$0.01 + 0.001$

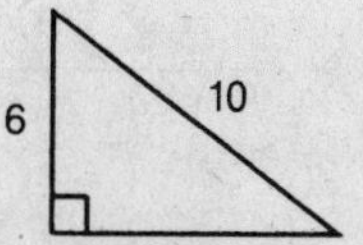

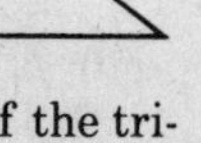

9. Perimeter of the triangle | Perimeter of the rectangle

$xy = z$

$z \neq 0$

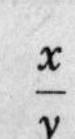

10. $\frac{x}{y}$ | $\frac{z}{y^2}$

Column A | Column B

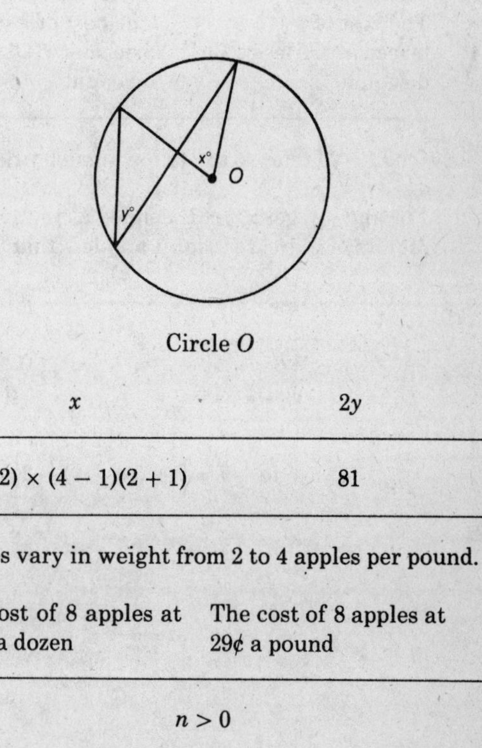

Circle O

11. x | $2y$

12. $3(5 - 2) \times (4 - 1)(2 + 1)$ | 81

Apples vary in weight from 2 to 4 apples per pound.

13. The cost of 8 apples at \$1.19 a dozen | The cost of 8 apples at 29¢ a pound

$n > 0$

$n \neq 1$

14. $\sqrt{n}$ | $\sqrt[3]{n}$

GO ON TO THE NEXT PAGE

	Column A	Column B
15.	The largest prime integer less than 20	The largest even integer less than 20

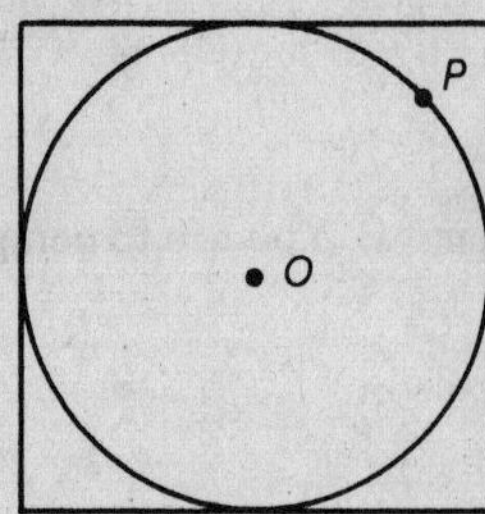

Circle O is inscribed in the square. Q is a point, not shown, located on one side of the square.

	Column A	Column B
16.	Length OP	Length OQ
17.	The average (arithmetic mean) of r, 0, $2r$, and $r + 4$	$r + 1$
18.	The cost of a jacket priced at \$90 less a 10% discount	The cost of a jacket priced at \$120 less a 33% discount

Questions 19–20 refer to the following definition.

For any integer x, $)x($ is defined as the sum of all factors of x greater than 1 and less than x.

	Column A	Column B
19.	$)18($	$)21($
20.	$\frac{)17(}{)8(}$	$\frac{)12(}{)4(}$

$$4a + 7 = 9 + (8a \div 2) - 2$$

	Column A	Column B
21.	a	4

Column A	Column B
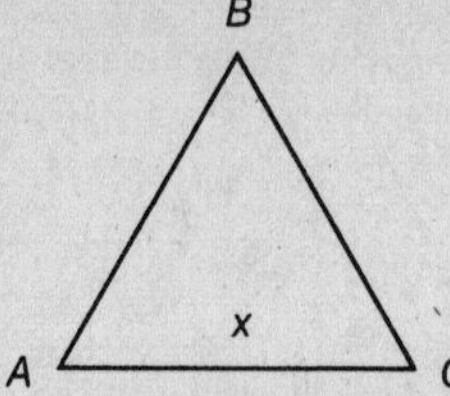	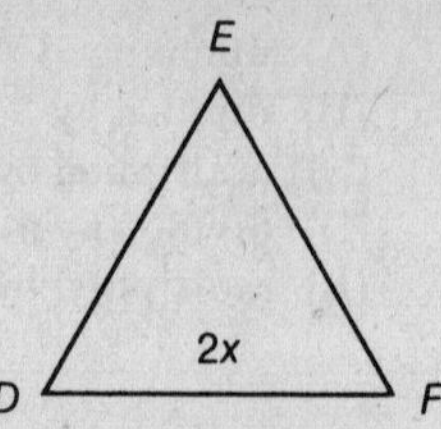

Note: Figures not drawn to scale.

	Column A	Column B
22.	Area $\triangle ABC$	Area $\triangle DEF$

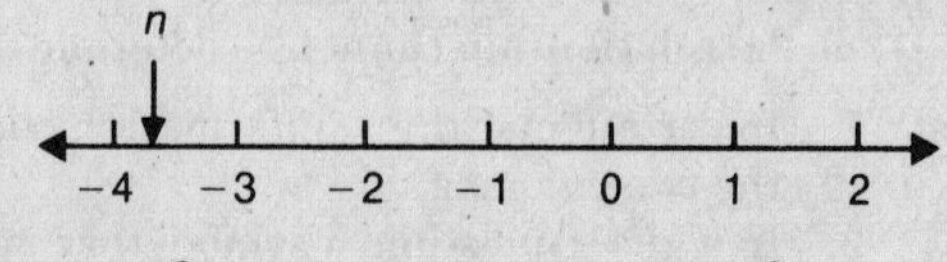

	Column A	Column B
23.	$-3 - n$	0

$$y > 1$$

$$x = \frac{y}{2}$$

	Column A	Column B
24.	$(x + 2y)^2$	$(2x + y)^2$

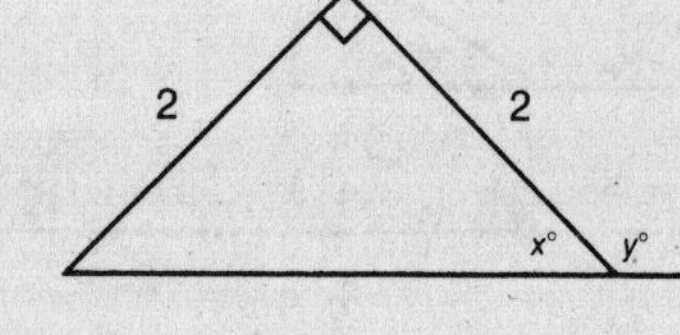

	Column A	Column B
25.	$3x$	y

$$\frac{1}{x} > 1$$

	Column A	Column B
26.	x	1

$$x^2 + 4x + 7 = 13$$

	Column A	Column B
27.	$8x + 14 + 2x^2$	26

GO ON TO THE NEXT PAGE

Solve each of the remaining problems in this section using any available space for scratchwork. Then indicate the one correct answer in the appropriate space on the answer sheet.

28. If x is a prime number greater than 10 and less than 20, then $2x + 1$ may equal any of the following EXCEPT

(A) 23 (B) 27 (C) 33 (D) 35 (E) 39

Candidate	Votes
A	86
B	60
C	x
D	58

29. In an election for two council members, each voter voted for exactly two of the four candidates on the ballot. If a total of 140 voters cast ballots, with the results shown above, how many votes did Candidate C receive?

(A) 16 (B) 38 (C) 46 (D) 58 (E) 76

30. If $\frac{x}{y} < 0$, which of the following must be FALSE?

I. $x > y$
II. $x = 0$
III. $x - y > 1$

(A) None (B) I only (C) II only
(D) III only (E) I and II only

31. If the operation $*n$ is defined as $*n = n(n + 1)$, then $(*2)(*3)(*4) =$

(A) 120 (B) 240 (C) 360
(D) 720 (E) 1440

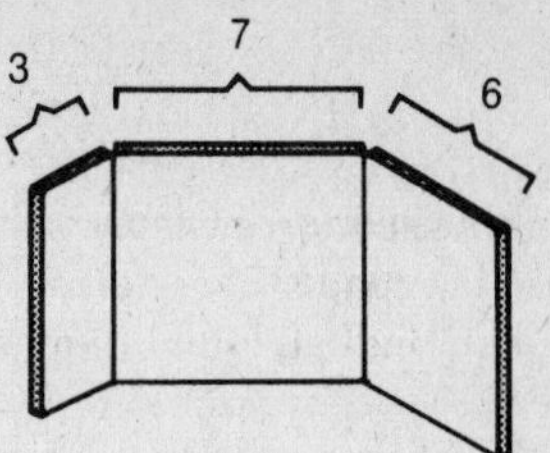

32. A folding screen is made of three sections respectively 3, 7, and 6 feet wide, as shown in the above figure. What is the difference between the width of the screen when folded into the narrowest possible space and the width of the screen when completely unfolded?

(A) 6 feet (B) 7 feet (C) 9 feet
(D) 13 feet (E) 16 feet

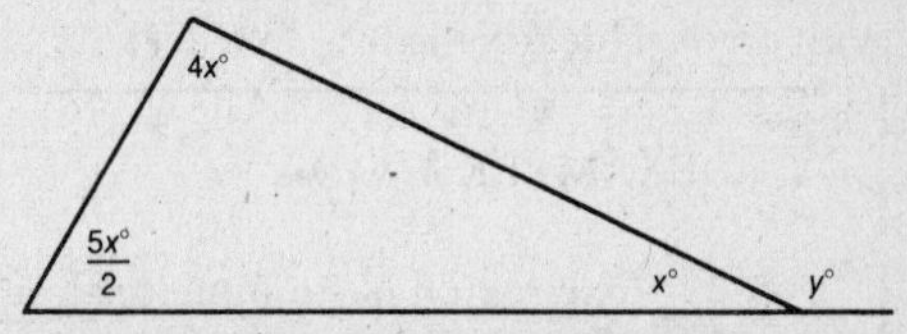

33. If the degree measures of the interior angles of the above triangle are as shown, then $y =$

(A) 120 (B) 148 (C) 156
(D) 160 (E) 172

34. If $x < -1$, then which of the following expressions has the greatest value?

(A) $\frac{1}{x^2}$ (B) x^5 (C) $\left(\frac{1}{x}\right)^3$ (D) x^2 (E) x^4

35. In a coordinate graph system, two of the vertices of a square are located at points with coordinates (2, 1) and (6, 1). A third vertex of the square could be located at any of the following points EXCEPT

(A) (4, 2) (B) (2, 5) (C) (6, −3)
(D) (2, −3) (E) (4, 3)

S T O P

IF YOU FINISH BEFORE TIME IS CALLED, YOU MAY CHECK YOUR WORK ON THIS SECTION ONLY. DO NOT WORK ON ANY OTHER SECTION IN THE TEST.

SECTION 3

Time—30 minutes

50 QUESTIONS

The questions in this section measure skills that are important to writing well. In particular, they test your ability to recognize and use language that is clear, effective, and correct according to the requirements of standard written English, the kind of English found in most college textbooks.

Directions: The following sentences contain problems in grammar, usage, diction (choice of words), and idiom.

Some sentences are correct.
No sentence contains more than one error.

You will find that the error, if there is one, is underlined and lettered. Assume that elements of the sentence that are not underlined are correct and cannot be changed. In choosing answers, follow the requirements of standard written English.

If there is an error, select the one underlined part that must be changed to make the sentence correct and blacken the corresponding space on your answer sheet.

If there is no error, blacken answer space Ⓔ.

EXAMPLE:

The region has a climate so severe that (A) plants growing there (B) rarely had been (C) more than twelve inches high. (D) No error (E)

SAMPLE ANSWER

Ⓐ Ⓑ ● Ⓓ Ⓔ

1. Scientific discoveries are rarely (A) predictable (B); chance, along with many other factors, play a part (C) in the birth of (D) a new theory. No error (E)

2. Though ineffective at times, (A) those who attack (B) the United Nations forget that (C) it has played a vital peacekeeping role in many regions (D) of the world. No error (E)

3. With the influx (A) of tourists, many of the quaint (B) old houses in the area have been reverted (C) into souvenir shops and boutiques catering to (D) affluent summer visitors. No error (E)

4. Until modern times, percussion instruments were relatively (A) unimportant in Western music, but they (B) have always been (C) widely used in countries such as (D) Java, Thailand, and India. No error (E)

5. Those who favor (A) a strict separation between church and state, as mandated by (B) the Constitution, are encouraged with (C) the latest (D) decision of the Supreme Court. No error (E)

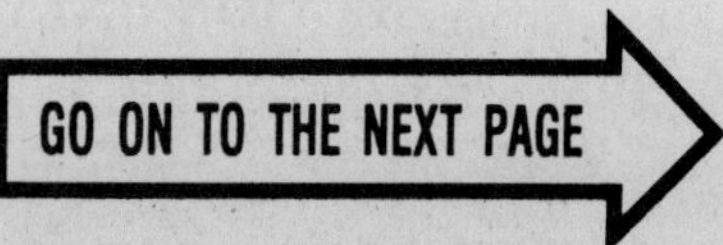

6. Originally ran from the garage of Anderson's home,
A
the company quickly grew into a million-dollar
B
operation employing seventy and occupying
C
a handsome new suite of offices. No error
D E

7. If one intends to pursue an exercise program
A
consistently, you had better make it one that
B C
realistically fits your current condition and your
D
available time. No error
E

8. It is time for we, the future leaders of the
A B
free world, to reevaluate the military doctrines
C
that have led us to the brink of nuclear war.
D
No error
E

9. Both cost and nutritional value seem to underlie
A B
the recent tendency among Americans to eat
C D
less beef and pork and more chicken and fish.

No error
E

10. Under the heading of external influences falls
A B
such forces as family makeup, educational
C
advantages, and the home environment. No error
D E

11. Ski equipment sales have leveled off,
A B
indicating that it is no longer one of the nation's
C D
fastest-growing sports. No error
E

12. The emphasis lain on the virtue of
A
hospitality to travelers in the poetry of Homer
B
may be explained by certain features of the
C
society in which he wrote. No error
D E

13. The class includes several budding scientists

besides Karen, but none has pursued her goal as
A B C
single-mindedly as her. No error
D E

14. If the teachers' union was willing to support
A B
it, the plan would have a far greater chance of
C D
acceptance by the state legislature. No error
E

15. With its several keyboards, its astonishing variety
A B
of tones and textures, and its range of volume from
C
a whisper to a roar, the organ was the greatest
D
musical achievement of Bach's day. No error
E

16. The weather on election day was good, but that by
A B
itself cannot explain neither the large turnout of
C
voters nor the closeness of the vote. No error
D E

17. One cannot help admiring the grandeur of
A
these ancient relics at the same time as you wonder
B C
what unknown purpose they were supposed to
D
serve. No error
E

18. By the time today's fifth graders enter college,
A B
the number of computers in American homes
C
has increased tenfold. No error
D E

19. Traditionally, music has been to play
A B
an important role in the devotional practices
C
of many of the world's religions. No error
D E

GO ON TO THE NEXT PAGE

20. A true stamp collector approaches the hobby
A
methodically; a mere "accumulator" saves them
B C D
casually and indiscriminately. No error
E

21. Within this hall has occurred many of
A B C
the most notable events in our city's colorful
D
history. No error
E

22. In attempting to measure the unprecedented power
A
of modern man, one should remember that the
B
greatest cities of the world can be brought to a
C
standstill by nothing more than a few inches of
D
snow. No error
E

23. Either the president or the leaders of the
A
congressional opposition is sure to suffer
B C
politically, whichever way the final vote
D
swings. No error
E

24. One may wish to consult with an attorney before
A B C
investing in any security that claims to offer tax
D
advantages. No error
E

25. A period of high interest rates tends to
A
mitigate against the prospects of businesses that
B C
operate on a seasonal basis, such as textbook
D
publishers. No error
E

Directions: In each of the following sentences, some part or all of the sentence is underlined. Below each sentence you will find five ways of phrasing the underlined part. Select the answer that produces the most effective sentence, one that is clear and exact, without awkwardness or ambiguity, and blacken the corresponding space on your answer sheet. In choosing answers, follow the requirements of standard written English. Choose the answer that best expresses the meaning of the original sentence.

Answer (A) is always the same as the underlined part. Choose answer (A) if you think the original sentence needs no revision.

EXAMPLE:

Laura Ingalls Wilder published her first book and she was sixty-five years old then.

(A) and she was sixty-five years old then
(B) when she was sixty-five years old
(C) at age sixty-five years old
(D) upon reaching sixty-five years
(E) at the time when she was sixty-five

SAMPLE ANSWER

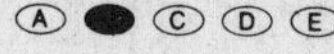

26. Flight is not a distinguishing characteristic of birds; many animals that are not in the category of birds can fly, and many birds cannot.

(A) that are not in the category of birds
(B) other than birds
(C) of the nonbird type
(D) which are not considered as birds
(E) not known to be birds

27. Among the ideas periodically rejected by the Treasury are plans for currency of different sizes, various colors, and shapes that are unusual.

(A) and shapes that are unusual
(B) and shapes
(C) as well as unusual shapes
(D) and shapes that are unusual also
(E) and unusual shapes

GO ON TO THE NEXT PAGE

28. The economics of television news differs from that of the newspaper business, the number of television networks is limited by technology.

(A) business, the
(B) business; and the
(C) business, although the
(D) business because the
(E) business; since the

29. Although trees are no longer widely used for fuel, they are still harvested for use in building houses, in making furniture, and paper is made from wood.

(A) paper is made from wood
(B) to manufacture paper
(C) in manufacturing paper
(D) for paper manufacture
(E) for paper

30. Most fashion experts warn against wearing two different patterns together, and all agreeing that wearing three patterns is never acceptable.

(A) and all agreeing
(B) and all are agreeing
(C) all agree
(D) and are all in agreement
(E) and all agree

31. Free access for reporters even to battlefront areas has generally been allowed by democratic nations.

(A) Free access for reporters even to
(B) Freedom for reporters even of access to
(C) Free access of reporters for even
(D) Even free access for reporters in
(E) Freedom of access of reporters in

32. Anyone can learn to make simple auto repairs, all it takes is a few tools and a little patience.

(A) repairs, all it takes is
(B) repairs, however, all it takes is
(C) repairs; but all it takes is
(D) repairs; needing only
(E) repairs; all it takes is

33. Nearly all of the students signed the petition, many of the teachers supported it, and it was endorsed by several of the deans.

(A) it was endorsed by several of the deans
(B) it received the endorsement of several deans
(C) several of the deans endorsed it
(D) so also did several of the deans
(E) several deans did as well

34. Inevitably, some political motivation must underlie any action, no matter how meritorious it is, by a public official in a democracy.

(A) no matter how meritorious it is
(B) whether meritorious or no
(C) despite its merit
(D) meritorious though it may be
(E) however meritorious

35. Konrad Lorenz spent a lifetime studying animal behavior, yet his home was generally shared with several unusual pets.

(A) behavior, yet his home was generally shared
(B) behavior, so his home was generally shared
(C) behavior, thus his home generally was shared
(D) behavior, with the sharing of his home
(E) behavior; and his home generally was shared

36. Needing only one more vote to pass, the supporters of the bill reintroduced it the next day.

(A) the supporters of the bill reintroduced it
(B) the bill's supporters reintroduced it
(C) the supporters reintroduced the bill
(D) the bill's reintroduction by its supporters occurred
(E) the bill was reintroduced by its supporters

37. Journalists consider themselves defenders of the public, but surveys show that many of the persons that make up the public dislike modern journalism.

(A) many of the persons that make up the public dislike
(B) those who comprise the public dislikes
(C) much of the public dislikes
(D) many of the public have a dislike for
(E) the public itself, on the whole, dislikes

38. Aviation officials have not only failed to determine the cause of the crash but also ignored demands by the pilots' union that the investigation be expedited.

(A) but also ignored
(B) but also have ignored
(C) but they have ignored
(D) and have also ignored
(E) as well as ignoring

GO ON TO THE NEXT PAGE

39. To avoid offending speakers of any of Switzerland's three languages, consequently the nation adopted the Latin *Helvetia* as its official name.

(A) languages, consequently the nation
(B) languages, and so the nation
(C) languages; the nation
(D) languages, the nation
(E) languages; they

40. Advertising aimed at children is controversial, children have not yet learned to interpret its claims.

(A) controversial, children
(B) controversial, so children
(C) controversial: since children
(D) controversial because children
(E) controversial, and children

Directions: The remaining questions are like those at the beginning of the section. For each sentence in which you find an error, select the one underlined part that must be changed to make the sentence correct and blacken the corresponding space on your answer sheet. If there is no error, blacken answer space E.

41. For any person who has not spoke before a group,
A B C
the prospect of addressing a large audience can be
D
highly intimidating. No error
E

42. The federal government has rushed emergency
A
help into the area, offering food, clothing, and
B C
shelter to whomever needs them. No error
D E

43. Even though organized labor is making some
A
inroads in industries formerly nonunionized, it is
B C
suffering greater losses in fields where it once
D
held sway. No error
E

44. Shakespearean heroes have been portrayed
A
with more passion than Mr. Keating shows, but
B
there can scarcely have been a more nobler or
C D
sincere Marc Antony than his. No error
E

45. The members of the mayor's committee
A
charged with investigating the problem of street
B
crime was unsure about the legal scope
C
of their inquiry. No error
D E

46. Few works of literature are as pessimistic
A
in their assessment of the human condition
B
the way the biblical Book of Ecclesiastes is.
C D
No error
E

47. Neither the financial community or the leaders
A
of industry were completely satisfied with the
B C D
final form of the budget resolution. No error
E

48. The artificial playing surface was developed only
A
after research indicated that one of the first
B
domed stadiums did not permit enough light to
C
enter for real grass to grow. No error
D E

49. It would be shortsighted, as well as selfish, to deny
A B
from our children an education at least equal to
C D
the education that we enjoyed ourselves. No error
E

50. John F. Kennedy was not the first Roman Catholic
A
to run for president; Governor Alfred E. Smith of
B
New York was running as the Democratic
C D
candidate in 1928. No error
E

S T O P

IF YOU FINISH BEFORE TIME IS CALLED, YOU MAY CHECK YOUR WORK ON THIS SECTION ONLY. DO NOT WORK ON ANY OTHER SECTION IN THE TEST.

SECTION 4

Time—30 minutes

45 QUESTIONS

For each question in this section, choose the best answer and blacken the corresponding space on the answer sheet.

Each question below consists of a word in capital letters, followed by five lettered words or phrases. Choose the word or phrase that is most nearly opposite in meaning to the word in capital letters. Since some of the questions require you to distinguish fine shades of meaning, consider all the choices before deciding which is best.

Example:

GOOD: (A) sour (B) bad (C) red (D) hot (E) ugly

Ⓐ ● Ⓒ Ⓓ Ⓔ

1. ABBREVIATE: (A) spell (B) measure (C) widen (D) prolong (E) delay
2. GLIB: (A) forthright (B) uninformed (C) tactless (D) impressive (E) inarticulate
3. DESPONDENT: (A) energetic (B) noisome (C) exciting (D) hopeful (E) obdurate
4. FURTIVE: (A) overt (B) gay (C) proud (D) novel (E) sincere
5. INSENSIBLE: (A) conscious (B) well-planned (C) profound (D) sympathetic (E) knowledgeable
6. PUGNACIOUS: (A) generous (B) pacific (C) reticent (D) humble (E) thoughtful
7. ENTHRALL: (A) dull (B) bore (C) invade (D) offend (E) ignore
8. ABEYANCE: (A) normal condition (B) final appeal (C) failure to adhere (D) active state (E) illegal activity
9. COMPLACENT: (A) aggressive (B) uncertain (C) striving (D) uneasy (E) imaginative
10. DILAPIDATED: (A) shipshape (B) modernistic (C) fresh (D) presentable (E) formed
11. UNWITTING: (A) wary (B) definite (C) genuine (D) intelligible (E) intentional
12. CHIMERICAL: (A) solidified (B) real (C) nominal (D) known (E) ancient
13. CADAVEROUS: (A) sprightly (B) haughty (C) garrulous (D) wizened (E) corpulent
14. DEARTH: (A) favor (B) acceptance (C) plenty (D) volume (E) quantity
15. ACCEDE: (A) refute (B) supply (C) refuse (D) desist (E) consort

Each sentence below has one or two blanks, each blank indicating that something has been omitted. Beneath the sentence are five lettered words or sets of words. Choose the word or set of words that best fits the meaning of the sentence as a whole.

Example:

Although its publicity has been ----, the film itself is intelligent, well-acted, handsomely produced, and altogether ----.

(A) tasteless..respectable (B) extensive..moderate (C) sophisticated..amateur (D) risqué..crude (E) perfect..spectacular

● Ⓑ Ⓒ Ⓓ Ⓔ

16. Although the two poems attributed to Homer are noticeably ---- in style, most scholars continue to regard them as the work of a ---- author.
    (A) different..single
    (B) accomplished..talented
    (C) deficient..pagan
    (D) serious..professional
    (E) similar..skillful
17. Recent ---- helicopters have led many to question the suitability of the aircraft for travel over densely populated areas.
    (A) improvements in
    (B) decisions concerning
    (C) developments in
    (D) cost increases for
    (E) accidents involving
18. The tax system must be fair if the government is to raise expected revenues, for unless citizens believe that their tax burben is ----, they will find ways to ---- payment.
    (A) substantial..delay
    (B) decreasing..avoid
    (C) proper..increase
    (D) reasonable..protest
    (E) equitable..evade

GO ON TO THE NEXT PAGE

19. Just as Germany's first attempt at democracy ---- in the wake of the Great Depression, so recent economic failures have pushed several nations in the direction of ----.

(A) failed..freedom
(B) occurred..modernization
(C) prevailed..bankruptcy
(D) collapsed..totalitarianism
(E) flourished..tyranny

20. In such forms as defense-related experiments aboard spacecraft and satellite surveillance of troop movements, the ---- exploitation of ---- has already begun.

(A) political..national security
(B) military..outer space
(C) capitalist..aviation science
(D) violent..space flight
(E) governmental..scientific technology

Each passage below is followed by questions based on its content. Answer all questions following a passage on the basis of what is stated or implied in that passage.

One highly important fact about Greek architecture is the liberal use it made of color. The ruins of Greek temples are today monochromatic—either a glittering white, like the temple at Sunium, or a golden brown, like the Parthenon and other buildings of Pentelic marble, or a still warmer brown, like the limestone temples at Paestum and Girgenti. But this uniformity of tint is due only to time. A colorless city would have been unimaginable to an ancient Greek.

Even today, the attentive observer may sometimes see upon old Greek buildings, as, for example, upon ceiling beams of the Parthenon, traces left by patterns from which the color has vanished. In other instances, remains of actual color exist. So specks of blue paint may still be seen, or might have been seen a few years ago, on blocks belonging to the Athenian Propylaea.

During the excavation of Olympia (1875–1881), this matter of the coloring of architecture was constantly in mind, and a large body of facts relating to it was accumulated. It appears that just as the forms and proportions of a building and of all its details were determined by precedent, yet not so absolutely as to leave no scope for the exercise of individual genius, so there was an established system in the coloring of a building, yet a system which varied somewhat according to time and place and the taste of the architect. The main colors were dark blue (sometimes almost black) and red, but green and yellow were also used, and some details were gilded. The coloration of the building was far from total. Plain surfaces, such as walls, were unpainted. So, too, were the columns, including, probably, their capitals, except between the annulets.

If it is asked what led the Greeks to a use of color so strange to us and, on first acquaintance, so little to our taste, it may be answered that possibly the example of their neighbors had something to do with it. The architecture of Egypt, Mesopotamia, and Persia was polychromatic. But the practice of the Greeks was probably, in the main, an inheritance from the early days of their own civilization. According to a well-supported theory, the Doric temple of the historical period is a translation into stone or marble of a primitive edifice whose walls were of sun-dried bricks and whose columns and entablature were of wood. Now, it is natural and appropriate to paint wood, and we may suppose that the taste for a partially colored architecture was thus formed.

This theory does not explain everything. It does not, for example, explain why the columns should be uncolored. In short, the Greek system of polychromy presents itself to us as a largely arbitrary system.

21. According to the passage, the present coloration of the ancient Greek temples was caused by

(A) vandals who effaced the original colors
(B) the effects of aging
(C) incompetent modern art restorers
(D) damage in warfare
(E) later architects who altered the early designs

22. The passage implies that the excavation of Olympia yielded information concerning

(A) the reasons behind the use of color in Greek architecture
(B) how colors were used on different parts of Greek buildings
(C) the transition in Greek architecture from wood and brick to stone
(D) the similarity of Greek architecture to that of neighboring countries
(E) engineering methods used by ancient Greek architects

23. The author implies that if the Greek temples were rebuilt in their original condition, most modern viewers would find their coloration

(A) warm and appealing
(B) primitive and crude
(C) natural and appropriate
(D) brilliant and vivid
(E) strange and unattractive

GO ON TO THE NEXT PAGE

24. Which of the following is assumed to be true by the author of the passage?

(A) Modern attitudes toward the use of color in architecture derive from those of the Greeks.
(B) Greek architects had some definite reason for the patterns of colors they used.
(C) It is more natural to paint a wooden building than a stone building.
(D) Compared to other artistic styles, architectural styles are slow to change.
(E) Ancient art loses much of its beauty when its condition is allowed to change over time.

25. According to the passage, the theory that the Greek use of color was inherited from an earlier stage of Greek history is

(A) significant but not fully adequate
(B) an ingenious solution to a historical dilemma
(C) in need of more substantial supporting evidence
(D) confusing and arbitrary
(E) likely to be supplanted soon by some superior theory

The time was late in the summer, the place a ranch in southwestern Kansas, and Sam Lewiston and his wife Emma were two of a vast population of farmers, wheat growers, who at that moment were passing through a crisis. Wheat was down to sixty-six.

Emma Lewiston spoke. "Well," she hazarded, looking vaguely out across the ranch toward the horizon, leagues distant. "Well, Sam, there's always that offer of brother Joe's. We can quit, and go to Chicago, if the worst comes."

"And give up!" explained Lewiston. "Leave the ranch! After all these years!"

His wife made no reply. Lewiston climbed into the wagon and gathered up the reins. "Well, here goes for the last try, Emma," he said. "Good-bye, girl. Maybe things will look better in town today."

"Maybe," she said gravely. She kissed her husband good-bye and stood for some time looking after the wagon traveling toward the town in a moving pillar of dust.

"I don't know," she murmured at length. "I don't know just how we're going to make out."

When he reached town, Lewiston tied up the horse and went up the stairway of a building of brick and granite—quite the most pretentious structure of the town. He knocked at a door on which, in gold letters, was inscribed "Bridges & Co., Grain Dealers."

Bridges himself, a middle-aged man smoking a Pittsburgh stogie, met the farmer at the counter, and the two exchanged perfunctory greetings.

"Well," said Lewiston, tentatively, after a while.

"Well, Lewiston," said the other, "I can't take that wheat of yours at any better than sixty-two."

"Sixty-*two*."

"It's the Chicago price that does it, Lewiston. It's Truslow and his clique that stick the knife into us. The price broke again this morning. We've just got a wire."

"Good heavens," murmured Lewiston, looking vaguely from side to side. "Sixty-two cents a bushel! Why, man, what with this and with that, it's cost me nearly a dollar a bushel to raise that wheat, and now Truslow—"

He turned away abruptly with a quick gesture of infinite discouragement.

He went down the stairs, and making his way to where the wagon was hitched, got in, and, with eyes vacant, drove slowly back to the ranch. His wife met him as he drew up before the barn.

"Well?" she demanded.

"Emma," he said as he got out of the wagon, laying his arm across her shoulders. "Emma, I guess we'll take up with Joe's offer. We'll go to Chicago."

26. The passage primarily concerns

(A) the exploitation of Kansas wheat farmers by banking interests of the East
(B) how a farming family loses its home because of a disastrously poor crop
(C) a farmer's decision to leave his rural home and seek his fortune in the city
(D) the devastating effect on a wheat-farming family of a drop in the price of grain
(E) the effects of a financial crisis on the relationship of a husband and wife

27. The reference to "the most pretentious structure of the town" (lines 26–27) most clearly suggests

(A) Lewiston's anxiety as he approaches a crucial interview
(B) the haughty attitude taken by Bridges toward Lewiston
(C) the prominent social and economic position held by the local grain dealer
(D) the helplessness of the wheat farmer in opposition to the grain-dealing interests
(E) the financial power that had been wielded in better days by the wheat farmer

28. The author suggests Lewiston's reaction to the news from Bridges primarily by

(A) the use of interior monologue
(B) presenting an allegorical scene
(C) the use of metaphor and simile
(D) the use of symbols drawn from nature
(E) relating Lewiston's words and describing his gestures

GO ON TO THE NEXT PAGE

29. It can be inferred that during his ride back to the ranch Lewiston

(A) decides to withhold from his wife the truth about their plight
(B) vows revenge on the Chicago interests that he feels have victimized him
(C) resolves to struggle on in his present situation
(D) decides to give up on his efforts to save the ranch
(E) lapses into a state of indifference and despair

30. The passage suggests that Lewiston's plight is primarily due to

(A) price manipulation by a syndicate in Chicago
(B) the greed of Bridges and other small grain dealers
(C) a bad harvest caused by unfavorable weather
(D) poor planning on the part of Lewiston and his wife
(E) the high cost of supplies and tools for the farmer

Select the word or set of words that best completes each of the following sentences.

31. The political crises of our time are inevitably the most ---- in history, for today we are responsible, for the first time, for deciding whether or not humanity shall survive.

(A) fascinating (B) crucial (C) tragic
(D) violent (E) instructive

32. Although the heavy rainfalls of this spring ---- the reservoirs, the long-term threat of a water shortage remains ----.

(A) damaged..real
(B) drenched..plausible
(C) replenished..minuscule
(D) filled..genuine
(E) overflowed..remote

33. Popular conceptions of science are more strongly influenced by technological ---- of scientific principles than by the pure research that is the ---- of scientific activity.

(A) developments..goal
(B) misuse..focus
(C) extensions..purpose
(D) distortions..source
(E) applications..heart

34. If, as these studies suggest, mere geographical proximity is the main factor in determining one's choice of a ----, then our romantic belief that each person has one destined mate is probably ----.

(A) life-style..fallacious
(B) career..questionable
(C) wife..accurate
(D) home..untrue
(E) spouse..incorrect

35. The general public was unwilling to support black music in its pure original form; only after it had been ---- by ---- white musical styles did it achieve wide popularity.

(A) improved..comparison with
(B) adulterated..blending with
(C) spoiled..separation from
(D) clarified..mingling with
(E) modified..reaction to

GO ON TO THE NEXT PAGE

Each question below consists of a related pair of words or phrases, followed by five lettered pairs of words or phrases. Select the lettered pair that best expresses a relationship similar to that expressed in the original pair.

Example:

YAWN:BOREDOM:: (A) dream:sleep (B) anger:madness (C) smile:amusement (D) face:expression (E) impatience:rebellion Ⓐ Ⓑ ● Ⓓ Ⓔ

36. ANXIETY:CALM::
(A) embarrassment:composure
(B) fear:determination
(C) worry:reassurance
(D) lethargy:strength
(E) terror:disgust

37. HIRE:EMPLOYEE:: (A) enroll:member
(B) sue:attorney (C) dismiss:supervisor
(D) obey:ruler (E) pay:salary

38. EXCERPT:ARTICLE:: (A) portion:meal
(B) headline:story (C) clip:film
(D) chapter:encyclopedia (E) detail:story

39. STORM:SHOWER:: (A) river:pond
(B) torrent:trickle (C) gust:squall
(D) tornado:hurricane (E) wind:rain

40. VINDICTIVE:REVENGE::
(A) belligerent:territory
(B) repentant:guilt
(C) ravenous:satiation
(D) hostile:brutality
(E) forgiving:clemency

41. COMPOSITION:PERFORM::
(A) symphony:conduct
(B) comedy:laugh
(C) script:rehearse
(D) drama:enact
(E) music:write

42. SHEAF:GATHERED:: (A) collection:selected
(B) lawn:mowed (C) bouquet:scented
(D) crop:planted (E) stack:piled

43. LINE:REEL:: (A) thread:spool
(B) rod:tackle (C) rein:harness
(D) tape:wheel (E) rope:knot

44. HISTORIOGRAPHER:PAST::
(A) philosopher:science
(B) linguist:pronunciation
(C) entomologist:insects
(D) cartographer:terrain
(E) archaeologist:artifacts

45. POTENTIAL:UNTAPPED::
(A) aptitude:proven
(B) possibility:realized
(C) ability:unappreciated
(D) capital:accumulated
(E) talent:exploited

S T O P

IF YOU FINISH BEFORE TIME IS CALLED, YOU MAY CHECK YOUR WORK ON THIS SECTION ONLY. DO NOT WORK ON ANY OTHER SECTION IN THE TEST.

SECTION 5

Time—30 minutes

25 QUESTIONS

In this section solve each problem, using any available space on the page for scratchwork. Then indicate the one correct answer in the appropriate space on the answer sheet.

The following information is for your reference in solving some of the problems.

Circle of radius r: Area $= \pi r^2$; Circumference $= 2\pi r$
The number of degrees of arc in a circle is 360.
The measure in degrees of a straight angle is 180.

Definitions of symbols:

$=$	is equal to	$\leq$	is less than or equal to
$\neq$	is unequal to	$\geq$	is greater than or equal to
$<$	is less than	$\parallel$	is parallel to
$>$	is greater than	$\perp$	is perpendicular to

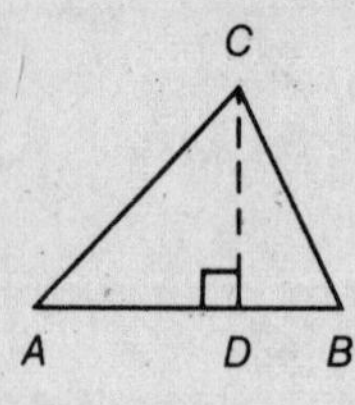

Triangle: The sum of the measures in degrees of the angles of a triangle is 180.

If $\angle CDA$ is a right angle, then

(1) area of $\triangle ABC = \frac{AB \times CD}{2}$

(2) $AC^2 = AD^2 + DC^2$

Note: Figures which accompany problems in this test are intended to provide information useful in solving the problems. They are drawn as accurately as possible EXCEPT when it is stated in a specific problem that its figure is not drawn to scale. All figures lie in a plane unless otherwise indicated. All numbers used are real numbers.

---

1. If $a = 4$ and $b = 3$, then $10(ab) =$

   (A) 10 (B) 70 (C) 90 (D) 120 (E) 240

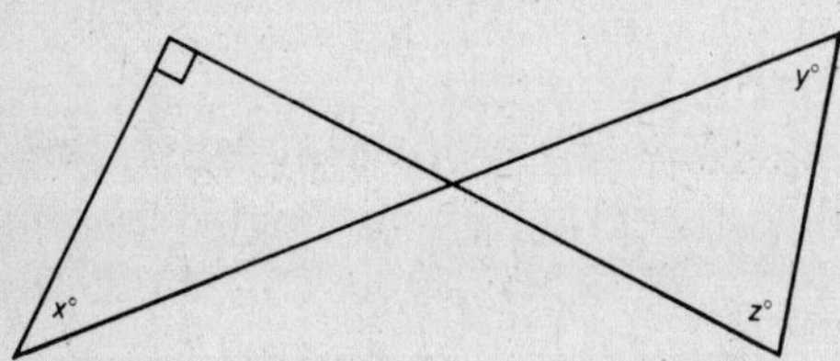

2. In the figure above, what is the sum of y and z in terms of x?

   (A) $2x$ (B) $90 + x$ (C) $180 - x$
   (D) $180 - 2x$ (E) $180 - (x + 90)$

3. A football team has jerseys in 3 different colors and pants in 4 different colors. How many different color combinations of jerseys and pants are possible?

   (A) 8 (B) 9 (C) 10 (D) 12 (E) 16

4. In a coordinate graph system, a circle is drawn whose center is at the origin and whose radius is 4. All of the points described by the following coordinates will fall within the circle EXCEPT

   (A) $(0, 3)$ (B) $(-2, -2)$ (C) $(3, 4)$
   (D) $(-1, 2)$ (E) $(-3, 0)$

5. If $0 < x < 1$, then which of the following must be true?

   (A) $x^2 < 0$ (B) $x^2 > 1$ (C) $x^2 < x$
   (D) $x^2 = x$ (E) $x^2 > x$

6. What is the average (arithmetic mean) of 27.4, 32.6, 30.2, and 19?

   (A) 24.7 (B) 25.3 (C) 26.8
   (D) 27.3 (E) 30.1

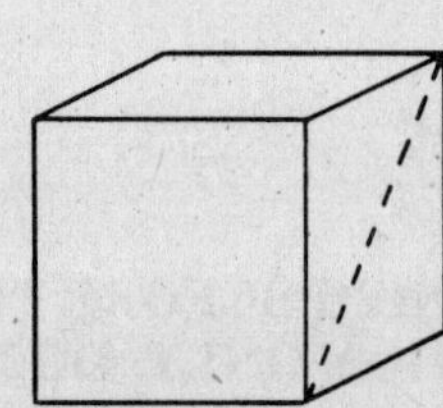

7. If the length of the dashed line connecting two vertices of the cube shown above is 2, then the volume of the cube equals

   (A) $2\sqrt{2}$ (B) $\frac{6}{\sqrt{2}}$ (C) $4\sqrt{2}$
   (D) 4 (E) $8\sqrt{2}$

GO ON TO THE NEXT PAGE

8. If A is the set of 6 consecutive integers whose sum is 9, and B is the set of 6 consecutive integers whose sum is -3, how many integers are members of both set A and set B?

(A) 0 (B) 1 (C) 2 (D) 3 (E) 4

9. If $x - y = 6$, then $9 - (x - y) =$

(A) 15 (B) 12 (C) 9 (D) 6 (E) 3

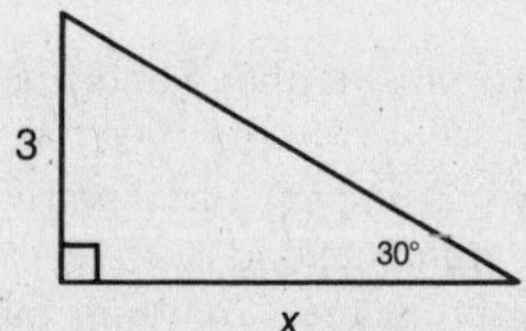

10. In the triangle above, what is the value of x?

(A) $3\sqrt{2}$ (B) $3\sqrt{3}$ (C) $\frac{3}{2}$ (D) 6

(E) It cannot be determined from the information given.

11. City A lies 30 miles due north of City B along a railroad line. A train leaves City A at 2 P.M. and travels north at a rate of 48 miles per hour. A second train leaves City B at 3:30 P.M. on the same day and travels north along an adjacent track at a rate of 60 miles per hour. At what time will the second train overtake the first?

(A) 12 midnight (B) 1:30 A.M. (C) 2:30 A.M.
(D) 4:00 A.M. (E) 5:30 A.M.

12. If each of the following numbers is rounded to the nearest tenth, all will have the same value EXCEPT

(A) 2.2374 (B) 2.02 (C) 2.19
(D) 2.2009 (E) 2.165

13. If $x = 12 - y$ and $\frac{y}{5} = 2$, then $x =$

(A) 10 (B) 5 (C) 4 (D) 2 (E) 1

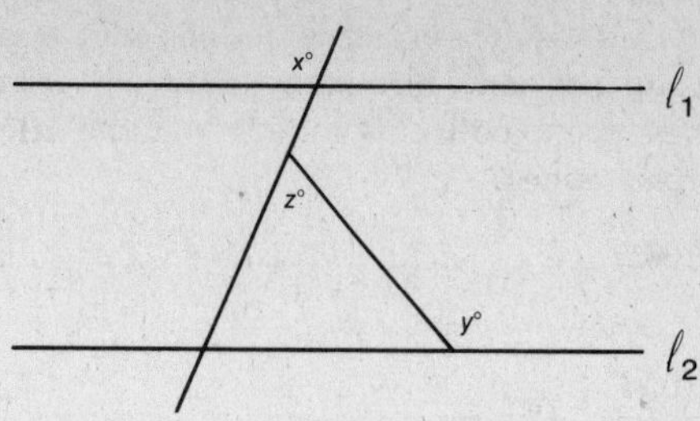

14. In the figure above, if $\ell_1 \parallel \ell_2$, what is the value of z?

(A) $180 - y$ (B) $x - y$ (C) $180 - x$
(D) $90 + x - y$ (E) $x + y - 180$

15. In a class of 25 students, the first 10 received test scores averaging 92, while the second 10 received scores averaging 84. If the average score for the entire class was 86, what was the average score for the last 5 students?

(A) 64 (B) 66 (C) 71 (D) 74 (E) 78

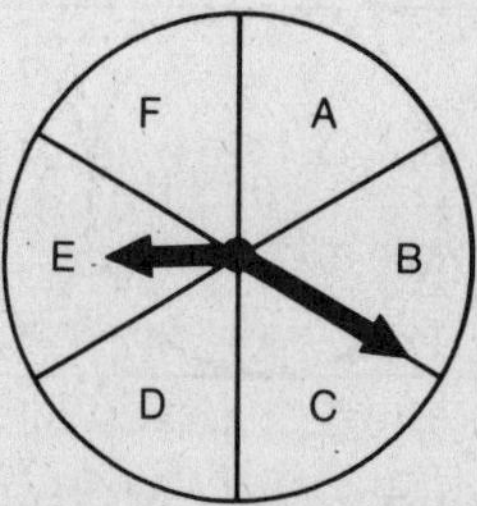

16. The clock above operates in the same manner as a conventional 12-hour clock. However, its dial is divided into six equal regions marked A, B, C, D, E, and F. Exactly 6 hours and 45 minutes after the time shown, in which two regions will the hour and minute hand, respectively, be found?

(A) B, D (B) C, A (C) D, E
(D) A, F (E) C, C

17. A set of weights for use with a balance scale includes one weight in each of the following sizes: 1 pound, 3 pounds, 5 pounds, 7 pounds, and 10 pounds. With exactly three weights from this set, it is possible to measure each of the following weights EXCEPT

(A) 8 pounds (B) 9 pounds (C) 13 pounds
(D) 16 pounds (E) 18 pounds

GO ON TO THE NEXT PAGE

18. If a store sells i ice-cream cones per hour at a price of c cents per cone, how many hours will it take for the store to collect d dollars from the sale of ice-cream cones?

(A) $\frac{100dc}{i}$ (B) $\frac{dci}{100}$ (C) $\frac{dc}{100i}$

(D) $\frac{100d}{ci}$ (E) $\frac{c}{100di}$

$P = \{\text{all integers smaller than } \pi\}$

$Q = \{\text{all numbers greater than } 0\}$

19. Given the definitions above, which of the following numbers is a member of both set P and set Q?

(A) -2 (B) 0 (C) 1.6 (D) 3 (E) 4

20. If $3x + y = 14$ and $y - x = 2$, then $2x - 2y =$

(A) 8 (B) 3 (C) 2 (D) 0 (E) -4

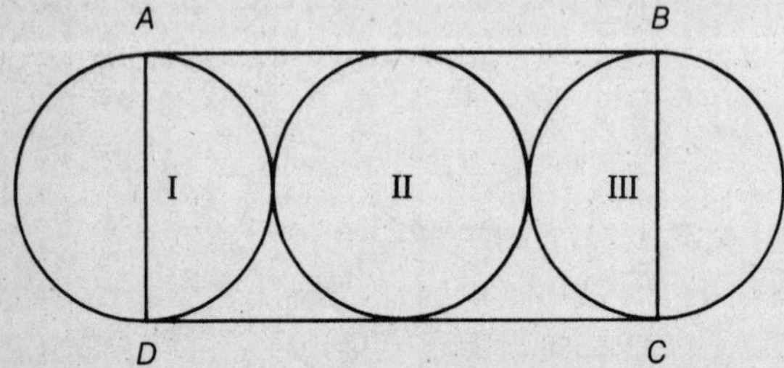

21. Sides AD and BC of rectangle $ABCD$ pass through the centers of circles I and III. If the circumference of each circle is 7π, what is the area of rectangle $ABCD$?

(A) $24\frac{1}{2}$ (B) 35 (C) 49 (D) 63 (E) 98

22. If $n - 3$ is an even integer, which of the following must be an odd integer?

(A) $2n + 1$ (B) $4n$ (C) $\frac{n}{2}$

(D) $n - 1$ (E) $2n$

23. If $x = 2z$ and $y = \frac{z}{3}$, then $\frac{x}{y} =$

(A) 6 (B) 3 (C) 2 (D) $2z$ (E) $3z + 1$

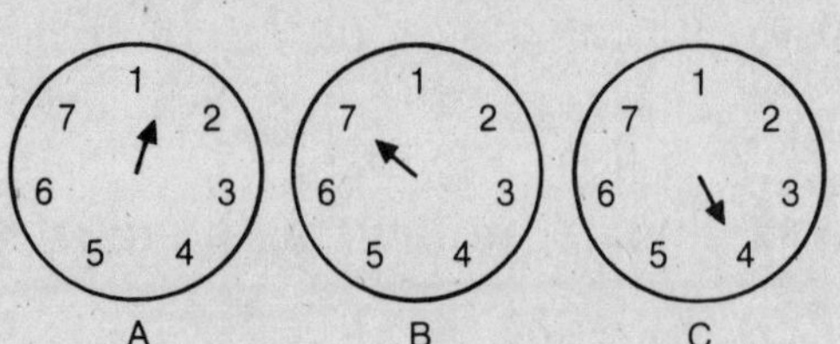

24. The three dials shown above operate in such a way that each time the pointer on dial A completes a revolution by passing the number 1, dial B advances one number; and each time dial B completes a revolution by passing the number 1, the pointer on dial C advances one number. After the pointer on dial A makes ten complete revolutions beginning at the reading shown, the pointer on dial C will be closest to which number?

(A) 2 (B) 4 (C) 5 (D) 6 (E) 7

25. In a coordinate graph system, a triangle is drawn with vertices located at points with coordinates $(-2, -1)$, $(10, 4)$, and $(-2, 4)$. What is the length of the longest side of the triangle?

(A) 12 (B) 13 (C) $5\sqrt{20}$

(D) 17 (E) $\sqrt{389}$

S T O P

IF YOU FINISH BEFORE TIME IS CALLED, YOU MAY CHECK YOUR WORK ON THIS SECTION ONLY. DO NOT WORK ON ANY OTHER SECTION IN THE TEST.

SECTION 6

Time—30 minutes

40 QUESTIONS

For each question in this section, choose the best answer and blacken the corresponding space on the answer sheet.

Each question below consists of a word in capital letters, followed by five lettered words or phrases. Choose the word or phrase that is most nearly opposite in meaning to the word in capital letters. Since some of the questions require you to distinguish fine shades of meaning, consider all the choices before deciding which is best.

Example:

GOOD: (A) sour (B) bad (C) red (D) hot (E) ugly

Ⓐ ● Ⓒ Ⓓ Ⓔ

1. STATIC: (A) innumerable (B) changing (C) disparate (D) visceral (E) soundless

2. RADICAL: (A) ordinary (B) acceptable (C) superficial (D) logical (E) prudent

3. DOFF: (A) put on (B) look up to (C) give up (D) play down (E) hold forth

4. ENCUMBERED: (A) empty-headed (B) weightless (C) simple (D) unburdened (E) rapid

5. BUTTRESS: (A) fault (B) depose (C) collapse (D) dissemble (E) undermine

6. GROVEL: (A) salute (B) adjure (C) grimace (D) abut (E) strut

7. FALLOW: (A) desiccated (B) rich (C) unripe (D) cultivated (E) harvested

8. JOCULAR: (A) grave (B) significant (C) literal (D) religious (E) straight

9. GRATIS: (A) unworthy of thanks (B) offered for sale (C) taken for granted (D) freely chosen (E) easily obtained

10. HALCYON: (A) cloudy (B) turbulent (C) immemorial (D) refulgent (E) barren

Each sentence below has one or two blanks, each blank indicating that something has been omitted. Beneath the sentence are five lettered words or sets of words. Choose the word or set of words that best fits the meaning of the sentence as a whole.

Example:

Although its publicity has been ----, the film itself is intelligent, well-acted, handsomely produced, and altogether ----.

(A) tasteless..respectable (B) extensive..moderate (C) sophisticated..amateur (D) risqué..crude (E) perfect..spectacular

● Ⓑ Ⓒ Ⓓ Ⓔ

11. In the years before the invention of modern methods of ----, cutting ice from frozen lakes in the north and shipping it to warmer climes was an industry in itself.

(A) transportation (B) heating (C) refrigeration (D) communication (E) food preparation

12. The literature of the nursery is largely grown-up fare that has been relegated to the use of ----; the fairy tales of Grimm, for instance, were originally told and enjoyed by ----.

(A) schoolteachers..poets
(B) the young..amateurs
(C) children..adults
(D) infants..authors
(E) writers..troubadours

13. Darwin was not the first to advance a theory of evolution; his tremendous originality lay in the fact that he ---- the idea of natural selection as the means by which evolution worked.

(A) discredited (B) elaborated (C) proposed (D) modified (E) supported

14. Arousal level can be affected by such ---- drives as hunger and thirst or by such external ---- as the aroma of food or the clang of a bell.

(A) internal..stimuli
(B) basic..episodes
(C) aberrant..factors
(D) antisocial..incentives
(E) biological..conflicts

GO ON TO THE NEXT PAGE

15. It is not only the ---- who accepts things on ----; most people believe in countless things they have heard about but have not seen for themselves.

(A) scientist..the evidence
(B) student..intuition
(C) tribesman..condition
(D) mystic..faith
(E) expert..instinct

Each question below consists of a related pair of words or phrases, followed by five lettered pairs of words or phrases. Select the lettered pair that best expresses a relationship similar to that expressed in the original pair.

Example:

YAWN:BOREDOM:: (A) dream:sleep (B) anger:madness (C) smile:amusement (D) face:expression (E) impatience:rebellion

16. SCRIBBLE:WRITE:: (A) daub:paint (B) chuckle:speak (C) mumble:explain (D) titter:laugh (E) batter:build

17. DOLPHIN:MAMMAL:: (A) bird:creature (B) tomato:bush (C) toad:amphibian (D) caterpillar:butterfly (E) whale:fish

18. INGENUE:NAIVE::
(A) simpleton:sincere
(B) sophisticate:vicious
(C) innocent:pious
(D) scientist:profound
(E) sage:wise

19. ABRIDGEMENT:BOOK::
(A) interruption:speech
(B) correction:error
(C) sequel:film
(D) punctuation:sentence
(E) abbreviation:word

20. ORCHESTRA:CONDUCTOR::
(A) classroom:teacher
(B) company:commander
(C) music:composer
(D) team:athlete
(E) audience:performer

21. MALINGERER:SHIRK::
(A) benefactor:please
(B) sensualist:demand
(C) procrastinator:postpone
(D) misanthrope:disgust
(E) dissembler:reveal

22. FIELD:CULTIVATE:: (A) mountain:scale (B) ocean:navigate (C) farm:subdivide (D) lake:stock (E) crop:harvest

23. UNPARALLELED:ROUTINE::
(A) unique:unusual
(B) singular:multifarious
(C) inimitable:commonplace
(D) curious:unprecedented
(E) unlike:dissimilar

24. GRIMACE:EXERTION:: (A) frown:fear (B) sneer:horror (C) smile:companionship (D) murmur:exclamation (E) contortion:pain

25. ATTORNEY:LITIGATION::
(A) surgeon:operation
(B) lawyer:negotiation
(C) agent:compromise
(D) educator:knowledge
(E) clergyman:salvation

Each passage below is followed by questions based on its content. Answer all questions following a passage on the basis of what is stated or implied in that passage.

Assigned the task of establishing new and more accurate time standards, physicists and engineers have become members of the clock-making profession. They share little of the trade's traditional vocabulary and methodology. Instead of "escapement," "pendulum," and "mainspring," these new clockmakers speak in terms of "microwave interaction cavities" and "atomic resonances." Nonetheless, atomic clocks are identical in function with the mechanical clocks used for centuries. Both kinds of clocks have means of providing a repetitious, periodic, or cyclical phenomenon (a pendulum, a balance wheel, or an electric motor corresponding to the resonance or

"vibration" of an atom or molecule); that is, each has a "frequency standard" associated with it. Both kinds of clocks have means of counting and displaying the accumulation of these periodic phenomena (the gears and hands corresponding to electronic circuits and digital displays).

In both traditional and atomic clocks, the accuracy of timekeeping depends on how stable the frequency of the periodic phenomenon is, not on how fast the phenomenon repeats. For example, a quartz crystal, which may oscillate millions of times a second, keeps time more accurately than the pendulum on a grandfather clock, which may swing only once every two seconds, not because the former has a higher frequency, but because its frequency is more stable. Similarly, an atomic clock is more accurate than a quartz crystal clock, at least for long periods of time, not because its frequency may be higher, but because individual atoms and molecules maintain their resonant frequency more constantly than a crystal can.

As long ago as the 1920s, scientists at the National Bureau of Standards (NBS) were among those suggesting future applications of atomic and molecular beams to determine precise frequencies. The second director of NBS, Dr. George K. Burgess, noted in the 1928 *Standards Yearbook*, "Any radiation frequency emitted by an atom is the ticking of an atomic clock, the oscillation mechanism of which causes hundreds of trillions of waves per second. The accurate standardization of these frequencies ... is the basis of spectroscopy, which has created a new astronomy, a new chemistry, and a new physics."

However, it was not until 1949 that NBS announced the development of its first time source linked to the natural frequency of an atom or a molecule. The first NBS atomic clock relied on the ammonia molecule to regulate its rate. Ammonia molecules strongly absorb microwave radiation when this radiation precisely matches the molecules' natural resonance frequency of 23,870 million hertz (cycles per second). The ammonia was contained in a waveguide absorption cell where it could be irradiated by the microwaves. The microwaves were generated by a quartz crystal oscillator and a frequency multiplier and were tuned until the absorption was maximized. The tuning was done manually, not automatically, so that the system had a short-term stability similar to the quartz crystal itself; long-term stability was provided by the ammonia absorption line. The overall accuracy of this system was no better than the astronomical time maintained by several observatories around the world, but it was a significant first step toward linking time with the atom.

26. The passage deals primarily with the

(A) practical application of a scientific concept
(B) steps in the development of a theory
(C) implications for pure research of a technological advance
(D) role of government in supporting a scientific project
(E) general theory underlying a particular scientific idea

27. According to the passage, the most fundamental difference between atomic and mechanical clocks is the

(A) use of the principles of physics in the design of atomic clocks
(B) absence of mechanical parts in atomic clocks
(C) type of periodic phenomenon used as a frequency standard
(D) vocabulary used in discussing the clock-making craft
(E) use of electronic circuits in atomic clocks

28. According to the passage, each of the following has been used as the frequency standard in clocks EXCEPT

(A) the "vibration" of atoms
(B) changes in a digital display
(C) the movement of a balance wheel
(D) the resonance of a crystal
(E) the swinging of a pendulum

29. It can be inferred from the passage that the term *atomic clock*, as used by Dr. Burgess (line 43), refers to the

(A) earliest attempts by the NBS to develop an atomic time source
(B) use of atomic radiation as a basis for accurate timekeeping
(C) remarkable stability of the frequency of atomic resonances
(D) possibility of using quartz crystal vibrations as a timekeeping mechanism
(E) revolutionary effects of spectroscopy on studies in chemistry and physics

30. According to the passage, the first atomic timekeeping device was significant mainly because of its

(A) high short-term stability
(B) use of a molecular frequency
(C) extreme accuracy
(D) use of microwave radiation
(E) reliance on the ammonia atom

GO ON TO THE NEXT PAGE

In the eighteenth century, crime was seen largely as a deliberate choice among alternative courses of action. Motivated by lust, greed, or malice—the inevitable wellsprings of much human conduct—people would select the criminal path if the pains did not outweigh the pleasures. According to Beccaria, Bentham, and other founders of the classical school of criminology, it was the responsibility of the state to make punishment so quick and certain that law-abiding behavior would be obviously preferable.

In the latter part of the nineteenth century, after the publication of Darwin's *Origin of Species* and *Descent of Man*, biological characteristics played a large part in the explanation of human behavior. The theories of Cesare Lombroso, with their depiction of the criminal as bearing the primitive characteristics of an earlier human form, found an enthusiastic worldwide audience. Many people became convinced that the sources of crime were to be found not in the uncontrolled will but in defects of the body.

After Lombroso's theories collapsed under the attacks of his critics, the electrifying ideas of Freudian psychiatry came to dominate the scene, and crime was seen as an expression of unconscious emotional conflicts bred in the traumas of childhood. In the 1930s, the popularity of this viewpoint began to wane—in part, perhaps, because the Great Depression helped to shift attention from individual failings to the malfunctioning of society as the source of social problems. In any event, crime increasingly came to be viewed as an outcome of the social environment, often in terms of inadequate socialization due to broken families.

Much of the present sociological theorizing about crime causation can be divided into three main categories. First, there are arguments clustered around the idea that crime is largely a function of the inability of the individual to achieve by legitimate means the goals set by society, coupled with an erosion of the restraining forces of social norms.

Second, the causes of crime are seen as rooted in the disorganization of agencies of social control, including both informal groups (such as the family, neighborhood, and friends) and the formal organizations of the larger society.

Third, there is the idea that crime is learned behavior that is acquired in an ordinary learning process when an individual happens to be associated with people who hold criminal values and attitudes.

31. Which of the following titles best describes the content of the passage?

(A) Theories of Crime from Darwin to Today
(B) Sociology's Contributions to the Control of Crime
(C) Modern Theories of the Causes of Crime
(D) Social and Psychological Roots of Crime
(E) Changing Theories of the Causes of Crime

32. Which theorist mentioned in the passage would be most likely to agree with the following statement: "Humanity has developed in such a way that the normal behavior of the past would be considered criminal today"?

(A) Beccaria
(B) Bentham
(C) Darwin
(D) Freud
(E) Lombroso

33. All of the present-day theories of crime discussed by the author have in common an emphasis on the

(A) breakdown of social norms as a cause of crime
(B) social forces that influence an individual to turn to crime
(C) role of the family in the development of criminal behavior
(D) moral responsibility of the individual for his or her criminal acts
(E) role of learning in the genesis of crime

34. It can be inferred from the passage that a member of the classical school of criminology would be most likely to favor which of the following as a means of reducing the crime rate?

(A) Strengthening the family as a source of stable social values
(B) A return to the stricter moral standards of the past
(C) Greater support for social norms by the organs of government
(D) More efficient prosecution and punishment of criminals
(E) Reassertion of the right of society to protect itself against violent behavior

35. Which of the following questions CANNOT be answered by information provided in the passage?

(A) Why did Freudian explanations of crime fall out of favor during the 1930s?
(B) Who was the leading theorist to apply Darwinian ideas to the study of crime?
(C) What basic motivations did the classical criminologists blame for the existence of crime?
(D) How widely are the theories of Lombroso accepted among sociologists today?
(E) Which one of the theories described most adequately explains the existence of crime in modern society?

GO ON TO THE NEXT PAGE

The American bison (*Bison bison*) was the one feature of the North American central grasslands that all historians, naturalists, trappers, and travelers mentioned in writings concerning the pristine conditions of the area. Based on a series of assumptions about carrying capacity, range area, habits, and population trends, Seton estimated a population of forty to sixty million bison in North America during the years previous to disturbance by the white man. Bison were spread over one-third of the North American continent, with the largest herds distributed along the Mississippi River Valley. The total area inhabited by bison was about three million square miles.

Overgrazing by bison, in association with trampling, rubbing, and wallowing, contributed to the creation and maintenance of environmental conditions favorable to a variety of other wildlife. Bison are primarily grazers, so they depend on herbaceous vegetation for food. Few herbivores possess the bison's capability for altering its environment. Bison require approximately thirty pounds of forage per day, so they can easily overgraze even large areas.

A dramatic change occurred on the Great Plains during the 1800s. Prior to this time, the American Indians were completely dependent on bison for their livelihood. Their hunting methods did not cause major changes in bison numbers and usually resulted in a harvest of surplus animals. It is estimated that approximately three hundred thousand Plains Indians existed primarily by hunting the bison herds from Mexico to Lake Winnipeg and from the Rocky Mountains to the Mississippi River. However, part-Arab horses, escaping from the Spaniards, gave the Indians additional hunting ability. Even with the horse and bow, the Indians could not seriously deplete their resources, as the gun and fence were to do later. Liquidation of the bison took about fifty years. By 1883, only a few animals remained.

36. According to the passage, prior to the arrival of the white man, bison had

(A) grown steadily in population for several centuries
(B) played a major role in shaping the natural conditions of their homeland
(C) destroyed vast areas of the middle American grasslands by their grazing
(D) spread into almost every corner of the North American continent
(E) driven most other forms of wildlife from the areas they inhabited

37. The author apparently regards the assumptions made by Seton in his study of bison population as

(A) possible but unlikely
(B) almost certainly false
(C) impossible to disprove
(D) probably accurate
(E) lacking in critical supporting evidence

38. It can be inferred from the passage that prior to the arrival of the white man, the density of the bison population, in animals per square mile within their range area, was probably

(A) ten to twelve
(B) thirteen to twenty
(C) eighteen to thirty
(D) thirty-six to forty-eight
(E) fifty to sixty-five

39. According to the passage, the destruction of the bison herds of the Great Plains was most significantly promoted by

(A) the introduction of firearms
(B) overgrazing
(C) the adoption of the horse by Indian hunters
(D) invasion of the area by predatory wildlife
(E) an increase in the Indian population

40. Based on the information in the passage, the decline of the bison during the 1800s might be considered ironic in that

(A) the destruction of the herds forced the Plains Indians to find another means of feeding themselves
(B) the horses used by the Indians in hunting the bison were descended from animals that had escaped from the Spanish
(C) an increase in the efficiency of Indian hunters ultimately helped diminish the Indians' ability to earn a livelihood
(D) the bison herds had supported themselves by grazing, without need of human care or feeding
(E) implements originated by the white man helped to destroy a major food source of the Indians

S T O P

IF YOU FINISH BEFORE TIME IS CALLED, YOU MAY CHECK YOUR WORK ON THIS SECTION ONLY. DO NOT WORK ON ANY OTHER SECTION IN THE TEST.

PRACTICE TEST 1: *Scoring Instructions*

1. Check your answers against the answer key on page 43.
2. To figure your SAT-verbal score:
   A. Count the total number of correct answers you chose in Sections 1, 4, and 6.
   B. Count the total number of incorrect answers you chose in Sections 1, 4, and 6. Multiply this number by 1/4. Ignore any questions you left blank.
   C. Subtract the result of Step B from the result of Step A. Round off the answer to the nearest whole number. This whole number is your SAT-verbal raw score.
   D. Find your raw score in the first column of the score conversion table on pages 44–45. Read across to the column headed SAT-verbal. The three-digit number there is your SAT-verbal score.
3. To figure your SAT-mathematical score:
   A. Count the total number of correct answers you chose in Sections 2 and 5.
   B. Count the total number of incorrect answers you chose from questions 8–27 in Section 2. Multiply this number by 1/3. Ignore any questions you left blank.
   C. Count the total number of incorrect answers you chose from all other questions in Sections 2 and 5. Multiply this number by 1/4. Ignore any questions you left blank.
   D. Add the results of Step B and Step C. Subtract this total from the result of Step A. Round off the answer to the nearest whole number. This whole number is your SAT-mathematical raw score.
   E. Find your raw score in the first column of the score conversion table on pages 44–45. Read across to the column headed SAT-mathematical. The three-digit number there is your SAT-mathematical score.
4. To figure your Test of Standard Written English (TSWE) score:
   A. Count the total number of correct answers you chose in Section 3.
   B. Count the total number of incorrect answers you chose in Section 3. Multiply this number by 1/4. Ignore any questions you left blank.
   C. Subtract the result of Step B from the result of Step A. Round off the answer to the nearest whole number. This whole number is your TSWE raw score.
   D. Find your raw score in the first column of the score conversion table on pages 44–45. Read across to the column headed TSWE. The two-digit number there is your TSWE score.

Note: Allow for a margin of error of 30 points either way on your SAT-verbal and SAT-mathematical scores (3 points on your TSWE score). For instance, an SAT-verbal score of 470 really represents a range of scores from 440 to 500. Remember that test performance varies greatly from one day to the next and can be improved through study and practice. So don't consider your scores on any practice test as a perfect prediction of how you'll do on the real SAT.

SECTION 1

1. C	6. B	11. A	16. B	21. A	26. B	31. E	36. A
2. A	7. B	12. D	17. C	22. D	27. A	32. C	37. E
3. C	8. D	13. D	18. E	23. A	28. D	33. D	38. B
4. E	9. A	14. B	19. E	24. B	29. D	34. C	39. A
5. A	10. E	15. B	20. C	25. C	30. B	35. D	40. E

SECTION 2

1. D	6. A	11. C	16. D	21. D	26. B	31. E
2. C	7. B	12. C	17. C	22. D	27. C	32. C
3. B	8. A	13. D	18. A	23. A	28. C	33. C
4. C	9. B	14. D	19. A	24. A	29. E	34. E
5. B	10. C	15. A	20. B	25. C	30. C	35. A

SECTION 3

1. C	8. B	15. E	22. E	29. C	36. E	43. E	50. C
2. A	9. E	16. C	23. B	30. E	37. C	44. D	
3. C	10. B	17. C	24. E	31. A	38. A	45. C	
4. E	11. C	18. D	25. B	32. E	39. D	46. C	
5. C	12. A	19. B	26. B	33. C	40. D	47. A	
6. A	13. D	20. D	27. E	34. E	41. C	48. E	
7. A	14. A	21. B	28. D	35. B	42. D	49. C	

SECTION 4

1. D	7. B	13. E	19. D	25. A	31. B	37. A	43. A
2. E	8. D	14. C	20. B	26. D	32. D	38. C	44. D
3. D	9. C	15. C	21. B	27. C	33. E	39. B	45. D
4. A	10. A	16. A	22. B	28. E	34. E	40. C	
5. A	11. E	17. E	23. E	29. D	35. B	41. D	
6. B	12. B	18. E	24. C	30. A	36. A	42. E	

SECTION 5

1. D	6. D	11. A	16. B	21. E
2. B	7. A	12. B	17. A	22. A
3. D	8. E	13. D	18. D	23. A
4. C	9. E	14. E	19. D	24. D
5. C	10. B	15. E	20. E	25. B

SECTION 6

1. B	6. E	11. C	16. A	21. C	26. A	31. E	36. B
2. C	7. D	12. C	17. C	22. D	27. C	32. E	37. D
3. A	8. A	13. C	18. E	23. C	28. B	33. B	38. B
4. D	9. B	14. A	19. E	24. E	29. C	34. D	39. A
5. E	10. B	15. D	20. B	25. A	30. B	35. E	40. C

PRACTICE TEST 1: *Score Conversion Table*

Raw Score	SAT-Verbal	SAT-Mathematical	TSWE
125	800		
124	790		
123	780		
122	770		
121	760		
120	750		
119	740		
118	730		
117	720		
116	710		
115	710		
114	700		
113	700		
112	690		
111	690		
110	680		
109	680		
108	670		
107	670		
106	660		
105	660		
104	650		
103	650		
102	640		
101	640		
100	630		
99	630		
98	620		
97	620		
96	610		
95	610		
94	600		
93	600		
92	590		
91	590		
90	580		
89	580		
88	580		
87	570		
86	570		
85	570		
84	560		
83	560		
82	560		
81	550		
80	550		
79	550		
78	540		
77	540		
76	530		
75	530		
74	520		
73	520		
72	510		
71	510		
70	500		
69	500		
68	490		
67	490		
66	480		
65	480		
64	470		
63	470		
62	460		
61	460		
60	450	800	
59	450	780	
58	450	770	
57	440	760	
56	440	750	
55	440	740	
54	430	730	
53	430	720	
52	430	710	
51	420	700	
50	420	690	60+
49	420	680	60+
48	410	670	60+
47	410	660	60+
46	410	650	60+
45	400	640	59
44	400	630	58
43	390	620	57
42	390	610	56
41	380	600	55
40	380	600	54
39	370	590	53
38	370	580	52
37	360	570	51
36	360	560	50
35	350	550	49
34	350	540	48
33	340	530	47
32	340	520	46
31	330	510	45
30	330	500	44
29	320	490	43
28	320	490	42
27	310	480	41
26	310	470	40
25	300	460	39
24	300	450	38
23	290	440	37
22	290	430	36
21	280	420	35
20	280	410	34
19	270	400	33
18	270	390	32
17	260	380	31
16	260	370	30

Raw Score	SAT-Verbal	SAT-Mathematical	TSWE
15	250	360	29
14	240	350	28
13	230	340	27
12	220	330	26
11	210	320	25
10	200	310	24
9	200	310	23
8	200	300	22
7	200	290	21
6	200	280	20

Raw Score	SAT-Verbal	SAT-Mathematical	TSWE
5	200	270	20
4	200	260	20
3	200	250	20
2	200	240	20
1	200	220	20
0 or less	200	200	20

PRACTICE TEST 1: *Explanatory Answers*

SECTION 1

1. **C** *Waver* means "to hesitate," so the best opposite is *act decisively*. Choice E is a subtle wrong answer. The point is not how quickly a person acts, but how resolutely.

2. **A** Something *intangible* cannot be touched. Love, freedom, fear—these are *intangible* things. By contrast, *corporeal* means "having a physical body." Remember the word root *corp*, as in *corpse* and *corpulent*.

3. **C** To *forgo* something is to pass it up or to give it up willingly. The opposite would be to demand it or to insist upon it. *Accept*, choice D, is wrong because it is not "opposite enough."

4. **E** Something *passé* is out of fashion or outmoded. The best opposite is *modish*, which means "stylish" or "up-to-date." *Present-day*, choice C, is wrong because it isn't related to the idea of being up-to-date.

5. **A** You might automatically think of the political meaning of *impeach*, as in "*impeaching* the president," but the word also has the more general meaning of "to accuse, challenge, or blame." The best opposite for this meaning is *exonerate*, which means "to clear of blame" or "to prove innocent."

6. **B** *Sobriety* is the state of being sober. The opposite is *inebriation*, the state of being drunk. Choice A, *lassitude*, means "lethargy" or "lack of energy." Choice E, *conviviality*, means "sociability."

7. **B** *Invaluable* is a tricky word. It doesn't mean "not valuable," as you might expect. Instead, it means "unable to be measured in value" and therefore "very valuable." The best antonym, then, is *worthless*. Choice C is off target, as you can tell by working backward: the opposite of *cheapened* would not be *valuable* but *made more costly*, which is not exactly the same thing.

8. **D** *Sporadic* means "occasional, irregular." "*Sporadic* showers," for example, are on-again, off-again rainfalls. Choice D is a better answer than choice C because something *sporadic* may also be *repetitious*.

9. **A** To *infringe* on someone's rights is to fail to honor them; thus, *honor* is a good antonym.

10. **E** A *pariah* is an outcast, someone shunned and hated by a whole group or community. The opposite would be someone who is accepted. Choice D brings in an irrelevant issue: a *pariah* is not someone of low status in a community but someone who is completely outside the community.

11. **A** The *Small* Business Association would oppose any law that placed a burden on companies with *few* employees because most small businesses have small staffs.

12. **D** Choice D fits the cause-and-effect relationship suggested by the word *because*. If the prehistoric plants and animals on the two continents were *similar*, it is logical to conclude that the two continents were once *joined*.

13. **D** If we are all "guided by some set of values," then we all have some *philosophy*, whether we realize it or not. The first words in the other answer choices have nothing to do with values.

14. **B** The words *to be obeyed* and *inflexible dogmas* make it clear that Aristotle's comments were turned into *laws*. And the word *observations* is closely parallel to the word *comments* in the first part of the sentence.

15. **B** The key word *despite* signals a contrast; it indicates that the mayor's educational plan was *not* mainly concerned with the interests of the students. Choice B completes the contrast. (Choices D and E would support the mayor's claim, not contradict it.)

16. **B** Just as a *frame* is an underlying structure that supports and gives shape to a *house*, so a *skeleton* is an underlying structure that supports and gives shape to a *body*. *Air* supports and gives shape to a *balloon* (choice D), but it's not an underlying structure.

17. **C** You go to an *auditorium* to *hear* things, and you go to a *gallery* to *see* things (works of art, for instance). You don't go to a *studio* to *enjoy* things but to *create* them. You don't go to a *museum* to *buy* things but to *look at* them. And no one goes to a *library* to *refer* things—or to a *classroom* to *educate* things!

18. **E** Something *predestined* is decided by *fate*. Similarly, something *deserved* is decided by *merit*—that is, by what one has earned.

19. **E** A *pedant* carries *learning* to extremes; a *chauvinist* carries *patriotism* to extremes. (A *martinet*, choice B, is someone who believes in strict military discipline.)

20. **C** An *armistice* is an agreement that brings an end to *hostilities* just as a *settlement* is an agreement that brings an end to a *dispute*.

21. **A** A *bristle* is one part of the working end of a *brush*; a *straw* is one part of the working end of a *broom*. Choice D is close, but a *picket* is not used in the same way that a *bristle* or a *straw* is used.

22. **D** A person who *implores* is *earnest*, and a person who *commands* is *authoritative*. A person who *requests* may or may not be *deprived*; a person who *accepts* may or may not be *eager*; a person who *muses* may or may not be *wistful*; a person who *insists* may or may not be *anxious*.

23. **A** One uses the *tiller* to *steer* a boat. One uses the *ignition* to *start* an engine.

24. **B** A *tyro* is a greenhorn or a rookie; he or she lacks *experience*. Similarly, an *ignoramus* lacks *knowledge*. A *novice* (choice C) may or may not have *enthusiasm* just as an *amateur* (choice D) may or may not have *ability*.

25. **C** To *cross-examine* a *witness* is to grill her or him with questions. To *interrogate* a *suspect* is to do much the same thing.

26. **B** Nowhere in the passage is it implied that the Federal Theater Project sought to "organize *all* theatrical activity in the United States." Each of the other goals is mentioned somewhere in the passage.

27. **A** Critics of the Federal Theater Project would not agree with any of the adjectives in choices B through E. It is clear, however, that the project was "ambitious" by any measure: the sheer size and diversity of the program would show this.

28. **D** Of the projects described in the passage, the Living Newspaper dramas were clearly the most controversial and therefore probably the most objectionable on political grounds. (See the last sentence of paragraph 3.)

29. **D** Paragraph 4 states that the productions of *It Can't Happen Here* were undertaken to demonstrate "the potential scope of federal theater." The fact that the play was produced in seventeen states also fits answer D.

30. **B** Reread the last paragraph. The Federal Theater Project was ended because Congress refused to provide funds for its support.

31. **E** The main idea of the passage is how movements in the mantle rock affect the earth's surface. Only choice E states this whole idea.

32. **C** The second sentence of the passage states that the currents appear to be caused by the *difference* in temperature between the material near the core and the region near the crust. This has nothing to do with any temperature *changes* within the mantle rock, as choice A implies.

33. **D** The end of paragraph 2 states that "drifting continents" are being pushed apart.

34. **C** Reread paragraphs 2 and 6 if you have any doubts about what these men are doing in a small boat at sea.

35. **D** Although the men are probably suffering from many of the afflictions named in the answer choices, the passage is filled with references to their fatigue: "none had slept," "weary-faced oiler," "you'll need all your strength."

36. **A** The first paragraph makes a grim, ironic joke about how inconvenient shipwrecks are.

37. **E** Choice E summarizes the point of the whole passage effectively. The other answer choices are vague or off the point.

38. **B** The rise in specific heat at very low temperatures is first mentioned in paragraph 2, and the rest of the passage is devoted to explaining it. So it is an out-of-the-ordinary phenomenon (an "anomaly"), but not an "inexplicable" one (choice E).

39. **A** Paragraph 2 states that "the interactions between the tiny natural magnetic fields" cause the "bumps or peaks" (that is, the increases) in the specific heat values "at very low temperatures."

40. **E** Since the passage explains how the interactions of the tiny magnets become significant only when the temperature is extremely low, you can infer that a thermometer based on those interactions can be used only at low temperatures.

SECTION 2

1. **D** $x \div 2/5$ is the same as $x \times 5/2$. That works out to $5x/2$, or $2.5x$.

2. **C** If the company's sales averaged \$4.2 million per month for the first 9 months, then they totaled \$37.8 million for that period. For the whole year, if sales are to

average \$4.5 million per month, they must total \$54.0 million. Subtract \$37.8 million from \$54.0 million and you get the amount of sales that must be chalked up during that last quarter.

3. **B** Since the whole square is four units on a side, you can see that each smaller square must be one unit on a side. To find the answer to this question, just count the number of shaded squares and half-squares.

4. **C** Since square $ABCD$ has a side (s) of 2, its area (s^2) is 4. Since circle O has a radius (r) of 1, its area (πr^2) is π. To find the area of the shaded region, just subtract the area of half the circle from the area of the square: $4 - \pi/2$.

5. **B** If you set up the equation and multiply both sides by 4/3, you'll find that $a = 24$:

$$\frac{3}{4}a = 18$$

$$\frac{4}{3} \times \frac{3}{4}a = \frac{18}{1} \times \frac{4}{3}$$

$$a = 24$$

Thus, 1/3 of $a = 24/3 = 8$.

6. **A** If one factor is increased by a given amount and the other factor is decreased by the same amount, the net effect is nil.

7. **B** To arrive at the correct answer to this problem, you have to be careful not to count the 9 students who can play both the infield and the outfield twice. If 22 students can play the infield, 30 can play the outfield, and 9 can play both, then 13 can play only the infield and 21 can play only the outfield. Thus the infielders and outfielders account for 43 of the 60 students, leaving 17 who can't play either the infield or the outfield.

8. **A** Column A equals 0.018; Column B equals 0.011.

9. **B** If you know the standard right triangles, you can solve this problem very quickly because the right triangle in Column A is a multiple of the 3-4-5 right triangle. This means that its base must be 8 and its perimeter 24, which is less than the perimeter of the rectangle in Column B (28). If you don't know the standard right triangles, you can still solve the problem the long way—by applying the Pythagorean theorem to find the base of the right triangle:

$$\text{leg}^2 + \text{leg}^2 = \text{hypotenuse}^2$$
$$6^2 + x^2 = 10^2$$
$$36 + x^2 = 100$$
$$x^2 = 64$$
$$x = 8$$

10. **C** You know that $xy = z$. If you divide both sides of that equation by y^2, you get $xy/y^2 = z/y^2$, or $x/y = z/y^2$.

11. **C** An inscribed angle that cuts off the same arc as a central angle always has exactly half the degree measure of that central angle. Therefore $y = x/2$, or $2y = x$.

12. **C** Perform all the operations within parentheses first: $3(3) \times (3)(3) = 9 \times 9 = 81$.

13. **D** It's possible to figure out what the 8 apples in Column A would cost. But because the weight of apples varies, it's not possible to figure out what the 8 apples in Column B would cost. So the comparison is impossible.

14. **D** Don't assume that the square root of n must be greater than the cube root of n. If n is a fraction less than 1 (a possibility that is not ruled out), the cube root will be larger than the square root.

15. **A** Remember that a prime integer is one that cannot be divided by any other integer except itself and 1. The largest prime integer less than 20 is 19; the largest even integer less than 20 is 18.

16. **D** Point Q may be anywhere along the square. In most locations, OQ will be longer than OP. However, if Q is located at one of the four points where the square and the circle touch, then OQ will be equal to OP. Since two answers are possible, the correct choice is D.

17. **C** Just add up the four terms in Column A and divide by 4 (the number of terms). The sum is $4r + 4$; therefore the average is $r + 1$.

18. **A** Since 10% of \$90 is \$9, Column A equals \$81. Column B equals 67% of \$120, or \$80.40. (You can answer this question in your head by figuring that 33% is a little less than 1/3, and 1/3 of \$120 is \$40; so Column B is a bit more than \$80.)

19. **A** The factors of 18 greater than 1 and less than 18 are 2, 3, 6, and 9; their sum is 20. The factors of 21 greater than 1 and less than 21 are 3 and 7; their sum is 10.

20. **B** As defined,)17(= 0, since 17 is a prime number. This tells you that Column A equals 0. If you then note that neither the numerator nor the denominator in Column B is a prime number, you can conclude that the value of Column B must be greater than 0.

21. **D** First, simplify the equation. You'll get this:

$$4a + 7 = 9 + \frac{8a}{2} - 2$$

$$4a + 7 = 9 + 4a - 2$$

$$4a + 7 = 7 + 4a$$

An equation like this ($4a + 7 = 7 + 4a$) is true by definition. It tells you *nothing* about the value of a.

22. **D** All you know about these two triangles is that side DF is twice as long as side AC. However, since you know nothing about the lengths of any of the other sides, you can't compare the areas of the two triangles. The fact that both triangles look more or less equilateral means nothing: as the note says, these figures are *not* drawn to scale.

23. **A** Assign n some value between -3 and -4, such as -3.7, and then subtract that value from -3: $-3 - (-3.7) = -3 + 3.7 = 0.7$, which is greater than 0.

24. **A** You know that y is twice as great as x. This alone enables you to make the comparison. Because Column A has "more of y" while Column B has "more of x," Column A must work out to a larger value. Test this by assigning arbitrary values to x and y—say, $x = 2$ and $y = 4$.

25. **C** An isosceles right triangle has two angles of 45° each. If $x = 45$, then y must equal 135, which is exactly 3 times 45.

26. **B** A little experimentation will show you that x must be a fraction less than 1.

27. **C** Before getting involved in any multistep procedures with a quantitative comparison, look for a quick and simple way to find the right answer. In this question, for example, it's not necessary to solve for x. If you just write the expression in Column A in the customary order, $2x^2 + 8x + 14$, you can tell at a glance that it is exactly double the expression on the left side of the equation that you're given, $x^2 + 4x + 7 = 13$. So its value must be double 13, or 26.

28. **C** As defined, x may equal 11, 13, 17, or 19. Use these numbers to figure out the four possible values of $2x + 1$.

29. **E** If 140 voters each voted for two candidates, then 280 votes were cast. The chart shows that Candidates A, B, and D received a total of 204 votes, leaving 76 for Candidate C.

30. **C** If x/y is less than 0, then either x or y is negative—but not both. Given that fact, Statement I and Statement III *could* be true. Statement II must be false: if x were equal to 0, then x/y would also be equal to 0.

31. **E** As defined, *2 = 6, *3 = 12, and *4 = 20. The product of all three is 1440.

32. **C** When fully unfolded, the screen measures 16 feet. When fully folded, the screen is as narrow as its widest section, 7 feet. The difference is 9 feet.

33. **C** You know that the three interior angles of a triangle add up to 180°. So:

$$4x + \frac{5x}{2} + x = 180$$

$$\frac{8x}{2} + \frac{5x}{2} + \frac{2x}{2} = 180$$

$$\frac{15x}{2} = 180$$

$$x = 24$$

Then, since $x + y = 180$, $y = 156$.

34. **E** Suppose $x = -2$. Then $1/x^2 = 1/4$; $x^5 = -32$; $(1/x)^3 = -1/8$; $x^2 = +4$; and $x^4 = +16$.

35. **A** The dashed lines in the following diagram show the possible squares that could have the two given points as vertices. Note that $(4, 3)$ can be a vertex of the square if the square is drawn catty-cornered.

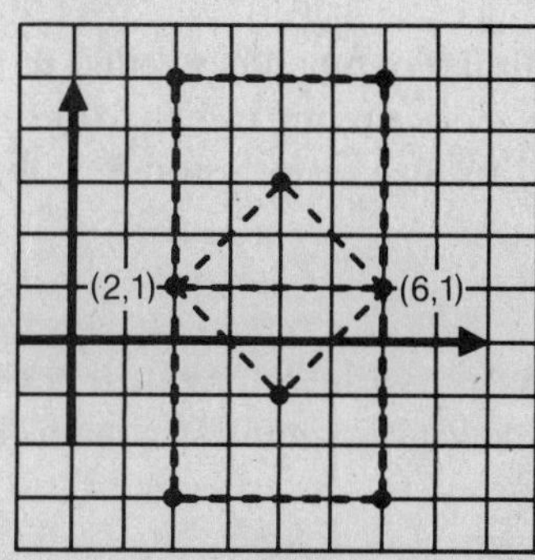

SECTION 3

1. **C** The verb *play* is plural, but its subject, *chance*, is singular. The two should agree: *chance plays.*

2. **A** The phrase at the beginning of the sentence is a misplaced modifier. Since it describes the United Nations, it should be next to the words *United Nations* (or the sentence should be rewritten in some other way).

3. **C** The word *reverted* is misused here. (Look it up.) The right word for this context is *converted.*

4. **E** No error here.

5. **C** An idiom error involving a preposition. Standard English usage demands "encouraged *by*," not "encouraged *with.*"

6. **A** The past participle of the irregular verb *run* is *run*, not *ran.*

7. **A** It's wrong to shift, as this sentence does, from *one* to *you*. Since the *you* phrases are not underlined, *if one intends* must be changed to *if you intend.*

8. **B** If you mentally eliminate the parenthetical phrase *the future leaders of the free world*, you'll quickly see the error in pronoun case. It should be "It is time for *us* to reevaluate," not "It is time for *we* to reevaluate."

9. **E** No error in this sentence.

10. **B** The verb is *falls*; the subject is *such forces*. Since the subject is plural, the verb should also be plural—*fall.*

11. **C** There is no clear reference for the pronoun *it*. What is *it*? Obviously, skiing is intended, but the word *skiing* doesn't appear in the sentence. (To correct the error, you'd have to change *it* to *skiing.*)

12. **A** *Lie* and *lay* are a troublesome pair of verbs. *Lie* means "to recline" or "to rest in place"; its principal parts are *lie, lay, lain*. *Lay* means "to put or place"; its principal parts are *lay, laid, laid*. This sentence clearly calls for the meaning "put or placed" ("the emphasis *put or placed* on the virtue of hospitality"), so the correct verb form is *laid*, not *lain.*

13. **D** If you were to complete the final clause, it would read "as single-mindedly as she has pursued her goal." Therefore, the shortened form of the comparison requires the pronoun *she*: "as single-mindedly *as she.*"

14. **A** A verb in the subjunctive mood is needed to describe a situation contrary to fact. In this case, since the sentence implies that the teachers' union is *not* willing to support the plan, the verb *was* should be subjunctive—*were.*

15. **E** No error here.

16. **C** The sentence contains a double negative: *cannot* and *neither ... nor*. Since *neither* is not underlined, *neither ... nor* cannot be changed. Therefore, *cannot* must be changed to *can.*

17. **C** Another shift from *one* to *you*. Since the third-person pronoun *one* is not underlined, it can't be changed and therefore should be used throughout the sentence.

18. **D** This is an error in verb tense. The sentence is discussing something that will have happened by a specified time in the future, so the future perfect tense should be used: *will have increased*.

19. **B** An idiom error. One would normally write "music *has played*," rather than the odd-sounding "music *has been to play*."

20. **D** The pronoun *them* has no clear antecedent since the word *stamps* doesn't appear in the sentence. You'd probably change *them* to *stamps* if you wanted to correct the error.

21. **B** Even though the subject of this sentence (*many*) follows the verb (*has occurred*), the two must still agree: *many have occurred*.

22. **E** No error here.

23. **B** In a sentence that contains two subjects joined by the conjunction *or*, the verb should agree with the closer subject. In this case, the closer subject, *leaders*, is plural, so the verb should also be plural: *are*.

24. **E** No error.

25. **B** A diction error. To *mitigate* something is to make it less severe. The word is being misused here, probably in place of *militate*, which sounds similar.

26. **B** The original version is very wordy. Choice B expresses the idea the most clearly and succinctly.

27. **E** Errors in parallel structure are very common in error correction items, so be prepared for them. In this sentence, the third element in the series should be parallel to the first two. In other words, it should be cast in the same grammatical form (adjective plus noun): "different sizes, various colors, and *unusual shapes*."

28. **D** The original sentence is a run-on. Choices B and C confuse the logical relationship between the two clauses. Choice E is improperly punctuated.

29. **C** Another error in parallelism. The last phrase must be in the same grammatical form as *in building houses* and *in making furniture*.

30. **E** In the original version, the verb *agreeing* is incomplete. Choices B and D are wordy and awkward, and choice C results in a run-on sentence.

31. **A** The original version is perfectly correct. The other versions are awkward, wordy, or confusing.

32. **E** Version A is a run-on sentence. Versions B and C use *but* and *however* in an illogical way, and versions C and D misuse the semicolon.

33. **C** The parallelism this time involves complete clauses: the students signed the petition, the teachers supported it, and the deans endorsed it.

34. **E** Choice E exhibits all the characteristics of good writing: it is clear, concise, and graceful. The other choices are awkward, wordy, or confusing in some way.

35. **B** *So* expresses the logical relationship between the two ideas in the sentence more precisely than any of the other connectives in the answer choices. *Thus* (choice C) would be acceptable, too, but in this context it must be preceded by a semicolon, not a comma. *Yet* (choice A) is illogical, choice D is clumsy, and choice E uses a semicolon where a comma will do.

36. **E** The underlined portion of the sentence must start with the words *the bill* because the opening phrase describes the bill, not its supporters or its reintroduction.

37. **C** Choice C is the most concise version.

38. **A** The original version preserves the parallelism required by the *not only ... but also* construction: they "not only failed ... but also ignored."

39. **D** Looking at the opening phrase as a modifier, you can see that the words *the nation* should follow immediately. Choices C and E use the semicolon where it doesn't belong.

40. **D** The original sentence is a run-on. Choices B and E distort or obscure the relationship between the two clauses. Choice C contains an unnecessary colon.

41. **C** *Speak* is a sometimes troublesome irregular verb. The correct form is *has spoken*, not *has spoke*.

42. **D** This is a pronoun case problem. The pronoun *whomever* is the subject of the verb *needs*. Therefore, it should be in the subjective case—*whoever*.

43. **E** No error here.

44. **D** The phrase *more nobler* is a double comparative. Either *more noble* or *nobler* would be acceptable, but *more noble* is preferable in this case because *more* also modifies *sincere*.

45. **C** Mentally eliminate all the words that come between the verb and the subject. The verb is *was*; the subject is *members*. The plural subject demands the plural verb—*were*.

46. **C** A comparison introduced by the word *as* must be completed by the word *as*. So the phrase *the way* in this sentence would have to be changed to *as*: "*as* pessimistic ... *as*."

47. **A** *Nor*, not *or*, should be used with *neither*.

48. **E** No error.

49. **C** The idiom is "deny *to*," not "deny *from*."

50. **C** In English the imperfect tense (for example, *was running*) is used only to emphasize the *continuity* of an action that took place during some specified period in the past, so in this sentence it is inappropriate. The point is not that Alfred E. Smith *was running* for president throughout 1928 but that he *did run* for president in 1928. *Was running* should be *ran* (simple past tense).

SECTION 4

1. **D** To *abbreviate* something is to make it shorter. The opposite is to make it longer, or *prolong* it.

2. **E** Someone *glib* speaks smoothly; someone *inarticulate* speaks awkwardly. Eliminate subtle wrong answers B and C by checking them backward: the opposite of *uninformed* is *well-informed*; the opposite of *tactless* is *tactful* or *polite*.

3. **D** *Despondent* means "depressed," "dejected," or "gloomy." *Hopeful* or *cheerful* would be a good antonym. *Energetic* doesn't quite work because the main idea is not how much energy one has but how high one's spirits are.

4. **A** A *furtive* action is secret or stealthy. An *overt* action is open and aboveboard.

5. **A** To be *insensible* is to be without feeling or awareness. To be *sensible* (the opposite) is to be *conscious* or *aware*.

6. **B** *Pugnacious* means "aggressive," "bellicose," "spoiling for a fight." *Pacific*, means "peaceful." (The Pacific Ocean is reputedly calm.)

7. **B** Literally, *enthrall* means "to capture or enslave." Figuratively—and more commonly—it means "to fascinate." So the best antonym here is *bore*. Choice A, *dull*, might be a good antonym for the adjective *enthralling*, but not for the verb *enthrall*.

8. **D** When something is in *abeyance*, it is in an inactive state. Therefore, the opposite is to be in an *active state*.

9. **C** To be *complacent* is to be self-satisfied or smug. The opposite is to be *striving*—that is, to be seeking improvement or self-betterment.

10. **A** A *dilapidated* house is in need of repairs; *shipshape* is an exact antonym. Choices C and D don't quite work: the opposite of *fresh* is *spoiled* or *old*, and the opposite of *presentable* is *bad-looking*, which is not exactly the same as *dilapidated*. Checking the choices backward like this will help you avoid choosing answers that are only partly right.

11. **E** *Unwitting* literally means "not knowing"; it is used to describe something done without awareness. Thus, a good opposite is *aware*, *intentional*, or *deliberate*.

12. **B** *Chimerical* comes from *Chimera*, a fabulous fire-breathing monster in Greek mythology with the head of a lion, the body of a goat, and the tail of a serpent. Appropriately enough, *chimerical* means "fantastic," "unreal," or "imaginary."

13. **E** *Cadaverous* means "extremely thin." There are many good antonyms; the best one here is *corpulent*, which means "fat."

14. **C** A *dearth* of something is a lack or a shortage. The opposite is *plenty*. Choices D and E aren't "opposite enough" to be correct.

15. **C** To *accede* to a demand is to give in to it or to agree; to *refuse* is the opposite.

16. **A** The two ideas in the sentence should contrast with one another. Choice A works because it seems contradictory to attribute two poems *different* in style to a *single* author.

17. **E** It seems likely that *accidents involving* helicopters would lead to questions about their use in areas where many people live.

18. **E** The point of the first half of the sentence is that the tax system must be fair or the government will not collect as much revenue (tax money) as it expects to collect. Choice E explains why: if a tax system is not *equitable*, or fair, people will *evade*, or find ways to avoid, payment of their taxes.

19. **D** Again, the two halves of the sentence must be consistent with one another. In both clauses, the point is that economic failures lead to a rise in totalitarianism.

20. **B** The first half of the sentence discusses military uses of outer space; hence choice B is best. Choice D is wrong because activities such as satellite surveillance, although military, are not violent.

21. **B** As the first paragraph states, the present "uniformity of tint is due only to time." Choice B paraphrases this statement.

22. **B** Look back at paragraph 3. It shows that the excavation of Olympia gave evidence concerning the system that the ancient Greeks followed when they colored their buildings.

23. **E** Reread the first sentence of paragraph 4, which describes the ancient Greek use of color as "so strange to us and, on first acquaintance, so little to our taste." Don't assume that answer B is correct just because the passage deals with architects of an ancient civilization.

24. **C** Look at the last sentence of paragraph 4. Choice A is wrong because the passage states that we would not like the ancient Greek style of coloring buildings. Choice B is contradicted by the last sentence of the passage. And choices D and E are simply unsupported by the passage.

25. **A** See the last paragraph: "This theory does not explain everything."

26. **D** Choice D sums up the passage well. Neither the idea of exploitation (choice A) nor the relationship between Lewiston and his wife (choice E) is significantly stressed. There is no evidence that the wheat crop has been poor (choice B). And choice C distorts the passage by making the decision sound voluntary.

27. **C** As the local wheat dealer, Bridges is plainly well-off and important. The style of building he works in reflects this. His attitude toward Lewiston is not "haughty" (choice B); he seems sorry for what has happened to the price of wheat. Some of the other answer choices may be vaguely suggested by the passage, but none very clearly at all.

28. **E** Look back at lines 41–50 in the passage.

29. **D** By the time Lewiston arrives home, his mind is made up. So we can infer that his trip home has been a time of decision making for him. Choice E is not supported by the tone of the end of the passage; after all, Lewiston does have a plan for the future.

30. **A** Lines 37–40 make this clear.

31. **B** If today's crises involve the very survival of humanity, then clearly they are the most *crucial* in history. Some of the other answers may seem applicable, but none is as directly relevant.

32. **D** Logically, heavy rainfalls would have *filled* the reservoirs. And if the two clauses contrast with one another, then *genuine* is a good word for the second blank, since it suggests something surprising or apparently contradictory.

33. **E** It would make little sense to refer to pure research as the *goal*, *focus*, or *purpose* of science. Both *source* and *heart* are plausible words for the second blank, but only *applications*, from choice E, really works in the first blank.

34. **E** Since the sentence is about finding one's destined mate, both *wife* and *spouse* would seem to be possible answers for the first blank in the sentence. But if mere geographical proximity (nearness) is the main factor in our choice of a mate, then our romantic belief is likely to be *incorrect*, not *accurate*.

35. **B** The first half of the sentence tells us that black music was unacceptable to the general public in its "pure original form." So before it achieved "wide popularity," it must have been changed. The words in choice B fit this idea. *Adulterated* means "watered down" or "spoiled by the addition of impurities."

36. **A** *Anxiety* and *calm* are opposites, as are *embarrassment* and *composure*. Choices C and D do not present true opposites: *reassurance* may calm someone's *worry*, but it is not the opposite of *worry*; *strength* is the opposite of *weakness*, not of *lethargy*.

37. **A** To *hire* an *employee* is to bring him or her into a company; to *enroll* a *member* is to bring her or him into a club.

38. **C** A portion of an *article* that is reprinted in another publication is called an *excerpt*. Similarly, a portion of a *film* that is shown on a TV program is called a *clip*.

39. **B** A *storm* is a heavier, wilder form of rainfall than a *shower*, just as a *torrent* is a heavier, wilder flow of water than a *trickle*.

40. **C** To be *vindictive* is to seek *revenge* eagerly. To be *ravenous* (very hungry) is to seek *satiation* (satisfaction or fullness) eagerly. A *belligerent* person wants a fight, but not necessarily to gain *territory*. And a *forgiving* person offers, rather than seeks, *clemency*.

41. **D** An orchestra *performs* a musical *composition*; a cast of actors *enacts* a *drama*.

42. **E** A *sheaf* is a bunch of wheat stalks *gathered* together; a *stack* of something (hay, for instance) is a bunch of separate pieces *piled* together.

43. **A** Fishing *line* is wound on a fishing *reel* in much the same way that *thread* is wound on a *spool*. One doesn't usually speak of *tape* being wound on a *wheel* (choice D).

44. **D** A *historiographer* is someone who records observations, or writes, about the *past*. Similarly, a *cartographer* (mapmaker) records observations about, or charts, the *terrain* (countryside). Other answer choices pair different kinds of scholars with the things they study, but they do not express the key relationship of recording observations on paper.

45. **D** *Untapped potential* is like *accumulated capital*: both are forms of wealth waiting to be developed and used.

SECTION 5

1. **D** Just multiply $10 \times 4 \times 3$.

2. **B** The third (unmarked) angle in the triangle on the left has a degree measure of $90 - x$. The degree measure of the vertical angle opposite it in the triangle on the right is the same (by definition). Thus we know that y and z must add up to 180 minus the degree measure of the third angle: $y + z = 180 - (90 - x) = 90 + x$.

3. **D** You can find the number of combinations by multiplying 3×4. Or you can list the possible combinations, calling the jersey colors A, B, and C and the pant colors W, X, Y, and Z: AW, AX, AY, AZ, BW, BX, BY, BZ, CW, CX, CY, and CZ.

4. **C** For a problem like this, you should sketch a grid in the margin of your test booklet and plot the points. If you do, you'll see that point (3, 4) falls just outside the circle, to the right and above. All the others fall inside.

5. **C** The inequality tells you that x is a fraction less than 1. When that is so, x^2 is always less than x.

6. **D** You can work the average out exactly by adding the four terms and dividing by 4, or you can round off each number to the nearest integer and (probably) do it in your head: $27 + 33 + 30 + 19 = 109$; $109 \div 4$ is a little over 27.

7. **A** The diagonal of a square equals the side of the square times $\sqrt{2}$. (You should remember this for the SAT.) So, in this case, each side of the square equals $2/\sqrt{2}$, or $\sqrt{2}$ (since 2 is equivalent to $\sqrt{2} \times \sqrt{2}$). To find the volume of the cube, multiply $\sqrt{2} \times \sqrt{2} \times \sqrt{2}$ and get $2\sqrt{2}$.

8. **E** By experimenting, you'll find that set $A = \{-1, 0, 1, 2, 3, 4\}$ and set $B = \{-3, -2, -1, 0, 1, 2\}$. The two sets have four common members.

9. **E** If $x - y = 6$, you can just substitute 6 for $(x - y)$ in the second equation: $9 - 6 = 3$.

10. **B** In a 30°-60°-90° triangle, the sides measure, proportionately, 1-$\sqrt{3}$-2. In the example shown, since the shortest side measures 3, you know that every length should be increased by a factor of 3. So the longer leg measures $3\sqrt{3}$.

11. **A** This is a long, complicated word problem, but you can work it out if you start with what you know. You know that train 1 travels at a rate of 48 miles per hour and train 2 at a rate of 60 miles per hour. You also know that train 2 starts traveling $1\frac{1}{2}$ hours after train 1. So if train 1 travels x hours (you don't know how many), then train 2 travels $x - 1\frac{1}{2}$ hours. With this information you can express the distance traveled by each train in terms of x:

	Rate	×	Time	=	Distance
Train 1	48	×	x	=	$48x$
Train 2	60	×	$x - 1\frac{1}{2}$	=	$60x - 90$

Finally, you know that train 2 starts out 30 miles "behind" train 1, so it has to travel the same distance as train 1 plus an extra 30 miles in order to overtake it. This means that when train 2 overtakes train 1, the distance traveled by train 1 ($48x$) is exactly 30 miles less than the distance traveled by train 2 ($60x - 90$). With this information you can set up an equation and solve for x:

$$48x = (60x - 90) - 30$$
$$120 = 12x$$
$$10 = x$$

Now, x is the number of hours train 1 travels before it is overtaken by train 2. So if train 1 travels 10 hours after departing at 2 P.M., the two trains will meet at 12 midnight.

12. **B** All of the numbers will round off to 2.2, except for 2.02, which will round off to 2.0.

13. **D** If $y/5 = 2$, then $y = 10$. So if $x = 12 - y, x = 2$.

14. **E** Again, start with what you know and gradually fill in what you don't know. The right base angle of the triangle is supplementary to the angle marked $y°$, so it must measure $180 - y$. The left base angle of the triangle corresponds to the angle next to the one marked $x°$ (since $\ell_1 \| \ell_2$), so it must measure $180 - x$. Now, since the three angles of a triangle always add up to 180°, you can find the value of z simply by subtracting the values of the two base angles from 180: $z = 180 - (180 - x) - (180 - y) = 180 - 180 + x - 180 + y = x + y - 180$.

15. **E** The first 10 students earned a total score of 920; the second 10 earned a total score of 840; together, the first 20 earned a total score of 1760. If all 25 students averaged 86, then the total score for the class was 2150. Subtract 1760 from 2150 and you see that the last 5 students earned a total score of 390, for an average of 78.

16. **B** The time shown is 9:20. In 6 hours and 45 minutes, it will be 4:05, and the hands will be in the C and A regions.

17. **A** Measure 9 pounds using the 1, 3, and 5; measure 13 pounds using the 1, 5, and 7; measure 16 pounds using the 1, 5, and 10; and measure 18 pounds using the 1, 7, and 10. You can measure 8 pounds, but not with exactly three weights.

18. **D** You can work out this kind of problem only by being methodical. Build up the formula step by step. The cents collected in an hour is ci (cents per cone times cones per hour). To turn that into dollars, simply divide by 100: $ci/100$. You now have dollars collected per hour. If you call x the number of hours it takes to collect d dollars, then d equals dollars per hour times x: $d = ci/100 \times x$. To solve for x, just multiply both sides of the equation by $100/ci$:

$$d = \frac{ci}{100} \times x$$

$$\frac{100}{ci} \times d = \frac{100}{ci} \times \frac{ci}{100} \times x$$

$$\frac{100d}{ci} = x$$

19. **D** Set P includes 3, 2, 1, 0, −1, and so on downward. Set Q includes all numbers, both fractions and integers, greater than 0. Of the five answer choices, only 3 is a member of both sets. Choice C (1.6) is greater than 0 (set Q), but it is not an integer (set P).

20. **E** There's a shortcut built into this problem. You don't have to solve for either x or y if you notice that you can get the answer you're looking for simply by multiplying the second equation through by −2:

$$y - x = 2$$
$$-2(y - x) = -2(2)$$
$$-2y + 2x = -4$$
$$2x - 2y = -4$$

Of course you can also take a longer route to the answer: Solve one equation for x or y (if $y - x = 2$, then $y = x + 2$), plug that value into the other equation, and work the problem out.

21. **E** The circumference of any circle equals π times the circle's diameter. If the circumference of each of these circles is 7π, then the diameter of each is 7. Rectangle $ABCD$ has a shorter side equal to one diameter (7) and a longer side equal to two diameters (14). Thus the area of $ABCD$ is $7 \times 14 = 98$.

22. **A** If $n - 3$ is even, then n itself must be odd. And if n is odd, the only expression that must also be odd is choice A. Try plugging in any odd value for n—say, $n = 5$—and figuring it out.

23. **A** Figure it out like this:

$$2z \div \frac{z}{3} = 2z \times \frac{3}{z} = \frac{6z}{z} = 6$$

24. **D** In ten revolutions, the pointer on dial A will pass 1 ten times. Therefore the pointer on dial B will move up ten numbers, to 3. In doing so, it will pass 1 twice, so the pointer on dial C will move up two numbers, to 6.

25. **B** Sketch the triangle and you'll see that it's a right triangle. If you know the standard right triangles, you'll recognize this one. It's the 5-12-13 right triangle, so its longest side must measure 13. If you don't know the standard right triangles, use the Pythagorean theorem to find the length of the longest side (the hypotenuse):

$$\begin{aligned} \text{leg}^2 + \text{leg}^2 &= \text{hypotenuse}^2 \\ 5^2 + 12^2 &= x^2 \\ 25 + 144 &= x^2 \\ 169 &= x^2 \\ 13 &= x \end{aligned}$$

SECTION 6

1. **B** *Static* means "unchanging"; the opposite, logically enough, is *changing*.

2. **C** A *radical* change tries to get at the root of a situation; by contrast, a *superficial* change attacks only the surface.

3. **A** *Doff* means "to take off" ("he *doffed* his hat"). The opposite is *put on*.

4. **D** To be *encumbered* is to be weighed down or burdened. *Unburdened* is thus a good antonym. Choice B is wrong because *encumbered* doesn't mean "heavy" but rather "bearing a heavy load."

5. **E** To *buttress* something is to support it or hold it up; to *undermine* something is to weaken it and make it fall. *Collapse* (choice C) is wrong because it doesn't refer to what one thing does to another, as both *buttress* and *undermine* do.

6. **E** When you *grovel*, you abase yourself and act with extreme humility. When you *strut*, you act high and mighty.

7. **D** A *fallow* field is one that is not being cultivated. Choice E is wrong because harvesting is something one does to a crop, not to a field.

8. **A** *Jocular* means "comic," "humorous." *Grave* means "serious," "somber."

9. **B** The root *grat*, which is related to *grace*, means "favor" or "gift." It is found in such common words as *grateful, ingratiate*, and *gratify*. It is also found in *gratis*, which means "given for free." The opposite of *gratis* is *offered for sale.*

10. **B** This question is about as tough as SAT antonyms get. The word *halcyon*, which is used mainly in the phrase "*halcyon* days," is an unusual word that means "peaceful." Its opposite, *turbulent*, means "disturbed," "troubled," or "agitated."

11. **C** Clearly, the cutting and shipping of ice was necessary before modern methods of *refrigeration* were invented.

12. **C** Both halves of the sentence say that the children's books of today were originally read by grown-ups.

13. **C** Of the verbs given, *proposed* is the only one that suggests "tremendous originality."

14. **A** *Internal, basic*, and *biological* are all good choices for the first blank, but only *stimuli* fits well in the second blank. (*Aberrant*, choice C, means "atypical," "unusual," or "abnormal.")

15. **D** The missing words should describe someone who believes in things he or she has not personally seen. Choice B is wrong because one doesn't usually think of a *student* as especially apt to believe in *intuition.*

16. **A** To *scribble* is to *write* in a casual, sloppy, hasty way. To *daub* is to *paint* in just the same way. *Mumbling* (choice C) is a form of speaking, not of *explaining.*

17. **C** A *dolphin* is classified as a *mammal*; a *toad* is classified as an *amphibian.*

18. **E** An *ingenue*, by definition, is innocent or *naive*. Similarly, a *sage*, by definition, is *wise.*

19. **E** Just as an *abridgement* is a shortened form of a *book*, so an *abbreviation* is a shortened form of a *word.*

20. **B** An *orchestra* is a group of people led by a *conductor*. A *company* (of soldiers) is a group of people led by a *commander*. Neither a *classroom* (choice A) nor *music* (choice C) is a group of people at all.

21. **C** A *malingerer* is someone who habitually *shirks* work. A *procrastinator* is someone who habitually *postpones* doing things.

22. **D** One *cultivates* a *field* in order to raise crops; one *stocks* a *lake* in order to raise fish. The idea in both cases is to encourage something to grow so that one can harvest it at maturity.

23. **C** The two words in the pair are opposites. Choice B doesn't work because *singular* and *multifarious* aren't really opposites; *singular* means "unusual" or "unique," while *multifarious* means "having many forms."

24. **E** A *grimace* is a facial expression that may reflect *exertion*. In the same tone, the *contortion* of one's face may reflect *pain*. A *smile* (choice C) may reflect pleasure in one's companion, but it doesn't reflect *companionship.*

25. **A** *Litigation* is the professional activity in which an *attorney* specializes, just as an *operation* is the special activity of a *surgeon.* Choices D and E are wrong because *knowledge* and *salvation* are not activities.

26. **A** The central focus here is not the theory behind atomic timekeeping, but the way in which the theory was used in developing a practical timekeeping device.

27. **C** Reread paragraph 2. The main difference between the two types of timepieces is that the frequency standard used in an atomic clock is more stable than that used in a mechanical clock.

28. **B** In the first two paragraphs, choices A, C, D, and E are all mentioned as examples of frequency standards. A digital display is merely a way of recording the progress of time, not of measuring it (see the last sentence of paragraph 1).

29. **C** Dr. Burgess's point is that the radiation frequency emitted by an atom is as regular as the ticking of a clock. He is using the word *clock* metaphorically, not describing an actual timepiece.

30. **B** Look at the last sentence of the passage. The first atomic timekeeping device was significant not because of its accuracy but because it was a first step in "linking time with the atom." Choice E is wrong because the clock relied on the ammonia *molecule*, not atom, to regulate its rate; there is no such thing as an ammonia atom.

31. **E** The crucial point is the *causes* of crime, not just crime in general. Choices A and C are too narrow, leaving out major chunks of the passage.

32. **E** As paragraph 2 explains, Lombroso thought that crime might be a throwback to the behavior of an earlier, primitive human being.

33. **B** Review the last three paragraphs. All of the modern theories discussed there relate crime to social causes.

34. **D** See the last sentence of paragraph 1. The classical criminologists believed in punishment as the primary means of controlling crime.

35. **E** The author describes the theories but does not evaluate or choose among them.

36. **B** Reread the third sentence of paragraph 2. Choice A sounds plausible, but it is not supported by the passage. Choices C and E are specifically rejected by paragraph 2.

37. **D** The author cites Seton's estimates without any critical comments and thus seems to accept them as accurate.

38. **B** If there were forty to sixty million bison spread over an area of three million square miles, then the bison density would have been somewhere between thirteen and twenty bison per square mile.

39. **A** According to the last paragraph, the gun and the fence were responsible for seriously depleting the bison herds. (See lines 37–39.)

40. **C** The facts described in answer C are ironic because they show that, in effect, the Indian hunters became so good that they hunted themselves right out of work. The other statements offered as answer choices aren't really ironic.

PART

3

SAT Study Program: Unit 1

LESSON 1
Basic Strategies for the SAT

OBJECTIVES

☐ To understand why the SAT requires special test-taking strategies

☐ To learn how to use your time and energy effectively when you take the SAT

☐ To develop the test-taking skills that will enable you to earn your highest possible scores on the SAT

How to Take a Standardized Test

1.1 What Is a Standardized Test?

Teachers and testing experts refer to the SAT as a *standardized* test. It's important for you to know what that means. Many students lose points on the SAT because they don't understand the nature of the test and what the test makers are looking for. They prepare ineffectively and waste time and energy while taking the test. This won't happen to you if you take the time now to learn a little about the nature of the SAT.

A standardized test is designed by test-making experts to be taken by many students at different times and in different places. The questions are designed to be fair to students of widely varying backgrounds. The method of administering the test is rigidly controlled. And the test is scored in such a way as to make up for differences in the difficulty level of different tests.

You can see the difference between a standardized test and a typical classroom test. A classroom test is given to twenty-five or thirty students in a single location; a standardized test is given to thousands of students all over the country. A classroom test is administered in accordance with flexible rules that vary from teacher to teacher and from class to class; a standardized test is administered in accordance with rigid rules that are carefully designed and strictly enforced. A classroom test is graded subjectively by hand; a standardized test is graded objectively by machine.

Because the SAT is a standardized test, you need to know certain special test-taking strategies. That's what this lesson is all about.

1.2 A Test of Skills

The SAT is taken by students from every kind of school—inner-city, suburban, rural, rich, poor, and so on. Some of the students have studied chemistry, physics, and geology; others may have had only one elementary science course. Some have studied foreign languages; others have not. The SAT is designed to be fair to all of these students.

Therefore, you'll find that the SAT is mainly a test of skills, not of factual knowledge. You don't need any specific information to answer most SAT questions. For example, if a reading comprehension passage deals with U.S. history, the questions will not assume that you know anything about U.S. history. They will deal only with what is discussed in the passage. Similarly, the TSWE will not expect you to know any terms of English grammar. It will just ask you to distinguish "good English" from "bad English" by using your ear.

Of course you do need to have some factual knowledge for the SAT-mathematical sections. However, that knowledge is limited, for the most part, to the basic rules of math. Nearly all the problems are drawn from arithmetic, elementary algebra, and plane geometry. So students who have taken advanced courses in trigonometry or calculus don't have any special advantage.

When preparing for the SAT, remember that the SAT tests skills, not knowledge. Memorizing facts, dates, formulas, names, or vocabulary words is not a good way to prepare for the SAT. You can't get high scores by spilling out facts. The SAT tests what you can do, not what you know.

1.3 No "Trick" Questions

Because the SAT is designed to be fair to all kinds of students, it usually does not test obscure skills, words, or ideas. This fact should influence how you prepare for the SAT. When studying math, for example, concentrate on the basic rules of arithmetic, algebra, and geometry. Don't spend time reviewing minor or advanced topics that your teacher or textbook may have touched upon. They won't appear on the SAT.

Many vocabulary study books give you hundreds of obscure words to learn. Some SAT study guides include such word lists. Don't waste your time with word lists like these. The vocabulary on the SAT consists only of words that a well-read twelfth grader should know.

Furthermore, the SAT doesn't include "trick" questions. Some of the questions are hard, and you have to read all of them carefully, but none are designed to trap you into making dumb mistakes. The test makers are not trying to prove how clever they are; nor do they want you to get a low score. They try hard to make the tests fair. So if a question on the SAT seems easy, don't worry. It's not a trap. Whatever seems obvious on the SAT usually *is*.

1.4 Varying Levels of Difficulty

You can expect questions at many levels of difficulty on the SAT. A few will probably seem surprisingly easy. A few will probably seem very hard. Most will fall somewhere in between. This is how standardized tests are normally made. The test makers want to sort out the students into various levels, from those who will earn very low scores to those who will earn very high ones. To do so, they must devise questions of varying levels of difficulty.

When you take the SAT, you'll find that each group of questions—a group of fifteen antonyms, say, or a group of twenty quantitative comparisons—will start out fairly easy and gradually get more difficult. (The exception is reading comprehension questions, which are not arranged in order of difficulty.) As you'll learn later, it's best to do the easier questions first.

In addition, the answer choices for each question—for each *verbal* question, at least—will vary in subtlety. Sometimes the right answer will be obvious. For many questions, though, more than one answer will be partly correct. It's important not to choose the first answer that seems right. Another answer may be "more right" than the first one. Remember, your job is to choose the *best* answer, not just a good one. So always read every answer to each question. One or two wrong answers may be very tempting.

1.5 Expect to Get Some Questions Wrong

Performance levels on a standardized test are very different from those on a classroom test. This can be alarming if you're not prepared for it.

On most classroom tests, you need to get at least sixty-five percent of the questions right to pass. A score of eighty percent right is a good one, and you need ninety percent right or more to earn an excellent grade.

Standardized tests are very different. On a typical SAT, the average student will get less than half of the questions right. If you get sixty or sixty-five percent of the questions right, you will score well above average. And seventy-five or eighty percent right will earn you a very high score. Very, very few students get ninety percent or more right.

You see, then, that you should expect to get several questions wrong on each test section. You mustn't become discouraged if you find that some of the questions are very hard. Just narrow your choices, select an answer, and move on. A few wrong answers will not hurt your score very much.

Using Your Time Effectively

1.6 The Time Factor on the SAT

Among test makers, the SAT is known as a moderately speeded exam. *Moderately speeded* means that time is a factor in how well students do, but not an overwhelming one. Most students finish most questions on the SAT.

If you pace yourself on exam day, you'll probably finish most of the questions, too. But you do have to pace yourself. In a mathematical section with thirty-five items, for example, you have less than 52 seconds to answer each question. In a TSWE section, which includes fifty items, you have only 36 seconds to answer each question. Some questions, of course, won't take you that long, and you can use your "extra" time on the harder ones. But the temptation to keep working on a difficult question until you find the correct or the "best" answer will be great. So you have to learn to budget your time efficiently. In this part of the lesson, you'll get some pointers on the "clock-wise" approach to the SAT.

1.7 Budgeting Your Time

To set up an effective time budget for each section of the SAT, you should *preview* the section. When the proctor gives the signal to start working, open your test booklet and spend a few seconds looking through the entire section. If you're familiar with the formats of the six test sections ahead of time (see Sections 0.15, 0.19, and 0.23), you should know the number and the kinds of questions you're facing, as well as the order in which they're arranged. Estimate the amount of time you have for each question, and, if you can, figure out which ones you can probably answer most quickly. Start with those—even if they don't come first in the section.

Since the time limit for each section is 30 minutes, you'll probably find it easier to keep track of your time if you reset your watch to 12:00 at the start of each section. Doing so will enable you to tell at a glance how many of your 30 minutes remain.

Check your watch every 5 minutes. Keep tabs on whether you're behind or ahead of schedule. For instance, if you're working on a verbal section with forty items, after 10 minutes you should have answered thirteen or fourteen questions. If you've answered only eight at that point, you should speed up. If you've answered eighteen, you can work more deliberately.

But remember: *Do the easy questions first.* You can do them faster, you have a much better chance of getting them right, and you get just as much credit for the correct answer to an easy question as you do for the correct answer to a hard one. The SAT doesn't reward you for perseverance; it rewards you for correct answers. The more correct answers you mark, the higher you score. So when you preview a test section, find the questions that look easiest to you, and start with them. Then if you run out of time, you may miss out on a few hard points, but you won't miss out on several easy ones.

Besides, starting out with the easy questions will boost your confidence. After reeling off a bunch of correct answers, you may not find the harder questions quite so intimidating.

1.8 Hit the Ground Running

When you take the SAT, you don't get any extra time to read the directions for each section. That time is included in the 30 minutes you're allowed to work on the section. It's good strategy, therefore, to learn the directions for all the sections *before* you take the test. Some of them—particularly the ones in the math sections—are long. If you learn them in advance, you won't have to waste precious time reading them on exam day. You can simply skim them—or, since they're always the same, just ignore them—and get right to work on the questions. (By the way, the directions in the practice tests in this book are the same as the directions on the real SAT. Study them until you know them well.)

1.9 Don't Get Bogged Down

The most important rule for using your testing time well is *keep moving*. Remember, it's not worth your while to spend 3 or 4 minutes puzzling out the answer to one tough question when you could be answering four or five easier ones instead. If you can't figure out the answer to a question quickly, put a check by it in your test booklet and move on. You can always go back to it later if you have time.

Remember this, too: The test makers know that you have only a short time to answer each question. Therefore, they write most of the questions—especially the math questions—with some simple "hook" by which the answer can be quickly unraveled. Very few SAT questions require lengthy study or calculation. So if you find yourself following a complicated procedure in an attempt to answer a question, *stop*. You're probably tackling the question in the wrong way. Step back and try to find a shortcut.

1.10 If Time Runs Out

Despite all your efforts, you may find yourself running short of time before you can finish all the questions in a section. If you do, don't panic. Follow these suggestions instead:

Suppose you discover that you have only 5 minutes left, and you still have fifteen questions to answer. Stop working and preview the remaining questions. Pick out those you can do most quickly and easily. In a verbal section, work only on antonyms or analogies, which don't take much time. In a math section, avoid word problems or questions based on graphs or charts. Before the clock runs out, tackle as many of the short-and-simple questions as you can.

What if there aren't any short-and-simple questions left? What if, for example, you're almost out of time on a verbal section and you still have three passages to read and fifteen reading comprehension questions to answer? Try this approach: First, glance at all three passages and choose the one that looks easiest. Second, preview that passage by skimming, rather than reading, it. (Lesson 3 explains how to preview reading passages.) It shouldn't take you more than 30 seconds or so to skim the passage. Third, make a good guess at as many of the questions as you can. Finally, if you still have a little time left, follow the same procedure with the second easiest passage. In only a few minutes, you can probably answer as many as eight or nine of the fifteen questions in this way, and you'll probably get five or six right. The skim-and-guess approach will also work with lengthy math questions such as graph or word problems.

Of course, if you budget your time effectively from the start, chances are you won't be faced with this kind of emergency situation.

1.11 Practice Working Efficiently

Since time is a factor on the SAT, practice working within the prescribed limits before the exam. When you take the practice tests in this book, spend only 30 minutes on each section. Use an alarm clock or a kitchen timer—and don't fudge the rules. Only through practice can you become comfortable with the time pressures you'll experience on the real SAT.

Effective Guessing

1.12 The Guessing Penalty

The SAT is scored with a so-called "guessing penalty." When your score is computed, a percentage of the number of wrong answers is subtracted from the number of right answers. The idea is to eliminate any advantage from purely lucky guessing.

Here's how it works: Suppose a test section contains forty questions, including ten questions you're not sure about. If you make purely random, wild guesses on those ten questions, the odds are you'll get two of them correct. (With five answer choices, you have a one-in-five chance of guessing correctly.) But with the guessing penalty, you'll lose a fourth of a point for each wrong answer. So your balance sheet for the ten questions will look like this:

2 correct	=	+2 points
8 incorrect × $\frac{1}{4}$-point deduction for each	=	−2 points
Net gain	=	0 points

As you can see, the guessing penalty takes away any advantage from purely random guessing. (On quantitative comparison questions, which have only four answer choices, the guessing penalty is a third of a point for each wrong answer.)

1.13 Guess Intelligently

Does the guessing penalty mean that you shouldn't guess? No! It just means that wild guessing probably won't increase your scores, but it probably won't decrease them, either. And, in any case, most of your guessing won't be wild.

You can almost always improve the odds on your guesses somewhat. On some questions, you may be able to eliminate one or two answers as clearly wrong. On others, you may be able to "guesstimate" an answer or figure out the general area in which an answer should fall, thereby narrowing the choices a little. On still others, you may have a strong hunch that one answer is right, even if you can't prove it. In any of these situations, you can and should make a "calculated" guess—and for good reason. Calculated guessing will usually improve your scores.

Consider again the example of ten questions that you're not sure how to answer. Suppose, with thought, you can eliminate two answer choices for each question as clearly wrong. This improves the odds of your guessing correctly from one in five to one in three. Therefore, you're likely to get three or four of the ten questions right, rather than just two. If you get four right, your balance sheet will look like this:

4 correct	=	+4 points
6 incorrect × $\frac{1}{4}$-point deduction for each	=	$-1\frac{1}{2}$ points
Net gain	=	$+2\frac{1}{2}$ points

A gain of a couple of points may sound small. But when these raw points are converted into your final scaled score, they may represent ten, twenty, or even thirty points. That's a chance worth taking.

1.14 Changing Answers

Students commonly believe that changing answers on a test usually results in a lower score. This belief is not true. Educational researchers have studied the question by looking at actual student test performances. They have found that, on the contrary, students who change answers during a test usually *improve* their scores.

The best strategy is this: If you are reviewing your answers and find an error you made or a fact you overlooked, go ahead and change the answer. Chances are your new answer is correct. On the other hand, if you've chosen an answer on the basis of a hunch, don't change it later just because you get a different hunch. Your original hunch is more likely to be right.

Marking Your Answers

1.15 Using the Answer Sheet

Standardized tests like the SAT use special answer sheets designed to be read by machines. Most students today are used to them, having taken standardized tests throughout their school years. If you're not, practice using the special fill-in-the-blank answer sheets before the exam. A carelessly marked answer sheet may cause correct answers to be scored as incorrect.

When you mark your answer sheet, remember three things: (1) Fill in the space for each answer that you choose *completely*. (2) Erase any stray marks that you make *completely*; otherwise, they may be counted as answers. (3) If you change an answer, erase the first answer *completely*; two answers for any one question are scored as no answer at all.

Don't do any figuring on the answer sheet. Use the margins of your test booklet for notes, calculations, diagrams, and so on. It's perfectly all right to do this. The test booklets are printed with wide margins for you to use as "scratch paper."

Be careful to keep your place on the answer sheet. Be sure that you don't accidentally skip an answer space or put two answers in one space. If you skip a question, be sure to skip an answer space as well. Check your place on the answer sheet regularly—every five questions or so. This will help you avoid mismarking the sheet.

1.16 If You Mismark Your Answers

If you find that you've mismarked your answer sheet, don't panic. Figure out where you went wrong. (For instance, you may find that all of your answers are one space off starting ten answers back.) Raise your hand and explain to the proctor what has happened. If you ask, you should be able to get a few minutes with your answer sheet at the end of the test to erase and correct your answers.

LESSON 2

Building Your Vocabulary for the SAT

OBJECTIVES

- ☐ To learn how to increase your vocabulary when you read
- ☐ To discover the best methods for understanding and remembering new words
- ☐ To learn how to use the dictionary as a tool for expanding and sharpening your vocabulary

Your Vocabulary and the SAT

2.1 The Importance of Vocabulary

A strong vocabulary—that is, knowledge of the meanings of words—is one of the basic tools for success on the SAT. Antonyms, of course, are a form of vocabulary question. Each antonym question includes six different words, some of them hard. The more words you recognize and understand, the more likely you are to answer the question correctly. The same is true of analogies and sentence completions. If you don't know the meaning of an important word in a question of either kind, you probably won't understand the question.

Vocabulary is important in reading comprehension as well. The stronger your knowledge of words, the easier it will be for you to understand the passages. Reading comprehension questions also may contain some difficult words. Even the TSWE is easier for those with strong vocabularies. Although the TSWE is a grammar test, some of the questions have to do with the correct use of words. The more you know about word meanings, the better you'll do.

There are two aspects to a strong vocabulary. One is the number of words you know. The other is how well you know them. It's important to be acquainted with a large number of words. The English language probably has the most extensive vocabulary of any language. The more of these words you know, the better.

Equally important, however, is making sure that you know well the words you do know. This means understanding exactly what they mean, what tone or feeling they usually convey, and how they are usually used in writing. Some SAT questions turn on subtle differences between words. So don't be concerned only about the size of your vocabulary; knowing words in depth is important, too.

2.2 Building Your Vocabulary with Word Lists

Some SAT study guides include lists of one thousand to three thousand vocabulary words. The authors recommend that you study as many of these words as possible every day. It's a big job.

Most experts on language and learning agree that this is a poor way of building your vocabulary. If you've ever tried to learn words this way, you probably agree, too. There are several reasons why most word lists are a bad way to prepare for the SAT.

First, many word lists, even those written especially for SAT preparation, contain words that would never appear on the SAT. These include archaic or obsolete words, technical terms, proper names, and foreign words. These words may be worth knowing, but they won't help you on the SAT.

Second, no word list in a book can exactly match your vocabulary-building needs. It will always contain many words that you already know and omit other words that you need to learn. Only a fraction of the words on any word list will be useful to you.

Third, and most important, it's very, very hard to learn words by memorization. Words on a word list can be learned only by constant repetition and practice. Words learned in this way tend to be forgotten quickly. It's an unnatural and inefficient way to learn words.

For these reasons, you won't find a word list in this book. Instead, you'll learn several better ways to build your vocabulary for the SAT. If you follow these suggestions, you'll probably learn more words than you would if you studied a vocabulary list. You'll have more fun, too.

One kind of list *is* helpful in learning vocabulary: a list of common word roots. Word roots are simple elements from which many words are built. Studying a list of word roots is worthwhile because each word root can help you learn a group of eight, ten, twelve, or more words. When you learn a word root, you are learning an *idea* that links together words in a meaningful way. Your mind can grasp and retain this kind of knowledge much better than it can absorb a set of unrelated words. Mastering the lists of word roots in Lessons 6 and 11 will help you to learn hundreds of useful vocabulary words.

Learning Words Through Reading

2.3 The Natural Method of Vocabulary Building

Chances are you already know well over ten thousand words. That's the size of the writing vocabulary of the average high school student. (The average reading vocabulary is even higher.) You probably learned almost all of those words without trying. How did you do it?

You learned them the natural way: by seeing or hearing them in their contexts. The *context* of a word is the setting in which it occurs in writing or speech. When you see or hear a word in a context, the context helps reveal the meaning of the word. You learn the word by observing or listening to how it is used and then using it yourself. This is how a baby learns to talk and how all of us learn new words throughout our lives. You do it every day, without even knowing it.

In order to expand and sharpen your vocabulary for the SAT, you can increase the efficiency of this natural method of vocabulary building. You can make sure that you encounter a larger number of new words in a variety of contexts and learn them in a way that will help you to remember them. Using this method, you can learn hundreds of new words within six or eight weeks.

2.4 Words in Contexts

How can the context of a word teach you its meaning? Let's look at an example.

We'll use an imaginary word: *snamor*. Obviously, it's impossible to tell what *snamor* might mean if you see it by itself. Even in a context, it may be hard to tell what *snamor* means if the context is brief or vague. From the sentence "The curtains were *snamor*," you can tell that *snamor* is probably an adjective (a word that describes a thing), but you can't guess what it means. It could mean "torn," "brightly colored," "lacy," "thick," "dusty," or many other things. But when the word appears in a more complete context, as it usually does in a story or a book, the context helps explain the word:

> Glancing through the window, Susan noticed a light shining in the garden. She could tell that the light was moving, but she couldn't tell what kind of light it was because of the *snamor* curtains covering the window.

This context suggests that the curtains are of a kind that admit light but diffuse it so that objects beyond cannot be clearly distinguished. So you can guess that *snamor* probably means something like "translucent," "gauzy," or "filmy." The context of the word reveals its meaning. Other uses of *snamor* elsewhere in the story, or in other stories, will add to your understanding of the word.

The example is artificial, but the point is real. You normally learn words by seeing or hearing them used in contexts. One way to increase your vocabulary is to develop your ability to learn new words from contexts. When you begin to do this, you'll find yourself learning new words almost every time you read. The key is learning to use the clues to word meanings that are usually built into their contexts.

2.5 Using Context Clues

There are four kinds of contextual clues to word meanings: straightforward definitions, synonyms or paraphrases, antonyms or opposites, and implied definitions. When you see a new word in any context, look for one or more of these kinds of clues. Here's how the process works:

1. *Straightforward definitions.* Sometimes, when an unusual word is introduced, a definition is provided nearby. When this happens, study the definition, make sure that you understand it, and reread the sentence containing the unfamiliar word. Try to see how the definition fits into the context. For example:

> The results of experiments with new drugs are often affected by patients' expectations. If patients believe that a drug will improve their condition, they often experience an improvement, even though the improvement may be only psychological and not physiological. To guard against this, researchers use a control group as well as an experimental group when they test a new drug. To the subjects in the control group, they give a placebo, that is, a pill or other medication that looks just like the drug but contains no active ingredient (it may be made of plain sugar or salt, for instance). Any improvement caused by the placebo is considered purely psychological.

In this passage, the unusual word *placebo* is used. Knowing that some readers will not recognize the word, the author defines it. Applying the definition to the word in its context, you can see what the passage is saying. The *placebo* is a "dummy" drug used to detect any psychological effects caused by patients' expectations of improvement.

2. *Synonyms or paraphrases.* Sometimes, when an unusual or unfamiliar word is introduced, the context contains another word that means the same (a synonym) or a group of words that mean the same (a paraphrase). Look for a synonym or a paraphrase when you come across an unfamiliar word. For example:

> Mr. Callahan's promotion to office manager brought out the martinet in him. He tried to create an atmosphere of rigid military discipline among his employees, and he flew into a rage over any error or misunderstanding, no matter how small.

Martinet is a hard word, but the second sentence paraphrases its meaning. A *martinet* is someone who believes in "rigid military discipline."

3. *Antonyms or opposites.* In some passages, an unfamiliar word is contrasted with some other, more familiar word or idea. By examining the context, you can find out what the unknown word does *not* mean, and this can help you understand what it *does* mean. For example:

> A painting, a sculpture, or a work of architecture has solidity and permanence. Once it is created, it normally lasts a long time and gives pleasure to many generations of viewers. Even a book is a relatively long-lasting object. By contrast, the beauty of a piece of music is ephemeral.

This passages draws a contrast between music and other kinds of art—painting, sculpture, architecture, and books. It says that those other kinds of art are solid and long-lasting, whereas music is *ephemeral.* Because of the contrast, you can tell what *ephemeral* means, even if you've never seen the word before. It means "short-lived," "quickly vanishing," "fleeting."

4. *Implied definitions.* This is the subtlest kind of contextual clue. In some contexts, only indirect clues to the meaning of a difficult word are given. You may not be able to determine the exact meaning of the new word. However, you can usually make a reasonable guess at its general meaning. For example:

> The sunlight drifting down through many layers of leaves, grass, and branches, moving to and fro in the ever-shifting breezes, transformed the forest floor into a variegated carpet of light and shadow.

You may not know the word *variegated.* It isn't defined in the sentence. If you think about the context, though, you may be able to guess what *variegated* means. Try to picture the scene described. You are told that the forest floor is a "carpet of light and shadow." This suggests that light and dark areas are scattered over the forest floor. You can guess, then, that *variegated* probably means "irregular," "multicolored," or "varied." A dictionary will show that this definition is almost exactly right.

As you can see, the context of an unknown word may give you direct or indirect clues to the meaning of the word. Practice looking for contextual clues every time you read. Such practice will prepare you for the SAT in several ways. It will help you learn new words. It will encourage you to analyze the meaning of what you read, which is a major skill tested on the exam. Most important, it will get you used to thinking carefully about words and their meanings.

Using the Dictionary in Building Your Vocabulary

2.6 Getting to Know the Dictionary

Contextual clues alone may not enable you to define every new word you meet. Another important step in expanding your vocabulary is learning to use the dictionary as a vocabulary-building tool.

First, be sure that you have a good dictionary. You need the kind known as a *college dictionary*. It will be a hardcover, not a paperback. It will probably have the word *college* in the title or on the cover. It will probably cost from twelve to twenty dollars (an important and worthwhile investment that will benefit you for years to come).

You need a college dictionary because some other kinds of dictionaries, such as the paperback ones, are not complete enough, accurate enough, or timely enough. The words and meanings you most need to find may be omitted to keep the dictionary small and inexpensive. Buying one of these dictionaries is a false economy.

Use your dictionary often. Every time you sit down to read—whether you're reading a textbook, a novel, a magazine, or anything else—get the dictionary off the shelf and put it next to you. There's a psychological reason for this. If you're sitting in a comfortable chair—perhaps with a snack in your lap—you probably won't get up to grab the dictionary when you find an unfamiliar word in your reading. If the dictionary is within arm's reach, you'll be much more likely to use it.

Learn to use all the information that's included in a dictionary entry. Make sure that you understand the pronunciation symbols, and practice saying each new word. Although you don't have to pronounce words on the SAT, you'll feel more at home with a new word if you know how to say it.

Read *all* the definitions for each word you look up. Often the most important meaning of a word—the one you need in order to understand a particular passage—will come near the end of the entry. And it's interesting and useful to see how the different meanings of a word are related.

Be sure to read the preface to your dictionary, too. It explains the order in which the definitions of a word are given. Some dictionaries list definitions in order of importance. In these dictionaries, the most common meaning comes first. In other dictionaries, the definitions are listed in historical order, with the oldest meaning first. Historical order can be confusing because the first definition of a word may be one that is no longer in use. For instance, the first definition of *awful* may be "inspiring awe"; the first definition of *nervous*, "strong, vigorous"; and the first definition of *condescending*, "gracious." All of these definitions are obsolete; they used to be common, but they aren't any longer.

2.7 Synonyms and Antonyms

Synonyms are words that are almost the same in meaning; antonyms are words that are almost opposite in meaning. For the word *brave*, *bold* and *courageous* are synonyms; *cowardly* and *timid* are antonyms.

Many dictionaries list both synonyms and antonyms for some words. Be sure to make a note of them. A synonym may be given as one definition of a word. If you know the synonym, you can remember the meaning of the new word more easily. If you don't, you can learn two words for the price of one. Antonyms, when given, usually appear at the end of an entry, often preceded by the abbreviation *ANT.* Try to learn these when you learn a new word from the dictionary. Remember, SAT vocabulary questions require you to recognize antonyms.

A very useful feature of some dictionaries is the synonym study. A *synonym study* is a one-paragraph discussion of several related synonyms. Whenever you come across a synonym study, read it carefully. It discusses in detail the exact meaning of each synonym and explains how the synonyms differ. No two words have *exactly* the same meaning; there are always subtle differences. A synonym study highlights those differences, which may prove to be very important on the SAT. Subtle antonym questions often turn on different shades of meaning in closely related words.

Here's an example of a synonym study from *The American Heritage Dictionary of the English Language*. Notice how precisely it distinguishes the various synonymous words.

> **Synonyms:** *brave, courageous, fearless, intrepid, bold, daring, audacious, gallant, valiant, valorous, doughty, game, gritty, mettlesome, plucky, dauntless, undaunted.* These adjectives all apply to admirable human action in difficult conditions. *Brave*, the least specific, is frequently associated with an innate quality, and *courageous* with the act of consciously rising to a specific test by drawing on a reserve of moral strength and righteousness. *Fearless* emphasizes, besides absence of fear, resolute self-possession; *intrepid* adds to this the sense of invulnerability to fear in any situation. *Bold* and *daring* stress not only readiness to meet danger but a desire to seize initiative; *audacious* intensifies those qualities, often to the point of recklessness. *Gallant* also implies indifference to danger, together with a noble display of courage, often in a losing cause. *Valiant*, said principally of persons, pertains to the bravery or courage of heroes, and *valorous* to their deeds. On a lower and perhaps more contemporary plane, *doughty* suggests formidableness (now usually humorously), and *game* and *gritty* imply dogged persistence and capacity for resisting pain. *Mettlesome* stresses spirit and love of challenge; *plucky* stresses spirit and heart in the face of unfavorable odds. *Dauntless* refers to courage that resists subjection or intimidation; *undaunted* more strongly suggests such courage that has been put to actual test.

By the way, because there are always subtle differences between words, even when they are close synonyms, a thesaurus can be a dangerous book to use. A thesaurus doesn't define words. It just lists synonyms and antonyms for them. And since it does nothing to indicate the differences among those synonyms and antonyms, it may misguide you. As a writing tool, a thesaurus may lead you to select a word that doesn't really fit the context in which you want to use it. As a vocabulary-building tool, a thesaurus may blur rather than sharpen your knowledge of words. A thesaurus can help add color to your writing by reminding you about words you already know, but it is not a very helpful study tool.

2.8 Etymologies

The *etymology* of a word is its history—where it came from, what its original meaning was, and how that meaning has changed over time. Dictionary entries usually list each word's etymology in brackets, immediately following its pronunciation and part of speech. A typical etymology includes the word's *source*—that is, the language from which it is derived—and *original meaning*. Learn to read etymologies, and study them when you look up new words. You'll discover that certain words from languages like Latin and Greek are sources of large numbers of English words. If you learn to recognize these word roots, you'll begin to see connections among many English words. These connections will make it easier for you to understand the words and remember their meanings.

Here's one example: If you look up the word *revolve* in the dictionary, you'll find that it comes from the Latin verb *volvere*, which means "to turn" or "to roll." It's not hard to see the connection between the meaning of *volvere* and that of the English word *revolve*. The same root—*vol*—also appears in other English words. For example, something *convoluted* is something turning, twisted, and confusing. *Evolution* is how something changes over time, how it "turns" into something else. And when something *devolves*, it "rolls" down or passes on to someone else. The basic idea of turning or rolling changes slightly in each word, but the connection is still there. Remembering the root *vol* can help you remember all the related words.

2.9 Making Your Own Word List

As you've learned, the best way to increase your vocabulary is by mastering the words you encounter in your reading. You've seen how contextual clues can help you decipher the meanings of new words. You've also seen how the dictionary can help you learn new words. Now, here is a method for putting these two techniques together to learn many new words before you take the SAT.

Get a notebook especially for vocabulary study. In this notebook, you'll create your own personalized word list. This list will not have most of the weaknesses of word lists in books. Because you create it, it will contain only words you don't already know. And because it is based on your reading, it will contain only words that contemporary writers really use—the kinds of words most often tested on the SAT.

Keep this notebook at your side, next to your dictionary, whenever you read. When you come across a new word, jot it down in your notebook, along with the sentence or the phrase in which you found it. Try to figure out the meaning of the word from its context. Make up your own definition.

Then look up the word in your dictionary. Find the relevant definition. See how close your guess was. Plug the dictionary definition into the context and see how it fits. Copy the dictionary definition into your notebook. Also copy down the root from which the word is derived. Try to see how the root gave rise to the English word.

Finally, make up your own sentence using the word. Make sure that the dictionary definition fits into your sentence. Write the sentence in your notebook to complete your entry for the word. This is the most important step in the whole method. You'll find that your recollection of any word is much stronger when you've used the word yourself. And the simple act of writing it down with your own hand helps you remember the word and its meaning.

Try to add to your word list every day. In no time at all you'll have a few hundred words. Review the words every so often. Quiz yourself by covering the definitions with a card and trying to define the words. After several repetitions, you'll know most of the words quite well.

This whole procedure should take you just a few minutes every day. Get into the habit of doing it regularly—the sooner the better. You'll learn many new words this way, and you'll boost your SAT scores as a result.

2.10 Use Your New Words

One point in the preceding section bears repeating: Using new words yourself is the most important step in learning them. If you take the trouble to use the words on your personalized vocabulary list when you're speaking or writing, whether in school or out, you'll quickly make the words your own. As an additional benefit, your writing style will probably improve, too.

LESSON 3
Techniques for Reading Comprehension

OBJECTIVES

☐ To learn what SAT reading comprehension passages and questions are like

☐ To understand the best methods of improving your reading comprehension skills for the SAT

☐ To recognize the most common structures of SAT reading passages

Reading Comprehension on the SAT

3.1 How Reading Skills Are Tested on the SAT

Every SAT-verbal section contains either ten or fifteen reading comprehension questions. These questions are based on two, three, or four reading passages, so you have to answer anywhere from two to five questions on each passage.

The passages range in length from about one hundred to about five hundred words (one to five paragraphs). They are drawn from the kinds of books and magazines that college freshmen are usually expected to read. So the passages you see on the exam will probably remind you of excerpts from textbooks, high-quality magazines, books on current events or social issues, or serious novels and short stories. They are written in a challenging style, with some hard words and some subtle or complicated ideas. However, there's nothing in any SAT passage that an intelligent high school student can't understand.

Passages fall into four main subject categories:

1. *Natural science.* This category includes such subjects as biology, chemistry, physics, geology, and astronomy. In a typical natural science passage you might read about what black holes are, how DNA works, or why earthquakes occur.

2. *Social science.* This category includes psychology, history, sociology, anthropology, and archaeology. A typical social science passage might deal with the treatment of mental illness, the causes of World War I, or the culture of a certain African tribe.

3. *The humanities.* This category includes literature, music, art, architecture, and philosophy. Typical humanities passages cover such topics as the novels of Herman Melville, the design of a certain cathedral, and romanticism in nineteenth-century music.

4. *Fiction.* This category includes stories about made-up characters. Fictional passages are often excerpts from novels or short stories.

In addition, the SAT occasionally includes a "wild-card" passage that doesn't exactly fit into any of these categories. It might be an excerpt from a speech, a portion of someone's memoirs, or a political manifesto. Such wild-card passages are rare. The verbal sections of the SAT normally include passages that fall into each of the four main subject categories.

You'll learn about what reading comprehension questions are like in Lesson 8. In this lesson, you'll study the art of reading itself.

3.2 Practicing Reading Comprehension

An important part of preparing for reading comprehension on the SAT is reading often and widely in the weeks before the exam. Practice reading every day. Get used to reading difficult material about challenging topics. This mental stretching will help you get in shape for the SAT.

There are many good materials to use in practicing reading for the SAT. Certain magazines are especially useful because they cover a wide array of topics. Get a few issues of *The New*

Yorker, the *Atlantic*, *Harper's*, the *New York Times Book Review*, *The New York Review of Books*, *Scientific American*, *Science*, and *Psychology Today*. Articles in these magazines are similar in style and content to the reading passages on the SAT.

Look for challenging books to read as well. There are many fascinating collections of essays on natural science, the social sciences, and the humanities. Your school or public librarian can suggest titles on topics that are new and challenging for you.

You will find this unfamiliar reading difficult at first. You may understand only a little of what you read. That's all right. Your comprehension will increase with practice. The main thing is to become comfortable reading material that you previously found intimidating.

Practice this difficult reading in half-hour sessions. You don't have to read a whole book; practice with single chapters, essays, or magazine articles. They're closer in length to the passages you'll be reading on the SAT, anyway. And don't feel that you must settle down in a library or a quiet room at home each time you practice reading. Use the bus, a cafeteria, or a park bench sometimes. The classroom where you take the SAT may not be quiet or comfortable, so your ability to concentrate despite distractions can be a valuable test-taking skill.

After you finish reading an article or chapter, quiz yourself on what you've read. Try to summarize the selection in your own words without referring to it. Write two or three sentences that sum up the passage. Also try to answer these questions:

What was the one most important idea or fact in the passage?

What was the author's purpose in writing the passage?

How did the author attempt to prove his or her point—through examples, through statistics, through quotations, through anecdotes, or through logic?

What was the author's attitude toward the subject?

If you can answer these questions, you've understood the passage.

It's worth taking the trouble to *write* your answers during these self-quizzing sessions. Even jotting a sentence or two on a piece of paper will be worthwhile. Putting the answers in writing forces you to focus and clarify your thoughts. Again, try to write your answers without looking back at the passage. On the SAT, you're allowed to look at the passages when you're answering the questions about them. However, it's very helpful to develop your memory through practice of this kind. The more you can remember about a passage on the SAT without referring back to it, the more quickly you can answer the questions about it.

3.3 Reading Speed

Many students wonder whether it's necessary to speed-read to do well on the SAT. The answer is no. The average person reads about 250 words per minute. At that rate, you can read all the reading passages in an SAT-verbal section in 4 to 6 minutes, which leaves you more than enough time to answer the questions. However, reading as fast as you can comfortably read will help you on the exam. It will give you more time to spend on the passage you find most difficult, as well as on any especially difficult questions. Reading fairly quickly also improves your concentration. Slow reading gives your mind time to wander. So you may want to work on increasing your reading speed as you practice reading.

First, figure out how fast you read now. Read some fairly difficult material, such as a textbook, for 5 minutes, and figure out how many words you read a minute. Then, each time you practice reading, aim at increasing your speed slightly. If you now read at 230 words a minute, for example, you might try to read a 2,000-word article in 8 minutes—250 words a minute. After a week or two, aim for 260 or 270 words a minute. A good final goal is about 350 words a minute. That's a fairly rapid speed which most people can reach pretty easily.

Using your finger or a pencil tip as a marker may help you increase your reading speed. As you read, move the marker down the center of the page slightly faster than you can easily read. Move the marker at a smooth, steady pace, and do your best to keep up with your reading. This will train you to read more quickly. It will also help you get used to making steady progress as you read, rather than starting and stopping frequently, which people often do without realizing it.

If you're a slow reader, you may have trouble with *reading regression*—that is, your eyes may slip back up the page after you've finished a line of print. If you sometimes find yourself reading the same line twice, this is your problem. Reading regression is easy to cure. Get a blank card a little wider than the page you're reading. Hold it across the page, covering what you've already read. Move the card downward as you read, as if a curtain were descending. Covering the material you've already read will prevent your eyes from slipping back up the page. A few sessions with the card should cure your reading regression.

The card has another value as a reading practice tool. It allows you to read each sentence only once, forcing you to concentrate on the meaning of each sentence. (Don't you concentrate better in class when your teacher announces, "'Now, listen up—I'm only going to say this once"?) Like anything else, concentration becomes easier with practice. After a while, it will be second nature.

The Three-Step Approach to Reading Comprehension

3.4 The Importance of Effective Reading

You have two jobs to do in tackling the reading comprehension items on the SAT. The first is reading the passage. The second is answering the questions about the passage. Of the two, the first is more important. If you read the passage effectively, you won't have much difficulty answering the questions. Therefore, don't rush through the reading stage. If your reading is hasty, chances are you won't be able to answer the questions correctly. A thorough, careful reading will earn more points and save you time in the long run.

Reading teachers have long suggested a three-step approach to reading comprehension: (1) previewing, (2) reading actively, and (3) reviewing. With some special changes to fit the requirements of the exam, the three-step approach to reading works very well on the SAT. Thousands of test takers have used it successfully.

In the rest of Lesson 3, you'll learn how to use the three-step approach on SAT reading passages. You'll find that it enables you to uncover and understand the full meaning of any passage more easily than ordinary reading can.

3.5 Step 1: Previewing the Passage

Before you actually start reading a passage on the SAT, you should preview both the passage and the question stems. To preview the passage, glance through it quickly. Read only the first sentence of each paragraph and the last sentence of the entire passage. The most important ideas in the passage often appear in these locations. Try to get a general idea of what the passage is about, what its main idea is, and how its content is organized. Don't try to understand any details at this point; just get a feel for what the passage says. You'll find that this procedure will prepare you effectively to read the passage with understanding.

Here's an example of how previewing works. On pages 78–79 you'll find the full text of a fairly long reading passage similar to the ones you'll find on the SAT. Just glance at it now—*don't* read it. You can see that it deals with Indian life, but you really can't tell much more about it at a glance. This is where previewing comes in. On the SAT, you would preview this passage by reading the first sentence of each paragraph and the last sentence of the passage. Here's what you'd read:

> From the time they first acquired the horse in the eighteenth century, the three tribes of the Blackfeet nation—Blackfeet, Bloods, and Peigans—turned to horse raiding as one of their main vocations.
>
> Blackfeet war parties were usually organized for one of two purposes: either to capture horses from enemy tribes or to revenge an attack suffered by their own people.
>
> The taking of human life was not usually one of the objectives of a horse raid.

The intertribal raiding for horses ended during the 1880s.

The last raid among the Montana Blackfeet seems to have occurred as late as 1892.

By this time, the country between the various Indian reservations was becoming too heavily populated for the raiders to travel undetected.

The lack of sympathy from the chiefs, the increased military and police protection, and the expanding white population were all factors that finally ended the horse-raiding careers of the Blackfeet.

Notice how much you can tell about the passage from those few sentences. You now know the topic of the passage: horse raiding among the Blackfeet Indians. You know many of the specific details discussed in the passage, such as how and why the horse raids were conducted. And you see how the passage ends: with a description of when and why the raids ceased. Thus, before you actually read the passage, you have a clear idea of what you will be learning and how the facts are organized. As you'll see, this will make reading the passage much easier. (If you like, go ahead and read the passage now.)

After you've previewed the passage, preview the stem of each question that follows. The *stem* is the part of the question that comes before the answer choices. It is usually a short sentence or a sentence fragment, such as "The main idea of the passage is," "The author regards Matisse as the most important nineteenth-century artist mainly because," or "According to the passage, which of the following is the most important cause of tidal waves?" Previewing the question stems will give you an idea of how detailed the questions are and what aspects of the passage they focus on. Don't read the answer choices yet. There are too many of them, and four out of five of them are wrong, anyway, so they may confuse you. Don't try to *remember* the question stems, either. If you do, you may not be able to concentrate while you're reading. Just skim the question stems quickly to help set yourself up for an effective reading of the passage.

Previewing shouldn't take much time. In fact, with a little practice, you should be able to preview a reading passage and a set of question stems in 30 or 40 seconds at the most. Work on this technique when you take the practice tests in this book, and you'll find that your previewing time is well spent.

Sample Passage

From the time they first acquired the horse in the eighteenth century, the three tribes of the Blackfeet nation—Blackfeet, Bloods, and Peigans—turned to horse raiding as one of their main vocations. Any of their enemies were possible prey for small war parties, but the transmountain tribes, such as the Nez Perce, Flathead, and Shoshone, were particular targets because of their fine breed of horses.

Blackfeet war parties were usually organized for one of two purposes: either to capture horses from enemy tribes or to revenge an attack suffered by their own people. A horse-raiding party was often made up of small groups of young warriors from different camps. Their party had no permanent organization but was usually formed for a single raid and then disbanded. A revenge party, on the other hand, was usually a large, well-organized group of warriors who were bent on killing their enemies. Their victims did not have to be the same persons who had attacked them; more often, the victims were not even from the same tribe. Any enemy death satisfied the need for revenge.

The taking of human life was not usually one of the objectives of a horse raid. The raiders preferred to creep into enemy territory undetected, take their booty of horses, and return to their own camps. They were often able to seize enemy herds grazing on the prairies, but the prized buffalo runners and racehorses were usually kept under closer guard within the enemy camp. These horses were tied to the owner's tepee—or, in some cases, even to the owner's wrist—by a long rope. It was considered a great feat if a raider could successfully creep into camp, cut this rope, and take the animal.

The intertribal raiding for horses ended during the 1880s. The last recorded raid in which a human life was taken occurred in 1889, when a war party of Bloods took forty horses from the Crow Indians. While returning north to their own reservation, they were suddenly attacked by Assiniboine Indians and managed to kill and scalp at least one of their attackers.

The last raid among the Montana Blackfeet seems to have occurred as late as 1892. The leader in this case was White Quiver, perhaps the greatest of all Blackfeet raiders. He stood trial before the Indian Court but, having turned over four horses alleged to have been stolen from the Crows, was released for lack of evidence.

By this time, the country between the various Indian reservations was becoming too heavily populated for the raiders to travel undetected. Therefore, they turned their attention to horses of white ranchers and farmers. For the next several years, young men unwilling to give up their old customs conducted raids against the whites, but they met with little success. The lack of sympathy from the chiefs, the increased military and police protection, and the expanding white population were all factors that finally ended the horse-raiding careers of the Blackfeet.

3.6 Step 2: Active Reading

The second step in effective reading for the SAT is active reading. Most people usually read passively. When you glance through a newspaper or zip through the latest thriller or romance, you are reading passively. The words and ideas simply flow by. If any are especially interesting, you may notice them. Otherwise, you quickly forget what you've read.

Active reading is a more concentrated and disciplined way of reading. It involves 2 to 3 minutes of focused study for each reading passage. As you read, you will be taking apart the content and structure of the passage. You will be deliberately searching out the most important ideas in the passage and determining the connections among the various details. Active reading means getting inside the passage to dig out the information it contains.

Here are the most important things to search for as you read each SAT passage.

First, find the *main idea of the passage as a whole.* This is not just what the passage is *about*, but what the passage *says*. The main idea can usually be stated in sentence form. For example, a given passage may be about Abraham Lincoln as a writer. That is its topic, but not its main idea. The main idea *says* something about the topic. In this instance, the main idea might be "Contrary to popular opinion, Lincoln's prose was the product of a skilled and deliberate literary craftsman, not a simple, untutored genius." Once you find the main idea, you have a key to understanding most of the passage.

The main idea of a passage ties together most or all of its content. Everything in the passage should relate in some way to the main idea. If large sections of the passage don't relate to what you think is the main idea, you have probably misunderstood the passage.

The main idea of a passage is often stated in a sentence at or near the beginning. (In the sample passage about horse raiding, for example, the main idea is stated in the very first sentence.) Look for this sentence, sometimes called the *thesis statement*, and underline it with your pencil. Underlining the thesis statement will enable you to refer to it later and will also fix the main idea of the passage in your memory. Reading with pencil in hand is one key to the active reading approach.

Second, look for the *main idea of each paragraph* in the passage. Typically, an SAT reading passage focuses on one main idea and includes several less important ideas that support, explain, develop, or modify the main idea. In most cases, each of these secondary ideas will be developed in a paragraph. Look for a statement of each secondary idea in the *topic sentence* of each paragraph. Like a thesis statement, a topic sentence usually appears at or near the beginning of a paragraph. You may want to underline each topic sentence as you find it. The underlined thesis statement and topic sentences will form a neat, easy-to-review summary of the entire passage.

Third, look for the *structure of the passage*. Structure refers to the way in which the various ideas in a passage are related to one another. Sometimes an idea in one paragraph supports or gives evidence for an idea in another paragraph; sometimes it provides an example of an idea stated elsewhere; sometimes it presents an opposing or contradictory argument. Note how the various ideas relate to one another. As you'll learn later in this lesson, understanding the structure of a passage will help you grasp the full meaning of the passage.

If you read each passage actively, looking for its main idea and structure and the main idea of each paragraph, you'll dig out the meaning of the passage very effectively.

Don't get bogged down in the minor details of the passage. They are much less important than the main ideas. There may be ten or twenty specific facts in a passage, and some of them may be confusing. Don't worry. Remember that the number of questions on any one passage is small, so you're not likely to be asked about more than a few specific facts. Chances are any detail you spend time agonizing over will not even be important in answering the questions. Time on the SAT is precious. Don't waste it by puzzling over details. If you feel confused, try to get the gist of what is being said. Then move on.

3.7 Common Structures for SAT Reading Passages

As you've learned, it's important to look for the structure of a reading passage as you read it. Paying attention to the structure of a reading passage is important for several reasons. First, some questions on the passage may relate directly to its structure. For example, a question may ask, "What is the relationship between X and Y as described in the passage?" Second, understanding the structure will help you recognize which ideas in the passage are most important. Ideas that simply support others are usually not as important as the ideas they support. The most important ideas in a passage will deserve more of your attention and time. Third, understanding the structure will often help you understand the meaning of particular details. Once you recognize, for instance, that a particular idea has been included to serve as an example of some other idea, you'll be better able to understand what it means.

Several structures are common in SAT reading passages. It's good to know them and be able to recognize them when you read. Here they are:

1. A reading passage may be based on a *contrast or comparison* between two things. For example, a science passage might discuss two different theories about how the universe came into existence, explaining the similarities and differences between them. The passage might compare the two theories as wholes, with one or two paragraphs devoted to the first theory and one or two paragraphs devoted to the second one. Or it might compare the two theories on a point-by-point basis, with a paragraph devoted to each of the main similarities or differences between them.

2. A passage may consist of a *main idea plus examples*. In this type of passage, the main idea usually appears in the first paragraph, and the other paragraphs contain examples illustrating that idea. In reading a passage of this type, notice how the examples help to clarify the meaning of the main idea.

3. Another reading passage may consist of a *main idea plus supporting arguments*. This type of passage presents a main idea along with several arguments, facts, or pieces of evidence to prove the truth of that idea. As you read this kind of passage, consider the strength of the evidence given. Is it logical and convincing? Are there holes in the argument?

4. Some passages consist of *several different aspects of one idea*, with each aspect covered in a separate paragraph. For instance, a passage about crime in the nineteenth century might contain one paragraph discussing common patterns of crime, another paragraph discussing the causes of crime, and a third paragraph discussing how lawmakers tried to deal with crime.

5. Other passages have a *pro-and-con* structure. This kind of passage deals with a topic about which there is some controversy or disagreement. The author usually takes a particular position and then presents arguments both for and against that position. A passage organized in this way typically contains separate sections presenting the author's point of view and the opposing point of view. In reading a passage of this type, be sure that you understand whose point of view is being presented at all times.

6. A final common structure for reading passages is *chronological*. In a passage with this structure, events are presented in the order in which they happened. A history passage, for example, might recount historical events chronologically. A science passage might describe a series of experiments or give an account of how ideas related to the topic have changed over time. As you read, note the cause-and-effect relationships among the events—how one event leads to another. There will probably be a question about causal relationships.

Not every SAT reading passage will have one of these structures, but most will. You may find that some passages combine elements of two or more structures. For example, the structure of the passage about horse raiding is basically chronological (structure 6). It starts by mentioning when the horse raiding began and ends by telling when and how it ceased. Events are recounted in the order in which they happened. However, part of the passage has a different-aspects structure (structure 4). The first three paragraphs discuss different aspects of horse raiding: who did it, why it was done, and how it was carried out. So this passage really combines two different structures. That's not unusual.

The structures we've considered aren't followed rigidly by the SAT. And it's not necessary to fit every passage neatly into one of those structures. Nevertheless, a knowledge of the six common structures is a handy mental tool that will help you recognize how writers organize information in an SAT reading passage.

3.8 Step 3: Reviewing the Passage

Reviewing is the final step in the three-step reading process. It is also the simplest. After you finish your active reading of the passage, skim it again, reading only those portions that you've underlined with your pencil. If you did a good job of picking out the most important ideas in the passage, your review will solidify them in your mind.

Reviewing the passage helps you in several ways. It helps you understand the passage by giving you a chance to see how it all fits together. It helps you remember the ideas in the passage, which will save you time when you're answering the questions. And it helps you remember where each fact or detail appears in the passage. If you know where to look, you'll be able to find the answers to factual questions more easily.

Reviewing should take you no more than 30 seconds. For a long reading passage (four hundred to five hundred words), the three-step reading process should follow this schedule:

Step 1:	Previewing	30 seconds
Step 2:	Active reading	120–180 seconds
Step 3:	Reviewing	30 seconds
	Total time	180–240 seconds

That's 3 or 4 minutes altogether, which will leave you plenty of time for the four or five questions that follow. For shorter passages, of course, the time you spend on each step should be shorter.

Don't skip the previewing and reviewing steps. They take up some of your valuable test-taking time, but they are important. They will help you do the reading more quickly and effectively, and they will help you answer the questions more easily and accurately. In the long run, these "extra steps" will help you save time.

Reading Comprehension Questions

3.9 Basic Techniques for Reading Comprehension Questions

Answering reading comprehension questions is an art. You'll learn many useful approaches to this art in Lesson 8. For now, here are a few basic techniques that you should practice.

Read every question and answer choice carefully. Watch out for small words that drastically change the meaning of a statement. Remember that many questions have two or three answers that are partially correct. So even if one answer seems good, take the time to check all the other choices as well. Another answer may be slightly better.

Don't assume that certain words or phrases are signs of right or wrong answers. You may have heard, for example, that answers containing words such as *all, always, never, none, no,* and *every* are almost always wrong. This is not so. Judge each answer on its merits.

Base your answers only on what is stated or implied in the passage. Don't base them on your own ideas or your own knowledge of a topic. If a passage deals with a topic that you have strong opinions or feelings about, try to put them aside while you answer the questions.

Make sure that the answer you choose actually answers the question. An answer choice may be true, but if it isn't relevant to the question, it's not the correct answer.

Refer to the passage as often as you need to. If you can answer a question without looking back at the passage, fine. For most questions, however, you'll find that you need to locate a particular part of the passage and review it. If you understand the structure of the passage, you should be able to find a necessary detail quickly and easily.

LESSON 4
Tackling the SAT-Mathematical Sections

OBJECTIVES

- ☐ To recognize the math skills that are tested on the SAT
- ☐ To understand the best test-taking strategies for both math problems and quantitative comparisons
- ☐ To learn problem-solving techniques that can save you time and help you approach SAT math questions more efficiently

Overview of the SAT-Mathematical Sections

4.1 Format and Timing

As you known, the mathematical sections of the SAT consist of two types of questions: math problems and quantitative comparisons. You learned a little about each type in Lesson 0, Sections 0.16–0.18.

Not all mathematical sections contain both types of questions. Some contain only math problems—twenty-five of them to be done in 30 minutes. These sections allow you a bit more than a minute for each problem (72 seconds, to be exact). You'll find that some problems can be solved much more quickly than that, while a few take longer—2 or 3 minutes, perhaps. Your average working time per problem should be around 1 minute.

When a mathematical section includes both types of questions, you can expect seven math problems at the beginning, twenty quantitative comparisons in the middle, and eight more math problems at the end. Each group of math problems should take you about 10 minutes, leaving you 10 minutes for the twenty quantitative comparisons. A rate of two quantitative comparisons a minute is about right. As you'll see, quantitative comparisons can usually be done quickly. Many of them require no calculations, and none of them require exact answers. So the amount of time-consuming work on a typical quantitative comparison is quite small.

When a mathematical section includes quantitative comparisons, do them first. In other words, turn to the middle of the section to start with. When you're finished with the quantitative comparisons, go back to the beginning of the section and do the first batch of problems. Then tackle the batch of problems at the end. This plan fits the general rule that you should always do the easier questions first and save the longer and harder ones for later.

You'll notice that within each group of questions the items will usually become progressively harder. Not every student will find the same questions difficult, of course, but you'll probably find the last five quantitative comparisons in a section harder than the first five. So don't be alarmed if the questions seem to get tough toward the end. They're supposed to.

4.2 Math Skills Tested on the SAT

In tackling the mathematical sections on the SAT, there's no substitute for strong basic math skills. So if your math skills are shaky or you haven't been taking a math class this year, review your high school math before the exam. Here are some guidelines you should follow.

First, be sure that you feel very comfortable with the basic operations of arithmetic: addition, subtraction, multiplication, and division. You should be good at working with negative numbers, decimals, fractions, percentages, ratios, and proportions. You should understand basic number properties and types of numbers, including primes, even numbers, odd numbers, and zero. And you should be able to read and interpret graphs and charts.

Second, polish your skills in elementary algebra. You should be able to perform computations that include unknowns, solve equations, set up equations to solve word problems, and so on. You should understand how radicals and exponents work, and you should be able to solve pairs of simultaneous equations and simple quadratic equations as well.

Third, review plane geometry. You need to know and be able to apply your knowledge of the basic properties of lines, angles, triangles, quadrilaterals, and circles. You should be able to read and use coordinate graphs, the kind drawn on graph paper against an x-axis and a y-axis. It's also useful if you have some knowledge of simple three-dimensional figures such as cubes, spheres, and cylinders.

A few SAT math questions deal with topics other than these. There may be three or four questions dealing with set theory, the basic rules of probability, or inequalities. However, if you are strong in the three basic areas of arithmetic, elementary algebra, and plane geometry, you'll be ready to handle most SAT math questions.

Notice that some topics you may have studied in math classes—especially if you're an advanced math student—are not included on the SAT. Major areas such as trigonometry and calculus aren't even touched upon. If you never got very far in math, don't worry. Your classmate who has taken college-level math subjects has no advantage over you. You may, however, be at a disadvantage if you haven't studied basic math recently. Most students find it necessary to review their ninth- and tenth-grade math before taking the SAT.

A thorough review of math is a big job. This book, which is designed to help you prepare for all areas of the SAT, doesn't cover the SAT math topics in as much detail as a textbook devoted only to math can do. If you're very weak in one or more math areas, you may need to study a review book on your weak subject.

If you're an average math student, though, you should find the review material in Lessons 9 and 14 of this book sufficient preparation for the SAT. In those two lessons, you'll review the basic concepts of arithmetic, elementary algebra, and geometry, along with some miscellaneous topics that often appear on the SAT. You'll also learn some problem-solving techniques that will help you apply the math concepts to test taking. Review questions are also included.

The remainder of this lesson covers test-taking techniques and principles that will help you use your math knowledge on the exam. Practice using them every time you tackle math questions between now and the SAT.

Tackling Math Problems

4.3 Basic Techniques for Math Problems

When you approach *any* math problem on the SAT, there are two basic techniques that you should apply.

First, read the question carefully. Focus on the words that actually pose the question, and make sure that you understand what you're being asked. Make sure that you know, for example, whether you need to express your answer in inches, feet, or yards, or whether you need to find out the total time that Joe worked, the time that Joe worked after Laura stopped working, or the total time that Joe and Laura worked together. Very often the "obvious" question that you expect is not the question that you're really asked.

Second, avoid long calculations. Most SAT math problems are set up to make much figuring unnecessary. The test makers aren't much interested in how well you can multiply a long string of numbers, for instance; they're interested in seeing whether you can figure out which numbers need to be multiplied in the first place. Most SAT math problems are *thinking* problems, not calculation problems. So if you begin work on a problem and find yourself starting a long series of computations, *stop*. You're probably on the wrong track. Go back and reconsider the problem. You may have set up your equation incorrectly. Perhaps you're overlooking a simple "trick" solution or an easy way to estimate the right answer. Remember, even on the more difficult problems, your path to the right answer should be fairly direct.

4.4 Techniques for Special Kinds of Math Problems

There are certain specific kinds of math problems that call for special techniques of their own. Here are some you'll find useful.

When a word problem involves several different units of measure, begin by converting all the quantities into the same units—preferably the ones in which the question is expressed. For example, a problem might refer to different quantities in terms of grams, milligrams, meters, and centimeters. Find the words that state the question: "What is the density of the mixture in grams per centimeter?" Before you do any other figuring, convert all units into grams and centimeters. Converting will save you time at the end and will also prevent you from carelessly confusing units of measure.

When a geometry problem does not include a diagram, sketch your own in the margins of your test booklet. Sometimes merely looking at the geometric figure described in a question—the triangle, rectangle, circle, or whatever—will make the answer, or a way of finding it, obvious. Also feel free to add to any diagrams given by the test makers. If the problem assigns lengths or degree measures to certain parts of the diagram, mark them in as you read. You'll be able to see more clearly how the facts that you're given are interrelated and how they lead to a solution.

Some math problems follow the so-called "multiple-option" format. Here's an example:

> If x, y, and z are consecutive odd integers, not necessarily in that order, which of the following statements must be true?
>
> I. $x + y + z$ is odd.
>
> II. xyz is even.
>
> III. $\frac{xy}{z}$ is odd.
>
> (A) I only (B) II only (C) III only
>
> (D) I and III only (E) I, II, and III

The multiple-option format may look confusing, but it can help you make the most of incomplete knowledge. For instance, if you're sure that Statement I is true but you're not sure about II and III, don't despair. What you do know will immediately allow you to eliminate choices B and C, since they don't include Statement I. This leaves only A, D, and E to choose from, and a one-in-three guessing chance is good odds on the SAT. So try never to omit a multiple-option item, even if you know very little about the question. You can usually use what you know to establish a good chance of making an accurate guess. (By the way, the correct answer for this example is choice A.)

4.5 If You Feel Stumped

If you are at a loss as to how to solve a particular problem, don't just sit there—try something. Set up an equation, even if you're not sure it's the correct one. Fill in as many angle sizes, line lengths, and other facts as you can figure out, even if they don't seem immediately relevant. Reduce the terms of an equation, simplify or expand an expression, change decimals into fractions or vice versa—do almost anything rather than give up. You'll find that sometimes—not always, but often enough to be worthwhile—a method for solving a problem will pop out at you from these experiments.

Of course you shouldn't spend a lot of time in this kind of experimentation. If no road to a solution is apparent after 20 or 30 seconds, give up and go on. But give every problem at least a try. You'll probably pick up a few points in this way—and every point counts.

4.6 Timesaving Strategies for Math Problems

As you've already learned, you have only a little more than a minute to solve each SAT math problem. Since your time is so limited, you must use any timesaving strategies you can. Many students are trained to feel that taking shortcuts is wrong. Math teachers often give you full credit for an answer only if you show every step of your calculations. They sometimes take away points for a right answer you got in the "wrong" way. This is a valid approach to teaching math, but not to taking the SAT. The SAT rewards the student who uses shortcuts and finds answers by "seat-of-the-pants" reasoning. If you're in the habit of using only slow-and-steady math techniques, try to change that habit for the exam.

Get used to "guesstimating." Practice rounding off numbers and making thumbnail calculations. These shortcuts will often get you close enough to pick the correct answer. In some cases, looking at the answer choices will tell you how precise your answer needs to be. For example, suppose a problem asks, "How many theater tickets must be sold at a profit of \$2.40 each to obtain a total profit of \$1,500?" Glance at the answers before you begin your figuring. If the answers are

(A) 615 (B) 625 (C) 630 (D) 638 (E) 640

then you know that you need a precise answer, since all five answers are close together. However, if the answers are

(A) 525 (B) 625 (C) 700 (D) 850 (E) 1000

then you don't need to be very precise. The answers are so far apart that even an approximation will allow you to pick the correct one. If you know, for instance, that the right answer is somewhere around 600, it's easy to see that choice B is correct.

Even when a problem seems to demand a precise answer, it pays to look at the problem in broad terms first and get a general idea of where the answer should fall. This tactic will help you avoid many careless errors. For example, suppose a problem involves a car traveling for a period of, say, 11 hours. You should first see that the distance traveled will probably be somewhere between 450 and 700 miles, since cars usually travel between 40 and 65 miles per hour. So an answer of 200 miles or 1100 miles is almost certainly wrong. When you do your exact figuring, it's easy to let a decimal point slip or to make a careless error such as $3 \times 4 = 21$. This can throw your answer way off. Having a ballpark figure in mind before you start will alert you to any error of this type.

4.7 Tips on Rounding Off

When rounding off seems like a good timesaving tactic for a math problem, follow these principles.

Round off numbers to the nearest whole or to the nearest easy-to-use number. For example, if a problem involves numbers like 41, 78, and 119, round them off to 40, 80, and 120. If a problem involves a dollar amount like $4.09, round it off to $4.10 or even $4.00. (If you round it off to $4.00, make a mental note that you rounded it *down*. Keep in mind that your "round" answer will be a little less than the true answer.)

In some cases, the easiest unit to use isn't a whole number at all. For example, if a problem calls for multiplying 693 by 34%, the best approach is to realize that 34% is very close to $33\frac{1}{3}\%$, the equivalent of the fraction $\frac{1}{3}$. Therefore, the question is really asking for a little more than $\frac{1}{3}$ of 693. That's easy to figure out; you may even be able to do it in your head. So for this problem, $33\frac{1}{3}$ is a round, easy-to-use number. Percentages like 25% (equivalent to $\frac{1}{4}$) and $66\frac{2}{3}\%$ (equivalent to $\frac{2}{3}$) are also easy to use and are therefore "round" numbers.

When rounding off two or more numbers in a single problem, try to round them so they compensate for one another. When the numbers are to be added or multiplied, it's best to round them in opposite directions—that is, make one a little larger and the other a little smaller. Then the combined value of the two numbers together will work out about right. If the numbers are to be subtracted or divided, it's best to round both numbers in the same direction. Again, the result will be closer to the exact answer.

For example, if a problem calls for you to *multiply* 588 by 65, round the two numbers in *opposite* directions: multiply 600 by 60. If the problem calls for you to *divide* 588 by 65, round the two numbers in the *same* direction: divide 600 by 70. In both cases, your answer will not be exactly right, but it will probably be close enough for you to work with.

Tackling Quantitative Comparisons

4.8 The Quantitative Comparison Format

Quantitative comparisons may strike you as the strangest questions on the SAT. You've probably never faced questions like these on any classroom test. Once you get used to them, though, you'll find that they're really not very hard.

Studying the quantitative comparison format is important because it may be confusing at first. To review: Your job is to compare the quantities given in two columns, labeled "Column A" and "Column B." If the quantity in Column A is greater, the answer is A; if the quantity in Column B is greater, the answer is B; if the two quantities are equal, the answer is C; and if the information given isn't enough to allow you to determine which quantity is greater, the answer is D. Be sure to learn this classification scheme before the exam. On SAT day, you should be able simply to skim the instructions and get right to work, without having to refer back to the explanation of what each answer choice means.

As you've already learned, you should be able to complete each quantitative comparison in about 30 seconds. This rate sounds very fast. But remember, it isn't necessary to solve any problems; all you have to do is tell which quantity is greater. In many cases, as you'll see, it's not necessary to figure out the exact values of the quantities involved. Rough calculations will do.

4.9 Techniques for Quantitative Comparisons

Here are some basic principles to follow in tackling quantitative comparisons.

As the old saying goes, you can't compare apples with oranges. So always try to make the two quantities resemble one another as closely as possible. For instance, you may need to translate differing units of measure (such as seconds and minutes) into a common unit before you can compare the two quantities. You may need to reduce fractions in one or both in order to make the two quantities more alike. You may need to turn decimals into fractions or fractions into percentages. You may need to simplify algebraic expressions or restate them in terms of the same unknown. Or you may need to carry out some calculation (for instance, a series of multiplications or divisions) to reduce two complex expressions into single values, which you can then readily compare. This process of making the two quantities resemble one another as closely as possible is the basic tactic for most quantitative comparisons.

You'll often find it helpful to eliminate any elements that appear in both columns. Then you can compare what's left. For example, let's compare these two quantities:

Column A	**Column B**
$\frac{1}{2} \times \frac{1}{3} \times \frac{1}{4} \times \frac{1}{5}$	$\frac{1}{3} \times \frac{1}{4} \times \frac{1}{5} \times \frac{1}{6}$

Notice that both sides include the factors 1/3, 1/4, and 1/5. Since these factors appear in both columns, they cannot make the difference between the value of one column and that of the other. Therefore, you can eliminate them. Cross them out. Now you're left with the two quantities 1/2 and 1/6, and you can easily see that 1/2 is greater. So the correct answer is A. *Notice that no computations are necessary.* Many quantitative comparisons are constructed in such a way that you don't have to do any calculating.

Let's look at some other examples of how this technique works.

Column A	**Column B**
The cost of 6 pounds of apples sold at 69¢ a pound	The cost of 30 oranges sold at \$1.79 a dozen

Here the basic problem is that the two sides of the comparison describe different ways of selling fruit—by the pound and by the dozen. Nevertheless, the two quantities can be expressed in the same terms—that is, in dollars and cents. A little figuring shows you that the quantity in Column A can be expressed as \$4.14 and the quantity in Column B as \$4.48. Thus you can easily see that Column B is greater.

Column A	**Column B**
4×3^3	4×5^2

Again, the two quantities aren't directly comparable because they aren't in the same terms. You can make them more comparable by multiplying them out and so turning them into simple numbers that you can then compare. Before multiplying, however, note the built-in shortcut: the term 4 appears on both sides of the comparison. This means that you can eliminate the 4 and simply compare 3^3 with 5^2. Since $3 \times 3 \times 3 = 27$, while $5 \times 5 = 25$, Column A is greater.

$$x \neq 0$$

Column A	**Column B**
$\frac{1}{x}$	$\frac{x^2 + x}{x^2(x + 1)}$

This is a more difficult example. The fraction in Column A is much simpler in form than the one in Column B. To make them directly comparable, you need to simplify the fraction in Column B. Start by looking for a factor that is common to both the numerator and the denominator so that you can reduce the fraction to lowest terms. The most likely possibility is $x + 1$. Is $x + 1$ a factor of $x^2 + x$? Yes, $x^2 + x = x(x + 1)$. So you have

$$\frac{x(x + 1)}{x^2(x + 1)}$$

which reduces to

$$\frac{x}{x^2}$$

Now, simplify further by dividing both the numerator and the denominator by the common factor of x. You get

$$\frac{1}{x}$$

As this process of simplification reveals, the two columns are equal, so the correct answer is choice C.

You needed a bit of algebraic insight to solve that problem. However, your solution began with the impulse to make Column B look more like Column A. After you've done a great many quantitative comparisons, that impulse will become an instinct.

4.10 Avoiding Unsound Assumptions

On quantitative comparisons, never assume anything that's not stated. Remember, about one-fourth of all quantitative comparisons are correctly answered with choice D: the information given to compare the two quantities is *not* sufficient. These D items can be somewhat tricky, especially if you assume some fact that's not actually given on the test. For example, suppose you're told that the average price of ten different shirts is $16. You're then asked to compare these two quantities:

Column A	Column B
The total price of two shirts	$32

Your first reaction may be to choose answer C. But think again. The *average* price of the ten shirts is $16, but not every shirt necessarily costs $16. One may cost only $8 or $10 while another may cost $20 or $25. And you don't know the prices of the two specific shirts referred to in Column A. So this is a D item.

Be especially careful with geometry items because the figures that accompany some of them may lead you to make false assumptions. For instance, look at the following figure and the comparison that goes with it:

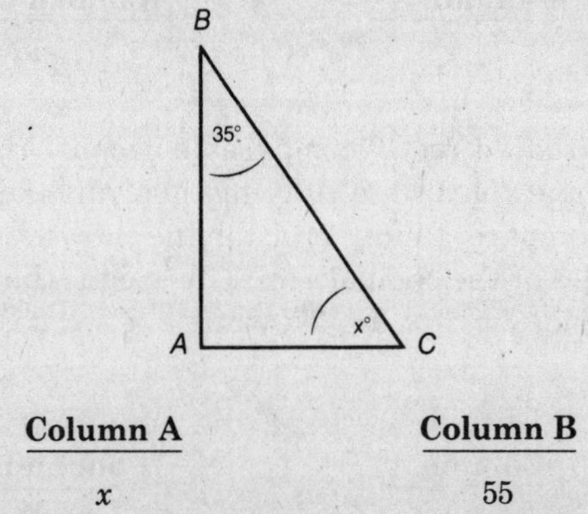

Column A	Column B
x	55

Angle A certainly looks like a right angle in the diagram, which would make angle C equal to 55°. But you haven't been told that angle A is in fact a right angle. It *might* measure 89° or 91°. So, again, the answer must be choice D. The test makers want to see whether you know how to distinguish facts from assumptions, which may or may not be well founded. Of course, if the diagram looked like this, choice C would be correct:

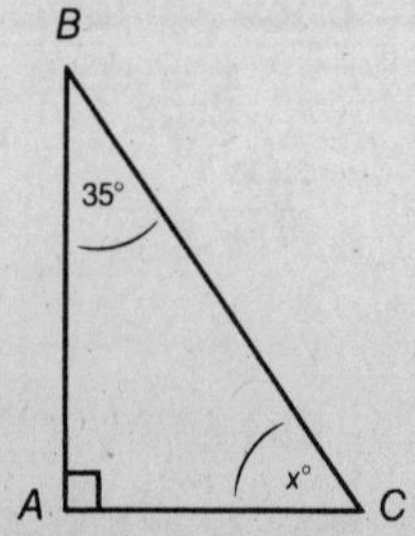

4.11 Dealing with Unknowns

Many quantitative comparisons include unknown quantities, usually represented by letters—x, a, n, and so on. You may or may not be given some information about the unknowns in a particular comparison. For example, if you are told that $x \neq 0$ or that $x > 1$, you know something about the value of x. But if you *aren't* given such information, don't assume anything about an unknown. We tend to think of numbers in terms of positive integers—1, 2, 3, and so on. But an unknown may represent any type of number, including a fraction, a negative number, a negative fraction, 0, and 1. Any of these possibilities may change an answer.

For instance, suppose you are told

$$x > y$$

and you are then asked to compare these two quantities:

Column A	Column B
$\frac{x}{y}$	1

If you think of x and y as positive integers—say, 3 and 2—then your assumption will be that Column A is greater (since 3/2 is greater than 1). But what if x and y are negative integers? If x is -2 and y is -3, for instance, then x/y will equal $-2/-3$, which is equivalent to 2/3, which is less than 1. In that case, Column B will be greater. Since two answers are possible, depending on where the values of x and y fall, the correct answer is choice D—the information given is not sufficient.

The moral is this: Whenever an unknown is not narrowly defined, consider *all* its possible values.

Two final points to remember: First, if a quantitative comparison contains no unknowns—that is, if the problem involves numbers only—never pick choice D. It is always possible under such circumstances to determine the value of each quantity, even if you can't figure out how to do it at the time. So D cannot be the correct answer. Second—this seems obvious, but it's easy to forget—if you have to guess on a quantitative comparison, never pick choice E. On quantitative comparisons, unlike other SAT questions, there are only four answer choices.

LESSON 5
Strategies for the TSWE

OBJECTIVES

☐ To understand the two types of TSWE questions and recognize their similarities and differences

☐ To learn effective test-taking strategies for both types of TSWE questions

☐ To discover which grammar and usage errors appear most frequently on the TSWE

Overview of the TSWE

5.1 Skills Tested on the TSWE

As you already know, TSWE scores aren't used to determine who will gain admission to a college and who won't. Instead, they're used to place students in appropriate English classes after they've been admitted. But a good TSWE score certainly can't hurt your chances of admission. Colleges today are more concerned than ever about the basic skills of their incoming students. Almost all colleges stress writing as a crucial skill. So doing your best on the TSWE is a very good idea.

Of course, no multiple-choice test can fully measure a student's writing skills. The TSWE doesn't test originality, creativity, organizational skill, clear thinking, self-discipline, and many other qualities that a good writer possesses. It tests only the rules of grammar and usage—in particular, certain rules that lend themselves readily to the format of the two types of questions on the TSWE.

Don't worry if you're not an expert on the fine points of English grammar and usage. The TSWE tests only the common, hard-and-fast rules of standard written English. It doesn't test obscure or subtle rules like the difference between *that* and *which*. (There's supposed to be a distinct difference in the two relative pronouns, and your English teacher may have discussed it. But in practice, only professional writers and editors usually make the distinction—and even they have to look up the rule sometimes.)

The TSWE doesn't test rules that are changing or rules that vary from place to place, either. So you're not likely to be asked whether *shall* or *will* is more appropriate in a certain context, whether it's acceptable to split an infinitive or to end a sentence with a preposition, or whether it's correct to use *hopefully* to mean "it is hoped that," as in "*Hopefully*, it won't rain today." (Most scrupulous writers use *hopefully* only to mean "in a hopeful way," as in "He gazed at the horizon *hopefully*, looking for the rescue plane." However, this rule is changing. Today, more and more writers, including many good writers, feel that both uses of *hopefully* are acceptable.) When rules are in flux, the TSWE doesn't test them.

A typical TSWE section contains thirty-five usage questions and fifteen error corrections, for a total of fifty questions to be answered in 30 minutes. The usage questions are short; you should be able to do them quickly—about two a minute. So the thirty-five usage questions should take you about 17 or 18 minutes. The error corrections involve more reading and are sometimes more subtle as well. They take longer—about 45 or 50 seconds each, on the average. So the set of fifteen error corrections should take you between 12 and 13 minutes. You may spend more or less time on any given question, but these estimates give you a rough idea of how fast you'll need to work.

Usage Questions

5.2 Tactics for Usage Questions

If you're insecure about your writing skills, you've got one big thing going for you on the Test of Standard Written English: you don't have to do any writing. All you have to do is recognize the difference between good writing and bad.

On usage items, you have a further advantage: you don't have to be able to tell how an error should be corrected. All you have to do is find the error.

Of course, the two things usually go together. Once you find the error, you can usually tell how to correct it. But you don't need to correct it, and you shouldn't waste any time on the exam wondering about it. Here are two basic techniques that will help you locate the errors on usage questions.

First, as you read each sentence, listen to how it sounds in your "mind's ear." If you grew up speaking and hearing English, chances are most grammar errors will sound wrong to you. Remember that it doesn't matter whether or not you can explain exactly what is wrong; as long as you know it sounds wrong, you can get the question right. Just pick the underlined word or phrase that sounds wrong to you.

Of course, what sounds wrong to you isn't always wrong. If you can, try to identify the error in your mind; give it a name or relate it to a particular grammatical rule. This will prevent you from picking as an error a word or a phrase that is correct but unfamiliar to you.

Second, remember that any part of the sentence that is not underlined cannot be changed. You must assume that it's correct. So if some parts of the sentence don't seem to work together, you must find an underlined part that could be changed to fit the nonunderlined parts. The following example contains a common type of error, disagreement between subject and verb:

> This novel, along with his award-winning plays
> (A: This; B: his award-winning plays)
> and two volumes of insightful essays, have made
> (C: have made)
> the author one of our best-known writers. No error
> (D: our; E: No error)

The subject is *novel*, which is singular; the verb is *have made*, which is plural. In real life, the error could be corrected in any of several ways. For example, the sentence could be rewritten to have a compound (plural) subject:

> This novel, his award-winning plays, and his two volumes of insightful essays have made the author one of our best-known writers.

Or a more drastic revision could be made:

> Many books by the author—this novel, his award-winning plays, and his two volumes of insightful essays—have made him one of our best-known writers.

On the TSWE, however, you can choose only one underlined word or phrase to be changed. In this case, the verb phrase *have made* would have to be changed to the singular *has made*. Focus only on the underlined parts of the sentence; the rest cannot be touched.

5.3 Common Error Types in Usage Questions

Be on the lookout for certain basic errors in grammar and diction that crop up frequently in usage questions. Here's a list of them:

1. *Errors in subject-verb agreement.* Singular verbs must have singular subjects; plural verbs must have plural subjects.

2. *Errors in tense and tense sequence.* The tenses of verbs should make clear the time of each action and the order in which the actions occur.

3. *Errors in irregular verb forms.* Irregular verbs form the past tense and past participle in unusual ways. Faulty verb forms like "I have went," "they seen," and "he had ate" will probably crop up on the TSWE.

4. *Errors in pronoun reference.* Every pronoun should refer clearly to a particular noun, usually one that precedes it.

5. *Errors in pronoun case.* The form a pronoun takes should reflect its use in a sentence. Errors in pronoun case usually involve the use of the objective case of a pronoun when the subjective case is needed, or vice versa. "I went with he and she" is wrong, for instance; "I went with him and her" is correct.

6. *Errors in diction.* Word choice must be consistent with the meaning of a sentence. Errors in diction usually involve confusion between two words that look or sound alike. Examples include the use of *effect* for *affect*, *illusion* for *allusion*, *defer* for *deter*, and *comprise* for *compose*.

7. *Errors in idiomatic usage.* An *idiom* is an established expression—the customary way of saying something in a language, whether or not that way is logical or even grammatical. "She really *looks down on him*" is an example of an idiom. Errors in idiomatic usage produce phrases that sound odd or foreign.

8. *Errors in the idiomatic usage of prepositions. Prepositions* are connecting words, usually little ones like *in*, *to*, *of*, *for*, *from*, and *by*. Errors in the idiomatic usage of prepositions, like other idiom errors, produce phrases that sound odd or foreign. For example: "They trusted *on* him" rather than "They trusted *in* him."

9. *Faulty comparisons.* Comparisons must be clear and complete. Faulty comparisons include a variety of errors found in phrases or clauses that compare one thing to another. Misuse of *than* and *as*, double comparatives, and incomplete comparisons are examples.

Most usage errors on the TSWE fall into one of these nine categories. You'll find a discussion of these errors, with examples, in Lesson 15 of this book, but you may also want to review selected parts of an English grammar text or writing handbook before you take the exam. Look up the nine basic types of errors and make sure that you understand the rules that apply to them. Don't worry about most of the other topics covered in grammar or writing texts. They are important in learning how to write well, but they're not very important in answering usage questions on the TSWE.

Error Corrections

5.4 How Usage Questions Differ from Error Corrections

In some ways, error correction questions resemble usage questions. Both are tests of writing ability. Both test some of the same rules of grammar and usage. And for both, your ear for correct English will be a valuable guide. But there are important differences as well.

The main difference is that for error corrections, you must not only locate any error in a sentence but also decide which of several versions of the sentence is best. For this reason, error corrections take longer to do.

In addition, more subtle distinctions are required on error corrections. You must do more than find an answer that is grammatically correct. You must also find the one answer that expresses an idea most *effectively*. In other words, even if two or more versions of a sentence are technically correct, one version will be more effective than the others. That is the answer you must choose.

5.5 Tactics for Error Corrections

What makes an "effective" sentence? Several qualities are involved. First, an effective sentence is concise. It contains no unnecessary words. This doesn't necessarily mean that the shortest answer is best. Sometimes the shortest version of a sentence will leave out part of its meaning. However, any version that contains unnecessary words, words that do not add to the meaning of the sentence, is ineffective and probably wrong. For instance, of the two sentences "He was late as a result of the fact that his car broke down" and "He was late because his car broke down," the second is more concise and therefore more effective.

An effective sentence is also easy to understand. On the TSWE, if one answer choice is confusing or vague while another is clear and specific, the right answer is the second one, even if both are technically correct.

An effective sentence contains no awkward phrases. If an answer choice sounds odd, is hard to read, or contains words that seem out of place, it is probably not the correct answer.

As you can see, on error correction items, you can't just pick the first answer that doesn't contain a grammatical error. You must also read all the answers and find the one that is written best.

5.6 Common Error Types in Error Corrections

When tackling an error correction, first read the original version of the sentence carefully. The underlined portion will probably contain an error. Try to figure out what the error is. Here are the most common errors to look for in error correction questions:

1. *Wordiness. Wordiness* is the use of unnecessary words, as in the earlier sentence about the car breakdown.

2. *Run-on sentences.* A run-on sentence is two complete sentences run together as one sentence without a connecting word (such as *and*), a semicolon (;), or a colon (:) to separate them. Two complete sentences joined only by a comma make a run-on sentence, the sentence you are now reading is an example.

3. *Errors in parallelism.* The rules of parallelism in English are fairly complex. For this reason, they're worth reviewing in a grammar text or writing handbook. Basically, parallelism means that all parts of a sentence with similar meanings or similar roles in the sentence should be in the same grammatical form. A simple example of faulty parallelism is "Her favorite pastimes are *swimming*, *boating*, and *to water-ski*." The sentence should read "Her favorite pastimes are *swimming*, *boating*, and *waterskiing*."

4. *Dangling or misplaced modifiers.* A word, phrase, or clause that describes something else in a sentence is known as a *modifier*. A modifier should be placed as close as possible to the word or words it describes. For example, it is incorrect to write "Painted a bright shade of red, Frank drove his sports car down the street." The phrase that begins the sentence is misplaced; it should be close to the word *car* because it describes Frank's car, not Frank. A dangling modifier is a modifying phrase or clause with *no* word or words to modify.

5. *Fragments.* Fragments are sentences that do not contain both a subject and a predicate. Like this one.

6. *Errors in logic.* This is a grab-bag category of errors that includes any illogical connection between one part of a sentence and another.

Notice that the kinds of errors common in error corrections differ markedly from the kinds of errors common in usage questions. Error correction questions, for example, rarely test your ability to distinguish between words that look or sound alike. They rarely test your knowledge of the rules of pronoun reference or subject-verb agreement, either. So when you're answering error correction questions on the TSWE, don't waste your time looking for these types of errors. Though they're very common in usage questions, they're very uncommon in error corrections.

In Lesson 10 of this book you'll review the types of errors that frequently appear in error correction questions on the TSWE. The review will sharpen your ability to detect and correct these types of errors.

5.7 Choosing the Best Answer for an Error Correction

Naturally, the first step you should take in approaching an error correction question is to examine the original version of the sentence carefully. Try to find the error in that version first. If you do, your job will be easier. Then *glance* at answer choices B, C, D, and E—the four rewritten versions of the sentence. (Don't bother reading choice A. It's always the same as the original version.) Some of the answer choices may contain the same error as the original. You can usually spot these answers right away. Mentally eliminate them.

Read through the answers that remain. Make sure that they do not contain different errors. If any do, eliminate them as well.

Also make sure that the rewritten versions do not change the meaning of the original version. For example, one of the rewritten versions may leave out an idea in the original version, distort part of its meaning, or drag in some new idea that was not there in the first place. If so, eliminate that answer.

Read the answers that remain for their "sound." Does one make the point especially forcefully and clearly? Do any contain awkward or confusing phrases? These considerations will narrow your choices still further.

After all this, if you're still left with two or three answers that seem equally correct and effective, choose the shortest version. It's the most succinct and therefore probably the best answer.

PART 4

Practice Test 2

PRACTICE TEST 2: *Directions*

This practice test is for you to take after you have studied Lessons 1–5 in this book. Because you have previously taken one practice test and have now studied a number of important SAT skills, your scores on Practice Test 2 should show some improvement over your scores on Practice Test 1 (the pretest). The answers and scoring instructions for this test, which begin on page 123, will help you measure your progress so far and determine which SAT skills need special attention as you continue your study program.

Directions: Set aside $3\frac{1}{2}$ hours without interruption for taking this test. The test is divided into six 30-minute sections. You may wish to use a timer or an alarm to time yourself on each section. Do not work past the 30-minute limit for any section. If you finish a section before time is up, you may check your work on that section, but you are not to work on any other section. You may take a 5-minute break between sections.

Do not worry if you are unable to finish a section or if there are some questions you cannot answer. Do not waste time puzzling over a question that seems too difficult for you. You should work as rapidly as you can without sacrificing accuracy.

Students often ask whether they should guess when they are uncertain about the answer to a question. Your test scores will be based on the number of questions you answer correctly minus a fraction of the number you answer incorrectly. Therefore, it is improbable that random or haphazard guessing will change your scores significantly. If you have some knowledge of a question, you may be able to eliminate one or more of the answer choices as wrong. It is generally to your advantage to guess which of the remaining choices is correct. Remember, however, not to spend too much time on any one question.

Mark all your answers on the answer sheet on the facing page. (For your convenience, you may wish to remove this sheet from the book and keep it in front of you throughout the test.) Mark only one answer for each question. Be sure that each mark is dark and that it completely fills the answer space. In each section of the answer sheet, there are 5 answer spaces for each of 50 questions. When there are fewer than 5 answer choices for a question or fewer than 50 questions in a section of your test, leave the extra answer spaces blank. Do not make stray marks on the answer sheet. If you erase, do so completely.

You may use any available space on the pages of the test for scratchwork. Do not use books, dictionaries, reference materials, calculators, slide rules, or any other aids. Do not look at the answer key or any other parts of this book. It is important to take this practice test in the same way that you will take the actual SAT.

When you have completed all six test sections, turn to the answers and scoring instructions that follow the test.

REMOVE ANSWER SHEET BY CUTTING ON DOTTED LINE

PRACTICE TEST 2: *Answer Sheet*

Directions: Use a No. 2 pencil only for completing this answer sheet. Be sure each mark is dark and completely fills the intended space. Completely erase any errors or stray marks. Start with number 1 for each new section. If a section has fewer than 50 questions or if a question has fewer than 5 answer choices, leave the extra answer spaces blank.

	SECTION 1	SECTION 2	SECTION 3	SECTION 4
1	A B C D E	A B C D E	A B C D E	A B C D E
2	A B C D E	A B C D E	A B C D E	A B C D E
3	A B C D E	A B C D E	A B C D E	A B C D E
4	A B C D E	A B C D E	A B C D E	A B C D E
5	A B C D E	A B C D E	A B C D E	A B C D E
6	A B C D E	A B C D E	A B C D E	A B C D E
7	A B C D E	A B C D E	A B C D E	A B C D E
8	A B C D E	A B C D E	A B C D E	A B C D E
9	A B C D E	A B C D E	A B C D E	A B C D E
10	A B C D E	A B C D E	A B C D E	A B C D E
11	A B C D E	A B C D E	A B C D E	A B C D E
12	A B C D E	A B C D E	A B C D E	A B C D E
13	A B C D E	A B C D E	A B C D E	A B C D E
14	A B C D E	A B C D E	A B C D E	A B C D E
15	A B C D E	A B C D E	A B C D E	A B C D E
16	A B C D E	A B C D E	A B C D E	A B C D E
17	A B C D E	A B C D E	A B C D E	A B C D E
18	A B C D E	A B C D E	A B C D E	A B C D E
19	A B C D E	A B C D E	A B C D E	A B C D E
20	A B C D E	A B C D E	A B C D E	A B C D E
21	A B C D E	A B C D E	A B C D E	A B C D E
22	A B C D E	A B C D E	A B C D E	A B C D E
23	A B C D E	A B C D E	A B C D E	A B C D E
24	A B C D E	A B C D E	A B C D E	A B C D E
25	A B C D E	A B C D E	A B C D E	A B C D E
26	A B C D E	A B C D E	A B C D E	A B C D E
27	A B C D E	A B C D E	A B C D E	A B C D E
28	A B C D E	A B C D E	A B C D E	A B C D E
29	A B C D E	A B C D E	A B C D E	A B C D E
30	A B C D E	A B C D E	A B C D E	A B C D E
31	A B C D E	A B C D E	A B C D E	A B C D E
32	A B C D E	A B C D E	A B C D E	A B C D E
33	A B C D E	A B C D E	A B C D E	A B C D E
34	A B C D E	A B C D E	A B C D E	A B C D E
35	A B C D E	A B C D E	A B C D E	A B C D E
36	A B C D E	A B C D E	A B C D E	A B C D E
37	A B C D E	A B C D E	A B C D E	A B C D E
38	A B C D E	A B C D E	A B C D E	A B C D E
39	A B C D E	A B C D E	A B C D E	A B C D E
40	A B C D E	A B C D E	A B C D E	A B C D E
41	A B C D E	A B C D E	A B C D E	A B C D E
42	A B C D E	A B C D E	A B C D E	A B C D E
43	A B C D E	A B C D E	A B C D E	A B C D E
44	A B C D E	A B C D E	A B C D E	A B C D E
45	A B C D E	A B C D E	A B C D E	A B C D E
46	A B C D E	A B C D E	A B C D E	A B C D E
47	A B C D E	A B C D E	A B C D E	A B C D E
48	A B C D E	A B C D E	A B C D E	A B C D E
49	A B C D E	A B C D E	A B C D E	A B C D E
50	A B C D E	A B C D E	A B C D E	A B C D E

SECTION 5

1	A	B	C	D	E	26	A	B	C	D	E
2	A	B	C	D	E	27	A	B	C	D	E
3	A	B	C	D	E	28	A	B	C	D	E
4	A	B	C	D	E	29	A	B	C	D	E
5	A	B	C	D	E	30	A	B	C	D	E
6	A	B	C	D	E	31	A	B	C	D	E
7	A	B	C	D	E	32	A	B	C	D	E
8	A	B	C	D	E	33	A	B	C	D	E
9	A	B	C	D	E	34	A	B	C	D	E
10	A	B	C	D	E	35	A	B	C	D	E
11	A	B	C	D	E	36	A	B	C	D	E
12	A	B	C	D	E	37	A	B	C	D	E
13	A	B	C	D	E	38	A	B	C	D	E
14	A	B	C	D	E	39	A	B	C	D	E
15	A	B	C	D	E	40	A	B	C	D	E
16	A	B	C	D	E	41	A	B	C	D	E
17	A	B	C	D	E	42	A	B	C	D	E
18	A	B	C	D	E	43	A	B	C	D	E
19	A	B	C	D	E	44	A	B	C	D	E
20	A	B	C	D	E	45	A	B	C	D	E
21	A	B	C	D	E	46	A	B	C	D	E
22	A	B	C	D	E	47	A	B	C	D	E
23	A	B	C	D	E	48	A	B	C	D	E
24	A	B	C	D	E	49	A	B	C	D	E
25	A	B	C	D	E	50	A	B	C	D	E

SECTION 6

1	A	B	C	D	E	26	A	B	C	D	E
2	A	B	C	D	E	27	A	B	C	D	E
3	A	B	C	D	E	28	A	B	C	D	E
4	A	B	C	D	E	29	A	B	C	D	E
5	A	B	C	D	E	30	A	B	C	D	E
6	A	B	C	D	E	31	A	B	C	D	E
7	A	B	C	D	E	32	A	B	C	D	E
8	A	B	C	D	E	33	A	B	C	D	E
9	A	B	C	D	E	34	A	B	C	D	E
10	A	B	C	D	E	35	A	B	C	D	E
11	A	B	C	D	E	36	A	B	C	D	E
12	A	B	C	D	E	37	A	B	C	D	E
13	A	B	C	D	E	38	A	B	C	D	E
14	A	B	C	D	E	39	A	B	C	D	E
15	A	B	C	D	E	40	A	B	C	D	E
16	A	B	C	D	E	41	A	B	C	D	E
17	A	B	C	D	E	42	A	B	C	D	E
18	A	B	C	D	E	43	A	B	C	D	E
19	A	B	C	D	E	44	A	B	C	D	E
20	A	B	C	D	E	45	A	B	C	D	E
21	A	B	C	D	E	46	A	B	C	D	E
22	A	B	C	D	E	47	A	B	C	D	E
23	A	B	C	D	E	48	A	B	C	D	E
24	A	B	C	D	E	49	A	B	C	D	E
25	A	B	C	D	E	50	A	B	C	D	E

SECTION 1

Time—30 minutes

40 QUESTIONS

For each question in this section, choose the best answer and blacken the corresponding space on the answer sheet.

Each question below consists of a word in capital letters, followed by five lettered words or phrases. Choose the word or phrase that is most nearly opposite in meaning to the word in capital letters. Since some of the questions require you to distinguish fine shades of meaning, consider all the choices before deciding which is best.

Example:

GOOD: (A) sour (B) bad (C) red (D) hot (E) ugly

Ⓐ ● Ⓒ Ⓓ Ⓔ

1. VACATE: (A) adhere (B) rent (C) grasp (D) occupy (E) expel
2. AUTHENTIC: (A) bogus (B) ephemeral (C) allusive (D) perjured (E) altered
3. DISCLOSE: (A) murmur (B) confer (C) write (D) open (E) conceal
4. APEX: (A) nadir (B) extremity (C) goal (D) dearth (E) failure
5. WHET: (A) barter (B) desiccate (C) satiate (D) thicken (E) blunt
6. IMPEDIMENT: (A) regulation (B) aid (C) consequence (D) foresight (E) ease
7. ACUMEN: (A) sloth (B) error (C) carelessness (D) boredom (E) obtuseness
8. NEOPHYTE: (A) native (B) junior (C) instructor (D) veteran (E) director
9. DERELICT: (A) holy (B) willful (C) dutiful (D) considerate (E) sober
10. SALIENT: (A) unsavory (B) inconspicuous (C) mysterious (D) commonplace (E) undistinguished

Each sentence below has one or two blanks, each blank indicating that something has been omitted. Beneath the sentence are five lettered words or sets of words. Choose the word or set of words that best fits the meaning of the sentence as a whole.

Example:

Although its publicity has been ----, the film itself is intelligent, well-acted, handsomely produced, and altogether ----.

(A) tasteless..respectable (B) extensive..moderate (C) sophisticated..amateur (D) risqué..crude (E) perfect..spectacular

● Ⓑ Ⓒ Ⓓ Ⓔ

11. Recent studies show that although school-based programs and mass media support can encourage preschool learning, the major influence on early childhood education is ----.

(A) the home environment
(B) television viewing
(C) teacher training
(D) grammar school experiences
(E) still unknown

12. Federal insurance programs have greatly increased the ---- of individual bank deposits, and few experts fear any repetition of the widespread loss of ---- that occurred during the Great Depression.

(A) safety..savings
(B) number..capital
(C) practicality..homes
(D) popularity..incomes
(E) volume..property

13. An amazing gulf separates our culture from that of the world before the invention of printing; a studious man of the year 1300 would have considered himself ---- if he could have amassed a collection of just twenty books in a lifetime.

(A) unlucky
(B) impoverished
(C) scholarly
(D) fortunate
(E) grateful

GO ON TO THE NEXT PAGE

14. Like primitive peoples, the small child believes in the magical power of ----; to wish for something, the child feels, is to make it ----.

(A) death..exist
(B) thought..intelligible
(C) belief..visible
(D) desire..happen
(E) words..real

15. Although Babbage's early plans for a computing machine were highly ----, they proved to be ----, for the machine was never built.

(A) workable..unnecessary
(B) impractical..insignificant
(C) ingenious..impracticable
(D) technical..manageable
(E) impressive..useful

Each question below consists of a related pair of words or phrases, followed by five lettered pairs of words or phrases. Select the lettered pair that best expresses a relationship similar to that expressed in the original pair.

Example:

YAWN:BOREDOM:: (A) dream:sleep (B) anger:madness (C) smile:amusement (D) face:expression (E) impatience:rebellion
Ⓐ Ⓑ ● Ⓓ Ⓔ

16. HUMILITY:BRAGGART::
(A) generosity:misogynist
(B) violence:overlord
(C) kindliness:boor
(D) warfare:pacifist
(E) selflessness:egotist

17. DETECTIVE:FINGERPRINT::
(A) geologist:continent
(B) philologist:language
(C) composer:sonata
(D) philatelist:stamp
(E) biologist:specimen

18. WRECK:VESSEL:: (A) lemon:automobile
(B) feathers:bird (C) carcass:animal
(D) skeleton:bones (E) graveyard:body

19. UNFORMED:EMBRYO:: (A) partial:organ
(B) lifeless:creature (C) shapeless:seed
(D) chaotic:form (E) mature:adult

20. ARGUMENT:REFUTE::
(A) fact:reveal
(B) agreement:establish
(C) contention:disprove
(D) belief:accept
(E) rebuttal:respond

21. STACCATO:MUSIC:: (A) thunderous:ovation
(B) graceful:dance (C) brittle:sculpture
(D) clipped:speech (E) vigorous:painting

22. BOXER:PUGILISM::
(A) teacher:pedagogy
(B) musician:instrumentation
(C) driver:exploration
(D) actor:emotion
(E) detective:crime

23. PATIENT:QUACK:: (A) prank:hoaxster
(B) victim:bully (C) suspect:officer
(D) prospect:salesperson (E) client:shyster

24. GRATITUDE:THANK:: (A) friendship:repay
(B) generosity:offer (C) admiration:applaud
(D) obligation:resent (E) annoyance:snub

25. JINGOISM:PATRIOTISM::
(A) selfishness:conceit
(B) arrogance:pride
(C) belligerence:amity
(D) tyranny:democracy
(E) chauvinism:xenophobia

Each passage below is followed by questions based on its content. Answer all questions following a passage on the basis of what is stated or implied in that passage.

In the late 1930s and early 1940s, a group of blacks in Washington, D.C., resorted to direct action to try to break the economic discrimination that continued to deny them jobs. The New Negro Alliance began in 1933 when three or four young men saw the management of a hamburger grill discharging black employees and replacing them with whites, although the cafe's entire trade came from blacks. A campaign developed to bring consumer pressure on businesses in black neighborhoods. The idea of using black purchasing power to try to get and keep black jobs was not new in Washington. Andrew Hilyer's Union League had stood for the same approach. Now the New Negro Alliance urged, "Don't buy where you can't work. Buy where you work—buy where you can clerk."

Through picketing and boycotts, the New Negro Alliance forced some Washington businesses to hire blacks. Although some businesses obtained injunctions against the alliance, the Supreme Court eventually ruled in its favor. The alliance also attacked the city government on its hiring policies, decrying the decrease over the years in the proportion of municipal jobs held by blacks. Pointing out that there were only 36 blacks on the police force in 1938, the alliance insisted that the city needed 373 black officers to give blacks fair representation. In like manner, the alliance attacked the fire department, which employed only 17 black fire fighters.

GO ON TO THE NEXT PAGE

26. According to the passage, the New Negro Alliance fought against racial discrimination primarily in the area of

(A) access to public facilities
(B) governmental policies
(C) voting rights
(D) employment opportunities
(E) salaries and working conditions

27. It can be inferred that the New Negro Alliance's efforts to force businesses to hire blacks were probably most effective with businesses

(A) whose clientele was mostly or entirely black
(B) that had previously demonstrated a willingness to hire some black workers
(C) located in neighborhoods with a low rate of unemployment
(D) that had few or no black customers
(E) owned and managed by whites

28. The passage states that some business owners responded to the campaign of the New Negro Alliance with

(A) threats of physical violence
(B) firings of black employees
(C) legal challenges
(D) shutdowns of stores and factories
(E) even greater antiblack discrimination

Line

Mr. Riley was a man of business, and suitably concerned with his own interest, yet he was more under the influence of small promptings than of farsighted designs. He had no private understanding with Walter Stelling; on the contrary, he knew very little of that man and his acquirements—not quite enough perhaps to warrant so strong a recommendation of him as he had given to his friend Tulliver. But he believed Mr. Stelling to be an excellent Latin tutor, for Gadsby had said so, and Gadsby's first cousin was an Oxford tutor, which was better ground for the belief even than Mr. Riley's own observation would have been; for though Mr. Riley had received a touch of the classics at the great Mudport Free School and had a sense of understanding Latin generally, his comprehension of any particular Latin was not strong.

Then, too, Stelling was an Oxford man, and a man who had had a university education could teach anything he liked, especially a man like Stelling, who had made a speech at a Mudport dinner on a political occasion and had done so well that it was generally remarked that this Stelling was a sharp fellow. Moreover, Mr. Riley knew of no other schoolmaster whom he had any ground for recommending instead; why, then, should he not recommend Stelling? His friend Tulliver had asked him for an opinion; it is always chilling in friendly conversation to say that you have no opinion to give. And if you deliver an opinion at all, it is mere stupidity not to do it with an air of conviction and well-founded knowledge. You make it your own in uttering it, and naturally get fond of it. Thus Mr. Riley, knowing no harm of Stelling to begin with and wishing him well, so far as he had any wishes at all concerning him, had no sooner recommended him than he began to think with admiration of a man recommended on such high authority.

29. The passage is primarily concerned with describing

(A) the interrelationships among a group of small-town citizens
(B) one man's reasons for recommending another for a job
(C) how one man persuades another to agree to a disadvantageous contract
(D) the author's opinions on the importance of a classical education
(E) the shrewd manipulation of a friend by an unscrupulous businessman

30. It can be inferred from the passage that Mr. Riley is very adept at

(A) persuading others to his point of view
(B) rationalizing his actions
(C) judging people by their conduct
(D) formulating well-reasoned opinions
(E) promoting the careers of his friends

31. It can be inferred from the passage that Mr. Riley's opinion of Mr. Stelling's abilities is based on all of the following EXCEPT

(A) the fame of Oxford University
(B) hearsay
(C) personal experience
(D) Mr. Stelling's educational background
(E) the opinion of a friend

32. The author's reference to "such high authority" (line 40) suggests Mr. Riley's

(A) status in the community
(B) objectivity
(C) respect for the learned
(D) cleverness
(E) egotism

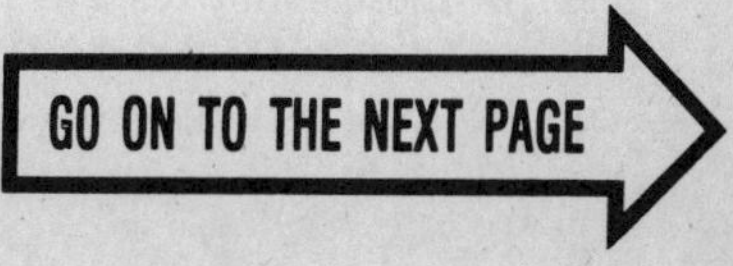

Although democratic theory attaches primary importance to the discussion of public issues by the mass media, it is clear that some segments of the media see themselves primarily as entertainers. The economic bases upon which each survives have much to do with whether the particular medium produces "educational," "informative," or "entertaining" content. Television, for example, is an oligopoly and acts in accordance with the expected behavior of such an economic structure. It has a restricted number of suppliers and distributors, few channels, and a focus on a national market, and it produces programs based on a small number of familiar formats, genres, and plots. Television, in particular, writes Professor Paul Hirsch, "is less distracted than any other mass medium by loyalties to such noneconomic goals as editorial policy and standards, generations of family ownership, or idiosyncratic decisions based on personal taste. It is an economic institution, first and foremost, responsive to market forces and concerned only incidentally with questions about its broader cultural role or possible effects on a nation of viewers."

Newspapers can also be viewed through an economic lens. Many are local monopolies, and an increasing number are owned by chains. Craft traditions and occupational norms must now interact with new economic and organizational conditions that may not provide an adequate climate for the broadest and most representative expression of views in a community or an adequate description of public events. For example, if circulation expansion is possible only in affluent suburbs, urban news must be balanced against suburban news not because of "objective" news criteria but because of marketing decisions made at national chain headquarters.

Obviously, the political and economic system of the United States provides a different set of media structures than may be found in other countries. In Canada, for example, commercial television coexists with the government-financed Crown Corporation, which has a national mandate to provide information and cultural content bearing on national identity. In Mexico, private activity dominates communication, and the government rarely interferes with the market. In Eastern European countries, the state controls television. There are also differences among the magazine, newspaper, radio, and book publishing industries in each of these countries. The point is that there is no way to separate the mass media system of a country from its larger social system.

33. The passage is primarily concerned with

(A) the influence of economics on the coverage of news by the mass media
(B) how effective the mass media are in keeping the public fully informed
(C) differences between television and newspapers in their treatment of public affairs
(D) the role of television news coverage in a democracy
(E) social and political pressures that affect news coverage by the mass media

34. According to the passage, television differs from other mass media in that it is

(A) more closely attuned to the needs of an urban audience
(B) less concerned with the preferences of a national market
(C) more directly responsive to economic influences
(D) less closely subject to governmental control
(E) more open to influence by the personal tastes of a few individuals

35. The author's description of how decisions are made at the national newspaper chains would best be illustrated by which of the following incidents?

(A) An editor orders a reporter to write a favorable story about a company that has purchased substantial advertising space in the newspaper.
(B) A newspaper is ordered by its chain's central office to print more news of interest to young professional people because circulation among that group has declined.
(C) The publisher of a newspaper fires the editor-in-chief because the newspaper's sales have fallen sharply over the last several years.
(D) A newspaper is ordered by its chain's central office to print more stories about sports because the television networks are broadcasting more sports coverage than ever before.
(E) An editor is asked by the publisher to print a story favorable to a political candidate whom the publisher personally supports.

GO ON TO THE NEXT PAGE

36. The passage suggests that the public's need for information on current affairs

(A) is likely to be met only by publicly funded branches of the mass media
(B) has been ignored or underestimated by past critics of the mass media
(C) is more likely to be met by media whose focus is on national rather than local concerns
(D) may be inadequately met by mass media that view themselves primarily as entertainers
(E) is most likely to be met through the influence of the free market on the mass media

37. The "craft traditions and occupational norms" to which the author refers (lines 27–28) would most likely include

(A) work rules laid down by newspaper printers' unions
(B) legal restrictions on newspaper treatment of controversial issues
(C) customs handed down through generations of a newspaper-owning family
(D) local preferences for particular types of news coverage
(E) traditional standards of journalistic ethics

For the archaeologist, changes in the earth's magnetic field provide an important opportunity for dating past cultural events. Magnetic observatories have noted fairly regular fluctuations in the earth's magnetic field over 12-hour, 24-hour, 1-month, 1-year, and 11-year cycles. These cyclic changes are minor (less than 0.1% of the observed field) and as such are irrelevant to the archaeologist. At the other extreme of periodicity and magnitude, actual reversals in the polarity of the earth's field have been recorded, occurring at intervals of approximately 200,000 years. Such long-term shifts have been found to be of some use in dating relics of hominid evolution, but by and large the period of change is too great for accurate age determination in archaeology. Between these two extremes, fluctuations in the earth's field, called secular variation, have been found to be great enough to be observable and short enough to be of use in precise age determination. Records of secular variation have been kept at various magnetic observatories for the past 400 years. From these records it is known that the direction of the earth's field changes at a rate of about 1 degree every 10 to 20 years. Movement at this order of magnitude provides the archaeologist with the opportunity to use the earth's field as the basis of a dating technique.

38. The author is mainly concerned with the use of magnetic variations in studying

(A) the evolution of the human species
(B) changes in human culture
(C) geological processes
(D) human migrations
(E) changes in the earth's magnetic field

39. According to the passage, evidence of reversals in the earth's magnetic field is not useful to archaeologists because such reversals

(A) cannot be dated accurately
(B) have not been directly recorded by magnetic observatories
(C) occur too infrequently
(D) leave little trace in human relics
(E) do not take place at regular intervals

40. It can be inferred that the use of secular variation in archaeological dating is based on the assumption that

(A) changes in the earth's magnetic field occur at a roughly constant rate
(B) human activity has influenced the strength and direction of the earth's magnetic field
(C) future changes in the earth's magnetic field are likely to resemble those of the past
(D) early humans were aware of the existence of the earth's magnetic field
(E) human evolution is continuing at the present time at about the same rate as in the past

S T O P

IF YOU FINISH BEFORE TIME IS CALLED, YOU MAY CHECK YOUR WORK ON THIS SECTION ONLY. DO NOT WORK ON ANY OTHER SECTION IN THE TEST.

SECTION 2

Time—30 minutes

35 QUESTIONS

In this section solve each problem, using any available space on the page for scratchwork. Then indicate the one correct answer in the appropriate space on the answer sheet.

The following information is for your reference in solving some of the problems.

Circle of radius r: Area $= \pi r^2$; Circumference $= 2\pi r$
The number of degrees of arc in a circle is 360.
The measure in degrees of a straight angle is 180.

Definitions of symbols:

$=$ is equal to $\leq$ is less than or equal to
$\neq$ is unequal to $\geq$ is greater than or equal to
$<$ is less than $\parallel$ is parallel to
$>$ is greater than $\perp$ is perpendicular to

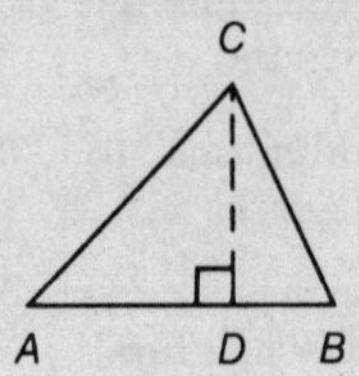

Triangle: The sum of the measures in degrees of the angles of a triangle is 180.

If $\angle CDA$ is a right angle, then

(1) area of $\triangle ABC = \frac{AB \times CD}{2}$

(2) $AC^2 = AD^2 + DC^2$

Note: Figures which accompany problems in this test are intended to provide information useful in solving the problems. They are drawn as accurately as possible EXCEPT when it is stated in a specific problem that its figure is not drawn to scale. All figures lie in a plane unless otherwise indicated. All numbers used are real numbers.

---

1. If $\frac{2}{5}$ of n is 12, then $n =$

(A) 30 (B) 24 (C) 18 (D) 15 (E) 8

2. A newsstand sells x newspapers per hour at a price of y cents each. If the newsstand is open z hours, how much money in dollars will it take in from the sale of newspapers?

(A) xyz (B) $\frac{xy}{100z}$ (C) $\frac{xyz}{100}$

(D) $\frac{y}{100} \times \frac{x}{z}$ (E) $\frac{100xy}{z}$

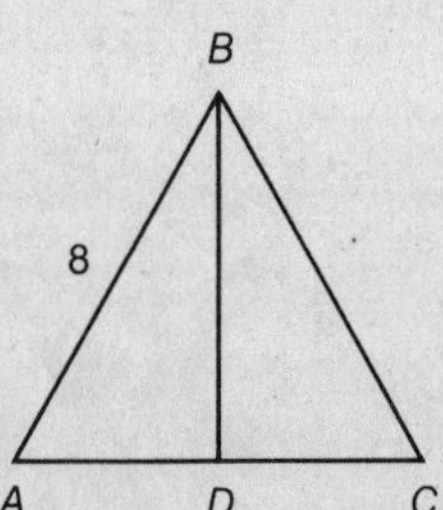

3. Triangle ABC above is an equilateral triangle. If $BD \perp AC$, what is the area of triangle ABD?

(A) $4\sqrt{3}$ (B) 16 (C) $6\frac{\sqrt{2}}{8}$

(D) $8\sqrt{3}$ (E) 32

4. If $x^2 - 9 = 4^2 \times 10$, then $x =$

(A) 10 (B) 11 (C) 12 (D) 13 (E) 14

5. A 12-liter solution of ammonia and water is 25% ammonia. How many liters of water must be added to reduce the concentration of ammonia in the solution to 20%?

(A) 3 (B) $2\frac{1}{2}$ (C) $2\frac{1}{4}$ (D) 2 (E) $1\frac{1}{2}$

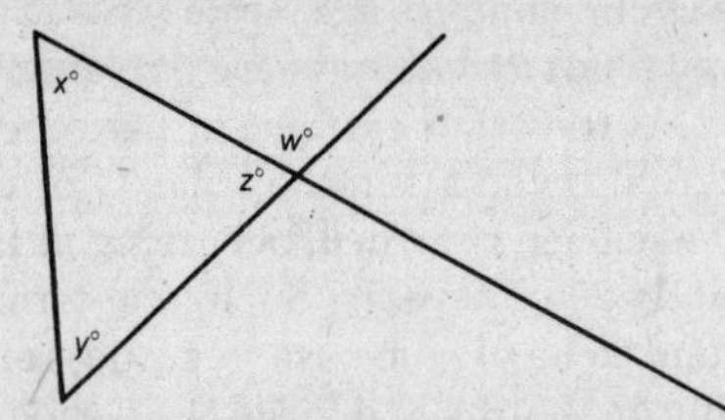

6. In the figure above, if $w = 110$, then $x =$

(A) $110 - y$ (B) 70 (C) $z + y - 70$

(D) $70 + y$ (E) $110 - z$

7. If exactly two of the three integers l, m, and n are odd, which of the following must be even?

I. $l + m + n$

II. lmn

III. $\frac{lmn}{2}$

(A) I only (B) II only (C) I and II only

(D) II and III only (E) I, II, and III

GO ON TO THE NEXT PAGE

Questions 8-27 each consist of two quantities, one in Column A and one in Column B. You are to compare the two quantities and on the answer sheet blacken space

A if the quantity in Column A is greater;
B if the quantity in Column B is greater;
C if the two quantities are equal;
D if the relationship cannot be determined from the information given.

Notes: 1. In certain questions, information concerning one or both of the quantities to be compared is centered above the two columns.
2. In a given question, a symbol that appears in both columns represents the same thing in Column A as it does in Column B.
3. Letters such as x, n, and k stand for real numbers.

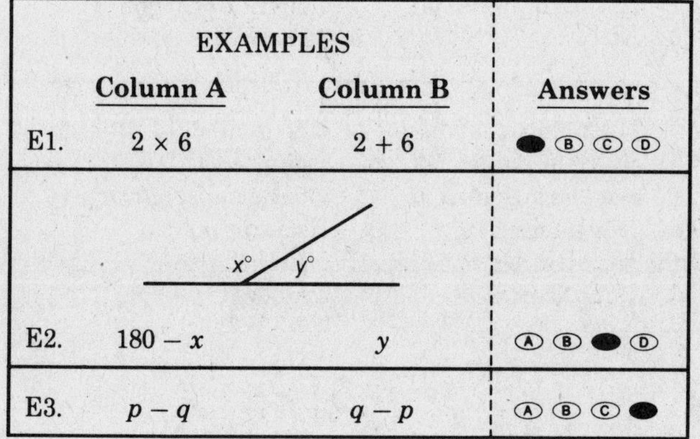

EXAMPLES

	Column A	Column B	Answers
E1.	2×6	$2 + 6$	● Ⓑ Ⓒ Ⓓ
E2.	$180 - x$	y	Ⓐ Ⓑ ● Ⓓ
E3.	$p - q$	$q - p$	Ⓐ Ⓑ Ⓒ ●

	Column A	Column B
8.	$\frac{1}{2} \times \frac{2}{3} \times \frac{3}{4} \times \frac{4}{5}$	$\frac{1}{2} + \frac{2}{3} + \frac{3}{4} + \frac{4}{5}$

$x - y = 3$

9.	$3x - 3y$	3

Mike's car travels 24 miles on a gallon of gas. Gas costs $1.20 per gallon.

10.	Cost of gas for traveling 120 miles in Mike's car	$6.00
11.	$\frac{19,390}{100}$	$\frac{2,166}{10}$

$x > 0$

12.	x	$\frac{1}{x}$

	Column A	Column B

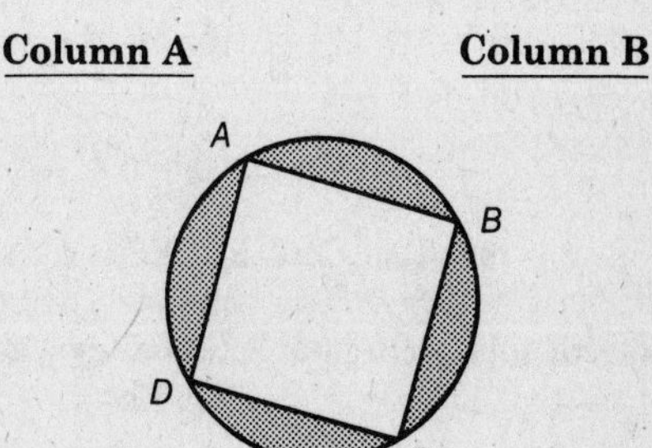

$ABCD$ is a square inscribed in the circle.

13.	Area of the shaded region	Area of square $ABCD$

$x = 4$
$y = -4$

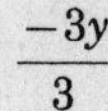

14.	$\frac{3x}{-3}$	$\frac{-3y}{3}$

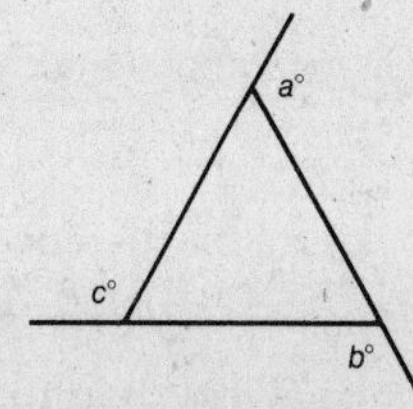

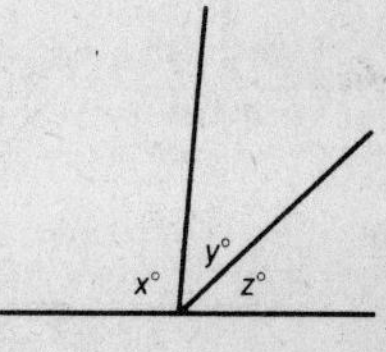

15.	$a + b + c$	$x + y + z$

For any real number n, $\textcircled{n} = \frac{n+1}{n-1}$.

16.	$\textcircled{2}$	$\textcircled{5} \times \textcircled{3}$
17.	The number of days in a month	Half the number of minutes in an hour

GO ON TO THE NEXT PAGE

	Column A	Column B

r, s, and t are integers.

$0 < r < s < t < 6$

18.	$2r$	t

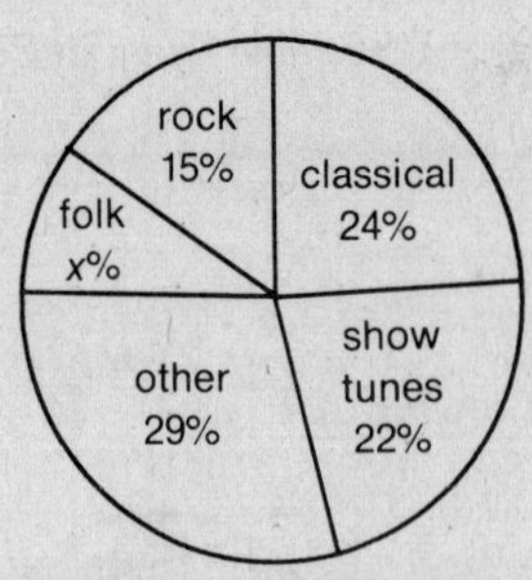

1984 RECORD SALES BY TYPE

19.	Sales of folk records for 1984	Sales of comedy records for 1984

$x + 6 = 10 - 3x$

20.	$3x + 3$	5

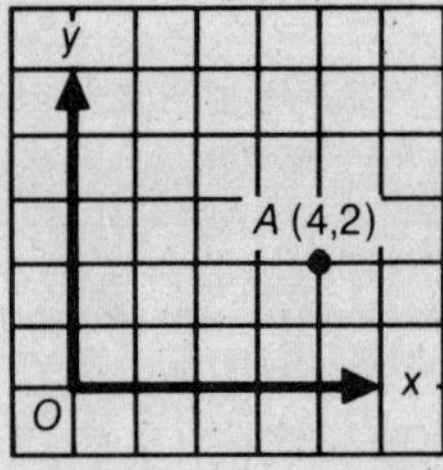

Point B to be placed on the grid above has coordinates (3, 4).

21.	Distance OA	Twice the distance AB

$P = \{\text{all positive odd integers less than } 13\}$

$Q = \{\text{all integers greater than 1 but less than } 8\}$

22.	The number of members of set P that are also members of set Q	3

$$\frac{3}{n} = 1$$

23.	$\frac{n}{2}$	$\frac{2}{n}$

	Column A	Column B

A 8 B, 6, D C — Rectangle $ABCD$

W 7 X, Z Y — Square $WXYZ$

24.	Length of diagonal AC	Length of diagonal WY
25.	The number of different pairs that can be chosen from four items	The number of different groups of three that can be chosen from five items

x is a negative number.

26.	$\frac{x^6}{x^3}$	$\frac{x^4}{x^2}$

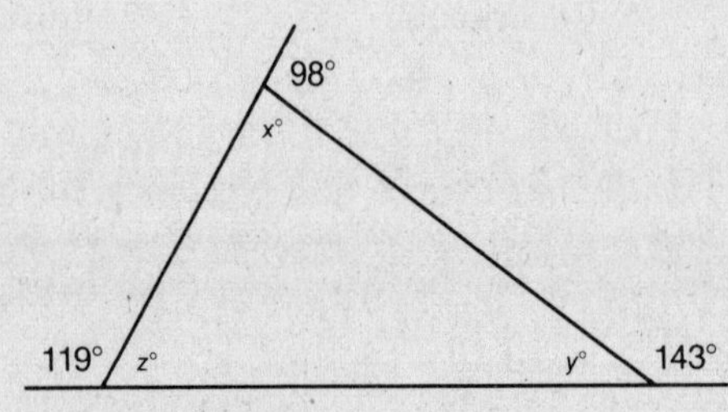

27.	The average (arithmetic mean) of x, y, and z	75

GO ON TO THE NEXT PAGE

Solve each of the remaining problems in this section using any available space for scratchwork. Then indicate the one correct answer in the appropriate space on the answer sheet.

28. If $5x + 2y = 25$ and $42 - 4x = 6y$, then $3y + 2x =$

(A) 16 (B) 18 (C) 21 (D) 24 (E) 28

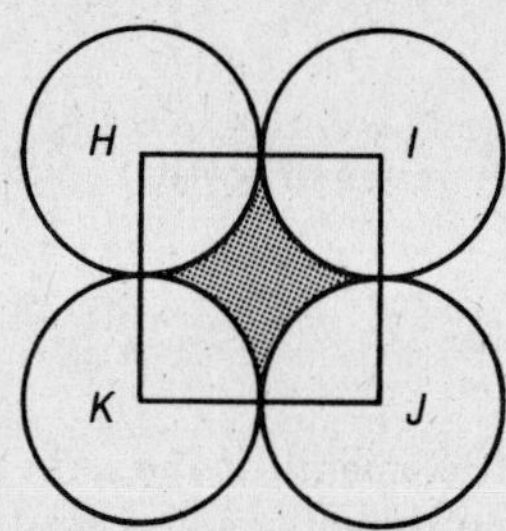

29. In the figure above, the vertices of square $HIJK$ are the centers of circles H, I, J, and K. If the area of the square is 36, what is the area of the shaded region?

(A) $36 - 9\pi$ (B) $18 - 4\pi$ (C) $6 - \pi$

(D) 9π (E) $36 - \frac{9\pi}{4}$

Questions 30–31 refer to the following figure, which represents the circular board used in a certain game. In that game, each player advances a token clockwise around the board. On each turn, the player moves her or his token the number of spaces indicated on the starting space for that move. A player who lands on space 0 takes no more turns.

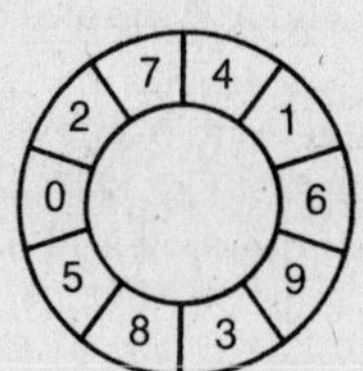

30. How many turns can a player who starts on space 1 take?

(A) 3 (B) 4 (C) 5 (D) 6 (E) 7

31. Five players begin the game. The player who starts on which of the following spaces will take the fewest turns?

(A) 2 (B) 3 (C) 5 (D) 7 (E) 9

32. In a coordinate graph system, a circle is drawn whose center is at (1, 3) and whose radius is 3. The following pairs of coordinates define other points lying in the same graph system. Which point lies closest to the edge of the circle?

(A) (2, 3) (B) (3, −2) (C) (5, 0)

(D) (−2, −1) (E) (4, 2)

33. If $2(a + 3) < 8$, which of the following must be true?

(A) $a > \frac{2}{3}$ (B) $a < 1$ (C) $5a < 2$

(D) $a < 0$ (E) $a > 3$

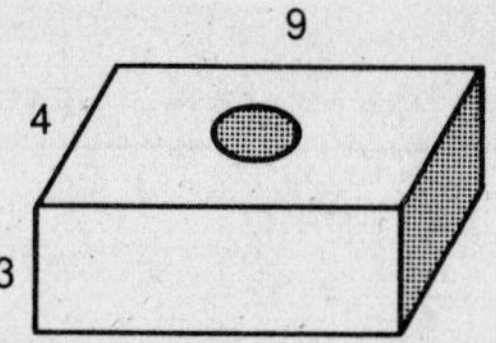

34. The rectangular solid above has a length of 9, a width of 4, and a height of 3, as shown. If a cylindrical section with a radius of 1 is removed from the solid, what is the total remaining volume of the solid?

(A) $108 - \pi^2$ (B) $36 - 4\pi$ (C) $54 + 16\pi$

(D) $108 - \pi$ (E) $108 - 3\pi$

35. A club had \$35.00 in its treasury. The club members decided to hold a raffle to raise money. They sold raffle tickets at \$1.50 each; they spent \$225.00 on prizes. If the club treasury showed a final balance of \$200.00, how many raffle tickets did the members sell?

(A) 133 (B) 175 (C) 225

(D) 260 (E) 340

S T O P

IF YOU FINISH BEFORE TIME IS CALLED, YOU MAY CHECK YOUR WORK ON THIS SECTION ONLY. DO NOT WORK ON ANY OTHER SECTION IN THE TEST.

SECTION 3

Time—30 minutes

50 QUESTIONS

The questions in this section measure skills that are important to writing well. In particular, they test your ability to recognize and use language that is clear, effective, and correct according to the requirements of standard written English, the kind of English found in most college textbooks.

Directions: The following sentences contain problems in grammar, usage, diction (choice of words), and idiom.

Some sentences are correct.
No sentence contains more than one error.

You will find that the error, if there is one, is underlined and lettered. Assume that elements of the sentence that are not underlined are correct and cannot be changed. In choosing answers, follow the requirements of standard written English.

If there is an error, select the one underlined part that must be changed to make the sentence correct and blacken the corresponding space on your answer sheet.

If there is no error, blacken answer space Ⓔ.

EXAMPLE:

The region has a climate so severe that plants
A
growing there rarely had been more than twelve
B C
inches high. No error
D E

SAMPLE ANSWER

Ⓐ Ⓑ ● Ⓓ Ⓔ

1. Sherlock Holmes, the detective hero created by
A
Arthur Conan Doyle, is probably more readily
B
recognized in more countries of the world than
C
any fictitious character. No error
D E

2. Johnson's *Dictionary* is not only a remarkable
A
feat of scholarship but also a storehouse
B C
of examples of his famous style and wit.
D
No error
E

3. Neither federal deregulation of the airlines
A
nor the effects of the lingering recession has proven
B C
fatal to the aeronautics industry. No error
D E

4. Other presidents have achieved greater things
A
than Grover Cleveland, but few have had
B C
greater personal integrity and honesty

than him. No error
D E

5. A row of quaint cottages, houses, and apartments
A B
are visible from the hilltop. No error
C D E

6. Public buildings resembling a Greek temple
A
were typical of the so-called Greek revival
B
style, which flourished in the mid-nineteenth
C D
century. No error
E

GO ON TO THE NEXT PAGE

7. Until well into the Renaissance, all knowledge
A
was regarded as unified; thus, a medieval
B C
textbook on rhetoric might include information
that we would classify as scientific, historical,
D
or religious. No error
E

8. The genre of the novel had its first emerging
A B
in England and France in the middle decades
C
of the eighteenth century. No error
D E

9. Despite the disadvantages of the high-technology
A
approach to modern medicine, most American
B
hospitals seem to have chose that route
C
rather than a less costly one. No error
D E

10. The project intrigued Greenspan, but she was
A
reticent to commit herself to a task that she knew
B C D
would require several years of her life. No error
E

11. If one is planning a summer vacation in
A
San Francisco, they should be sure to pack a
B C
warm jacket for those chilly evenings by the bay.
D
No error
E

12. Published in 1954–55, most critics consider
A B
Tolkien's greatest work to be *The Lord of the*
C
Rings, a multivolume epic fantasy that combines
ancient legends with an inventiveness that is
D
Tolkien's own. No error
E

13. There are, in the opinion of most anthropologists
A
who have studied the phenomenon of mass
B C
migrations, no single cause for most such
D
movements. No error
E

14. The earliest domesticated animals were
A
probably dogs that followed bands of hunters
B
from place to place, eventually making friends
C
with the humans. No error
D E

15. Dante has been called the European poet
from who writers of every language can
A B
most profitably learn. No error
C D E

16. By her comments, the chairperson
A
quietly sought to discourage the Langleys and
B
we from entering the competition. No error
C D E

17. Shortened by rain, most of the fans
A
were disappointed by the game, which ended
B C
after only six innings of play. No error
D E

18. One drawback of using fines to punish
A
corporate wrongdoing is that companies generally
B
find some means of passing the costs incurred
C
out to their customers. No error
D E

19. An executive for an insurance company
A
as well as an artist, Montgomery works on his
B C
canvases in odd moments stole from his other
D
responsibilities. No error
E

GO ON TO THE NEXT PAGE

20. No system of diplomacy that human beings have yet (A) been able (B) to device (C) is capable of ensuring (D) complete freedom from the possibility of war. No error (E)

21. Profoundly pessimistic, (A) a marked contrast to most other (B) parts of the Bible is offered (C) by the Book of Ecclesiastes, part of (D) the so-called wisdom literature of the ancient Jews. No error (E)

22. Not every American is (A) enthusiastic about sports, but (B) they are all inclined to think (C) in ways colored by (D) the competitive mores of sport. No error (E)

23. Although they are (A) cousins, Angela and Carol do not greatly (B) resemble each other (C) in appearance, mannerisms, nor (D) speech. No error (E)

24. Belief (A) in an afterlife is not necessarily a primitive concept (B); in some religions, it appears to have been (C) a relatively late (D) philosophical development. No error (E)

25. The idea of tourism did not develop (A) until the nineteenth century, when industrialization had advanced (B) to the point (C) where large numbers of people were both (D) mobile enough and wealthy enough to travel for amusement. No error (E)

Directions: In each of the following sentences, some part or all of the sentence is underlined. Below each sentence you will find five ways of phrasing the underlined part. Select the answer that produces the most effective sentence, one that is clear and exact, without awkwardness or ambiguity, and blacken the corresponding space on your answer sheet. In choosing answers, follow the requirements of standard written English. Choose the answer that best expresses the meaning of the original sentence.

Answer (A) is always the same as the underlined part. Choose answer (A) if you think the original sentence needs no revision.

EXAMPLE:

Laura Ingalls Wilder published her first book and she was sixty-five years old then.

(A) and she was sixty-five years old then
(B) when she was sixty-five years old
(C) at age sixty-five years old
(D) upon reaching sixty-five years
(E) at the time when she was sixty-five

SAMPLE ANSWER

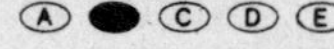

26. Success in law school requires an analytical mind, skill in speaking and writing, and one must be intelligent.

(A) and one must be intelligent
(B) along with being intelligent
(C) together with intelligence
(D) and intelligence
(E) and intellectual ability

27. During the 1970s, financial experts rose to head many major corporations, analysts considered the trend unfortunate for business.

(A) During the 1970s,
(B) During the 1970s, since
(C) In the 1970s, as
(D) As when, through the 1970s,
(E) When, during the 1970s,

GO ON TO THE NEXT PAGE

28. Angered by the president's recent foreign policy decisions, the speech was picketed by a group of protesters.

(A) the speech was picketed by a group of protesters
(B) a group of protesters picketed the speech
(C) the picketing of the speech was done by a group of protesters
(D) protesters grouped to picket the speech
(E) it fell to a group of protesters to picket the speech

29. When laying floor tiles decorated with a pattern, it is best that the direction of the pattern be laid in alternate fashion from tile to tile.

(A) it is best that the direction of the pattern be laid in alternate fashion
(B) you ought to lay the tiles alternately, pattern-wise,
(C) one should alternate the direction of the pattern
(D) the pattern is best laid alternately in direction
(E) it is best to lay the direction of the pattern in alternation

30. Far from being a threat to western sheep farmers, the wolves are themselves an endangered species.

(A) Far from being a threat to
(B) Other than a threat to
(C) Not to threaten
(D) Despite a threat to
(E) Nonthreatening to

31. Scott Joplin was a classically trained musician, so during his lifetime blacks had few career opportunities in classical music.

(A) so
(B) and so
(C) however,
(D) but
(E) for

32. Although petroleum products are used mainly for fuel, many synthetic materials, such as plastics, are also made from them.

(A) many synthetic materials, such as plastics, are also made from them
(B) they are also used in making many synthetic materials, such as plastics
(C) plastics, and other synthetic materials, are also made from them
(D) many plastics, like other synthetic materials, are made from them as well
(E) they are used, too, to make such synthetic materials as, for instance, plastics

33. The first phonograph records were not made as discs but rather in that of cylinders.

(A) made as discs but rather in that of
(B) disc-shaped but rather
(C) discs but
(D) made into discs but into
(E) in the form of discs but

34. The Puritans did not actually close the theaters until 1642, nevertheless, public attacks on the theater had begun long before.

(A) until 1642, nevertheless,
(B) until 1642, however,
(C) prior to 1642, when
(D) before 1642; furthermore,
(E) until 1642, although

35. Writing each day in the attic of her farmhouse, Edgeworth's novel was completed in about a year.

(A) Edgeworth's novel was completed in about a year
(B) the novel was completed by Edgeworth in about a year
(C) it took about a year for Edgeworth to complete her novel
(D) a year passed before Edgeworth's novel was completed
(E) Edgeworth completed her novel in about a year

36. Great Britain emerged victorious from the French and Indian Wars, and this victory ensuring British supremacy in North America.

(A) and this victory ensuring
(B) this victory ensured
(C) so ensured
(D) and this victory assuring
(E) thus ensuring

37. The North possessed not only advantages due to geography but also a greater population and a stronger industrial base.

(A) but also a greater
(B) but also possessed a larger
(C) as well as a greater
(D) and also a greater
(E) along with more

38. The educated man of the Middle Ages was well aware that the earth is not the center of the universe.

(A) that the earth is not
(B) of the earth not being
(C) of the fact that the earth is not
(D) that it is not true that the earth is
(E) of the earth's status as other than

GO ON TO THE NEXT PAGE

39. Garrison has the political instincts, the dynamic speaking style, and he also has the boundless egotism of the born candidate.

(A) he also has the boundless egotism of
(B) the boundless egotism of
(C) he is boundlessly egotistical, as is
(D) boundless egotism, of
(E) the same boundless egotism, as

40. The gold coin issued to commemorate the Olympic Games is the first one of such coins to be issued by the U.S. government in eighty years.

(A) one of such coins to be issued
(B) coin like this to be issued
(C) coin of such a type issued
(D) such coin issued
(E) coin produced

Directions: The remaining questions are like those at the beginning of the section. For each sentence in which you find an error, select the one underlined part that must be changed to make the sentence correct and blacken the corresponding space on your answer sheet. If there is no error, blacken answer space E.

41. Senator Clark, along with three members of his
A
staff, were reportedly among those taken
B C D
hostage on the airliner. No error
E

42. The charge of stealing club property is
A
so serious that it may not be sufficient
B
merely to censor a member found guilty of that
C D
charge. No error
E

43. Ambassador Kirkpatrick is presently en route
A B
to Pakistan; she is arrived there by this time
C D
tomorrow afternoon. No error
E

44. It sometimes takes a tragedy, like a bridge
A B
collapse or a tunnel cave-in, to remind people
of the importance of maintaining our public
C D
structures. No error
E

45. Him and Roberta, although they lived
A B C
only a few blocks away, were among the last
D
guests to arrive. No error
E

46. Unless some more final offer is
A B
received through our emissaries in Peking,
it must be assumed that the negotiations
C
are at an impasse. No error
D E

47. Greatly outnumbered, the small party of
A B
advance scouts was easily took prisoner by the
C
contingent of enemy cavalry. No error
D E

48. The effects of Miss Wozniak's action are
A B
apparent, but her motives of taking such a
C
drastic step remain difficult to fathom. No error
D E

49. Scarcely none of those trying out for the
A B
team had even seen a rugby match, let alone
C D
played the sport. No error
E

50. The Inuit people of Alaska are among the most
A B
ancient of the peoples which inhabit North
C D
America. No error
E

S T O P

IF YOU FINISH BEFORE TIME IS CALLED, YOU MAY CHECK YOUR WORK ON THIS SECTION ONLY. DO NOT WORK ON ANY OTHER SECTION IN THE TEST.

SECTION 4

Time—30 minutes

45 QUESTIONS

For each question in this section, choose the best answer and blacken the corresponding space on the answer sheet.

Each question below consists of a word in capital letters, followed by five lettered words or phrases. Choose the word or phrase that is most nearly opposite in meaning to the word in capital letters. Since some of the questions require you to distinguish fine shades of meaning, consider all the choices before deciding which is best.

Example:

GOOD: (A) sour (B) bad (C) red (D) hot (E) ugly

Ⓐ ● Ⓒ Ⓓ Ⓔ

1. FICKLE: (A) steadfast (B) fated (C) certain (D) secure (E) valorous

2. BRAZEN: (A) cowardly (B) modest (C) placid (D) disingenuous (E) retired

3. PAROCHIAL: (A) tolerant (B) magnanimous (C) irreligious (D) urbane (E) omnivorous

4. SYMMETRY: (A) deformity (B) imbalance (C) harmony (D) ambiguity (E) depression

5. CONGEAL: (A) blacken (B) intensify (C) decay (D) adhere (E) dissolve

6. OMINOUS: (A) casual (B) avoidable (C) positive (D) fortunate (E) propitious

7. IRREPRESSIBLE: (A) dull and unimpressive (B) harshly restrained (C) easily controlled (D) deeply moved (E) listless and weak

8. CONDONE: (A) abuse (B) profane (C) withdraw (D) condemn (E) waive

9. HETEROGENEOUS: (A) innumerable (B) uniform (C) relative (D) multiple (E) equivalent

10. TRACTABLE: (A) fallow (B) intransigent (C) permanent (D) invidious (E) compromising

11. PRODIGAL: (A) thrifty (B) domestic (C) minuscule (D) amiable (E) docile

12. SURFEIT: (A) quantity (B) request (C) lack (D) outpouring (E) waste

13. OSTRACIZE: (A) rebut (B) deploy (C) accept (D) indict (E) enjoin

14. TRUCULENT: (A) gifted (B) noble (C) generous (D) gallant (E) mild

15. INIQUITY: (A) pride (B) rationale (C) fairness (D) norm (E) concern

Each sentence below has one or two blanks, each blank indicating that something has been omitted. Beneath the sentence are five lettered words or sets of words. Choose the word or set of words that best fits the meaning of the sentence as a whole.

Example:

Although its publicity has been ----, the film itself is intelligent, well-acted, handsomely produced, and altogether ----.

(A) tasteless..respectable (B) extensive..moderate (C) sophisticated..amateur (D) risqué..crude (E) perfect..spectacular

● Ⓑ Ⓒ Ⓓ Ⓔ

16. Like Senator Muskie in 1972, who "lost" the primary when his winning margin was smaller than expected, this year's front-runner needs ---- victory to maintain his position.

(A) a nominal (B) a decisive (C) a technical (D) a narrow (E) an official

17. Despite Gandhi's stature as India's most respected leader, his pleas for intercommunal peace went unheeded; ---- between Hindus and Moslems ---- all over the country.

(A) warfare..subsided
(B) mistrust..diminished
(C) friendship..deepened
(D) misgivings..spread
(E) violence..erupted

18. Although separate studies of human and animal perceptions of time have long been pursued, only recently have the two areas of research begun to be ----.

(A) understood (B) well known (C) discussed (D) interconnected (E) analyzed

GO ON TO THE NEXT PAGE

19. As the reporters continued their ---- questioning, the governor's hands began to tremble, suggesting the ---- he felt over their line of inquiry.

(A) hostile. .anxiety
(B) journalistic. .fatigue
(C) intense. .resentment
(D) respectful. .hostility
(E) routine. .alarm

20. Beverage retailers have ---- the new bottle-deposit bill, saying that it will cause a ---- in sales of bottled soft drinks.

(A) criticized. .change
(B) ignored. .drop
(C) attacked. .surge
(D) opposed. .decline
(E) favored. .diminution

Each passage below is followed by questions based on its content. Answer all questions following a passage on the basis of what is stated or implied in that passage.

Few of Virginia's early settlers were born gentlemen. Shipping people, sons of merchants, squires, or yeomen were the highest among them, and men who arrived as servants later became burgesses. Still, if life in America could change English townsfolk into rough frontiersmen, it could also change English tradesmen and even bondsmen into plantation owners. As early Virginians began to acquire land and from the land gained wealth, they also began to hanker after the ways of England's landed gentry. Even before the seventeenth century was out, ships that came up the waterways to the thriving tobacco plantations brought lutes, virginals, violins, oboes, and flageolets for the planters' pleasure.

The transplanting of English music at fullest flower to a scattering of plantations in America was nevertheless a patent impossibility. No doubt music—whether madrigals or psalms—afforded the lonely planters, their families, and their servants grateful relief from the monotony of life in so remote a place. No doubt they sang, too, familiar songs and ballads, inventing new verses (or whole new versions) reflecting their American experience. And as Negro servants or slaves became part of the plantation scene they were quickly encouraged to learn to fiddle jigs and reels for dancing. But even 170 years after the founding of the Jamestown colony, one of the new planter aristocracy to whom music was most dear, Thomas Jefferson, lamented in a letter the "state of deplorable barbarism" in which music found itself in Virginia.

For music, as for the people who came to America, there would have to be a new beginning in the new land. It would not be made in Virginia from the heights of Tudor church music or the instrumental music of fashionable England, but from simple psalmody and the homely musical practice of families settling a wilderness.

21. Which of the following titles best describes the content of the passage?

(A) Foreign Influences on Early American Music
(B) Music and the Class System in Colonial Virginia
(C) Music in Early Virginia: New Music for a New Land
(D) The First Musicians in the New World
(E) Music in Colonial America: A Hardy Transplant

22. According to the passage, the Virginia colonists began to import musical instruments when

(A) their increased wealth permitted it
(B) the loneliness of the frontier became almost unbearable
(C) Negro slaves become part of their households
(D) music reflecting American experience began to be composed
(E) a landed aristocracy had developed

23. All of the following are mentioned in the passage as types of music enjoyed by the early settlers in Virginia EXCEPT

(A) madrigals
(B) reels
(C) psalms
(D) symphonies
(E) ballads

24. It can be inferred that the "barbarism" referred to by Jefferson (line 32) was attributable mainly to the

(A) lower-class origins of most of the early settlers of Virginia
(B) absence of musically trained individuals among the Virginia colonists
(C) impossibility of bringing English musical culture in its entirety to America
(D) monotony of life in a relatively crude frontier setting
(E) lack of inherited wealth with which to support an advanced musical culture

25. The passage implies that the development in Virginia of a distinctly American type of music was

(A) an unfortunate necessity
(B) astonishingly rapid
(C) retarded by colonial attitudes
(D) a slow process
(E) a result of political and religious changes

GO ON TO THE NEXT PAGE

Plankton is a collective term applied chiefly to all those small, extremely diverse forms of plants and animals that drift aimlessly with the currents in all natural waters and in artificial impoundments. Most of the forms swim feebly and are incapable of making long horizontal journeys except as they are swept along by persistent winds and currents. Some, nevertheless, make extended vertical migrations in response to stimuli not clearly understood. These movements have been partially correlated with diurnal changes in the intensity of light and the salinity, temperature, and density of the water at different levels. Community pressures may also be important factors. Most planktonic organisms, especially the one-celled plants and animals, are extremely small and were unknown prior to the invention of the compound microscope late in the seventeenth century.

The distribution of planktonic organisms is almost universal in aquatic environments. Some cosmopolitan forms of plankton are found at all latitudes, while other forms have disconnected distributions and occur in scattered, discrete areas where conditions favor their existence. No climate is too warm or too cold to support plankton of one type or another. The greatest concentration of phytoplanktons (plants) occurs in the upper layers of water down to the limit of effective penetration by light (100 to 130 feet). Maximum density of zooplankton (animals) also occurs in the surface strata, where the herbivorous species feed on the phytoplankton. Some forms, primarily zooplankton, inhabit the bottom zones of lakes and streams and also the depths of the oceans.

Especially dense concentrations of a single species of zooplankton or phytoplankton are population explosions known as swarms, flowers, or blooms. They occur seasonally or at irregular intervals when environmental conditions are exceptionally favorable for the growth and reproduction of a particular species. Swarming or flowering communities occur most often when the water is enriched by runoff from agricultural land, by upwelling from the bottom, by overturn of a body of water due to wind and thermal changes, or by the addition of small quantities of organic wastes from urban communities.

A bloom in the Vermillion River, South Dakota, lasted two or three days after the spring runoff in 1923. It formed a thick red scum from bank to bank for many miles along the river's course. Under the microscope, the scum was seen to be made up of *Euglena*, a single-celled organism. The blooming or swarming of *Euglena* was not an annual occurrence, and large crowds gathered to view this unusual phenomenon. Most of these people had lived near the river many years but had never seen the red scum before. A similar occurrence at some earlier time probably gave the river its name.

26. According to the passage, by contrast with their horizontal movements, the vertical movements of plankton appear to be

(A) more rapid
(B) more frequent
(C) less random
(D) more comprehensible
(E) less significant

27. It can be inferred from the passage that the plankton population of a body of water may not be observed with the naked eye UNLESS

(A) the light is of an unusual intensity
(B) a swarm of plankton has developed
(C) seasonal conditions are appropriate
(D) several different species of plankton are present
(E) the water is especially warm

28. In the passage, the word *cosmopolitan* (line 22) is used to mean

(A) many-celled
(B) dwelling near cities
(C) living in groups
(D) of various types
(E) widely adaptable

29. According to the passage, both zooplankton and phytoplankton

I. are herbivorous
II. may form swarming communities
III. are most dense in surface waters

(A) II only
(B) III only
(C) I and III only
(D) II and III only
(E) I, II, and III

30. It can be inferred from the passage that the Vermillion River bloom of 1923 was most probably produced by

(A) a runoff of water from nearby farmlands
(B) the proximity of an urban community
(C) upwelling of dirt and silt from the riverbed
(D) an overturn of water caused by temperature changes
(E) the gathering of crowds of people on the riverbanks

GO ON TO THE NEXT PAGE

Select the word or set of words that best completes each of the following sentences.

31. Everyone knows that the Gettysburg Address is a masterpiece of prose style, but few people realize that many of Lincoln's other mature writings reveal a similar ----.

(A) historical understanding
(B) moral greatness (C) sense of occasion
(D) political adroitness (E) literary ability

32. Because of the ---- of observing the whale in its natural habitat, its gestation period is still ----.

(A) excitement..mysterious
(B) opportunity..variable
(C) demands..lengthy
(D) importance..uncertain
(E) difficulty..unknown

33. Just as higher ---- rates encourage letter writers to turn to private delivery services, so higher subway fares lead to ---- use of other means of transportation.

(A) telephone..greater
(B) mail..daily
(C) postal..increased
(D) tax..widespread
(E) messenger..excessive

34. The primary argument in favor of extraterrestrial life is a negative one: most scientists can see no valid reason to assume that life is ---- our planet.

(A) necessary for (B) unique to
(C) important on (D) found upon
(E) created on

35. In every nation and era, acts of human ---- have occurred; yet, at the same time, some voice has usually been raised in protest to affirm the essential ---- of humanity.

(A) depravity..nature
(B) cruelty..goodness
(C) violence..wickedness
(D) compassion..dignity
(E) folly..generosity

Each question below consists of a related pair of words or phrases, followed by five lettered pairs of words or phrases. Select the lettered pair that best expresses a relationship similar to that expressed in the original pair.

Example:

YAWN:BOREDOM:: (A) dream:sleep
(B) anger:madness (C) smile:amusement
(D) face:expression (E) impatience:rebellion

Ⓐ Ⓑ ● Ⓓ Ⓔ

36. CHISEL:STONE:: (A) spade:clay
(B) blade:handle (C) knife:wood
(D) brush:painting (E) needle:thread

37. HAUGHTY:PRIDE:: (A) timid:boldness
(B) gay:frivolity (C) grandiose:beauty
(D) humble:honesty (E) brash:bravery

38. PROWESS:INEFFECTUAL::
(A) courage:realistic
(B) suavity:oafish
(C) gallantry:daring
(D) profundity:careless
(E) exuberance:scholarly

39. ARTERY:CAPILLARY:: (A) river:pond
(B) bough:twig (C) branch:root
(D) nerve:impulse (E) highway:railroad

40. PLEASURE:EXHILARATION::
(A) worry:despair
(B) gladness:happiness
(C) misery:gloom
(D) optimism:pessimism
(E) rapture:exaltation

41. PRISM:REFRACT:: (A) chemist:analyze
(B) soloist:interpret (C) jurist:uphold
(D) novelist:relate (E) professor:lecture

42. HISS:THREATENED:: (A) bark:noisy
(B) snarl:vicious (C) purr:contented
(D) whinny:equine (E) rattle:poisonous

43. RIND:CENTER:: (A) crust:core
(B) skin:form (C) edge:surface
(D) facade:wall (E) perimeter:radius

44. SQUELCH:RUMOR:: (A) deny:allegation
(B) obscure:deception (C) edit:manuscript
(D) quash:investigation (E) quench:thirst

45. BIGOT:PREJUDGE:: (A) criminal:condone
(B) bully:domineer (C) braggart:praise
(D) boor:badger (E) dolt:err

S T O P

IF YOU FINISH BEFORE TIME IS CALLED, YOU MAY CHECK YOUR WORK ON THIS SECTION ONLY. DO NOT WORK ON ANY OTHER SECTION IN THE TEST.

SECTION 5

Time—30 minutes

25 QUESTIONS

In this section solve each problem, using any available space on the page for scratchwork. Then indicate the one correct answer in the appropriate space on the answer sheet.

The following information is for your reference in solving some of the problems.

Circle of radius r: Area $= \pi r^2$; Circumference $= 2\pi r$
The number of degrees of arc in a circle is 360.
The measure in degrees of a straight angle is 180.

Definitions of symbols:

$=$	is equal to	$\leq$	is less than or equal to
$\neq$	is unequal to	$\geq$	is greater than or equal to
$<$	is less than	$\parallel$	is parallel to
$>$	is greater than	$\perp$	is perpendicular to

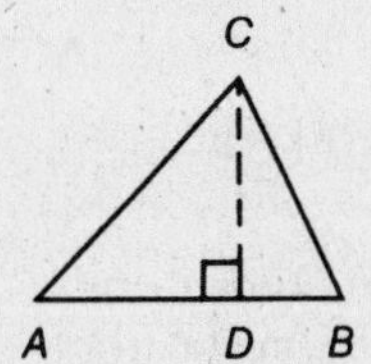

Triangle: The sum of the measures in degrees of the angles of a triangle is 180.
If $\angle CDA$ is a right angle, then

(1) area of $\triangle ABC = \dfrac{AB \times CD}{2}$

(2) $AC^2 = AD^2 + DC^2$

Note: Figures which accompany problems in this test are intended to provide information useful in solving the problems. They are drawn as accurately as possible EXCEPT when it is stated in a specific problem that its figure is not drawn to scale. All figures lie in a plane unless otherwise indicated. All numbers used are real numbers.

---

1. A store sells apples at a price of 8 apples for \$1.00. If it changes the price to 10 apples for \$1.50, what is the percent increase in price per apple?

(A) $2\frac{1}{2}\%$ (B) 5% (C) $12\frac{1}{2}\%$
(D) 20% (E) 25%

2. If $2y - x = 12$ and $y + 6 = 3x + 2y - 7$, then $x + y =$

(A) 9 (B) 7 (C) 6 (D) 5 (E) 4

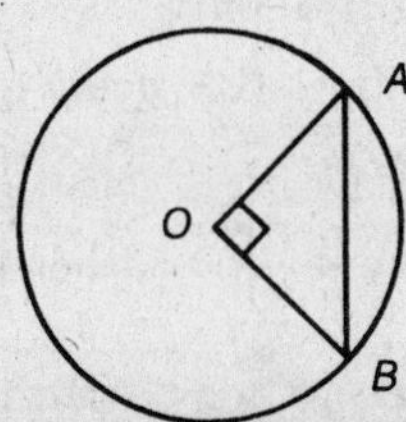

3. In the figure above, triangle AOB is drawn inside circle O, as shown. If the length of side AO is 6, what is the length of arc AB?

(A) $\frac{3}{2}\pi^2$ (B) $\frac{12}{5\pi}$ (C) $\frac{3\pi}{2}$
(D) 3π (E) 6π

4. An auto dealer sells 40 cars, of which some are compacts, others are sedans, and still others are station wagons. Any of the following could be the ratio of compact cars to sedans to station wagons EXCEPT

(A) 2:1:1 (B) 3:1:1 (C) 3:2:1
(D) 3:2:3 (E) 5:3:2

5. If $(a + b)^2$ is odd and b^2 is even, then which of the following expressions must be odd?

I. a
II. a^2
III. ab

(A) II only (B) III only (C) I and II only
(D) II and III only (E) I, II, and III

6. Roberta bicycles due north for 7 miles and then due east for 24 miles. She then bicycles straight back to her starting point. What is the total mileage for her trip?

(A) 38 miles
(B) 42 miles
(C) 49 miles
(D) 56 miles
(E) It cannot be determined from the information given.

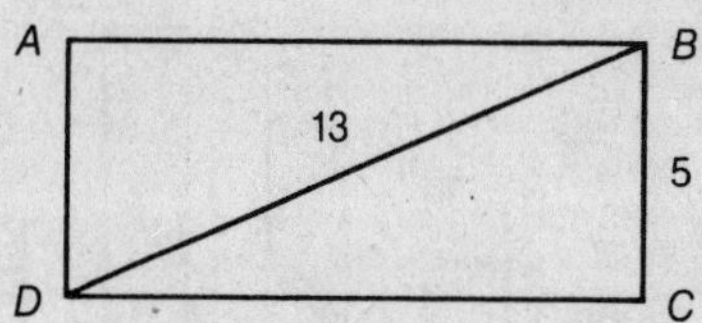

7. In the figure above, DB is a diagonal of rectangle $ABCD$. What is the area of the rectangle?

(A) 48 (B) 55 (C) 60 (D) 65 (E) 72

GO ON TO THE NEXT PAGE

8. Each hen on a farm lays l eggs per week. If there are m hens on the farm, how many weeks will it take them to lay n eggs?

(A) $\frac{l}{mn}$ (B) $\frac{n}{lm}$ (C) lmn

(D) $\frac{m}{ln}$ (E) $\frac{lm}{n}$

9. If $\frac{4 + x}{3 - x} = 6$, then $x =$

(A) 1 (B) 2 (C) 3 (D) 6 (E) 12

10. At a certain college, 40 percent of the students in the freshman class are enrolled in a chemistry class, and 80 percent are enrolled in an English class. If there are 150 students in the freshman class, what is the maximum number of students that can be enrolled in a chemistry class but not in an English class?

(A) 12 (B) 18 (C) 20 (D) 30 (E) 40

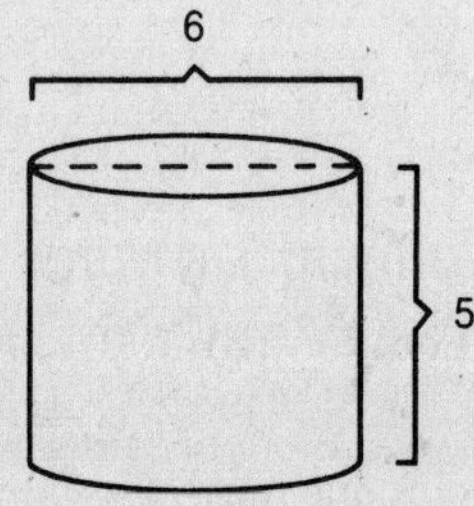

11. The closed cylinder above has a diameter of 6 and a height of 5, as shown. What is the total surface area of the cylinder?

(A) 30π (B) $36\pi + 30$ (C) 60π

(D) 48π (E) $18\pi + 120$

Questions 12–13 refer to the following graph.

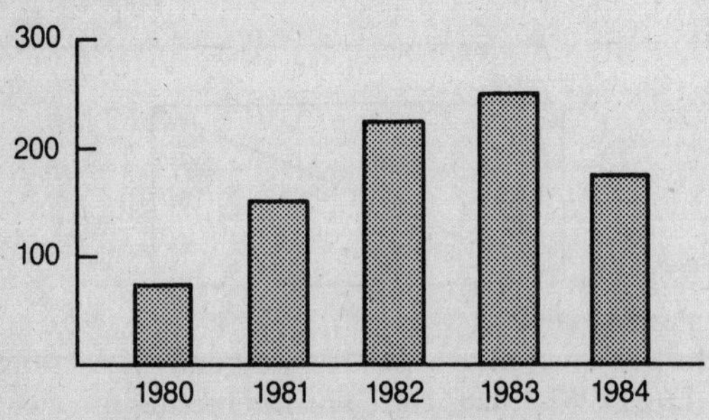

HOUSES BUILT IN SOMERVILLE
1980–1984

12. The difference between the number of houses built in the year when the most houses were built and the number built in the year when the fewest houses were built is about

(A) 75 (B) 160 (C) 175 (D) 190 (E) 215

13. The total number of houses built in Somerville during the period shown on the graph is about how many times the number built during 1983?

(A) $11\frac{2}{3}$ (B) 9 (C) 7 (D) 5 (E) 3.5

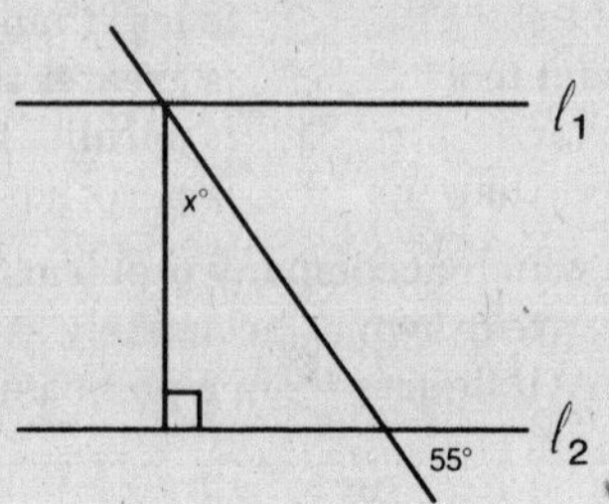

14. In the figure above, if $\ell_1 \| \ell_2$, then $x =$

(A) 15 (B) 25 (C) 35 (D) 45 (E) 55

15. If $\frac{x}{y}$ is positive, then which of the following must be positive?

I. xy
II. $x + y$
III. $x - y$

(A) I only (B) II only (C) III only

(D) I and II only (E) II and III only

16. If $\frac{a + b}{a - b} = 1$ and $\frac{a + c}{a - c} = 5$, then $\frac{abc}{a} =$

(A) 5 (B) 3 (C) 2 (D) 1 (E) 0

17. Points A, B, C, and D lie on a number line in that order. Given the lengths $BD = 11$, $AC = 8$, and $CD = 6$, what is the length AB?

(A) 3 (B) 4 (C) 5 (D) 6 (E) 7

GO ON TO THE NEXT PAGE

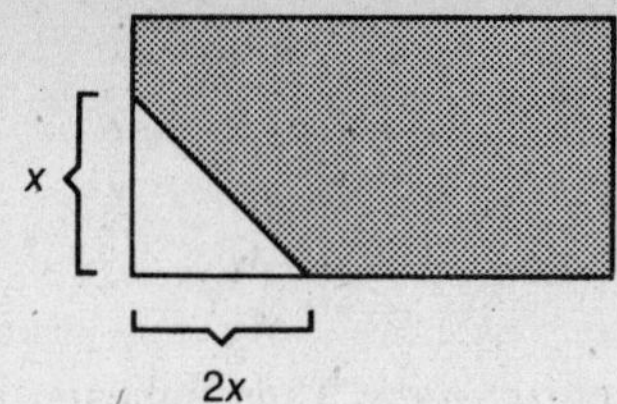

Note: Figure not drawn to scale.

18. If the shaded region of the rectangle above has an area of $5x^2$, which of the following could be the lengths of the sides of the rectangle in terms of x?

(A) $2x, 3x$ (B) $3x, 4x$ (C) $4x, 5x$
(D) $2x, 4x$ (E) $3x, 5x$

Sun.	Mon.	Tues.	Wed.	Thu.	Fri.
			1	2	3
4	5	6	7	8	9

19. In a certain mythical country, a week consists of 6 days, as indicated by the partial calendar above. If the month shown in the calendar contains 31 days, the first day of the following month will fall on a

(A) Sunday (B) Monday (C) Wednesday
(D) Thursday (E) Friday

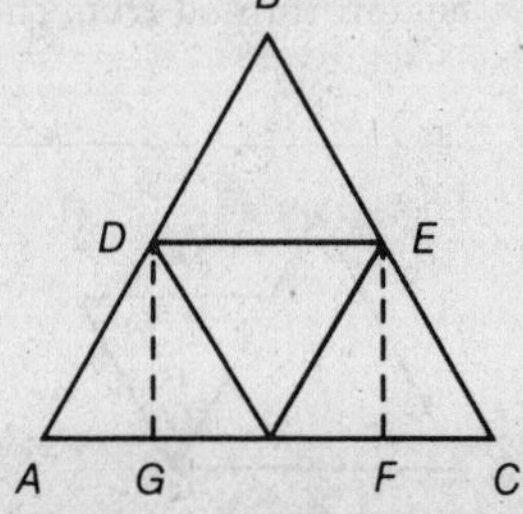

20. In the figure above, triangle ABC is an equilateral triangle divided into four smaller equilateral triangles, as shown. If the perimeter of triangle ABC is 12, what is the area of rectangle $DEFG$?

(A) 3 (B) $2\sqrt{3}$ (C) 4 (D) $4\sqrt{3}$ (E) $6\sqrt{3}$

21. If the operation $\boxed{n}$ is defined as $\frac{n+2}{n^2}$, then $\boxed{4} =$

(A) $\frac{3}{8}$ (B) $\frac{1}{2}$ (C) 4 (D) $\frac{6}{14}$ (E) $\frac{3}{4}$

22. If the area of a rectangle is 36, which of the following could be its perimeter?

I. 20
II. 24
III. 26

(A) I only (B) II only (C) III only
(D) II and III only (E) I, II, and III

23. A dress is put on sale on Monday. On Tuesday, the price of the dress is reduced by 10%. On Wednesday, the second price is reduced by $\frac{1}{3}$. On Thursday, the third price is reduced by 25%. The dress is then sold for \$18. What was the price of the dress on Monday?

(A) \$26 (B) \$30 (C) \$33
(D) \$37 (E) \$40

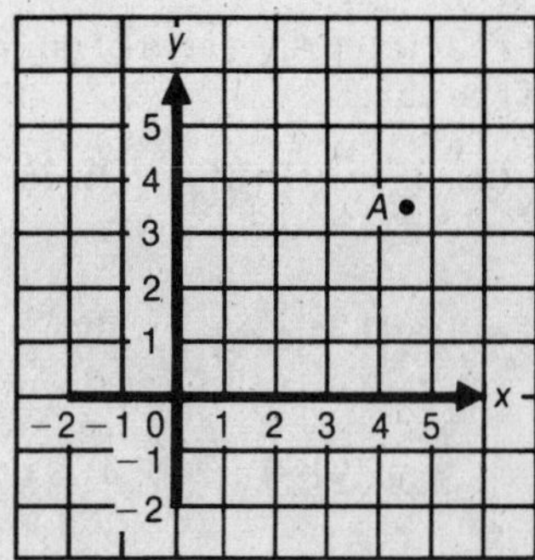

24. In the coordinate graph system above, a circle is drawn with its center at point A. What is the least possible radius circle A can have if circle A includes parts of at least three of the four quadrants of the system?

(A) 2 (B) 4 (C) 5 (D) 6 (E) 7

List A: −2, 0, 2, 4
List B: −1, 1, 3, 5

25. If a is any number from List A above, and b is any number from List B, how many different values are possible for $a + b$?

(A) 5 (B) 7 (C) 9 (D) 11 (E) 16

S T O P

IF YOU FINISH BEFORE TIME IS CALLED, YOU MAY CHECK YOUR WORK ON THIS SECTION ONLY. DO NOT WORK ON ANY OTHER SECTION IN THE TEST.

SECTION 6

Time—30 minutes

25 QUESTIONS

In this section solve each problem, using any available space on the page for scratchwork. Then indicate the one correct answer in the appropriate space on the answer sheet.

The following information is for your reference in solving some of the problems.

Circle of radius r: Area $= \pi r^2$; Circumference $= 2\pi r$
The number of degrees of arc in a circle is 360.
The measure in degrees of a straight angle is 180.

Definitions of symbols:

$=$	is equal to	$\leq$	is less than or equal to
$\neq$	is unequal to	$\geq$	is greater than or equal to
$<$	is less than	$\parallel$	is parallel to
$>$	is greater than	$\perp$	is perpendicular to

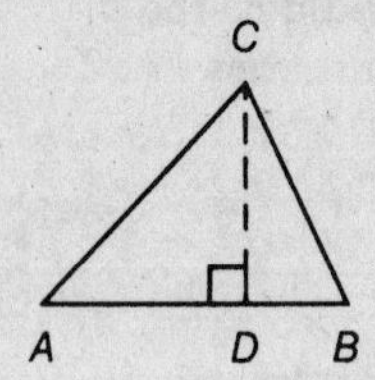

Triangle: The sum of the measures in degrees of the angles of a triangle is 180.

If $\angle CDA$ is a right angle, then

(1) area of $\triangle ABC = \frac{AB \times CD}{2}$

(2) $AC^2 = AD^2 + DC^2$

Note: Figures which accompany problems in this test are intended to provide information useful in solving the problems. They are drawn as accurately as possible EXCEPT when it is stated in a specific problem that its figure is not drawn to scale. All figures lie in a plane unless otherwise indicated. All numbers used are real numbers.

---

1. A cube has a total surface area of 96. What is the volume of the cube?

   (A) 16 (B) 48 (C) 64 (D) 78 (E) 96

2. If $3a - 4b = 6$, and $2a + b = \frac{19}{2}$, then $a - b =$

   (A) $\frac{3}{2}$ (B) $\frac{5}{2}$ (C) 3 (D) 4 (E) 5

3. A student's average score on six tests is 83. When the lowest score is dropped, the average increases to 87. What was the lowest score?

   (A) 63 (B) 65 (C) 67 (D) 71 (E) 73

4. $\frac{3}{4} \times \frac{2}{3} \times \frac{1}{2} \times \frac{4}{9} \times \frac{3}{4} =$

   (A) $\frac{1}{12}$ (B) $\frac{3}{8}$ (C) $\frac{1}{3}$ (D) $\frac{4}{9}$ (E) $\frac{9}{16}$

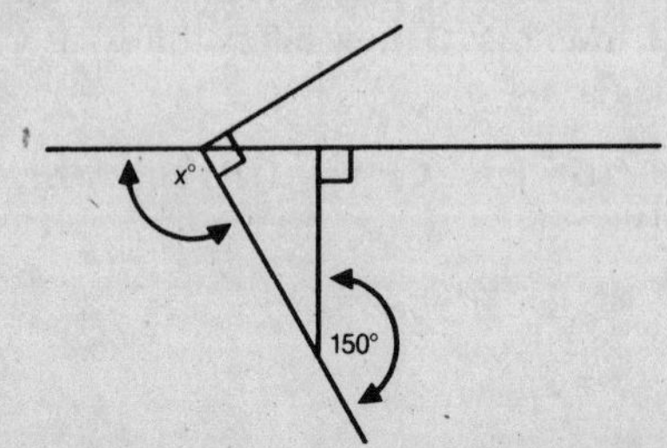

5. In the figure above, $x =$

   (A) 90 (B) 110 (C) 120
   (D) 150 (E) 165

6. If x and y are integers, and $12 > x \geqq y \geqq 4$, then each of the following is a possible value of x EXCEPT

   (A) 12 (B) 11 (C) 7 (D) 5 (E) 4

7. If $\left(\frac{x}{y}\right)\left(\frac{y}{z}\right)\left(\frac{z}{a}\right) = -1$, then $x + a =$

   (A) -1 (B) 0 (C) 1 (D) 2
   (E) It cannot be determined from the information given.

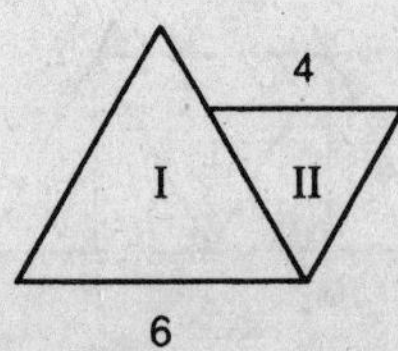

8. Triangles I and II above are equilateral triangles with the sides shown. The ratio of the area of triangle I to the area of triangle II is

   (A) 2:3 (B) 4:3 (C) 3:2
   (D) 2:1 (E) 9:4

GO ON TO THE NEXT PAGE

Questions 9–10 refer to the operation defined by the equation $x \mathbin{@} y = \frac{xy}{2}$.

9. $3 \mathbin{@} 5 =$

(A) 4 (B) 8 (C) $\frac{5}{2}$ (D) $\frac{15}{2}$ (E) 15

10. $7 \mathbin{@} (4 \mathbin{@} 3) =$

(A) 14 (B) 18 (C) 21 (D) 28 (E) 42

11. If $x = \sqrt[3]{27}$, then $x^2 =$

(A) 3 (B) 9 (C) 18 (D) 27 (E) 81

12. The number 660 is evenly divisible by each of the following EXCEPT

(A) 2 (B) 3 (C) 5 (D) 7 (E) 11

13. If $a + b + c = 0$, then which of the following must be true?

I. $abc = 0$

II. $\frac{ab}{c} < 0$

III. $\frac{a}{bc} > 0$

(A) None (B) I and II only (C) I and III only (D) II and III only (E) I, II, and III

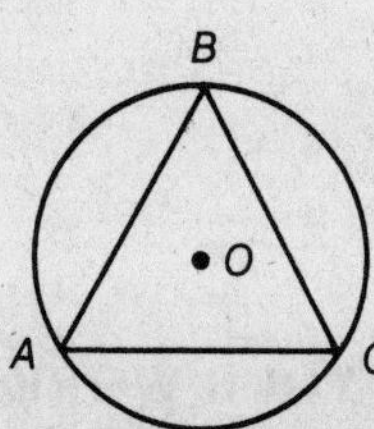

14. In the figure above, triangle ABC is an equilateral triangle inscribed in circle O. If the area of circle O is 9π, what is the length of arc BCA?

(A) $\frac{9\pi}{4}$ (B) 2π (C) $3\pi^2$ (D) 6 (E) 4π

15. A store owner buys wristwatches for x dollars per dozen. She sells them for y dollars each. If other costs are disregarded, what is her total profit on sales of z wristwatches?

(A) $\frac{xyz}{12}$ (B) $\frac{x}{12} - yz$ (C) $12xy - z$

(D) $z\left(\frac{x}{y} - 12\right)$ (E) $yz - \frac{xz}{12}$

16. If $t + 12 = 3t - 3 - \frac{t}{2}$, then $t =$

(A) 4 (B) 6 (C) 10 (D) 12 (E) 18

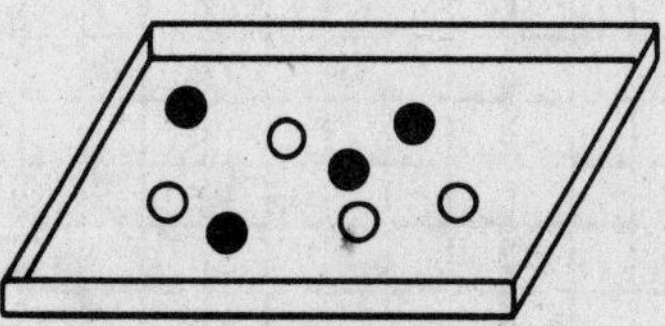

17. In a certain game, a player shuts his or her eyes and draws either a black token or a white token from a box. The player does not replace the token after drawing. If the box contains the tokens shown above, what is the chance that a player will choose black tokens on each of two consecutive draws?

(A) $\frac{3}{14}$ (B) $\frac{1}{4}$ (C) $\frac{2}{7}$ (D) $\frac{1}{8}$ (E) $\frac{3}{7}$

18. 50 percent of 75 percent of 20 percent of 20 =

(A) 1.5 (B) 3 (C) 4 (D) 6 (E) 7.5

19. If $x^2 + 3x = 10$, then which of the following is a possible value of x?

(A) -5 (B) -2 (C) 0 (D) 5 (E) 7

GO ON TO THE NEXT PAGE

20. Water flows into a 90-gallon tank through a pipe at the rate of 3 gallons per minute. Water leaks out of the tank through a hole at the rate of 1 gallon every 2 minutes. If the tank is empty when water starts flowing in, after how many minutes will it be $\frac{1}{3}$ full?

(A) 6 (B) 9 (C) 12 (D) 15 (E) 16

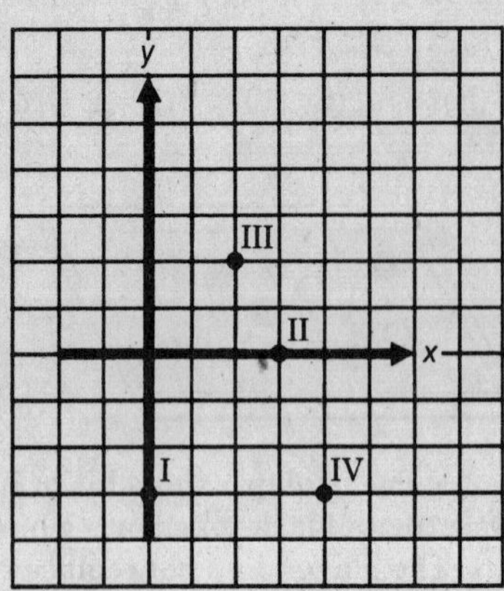

21. On the graph above, a square is drawn with an area of 25. The center of the square is at (2, −1). Which of the four points shown on the graph could be located within the square?

(A) I and II only (B) II and IV only
(C) III and IV only (D) I, II, and IV only
(E) I, II, III, and IV

22. Tickets for a play are sold for \$2, \$3, and \$5. Total receipts on sales of 305 tickets are \$925. If 140 \$2 tickets are sold, how many \$5 tickets are sold?

(A) 45 (B) 60 (C) 75 (D) 90 (E) 150

23. If $3a + \frac{a}{2} + 4 = 6$, then $\frac{a}{2} =$

(A) $\frac{12}{5}$ (B) $\frac{7}{4}$ (C) $\frac{4}{3}$ (D) $\frac{3}{4}$ (E) $\frac{2}{7}$

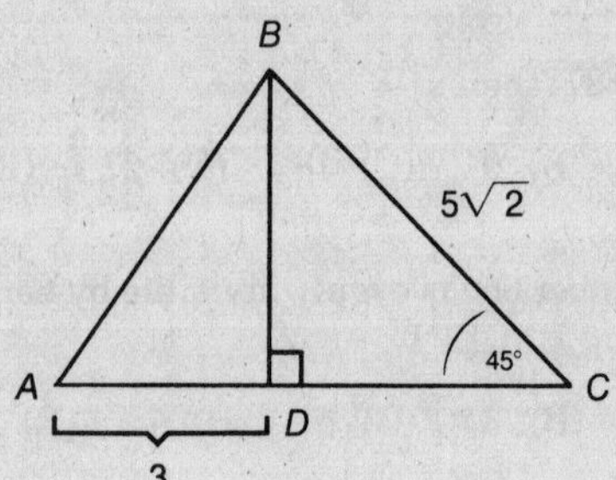

24. What is the area of $\triangle ABC$ in the figure above?

(A) $10\sqrt{2}$ (B) 20 (C) $15\sqrt{2}$
(D) 24 (E) $\frac{15}{2}$

25. Lynda is six years younger than John. In seven years, Lynda's age will be $\frac{3}{4}$ of John's age. How old is John?

(A) 7 (B) 11 (C) 13 (D) 17 (E) 24

S T O P

IF YOU FINISH BEFORE TIME IS CALLED, YOU MAY CHECK YOUR WORK ON THIS SECTION ONLY. DO NOT WORK ON ANY OTHER SECTION IN THE TEST.

1. Check your answers against the answer key on page 124.
2. To figure your SAT-verbal score:
   A. Count the total number of correct answers you chose in Sections 1 and 4.
   B. Count the total number of incorrect answers you chose in Sections 1 and 4. Multiply this number by 1/4. Ignore any questions you left blank.
   C. Subtract the result of Step B from the result of Step A. Round off the answer to the nearest whole number. This whole number is your SAT-verbal raw score.
   D. Find your raw score in the first column of the score conversion table on page 125. Read across to the column headed SAT-verbal. The three-digit number there is your SAT-verbal score.
3. To figure your SAT-mathematical score:
   A. Count the total number of correct answers you chose in Sections 2, 5, and 6.
   B. Count the total number of incorrect answers you chose from questions 8–27 in Section 2. Multiply this number by 1/3. Ignore any questions you left blank.
   C. Count the total number of incorrect answers you chose from all other questions in Sections 2, 5, and 6. Multiply this number by 1/4. Ignore any questions you left blank.
   D. Add the results of Step B and Step C. Subtract this total from the result of Step A. Round off the answer to the nearest whole number. This whole number is your SAT-mathematical raw score.
   E. Find your raw score in the first column of the score conversion table on page 125. Read across to the column headed SAT-mathematical. The three-digit number there is your SAT-mathematical score.
4. To figure your Test of Standard Written English (TSWE) score:
   A. Count the total number of correct answers you chose in Section 3.
   B. Count the total number of incorrect answers you chose in Section 3. Multiply this number by 1/4. Ignore any questions you left blank.
   C. Subtract the result of Step B from the result of Step A. Round off the answer to the nearest whole number. This whole number is your TSWE raw score.
   D. Find your raw score in the first column of the score conversion table on page 125. Read across to the column headed TSWE. The two-digit number there is your TSWE score.

Note: Allow for a margin of error of 30 points either way on your SAT-verbal and SAT-mathematical scores (3 points on your TSWE score). For instance, an SAT-verbal score of 470 really represents a range of scores from 440 to 500. Remember that test performance varies greatly from one day to the next and can be improved through study and practice. So don't consider your scores on any practice test as a perfect prediction of how you'll do on the real SAT.

PRACTICE TEST 2: ***Answer Key***

SECTION 1

1. **D**	6. **B**	11. **A**	16. **E**	21. **D**	26. **D**	31. **C**	36. **D**
2. **A**	7. **E**	12. **A**	17. **E**	22. **A**	27. **A**	32. **E**	37. **E**
3. **E**	8. **D**	13. **D**	18. **C**	23. **E**	28. **C**	33. **A**	38. **B**
4. **A**	9. **C**	14. **D**	19. **E**	24. **C**	29. **B**	34. **C**	39. **C**
5. **E**	10. **B**	15. **C**	20. **C**	25. **B**	30. **B**	35. **B**	40. **A**

SECTION 2

1. **A**	6. **A**	11. **B**	16. **C**	21. **C**	26. **B**	31. **B**
2. **C**	7. **C**	12. **D**	17. **D**	22. **C**	27. **B**	32. **E**
3. **D**	8. **B**	13. **B**	18. **D**	23. **A**	28. **C**	33. **B**
4. **D**	9. **A**	14. **B**	19. **D**	24. **A**	29. **A**	34. **E**
5. **A**	10. **C**	15. **A**	20. **A**	25. **B**	30. **C**	35. **D**

SECTION 3

1. **D**	8. **B**	15. **A**	22. **A**	29. **C**	36. **E**	43. **C**	50. **D**
2. **E**	9. **C**	16. **C**	23. **D**	30. **A**	37. **A**	44. **E**	
3. **C**	10. **B**	17. **A**	24. **E**	31. **D**	38. **A**	45. **A**	
4. **D**	11. **B**	18. **D**	25. **E**	32. **B**	39. **B**	46. **B**	
5. **C**	12. **A**	19. **D**	26. **D**	33. **C**	40. **D**	47. **C**	
6. **A**	13. **A**	20. **C**	27. **E**	34. **E**	41. **B**	48. **C**	
7. **E**	14. **E**	21. **A**	28. **B**	35. **E**	42. **C**	49. **A**	

SECTION 4

1. **A**	7. **C**	13. **C**	19. **A**	25. **D**	31. **E**	37. **E**	43. **A**
2. **B**	8. **D**	14. **E**	20. **D**	26. **C**	32. **E**	38. **B**	44. **D**
3. **D**	9. **B**	15. **C**	21. **C**	27. **B**	33. **C**	39. **B**	45. **B**
4. **B**	10. **B**	16. **B**	22. **A**	28. **E**	34. **B**	40. **A**	
5. **E**	11. **A**	17. **E**	23. **D**	29. **D**	35. **B**	41. **A**	
6. **E**	12. **C**	18. **D**	24. **C**	30. **A**	36. **C**	42. **C**	

SECTION 5

1. **D**	6. **D**	11. **D**	16. **E**	21. **A**
2. **A**	7. **C**	12. **C**	17. **A**	22. **D**
3. **D**	8. **B**	13. **E**	18. **A**	23. **E**
4. **C**	9. **B**	14. **C**	19. **D**	24. **C**
5. **C**	10. **D**	15. **A**	20. **B**	25. **B**

SECTION 6

1. **C**	6. **A**	11. **B**	16. **C**	21. **E**
2. **B**	7. **B**	12. **D**	17. **A**	22. **C**
3. **A**	8. **E**	13. **A**	18. **A**	23. **E**
4. **A**	9. **D**	14. **E**	19. **A**	24. **B**
5. **C**	10. **C**	15. **E**	20. **C**	25. **D**

PRACTICE TEST 2: *Score Conversion Table*

Raw Score	SAT-Verbal	SAT-Mathematical	TSWE
85	800	800	
84	780	780	
83	760	760	
82	750	740	
81	740	730	
80	730	720	
79	720	710	
78	710	700	
77	700	690	
76	690	680	
75	680	670	
74	670	660	
73	660	650	
72	650	640	
71	640	630	
70	630	630	
69	630	620	
68	620	620	
67	620	610	
66	610	610	
65	610	600	
64	600	600	
63	600	590	
62	590	590	
61	590	580	
60	580	570	
59	580	570	
58	570	560	
57	570	560	
56	560	550	
55	550	550	
54	550	540	
53	540	540	
52	540	530	
51	530	520	
50	520	510	60+
49	520	510	60+
48	510	500	60+
47	500	500	60+
46	500	490	60+
45	490	480	59
44	490	470	58
43	480	470	57
42	470	460	56
41	470	460	55
40	460	450	54
39	450	450	53
38	450	440	52
37	440	440	51
36	440	430	50
35	430	430	49
34	430	420	48
33	420	420	47
32	420	410	46
31	410	400	45

Raw Score	SAT-Verbal	SAT-Mathematical	TSWE
30	400	400	44
29	400	390	43
28	390	380	42
27	380	370	41
26	370	370	40
25	370	360	39
24	360	350	38
23	350	350	37
22	350	340	36
21	340	330	35
20	330	330	34
19	330	320	33
18	320	310	32
17	310	300	31
16	300	290	30
15	290	280	29
14	280	270	28
13	280	270	27
12	270	260	26
11	260	250	25
10	250	240	24
9	250	240	23
8	240	230	22
7	230	220	21
6	220	210	20
5	210	200	20
4 or less	200	200	20

PRACTICE TEST 2: *Explanatory Answers*

SECTION 1

1. **D** To *vacate* a place is to empty it or leave it. The opposite is to *occupy* a place or fill it. The word *rent* (choice B) is too specific to make a good antonym.

2. **A** *Authentic* means "genuine" or "real." *Bogus* means "false" or "fake." *Perjured* (choice D) is a legal term that refers to someone who has lied under oath. *Altered* (choice E) means "changed," with no implication of falseness.

3. **E** To *disclose* something is to reveal it. The opposite is *conceal*. You can eliminate choice D by working backward: the opposite of *open* is not *disclose* but *close*.

4. **A** The *apex* of something is its highest point; its lowest point is its *nadir*. Since *apex* doesn't necessarily imply success at something, *failure* (choice E) is slightly off target.

5. **E** *Whet* literally means "sharpen" (a *whetstone* is a tool-sharpening implement); it is also used to mean "heighten" (as in the phrase "*whet* one's appetite"). Its opposite is *blunt*. Choice C (*satiate*) ties in with the idea of appetite but does not relate to the basic meaning of *whet*.

6. **B** An *impediment* is anything that hinders or thwarts. The opposite is an *aid* or a help.

7. **E** *Acumen* means "keenness of perception." Its opposite is *obtuseness*. Choice B is a weak antonym: *error* does not refer to a personal quality but to a specific mistake or failure.

8. **D** A *neophyte* is someone who is new at doing something. *Tyro* would be a close synonym. By contrast, a *veteran* is an old-timer.

9. **C** As an adjective, *derelict* means "negligent" or "remiss"; to be *derelict* in one's duties is to fall down on the job. Work backward to eliminate choices D and E; *considerate* and *sober* suggest vaguely related, but different, ideas.

10. **B** Something *salient* is conspicuous or noticeable; the most obvious feature of something is often called its *salient* feature.

11. **A** The phrase that belongs in the blank must describe something other than school-based or mass media programs since the key word *although* indicates that a contrast is being developed. Choices B, C, and D don't complete that contrast. Neither does choice E; it just leaves the sentence hanging in midair.

12. **A** If "few experts fear any repetition of the widespread loss," then it must be the *safety* of bank deposits that has increased. Furthermore, *savings* is the only logical choice for the second blank since the other words don't relate to "individual bank deposits."

13. **D** The missing word must demonstrate how different the world was before printing. Choice D does that.

14. **D** The two halves of the sentence say much the same thing. The word *desire* in the first blank corresponds to the idea of wishing for something in the second half of the sentence; the word *happen* in the second blank corresponds to the idea of magical power in the first half.

15. **C** If Babbage's machine was never built, then the plans must have proved *impracticable*. The word *ingenious* ("clever") sets up the contrast implied by the word *although*.

16. **E** *Humility* is the quality a *braggart* does *not* have: *selflessness* is the quality an *egotist* does not have. *Warfare* (choice D) is not a quality.

17. **E** A *detective* examines a *fingerprint* not for its intrinsic beauty or interest but for what it can reveal about a crime. In the same way, a *biologist* studies a *specimen* for what it can reveal about plant or animal life.

18. **C** A *wreck* is the ruined remains of a *vessel* (that is, a boat). A *carcass* is the ruined remains of an *animal*.

19. **E** An *embryo* is an animal in the *unformed* state before birth; an *adult* is an animal that has reached the *mature* state. A *seed* is not normally described as *shapeless* (choice C).

20. **C** To show that an *argument* is wrong is to *refute* it. In the same way, to show that a *contention* is wrong is to *disprove* it.

21. **D** *Staccato music* is similar to *clipped speech*: both are composed of abrupt, distinct sounds.

22. **A** *Pugilism* is a fancy word for what a *boxer* does. Similarly, *pedagogy* (which means, strictly speaking, "the methods of teaching") is a fancy word for what a *teacher* does.

23. **E** A *quack* is an incompetent, fraudulent doctor who victimizes an unfortunate *patient*. A *shyster* is an incompetent, fraudulent lawyer whose victim is a *client*. A *bully* (choice B) is neither incompetent nor fraudulent.

24. **C** To *thank* someone is to express a feeling of *gratitude*. In the same way, to *applaud* someone is to express a feeling of *admiration*.

25. **B** *Jingoism* is an extreme, often bellicose form of *patriotism*. *Arrogance* is an extreme, often offensive form of *pride*. *Chauvinism* and *xenophobia* (choice E) are almost synonymous: both words refer to excessive love of one's country and dislike of foreigners.

26. **D** The entire passage focuses on efforts to secure more jobs for black people.

27. **A** Since the alliance tried to use the buying power of black consumers as an economic weapon, it is logical to assume that its efforts would have been most successful with businesses patronized primarily by blacks.

28. **C** See the second sentence of paragraph 2. *Injunctions* are court rulings forbidding certain activities.

29. **B** The whole passage is a detailed discussion of Mr. Riley's various reasons for recommending Mr. Stelling as a Latin tutor to his friend Tulliver.

30. **B** The passage provides ample evidence that Mr. Riley is very adept at rationalizing his actions. Although he has only the most trivial of reasons for recommending Mr. Stelling, he persuades himself that his strong recommendation is based on "high authority."

31. **C** The passage states that Mr. Riley's opinion of Mr. Stelling is based on the fact that Mr. Stelling was an Oxford man (choices A and D) and on things that he has heard from others (choices B and E). But as the second sentence of the passage states, he has no personal knowledge of Mr. Stelling.

32. **E** The "high authority" referred to is Mr. Riley's own. The author is saying that Mr. Riley thinks a great deal of himself and will stick to his opinions for no other reason than the fact that they are his.

33. **A** All five answer choices describe topics that are touched upon in the passage, but nearly the entire passage focuses on the economic considerations that affect news coverage by television, newspapers, and other mass media.

34. **C** As Paul Hirsch states near the end of paragraph 1, television "is less distracted than any other mass medium by loyalties to . . . noneconomic goals." In other words, economic considerations are more dominant in television than in any other mass medium.

35. **B** Reread the last sentence of paragraph 2. Choice B is an illustration of "marketing decisions made at national chain headquarters."

36. **D** Choice D accurately summarizes the points made in paragraph 1 about television—and, by extension, about other mass media.

37. **E** The passage discusses newspaper "craft traditions and occupational norms" in the context of an analysis of the forces influencing the handling of news stories by the media. Only choice E relates directly to the handling of news stories within a set of occupational standards.

38. **B** Look at the first sentence of the passage. The topic is the dating of "past cultural events."

39. **C** This point is discussed in the middle of the passage, where we are told that "the period of change is too great for accurate age determination in archaeology."

40. **A** The last third of the passage discusses secular variation. It states that observations over the past 400 years have determined that the direction of the earth's magnetic field changes by 1 degree every 10 to 20 years. This change is used in dating relics from thousands of years ago. Obviously, the archaeologists are assuming that the rate of secular variation was about the same during those thousands of years; otherwise, this dating method would be useless.

SECTION 2

1. **A** If $2n/5 = 12$, then $2n = 60$ and $n = 30$.

2. **C** If the newsstand sells x newspapers at a price of y cents each, then it will take in xy cents an hour. Multiply xy cents by the number of hours and you have the total number of cents the newsstand will take in (xyz). Divide by 100 to convert this into dollars.

3. **D** If triangle ABC is an equilateral triangle, then angle A measures 60°. This means that triangle ABD is a 30°-60°-90° triangle whose sides measure, proportionately, 1-$\sqrt{3}$-2. We know that the longest side (the hypotenuse) measures 8 and the shortest side (the base) measures 4, so the third side (the height) must measure $4\sqrt{3}$. Applying the formula for the area of a triangle (1/2 × base × height), we get $1/2 \times 4 \times 4\sqrt{3} = 8\sqrt{3}$.

4. **D** Multiplying $4^2 \times 10$ gives you 160. If $x^2 - 9 = 160$, then $x^2 = 169$ and $x = 13$.

5. **A** If the original solution is 25% (1/4) ammonia, then 3 of its 12 liters are ammonia. To create a 20% (1/5) solution containing 3 liters of ammonia, we need a total of 15 liters, so 3 liters of water must be added.

6. **A** If you know that an exterior angle of a triangle is equal to the sum of the two remote interior angles, you can make short shrift of this problem. If you don't, you can still figure out the answer pretty quickly: If $w = 110$, then $z = 70$ (since the two angles are supplementary). If $z = 70$, then $x = 180 - 70 - y$ (since the three angles of a triangle add up to 180). This simplifies to $110 - y$.

7. **C** Test this out by using any values for l, m, and n. For Statement I, two odd numbers plus an even number must produce an even sum. For Statement II, two odd numbers multiplied by an even number must produce an even product. For Statement III, however, that same even product, when divided by 2, may produce a result that is either odd or even.

8. **B** No need to do any calculations. In Column A, the amounts will grow smaller as you multiply the fractions together; in Column B, however, the amounts will increase as you add the fractions together.

9. **A** If $x - y = 3$, then $3x - 3y = 9$. No tricks here.

10. **C** Mike's car will need 5 gallons of gas to travel 120 miles. At $1.20 a gallon, that will cost $6.00.

11. **B** Dividing by 100 or by 10 is easy: just put in a decimal point at the right place. Column A then equals 193.90, while Column B equals 216.6.

12. **D** Whether x is greater than $1/x$ depends on what kind of number x is. If x is a fraction less than 1, then $1/x$ is greater. If $x = 1$, then the two are equal. Since no one answer can be determined, this is a D item.

13. **B** Your eyes are sometimes your most valuable asset when you're tackling geometry problems on the SAT. If you just look at the figure in this question, you can probably see that the area of square $ABCD$ is greater than the area of the shaded region. If you want to be sure, notice that the diagonal of the square and the diameter of the circle are identical. You know (or should know for the SAT) that the diagonal of a square equals the side of the square times $\sqrt{2}$. So you can assign an arbitrary length of, say, $2\sqrt{2}$ to this diagonal. Then the length of each side of the square is 2 and its area is 4. For the circle, use the area formula of πr^2. If the diameter of the circle is $2\sqrt{2}$, then the radius, which is half of that, is $\sqrt{2}$ in length. Therefore, the area of the circle equals $\pi(\sqrt{2^2})$, or 2π. The area of the shaded region, then, is 2π minus the area of the square. Since π equals about 3.14, 2π equals about 6.28, and $6.28 - 4 = 2.28$, which is much less than the area of the square itself.

14. **B** You can probably work this problem out very quickly in your head, but you don't have to. If x is positive, then $3x/-3$ will be negative. If y is negative, $-3y/3$ will be positive. So Column B is greater.

15. **A** The three angles shown in Column A add up to 360° (no matter what size each angle is). The three angles shown in Column B add up to 180°.

16. **C** Finding the value of Column A takes only one step: just substitute 2 for n in the definition and get 3/1, or 3. Finding the value of Column B takes three steps: (1) substitute 5 for n in the definition and get 6/4, or 3/2; (2) substitute 3 for n in the definition and get 4/2, or 2; (3) multiply 3/2 by 2 and get 3. As you can see, the two columns are equal.

17. **D** There are always 30 minutes in a half hour, but the number of days in a month varies from 28 to 31.

18. **D** Given the inequality, r may have a value anywhere from 1 to 3, while t may have a value anywhere from 3 to 5. Therefore, $2r$ could be greater than, equal to, or less than t, making this a D item.

19. **D** By subtraction, you could find that folk records accounted for 10% of total sales in 1984. However, comedy records are included in the "other" category, so you have no idea whether they accounted for more or less than 10% of total sales.

20. **A** From the equation given, you can figure out that $4x = 4$, and therefore $x = 1$. This means that $3x + 3$ (Column A) equals 6, which is greater than Column B.

21. **C** Plot point B on the grid provided and sketch in lines OA and AB. You can probably see that line OA is twice the length of line AB. If not, notice that OA is the diagonal of a rectangle with sides 2 and 4 and that AB is the diagonal of a rectangle with sides 1 and 2. Since the sides of the rectangle of which line OA is the diagonal are exactly twice the length of the sides of the rectangle of which line AB is the diagonal, OA must be twice as long as AB.

22. **C** Set P consists of the integers 1, 3, 5, 7, 9, and 11. Set Q consists of the integers 2, 3, 4, 5, 6, and 7. Three integers—3, 5, and 7—are members of both sets.

23. **A** If $3/n = 1$, then $n = 3$. So Column A equals 3/2, which is greater than 2/3 (Column B).

24. **A** Each triangle in rectangle $ABCD$ is a double-sized variant of the standard 3-4-5 right triangle. Therefore, the length of diagonal AC is 10. In square $WXYZ$, since the diagonal of a square always equals the side of the square times $\sqrt{2}$, the length of diagonal WY is $7\sqrt{2}$. Since $\sqrt{2}$ is about 1.414, $7\sqrt{2}$ equals about 9.898, which is a little less than 10.

25. **B** For Column A, call the four items A, B, C, and D, and list all the possible combinations. There are six of them: AB, AC, AD, BC, BD, and CD. For Column B, call the five items V, W, X, Y, and Z, and list the possible trios: VWX, VWY, VWZ, VXY, VXZ, VYZ, WXY—*stop!* You already have seven, which is more than the six in Column A.

26. **B** If x is a negative number, then x to an odd power is negative and x to an even power is positive. Since the denominator in Column A is negative, while both the numerator and the denominator in Column B are positive, Column B must be greater.

27. **B** Don't bother to figure out the actual values of x, y, and z. Since the three angles of a triangle always add up to 180, their average value is always 60.

28. **C** Rearranging the second equation will give you $6y + 4x = 42$. *Stop!* This is exactly double what you're looking for—namely, $3y + 2x$. So you can quickly see that the value you're seeking is half of 42, or 21.

29. **A** If the area of the square is 36, then each side of the square is 6. You can see that each side of the square is twice the radius of each circle. With a radius of 3, each circle has an area of 9π; and, of course, the four quarter-circles inside the square add up to the area of one full circle. So the shaded region equals the area of the square minus the area of one circle, or $36 - 9\pi$.

30. **C** A player who starts on space 1 will land, in succession, on spaces 6, 2, 4, 3, and 0—five moves in all.

31. **B** The player who starts on space 3 will make only one move since that move takes her or him directly onto space 0.

32. **E** Make a sketch:

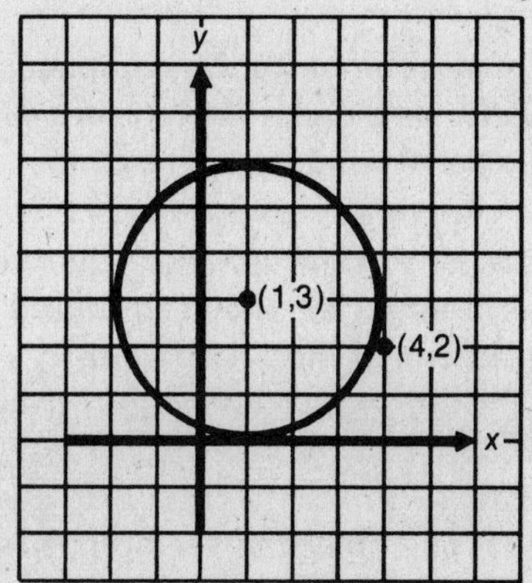

Of the five points given, only (4, 2) is at all close to the edge of the circle.

33. **B** If $2(a + 3) < 8$, then $2a + 6 < 8$, $2a < 2$, and $a < 1$.

34. **E** The volume of the rectangular solid is $9 \times 4 \times 3 = 108$. The volume of the cylinder is πr^2 times the height, or $1\pi \times 3 = 3\pi$. So the volume of the rectangular solid minus the volume of the cylinder is $108 - 3\pi$.

35. **D** The club spent $225.00 on prizes and ended up with $200.00, for a total of $425.00. But $35.00 of that total had been in the treasury to begin with, so the members took in $390.00 from ticket sales. Divide $390.00 by $1.50 per ticket, and you find that they sold 260 tickets.

SECTION 3

1. **D** Since Sherlock Holmes is himself a fictitious character, he cannot be compared to *any* fictitious character. Instead, he must be compared to any *other* fictitious character.

2. **E** No error here.

3. **C** When two subjects are joined by *or* or *nor*, the verb agrees with whichever subject is closer. Since *effects* is the closer subject, the verb should be plural—*have proven*.

4. **D** The phrase should be *than he* because the implied clause is *than he had*.

5. **C** The subject is the singular *row*, so the verb should be the singular *is*.

6. **A** *Public buildings* (plural) logically resemble *Greek temples* (plural), not *a Greek temple* (singular).

7. **E** No error in this sentence.

8. **B** *Had its first emerging* is nonidiomatic. The normal phrase is simply *first emerged*.

9. **C** The irregular verb *choose* is used incorrectly here. The proper form is *have chosen*, not *have chose*.

10. **B** This is a diction error. The word *reticent* is used in place of *reluctant*, which it somewhat resembles.

11. **B** The shift from the singular *one* to the plural *they* is awkward and incorrect. The same pronoun should be used throughout the sentence.

12. **A** The phrase that starts the sentence is a misplaced modifier. Grammatically, it describes *most critics*; logically, it describes *The Lord of the Rings*. Either it must be moved or the sentence must be rewritten.

13. **A** It is not until quite late in the sentence that you find the subject: *no single cause*. Since that subject is singular, the verb should be, too. Instead of *there are*, the first two words of the sentence should be *there is*.

14. **E** No error here.

15. **A** The pronoun *who* is the object of the preposition *from*. Therefore, it should be in the objective case: *whom*.

16. **C** This is another error in pronoun case. Try dropping the words *the Langleys and* from the sentence; you'll see that the sentence should read "the chairperson . . . sought to discourage *us*."

17. **A** The opening phrase, *shortened by rain*, is a misplaced modifier. It should modify *the game* but, as the sentence is written, it modifies *most of the fans*.

18. **D** Idiomatically, costs are passed *on*, not *out*.

19. **D** The past participle of the irregular verb *steal* is *stolen*.

20. **C** This is a diction error. The sentence clearly calls for the verb *devise*, not the noun *device*.

21. **A** The opening phrase here is a misplaced modifier. It should be next to *the Book of Ecclesiastes*, which it modifies, not next to *a marked contrast*, which it doesn't modify.

22. **A** The pronoun *they* has no clear antecedent. However, since it is not underlined, it cannot be changed. Therefore, *every American is* would have to be changed to *all Americans are*.

23. **D** Because *not* makes the sentence negative, a second negative is unnecessary and incorrect. The word *nor* should be changed to *or*.

24. **E** No error here.

25. **E** Also correct.

26. **D** Items in a series should be both logically and grammatically parallel. In this case, since the series begins with two noun phrases, it should end either with a third noun phrase or with a single noun. Choice *D* is better than choice *E* because *intelligence* is the concise equivalent of *intellectual ability*.

27. **E** As originally written, the sentence is a run-on. Choice E corrects the run-on by adding the subordinating conjunction *when*, which makes the first clause into a dependent one. It is also clearer and more logical than the other answer choices.

28. **B** The first half of the sentence is a long modifying phrase that describes the protesters. Therefore, the words that immediately follow it must refer to the protesters. Choice D alters the meaning of the original sentence.

29. **C** The correct answer must begin with a word that refers to a person because only a person can lay floor tiles. Choices B and C both begin with a word that refers to a person (*you* and *one*, respectively), but C is clearer and more graceful.

30. **A** The original version is the clearest and most logical of the five.

31. **D** *But* expresses the logical relationship between the two clauses. Choice C is a run-on sentence.

32. **B** The sentence is clearer and more graceful when the same grammatical structure is used in both clauses: *petroleum products are used ... they are also used.*

33. **C** Choice C is concise and clear. It also exhibits good parallel structure.

34. **E** Choices A and B are both run-on sentences; choices C and D confuse the logical relationship between the two clauses.

35. **E** The opening phrase describes the writer. Therefore, the first word that follows that phrase should be *Edgeworth* (the writer's name).

36. **E** Choice E is the only sentence that is complete, concise, logical, and properly punctuated.

37. **A** The original version is the best. When *not only* is used, it should be followed by either *but* or *but also*. Furthermore, the two elements joined by *not only* and *but* or *but also* should be parallel in form, as they are in choice A but not in choice B.

38. **A** The other choices are wordy or clumsy or both.

39. **B** Only in choice B are the three elements in the series grammatically parallel, as they should be: *the political instincts*, *the dynamic style*, and *the boundless egotism.*

40. **D** Choice D is the most concise. Choice E alters the meaning of the sentence radically.

41. **B** The subject of the sentence is *Senator Clark*. Therefore, the singular verb *was* is required.

42. **C** Two similar words are being confused here: *censor*, which means "to remove objectionable material from documents or films," and *censure*, which means "to criticize or condemn."

43. **C** Since the ambassador's arrival will have taken place by a specified time in the future, the future perfect tense is needed—she *will have arrived*.

44. **E** This sentence is correct as written.

45. **A** *Him* is part of the compound subject of the sentence. It should be in the subjective case—*he*.

46. **B** *Final* is one of several adjectives that have no comparative or superlative form. Something is either final or not final; it cannot be either more or less final. So the phrase *more final* has to be changed, either to a simple *final* or to something like *later*.

47. **C** The past participle of the irregular verb *take* is *taken*, not *took*.

48. **C** Idiomatically, a person has motives *for* taking a step, not motives *of* taking a step.

49. **A** The word *scarcely* is considered a negative. Therefore, *scarcely none* is a double negative. *None* should be changed to *any*.

50. **D** *Which* refers to things; *who* refers to people.

SECTION 4

1. **A** *Fickle* means "changeable" or "unsteady." *Steadfast* means "reliable" or "dependable" and is the best antonym.

2. **B** *Brazen*, literally "of or like brass," means "bold," "shameless," "lacking modesty." The best opposite, therefore, is *modest*, meaning "shy" or "reserved," "not forward." (Choice A, *cowardly*, is close, but if you check it backward, you'll see that its opposite is *brave* or *courageous*, not *brazen*.)

3. **D** The basic meaning of *parochial* is "related to a parish" (as in *parochial school*). From that meaning comes an associated meaning: "confined to a parish"—that is, "narrow" or "local." *Urbane*, which means "sophisticated" or "cosmopolitan," is a good antonym.

4. **B** *Symmetry* is balance. Choice A, *deformity*, is too extreme to be a good antonym: something can be asymmetrical without being deformed.

5. **E** To *congeal* is to thicken or harden. (Think of gelatin hardening in your refrigerator.) The opposite is to become thin or liquefy—to *dissolve*.

6. **E** *Ominous* means "foreboding evil." *Propitious* means "foretelling good."

7. **C** A person or thing that is *irrepressible* is impossible to control or repress.

8. **D** To *condone* an action is to accept it without protest. One speaks of apathetic bystanders *condoning* criminal acts by failing to object. The opposite is *condemn*.

9. **B** *Heterogeneous* means "varied in kind." *Uniform* means "all of one kind."

10. **B** A *tractable* person (or animal) is easily led or taught; a well-behaved horse, for instance, is *tractable*. An *intransigent* person (or animal) is stubborn and willful, like a donkey.

11. **A** *Prodigal* means "wasteful."

12. **C** *Surfeit* means "more than enough," while *lack* means "not enough."

13. **C** To *ostracize* someone is to cast out or reject that person. An antonym is *receive, welcome*, or *accept*.

14. **E** *Truculent* means "fierce," "ferocious," or "rough."

15. **C** The word root *equi* or *iqui* generally means "equal" or "fair." Thus *iniquity* means "unfairness" or "injustice."

16. **B** The first half of the sentence says that a candidate may "lose" by achieving only a narrow victory, so this year's front-runner must need a *decisive* victory (that is, a victory by a large margin) to be considered a real winner.

17. **E** If Gandhi's pleas for peace went *unheeded*, then the rest of the sentence should describe how war broke out.

18. **D** The key word *although* establishes a contrast between the *separate* studies referred to in the first half of the sentence and the *interconnected* studies mentioned at the end.

19. **A** If the reporters' questions are causing the governor's hands to tremble, we can infer that their questioning is probably *hostile*. Trembling hands are not a typical sign of *resentment* (choice C).

20. **D** The two missing words must be consistent with one another and with what beverage retailers would want. If the bill would cause sales of soft drinks to fall, then the retailers would oppose it; if it would cause sales to rise, the retailers would favor it. Choice D is the only one that works out logically.

21. **C** The central theme of the passage is that it was impossible to "transplant" English music to America because the conditions of life in the New World were so different. Choice C conveys this idea.

22. **A** Refer to the middle of paragraph 1. The early Virginians began to think about music as they "began to acquire land and from the land gained wealth." Choice E is tempting, but the passage does not suggest that the acquisition of land and wealth is equivalent to the development of a "landed aristocracy."

23. **D** Madrigals, reels, psalms, and ballads are all mentioned in paragraph 2. Symphonies are not.

24. **C** Reread the first sentence of paragraph 2.

25. **D** As paragraph 2 states, "even 170 years after the founding of the Jamestown colony," music in Virginia was still in a rudimentary state.

26. **C** The first paragraph explains that most plankton make horizontal journeys only at random, driven simply by winds and currents. By contrast, their vertical migrations appear to be in response to definite stimuli, though exactly why the movements occur is uncertain.

27. **B** The last sentence of paragraph 1 explains that plankton are too small to be seen with the naked eye. However, the last two paragraphs make it clear that swarms

or blooms of plankton are definitely visible; otherwise, people would not gather to see them.

28. **E** *Cosmopolitan* plankton are those that are found in many different regions of the world.

29. **D** The next-to-last sentence of paragraph 2 states that *zooplankton* are sometimes herbivorous; but phytoplankton, because they are plants, are neither herbivorous nor carnivorous. Statements II and III are applied in the passage to both zooplankton and phytoplankton.

30. **A** See the first sentence of the last paragraph.

31. **E** You are told that the Gettysburg Address is "a masterpiece of prose style" and that Lincoln's other writings are *similar* in some way.

32. **E** The two missing words must suggest a cause-and-effect relationship. If it is difficult to observe the whale, it is logical to conclude that certain facts about it would still be unknown.

33. **C** In both halves of the sentence, the idea is that higher costs drive customers away. Since the first half refers to letter writers, the logical adjective to be inserted is *postal*.

34. **B** The missing phrase must fit into an argument in favor of life on other planets.

35. **B** The key word *yet* shows that a contrast is being established. The words *cruelty* and *goodness* fit such a contrast.

36. **C** Just as a *chisel* is used to carve *stone*, so a *knife* is used to carve *wood*.

37. **E** A *haughty* person is characterized by excessive *pride*; a *brash* person is characterized by excessive *bravery*.

38. **B** To be *ineffectual* is to be completely lacking in *prowess*. Similarly, to be *oafish* is to be completely lacking in *suavity*.

39. **B** An *artery* is a large blood vessel from which many small *capillaries* branch off. In the same way, a *bough* is a large limb from which many small *twigs* branch off.

40. **A** *Exhilaration* is an extreme form of *pleasure*, just as *despair* is an extreme form of *worry*. The two words in choices B, C, and E are near synonyms, and the two words in choice D are antonyms.

41. **A** When a *prism refracts* light, it breaks the light up into its component parts. Similarly, when a *chemist analyzes* a compound, he or she breaks the compound up into the elements that compose it.

42. **C** An animal that feels *threatened* may *hiss*, and an animal that feels *contented* may well *purr*. Choice B is wrong because *vicious* is how we might describe an animal, not how an animal feels.

43. **A** The *rind* or skin of a fruit is outside the *center*, just as the *crust* of something (such as the earth) is outside the *core*.

44. **D** To *squelch* a *rumor* is to suppress it. Similarly, to *quash* an *investigation* is to suppress it, or keep it from continuing.

45. **B** A *bigot* is someone who constantly *prejudges* others; a *bully* is someone who constantly *domineers* over others.

SECTION 5

1. **D** At the original price, the apples cost $12\frac{1}{2}$ cents each. At the new price, they cost 15 cents each. The $2\frac{1}{2}$-cent price increase represents 1/5 of the original price, or a 20% increase.

2. **A** Use the first equation to solve for x in terms of y: $x = 2y - 12$. Substitute $2y - 12$ for x in the second equation and solve for y: $y = 7$. Substitute 7 for y in the first equation and solve for x: $x = 2$. Thus $x + y = 2 + 7 = 9$.

3. **D** Side AO is a radius of circle O. If the radius of the circle is 6, then the circumference of the circle is 12π, since the circumference always equals $2\pi r$. Triangle AOB is a right triangle, so arc AB is a 90° arc, representing 1/4 of the entire circle. Its length is therefore 1/4 of 12π, or 3π.

4. **C** Forty cars can be divided evenly into any of the ratios listed except 3:2:1. Note that 3, 2, and 1 add up to 6, and there is no way to divide 40 items into 6 equal groups.

5. **C** If $(a + b)^2$ is odd and b^2 is even, then b must be even and a, odd. If a is odd, then the first two expressions listed must be odd. However, the third expression, ab, must be even because the product of an odd number and an even number is always even. Insert any values for a and b and try it out.

6. **D** Make a simple sketch of Roberta's trip. You'll see a right triangle that happens to be the "standard" 7-24-25 right triangle. So Roberta bicycles a total of $7 + 24 + 25 = 56$ miles on her trip.

7. **C** Another "standard" right triangle, the 5-12-13, is involved here. Since the shorter leg of the triangle measures 5 and the hypotenuse measures 13, the longer leg must measure 12. Thus the area of the rectangle is $5 \times 12 = 60$.

8. **B** If there are m hens and each one lays l eggs a week, they will lay a total of lm eggs a week. To find out how many weeks it will take them to lay n eggs, divide n by lm.

9. **B** Start with the equation given and cross multiply to get $4 + x = 18 - 6x$. Rearrange the terms and simplify to get $7x = 14$. Therefore, $x = 2$.

10. **D** If 80 percent are enrolled in an English class, then 20 percent are *not* enrolled in an English class and may be enrolled in chemistry but not English. Twenty percent of 150 is 30.

11. **D** First, find the area of the two circles at the ends of the cylinder. Since each circle has a radius of 3, each one has an area of 9π. So the area of the two circles together is 18π. Second, find the area of the rest of the cylinder. If you imagine it unrolled and laid out on a flat surface, you should be able to see that it's a rectangle with a length equal to the circumference of the circle at either end and a width equal to the height of the cylinder. The circumference of the circle is 6π, and the height of the cylinder is given as 5. So the area of the rectangular part of the cylinder is 30π. Finally, combine the area of the two circles with the area of the rectangular part of the cylinder, and you get a total surface area of $18\pi + 30\pi = 48\pi$.

12. **C** In 1983, 250 houses were built; in 1980, 75 houses were built. The difference between these two numbers is 175.

13. **E** The total number of houses built in the period shown on the chart is about 875. If you divide 875 by 250, the number of houses built in 1983, you get 3.5.

14. **C** There are several ways to find the value of x. Here's one: The right base angle of the triangle is a vertical angle directly opposite the angle marked 55°. By definition, this angle must also measure 55°. Since the second angle in the triangle is a right angle measuring 90°, the third angle must measure $180° - 90° - 55° = 35°$.

15. **A** If x/y is positive, then x and y are either both positive or both negative. Either way, xy will also be positive. However, depending on the actual values of x and y, $x + y$ and $x - y$ may be either positive or negative.

16. **E** If $(a + b)/(a - b) = 1$, then $a + b = a - b$. And if that is so, then b must equal 0. Therefore, the second equation given is irrelevant. If $b = 0$, then any expression including b as a factor must also equal 0.

17. **A** Draw the number line:

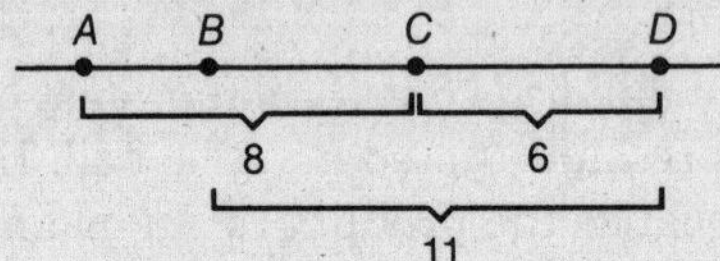

If $AD = 8 + 6 = 14$ and $BD = 11$, then AB must equal 3.

18. **A** The unshaded area in the lower left-hand corner of the rectangle is, of course, a right triangle. The formula for the area of a right triangle is $1/2 \times \text{leg} \times \text{leg}$. Therefore, the area of that triangle is $1/2 \times 2x \times x$, or x^2. Add this to $5x^2$, the area of the shaded portion, and you know that the total area of the rectangle is $6x^2$. Of the lengths given in the answer choices, the only pair that yields an area of $6x^2$ is $2x$, $3x$.

19. **D** Silly as it may seem, just count through the days of the month. The 31st will fall on a Wednesday, so the next month will begin on Thursday.

20. **B** If all the triangles are equilateral and the perimeter of ABC is 12, then DE must be 2, as shown in the following figure:

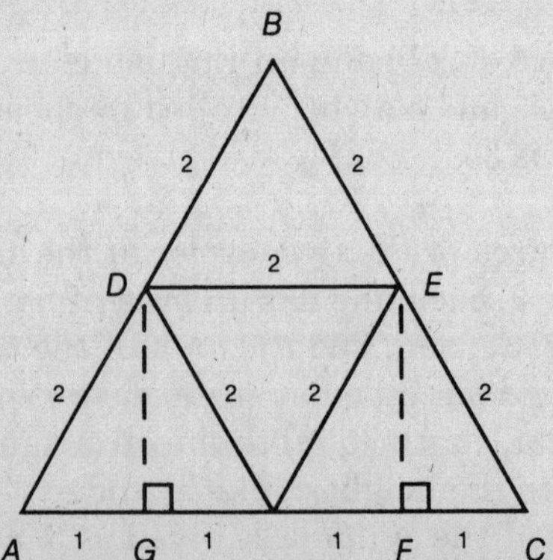

To find EF, either recognize that triangle ECF is a "standard" 30°-60°-90° triangle whose sides measure, proportionately, 1-$\sqrt{3}$-2, or apply the Pythagorean theorem:

$$FC^2 + EF^2 = EC^2$$
$$1^2 + EF^2 = 2^2$$
$$EF^2 = 3$$
$$EF = \sqrt{3}$$

Therefore, the area of *DEFG* is $2 \times \sqrt{3} = 2\sqrt{3}$.

21. **A** Just substitute 4 for n in the definition: $(4 + 2)/(4^2) = 6/16 = 3/8$.

22. **D** If the area of the rectangle is 36, its perimeter could be 26 or 24. With a perimeter of 26, the rectangle would be 4 by 9. With a perimeter of 24, it would be 6 by 6. (A square is one type of rectangle.) However, there is no way that its perimeter could be as small as 20.

23. **E** There are several ways of solving this problem. One way is to work backward. The final price, $18, was 1/4 less than the third price, which means that the third price was $24. The third price was 1/3 less than the second price, which means that the second price was $36. The second price was 1/10 less than the first price, which means that the first price was $40.

24. **C** Look at the diagram provided. The center of the circle is just $3\frac{1}{2}$ units away from the edge of the lower right quadrant. However, it is $4\frac{1}{2}$ units away from the edge of the upper left quadrant. Therefore, to reach into that upper left quadrant (and thus automatically into the lower right quadrant as well), the circle would have to have a radius greater than $4\frac{1}{2}$. Of the choices listed, the smallest one that still is greater than $4\frac{1}{2}$ is 5.

25. **B** Just work your way through the possibilities, pairing values from each list and adding them up. Count the same sum only once, of course. There are seven possible sums: -3, -1, 1, 3, 5, 7, and 9.

SECTION 6

1. **C** If the total surface area of the cube is 96, then the surface area of each of its six faces must be 16. Therefore, each edge of the cube must have a length of 4, and the volume of the cube must be $4 \times 4 \times 4 = 64$.

2. **B** Using the second equation, solve for b in terms of a: $b = 19/2 - 2a$. Substitute this value for b in the first equation:

$$3a - 4\left(\frac{19}{2} - 2a\right) = 6$$

$$3a - 38 + 8a = 6$$

$$11a = 44$$

$$a = 4$$

Substitute this value for a in either equation and you'll soon figure out that $b = 3/2$. Therefore, $a - b = 5/2$.

3. **A** On all six tests, the student's total score was $6 \times 83 = 498$. On the five best tests, the student's total score was $5 \times 87 = 435$. The difference between 498 and 435 is 63, which was the student's lowest test score.

4. **A** If you cancel as many terms as you can (which is most of them) before you multiply, you can find the product, 1/12, very quickly.

5. **C** There are several ways to figure this out. Here's one: The angle within the triangle that is next to the 150° angle must be a 30° angle, since the two are supplementary. A second angle in that triangle is a right angle, since it is supplementary to a right angle. That leaves 60° for the remaining angle in the triangle, which in turn is supplementary to the angle marked $x°$. Therefore, $x = 120$.

6. **A** Since the symbol > means "is greater than," x cannot possibly be equal to 12.

7. **B** Cancel the y's and z's and you get $x/a = -1$. Cross multiply and you get $x = -a$. If this is so, then the sum of x and a must be 0.

8. **E** A handy rule of thumb: If you know the ratio of the lengths of two congruent figures (figures with equal internal angles), you can find the ratio of their areas by squaring the ratio of their lengths. In this case, the ratio of lengths is 6:4, which reduces to 3:2. Therefore, the ratio of areas is $3^2:2^2$, or 9:4.

9. **D** Plug the numbers into the equation that you're given: $3 @ 5 = (3 \times 5)/2 = 15/2$.

10. **C** Again, plug the numbers into the equation. Start with the operation inside parentheses: $4 @ 3 = (4 \times 3)/2 = 12/2 = 6$. Then, $7 @ 6 = (7 \times 6)/2 = 42/2 = 21$.

11. **B** If x is the cube root of 27, then $x = 3$, since $3 \times 3 \times 3 = 27$. That means that $x^2 = 9$.

12. **D** Try it. The number 660 divided by 7 equals 94 with a remainder of 2.

13. **A** All you know for sure from $a + b + c = 0$ is that, of the three unknowns, one or two are negative and one or two are positive. You don't know which one or ones are negative or positive. Therefore, you can't evaluate the truth of any of the three statements.

14. **E** Since the area of a circle always equals πr^2, the radius of circle O must be 3 (the square root of 9). Since the circumference of any circle equals $2\pi r$, the circumference of circle O must be 6π. The three sides of equilateral triangle ABC divide the circumference of circle O into three equal arcs. Since arc BCA represents two of those three equal arcs, its length must be 2/3 of the circumference of circle O, or 4π.

15. **E** The store owner buys the watches at a cost of $x/12$ dollars each. She sells them for y dollars each. Therefore, her profit per watch is $y - x/12$. To find her total profit on z watches, multiply her profit per watch by z: $z(y - x/12) = yz - xz/12$.

16. **C** Just get all the t's on one side of the equation and all the numbers on the other side. Then solve for t:

$$t + 12 = 3t - 3 - \frac{t}{2}$$

$$15 = 2t - \frac{t}{2}$$

$$15 = \frac{3}{2}t$$

$$10 = t$$

17. **A** The box contains eight tokens, four black ones and four white ones. So a player's chance of picking a black token on the first draw is exactly 4/8, or 1/2. After the player chooses a black token, the box contains only seven tokens, three black

ones and four white ones. So the player's chance of picking a black token on the second draw is 3/7. To find the combined probability of the player's choosing two black tokens in succession, multiply the two figures: $1/2 \times 3/7 = 3/14$.

18. **A** You can do this type of problem easily if you set it up as a series of fractions to be multiplied: $1/2 \times 3/4 \times 1/5 \times 20/1$. Cancel whatever you can, and then complete the multiplication. The answer is 3/2, or 1.5.

19. **A** To solve a quadratic equation, rearrange it in this form: $x^2 + 3x - 10 = 0$. Then factor the expression on the left-hand side of the equation: $(x - 2)(x + 5) = 0$. This yields two possible values of x: 2 and -5. (You can also solve this problem quickly through the process of elimination. Simply plug each of the five possible values of x into the equation and see whether it works out.)

20. **C** Every 2 minutes, 1 gallon leaks out of the tank while 6 gallons pour in. At a rate of 5 gallons every 2 minutes, it will take 12 minutes for 30 gallons to accumulate, filling 1/3 of the 90-gallon tank.

21. **E** If the square has an area of 25 units, it is 5 units on a side. Any of the points shown could be located within such a square. Note that point III will be inside the square only if the square is drawn so that its diagonal is parallel to the y-axis.

22. **C** The \$2 tickets account for 140 tickets and \$280 in receipts, leaving 165 tickets and \$645 in receipts to be accounted for by the \$3 and \$5 tickets. Call the number of \$5 tickets x; then the number of \$3 tickets will be $165 - x$. The \$5 tickets will account for $5x$ dollars' worth of receipts; the \$3 tickets will account for $3(165 - x)$ dollars' worth of receipts; together they will account for \$645 worth of receipts. Set up the equation and solve for x:

$$5x + 3(165 - x) = 645$$
$$5x + 495 - 3x = 645$$
$$2x = 150$$
$$x = 75$$

23. **E** If $3a + a/2 + 4 = 6$, then $7a/2 = 2$. Divide both sides by 7 and you get $a/2 = 2/7$.

24. **B** To find the area of triangle ABC, you first need to find its base and its height. Its base is 3 plus DC, which is one leg of right triangle BCD. Its height is BD, which is the other leg of right triangle BCD. Triangle BCD is a multiple of the standard 45°-45°-90° right triangle whose sides measure, proportionately, 1-1-$\sqrt{2}$. Since hypotenuse BC measures $5\sqrt{2}$, legs DC and BD each measure 5. Plug this information into the formula for the area of a triangle and you get $1/2 \times (3 + 5) \times 5 = 1/2 \times 40 = 20$.

25. **D** Let J stand for John's age now (since that's what you need to find). Then, Lynda's age now is $J - 6$ (since Lynda is six years younger than John is), and, in seven years, John's age will be $J + 7$ and Lynda's age will be $J - 6 + 7$, or $J + 1$. The problem tells you that in seven years Lynda's age will be 3/4 of John's age, so set up the equation and solve for J:

$$\frac{3}{4}(J + 7) = J + 1$$

$$\frac{3}{4}J + \frac{21}{4} = J + 1$$

$$\frac{17}{4} = \frac{1}{4}J$$

$$17 = J$$

PART 5

SAT Study Program: Unit 2

LESSON 6
Vocabulary Building Through Word Roots, Part 1

OBJECTIVES

- ☐ To understand how knowledge of common word roots can help you learn and remember word meanings
- ☐ To learn some of the most important word roots and their meanings
- ☐ To learn the meanings of some of the words based on these word roots that are likely to appear on the SAT

Word Roots as Vocabulary-Building Tools

6.1 Word Roots in English

The vocabulary of English is the most extensive and diverse of any language in the world. Fortunately, though, you won't have to learn thousands of obscure words in order to prepare for the SAT. Why? Because most of the words tested on the SAT tend to be of a certain type. First, they are usually "hard" words—words you don't normally hear or use in everyday speech. Second, they are usually "bookish" words—words like those used in textbooks or serious, scholarly writing. Third, they are often words that signify abstractions rather than concrete things.

The single best way to build your vocabulary for the SAT is to study the roots from which many of the hard, bookish, abstract words of English are derived. These roots come from a number of foreign sources that contributed to the growth of the English language. Most, however, come from Latin. There's a reason for this. During the Renaissance—that is, during the fifteenth, sixteenth, and early seventeenth centuries—hundreds of Latin words were introduced into the English language. Scholars and writers of the period used Latin regularly, and they borrowed Latin words to form English ones. Moreover, many of the philosophical, scientific, religious, and political ideas we still discuss were being formulated during this period. Thus, many of the scholarly words of today were first used during the Renaissance, and these words still bear the marks of their Latin origins.

In this lesson and in Lesson 11, you'll study a number of Latin word roots, and a few Greek ones, that are common to many English words. Each of these word roots will help you learn a number of related English words. You'll find that the study of word roots, because it relates words to one another in families, makes the learning of new words easy.

6.2 Studying Word Roots

The word roots in this lesson are grouped according to meaning. This method of organization should enable you to learn and remember several roots (and dozens of words) at a time. For example, the first group includes word roots related to the general idea of "life." Each root in that group has something to do with life.

Of course, when the word roots were adopted into English, their meanings were sometimes modified. You might not always see at first glance how a particular English word grew from its word root. However, the connection is always there. Once you uncover it, you'll find it hard to forget either the word or its root.

Study the word roots and their offspring over a period of weeks, if you can. Try to learn a few word roots each day. Review the ones you've learned on previous days, and make an effort to use your new words in speech and writing. By the time you complete this lesson and Lesson 11, you'll have learned several hundred new words, all examples of the types of words commonly tested on the SAT.

Each list of word roots includes the root, its meaning, and a selection of words that contain the root. The entry for each word includes its most usual part of speech, its one or two most important definitions, and, in some cases, a phrase or sentence to illustrate its meaning. Many words can be used as more than one part of speech, and many words have multiple meanings. Your dictionary can provide this kind of additional information about the words listed here.

The Word Roots

6.3 Word Roots Related to "Life": *Gen, Vi, Cre, Anim, Mor*

The word root *gen* is derived from *genesis*, which is a word in both Latin and Greek. *Genesis* means "birth." (The first book of the Bible is called Genesis because it tells a story of the birth, or creation, of the universe.) English words that contain the root *gen* are all related to the idea of birth. Here are some that you should know:

genesis (*n*) the origin or beginning of anything.
generation (*n*) the act of creating or producing something; also a group of people born or living at about the same time.
gene (*n*) a unit on a chromosome that carries the biological codes determining the hereditary traits of offspring.
genetics (*n*) the study of the inheritance of biological traits.
genius (*n*) great creative power; also, a person gifted with such power.
congenital (*adj*) biologically inherited: Hemophilia is a *congenital* disease.
engender (*v*) to produce or create: Tyranny and oppression usually *engender* rebellion.
progenitor (*n*) a creator or founder, especially of a family or nation: Abraham was the *progenitor* of the Jewish people.
progeny (*n*) children or offspring.
eugenics (*n*) a science that deals with the improvement of the inherited traits of a species: The test-tube babies in *Brave New World* are an extreme example of *eugenics*.
degenerate (*v*) to become worse; to become corrupted; to decline from a position of excellence.
gentry (*n*) well-born, upper-class people, especially in England: The English *gentry* are said to enjoy fox hunting.
gentility (*n*) the quality of being well-mannered or well-bred.

The word root *vi* refers to life; it comes from the Latin word *vita*, meaning "life." Here are some examples of its use in English:

vital (*adj*) full of life; also, essential to existence, necessary, crucial.
viable (*adj*) capable of living; capable of existence or development; capable of working or functioning adequately.
revive (*v*) to bring back to life: The doctor *revived* the dying man.
survive (*v*) to outlive someone; to live through something, especially a difficult ordeal.
vivacious (*adj*) full of life, lively: She is a charming and *vivacious* hostess.
convivial (*adj*) fond of company, sociable. (The word combines *vi* with the prefix *con-*, meaning "with"; it literally means "good for living with.")
vivid (*adj*) full of life, lively; bright, intense, or clear: *vivid* colors, a *vivid* imagination.
viviparous (*adj*) bearing live babies rather than eggs. (The word describes mammals, as opposed to most fish, birds, and reptiles.)
vivisection (*n*) the practice of performing experimental surgery on living animals. (The word combines *vi* with the root *sec*, meaning "to cut.")

The word root *cre* means "grow"; it also appears in the forms *cres* and *cru*. It comes from the Latin verb *crescere*, "to grow."

increase (*v*) to grow in number or size.
decrease (*v*) to grow less; opposite of *increase*.

increment (*n*) the amount of an increase: The stock's value grew by an annual *increment* of 10 percent.
accrue (*v*) to grow or increase; used mainly in reference to money: Profits on this investment will *accrue* as a result of higher interest rates.
accretion (*n*) growth or enlargement; the process of increasing by external addition or accumulation.
excrescence (*n*) an outgrowth or enlargement, often excessive or abnormal.
crescendo (*n*) in music, a gradual increase in volume.
decrescendo (*n*) in music, a gradual decrease in volume; opposite of *crescendo*.

In Latin, the word *anima* originally meant "air" or "breath"; it came to mean "soul" or "spirit," the idea being that breath and the soul go together. In English, the root *anim* is used in words related to life or to the spirit of a living thing.

animal (*n*) any living thing that is not a plant.
animate (*v*) to bring to life.
animated (*adj*) lively or lifelike: An *animated* conversation is a lively one; an *animated* cartoon is a film in which cartoon characters move as if alive.
animus (*n*) unfriendly spirit; dislike, hatred, odium.
animosity (*n*) dislike, unfriendliness, hatred.
unanimity (*n*) complete agreement in a group. (The idea is that everyone is "of one spirit.")
equanimity (*n*) calm, placidity. (The idea is that one's spirit remains "equal"—the same—despite outside events.)
magnanimous (*adj*) great in spirit, forgiving, generous. (The word combines *anima* with *magna*, which means "great.")
pusillanimous (*adj*) cowardly, fainthearted: The *pusillanimous* prince fled from the battlefield.
animadversion (*n*) blame, criticism: She resented the critics' *animadversions* on her work.

In Latin, the word *mors* means "death." In English, the word root *mor* forms the basis of several words having to do with death or dying.

mortal (*adj*) doomed to die: All people are *mortal*; only the gods are immortal.
mortality (*n*) the condition of being mortal; also, the death rate among a group of people: Better health care has lowered infant *mortality*.
mortuary (*n*) a place where the dead are kept before burial.
morbid (*adj*) sickly or diseased: *Morbid* ideas are the product of a troubled mind.
moribund (*adj*) feeble, dying: By the 1850s, the Whig Party was *moribund*, though not yet dead.
mortify (*v*) to humiliate or shame. (The word originally meant "to kill pride" through punishment, self-denial, or shame.)

You've now studied five Latin word roots, which have unlocked the meanings of nearly fifty words. Many more words contain these roots; the words listed here are the ones most likely to appear on the SAT. You can now begin to see how the study of word roots naturally assists the learning of vocabulary.

6.4 Word Roots Related to "Movement": *Ven, Vol, Flu, Ver*

The next four word roots you'll study refer to various kinds of movement.

The root *ven* means "come." You may have heard of Julius Caesar's famous remark "*Veni, vidi, vici*," which means "I came, I saw, I conquered." In English, the root *ven* appears in many words. Here are some of them:

convene (*v*) to come together or gather, as for a meeting.
advent (*n*) the coming or arrival of something or someone: The *advent* of white settlers led to the destruction of Indian culture.

adventitious (*adj*) literally, "coming from outside"; extraneous; accidental, unintentional: Any merits that this trashy novel possesses are purely *adventitious*.
intervene (*v*) literally, "to come between"; to become involved in a dispute, problem, or conflict.
contravene (*v*) literally, "to come against"; to oppose or to conflict with: The strike *contravened* the judge's order.
circumvent (*v*) to go around, to avoid: He *circumvented* the law by falsifying his tax return.
covenant (*n*) literally, "a coming together"; a binding agreement or contract: God's promise to His people is considered a holy *covenant*.

In Latin, *volvo* is not a brand of car; it means "roll," "wind," "turn around," or "twist around." Many English words contain the word root *vol*; all have to do with rolling, winding, turning, or twisting.

revolve (*v*) to turn or roll.
evolve (*v*) literally, "to turn into something else"; to change gradually.
devolve (*v*) literally, "to turn over"; to pass on to another: If the president dies, the duties of the office *devolve* on the vice-president.
involve (*v*) literally, "to roll up or wrap up": to be *involved* in something is to be "wrapped up" in it.
convolution (*n*) an intricate rolling, twisting, turning, or coiling: It was hard to follow the *convolutions* of his long, confusing speech.
voluble (*adj*) literally, "letting the words roll out"; talkative, glib, and fluent: After a few drinks, he became extremely *voluble*.

Fluere, in Latin, means "to flow." (The word *flow* itself is related to the Latin, as you can see.) Many English words use the word root *flu* to suggest the idea of flowing. Here are some of them:

fluid (*adj*) flowing, liquid.
fluent (*adj*) flowing; able to speak in a flowing, practiced style.
flux (*n*) change, movement: The universe is in a state of continual *flux*.
influx (*n*) a flowing in of something: The seaside town expects a steady *influx* of tourists throughout the summer.
fluctuate (*v*) to vary; to rise and fall, as flowing waves do: Oil prices have *fluctuated* over the last few years.
affluent (*adj*) prosperous, well-to-do. (The word comes from the idea of wealth "flowing" toward a person or place.)
confluence (*n*) a flowing-together: Pittsburgh stands at the *confluence* of three rivers.
influence (*n*) the effect or power of something. (The word comes from the idea of an effect "flowing" from one thing to another.)
effluvium (*n*) anything that flows out of something else, especially sewage or other waste.
superfluous (*adj*) literally, "flowing over"; excessive, unnecessary: Once the job is completed, further work is *superfluous*.

The word *vertere* means "to turn" in Latin. In English, the root *ver* appears in many words. Here are some that you should know for the SAT:

reverse (*v*) to turn back or turn around.
versatile (*adj*) literally, "able to turn to a wide variety of activities"; able to do many different kinds of things.
aversion (*n*) literally, "a turning away from something"; a strong dislike.
versus (*prep*) against.
adversary (*n*) literally, "one whom one has turned against"; an enemy or opponent: Republicans and Democrats are perennial *adversaries*.
convert (*v*) to turn, change, or alter.
controvert (*v*) literally, "to turn in the opposite direction"; to dispute, deny, or disagree.

advert (*v*) literally, "to turn to"; to refer to; to pay attention to.
advertent (*adj*) giving attention; intentional.
inadvertent (*adj*) accidental or unintended; opposite of *advertent*.
vertex (*n*) literally, "a turning point"; a point or corner, as in a triangle.
vertical (*adj*) running straight up and down (from the idea of pointing toward a vertex).
vertigo (*n*) dizziness, as from turning around and around.

6.5 Word Roots Related to "Importance": *Prim, Arch, Reg, Magna*

In Latin, the word *primus* means "first." A number of English words use the root *prim* to mean either "first in time" or "first in importance."

primary (*adj*) first in time: The first school you attend is *primary* school. Also, first in importance: The *primary* reason for something is the main reason.
prime (*adj*) first; major, main; best.
primal (*adj*) earliest, first: Hunting and gathering were two of mankind's *primal* activities.
primeval (*adj*) of the earliest times: the *primeval* forest, *primeval* civilization.
primordial (*adj*) earliest, first: the *primordial* chaos before creation.
primitive (*adj*) earliest, first; also, crude or rudimentary: *primitive* technology.
primer (*n*) a book designed to teach children how to read (a "first" reader); also, any book that teaches the first principles of a subject.
primacy (*n*) importance, precedence.
primogeniture (*n*) the legal right of a first-born son to inherit his father's estate.

The word root *arch* comes originally from Greek. It means "chief" or "first." Here are some of the English words that contain it:

monarchy (*n*) rule by a king or queen. (The word combines *arch* with the root *mon*, which means "one"; the word literally means "rule by one person.")
oligarchy (*n*) rule by a few: A society ruled by a small group of powerful people is called an *oligarchy*.
hierarchy (*n*) a ranking of things or people in order of importance.
patriarch (*n*) the father and ruler of a tribe, nation, or family.
anarchy (*n*) a state of lawlessness: If all government were abolished, there would be *anarchy*.
archaic (*adj*) from the first or earliest times: An *archaic* word is one that is no longer used.
archive (*n*) a place where old records or documents are kept.
archaeology (*n*) literally, "the study of beginnings"; the study of the artifacts of ancient peoples.
archetype (*n*) an original pattern or model; a perfect image or symbol: Paul Bunyan is an *archetype* of the frontier hero.

In Latin, the word *rex* means "king." (The dinosaur name *Tyrannosaurus rex* means "tyrant king.") In the form of *reg*, this word root appears in a number of English words relating to kingship or rule.

regime (*n*) a particular political system or ruling body: Revolutionaries overthrew the old *regime*.
regal (*adj*) kingly or having to do with a king.
regnant (*adj*) ruling, holding power: Queen Elizabeth I was not a figurehead but a queen *regnant*.
regimen (*n*) a rule of life; especially, a prescribed system of diet and exercise.
regicide (*n*) the killing of a king. (The word combines *reg* with *-cide*, which means "to kill," as in *homicide* or *suicide*.)
regulate (*v*) to rule, control, or direct.
interregnum (*n*) the period of time between two rulers or two regimes.

regalia (*n*) originally, things associated with a king; now, fancy clothes, banners, and other ceremonial trappings.

The word *magnus* in Latin means "large" or "great." (Think of the famous emperor Charlemagne, whose name means "Charles the Great," or the English Magna Carta, which means "Great Charter.") You've already learned the word *magnanimous*, which means "great in spirit, forgiving, generous." Here are some other English words that contain the root *magna* or *magni*:

magnify (*v*) to make greater or larger.
magnitude (*n*) size or greatness.
magnificent (*adj*) great, grand, splendid, gorgeous.
magniloquent (*adj*) pompous, grandiose, or overfancy in speech. (The word combines *magni* with the root *loq*, which means "speech.")
magnate (*n*) an important or influential person, especially in business: J. R. Ewing is a fictional oil *magnate.*
magnanimity (*n*) greatness or loftiness of spirit; nobility or generosity of mind: The citizens were impressed by the *magnanimity* of the general, who ordered that all prisoners be freed.

6.6 Word Roots Related to "Good" and "Bad": *Bene, Mal, Mis-*

In Latin, *bene* means "well." (If you've studied French or Spanish, you'll recognize the word.) Here are several English words containing the root *bene*:

benefit (*n*) advantage, profit; anything that does one good.
beneficial (*adj*) helpful, profitable, advantageous; giving a benefit.
beneficent (*adj*) kindly, charitable, generous: The *beneficent* queen was adored by her people.
benevolent (*adj*) inclined to do good, wishing others well: A *benevolent* person wants everyone to be happy. (Note that to be *beneficent*, one must do good; to be *benevolent*, one need only wish good things for others.)
benign (*adj*) kind, favorable, friendly; used in medicine to mean harmless: The patient was relieved to learn that the tumor was *benign.*
benefactor (*n*) one who does good; especially, one who gives money to help others.
benediction (*n*) literally, a good-saying; a blessing: The priest pronounced a *benediction* on the newlyweds.

In Latin, *male* means "badly." (Again, the related words in French and Spanish are very close.) Here are some English words with *mal* as a root. Notice that some of them are exact opposites of the *bene* words.

malice (*n*) hatred, hostility, spite, ill will.
malicious (*adj*) given to, arising from, or marked by malice.
maleficent (*adj*) doing evil; harmful; mischievous: *Maleficent* spirits come out on Halloween.
malign (*adj*) evil, malicious: The plot centers on the *malign* influence of the evil counselor.
malignant (*adj*) causing harm, injurious: The patient was distraught to learn that the tumor was *malignant.*
malevolent (*adj*) wishing evil; spiteful, malicious.
malefactor (*n*) one who does evil; a criminal or culprit.
malediction (*n*) a curse.
maladroit (*adj*) clumsy, awkward; opposite of *adroit.*
malady (*n*) a sickness or disease.
malinger (*v*) to pretend to be ill in order to avoid work.
malcontent (*n*) someone who is habitually dissatisfied or rebellious.

Mis- is one of many prefixes that can be attached to the beginning of a word to change its meaning. It comes from Old English, and it means "wrong" or "bad." *Mis-* is used in scores of English words. Here are just a few:

misbehave (*v*) to behave badly.
misuse (*v*) to use wrongly or for an evil purpose.
mislead (*v*) to lead astray; to fool or deceive.
misjudge (*v*) to judge wrongly or erroneously.
miscarry (*v*) to go wrong, to fail: The project *miscarried.* (From *miscarry* derives the word *miscarriage,* for the expulsion of a fetus that is not viable.)
misconstrue (*v*) to interpret wrongly; to misunderstand: The detective realized with dismay that she had *misconstrued* the evidence.
misadventure (*n*) bad luck; an unfortunate occurrence; an accident.
misnomer (*n*) a wrong or inappropriate name: The woman exhibited her playful sense of humor when she affixed the *misnomer* "Spot" to her snow-white dog.
misappropriate (*v*) to take or make use of something, such as money, without right or authority: The accountant was accused of *misappropriating* funds.
misdemeanor (*n*) literally, "wrong or bad behavior"; a crime less serious than a felony: If the lawyer is convicted of a *misdemeanor,* he will still be able to practice law; if he is convicted of a felony, he will be disbarred.
miscreant (*n*) literally, "one with wrong or bad beliefs"; heretic, infidel; also, one who behaves viciously or criminally.

6.7 Word Roots Related to "Love" and "Hate": *Am, Phil, Miso*

In Latin, the word *amare* means "to love" and the word *amicus* means "friend." Several English words that relate to love and friendship spring from the root *am.*

enamor (*v*) to inflame with love; charm; captivate: Although Catherine was *enamored* of Heathcliff, she had no intention of marrying him.
amorous (*adj*) of or relating to love; moved by love: *amorous* advances.
amiable (*adj*) lovable; good-natured; pleasant, agreeable; friendly, sociable.
amicable (*adj*) characterized by friendliness and goodwill; friendly or neighborly.
amity (*n*) friendship; friendly relations, especially between nations: After a long history of hostility, the two bordering countries finally established a lasting *amity.*
amateur (*n*) one who engages in an activity for the love of it (as a pastime) rather than for money (as a profession); also, one with little experience in an activity or little knowledge of a subject.

In Greek, *philein* means "to love." The root *phil* is used in many English words to refer to various kinds of love.

philosophy (*n*) literally, "love of wisdom"; the study of the basic principles of knowledge, ethics, and logic.
philanthropy (*n*) literally, "love of humankind"; generosity in giving to charity. (The word combines *phil* with *anthrop,* which means "human being.")
philology (*n*) the study of linguistics; the science of language.
philander (*v*) to engage in frequent, trivial love affairs, especially if one is a married man.
philately (*n*) the hobby of collecting and studying postage stamps.
philter (*n*) a love potion: Tristan and Isolde fell in love after drinking a *philter.*

The opposite of *phil* is *miso,* which comes from the Greek word *misein,* meaning "to hate." *Miso,* or sometimes *mis,* is a component of a few English words that you should know for the SAT:

misanthropy (*n*) hatred or distrust of humankind; opposite of *philanthropy.*
misanthrope (*n*) one who hates or distrusts humankind: Before he reformed, Scrooge was a *misanthrope.*

misogyny (*n*) hatred or distrust of women. (The word combines *miso* with *gyn*, which means "woman.")
misogynist (*n*) one who hates or distrusts women.
misogamy (*n*) hatred of marriage. (The word combines *miso* with *-gamy*, which means "marriage.")

6.8 Word Roots Related to "Communication": *Dic, Voc, Loq, Nom, Pet, Rog, Laud, Mand*

The Latin word *dicere* means "to say" or "to name." The root *dic* is the source of many English words (including *dictionary*). You have already learned *benediction* (a "good-saying," or blessing) and its opposite, *malediction* (a "bad-saying," or curse). Here are some other English words that grew out of the root *dic*:

diction (*n*) a writer's choice of words; also, a person's enunciation or manner of speaking.
predict (*v*) literally, "to say before"; to prophesy, to foretell.
edict (*n*) an official pronouncement, rule, or order.
contradict (*v*) literally, "to say against"; to deny or disagree with.
verdict (*n*) literally, "what is truly said"; the judgment in a legal case.
interdict (*v*) literally, "to speak between"; to forbid.
dictate (*v*) to command; also, to say aloud for someone else to write down: The mayor *dictated* a letter to her secretary.
predicate (*v*) to state or affirm; to imply; to cause to be based: The plans for the picnic are *predicated* upon the expectation of good weather.
abdicate (*v*) to give up or abandon, especially a kingship or other office.
valedictorian (*n*) literally, "one who says farewell"; one who gives the farewell address at a school's graduation ceremony.
dictum (*n*) a saying, especially an authoritative or respected one: Thoreau's essay on civil disobedience opens with the *dictum* "That government is best which governs least."

The Latin word *vocare* means "to call." In English there are many words derived from *vocare* that contain the root *voc* or *vok*. Here are some of them:

vocabulary (*n*) literally, "what things are called"; words and their meanings; all the words of a language.
vocal (*adj*) spoken, oral; freely expressing one's opinions: a *vocal* supporter of the bill.
advocate (*n*) someone who speaks out in favor of a cause or person: an *advocate* of tax reform.
vocation (*n*) a profession, especially when seen as a "calling" of special importance: Though she worked as a plumber, she considered music her *vocation*.
convocation (*n*) literally, "a calling together"; a meeting or assembly.
invocation (*n*) the calling forth of some spirit or force: The speech ended with an *invocation* of the spirit of democracy.
evocation (*n*) the calling forth of a mood or feeling: The *evocation* of strong emotions is a special power of music.
provoke (*v*) to call forth some feeling, action, or response by another.
revoke (*v*) literally, "to call back"; to take away some right or privilege: The state *revoked* his driver's license.
equivocal (*adj*) literally, "speaking with two equal voices"; ambiguous, having two or more meanings; undecided.
vociferous (*adj*) loud, noisy; outspoken.

The Latin word *loqui* means "to say" or "to speak." Here are some English words containing the roots *loq* and *loc*, derived from *loqui*:

eloquent (*adj*) speaking with grace and skill: John F. Kennedy was an *eloquent* speaker.
loquacious (*adj*) talkative, garrulous.

colloquy (*n*) literally, "a speaking together"; a conversation, a dialogue.
soliloquy (*n*) a speech by one person alone: Hamlet's *soliloquy* is perhaps the best-known speech in all of Shakespeare.
obloquy (*n*) a verbal attack on someone; verbal abuse, vituperation.
grandiloquent (*adj*) speaking in a pretentious, overfancy manner.
locution (*n*) a word or expression; a style of speech.
circumlocution (*n*) a roundabout or indirect expression: Many people use *circumlocutions* when referring to unpleasant subjects, such as death.

The Latin word *nomen* means "name." In the forms of *nom* and *nym*, the word has become a root for many English words having to do with names or with words in general. You have already learned *misnomer*, which means "wrong or inappropriate name." Here are some other words derived from *nomen*:

nominate (*v*) to name someone, especially as a candidate for office.
nominal (*adj*) in name only: A *nominal* charge is a price so low as to be virtually meaningless.
anonymous (*adj*) without a name; unsigned, of unknown authorship.
synonym (*n*) one of two or more words that have almost the same meaning.
antonym (*n*) one of two or more words that have almost opposite meanings.
homonym (*n*) one of two or more words that sound the same: *Sea* and *see* are *homonyms.*
cognomen (*n*) a family name or surname.
nomenclature (*n*) any system of naming things: Zoology has its own system of *nomenclature* for the various species of animals.

The Latin word *petere* means "to seek" or "to ask for." It also means "to rush at" or "to attack." A number of related words in English spring from the root *pet.*

appetite (*n*) a need or desire for something, usually food.
petition (*n*) a request, especially one in written form signed by a number of supporters.
compete (*v*) to seek victory over others.
petulant (*adj*) irritable, peevish, impatient, complaining.
impetuous (*adj*) rushing into actions; rash, heedless, impulsive.
impetus (*n*) a force or motive that stimulates action: The demands of his constituents were the *impetus* behind the senator's action.
centripetal (*adj*) literally, "seeking the center": *Centripetal* force is the tendency of a body to move toward the center of a system. (The opposite of *centripetal* is *centrifugal.*)

In Latin, *rogare* means "to question," "to ask for," or "to propose." Here are some English words that contain the root *rog*:

interrogate (*v*) to ask questions, especially of a witness in a trial.
arrogate (*v*) to claim or demand: The president has no right to *arrogate* that power.
prerogative (*n*) a prior, exclusive, or inherent right.
abrogate (*v*) to repeal, abolish, or nullify, especially a law.
surrogate (*n*) a substitute.
rogation (*n*) a prayer, supplication, or formal request.

Laudare means "to praise" in Latin. Several English words grew out of the root *laud.*

laud (*v*) to praise; to commend.
applaud (*v*) to praise, especially by clapping.
plaudit (*n*) any expression of praise or approval: The play won *plaudits* from the critics.
laudable (*adj*) worthy of praise: Her motives are *laudable,* though her actions are questionable.
laudatory (*adj*) expressing praise: The award was inscribed with many *laudatory* comments.

Latin *mandare* means "to entrust," "to commit," or "to order." The root *mand*, or sometimes *mend*, appears in English words that are related to the meaning of *mandare*.

command (*v*) to order or rule.
mandate (*n*) a formal order or commission: As expressed in an election, the wishes of the people may constitute a *mandate*.
mandatory (*adj*) commanded, required, obligatory: When you apply for a driver's license, an eye examination is *mandatory*.
remand (*v*) to order back; especially, to order a prisoner to be returned to prison.
countermand (*v*) literally, "to order against"; to issue an order that overrules an earlier one.
commend (*v*) to commit or entrust to someone's care; to mention with approval or praise: The soldier was *commended* for his bravery in battle.
recommend (*v*) literally, "to entrust with anew"; to propose as worthy of acceptance; to advise.

6.9 Word Roots Related to "Sight": *Spec, Vis*

The Latin word *specere* means "to look at" or "to see." It is closely related to another Latin word, *spectare*, which means "to look at carefully," "to contemplate," "to observe," or "to watch." The two words provide the basis for many English words, all of which contain the root *spec*, *spect*, or *spic*.

aspect (*n*) the way something appears from one side or from one point of view.
expect (*v*) to look for or to look forward to.
inspect (*v*) to examine carefully.
suspect (*v*) to consider as possible or probable; to believe someone to be guilty or at fault without sufficient evidence.
prospect (*n*) literally, "a looking forward to something"; something that is awaited or expected; in the plural, chances: Our *prospects* of developing enough alternate sources of energy are still doubtful.
prospective (*adj*) looked forward to, expected; possible.
retrospect (*n*) a backward look: Events often seem different in *retrospect* than they do when they are happening.
introspection (*n*) a looking inward at one's own mind and feelings.
specimen (*n*) an item to be examined, as in a laboratory or museum; an example.
spectator (*n*) one who watches an event.
spectacle (*n*) something watched, especially a show or exhibition.
specter (*n*) a vision or ghost.
spectral (*adj*) ghostlike; visionary.
speculate (*v*) to view inwardly; to wonder about or to try to explain; to theorize.
auspicious (*adj*) literally, "foretold by the watching of birds" (in ancient Rome it was believed possible to foretell the future by examining the flight patterns of birds); hence, boding well for the future, favorable, propitious: The good weather is *auspicious* for our journey.
conspicuous (*adj*) easy to see, standing out, noticeable.
perspicacious (*adj*) observant, noticing much; keen in understanding.

In Latin, *videre* means "to see," "to look at," or "to observe." Here are some English words related to the root *vid* or *vis*:

vision (*n*) the power of seeing; something seen.
visual (*adj*) related to sight or vision.
visible (*adj*) able to be seen.
supervise (*v*) literally, "to oversee"; to control, organize, or direct.
visage (*n*) someone's appearance; especially, the face.

envisage (*v*) to picture in the mind, imagine, or conceive.
visionary (*adj*) imaginative, far-seeing; imaginary, unreal.
vista (*n*) a view or outlook, especially over a far distance: From the mountaintop, the climbers enjoyed a wonderful *vista*.
evident (*adj*) able to be seen; apparent, clear.

This completes Lesson 6. You've learned seven groups of word roots and about 250 words related to those roots. In Lesson 11, you'll learn another set of word roots and some useful words they help to form.

LESSON 7
Techniques for Antonyms

OBJECTIVES

☐ To master the three-step approach to antonym questions

☐ To learn to distinguish between two or more antonym answer choices that are nearly correct

☐ To understand how subtle variations in the meanings of words can affect the answers to antonym questions

Approaching Antonyms

7.1 The Three-Step Approach

Antonyms are the simplest (though not necessarily the easiest) type of question on the SAT. As you know, each antonym consists of two parts: the original word, or the *stem word*, and five answer choices. Your job is to choose the answer that is most nearly opposite in meaning to the stem word.

There are three things you should know about the antonym questions on the SAT. First, they're always antonym questions; they're never synonym questions. That may seem obvious, but some test preparation books lead you to believe that the makers of the SAT sometimes substitute synonyms for antonyms. They don't—probably because antonyms require two mental steps, rather than one, and thus perhaps serve as better indicators of "aptitude."

Second, synonyms are never given as answer choices. Although many test preparation books tell you that synonyms are common "distractors" on antonym questions, they're not. The makers of the SAT aren't interested in "tricking" you into choosing a synonym rather than an antonym. They're interested in how well you understand the meaning of a word and its connotations. So they never present you with a word that has the same meaning as the stem word in an antonym question.

Third, the answer choices for antonym questions are always the same part of speech as the stem word. Again, many SAT preparation books warn you to watch out for answer choices that aren't the same part of speech as the stem word. Don't bother. If the stem word is an adjective, all five answer choices will be adjectives. If the stem word is a noun, all five answer choices will be nouns. Just as the test makers don't make it hard on you by giving synonyms as answer choices, so they don't make it easy on you by giving answer choices that are the "wrong" part of speech.

Naturally, the main requirement for scoring high on antonym questions is a good vocabulary. Lessons 2, 6, and 11 will help you strengthen and enlarge your vocabulary. In this lesson, you'll learn some techniques that will help you use your vocabulary knowledge effectively when you tackle antonyms. Specifically, you'll learn the three-step approach to antonyms: (1) define the stem word, (2) select an opposite, and (3) check your answer backward.

When you take the SAT, each verbal section will include some antonyms. Some verbal sections will have ten antonyms, others fifteen. On the average, you should do antonyms at a rate of about two a minute; a group of ten antonyms should therefore take you about 5 minutes and a group of fifteen about 7 minutes. With practice, you should have no trouble maintaining this pace.

You may wonder whether it's possible to complete the three-step approach to every antonym question within 30 seconds. Don't worry. You won't always have to take all three separate steps. Some antonym questions are quite easy. For these, you can safely omit the third step, and you can probably complete the first two steps in 10 seconds or less. So when you take the SAT, the time pressures will be manageable. Because the three-step approach is very helpful with the more difficult antonym items, it's a good idea to practice it beforehand.

7.2 Step 1: Define the Stem Word

When tackling an antonym, first consider the meaning of the stem word. Thinking of a phrase or a sentence that contains the word might help you remember its meaning. So might recognizing the root from which the word is derived. If you can, think of a synonym. Do all of this *before* you look at the answer choices.

This step is important for several reasons. First of all, the answer choices may be confusing or misleading. Remember, four of them are wrong; only one is right. If you approach the answer choices with only a vague idea about the meaning of the stem word, you may find yourself misled by the wrong answer choices.

Also, on many antonyms, more than one answer choice will be partly right, and the differences among the answers will be quite subtle. If your idea of the stem word is clearly focused beforehand, you'll find it easier to distinguish among several similar choices.

Here's an example of how you might approach a rather hard antonym. Suppose the stem word is *desecration.* You may know the meaning of the word right away. If you do, you're home free. You can go right on to the answer choices. However, if you're among the majority of test takers who find this a tough word, here are some ways you can use to figure out its meaning:

First, see whether you can think of a phrase or sentence containing the word. Thinking of a phrase or sentence will often help when a word seems vaguely familiar, but you can't pin down its meaning. In the case of *desecration*, you might recall seeing or hearing the word in news stories about vandalism of churches or synagogues. The painting of graffiti on a church, for example, is often described as an act of *desecration.* This kind of recollection might be enough to jog your memory of the meaning of the word.

Second, see if you can break the word down into its component parts, which may provide another clue. *Desecration* starts with the familiar prefix *de-*, which means "away from," "out of," or "not." (Think of the verb *desert*, which means "to go away from" or "to leave behind.") This is followed by *secr*, a variant of the root *sacr*, which might remind you of the word *sacred.* Other words with the same word root include *consecrate* and *sacrament*, both of which have to do with holy things. Combine this root with the prefix *de-*, and you can figure out that the word *desecration* has to do with "taking away the holiness of something."

Of course, this is just an example. You might not know the root of *desecrate*, and you may never have seen the word before. But in many cases, you can figure out a word you don't know by using what little you do know—by recollecting how you've seen the word used or by breaking the word down into its component parts.

Once you've figured out as best you can what the stem word means, you're ready for step 2.

7.3 Step 2: Select an Opposite

Before looking at the answer choices, think of what the opposite of the stem word would be. If one of the five answer choices is the same as the opposite you think of, you've found the right answer. If not, look for a synonym for the word you thought of. That will be the answer you want.

The point of trying to think of a suitable antonym *before* looking at the answer choices is, again, to avoid the confusion that may arise when you look at five new words, four of which are incorrect. If you know what you're looking for before you start looking for it, your chance of finding it is much better.

You have seen that the word *desecrate* means "to take away the holiness of something." What would the opposite of that be? Clearly, "to make something holy." The best answer choice will be a word with that meaning. *Sanctify* or *consecrate*, for example, would be good answers. Another possible answer is a phrase that means the same thing, such as "to make holy."

Here's another example: If the stem word is *pusillanimous*, meaning "cowardly," the answer should be a word meaning the opposite of "cowardly." You might think of *brave*, *courageous*, or *heroic*. With these possibilities in mind, look at the answer choices. If *brave* is one of them, you know you've found the answer. If not, you need to do some more thinking.

For instance, suppose the answer choices are these:

PUSILLANIMOUS: (A) noteworthy
(B) magnanimous (C) vindictive (D) intrepid
(E) grandiose

You might look at these five words and be uncertain about which is closest in meaning to *brave*. (The correct answer is choice D. *Intrepid* means "brave, facing danger with determination and valor.") You can start by eliminating any answers that you know are clearly wrong. Don't be tempted by choices that seem vaguely similar to what you want. For instance, choice B, *magnanimous*, has a positive meaning, just as *brave* does. However, *magnanimous* doesn't mean anything very close to *brave*; it means "generous, forgiving." Correct antonym answers will be much more directly on target than that. If you can eliminate at least one of the answers as clearly wrong, you'll have a better chance of choosing the right anwer from among the others.

Of course, you can use the same methods to figure out the meaning of any of the answer choices as you use to figure out the meaning of the stem word. For example, the root of *intrepid* is *trep*, which means "fear"; the prefix *in-* means "not." So you might be able to use your word-attack skills to figure out that *intrepid* means "not fearful."

If you're unable to figure out the answer to an antonym question, make an educated guess. Eliminate as many incorrect choices as you can; then choose one of the others. If you have a hunch about the right answer, follow it. Hunches are correct often enough to make them worth following whenever you must guess at an answer.

7.4 Step 3: Check Your Answer Backward

After choosing the answer you think is best, check your answer backward. In other words, look at the answer you've chosen and ask yourself this: "What would be the opposite of this word?" The answer should be the same as the original word. If it is, you've chosen correctly. If not, think again.

Here's an example of how this technique works. Look at the following antonym question:

INDIGENT: (A) capable (B) affluent
(C) celebrated (D) free-spending (E) miserly

The stem word means "poor, lacking money." Therefore, the correct antonym should mean something like "having a lot of money." A word like *rich* or *wealthy* would be a good choice.

Unfortunately, neither of these is among the answer choices. So you have to decide which of the five choices is closest in meaning to *rich*. You might be tempted by any of the five. All of them have some relation to the idea of wealth. However, only one choice is correct. Checking answer choices backward will help you differentiate the almost-right answers from the one that's completely right. Here's how:

Choice A, *capable*, means "competent, able to do things well." You might be tempted to choose this answer, even though it doesn't exactly mean "rich," because a rich person is able to do many things that a poor person can't. Now check this answer backward. What's the opposite of *capable*? Some possibilities are *incapable*, *incompetent*, or *unable*. Are any of these close in meaning to *indigent*? Not really.

Choice B, *affluent*, means "well-to-do, prosperous." The opposite of *affluent* is *poor*, which is much the same as *indigent*. So this looks like a good answer choice.

Choice C, *celebrated*, means "famous." Many famous people are rich, but if you check this answer backward, you'll see that the opposite of celebrated is *little-known* or *obscure*, neither of which means the same as *indigent*. So choice C is wrong.

Choice D, *free-spending*, describes a quality that a rich person might be more likely to have than a poor person. But again, check the answer backward. The opposite of *free-spending* is *tight-fisted*, *cheap*, or *stingy*. None of these are synonymous with *indigent*.

Finally, choice E, *miserly*, means "greedy" or "grasping." Some rich people are indeed miserly, but the backward check can eliminate this answer, too. The opposite of *miserly* is *generous* or *liberal*, which is not the same as *indigent*.

You won't have to use step 3 for every antonym. You may be confident enough of certain answers to skip this step. But whenever you're in doubt about an answer, use step 3. It will often resolve your doubts.

Now that you've studied the basic method for approaching antonyms, you're ready to learn some special techniques that are useful for answering certain antonym questions.

Advanced Antonym Techniques

7.5 Denotations and Connotations

When more than one answer to an antonym question seems right to you, consider the *connotations*, or feelings, of the words as well as their *denotations*, or literal meanings. For example, the word *shrewd* means "clever" or "smart." So a word meaning something like "foolish" or "dull" would be more or less opposite to *shrewd*. But *shrewd* also has the connotation of "tricky," "cunning," or "deceitful." So the *best* antonym would be a word that includes the connotation of "open," "innocent," or "sincere." A word like *simple* or *artless* would be a good choice.

Another example: *Servile* means "like a servant or slave." Its central meaning has to do with working under the commands of another. The opposite of *servile*, then, would have something to do with ruling or commanding others. However, *servile* has connotations that go beyond the basic idea of service. It implies a lack of dignity, an abject humility or slavishness. Therefore, the best antonym would include the idea of holding oneself above others in a haughty or proud way. Words like *arrogant*, *imperious*, and *haughty* capture this idea.

As you can see, it's helpful to be aware of emotional shades of meaning when tackling antonyms on the SAT.

7.6 Level of Specificity

Watch out for answers that are more general in meaning than the stem word in an antonym question. For instance, suppose the stem word is *vindictive*, which generally means "spiteful" or "malicious" but also has the specific meaning of "eagerly seeking revenge." A general word like *kindly* or *gentle* would not be a good antonym. A more specific word, one that focused on the idea of not seeking revenge, would be better. The correct answer would probably be a word like *forgiving*, *forbearing*, or *clement*.

Also watch out for answers that are more specific than the original word. For instance, suppose the stem word is *abet*, which means "to help." Specific words like *confuse* and *retard*, which refer to specific ways not to help someone, would not make good antonyms. A more general word like *hinder* or *encumber* would be better.

The basic principle underlying these two suggestions is the same. When you examine the stem word, take into account how general or specific it is. The best answer choice will be one at the same level of specificity.

7.7 Degree of "Oppositeness"

Make sure that the answer you choose for an antonym is directly opposed in meaning to the stem word. For example, if the stem word is *turbid*, meaning "cloudy" or "muddy," the opposite should be a word that means "very clear," such as *pellucid* or *crystalline*. Words like *translucent* and *milky*, which refer to partly cloudy substances, would be poor answers; they aren't "opposite enough."

Here is another example:

REVILE: (A) laud (B) ignore (C) tease
(D) describe (E) address

To *revile* someone is to attack or insult that person in a very harsh and vicious manner. You would *revile* only someone whom you hated or found repulsive. It's a very strong word. The answer should be an equally strong word—one meaning to praise someone in a highly respectful manner. So the best opposite is *laud*, choice A. The other answers are also opposed in meaning to *revile*, but they aren't "opposite enough." To *ignore* someone is to neither praise nor condemn that person. To *tease* someone is to criticize or mock that person in a gentle, humorous fashion. Teasing is quite different from reviling, but it isn't opposite to it. And the words *describe* and *address*, which refer to other ways of speaking to or about someone, don't convey either a strongly positive or a strongly negative feeling.

7.8 Secondary Meanings

When no answer to an antonym question seems correct, look at the stem word again. It may have a second meaning that you're forgetting. For example, *heighten* means "to raise." Its antonym would be a word like *lower*. But if you don't find an answer choice meaning "lower," a second meaning of *heighten* may be involved. *Heighten* is sometimes used to mean "to sharpen" or "to make more intense," as in the sentence "The sound of the bombs exploding nearby *heightened* the prisoners' fear." So another possible antonym for *heighten* would be a word meaning "to make less intense," such as *alleviate*, *mitigate*, or *relieve*.

Another example: *Decisive* means "self-assured, definite, determined"; a decisive person knows what she or he wants. A good opposite would be *hesitant*, *unsure*, *wavering*, or *indecisive*. You may find, however, that no words like these are included as answer choices. If that's the case, a second meaning of *decisive* could be intended: "crucial," "playing a deciding role." In this sense of the word, a decisive action is one that determines the course of future events. (Gettysburg was a *decisive* battle of the U.S. Civil War.) The best opposite for this meaning would be a word like *insignificant*, *minor*, or *unimportant*.

Remember, then, if no answer seems correct, consider whether the stem word has a second meaning. Try to find an answer choice that is an antonym for that second meaning.

LESSON 8
Tackling Reading Comprehension Questions

OBJECTIVES

- ☐ To distinguish the common types of reading comprehension questions
- ☐ To master effective techniques for answering each type of question
- ☐ To recognize the common types of incorrect answer choices and learn how to avoid them

Approaching Reading Questions

8.1 Format and Timing

In Lesson 3, you learned some techniques for effective reading on the SAT. Now it's time to study the other half of the task: answering reading comprehension questions.

As you learned, reading each passage on the SAT should be done in three steps: previewing, active reading, and reviewing. On a typical long passage, you should be able to go through these three steps in about 3 or $3\frac{1}{2}$ minutes. Only after completing this job should you go on to the questions.

The number of questions on a passage will vary. A short reading passage might have only two or three questions. A long passage will usually have four or five. The questions are designed to cover most or all of the major points in the passage. They will vary in content and style. You'll probably find some of them very hard and others quite easy. Unlike the questions in other parts of the SAT, reading comprehension questions are not arranged in order of difficulty. Instead, the questions usually follow the order in which the material asked about appears in the passage.

Plan on spending an average of 30 to 40 seconds on each question. Naturally, the time required will vary. You'll be able to do some easy questions in 20 seconds or less, while some hard ones may take you a minute or more. But your goal should be to complete about two questions a minute. Five questions on a passage should take you between $2\frac{1}{2}$ and 3 minutes. Add this to the 3 minutes you'll need to read the passage, and the whole task should take you about 6 minutes.

In this lesson, you'll learn about six common types of reading comprehension questions: main idea questions, detail questions, logic questions, inference questions, tone questions, and rhetoric questions. When you take the SAT, you'll probably encounter some of each.

First, read the following sample reading passage, using the three-step approach. Some of the sample questions discussed in this lesson will be based on this passage.

Experiments in sleep deprivation have been conducted for a number of years in an effort to determine the function of sleep. Theoretically, if sleep plays any biologically or psychologically essential role, that role should become apparent when a person has been deprived of sleep. The results of the experiments are not clear-cut, though. In some experiments, people deprived of sleep for periods of two hundred hours or more have been able to function almost normally. A few early studies had seemed to suggest that bizarre, psychotic-like symptoms would routinely occur after a long period without sleep. However, later studies have not borne out this hypothesis. These studies have revealed that most people who experience psychotic-like reactions to sleep deprivation have a history of mental illness. Furthermore, they have shown that the effects of sleeplessness rarely persist beyond a two-day period of recovery sleep.

Certain mild reactions to long periods without sleep usually do occur. For example, hand tremors, slurred speech, and sensory dullness are common. Subjects usually experience some loss of efficiency in performing tasks, although the nature and degree of the loss depend on the type of task imposed. Brief tasks may be affected only slightly. However, tasks requiring thirty minutes or more of continuous work are usually seriously affected, as are tasks requiring alertness. Some scientists believe that these difficulties can be explained by the occurrence of "microsleep," momentary lapses into sleep by an otherwise wakeful individual. Microsleep episodes, though brief and often undetected by the subject, may well cause errors in the performance of a task.

At the completion of a sleepless experimental period, most subjects sleep for twelve to fourteen hours, after which most effects are gone. For the first two or three nights after the vigil, the usual pattern of sleep stages is generally disrupted. The first recovery night includes a much greater amount than usual of stage-4 sleep (the deepest form of sleep). The second recovery night includes slightly more stage-4 sleep than usual, but it also shows a sharp increase in REM sleep, the type of sleep associated with dreaming. The marked increase in REM sleep after a period of wakefulness generally supports the idea that dreaming is necessary for full psychological health. It does not, however, explain exactly how or why this is so.

Types of Reading Questions

8.2 Main Idea Questions

One of the most common types of reading comprehension questions is the main idea question. There is usually one on each reading passage. As the name suggests, a question of this type focuses on the main idea of the passage. This means that as long as you can figure out the main idea of a passage, you'll probably get at least one question right. So never give up reading, even on a passage you find very difficult. If nothing else, you can usually catch its main idea and so earn a few points.

Main idea questions can take any of several forms. Here are some typical question stems:

The main idea of the passage is . . .
The author of the passage is primarily concerned with . . .
The purpose of the passage is to explain . . .
Which of the following best summarizes the main point of the passage?
Which of the following titles best expresses the central idea of the passage?

Although each of these stems is worded slightly differently, all of them seek the same basic information.

Make sure that the answer you choose for a main idea question relates to the entire passage, not to just one part of it. If necessary, scan the passage to make sure that the main idea you have selected is discussed throughout the entire selection. Wrong answer choices for main idea questions are often true statements that focus too narrowly on one paragraph or one detail.

Also read the answer choices carefully to make sure that the answer you choose describes the main idea precisely. Another common type of wrong answer is a slight distortion of the true main idea.

Here is a sample main idea question based on the sample reading passage you just read:

In this passage, the author is primarily concerned with

(A) explaining the function of sleep in human life
(B) describing the historical development of psychological knowledge about sleep
(C) disproving some common ideas about the effects of sleep deprivation
(D) discussing the studies of sleep deprivation conducted in recent years
(E) summarizing present knowledge about the effects of sleep deprivation

The correct answer is choice E. Each of the three paragraphs in the passage tells something about what is now known about sleep deprivation and its effects. Paragraph 1 explains that serious ill effects are rare. Paragraph 2 tells about the minor effects that occur. Paragraph 3 tells about how sleep is affected after the conclusion of the deprivation period. Choice E sums up these points.

Choices A and B are off the point. The passage doesn't discuss sleep in general, only the effects of sleep deprivation. The discussion may imply something about the nature of sleep, but the passage is more specific than choices A and B suggest. Choices C and D, by contrast, are too narrow. The first paragraph disproves some common ideas about sleep deprivation, but paragraphs 2 and 3 don't deal with this topic; so choice C is wrong. And choice D makes it sound as though the passage merely describes the experiments. In fact, the passage focuses mainly on what those experiments *show* about sleep deprivation; furthermore, paragraph 2 doesn't refer to the experiments at all.

8.3 Detail Questions

Almost every reading passage will have at least one detail question. As the name implies, detail questions deal with specific facts or details in a passage. Usually, a detail question focuses on one or two particular sentences in a passage. Find the relevant sentences and reread them. Make sure you understand them before you try to answer the question. Don't base your answer on a vague recollection of the passage. There will normally be one particular sentence that expresses the correct answer to the question.

The correct answer for a detail question will not necessarily contain the exact words or phrases that are used in the passage itself. More often, the answer choice will restate or paraphrase the idea. A common type of wrong answer for a detail question is one that includes a few words from the passage but distorts the basic idea.

Watch out for answer choices that state a fact mentioned in the passage but in a context different from that posed by the question. These answer choices may be tempting because they sound familiar, but they do not answer the question.

Here are two typical detail questions based on the passage about sleep deprivation:

According to the passage, experimental studies of sleep deprivation have been conducted mainly

(A) to explain the nature of psychotic symptoms
(B) to investigate problems of perception and problem solving
(C) to obtain clues to the role of sleep disorders in mental illness
(D) to help determine the psychological function of dreaming
(E) to gather information about the biological and psychological functions of sleep

According to the passage, psychotic-like symptoms in sleep-deprived individuals

(A) are relatively common but short-lived, rarely persisting beyond two days after the period of deprivation
(B) indicate the psychological necessity of sleep for the healthy functioning of an individual
(C) have occurred only in experimental subjects who went without sleeping for two hundred hours or longer
(D) have been found to occur mainly in those with prior mental problems
(E) have been found to occur in numerous, but not all, experimental studies

The correct answer to the first question is choice E. As usual, it can be found in a particular sentence of the passage—in this case, the very first one, which states that studies of sleep deprivation have been conducted "in an effort to determine the function of sleep." Choice E paraphrases this idea. The ideas stated in the other choices appear in the passage, but they don't answer the question, which asks about the *main* reason for the studies of sleep deprivation. The study of psychotic symptoms and mental illness (choices A and C) is mentioned in the passage but not as a major purpose of the studies. Perception and problem solving (choice B) are also mentioned (in paragraph 2), but only as activities affected by sleep deprivation. Dreaming (choice D) is mentioned only briefly at the end of the passage.

The second question can be answered on the basis of the fifth, sixth, and seventh sentences of the passage. Those sentences explain that psychotic-like symptoms did occur in some studies of sleep deprivation. However, they occurred mainly in people with "a history of mental illness." The correct answer—choice D—paraphrases this. Choices A and E are wrong because they imply that psychotic-like symptoms commonly arise in studies of sleep deprivation. That's false. Choice B sounds plausible, but the sentences that discuss psychotic-like symptoms don't mention the idea in choice B. Choice C twists what the passage says: people deprived of sleep for two hundred hours or longer functioned "almost normally" in the studies mentioned.

As you can see, detail questions test several skills: the ability to read and understand particular facts, the ability to understand what is being asked by a question, the ability to find a required fact quickly, and the ability to distinguish several slightly wrong answers from the one answer that states the required fact accurately.

8.4 Logic Questions

Like detail questions, logic questions focus on details in a passage. The difference is that logic questions ask about how the details are related to one another. Two particular details might be introduced to illustrate a *contrast*, or they might be two *examples* of the same idea, two *stages* in the same process, or two differing *interpretations* of the same fact. Whereas a detail question requires understanding of one particular detail, a logic question requires recognition of how two or more details fit into a pattern.

To answer a logic question, find the specific details being asked about. The answer is likely to be stated or strongly implied in the same paragraph—or even in the same sentence. Also look for words or phrases that describe the relationship between the details. Words and phrases like *however, nonetheless, despite, by contrast, on the other hand*, and *on the contrary* show that two details are being contrasted with one another. Words and phrases like *similarly, likewise, in the same way*, and *equally* show that two details are similar to one another. Words and phrases like *thus, hence, therefore, as a result, consequently*, and *so* express a cause-and-effect relationship between two details. Words like *before, after, prior, previous, later, then, next*, and *subsequently* indicate that two details are related chronologically. The answers to logic questions often turn on key words like these.

Here is a sample logic question based on the sample passage about sleep deprivation:

> Hand tremors, slurred speech, and sensory dullness are mentioned in the passage as
>
> (A) symptoms of a severe reaction to sleep deprivation
> (B) examples of the mild reactions that commonly follow a period of sleeplessness
> (C) results of momentary lapses into sleep by otherwise wakeful people
> (D) psychotic-like reactions that occasionally occur among the sleep-deprived
> (E) evidence for the belief that sleep plays an essential role in life

The question requires you to figure out how the details mentioned—hand tremors and so on—are related to the rest of the passage. First, locate the details. You'll find them in the second sentence of paragraph 2. Notice that the sentence begins with the phrase *for example.* This phrase indicates that the details are examples of what is discussed in the previous sentence—that is, the "mild reactions" that "usually do occur" after long sleeplessness. Choice B is the correct answer because it accurately summarizes that idea.

8.5 Inference Questions

Unlike the answer to a detail question, the answer to an inference question will not be found in any sentence in a reading passage. Instead, you must look for ideas that are implied—that is, stated indirectly—by the passage.

Inference questions generally contain either the word *implied* or the word *inferred.* "Which of the following is *implied* by the passage?" and "Which of the following can be *inferred* from the passage?" are two typical ways of asking the same question.

To find the answer to an inference question, you must decide what conclusion follows logically from the facts and ideas stated in a passage. Look for the underlying assumptions that haven't been put into words—that is, the ideas the author believes to be true but hasn't stated in so many words. Beware of answer choices that go beyond what you can logically infer from the passage. Wrong answers are often slightly too sweeping or overstated to be precisely correct.

Most reading passages will have one or two inference questions. Many students find them the hardest kind of reading comprehension question. Here are two examples based on the sample passage about sleep deprivation:

> It can be inferred from the passage that the adverse effects of prolonged sleep deprivation have been found to be
>
> (A) largely associated with the loss of stage-4 and REM sleep
> (B) confined mainly to those with a past history of mental disorders
> (C) so minor as to be negligible for nearly all practical purposes
> (D) very varied, even among psychologically healthy individuals
> (E) less serious than they were once thought to be
>
> Which of the following statements about microsleep can be inferred from the passage?
>
> (A) In a study of sleep deprivation, microsleep is generally prevented by the experimenter.
> (B) Microsleep occurs in all sleep-deprived persons.
> (C) The function of microsleep is to allow an individual to function adequately with little or no sleep.
> (D) Microsleep can be detected by an observer.
> (E) Microsleep has been shown to impair task performance by sleep-deprived individuals.

The correct answer to the first question is choice E. The passage doesn't make this statement in so many words. However, the first paragraph strongly implies that it is true. It states that some early studies of sleep deprivation suggested that psychotic-like symptoms were a common reaction, but later studies revealed only more minor and short-term effects. Thus, the effects of sleep deprivation are not as serious as was first thought. Choice A is a fabrication; nothing in the passage supports it. Choices B and C are overstated. Sleep deprivation adversely affects normal individuals as well as those who have been mentally ill, and although the adverse effects are not serious, they are not "negligible," either; task performance, for instance, is affected. Finally, choice D, though a bit tempting, is also wrong. Nowhere does the passage suggest that the adverse effects of sleep deprivation are "very varied." On the contrary, by mentioning only "common" reactions, it suggests just the opposite.

The second question focuses on an unstated assumption of the passage—something that must be true even though it is not mentioned in the passage. The correct answer is choice D. Microsleep must be detectable by an observer; otherwise no one would know that it was taking place. Remember, the passage states that microsleep is often not noticed by the person experiencing it. Therefore, it must be observable by others. The other answer choices can't be inferred from the passage. Choice A is wrong because if microsleep were prevented by experimenters, it wouldn't be used by them as an explanation for the effects of sleep deprivation. Choices B and C are not supported by anything in the passage. And choice E is wrong because microsleep has not been *shown* to be the cause of task performance errors; this is only one, unproven theory.

8.6 Tone Questions

The last two question types—tone questions and rhetoric questions—differ from the other four. First, they are less common. You will probably encounter only two or three questions from these categories on any given verbal section, as opposed to ten to thirteen of the other types. And they tend to appear in connection with passages on "softer" topics: fiction, the humanities, and sometimes the social sciences—topics in which the writer's feelings and opinions are usually more important than in natural science passages.

For this reason, the discussion of these last two question types will be based on a different reading passage—one that works well with tone and rhetoric questions.

King Alfred occupied and fortified London in 886. During the next few years, he began construction of his system of *burhs*, or fortresses, throughout Wessex. The surrounding villages and estates were responsible for providing men to defend the *burhs* in numbers determined by the amount of land their farmers cultivated. Though not completed until the reign of Alfred's son Edward, this system of fortresses did much to hamper the Danish invaders during the last great war of Alfred's reign.

This war began in 893, when Danish Vikings who had been repelled from Germany invaded England and joined forces with the by then well-established English Danes. For three years, Alfred and Ethelred of Mercia fought the Danes throughout southern England. On numerous occasions, Alfred's strategic skills turned away Danish advances, as when he marched on London unexpectedly during the harvest season of 894 to prevent the Danes from seizing the crops for use during the winter. Alfred then clinched the triumph with a fortress-and-dam blockade of the Thames. In 896, huge longboats of a new design devised by Alfred decimated and scattered a force of Danish raiding ships. By 897, the second invasion had been soundly defeated. This ended Alfred's military career, since the Danes did not renew their attempts to conquer Wessex until after Alfred died in 899.

Alfred's technique of combining imaginative innovations with highly practical administrative measures can also be seen in his nonmilitary career. His methodical nature is demonstrated by the organization of his court. Officeholders were divided into three groups who served rotating one-month shifts, thus freeing them to tend their farmlands two months out of every three. (Alfred had introduced a similar policy for his soldiers, largely eliminating the common problem of an army deserting at planting or harvest time.) Alfred's finances were also systematized. Taxes were divided into two shares for secular and religious purposes. Each share was in turn methodically subdivided into a number of preplanned spending categories.

Alfred won a name as a strict and fair overseer of the *ealdormen*, reeves, and other judges. His own reputation as a judge is suggested by a comment in a charter issued during his son's reign. In upholding one of Alfred's decisions, the anonymous author of the charter asked rhetorically, "When would any claim be decided if every judgment which Alfred made were in dispute?"

Alfred's major contribution to the legal system of his day was his systematization of the law code. Alfred's law book was compiled, significantly, from laws previously issued not only by one of his predecessors, King Ine of Wessex, but also by Offa of Mercia and Ethelbert of Kent. The use of all three sources reflects the increased unity among the English kingdoms forged by Alfred's unique prestige and power.

Tone questions focus on the attitudes or feelings expressed in a passage rather than on the facts it contains. The word *tone* refers to the feeling or mood of a piece of writing. Tone is almost always implied rather than explicitly stated in a passage. You must be on the lookout for loaded or emotional words that convey an author's opinion or feeling about a topic.

Typical tone questions on the SAT will take such forms as these:

The passage implies that the author's opinion of X is ...
The author's attitude toward X is mainly one of ...
The author's feelings concerning X could best be described as ...

Answer choices might include words such as *ironic*, *hostile*, *negative*, *positive*, *judgmental*, *adulatory*, *concerned*, *admonitory*, and *sarcastic*. Note that some of these are hard words in themselves. It's a good idea to learn them before the exam.

Watch out for answer choices that overstate or exaggerate the author's true attitude. A *slightly* negative opinion might be described in a wrong answer choice as "overwhelmingly disapproving" or "harshly condemnatory." In the same way, a *slightly* favorable opinion could be erroneously called "extremely positive."

Here are two typical tone questions based on the passage about King Alfred:

The passage implies that the author's attitude toward his subject could best be described as

(A) neutral and objective
(B) respectful and admiring
(C) both favorable and unfavorable
(D) scathingly critical
(E) lavishly adulatory

It can be inferred that the anonymous author of the charter quoted in the passage had adopted which of the following attitudes toward King Alfred?

(A) Concern over the excessive influence of his judicial methods
(B) Admiration for his methodical administrative style
(C) Respect for the wisdom of his legal decisions
(D) Deference toward his unique political and military power
(E) Despair at the prospect of overturning legal settlements he had made

The first question asks about the attitude of the author of the passage toward King Alfred. It should be fairly clear that the author admires King Alfred. He uses words such as *imaginative*, *methodical*, *practical*, and *fair* to describe Alfred, and he devotes the entire passage to a description of the king's various achievements and triumphs. Thus, the passage is not merely neutral or balanced, as choices A and C suggest, and it's certainly not "scathingly critical," as choice D states. On the other hand, the author is not "lavishly adulatory," either. Lavish adulation implies excessive praise, inspired by extreme, even blind, admiration. The author does admire Alfred, but he carefully gives specific factual reasons for his admiration; he doesn't simply heap up the compliments. So choice E is exaggerated. The best answer is choice B.

The second question focuses on the attitude expressed in the quotation near the end of the passage. The anonymous author of the charter is making the point that if one were to question King Alfred's decisions, no decisions would be safe. The implication is that Alfred's decisions carry a weight of authority matched by no others. Choice C summarizes this well. Choices A and E imply that the statement makes a negative comment about Alfred, which is false. And choices B and D focus on other qualities of King Alfred—his administrative style and his political and military power—rather than on his judicial reputation. So they are basically irrelevant.

Tone questions require you to notice the "sound" of a passage—that is, the feeling expressed by the author's "tone of voice." When reading a passage that expresses opinions or attitudes, as this passage does, listen for the sound of the author's voice. Listening for the sound of the author's voice will help you find the right answer for any tone question that may follow.

8.7 Rhetoric Questions

Rhetoric questions don't relate directly to the ideas or facts presented in a passage. Instead, they relate to the form and structure of a passage—that is, to the methods the author uses to put his or her point across. Typical rhetoric questions might begin as follows:

The author attempts to prove her point primarily by means of ...
Each of the following persuasive devices is used in the passage EXCEPT ...
The author mentions X primarily in order to ...

The answer choices are likely to include some of the terms you've read in Lesson 3 of this book, such as *comparison* and *example*, as well as terms for other common devices used in writing. These rhetorical devices include the following: (1) *argument by analogy*—suggesting a parallel between two similar situations; (2) *simile or metaphor*—using figurative language to suggest a comparison between unlike things; (3) *historical allusion*—referring to a well-known figure or event from history; (4) *appeal to authority*—bolstering an argument by quoting an expert; and (5) *illustrative anecdote*—telling a story to prove a point.

Most reading passages on the SAT will *not* be followed by a rhetoric question. However, you're likely to encounter one or two somewhere in your exam. Here is a sample rhetoric question based on the passage about King Alfred:

> The author suggests King Alfred's significance in English history by outlining
>
> (A) the gradual consolidation of English rule throughout the years of his reign
> (B) the ways in which Alfred improved upon the work of his immediate predecessors
> (C) his influence upon several later trends in the history of the nation
> (D) the contributions Alfred made in three different aspects of government
> (E) the differing views of Alfred espoused by various contemporary figures

To answer this question correctly, you must recognize the structure of the passage. That structure is one in which different aspects of the topic are discussed in separate paragraphs. The passage devotes its first two paragraphs to a discussion of Alfred's military career. Paragraph 3 discusses his administrative achievements. The last two paragraphs discuss his contributions to the legal system. These are the "three different aspects of government" referred to in choice D, which is the right answer. Choice A would be appropriate if the passage covered Alfred's career chronologically, but it doesn't. Choices B, C, and E sound plausible, but they don't accurately reflect the structure and content of the passage.

You've now learned about all six common types of reading comprehension questions. Look for them when you take the practice tests in this book. If you recognize the type of question you're facing, you'll know what kind of answer to choose.

Choosing an Answer

8.8 Types of Incorrect Answer Choices and How to Avoid Them

Earlier in this lesson you were introduced to some of the common types of incorrect answer choices for reading comprehension questions. In this section you'll review those types and learn how to avoid them.

1. *Answers drawn from the wrong part of the passage.* These answers are typical distractors in detail questions. They are true statements or facts that appear in the passage, but they do not answer the question. You may be tempted to choose one of these answers because it sounds familiar and because you can find it in the passage—"See, it says that right here." To avoid this temptation, find and review the sentence or sentences referred to in the question. Be sure you understand exactly which detail supplies the information demanded by the question.

2. *Distortions of the true answer.* These are answers that are almost correct but slightly twist the right idea. There are several ways to avoid choosing a wrong answer of this type. First, read the passage carefully to be sure you understand exactly what it says, not what you might assume it says. Second, read every answer choice. Several answers may be almost right, but only one will be completely correct. Third, read each answer carefully. Every word counts, and one or two words may turn a right answer into a wrong one. So don't rush through the answers. Read them quickly but deliberately.

3. *Overstatements and understatements.* Particular types of distortions include answers that overstate or understate the real answer. Again, careful reading is important. Watch out for words like *all, none, every, always, very, extremely, too,* and *entirely.* These words are not necessarily signs of wrong answers. However, they do change the meaning of the answer in which they appear. Make sure that extreme or all-inclusive words like these are used accurately before you choose an answer containing one of them.

4. *Answers that are too narrow or too broad.* These are especially common as wrong answers for main idea questions. Remember that the main idea of the passage should be stated or strongly implied in every paragraph of the passage. An answer that mentions a topic discussed in only one or two paragraphs is probably too narrow. On the other hand, a statement that is broad and vague isn't right, either. The answer to a main idea question should focus on the topic of the passage specifically. When you've selected an answer choice for a main idea question, ask yourself this: If I had read this statement before looking at the passage, would it lead me to expect the passage to contain the information it does?" If the answer is yes, you've chosen correctly.

5. *Answers that are true but irrelevant.* For each answer you choose, ask not only "Is it right?" but also "Does it answer the question?" Make sure that your answer fits logically with the question stem. If the stem is a fragment to be completed by the correct answer, read the stem and each answer choice together, as a complete sentence. This sentence should be logically coherent. The answer choice should complete the statement begun by the question stem. Some wrong answers are true statements in themselves but simply don't address the question asked. Watch out for these red herrings.

LESSON 9
Math Review: Arithmetic and Algebra

OBJECTIVES

- ☐ To review basic skills in arithmetic needed for success on the SAT
- ☐ To review concepts and operations of elementary algebra covered on the SAT
- ☐ To understand how skills in arithmetic and algebra are tested in math problems and quantitative comparisons on the SAT

9.1 Introduction

In this lesson and in Lesson 14, you'll review some of the math skills and concepts you learned during your elementary, junior high, and early high school years. Material beyond what is usually taught in tenth grade—that is, beyond elementary algebra and plane geometry—is not included because the SAT doesn't test any math knowledge past that point.

Each section in the two math review lessons covers one math topic. Within each section, you'll find a Math Capsule that briefly defines key terms and summarizes essential concepts, formulas, and operations. Study the concepts, formulas, and operations carefully, but don't bother memorizing the definitions. You need to know what a few of the terms mean for the SAT—terms like *integer, average, prime number*, and the like. But you won't be asked to define them, and you certainly shouldn't worry about them. The terms are included in the Math Capsules simply because you'll encounter them in the lessons, and you may want to refer to the definitions as you're reviewing.

Following each Math Capsule you'll find a discussion of how the information in the capsule is treated on the SAT, along with shortcuts and handy rules of thumb that you can try out when you take the practice tests in this book. In most sections, you'll also find a set of practice exercises that you can work if your skills need sharpening.

If you remember your math classes well, you may notice that some math topics are not covered in this review. That's because they're not tested on the SAT. You may also notice that some topics are presented in a different way than they were in your classes—with an emphasis on problem-solving skills rather than mathematical theory. That's because these lessons were designed with one practical purpose in mind: to prepare you for the mathematical sections of the SAT. To do well on those sections, you don't need a deep understanding of mathematical theory; you need to be able to solve problems quickly and accurately.

Remember, the SAT is a multiple-choice test. On a multiple-choice test, you're *given* the correct answer to every question, including math problems. In that sense, the SAT is different from most of the math tests you take in school. It doesn't ask you to find and write down the correct answer to each problem yourself. It doesn't ask you to demonstrate, step by step, that you know the "right" way to solve a problem. It doesn't even ask you to show your work. It just asks you to pick out the correct answer from four or five possible choices.

That doesn't mean, of course, that SAT math problems are easy. Some of them are; most of them aren't. It does mean that you have to approach the mathematical sections of the SAT in a different way than you would approach a regular classroom math test. Since your time is limited, you have to look for shortcuts—ways to simplify problems and identify correct answers quickly.

In fact, the most important thing to remember when you approach the mathematical sections of the SAT is this: *Keep it simple.* Most SAT math problems are set up to allow for a maximum of simplification. So if you ever find yourself embarking on a lengthy or complicated calculation, you should always stop and look at the problem again. You've probably missed a shortcut that the test makers deliberately built into the problem so that you could arrive at the correct answer more quickly than you could by going at it the "long" way—the way you've probably been taught is the "right" way. The "right" way is okay for your math classes, but it's not always the best way to approach the math questions on the SAT. That's why this review emphasizes practical problem-solving skills rather than mathematical theory. Sharpening those skills and learning how to "think SAT" should prepare you effectively for the exam.

Arithmetic

9.2 Basic Operations of Arithmetic

MATH CAPSULE

Operations and signs of arithmetic:

Addition: $a + b$
Subtraction: $a - b$
Multiplication: $a \times b$, $a \cdot b$, $a(b)$, or ab
Division: $a \div b$, $b\overline{)a}$, or a/b

Properties of multiplication and addition:

Associative:

$(a \times b) \times c = a \times (b \times c)$ $\quad$ $(a + b) + c = a + (b + c)$

Commutative:

$a \times b = b \times a$ $\qquad a + b = b + a$

Distributive:

$a(b + c) = ab + ac$

$(a - b)c = ac - bc$

Tests for divisibility:

A number is divisible by

2 if its last digit is even (0, 2, 4, 6, or 8)
3 if the sum of its digits is divisible by 3
4 if the number formed by its last two digits is divisible by 4
5 if its last digit is 0 or 5
6 if it is divisible both by 2 and by 3
9 if the sum of its digits is divisible by 9

By the time you take the SAT, you should be able to perform all four basic operations of arithmetic quickly and easily. Know your multiplication tables up to 12 × 12 backward and forward, and be able to add, subtract, multiply, and divide numbers of any length quickly and accurately. If you have trouble with any of these operations, don't miss an opportunity to practice them between now and the day of the exam.

Although few SAT math questions are designed to test these basic math skills exclusively, most problems require you to use them. If you can't do the arithmetic, you won't be able to solve the problems. Or you may take so long to solve them that you won't have time to complete the test section in the allotted time.

Here are some timesaving tips for use with the basic operations of arithmetic:

When adding a series of numbers, add the digits in pairs or groups. Look for pairs or groups of digits that add up to 10, as shown in the following example:

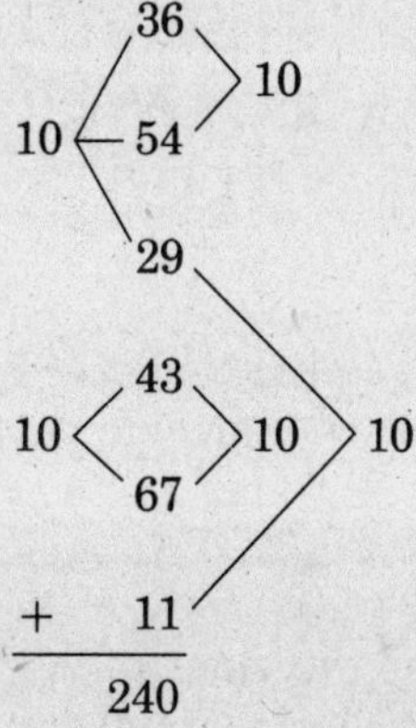

Add up all the 10s you can find; then add in any extra digits at the end. This is the fastest way to add up a large group of numbers.

You can usually multiply or divide numbers by 2 or by 3 in your head. Practice this skill between now and the day you take the SAT. Write down your results digit by digit as you determine them. When multiplying, work from the right-hand digit (the ones digit) toward the left. When dividing, work from left to right.

Multiplying or dividing by 10, 100, 1,000, or any other power of 10 is easy. Just move the decimal point one place to the right to increase the number by a power of 10 or one place to the left to decrease it by a power of 10. If no decimal point appears in the numbers, you can put one after the right-hand (ones) digit.

Example: To multiply 768 by 100, move the decimal point (which is after the 8) two places to the right: 76,800.

Example: To divide 768 by 10, move the decimal point one place to the left: 76.8.

MATH CAPSULE

Definitions:

A **positive number** is a number whose value is greater than 0.

A **negative number** is a number whose value is less than 0.

The **absolute value** of a number is its magnitude regardless of its sign: $|+6| = 6$; $|-6| = 6$.

Adding and subtracting signed numbers:

To add two numbers with the same sign, add their absolute values and prefix the sum with their common sign. For example: $(-3) + (-4) = -7$.

To add two numbers with different signs, subtract the smaller absolute value from the larger; then prefix the result with the sign of the number with the larger absolute value. For example: $(+3) + (-7) = -4$.

To subtract a negative number, add its opposite. For example: $(+7) - (-4) = (+7) + (+4) = +11$.

Multiplying signed numbers:

positive × positive = positive
negative × negative = positive
positive × negative = negative

Multiplying negative numbers:

An even number of negative factors yields a positive product. For example: $(-2)(-3) = +6$; $(-2)^2 = +4$.

An odd number of negative factors yields a negative product. For example: $(-2)(-3)(-4) = -24$; $(-2)^3 = -8$.

Dividing signed numbers:

positive ÷ positive = positive
negative ÷ negative = positive
positive ÷ negative = negative
negative ÷ positive = negative

Remember: In both division and multiplication, two numbers with the *same* sign yield a *positive* result; two numbers with *different* signs yield a *negative* result.

The image of numbers arranged on two sides of zero on a number line is a useful one for clarifying the nature of positive and negative numbers:

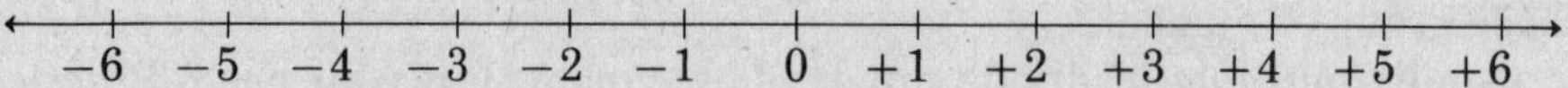

As you move to the right along the number line, the values become greater; as you move to the left, the values become smaller. Thus, for example, the value of -2 is greater than the value of -5.

Practice thinking of numbers in terms of the number line until you feel comfortable with it. You'll find that it will help you avoid some common errors. For example, when rushing through math questions on the SAT, you might easily look at two numbers such as -3 and -7 and say that, of the two, -7 is greater. Of course, that's wrong. To avoid such mistakes, picture the number line. Since -3 is closer to zero, and therefore farther to the right, -3 is greater than -7.

You may also find it useful to think of addition and subtraction as taking steps along the number line. Adding a positive number is like taking that many steps to the right along the line.

Adding a negative number is like taking that many steps to the left. For example, to add 6 and −10, you'd start at the point labeled 6 on the number line; then you'd take ten steps to the left and land on the point labeled −4, which is the correct answer.

Subtraction is just the opposite. Subtracting a positive number is like taking that many steps to the left along the number line. Subtracting a negative number is like taking that many steps to the right. For example, to subtract −8 from 2, you'd start at the point labeled 2 on the number line; then you'd take eight steps to the right and land on the point labeled 10. (Another good way to remember the "to subtract a negative number, add its opposite" rule is this: Minus a minus makes a plus—or, two negatives make a positive.)

If you find working with negative numbers confusing, try the number line approach a few times. After a while, the process will make more sense to you. (If you're still confused on exam day, just draw a number line in the margin of your test book. It's perfectly all right to do so.)

The number line won't help you with the multiplication and division of signed numbers, but the rules in the Math Capsule will, so study them carefully. They'll often allow you to short-cut problems on the SAT, especially in the quantitative comparison sections.

Example: Suppose you're asked to compare these two quantities:

Column A	Column B
$(11)(-3)(-9)(6)\left(-\frac{1}{2}\right)$	0

You don't need to multiply the numbers in Column A. Since the quantity in Column B is 0, all you have to do is determine whether the quantity in Column A is positive or negative. Notice that Column A includes two positive numbers and three negative numbers. Apply the rule: An odd number of negative factors yields a negative product. Therefore, the value of the quantity in Column A is negative, and the correct answer for the question is choice B.

PRACTICE EXERCISES

1. $(4) + (-7)$
2. $(11) + (-5)$
3. $(-4) + (-9)$
4. $(-5) + (-2)$
5. $(8) - (-4)$
6. $(19) - (-23)$
7. $(-9) - (-4)$
8. $(7) - (-8)$
9. $(-6) - (2)$
10. $(-10) + (13)$
11. $(5) \times (-8)$
12. $(-4) \times (11)$
13. $(12) \times (-\frac{1}{2})$
14. $(-3) \times (-9)$
15. $(\frac{1}{3}) \times (-21)$
16. $(28) \div (-4)$
17. $(-9) \div (3)$
18. $(-15) \div (-6)$
19. $(5) \div (-\frac{1}{4})$
20. $(-4) \div (-16)$

Answers

1. −3 2. 6 3. −13 4. −7 5. 12 6. 42 7. −5 8. 15 9. −8 10. 3 11. −40 12. −44 13. −6 14. 27 15. −7 16. −7 17. −3 18. $2\frac{1}{2}$ 19. −20 20. $\frac{1}{4}$

9.4 Fractions

MATH CAPSULE

Definitions:

A **fraction** is essentially a division problem expressed in the form a/b, which means "a divided by b."

A **numerator** is the top number in a fraction, such as a in a/b.

A **denominator** is the bottom number in a fraction, such as b in a/b.

A **proper fraction** is a fraction in which the numerator is less than the denominator, such as $\frac{1}{2}$. A proper fraction has a value less than 1.

An **improper fraction** is a fraction in which the numerator is greater than or equal to the denominator, such as $\frac{3}{2}$ or $\frac{2}{2}$. An improper fraction has a value greater than or equal to 1.

A **mixed fraction** is a numeral that consists of a whole number and a fraction, such as $1\frac{1}{2}$.

Equivalent fractions are fractions with the same value, such as $\frac{1}{2}$, $\frac{2}{4}$, $\frac{3}{6}$, and $\frac{4}{8}$. Two fractions are equivalent if their cross products are equal—that is, if the product of the numerator of the first and the denominator of the second is equal to the product of the denominator of the first and the numerator of the second. For example, $\frac{1}{2}$ is equivalent to $\frac{3}{6}$ because $1 \times 6 = 2 \times 3$.

The **lowest common denominator** of a group of fractions is the least common multiple of all the denominators—that is, the smallest number that all the denominators will divide evenly. For example, the lowest common denominator of $\frac{1}{2}$, $\frac{3}{4}$, $\frac{5}{9}$, and $\frac{7}{12}$ is 36 because 36 is the smallest multiple of 2, 4, 9, and 12.

Converting a mixed number to an improper fraction:

Before you perform any operations with a mixed number, first convert it to an improper fraction by following these three steps:

1. Multiply the whole number by the denominator of the fraction.
2. Add the product to the numerator.
3. Place the sum over the denominator.

Example: $2\frac{1}{3} = \frac{(2 \times 3) + 1}{3} = \frac{7}{3}$

Expressing a fraction in higher or lower terms:

To express a fraction in higher terms, multiply both the numerator and the denominator by the same number. The result is an equivalent fraction.

Example: $\frac{1 \times 3}{2 \times 3} = \frac{3}{6}$

To express a fraction in lower terms, divide both the numerator and the denominator by the same number. Again, the result is an equivalent fraction.

Example: $\frac{3 \div 3}{6 \div 3} = \frac{1}{2}$

Reducing a fraction to lowest terms:

To reduce a fraction to lowest terms, divide both the numerator and the denominator by the largest number that will divide both evenly.

Example: To reduce $\frac{6}{15}$ to lowest terms, divide both the numerator and the denominator by 3, the largest number that will divide 6 and 15 evenly:

$$\frac{6 \div 3}{15 \div 3} = \frac{2}{5}$$

Expressing a group of fractions in terms of their lowest common denominator:

To express a group of fractions in terms of their lowest common denominator, follow these three steps:

1. Find the least common multiple of all the denominators (the smallest number that all will divide evenly).
2. Multiply the denominator of each fraction by the number that will produce the least common multiple.
3. Multiply the numerator of each fraction by the same number as the denominator.

Example: The fractions $\frac{1}{2}$, $\frac{3}{4}$, $\frac{5}{9}$, and $\frac{7}{12}$ can all be expressed in terms of their lowest common denominator, 36:

$$\frac{1 \times 18}{2 \times 18} = \frac{18}{36} \qquad \frac{3 \times 9}{4 \times 9} = \frac{27}{36} \qquad \frac{5 \times 4}{9 \times 4} = \frac{20}{36} \qquad \frac{7 \times 3}{12 \times 3} = \frac{21}{36}$$

Adding and subtracting fractions:

To add or subtract fractions, follow these four steps:

1. Express all the fractions in terms of their lowest common denominator.
2. Add or subtract the numerators.
3. Place the result over the lowest common denominator.
4. Reduce the fraction to lowest terms.

Example: $\frac{1}{2}+\frac{3}{4}+\frac{5}{9}+\frac{7}{12}=\frac{18}{36}+\frac{27}{36}+\frac{20}{36}+\frac{21}{36}=\frac{86}{36}=\frac{43}{18}=2\frac{7}{18}$

Multiplying fractions:

To multiply fractions, follow these four steps:

1. Cancel wherever possible by dividing any numerator and any denominator by any number that will divide both evenly.
2. Multiply the numerators.
3. Multiply the denominators.
4. Place the product of the numerators over the product of the denominators.

Example: $\frac{\overset{2}{\cancel{6}}}{7}\times\frac{2}{\underset{1}{\cancel{3}}}=\frac{2\times 2}{7\times 1}=\frac{4}{7}$

Dividing fractions:

To divide by a fraction, invert the fraction you're dividing by; then multiply.

Example: $\frac{1}{3}\div\frac{3}{4}=\frac{1}{3}\times\frac{4}{3}=\frac{4}{9}$

Before you take the SAT, you should be as comfortable working with fractions as you are with whole numbers. In other words, you should be able to find the lowest common denominator for a group of fractions, you should be able to identify equivalent fractions, you should be able to convert mixed fractions to improper fractions (and vice versa), and you should be able to add, subtract, multiply, and divide fractions quickly and easily.

There are a few other things about fractions that you should know for the SAT, too. Here are some of them:

1. Since it's impossible to divide anything into zero parts, the denominator of a fraction can never equal 0.

2. A whole number can be expressed as a fraction simply by placing the whole number over a denominator of 1. For example:

$$120=\frac{120}{1}$$

3. Since fractions are essentially division problems, increasing the numerator of a fraction increases its value; increasing the denominator of a fraction decreases its value.

4. Proper fractions—fractions with a value less than 1—have peculiar properties. When you add two or more of them together, you end up with a larger fraction (as you would expect):

$$\frac{1}{2}+\frac{1}{4}=\frac{3}{4}$$

However, when you multiply two or more of them together, you end up with a smaller fraction:

$$\frac{1}{2}\times\frac{1}{4}=\frac{1}{8}$$

This means that the square of a proper fraction has a *smaller* value than the fraction itself:

$$\left(\frac{1}{2}\right)^2 = \frac{1}{4} < \frac{1}{2}$$

It also means that the square root of a proper fraction has a *greater* value than the fraction itself:

$$\sqrt{\frac{1}{4}} = \frac{1}{2} > \frac{1}{4}$$

You can answer some SAT math questions, particularly quantitative comparisons, very quickly if you remember this point. Here's an example:

Column A	**Column B**
The square of $\frac{9}{16}$	The square root of $\frac{9}{16}$

A question like this is intended to separate the sheep from the goats. The goats will either unthinkingly assume that the square of a number must be greater than its square root or waste time working the problem out. The sheep—like you—will remember that proper fractions behave differently than whole numbers:

$$\sqrt{4} < 4 < 4^2 \quad \textbf{BUT} \quad \sqrt{\frac{1}{4}} > \frac{1}{4} > \left(\frac{1}{4}\right)^2$$

5. The word *of*, when used with a fraction, usually calls for multiplication. For example,

$$\frac{1}{2} \text{ of } \frac{2}{3} \text{ of } \frac{4}{5} \text{ of } \frac{5}{6} \text{ of } 120$$

means

$$\frac{1}{2} \times \frac{2}{3} \times \frac{4}{5} \times \frac{5}{6} \times \frac{120}{1}$$

To solve a problem like this, set it up just as you see it here—that is, as a series of multiplications, with all whole numbers expressed as fractions. (Expressing whole numbers as fractions helps you remember that the whole numbers are numerators, not denominators.) Setting up the problem in this way enables you to cancel freely among the numerators and denominators and thus simplify the computation immensely:

$$\frac{1}{\cancel{2}_1} \times \frac{\cancel{2}^1}{3} \times \frac{4}{\cancel{5}_1} \times \frac{\cancel{5}^1}{\cancel{6}_1} \times \frac{\cancel{120}^{20}}{1} = \frac{80}{3}$$

Most SAT math questions of this sort are designed for maximum simplification.

6. A quick way to determine which of two fractions is greater is to compare their cross products—that is, to multiply the numerator of the first fraction by the denominator of the second and the numerator of the second fraction by the denominator of the first. The *numerator* that yields the greater product marks the larger fraction. For example, to determine whether $\frac{4}{7}$ is greater than $\frac{5}{9}$, first multiply 4 by 9 and get 36; then multiply 5 by 7 and get 35, as shown below:

$$\frac{4}{7} \times \frac{5}{9}$$

$$36 > 35$$

Since 36 is greater than 35, $\frac{4}{7}$ is greater than $\frac{5}{9}$.

This simple method of comparing fractions will come in handy on the SAT, especially with quantitative comparisons. So will an intuitive sense of the relative values of fractions. You have a feeling for the value of a common fraction like $\frac{1}{2}$, but you should also have a feeling for the value of less common fractions. Take, for example, the following group of fractions:

$$\frac{1}{3}, \frac{1}{4}, \frac{2}{5}, \frac{2}{7}, \frac{3}{8}$$

You should be able to tell quickly that $\frac{1}{4}$ is the smallest of these fractions and $\frac{2}{5}$ is the largest. If you get enough practice with fractions before you take the SAT, you'll develop this intuitive sense about their relative values.

Skill in working with fractions is crucial for success on the SAT. Not only is it necessary for many questions, but it's useful for others as well. As you'll discover, many SAT math questions are set up in such a way that they can be worked out with fractions, decimals, or percentages. In most cases, working with fractions is faster and easier than working with decimals and percentages. In the next section of this lesson you'll learn about translating decimals and percentages into fractions, and vice versa.

PRACTICE EXERCISES

Reduce the following fractions to lowest terms.

1. $\frac{3}{15}$	3. $\frac{30}{75}$	5. $\frac{12}{90}$
2. $\frac{24}{36}$	4. $\frac{6}{42}$	6. $\frac{21}{63}$

Rewrite the following sets of fractions in terms of their lowest common denominator.

7. $\frac{3}{4}, \frac{2}{3}$	9. $\frac{2}{5}, \frac{7}{15}, \frac{4}{9}$	11. $\frac{5}{12}, \frac{7}{16}$
8. $\frac{1}{6}, \frac{3}{8}$	10. $\frac{1}{2}, \frac{1}{4}, \frac{1}{6}, \frac{1}{8}$	12. $\frac{1}{3}, \frac{5}{6}, \frac{3}{7}, \frac{5}{14}$

Add or subtract the following fractions; reduce your answers to lowest terms.

13. $\frac{2}{3} + \frac{4}{3}$	15. $\frac{2}{5} + \frac{1}{3}$	17. $\frac{3}{4} + \frac{5}{6}$
14. $\frac{7}{8} - \frac{3}{8}$	16. $\frac{6}{7} - \frac{2}{5}$	18. $\frac{7}{9} - \frac{12}{27}$

Multiply or divide the following fractions; reduce your answers to lowest terms.

19. $\frac{2}{3} \times \frac{3}{4}$	21. $\frac{1}{2} \times \frac{1}{9}$	23. $3 \div \frac{6}{7}$
20. $\frac{3}{7} \times \frac{14}{15}$	22. $\frac{3}{14} \div \frac{6}{49}$	24. $\frac{3}{5} \div \frac{9}{10}$

Answers

1. $\frac{1}{5}$ 2. $\frac{2}{3}$ 3. $\frac{2}{5}$ 4. $\frac{1}{7}$ 5. $\frac{2}{15}$ 6. $\frac{1}{3}$ 7. $\frac{9}{12}, \frac{8}{12}$ 8. $\frac{4}{24}, \frac{9}{24}$ 9. $\frac{18}{45}, \frac{21}{45}, \frac{20}{45}$ 10. $\frac{12}{24}, \frac{6}{24}, \frac{4}{24}, \frac{3}{24}$ 11. $\frac{20}{48}, \frac{21}{48}$ 12. $\frac{14}{42}, \frac{35}{42}, \frac{18}{42}, \frac{15}{42}$ 13. 2 14. $\frac{1}{2}$ 15. $\frac{11}{15}$ 16. $\frac{16}{35}$ 17. $\frac{19}{12}$, or $1\frac{7}{12}$ 18. $\frac{1}{3}$ 19. $\frac{1}{2}$ 20. $\frac{2}{5}$ 21. $\frac{1}{18}$ 22. $\frac{7}{4}$, or $1\frac{3}{4}$ 23. $\frac{7}{2}$, or $3\frac{1}{2}$ 24. $\frac{2}{3}$

9.5 Decimals and Percentages

MATH CAPSULE

Definitions:

A **decimal fraction** is equivalent to a proper fraction whose denominator is a power of 10. A decimal fraction is written in the form 0.1, which means $\frac{1}{10}$. In a decimal fraction, the number to the right of the decimal point represents the numerator of the fraction, and the number of places to the right of the decimal point represents the power of 10 in the denominator. One place represents 10^1, or 10; two places represent 10^2, or 100; and so on. Thus, $0.42 = \frac{42}{100}$ and $0.607 = \frac{607}{1000}$.

A **mixed decimal** is equivalent to a mixed fraction; in other words, it is a numeral consisting of a whole number and a fraction whose denominator is a power of 10. A mixed decimal is written in the form 5.75, which means $5\frac{75}{100}$. In a mixed decimal, the number to the left of the decimal point represents the whole number, and the number to the right of the decimal point represents the decimal fraction.

A **percentage** is equivalent to a fraction whose denominator is 100. A percentage is written in the form 10%, which means $\frac{10}{100}$ (or, in decimal form, 0.10).

Converting a decimal into a fraction:

To convert a decimal into a fraction, follow these three steps:

1. Take the number to the right of the decimal point and make it the numerator of the fraction.
2. Count the number of places to the right of the decimal point, multiply 10 by itself that many times (raise 10 to that power), and write the result as the denominator of the fraction.
3. Reduce the fraction to lowest terms.

Example: $0.25 = \frac{25}{10^2} = \frac{25}{100} = \frac{1}{4}$

Converting a fraction into a decimal:

To convert a fraction into a decimal, just divide the numerator by the denominator.

Example: $\frac{4}{5} = 4 \div 5 = 0.8$

Converting a percentage into a fraction:

To convert a percentage into a fraction, follow these two steps:

1. Place the percentage over a denominator of 100.
2. Reduce the fraction to lowest terms.

Example: $75\% = \frac{75}{100} = \frac{3}{4}$

Converting a fraction into a percentage:

To convert a fraction into a percentage, use one of the following two-step methods:

Method 1

1. Multiply the fraction by 100.
2. Reduce the denominator to 1.

Example: $\frac{3}{4} \times \frac{100}{1} = \frac{300}{4} = \frac{75}{1} = 75\%$

Method 2

1. Divide the numerator by the denominator.
2. Move the decimal point in the result two places to the right.

Example: $\frac{2}{5} = 2 \div 5 = 0.40 = 40\%$

Converting a decimal into a percentage:

To convert a decimal into a percentage, just move the decimal point two places to the right.

Example: $0.01 = 1\%$; $0.10 = 10\%$; $1.00 = 100\%$

Converting a percentage into a decimal:

To convert a percentage into a decimal, just move the decimal point two places to the left.

Example: $1\% = 0.01$; $10\% = 0.10$ (or 0.1); $100\% = 1.00$ (or 1)

Adding and subtracting decimals:

To add or subtract decimals, follow these three steps:

1. Write the numbers vertically, making sure that the decimal points are lined up directly under one another.
2. Add or subtract as with whole numbers.
3. Place a decimal point in your answer directly below the decimal points in the numbers you're adding or subtracting.

Example:

$$\begin{array}{r} 0.347 \\ -\ 0.216 \\ \hline 0.131 \end{array}$$

Multiplying decimals:

To multiply decimals, follow these two steps:

1. Multiply as with whole numbers.
2. Count the total number of decimal places in the numbers you're multiplying, and put a decimal point that many places to the left in your product.

Example:

```
   4.426   (3 decimal places)
 × 0.34    (2 decimal places)
 -------
  17704
 1 3278
 -------
 1.50484   (5 decimal places)
```

Dividing decimals:

To divide decimals, follow these four steps:

1. Move the decimal point in the number you're dividing *by* enough places to the right to make it a whole number.
2. Move the decimal point in the number you're dividing the same number of places to the right.
3. Divide as with whole numbers.
4. Place a decimal point in your answer directly above the decimal point in the number you're dividing.

Example: $.15_{\wedge}\overline{).37_{\wedge}5} = 15\overline{)37.5}$ (quotient: 2.5)

Solving percentage problems:

To solve percentage problems, follow these four steps:

1. Express the problem in the general form "*a* is what percent of *b*." In this expression,

   is means "equals" (=)
   what percent means "$x/100$"
   of means "times" (×)

2. Translate the expression into an equation:

   $$a = \frac{x}{100} \times b$$

3. Substitute numerical values for two of the three unknowns (whichever ones you're given in the problem).
4. Solve for the remaining unknown.

Example: Maria runs three times a week: 12 miles on Monday, 21 miles on Wednesday, and 9 miles on Friday. What percent of her weekly mileage does she run on Wednesday?

Solution: Maria's weekly mileage is 12 + 21 + 9 = 42, so the problem can be restated as follows: 21 is what percent of 42? Thus:

$$21 = \frac{x}{100} \times 42$$

$$21 = \frac{42x}{100}$$

$$42x = 2100$$

$$x = 50\%$$

As the Math Capsule suggests, decimals and percentages are just different "names" for fractions. All three represent parts of a whole. In the case of percentages, the whole is always divided into 100 equal parts. In the case of decimals, the whole is always divided into a power of 10 equal parts. In the case of fractions, the whole may be divided into any number of equal parts.

Thinking of fractions, decimals, and percentages as different names for the same thing will help you in two specific ways on the SAT. First, it will allow you to work out fraction/decimal/percentage problems in the "language" that is easiest for you. (Fractions are generally easier to work with than decimals and percentages, but you should use whatever form you're most comfortable with.) Second, it will make it easier for you to recognize the correct answer to a question when it's written in a form other than the one in which you've expressed your own answer. (The makers of the SAT are fond of expressing answer choices in various forms.)

Of course, just thinking of fractions, decimals, and percentages as different names for the same thing won't be of much value on the SAT unless you can also "translate" easily from one "language" into the other. If you have trouble doing so, practice the conversion methods outlined in the Math Capsule until you've mastered them. And before you take the test, by all means learn the most common equivalencies among fractions, decimals, and percentages. Knowing these equivalencies will save you the time and trouble of calculating when you need or want to convert an expression from one form into another for an SAT math problem. Here are some of the common equivalencies you should know:

Fraction	Decimal	Percentage
$\frac{1}{2}$	.5	50%
$\frac{1}{3}$	.333...	$33\frac{1}{3}\%$
$\frac{2}{3}$	.666...	$66\frac{2}{3}\%$
$\frac{1}{4}$	.25	25%
$\frac{3}{4}$	.75	75%
$\frac{1}{5}$	.20	20%
$\frac{1}{6}$	.1666...	$16\frac{2}{3}\%$
$\frac{1}{7}$	.143...	$14\frac{2}{7}\%$
$\frac{1}{8}$	.125	$12\frac{1}{2}\%$
$\frac{1}{10}$	.1	10%

As the ellipses suggest, the decimal values for $\frac{1}{3}$, $\frac{2}{3}$, $\frac{1}{6}$, and $\frac{1}{7}$ in this list are not exact, but they're close enough for any problems you're likely to encounter on the SAT.

The great danger in working with decimals is the accidental loss or addition of decimal places. To avoid careless errors of this sort when you take the SAT, follow these guidelines:

1. Whenever you're working with decimals, be neat—don't be sloppy—and make a conscious effort to keep track of your decimal places. When you're adding or subtracting, for example, make sure that your columns are straight and that your decimal points are carefully aligned. Otherwise, you're apt to come up with a sum that's off by a power of 10. You might also find it helpful to "flesh out" some decimals so that all of them have the same number of digits to the right of the decimal point. For example, .7 + .062 + .12 is the same as

$$\begin{array}{r} .700 \\ .062 \\ +\ .120 \\ \hline .882 \end{array}$$

Using zeros as placeholders can help you avoid careless errors.

2. Remember that there's a decimal point after the last (or ones) digit of every whole number, even if it's not expressed. The number 365, for example, is exactly equivalent to 365.00 (just as the number .365 is exactly equivalent to 0.365).

3. If a problem involves numbers with three or more digits, guesstimate the answer *before* you work it out exactly. To guesstimate, round the numbers off, perform rough calculations in your head, and come up with a ballpark figure. Then, after you've worked out the exact answer, you can use your guesstimate as a check to make sure that you haven't added or lost a decimal place.

> **Example:** Suppose a problem requires you to multiply 97.8 by 3.18. Round off the two numbers to 100 and 3. You can easily multiply these in your head and get

300. Use this round number to check the result of your full-length calculation. If you arrive at an answer like 31.1004, you'll know that you've accidentally lost a decimal place. If you arrive at an answer like 3,110.04, you'll know that you've accidentally gained one.

You don't have to be quite as neat when you're solving percentage problems as you are when you're solving decimal problems, but you do have to be careful—and you do have to think. Most SAT percentage problems aren't presented in a straightforward manner: "What percent of a is b?" Instead, they're written in such a way that one or more of the unknowns—the a, the b, or the percent—are given only indirectly, and you have to figure out what they are before you can work the problem out.

Here are a couple of examples, one fairly easy, the second a little more difficult:

In its first year of business, a small bookstore took in $20,000 in sales. In its second year, it took in $50,000. By what percent did its sales increase the second year?

(A) 40% (B) $66\frac{2}{3}\%$ (C) $133\frac{1}{3}\%$

(D) 150% (E) 250%

The key word in this question is *increase*. A percentage problem that includes the word *increase*, *decrease*, or *change* is asking you first to find the *difference* between two quantities and then to find what percent the difference is of the *original* quantity. In this case, the difference is $30,000, so you can express the problem as follows: $30,000 is what percent of $20,000? The rest is simple. Just translate the problem into an equation, as explained in the Math Capsule, and solve for x:

$$30{,}000 = \frac{x}{100} \times 20{,}000$$

$$30{,}000 = 200x$$

$$150\% = x$$

During its annual white sale, a department store reduced the price of its finest bath towels 20 percent. If the sale price of one towel was D dollars, what was the original price of the towel?

(A) $\$0.80D$ (B) $\$1.20D$ (C) $\$1.25D$

(D) $\$1.75D$ (E) $\$1.80D$

This problem's difficult for several reasons, but mainly because it's abstract. Basically, what it's asking you is this: What do you have to multiply the sale price by in order to get the original price? In other words, what percent of the sale price is the original price?

If you have trouble working with abstractions (as most people do), the best way to approach a problem like this is to make it concrete. For simplicity's sake, say that the original price of the towel was $10. Then the sale price was 20 percent less, or $8: $10 - \frac{20}{100}(10) = 10 - 2 = 8$. Now, just rephrase the question ($10 is what percent of $8), translate it into an equation, and solve for x:

$$10 = \frac{x}{100} \times 8$$

$$10 = \frac{8x}{100}$$

$$8x = 1000$$

$$x = 125\%$$

If the original price was 125 percent of the sale price, then you have to multiply the sale price by $\frac{125}{100}$, or 1.25, in order to get the original price. Thus, the correct answer is choice C, $\$1.25D$.

PRACTICE EXERCISES

Solve each of the following decimal problems.

1. $3.27 + .06 + 12.99$
2. $.0045 + 19 + 2.2$
3. $24.1 + 3.006 + 2$
4. $12.056 - 3.023$
5. $10 - .054$
6. $.42 \times 10$
7. 7.95×1000
8. $.0435 \times 100$
9. $.27 \div 10$
10. $457 \div 100$
11. $.391 \div 2.3$
12. $10.01 \div 7.7$
13. $42 \div 2.1$
14. $.002 \div .05$
15. $.05 \div .002$

Solve each of the following percentage problems.

16. What percent of 24 is 16?
17. What percent of 17 is 51?
18. What percent of 48 is 12?
19. What percent of 18 is 3?
20. What percent of 16 is 20?
21. What is 24% of 50?
22. What is 75% of 300?
23. What is 50% of 50?
24. What is 23% of 150?
25. What is 120% of 45?
26. 52 is 50% of what number?
27. 17 is 25% of what number?
28. 400 is $12\frac{1}{2}$% of what number?
29. 6 is 200% of what number?
30. 56 is $33\frac{1}{3}$% of what number?

Convert each of the following into an equivalent fraction reduced to lowest terms.

31. .75
32. .125
33. .02
34. 3.4
35. .60
36. 2.5
37. $37\frac{1}{2}$%
38. $42\frac{6}{7}$%
39. 10%
40. 150%
41. 80%
42. $83\frac{1}{3}$%

Convert each of the following into an equivalent decimal.

43. $\frac{1}{4}$
44. $\frac{1}{2}$
45. $\frac{4}{5}$
46. $\frac{7}{10}$
47. $5\frac{3}{8}$
48. $\frac{3}{1000}$
49. $27\frac{1}{2}$%
50. 430%
51. 1%
52. $6\frac{1}{2}$%
53. $11\frac{3}{4}$%
54. $66\frac{2}{3}$%

Convert each of the following into an equivalent percentage.

55. $\frac{1}{3}$
56. $\frac{6}{5}$
57. $\frac{1}{6}$
58. $\frac{2}{7}$
59. $\frac{9}{100}$
60. $\frac{1}{1000}$
61. .003
62. .03
63. .3
64. 3.0
65. .625
66. .48

Answers

1. 16.32 2. 21.2045 3. 29.106 4. 9.033 5. 9.946 6. 4.2 7. 7950 8. 4.35 9. .027 10. 4.57 11. .17 12. 1.3 13. 20 14. .04 15. 25 16. $66\frac{2}{3}$% 17. 300% 18. 25% 19. $16\frac{2}{3}$% 20. 125% 21. 12 22. 225 23. 25 24. 34.5 25. 54 26. 104 27. 68 28. 3200 29. 3 30. 168 31. $\frac{3}{4}$ 32. $\frac{1}{8}$ 33. $\frac{1}{50}$ 34. $3\frac{2}{5}$, or $\frac{17}{5}$ 35. $\frac{3}{5}$ 36. $2\frac{1}{2}$, or $\frac{5}{2}$ 37. $\frac{3}{8}$ 38. $\frac{3}{7}$ 39. $\frac{1}{10}$ 40. $\frac{3}{2}$, or $1\frac{1}{2}$ 41. $\frac{4}{5}$ 42. $\frac{5}{6}$ 43. .25 44. .50 45. .8 46. .7 47. 5.375 48. .003 49. .275 50. 4.3 51. .01 52. .065 53. .1175 54. .666 . . . 55. $33\frac{1}{3}$% 56. 120% 57. $16\frac{2}{3}$% 58. $28\frac{4}{7}$% 59. 9% 60. .1% 61. .3% 62. 3% 63. 30% 64. 300% 65. $62\frac{1}{2}$% 66. 48%

9.6 Averages

MATH CAPSULE

An **average** is the sum of a group of values divided by the number of values in the group. For example, the sum of 29, 11, 18, 46, 3, 104, and 41 is 252; therefore the average of these seven numbers is $252 \div 7 = 36$.

Another name for the average of a group of values is the *mean*, or *arithmetic mean*. Don't confuse the average or mean of a group of values with the median or the mode. The *median* is the middle value—that is, the value above and below which there are an equal number of values. The *mode* is the most common value—that is, the value that occurs most frequently.

The mean, the median, and the mode of a set of numbers may be the same, or they may be quite different. Be sure to distinguish them. Look, for example, at the following set of numbers:

10, 5, 9, 10, 3, 2, 10

For this set of numbers, the average (or mean), the median, and the mode are all different. The average is 7, since the sum of the seven numbers is 49 and $49 \div 7 = 7$. The median is 9, since there are three numbers greater than 9 in the set and three numbers smaller than 9. The mode is 10, since 10 is the most common value in the set.

On the SAT, you're more likely to be asked about averages (or means) than you are about medians and modes. Since they're multiple-choice, many SAT average problems, you'll find, don't require exact calculations; they just require good approximations. To answer these questions—and to check your work on other average problems—follow these two guidelines for guesstimating averages:

First, the average of a set of values will always fall somewhere between the two extreme values—that is, it will always be greater than the lowest value and smaller than the highest value. So if any answer choices for an SAT average problem fall outside this range, eliminate them immediately.

Second, when a particular value appears twice as often in a set of values as some other value, the more common value will have twice as great an effect on the average as the less common value. In other words, the more common value will "pull" the average in its own direction. For example, look at this set of values:

11, 20, 2, 2, 12, 19, 2, 2

If you rewrite the values in order, you'll be able to see the relationships among them more clearly:

2, 2, 2, 2, 11, 12, 19, 20

Notice that the set includes four "small" values (the four 2s), two "big" values (the 19 and the 20), and two "in-between" values (the 11 and the 12). Since there are twice as many small values as there are big values, you know that the average will be pulled closer to the small values. A good guess, then, would be that the average is about 8 or 9. This turns out to be correct. The actual average is 8.75. As you can see, a careful inspection of a set of values can often enable you to make a very accurate estimate of the average value without doing any actual figuring.

Remember that the formula for computing an average works both ways. If you are given the average of a set of values together with some of the values, you can often figure out the missing value or values. Use the following formula:

$$\text{Sum of all values} = \text{Average value} \times \text{Number of values}$$

For example, if you know that the average weight of three students is 152 pounds and that one student weighs 131 pounds while another weighs 165 pounds, you can easily find the weight of the third. Just multiply the average weight times 3 to find the total weight of the three students: $152 \times 3 = 456$. Then subtract the combined weight of the first two students from the total weight: $456 - (131 + 165) = 456 - 296 = 160$. The third student must weigh 160 pounds.

PRACTICE EXERCISES

1. Mary's average on two tests is 65. What score must she obtain on a third test to raise her average to 70?
2. If each of four numbers is doubled, by how much is their average multiplied?
3. The average of four numbers is 28. If three of the numbers are 18, 28, and 36, what is the fourth number?
4. The average of four consecutive integers is 31.5. What is the largest integer?
5. If the average of four numbers is 6 and the average of six other numbers is 4, what is the average of all ten numbers?

Answers

1. To earn an average of 70 on three tests, Mary needs a total of $3 \times 70 = 210$ points. So far she has earned $2 \times 65 = 130$ points. So she needs to earn $210 - 130 = 80$ points on her third test.
2. Let x be the sum of the four numbers. Then their average is $x/4$. If each of the four numbers is doubled, then their sum will also be doubled and their average will be $2x/4$, or $x/2$, which is 2 times $x/4$.
3. If the average of the four numbers is 28, the sum of the four numbers must be $4 \times 28 = 112$. Therefore, the fourth number must be $112 - (18 + 28 + 36) = 112 - 82 = 30$.
4. Since the four integers are consecutive, you can represent them as x, $x + 1$, $x + 2$, and $x + 3$. You know that their sum $(4x + 6)$ divided by 4 equals 31.5, so set up the equation and solve for x:

$$\frac{4x + 6}{4} = 31.5$$
$$4x + 6 = 126$$
$$4x = 120$$
$$x = 30$$

   The largest integer is therefore $x + 3 = 33$.
5. Find the sum of all ten numbers: $4 \times 6 = 24$; $6 \times 4 = 24$; $24 + 24 = 48$. Then divide by 10: $48 \div 10 = 4.8$.

9.7 Ratios and Proportions

MATH CAPSULE

Definitions:

A **ratio** is a relationship between two quantities. The relationship can be expressed in three forms: $a \div b$, a/b, or $a:b$.

A **proportion** is a statement that two ratios are equal. It can be expressed in three forms: $a/b = c/d$, $a:b = c:d$, or $a:b::c:d$ (the form in which analogies in the verbal sections of the SAT are written).

The four elements in a proportion are called the **terms** of the proportion. In the proportion $a:b = c:d$, the middle terms (b and c) are known as the **means**; the outer terms (a and d) are known as the **extremes**.

Solving a proportion:

In any proportion, the product of the means is equal to the product of the extremes. Thus, if $a:b::c:d$, then $bc = ad$. This equality makes it possible to find the fourth term of any proportion if the other three terms are known.

If you're like most students, you'll find ratios easiest to work with if you set them up in fractional form. Then you can treat them just as you would any other fraction. You can raise them to higher terms by multiplying both the numerator and the denominator by the same number; you can reduce them to lower terms by dividing both the numerator and the denominator by the same number. Thus, the ratio 6:12 ($\frac{6}{12}$) is equivalent to the ratio 1:2 ($\frac{1}{2}$).

When you encounter a ratio problem on the SAT, read the question carefully. Be sure that you understand which quantities are related to one another. If you're not careful, you can easily confuse a part-to-part relationship with a part-to-whole relationship. For example, suppose you encounter the following question: If an auto dealer has four compact cars and five full-size cars on a lot, what is the ratio of compact cars to all cars on the lot? If you don't read the question carefully, you can easily make the mistake of selecting 4:5 as your answer instead of 4:9. Watch out for careless errors of this sort.

Setting up a proportion is often the best way to solve a word problem. Proportions are useful for any problem in which two quantities vary or change in relationship to one another. Situations of this sort come up continually, both on the SAT and in real life. The greater the number of hours you work, the larger your paycheck will be at the end of the week. The greater the number of workers sharing a job, the fewer hours the job will take to complete. The longer you study for the SAT, the higher your scores will be. Each of these situations can be represented mathematically by a proportion.

The first and most crucial step in working with a proportion is setting it up correctly. There are two types of proportion: direct proportion and inverse proportion. In a *direct proportion*, quantities vary in the same direction—that is, they increase or decrease together. The distance you travel, for example, will increase as the number of hours you travel increases (unless, of course, you're riding the subway in New York City). So time spent traveling and distance traveled are directly proportional. When you're working with a direct proportion, set up your equation so that the corresponding quantities are *directly* across from one another on either side of the equal sign:

$$\frac{\text{Fewer hours}}{\text{More hours}} \begin{matrix}\longleftrightarrow \\ = \\ \longleftrightarrow\end{matrix} \frac{\text{Shorter distance}}{\text{Longer distance}}$$

In an *inverse proportion*, quantities vary in opposite directions—that is, as one increases, the other decreases. For example, the number of hours it will take you to get somewhere will increase as the speed at which you travel decreases. So time spent traveling and speed of travel are inversely proportional. When you're working with an inverse proportion, you must *invert* one of the ratios—that is, you must set up your equation so that the corresponding quantities are *diagonally* across from one another on either side of the equal sign:

$$\frac{\text{Fewer hours}}{\text{More hours}} \begin{matrix}\nwarrow\ \nearrow \\ = \\ \swarrow\ \searrow\end{matrix} \frac{\text{Slower speed}}{\text{Faster speed}}$$

Once you have correctly set up a proportion in fractional form, you can solve it easily. Just cross multiply, set the two resulting products equal to one another, and solve for whatever is unknown (x).

Check your answer by using common sense. If you come up with an answer that seems to say that *more* workers will take *longer* to complete a job, then you know that you set up your proportion incorrectly. Look at the problem again and take another crack at it.

PRACTICE EXERCISES

1. In a small school, 25 students take science and 32 take math. If 18 students take both science and math, what is the ratio of students taking math only to students taking science only?
2. An inheritance is to be shared by two brothers in a 3 to 5 ratio. What part of the inheritance is the smaller share?
3. Two out of every 5 players on a baseball team are rookies. If the team has 15 players who are *not* rookies, what is the total number of players on the team?
4. In 6 hours, a painter can paint 21 wicker chairs. At the same rate, how many chairs can she paint in 15 hours?
5. Four workers can complete a certain task in 9 hours. At the same rate, how many hours will it take six workers to complete the task?

Answers

1. If 18 of the 25 science students also take math, only 7 take science alone. Similarly, if 18 of the 32 math students also take science, only 14 take math alone. The ratio of students taking math only to those taking science only is thus 14 : 7, or 2 : 1.
2. If one brother gets three parts of the inheritance and the other brother gets five, the estate must be divided into eight equal parts. The smaller share, therefore, is $\frac{3}{8}$.
3. From the one ratio you're given, you can derive two other ratios. If the ratio of rookies to all team members is 2 : 5, then the ratio of rookies to nonrookies is 2 : 3 and the ratio of

nonrookies to all team members is 3:5. Since you're given the number of nonrookies and you're asked to find the total number of players on the team, use the third ratio:

$$\frac{3}{5} = \frac{15}{x}$$
$$3x = 75$$
$$x = 25$$

4. The number of chairs painted is directly proportional to the number of hours worked. Therefore:

$$\frac{6}{15} = \frac{21}{x}$$
$$6x = 315$$
$$x = 52\frac{1}{2}$$

5. The number of workers is inversely proportional to the time it takes to complete a task. Therefore:

$$\frac{4}{6} = \frac{x}{9}$$
$$6x = 36$$
$$x = 6$$

9.8 Radicals and Exponents

MATH CAPSULE

Definitions:

In the expression a^b, which is read "a to the b power," a is called the **base** and b is called the **exponent**. The expression a^b means "multiply a times itself b times."

The **square root** of a number a, indicated by the form $\sqrt{a}$, is the number that when multiplied by itself equals a. For example, $\sqrt{16} = 4$, since $4 \times 4 = 16$. A square root is always expressed as a positive number. For example, $\sqrt{16} = +4$, even though -4×-4 also equals 16. (The negative square root of a number is designated by a negative sign: $-\sqrt{16} = -4$.)

The **cube root** of a number a, indicated by the form $\sqrt[3]{a}$, is the number that when multiplied by itself three times equals a. For example, $\sqrt[3]{27} = 3$, since $3 \times 3 \times 3 = 27$.

A **radical** is any expression that contains a square root, cube root, or any other root. For example, $\sqrt{a}$, $\sqrt[3]{a}$, and $1/\sqrt{a}$ are all radicals.

Laws of exponents:

$a^0 = 1$ (for all $a \neq 0$)

$a^1 = a$

$a^2 = a \times a$

$a^3 = a \times a \times a$

$a^2 \times a^3 = a^{(2+3)} = a^5$

$\frac{a^4}{a^2} = a^{(4-2)} = a^2$

$(a^4)^2 = a^{(4 \times 2)} = a^8$

Laws of radicals:

$\sqrt{a} \times \sqrt{a} = a$

$\sqrt{ab} = \sqrt{a} \times \sqrt{b}$

$\sqrt{\frac{a}{b}} = \frac{\sqrt{a}}{\sqrt{b}}$

$$\sqrt{a} + \sqrt{a} = 2\sqrt{a}$$

$$\frac{a}{\sqrt{b}} = \frac{a}{\sqrt{b}} \times \frac{\sqrt{b}}{\sqrt{b}} = \frac{a\sqrt{b}}{b}$$

Before you take the SAT, be sure you know the rules of exponents and radicals outlined in the Math Capsule. In other words, be sure you know how to multiply and divide numbers with exponents, how to simplify radicals, and so on. The SAT you take will almost certainly include several questions that test your knowledge of these operations.

You should also know how different types of numbers respond to these operations. For example, you probably realize that a number like 3 or 4 increases rapidly each time it is raised to a higher power: $3^2 = 9, 3^3 = 27, 3^4 = 81$, and so on. However, not all numbers respond in the same way. Neither 0 nor 1 changes at all no matter how large an exponent is tacked onto it. Fractions smaller than 1 *decrease* when raised to a power. For example, $(\frac{1}{2})^2 = \frac{1}{2} \times \frac{1}{2} = \frac{1}{4}$. And negative numbers follow an interesting pattern. A negative number squared yields a positive result: $(-2)^2 = +4$, for example. But the same negative number cubed yields a negative result: $(-2)^3 = -8$. The rule is this: When a negative number is raised to an *even* power, the result is *positive*. When a negative number is raised to an *odd* power, the result is negative. Remembering this will save you a good deal of time on certain test questions, especially on quantitative comparisons.

As the Math Capsule states, the square root of a number is always considered to be positive. (This is a mathematical convention.) Square roots are considered positive even though negative roots "work" just as well; for example, $(-2)^2 = 4$ just as surely as $(+2)^2 = 4$. Nonetheless, $\sqrt{4} = +2$ only.

You should know certain simple squares, cubes, and square roots by heart. You should know the squares of all the numbers from 2 through 10, and you should know them "backward" as well; for example, you should immediately recognize that $6^2 = 36$ and that $\sqrt{36} = 6$. You should also know the cubes and the approximate square roots of 2 and 3 by heart: $2^3 = 8$ and $3^3 = 27$; $\sqrt{2} \approx 1.414$ and $\sqrt{3} \approx 1.732$. As you'll see in Lesson 14, the approximate square roots of 2 and 3 figure in many SAT geometry problems.

PRACTICE EXERCISES

Give the value of the following expressions.

1. 3^3
2. 6^2
3. 4^3
4. 7^0
5. 5^1
6. $(\frac{2}{5})^2$
7. $\sqrt{25}$
8. $\sqrt{64}$
9. $\sqrt[3]{125}$
10. $\sqrt[3]{27}$
11. $\sqrt{81}$
12. $\sqrt{\frac{9}{16}}$

Simplify the following.

13. $a^2 \times a^5$
14. $a^3 \times a^6$
15. $a^7 \div a^4$
16. $a^6 \div a^2$
17. $(a^2)^5$
18. $(a^3)^4$
19. $\sqrt{a} + \sqrt{a} + \sqrt{a}$
20. $\sqrt[3]{8a}$
21. $\sqrt{3} \times \sqrt{3}$
22. $\sqrt{32}$
23. $\sqrt{54}$
24. $\sqrt{75}$

Answers

1. 27 2. 36 3. 64 4. 1 5. 5 6. $\frac{4}{25}$ 7. 5 8. 8 9. 5 10. 3 11. 9 12. $\frac{3}{4}$ 13. a^7 14. a^9 15. a^3 16. a^4 17. a^{10} 18. a^{12} 19. $3\sqrt{a}$ 20. $2\sqrt[3]{a}$ 21. 3 22. $4\sqrt{2}$ 23. $3\sqrt{6}$ 24. $5\sqrt{3}$

9.9 Number Properties

MATH CAPSULE

Types of numbers:

The set of **whole numbers** includes all the positive counting numbers and 0: $\{0, 1, 2, 3, 4, 5, \cdots\}$.

The set of **integers** includes all the whole numbers and their negatives: $\{\cdots -3, -2, -1, 0, 1, 2, 3, \cdots\}$.

The set of **even integers** includes all integers that are evenly divisible by 2: $\{\cdots -2, 0, 2, 4, 6, 8, \cdots\}$. (Notice that 0 is considered an even integer.)

The set of **odd integers** includes all integers that are not evenly divisible by 2: $\{\cdots -3, -1, 1, 3, 5, 7, 9, \cdots\}$.

The set of **prime numbers** includes all whole numbers that are evenly divisible by no other whole numbers except themselves and 1: $\{2, 3, 5, 7, 9, 11, 13, 17, 19, \cdots\}$. (Notice that 1 is not considered a prime number.)

Properties of odd and even numbers:

even × even = even	even + even = even
odd × odd = odd	odd + odd = even
even × odd = even	even + odd = odd

Properties of 0:

$a + 0 = a$

$a - 0 = a$

$a \times 0 = 0$

$a \div 0$ is undefined (can't be done)

$0^a = 0$

$\sqrt[a]{0} = 0$

Properties of 1:

$a \times 1 = a$

$a \div 1 = a$

$1^a = 1$

$\sqrt[a]{1} = 1$

Factoring:

Any number that is not prime can be represented as the product of two or more prime factors. For example, 4 can be represented as the product of 2×2; 18 can be represented as the product of $2 \times 3 \times 3$; 420 can be represented as the product of $2 \times 2 \times 3 \times 5 \times 7$. Finding the set of factors that can be multiplied together to yield a certain number is known as **factoring**.

Every SAT exam includes several questions on number properties. These questions test your understanding of the basic properties of odd and even numbers, prime numbers, and special numbers like 0 and 1. Here's an example:

> If x is even and y is odd, then which of the following must be even?
>
> (A) $xy + 1$ (B) $\frac{xy}{2}$ (C) $4xy + 2$ (D) $x^2 - 3$
>
> (E) $2(y^3) - 1$

To answer this question, you have to know the rules that govern both the multiplication and the addition of odd and even numbers. The correct answer is choice C. If x is even and y is odd, then xy must be even, since even × odd = even. If xy is even, then $4(xy)$ must be even, since even × even = even. Finally, if $4xy$ is even, $4xy + 2$ must be even, since even + even =

even. (If you selected choice B, remember that even ÷ even = even *or* odd, since both even × even = even and even × odd = even.)

Here's an example of how a question involving number properties can be adapted to the quantitative comparison format:

Column A	**Column B**
n is an odd whole number.	
Remainder when $3n$ is divided by 2	0

This is another question concerning the properties of odd and even numbers. If n is odd, then $3n$ must also be odd, since odd × odd = odd. If $3n$ is odd, then $3n$ divided by 2 will have a remainder of 1—any odd number will. Therefore, the correct answer for this question is A.

The Math Capsule includes some information about factoring a number. Factoring is essential for some SAT math problems. For others, it's the quickest and easiest way to find a solution. For example, suppose you're asked to add three fractions, one with a denominator of 28, one with a denominator of 42, and one with a denominator of 96. The easiest way to find the lowest common denominator for the three fractions is by factoring. First, find the prime factors of the three denominators by dividing each one by the prime numbers, beginning with 2:

```
2)28     2)42     2)96
2)14     3)21     2)48
   7        7     2)24
                  2)12
                  2) 6
                     3
```

Second, list the *different* prime factors of the three denominators. Include each prime factor the *greatest* number of times that it occurs in any *one* of the denominators: 2, 2, 2, 2, 2, 3, 7. Third, multiply the factors in the list to find the lowest common denominator: $2 \times 2 \times 2 \times 2 \times 2 \times 3 \times 7 = 672$.

PRACTICE EXERCISES

1. If x is an odd integer, which of the following must be an even integer?
   I. $\frac{x}{2}$
   II. $4x$
   III. $3x - 3$
2. If n is an integer, which of the following must be odd?
   I. $n + 1$
   II. $2n + 1$
   III. $3n + 1$
3. Which of the following must be true of the product of three consecutive integers?
   I. It is a multiple of 3.
   II. It is even.
   III. It is a multiple of 6.
4. All of the following are prime numbers EXCEPT
   (A) 13 (B) 23 (C) 37 (D) 39 (E) 47

List the prime factors of the following numbers.

5. 128
6. 140
7. 162
8. 212
9. 380
10. 1200

Answers

1. II and III 2. II only 3. I, II, and III 4. D (39) 5. 2, 2, 2, 2, 2, 2, 2 6. 2, 2, 5, 7
7. 2, 3, 3, 3, 3 8. 2, 2, 53 9. 2, 2, 5, 19 10. 2, 2, 2, 2, 3, 5, 5

Algebra

9.10 Algebraic Expressions

MATH CAPSULE

Definitions:

A **variable** is a letter that represents a number.

An **algebraic expression** is any variable, any number, or any combination of variables and numbers formed by the four basic operations of arithmetic: addition, subtraction, multiplication, and division. For example, a, $a + 1$, $2ab - 4a$, and a/b are all algebraic expressions.

A **term** is one of the quantities connected by a plus or minus sign in an algebraic expression. For example, the expression $2ab - 4a + 3$ consists of three terms: $2ab$, $4a$, and 3.

A **coefficient** (or **numerical coefficient**) is the numerical factor in an algebraic term. For example, in the term $-2a$, -2 is the coefficient; in the term $a/2$, which is equivalent to $\frac{1}{2}a$, $\frac{1}{2}$ is the coefficient. Every algebraic term has a coefficient, whether the coefficient is expressed or not. For example, in the term a, 1 is the coefficient; in the term $-a$, -1 is the coefficient.

Like terms are terms that contain exactly the same variable(s) raised to exactly the same power(s). For example, a and $2a$ are like terms; so are ab^2 and $4ab^2$. Like terms can be combined.

Unlike terms are terms that do not contain exactly the same variable(s) raised to exactly the same power(s). For example, $2a$ and $2ab$ are unlike terms; so are a and a^2, a^2b and ab^2. Unlike terms cannot be combined.

Combining like terms:

To combine like terms, follow these two steps:

1. Add or subtract their coefficients, as indicated.
2. Affix the result to the common variables.

Example: $ab + 2ab = 3ab$; $9a^2 - 8a^2 = a^2$

Simplifying an algebraic expression:

To simplify an algebraic expression, combine like terms.

Example: You can simplify the expression $4x + 3y + 2x$ by combining the two like terms, $4x$ and $2x$. The result is $6x + 3y$.

Evaluating an algebraic expression:

To evaluate (or find the value of) an algebraic expression, follow these two steps:

1. Substitute the numeric values given for the variables.
2. Perform the arithmetic operations indicated.

Example: To evaluate the expression $6x + 3y$, where $x = 2$ and $y = 3$, first substitute 2 for x and 3 for y. Then multiply and add as indicated: $6(2) + 3(3) = 12 + 9 = 21$.

Order of operations:

Arithmetic operations must be performed in the following order:

1. Perform any operations within *parentheses*.
2. Raise any numbers with exponents to the *powers* indicated.
3. Perform *multiplications* in order from left to right.
4. Perform *divisions* in order from left to right.

5. Perform *additions* in order from left to right.
6. Perform *subtractions* in order from left to right.

As a general rule, whenever you encounter an algebraic expression on the SAT, your first impulse should be to simplify it by combining like terms. As the Math Capsule explains, *like terms* are terms that contain the same variable(s) raised to the same power(s). For example, $3n$, $-2n$, and n are like terms because they all contain the variable n raised to the first power. Similarly, mn^2 and $4mn^2$ are like terms because they both contain the variable m raised to the first power and the variable n raised to the second power. When like terms appear together in the same algebraic expression, they can be combined. For example, $mn^2 + 4mn^2 = 5mn^2$.

By contrast, n and n^2 are unlike terms because one contains the variable n raised to the first power and the other contains the variable n raised to the second power. Similarly, n and mn are unlike terms because although they both contain the variable n raised to the first power, one contains the variable m and the other doesn't. Unlike terms cannot be combined.

When you're combining like terms or evaluating (finding the value of) an algebraic expression, be sure that you perform arithmetic operations in the correct order. You can remember the proper sequence by using this memory aid: *Pretty Please My Dear Aunt Sally*. The initial letters of this phrase—*PPMDAS*—will remind you of the proper sequence of operations: *Parentheses, Powers, Multiplication, Division, Addition,* and *Subtraction*. (The phrase is silly, but its silliness makes it harder to forget.)

The rule about the sequence of operations is important because the order in which you perform arithmetic operations often determines the final result that you get. Consider this simple example: $7 \times (2 + 3)$. If you follow the rule, you'll perform the operation in parentheses first: $2 + 3 = 5$. Then you'll multiply the result by 7 and get 35. If you don't follow the rule and instead perform the operations in the order in which you find them, you'll multiply 7×2, add 3 to the product, and get 17. Chances are your SAT will include some questions whose answers turn on the proper application of the "pretty please" rule.

PRACTICE EXERCISES

Find the value of each of the following expressions. (Be sure to perform the operations in the correct sequence.)

1. $2 + 3 \times 5 + 1$
2. $13 - 5 \times 2$
3. $2 \times 7 - 3 \times 4$
4. $10 + 8 \div 2 + 6$
5. $3 + (2 + 5^2) \div 3$
6. $(3 + 3)^2 \div 2 \times 9$

Simplify each of the following algebraic expressions.

7. $2x + 10y + 3x - 6y$
8. $-3x + x^2 + x + 2x^2$
9. $\frac{1}{2}x^2 + 4\frac{1}{2}x^2 - 1$
10. $9 - 1.6x^3 - 1.4x^3 - x^2 - 16$
11. $2x^2 - 6x + 7 - x^2 - x$
12. $7x + 3x^2 + x - 5 - x^2$

Given $a = 2$, $b = 3$, $d = 4$, and $e = 5$, evaluate each of the following expressions.

13. $ab + d$
14. d^2/a^3
15. $3e - 2ab$
16. $\sqrt{a^2e - d}$
17. $2a - 3b + e$
18. $a^2 - (e - ab)^2$

Answers

1. 18 2. 3 3. 2 4. 20 5. 12 6. 2 7. $5x + 4y$ 8. $3x^2 - 2x$ 9. $5x^2 - 1$
10. $-3x^3 - x^2 - 7$ 11. $x^2 - 7x + 7$ 12. $2x^2 + 8x - 5$ 13. 10 14. 2 15. 3 16. 4
17. 0 18. 3

9.11 Basic Algebraic Operations

MATH CAPSULE

Definitions:

A **monomial** is an algebraic expression that consists of only one term. For example, a, $7a^2$, $7a^3b$, 7, and $7a/b$ are all monomials.

A **polynomial** is the sum or difference of two or more monomials. For example, $a - 7$ and $a^2 + 2ab + bc^2$ are both polynomials.

A **binomial** is a polynomial that consists of exactly two terms. For example, $a + b$ is a binomial.

A **trinomial** is a polynomial that consists of exactly three terms. For example, $4a^2 + 12a + 9$ is a trinomial.

Adding polynomials:

To add two or more polynomials, simply combine like terms.

Example: $(3a + b + 7c) + (3b - 2c - a) = (3a - a) + (b + 3b) + (7c - 2c) = 2a + 4b + 5c$

Subtracting one polynomial from another:

To subtract one polynomial from another, follow these two steps:

1. Change the sign of each term in the polynomial being subtracted.
2. Combine like terms.

Example: $(6x + 3y + 8) - (2x - y + 4) = (6x + 3y + 8) - 2x + y - 4 = 4x + 4y + 4$

Multiplying a polynomial by a monomial:

To multiply a polynomial by a monomial, follow these two steps:

1. Multiply each term of the polynomial by the monomial.
2. Combine like terms.

Example: $3m(2n + 4n - 2) = 3m(2n) + 3m(4n) - 3m(2) = 6mn + 12mn - 6m = 18mn - 6m$

Dividing a polynomial by a monomial:

To divide a polynomial by a monomial, follow these two steps:

1. Divide each term of the polynomial by the monomial.
2. Combine like terms.

Example: $(3x - 2xy + x) \div x = (3x \div x) - (2xy \div x) + (x \div x) = 3 - 2y + 1 = -2y + 4$

Multiplying two binomials:

To multiply one binomial by another, follow these two steps:

1. Multiply each term of the first binomial by each term of the second binomial.
2. Combine like terms.

Example: $(3x + 2y)(x - y) = 3x(x) - 3x(y) + 2y(x) - 2y(y) = 3x^2 - 3xy + 2xy - 2y^2 = 3x^2 - xy - 2y^2$

This section of Lesson 9 concerns the application of the four fundamental operations of arithmetic—addition, subtraction, multiplication, and division—to algebraic expressions. Actually, the rules for performing these operations are the same in algebra as they are in arithmetic. However, since you've probably had less practice working with variables than you have with numbers, you may want to review the procedures outlined in the Math Capsule and brush up on your algebraic arithmetic before you take the SAT.

If you can recognize like terms when you see them, you should have little or no trouble adding polynomials, no matter how many terms they contain. Nor should you have any trouble subtracting them—providing, of course, that you remember to change the sign of each term in the polynomial you're subtracting. Otherwise, subtraction is just like addition—all you have to do is combine like terms. (The principle is this: To subtract a term, just add its opposite.)

> **Example:** To subtract $(-2x^2 + 5x - 3)$ from $(5x^2 - 2x + 7)$, first change the sign of $-2x^2$ to $+2x^2$, the sign of $+5x$ to $-5x$, and the sign of -3 to $+3$. Then

add like terms:

$$\begin{array}{rrrr} & +5x^2 & -2x & +7 \\ + & +2x^2 & -5x & +3 \\ \hline & +7x^2 & -7x & +10 \end{array}$$

The answer is $7x^2 - 7x + 10$.

The multiplication and division of polynomials require a little more care than addition and subtraction. The operations aren't particularly difficult, but if you don't approach them methodically, you can easily make careless mistakes. To multiply or divide a polynomial by a monomial, take up each term of the polynomial one at a time and multiply or divide it by the monomial. Write down each result as you determine it. Then combine the results to get your final answer. Proceeding in this step-by-step fashion will help you avoid confusion.

The same principle of working methodically applies to multiplying two binomials. First, multiply the *first* terms in each binomial:

$$(a + 1)(a + 1)$$

$$a \times a = a^2$$

Second, multiply the *outer* terms in each binomial:

$$(a + 1)(a + 1)$$

$$a \times 1 = a$$

Third, multiply the *inner* terms in each binomial:

$$(a + 1)(a + 1)$$

$$1 \times a = a$$

Fourth, multiply the *last* terms in each binomial:

$$(a + 1)(a + 1)$$

$$1 \times 1 = 1$$

Finally, combine the results of the four steps:

$$a^2 + a + a + 1 = a^2 + 2a + 1$$

The word *FOIL*—which stands for *First, Outer, Inner, Last*—may help you remember this step-by-step method of multiplying two binomials.

When you're multiplying binomials and other polynomials that contain the same variable, you'll usually end up with variables raised to the second power or higher. It's both conventional and convenient to arrange the resulting expression in order of decreasing powers—that is, to put all cubes (if any) first, then all squares, and then all terms raised to the first power (those with no exponents showing). Thus, you'd rearrange the expression $2a + a^3 + a^2$ to read $a^3 + a^2 + 2a$.

PRACTICE EXERCISES

1. $(2x^2 - 7y) + (3x + 5y)$
2. $(3a + 2b - 5c) + (b - a)$
3. $(15x^2y + 5) + (12y^2x - 5)$
4. $(2a^2b + ab - 5) + (3a^2b - 2ab + 7)$
5. $(-x^2 - 2x + 2) + (4x^2 + x - 9)$
6. $(6a - 3a^2 + a^3) + (2a^2 - 5 - 3a)$
7. $(5x - 7y) - (3z - 10y)$
8. $13x - (-24y + 7x)$
9. $(2a^2 + 2a - 5) - (a^2 + a - 3)$
10. $(6n^2 + 10n - 3) - (-2n^2 - 5)$
11. $(12 + 3a^2 - a^3) - (-2a - a^2 + 15)$
12. $(3n^3 - 5n^2 + 4) - (n^3 - 4n^2 - 3)$
13. $2x(x - 1)$
14. $-3(a^2 + 2ab + b^2)$
15. $x(-4x^2 - x - 5)$
16. $n^2(7n^2 - 9n - 16)$
17. $2ab(1 - a - b)$
18. $-\frac{1}{2}(2x^3 - 4x^2 - \frac{1}{2}x + 8)$
19. $(8x^2 + 10x) \div 2x$
20. $(0.8a^2 + 4.8a) \div 0.4a$

21. $(12n^3 - 6n^2 + 9n) \div -3n$
22. $(x^4 + x^2) \div x$
23. $(12a^3b + 18a^2c - 6ad) \div 6a$
24. $(-3m^4 - 21m^3 - 15m^2) \div -3m^2$
25. $(3x - 2)(x - 7)$
26. $(5 - 3a)(5 + 2a)$
27. $(3x - 4y)(4x - 3y)$
28. $(x + 2y)(x + 2y)$
29. $(5x + 7)(5x - 7)$
30. $(4x + 3)(2x - 1)$

Answers

1. $2x^2 + 3x - 2y$ 2. $2a + 3b - 5c$ 3. $15x^2y + 12y^2x$ 4. $5a^2b - ab + 2$ 5. $3x^2 - x - 7$ 6. $a^3 - a^2 + 3a - 5$ 7. $5x + 3y - 3z$ 8. $6x + 24y$ 9. $a^2 + a - 2$ 10. $8n^2 + 10n + 2$ 11. $-a^3 + 4a^2 + 2a - 3$ 12. $2n^3 - n^2 + 7$ 13. $2x^2 - 2x$ 14. $-3a^2 - 6ab - 3b^2$ 15. $-4x^3 - x^2 - 5x$ 16. $7n^4 - 9n^3 - 16n^2$ 17. $-2a^2b + 2ab - 2ab^2$ 18. $-x^3 + 2x^2 + \frac{1}{4}x - 4$ 19. $4x + 5$ 20. $2a + 12$ 21. $-4n^2 + 2n - 3$ 22. $x^3 + x$ 23. $2a^2b + 3ac - d$ 24. $m^2 + 7m + 5$ 25. $3x^2 - 23x + 14$ 26. $-6a^2 - 5a + 25$ 27. $12x^2 - 25xy + 12y^2$ 28. $x^2 + 4xy + 4y^2$ 29. $25x^2 - 49$ 30. $8x^2 + 2x - 3$

9.12 Factoring Algebraic Expressions

MATH CAPSULE

Factoring a polynomial:

To express a polynomial as the product of a monomial factor and another factor, follow these three steps:

1. Find a monomial factor that is common to all the terms of the polynomial. The common monomial factor may be a number, a variable, or a product of the two.
2. To find the second factor, divide each term of the polynomial by the common monomial factor.
3. Rewrite the polynomial as the product of the common monomial factor and the second factor.

Example: In the polynomial $3x^2 + 6xy + 12x$, the number 3 and the variable x are both common factors of $3x^2$, $6xy$, and $12x$. Therefore the polynomial can be rewritten as the product of $3x$ and another factor. To find the other factor, divide each term of the polynomial by $3x$: $3x^2 \div 3x = x$; $6xy \div 3x = 2y$; $12x \div 3x = 4$. The result is $x + 2y + 4$. Since the polynomial $3x^2 + 6xy + 12x$ is the product of $3x$ and $x + 2y + 4$, it can be rewritten as $3x(x + 2y + 4)$.

Factoring a trinomial of the form $x^2 + ax + b$:

To factor a trinomial of the form $x^2 + ax + b$, where x is a variable and a and b are any numbers, follow these three steps:

1. Set up two binomials with x as the first term in each: $(x + \quad)(x + \quad)$.
2. Through trial and error, find two numbers whose sum is a and whose product is b.
3. Make one of the numbers the second term of the first binomial; make the other number the second term of the second binomial.

Example: To factor $x^2 + 7x + 12$, start by setting up two binomials whose first terms are x: $(x + \quad)(x + \quad)$. Then, find two numbers whose sum is 7 and whose product is 12. Those numbers are 3 and 4. Make 3 the second term of one binomial (it doesn't matter which) and 4 the second term of the other: $(x + 3)(x + 4)$. To check your results, multiply the two binomials: $(x + 3)(x + 4) = x^2 + 4x + 3x + 12 = x^2 + 7x + 12$.

Factoring a binomial of the form $a^2 - b^2$:

A binomial that is the difference between two squares is the product of the sum and the difference of the two terms being squared. In other words, $a^2 - b^2 = (a + b)(a - b)$.

If you've forgotten how to factor algebraic expressions or if your factoring skills are a bit rusty, study the Math Capsule in this section of Lesson 9 and practice breaking down polynomials into their simpler component parts. Your study and practice will pay off when you take the SAT because factoring is often the fastest—and sometimes the only—way to solve some of the algebra problems that you're likely to encounter on the exam.

Here are some examples of the ways in which your factoring skills might be tested on the SAT:

Column A		**Column B**
	$6x + 36 = 20$	
$3x + 18$		10

You can work out a problem like this the long way and come up with the correct answer—choice C (the quantities in the two columns are equal). But to do so, you first have to solve $6x + 36 = 20$ for x; then you have to plug the numerical value of x into $3x + 18$ to determine the value of the quantity in Column A. Factoring is simpler and faster. (Remember, the SAT is a timed test, so taking shortcuts is smart strategy.) If you just step back and take a look at $6x + 36$ and $3x + 18$, you should be able to see that $3x + 18$ is a factor of $6x + 36$. The other factor is 2. That means that $3x + 18$ is half of 20, or 10.

If $a + b = x$, $a - b = \frac{1}{x}$, and $x \neq 0$, then $a^2 - b^2 =$

(A) 1 (B) 2 (C) x^2 (D) x (E) $\frac{1}{x}$

The key to this question is included in the Math Capsule for this section: A binomial of the form $a^2 - b^2$ has two factors, $a + b$ and $a - b$. (Remember this for the SAT.) Since the question tells you that $a + b = x$ and $a - b = 1/x$, all you have to do to find the value of $a^2 - b^2$ is multiply x times $1/x$. The answer is 1 (choice A).

If $a^2 - b^2 = 64$, then $2(a + b)(a - b) =$

(A) 16 (B) 32 (C) 64 (D) 68 (E) 128

This question is similar to the last one and can be solved just as quickly if you recognize $a + b$ and $a - b$ as the two binomial factors of $a^2 - b^2$: $2(a + b)(a - b) = 2(a^2 - b^2) = 2(64) = 128$. The correct answer is choice E.

A knowledge of factoring might even save you a little time on a question like this:

Column A	**Column B**
$\sqrt{n^4 + 6n^2 + 9}$	$n^2 + 3$

Notice that $n^4 + 6n^2 + 9$ is very similar to the trinomial of the general form $x^2 + ax + b$ cited in the Math Capsule (only the exponents are different). If you recall the three-step approach to factoring a trinomial of this form, you can answer this question without putting pencil to paper. Just ask yourself three questions: (1) Does $n^2 \times n^2 = n^4$? (2) Does $3 + 3 = 6$? (3) Does $3 \times 3 = 9$? If the answer to all three questions is yes (and it is), then $(n^2 + 3)(n^2 + 3)$ must equal $n^4 + 6n^2 + 9$, which means that $\sqrt{n^4 + 6n^2 + 9} = n^2 + 3$. Since the quantities in the two columns are equal, the correct answer is choice C.

As you can see, factoring can be very useful when you're tackling algebra problems on the SAT. And the best part is that you don't have to be particularly good at it—that is, you don't have to be able to factor especially complex or difficult expressions. The polynomials on the SAT tend to be of the "easily factorable" variety, so if you're just resourceful enough to think of factoring as the best way to solve or simplify a problem, you shouldn't have too much trouble finding your factors.

PRACTICE EXERCISES

Factor the following polynomials.

1. $2x + 4y$
2. $10x^2 + 15x$
3. $72a^2b^3 - 24ab^4 - 12ab$
4. $11ab - 22a$
5. $12x^2y - 16y^2 + 8y^3$
6. $-3n^4 - 9n^3 - 18n^2$
7. $x^2 + 3x + 2$
8. $x^2 + 23x + 22$
9. $y^2 - 13y + 42$
10. $a^2 + 3a - 18$
11. $n^2 - 11n - 26$
12. $x^2 - y^2$
13. $4a^2 - 9b^2$
14. $25x^6 - 16y^4$

Answers

1. $2(x + 2y)$ 2. $5x(2x + 3)$ 3. $12ab(6ab^2 - 2b^3 - 1)$ 4. $11a(b - 2)$ 5. $4y(3x^2 - 4y + 2y^2)$
6. $-3n^2(n^2 + 3n + 6)$ 7. $(x + 1)(x + 2)$ 8. $(x + 22)(x + 1)$ 9. $(y - 7)(y - 6)$
10. $(a + 6)(a - 3)$ 11. $(n - 13)(n + 2)$ 12. $(x + y)(x - y)$ 13. $(2a + 3b)(2a - 3b)$
14. $(5x^3 + 4y^2)(5x^3 - 4y^2)$

9.13 Solving Equations

MATH CAPSULE

Definitions:

An **equation** is a statement that two expressions are equal. Most equations include one or more variables, or unknowns.

To **solve an equation** is to find a numerical value for each variable that satisfies (or works out in) the equation. The basic principle for solving equations is this: You can always do the same thing to both sides of an equation without affecting its validity.

Techniques for solving equations:

1. *Isolating the variable on one side of the equal sign.* One of your first objectives in solving an equation is to isolate all the terms containing the variable (the unknown) on one side of the equal sign (usually the left) and all the numbers (the knowns) on the other side of the equal sign (usually the right). Ordinarily you can achieve this objective by adding the same quantity to both sides of the equation or by subtracting the same quantity from both sides of the equation.

   Example: To isolate the variable in the equation $4x = 15 - x$, add x to both sides:

   $$4x + x = 15 - x + x$$
   $$5x = 15$$

   To isolate the variable in the equation $3x = 2x + 5$, subtract $2x$ from both sides:

   $$3x - 2x = 2x + 5 - 2x$$
   $$x = 5$$

2. *Transposing a term from one side of an equation to the other.* Transposing is shorthand for adding and subtracting. To transpose a term from one side of an equation to the other, simply change its sign and move it to the other side.

   Example: To transpose -6 from the left to the right side of the equation $2x - 6 = 12 + x$, change its sign from -6 to $+6$ and move it:

   $$2x = 12 + x + 6$$
   $$2x = 18 + x$$

   (This operation is equivalent to adding 6 to both sides of the equation.) To transpose x from the right to the left side of the same equation, change its sign from $+x$ to $-x$ and move it:

$$2x - x = 18$$
$$x = 18$$

(This operation is equivalent to subtracting x from both sides of the equation.)

3. *Clearing an equation of fractions.* To clear an equation of fractions, multiply each term on both sides of the equation by the lowest common denominator of all the fractions.

   Example: The lowest common denominator of the fractions in the following equation is 15:

$$\frac{4x+1}{3} - \frac{2x+1}{5} = \frac{3}{5}$$

   To clear the equation of fractions, multiply each term on both sides by 15 (cancel before you multiply):

$$15\left(\frac{4x+1}{3}\right) - 15\left(\frac{2x+1}{5}\right) = 15\left(\frac{3}{5}\right)$$
$$5(4x+1) - 3(2x+1) = 3(3)$$
$$20x + 5 - 6x - 3 = 9$$

4. *Cross multiplying.* Cross multiplying is generally the simplest way of solving an equation that is set up in the form of a proportion. To cross multiply, multiply the numerator on each side of the equation by the denominator on the opposite side.

   Example: The following equation is set up in the form of a proportion:

$$\frac{x}{8} = \frac{11}{2}$$

   To solve it, multiply x by 2 and 8 by 11; then set the products equal and divide both sides of the equation by 2:

$$2x = 88$$
$$x = 44$$

5. *Multiplying an equation by* -1. Occasionally you will encounter (or end up with) an equation like the following: $-x = -7$. To find the value of $+x$ rather than $-x$, multiply both sides of the equation by -1. Multiplying an equation by -1 changes the sign of every term on both sides of the equation.

   Example: To find the value of x, given the equation $-x = -7$, multiply both sides of the equation by -1:

$$-1(-x) = -1(-7)$$
$$+x = +7$$

Your most common goal in algebra problems is solving equations—that is, finding numerical values for variables that will satisfy the equations. As you've probably discovered in your past study of algebra, the key to solving most equations is isolating the unknown term on one side of the equation. Doing this requires tinkering with the form of the equation until it begins "$x =$." However, you must tinker according to certain rules. Otherwise, you will destroy the validity of the equation. This section of Lesson 9 reviews those rules, which can be boiled down to a single principle: Whatever you do to one side of an equation you must do to the other side.

The basic procedure for solving an equation involves figuring out what you want to do to both sides of the equation in order to change the equation to the "$x =$ " form. You may need to add the same quantity to both sides of the equation or subtract the same quantity from both sides. You may have to multiply or divide each term on both sides of the equation by the same quantity. In some cases, you may find it useful to square both sides of the equation or take the square root of both sides of the equation. Any of these is a legitimate operation.

Transposing terms from one side of an equation to the other is one of the fastest ways of changing the form of the equation. The first step in solving many equations is simply to transpose all the unknowns to the left and all the known quantities to the right. Always be careful to change the sign of any terms you transpose. In essence, transposing is simply a faster way of adding or subtracting the same quantity on both sides of the equation. For example, if an equation reads $2x + 7 = 11 - x$, you'll want to transpose $+7$ to the right side of the equation (where it becomes -7) and $-x$ to the left side of the equation (where it becomes $+x$). This is exactly the same as subtracting 7 from both sides of the equation and adding x to both sides of the equation. Transposing is simply a mental shortcut—a faster and simpler way of thinking about the procedure.

One operation that's sometimes particularly helpful is multiplying both sides of an equation by -1. This has the effect of simply changing all the signs throughout the equation. It's a useful way of eliminating negative numbers and replacing them with positive ones, which are usually easier to work with. Don't forget that a term with no sign (including the first term in an expression) is positive, even though it doesn't have a plus sign in front of it. To transpose it or multiply it by -1, you have to change its sign from positive to negative.

Before attempting to solve an equation, you'll usually find it best to eliminate all fractions. As the Math Capsule explains, you can eliminate fractions from an equation by multiplying both sides by the lowest common denominator of all the fractions. (The technique for finding the lowest common denominator of a group of fractions is explained in Sections 9.4 and 9.9.) Doing so transforms all the fractions into whole numbers, which, like positive numbers, are much easier to work with.

PRACTICE EXERCISES

Solve each of the following equations for x.

1. $3x + 7 = 16$
2. $4 - 3x = 10$
3. $2x + 20 = 0$
4. $3x - 8 = 4$
5. $47 - 3x = -1$
6. $3x - 6 = 2 - x$
7. $x + 7 - 2x = 3$
8. $2 - x = 4 + x$
9. $5 + 3x + 1 = 5x + 2$
10. $2x - 5 - 8x = -x - 25$
11. $\frac{1}{2}x - \frac{1}{4} = \frac{3}{4}$
12. $x + 5 = \frac{3}{2}x$
13. $\frac{5}{7}x = 35$
14. $2x - \frac{7}{2} = \frac{3}{4}x + \frac{1}{4}$
15. $7 - 2x = \frac{1}{3}x$
16. $30 - \frac{2}{3}x = \frac{1}{6}x$

Answers

1. 3 2. −2 3. −10 4. 4 5. 16 6. 2 7. 4 8. −1 9. 2 10. 4 11. 2 12. 10
13. 49 14. 3 15. 3 16. 36

9.14 Solving Word Problems Algebraically

MATH CAPSULE

Two-step approach to solving word problems:

1. Translate the verbal statements in the problem into mathematical terms and set up an equation.
2. Solve the equation.

Hints for solving word problems:

1. Read the problem carefully, focusing on the words that actually pose the question. Make sure you understand exactly what you're being asked to find—whether it's Robert's age in 3 years, the area in square feet of Jane's room, or the number of pages that can be typed in 4 hours.
2. Use a "natural" letter to represent the unknown quantity you're looking for—a letter such as R for Robert's age, A for the area of Jane's room, P for the number of pages that can be typed in 4 hours.

3. If possible, represent other quantities that you're given in terms of the unknown you're looking for. For example, if you're asked to find R, Robert's age, and you're told that Teresa is twice as old as Robert, express Teresa's age as $2R$.
4. Convert all units that you're given (such as inches or feet) into the units in which you're asked to express your answer. For example, if you're given the number of pages that can be typed in 4 hours and you're asked to find the number of minutes that it will take to type three pages, first convert 4 hours to minutes and then do your figuring.

Translating words into mathematical expressions:

Certain words used in word problems are associated with mathematical operations. These words are clues to how you should set up and solve your equation. Here are some of them:

Addition: and, with, added to, in addition to, sum, together with, along with, plus, increased by, more than, greater than, exceeds

Subtraction: less than, fewer than, smaller than, without, take away, minus, difference, decreased by, diminished by, reduced by

Multiplication: times, each, multiplied by, product, of, twice, double, triple

Division: per, divided by, quotient, part of, fraction, ratio

Equality: is, equals, is the same as

As the Math Capsule points out, there are two basic steps to solving any word problem: (1) setting up an equation that expresses the relationships described in the problem and (2) solving the equation. Of the two steps, the harder is the first. Once you've translated the verbal statements into an equation, solving the equation is simply a matter of applying your algebraic skills. (That's why for some SAT word problems, you don't even have to solve the equation. You just have to set it up.)

The basic procedure for translating verbal statements into an equation is this: First, determine what you're being asked. Read through the entire problem and find the words that actually pose the question. (Underlining them may help to fix them in your mind.) After you figure out exactly what unknown quantity you're looking for, assign it a letter. (As the Math Capsule suggests, a "natural" letter, such as R for Robert's age, can help you keep things straight when you're translating complex word problems into mathematical terms. But x or n or a works just as well for simpler problems.) Then set up one or more equations that reflect the information you're given about the unknown in the rest of the problem.

When you're setting up the equation(s), look for the verbal clues listed in the Math Capsule—the words associated with particular mathematical operations. For instance, the term *greater than* generally calls for addition. So when you read "the average annual rainfall in Beaver Falls is 4 inches greater than the average annual rainfall in Hooterville," you should write "$B = H + 4$." Similarly, the word *each* usually implies multiplication. So when you read "each of the forty-two students in Professor Jones's class has completed three experiments this term," you should write, "$E = 42 \times 3$," where E stands for the total number of experiments.

Learn the verbal-mathematical associations listed in the Math Capsule and look for them when you're tackling the word problems in the practice tests in this book. Of course you can't simply memorize the associations and apply them unthinkingly. You have to read and understand the verbal statements in word problems to make sure that the equations you set up make sense. However, knowing the common associations should help you translate words into math.

Let's look at a couple of examples. Both of these word problems were used on a real SAT exam, which was published in the 1981 edition of *Taking the SAT*. The first one is fairly simple:

> In the United States in a certain year, food production per person was 15 per cent greater than food consumption per person. If the average daily consumption per person in the United States in that year was 3,000 calories, what was the average daily production (in calories) per person in that year?

First of all, notice that you're not given the population of the United States in the "certain year" mentioned in the question. Nor are you given the total food production for that year. So the phrase *per person* doesn't have to be reflected in your equation. You simply need to find a figure for food production, which you're told in the first sentence was 15 percent greater than food consumption. The words *greater than* call for addition, so you can start with the following equation:

$$P = C + 15\%C$$

This equation says that food production (P) equaled food consumption (C) plus an additional 15 percent.

Now you need to work on the right side of the equation. First, since C, by definition, equals 100 percent of C (just as 100 equals 100 percent of 100), you can combine C with $15\%C$ and get $115\%C$, or $\frac{115}{100}C$. Second, the problem tells you that the numeric value of C is 3,000, so you can substitute 3,000 for C in the equation:

$$P = \frac{115}{100}(3000)$$

The rest is easy. Just cancel the 100 and the 3,000, changing them to 1 and 30, and multiply:

$$P = \frac{115}{\underset{1}{\cancel{100}}} \times \frac{\overset{30}{\cancel{3000}}}{1}$$

$$= 3450$$

The second example is a little more complicated:

> Amy is twice as old as Bill. Five years ago she was 3 times as old as Bill was then. How old is Bill now?

First of all, notice that you're asked to find Bill's age now (not Amy's age now or Amy's age 5 years ago or Bill's age 5 years ago—all of which you can expect to be included as answer choices on a multiple-choice test). So let B stand for Bill's age now. Second, try to express the other information in the problem in terms of Bill's age now. The first sentence says that Amy presently is twice as old as Bill. *Twice* means "multiply by 2," so you can express Amy's age now as $2B$. The second sentence tells you how Bill's and Amy's ages were related 5 years ago. *Five years ago* means "subtract 5," so you can express Amy's age 5 years ago as $2B - 5$ and Bill's age 5 years ago as $B - 5$. Third, set up an equation. The second sentence tells you that 5 years ago, Amy was 3 times as old as Bill was then. *Was* means "equals"; *3 times* means "multiply by 3." Therefore:

$$2B - 5 = 3(B - 5)$$
$$2B - 5 = 3B - 15$$
$$-B = -10$$
$$B = 10$$

The key to solving a problem like this is expressing all the information in terms of a single unknown. You can call Amy's age A if you want to and still arrive at the correct answer. But then you have to set up and solve two simultaneous equations—not an impossible task, but a time-consuming one (see Section 9.16).

To summarize: Every word problem requires a different equation and a slightly different approach. However, the basic method is always the same: Carefully translate the verbal statements into equation form and then solve for the unknown value. At the end, check your answer by plugging it into the verbal statements to see if it makes sense. If it does, you're home free. If it doesn't, you probably set up the equation incorrectly. Go back and try to find your error. With practice, you won't make many mistakes.

PRACTICE EXERCISES

1. John borrows \$3,500 at the simple interest rate of 8 percent a year. How much interest will he owe in 2 years?
2. Four men take 18 days to complete a certain job. How long will it take nine men to complete the same job if they all work at the same rate?
3. A jet plane flies at 450 miles per hour from 2:30 P.M. to 6:00 P.M. How many miles does it fly?
4. A woman's will stipulates that her inheritance be divided between her two daughters in a 5 to 3 ratio. What is the larger share if the total of her inheritance is \$640,000?
5. If y is 16 and x exceeds y by the same amount that 7 exceeds 2, what is the value of x?
6. If half of a number is 7 more than a third of the same number, what is the number?
7. If Rita can walk 5 miles in 2 hours, how many miles can she walk at the same rate in 7 hours?
8. If it takes 20 minutes for 20 pounds of laundry to dry on a clothesline, how many minutes will it take for 50 pounds of similar laundry to dry under the same conditions on another clothesline?
9. The sum of three consecutive integers is 48. What are the three integers?
10. Half the sum of two numbers is 10. If one of the numbers is 4, what is the product of the two numbers?

Answers

1. At a simple interest rate of 8 percent a year, John will owe $2 \times 8 = 16$ percent in interest (I) after 2 years. Thus:

$$I = \frac{16}{100} \times \frac{3500}{1}$$
$$= 16 \times 35$$
$$= 560$$

The answer is \$560.

2. The number of workers is inversely proportional to the amount of time it takes to complete a job. Thus:

$$\frac{4}{9} = \frac{x}{18}$$
$$9x = 72$$
$$x = 8$$

It will take nine workers 8 days to complete the job.

3. The formula for distance problems is Distance = Rate × Time (or $d = rt$). The plane flies for $6{:}00 - 2{:}30 = 3\frac{1}{2}$, or $\frac{7}{2}$ hours. At a rate of 450 miles per hour, it will fly a distance of

$$d = \frac{7}{2} \times \frac{450}{1}$$
$$= 7 \times 225$$
$$= 1575 \text{ miles}$$

4. A ratio of 5 : 3 means that the inheritance is divided into eight equal parts. The larger share, then, is $\frac{5}{8}$ of \$640,000, or \$400,000.
5. *Exceeds* means "plus," so $x = y + 5$. If $y = 16$, then $x = 16 + 5 = 21$.
6. *Of* means "times," *is* means "equals," and *more than* means "plus." Thus, if x is the unknown number:

$$\frac{1}{2}x = \frac{1}{3}x + 7$$
$$3x = 2x + 42$$
$$x = 42$$

7. Distance and time are directly proportional. Thus:

$$\frac{5}{d} = \frac{2}{7}$$

$$2d = 35$$

$$d = 17\frac{1}{2}$$

8. Under the same conditions, similar laundry—no matter how much there is of it—will dry in the same amount of time, 20 minutes.
9. Let x be the first integer. Then the next two consecutive integers are $x + 1$ and $x + 2$. Thus:

$$x + x + 1 + x + 2 = 48$$

$$3x + 3 = 48$$

$$3x = 45$$

$$x = 15$$

The three integers are 15, 16, and 17.
10. Let x be the second number. Then:

$$\frac{1}{2}(x + 4) = 10$$

$$x + 4 = 20$$

$$x = 16$$

The product of 4 and 16 is 64.

9.15 Common Types of Word Problems

MATH CAPSULE

Travel problems:

In travel problems, one or more people, vehicles, or other things are set in motion. You are then asked to determine how far they travel, what their travel time is, what their rate of travel is, or something else. No matter how a travel problem is posed, you can use the same basic algebraic formula:

$$\text{Distance} = \text{Rate} \times \text{Time}$$

or, in shorthand:

$$d = rt$$

This formula has two variations, which may be more appropriate for some travel problems:

$$r = \frac{d}{t} \qquad t = \frac{d}{r}$$

Work problems:

In work problems, one or more people, groups, machines, or other things are set to work at a task. You are then asked to determine how much work they can do in a given time, what percentage of an entire job they can complete in a given time, what their rate of work is, or something else. Whatever the question, you can use the same basic algebraic formula:

$$J = \frac{T_A}{C_A} + \frac{T_B}{C_B} + \frac{T_C}{C_C} \cdots$$

where J is the fraction of the entire job completed, T is the length of time a particular worker works, and C is the worker's capacity—that is, the length of time it would take that worker to complete the entire job. A, B, and C represent three different workers; a problem could include more or fewer workers than that. In a case where an entire job is completed, J equals 1.

Age problems:

In age problems, the ages of two or more people (or things) are related to one another by a series of statements. To solve an age problem, assign a letter to represent one of the unknown ages—preferably the one you're asked to find. Try to express all of the other ages that you're given in terms of the unknown you're looking for. Add to it to represent a future age; subtract from it to represent a past age; multiply it to represent a statement like "twice as old"; divide it to represent a statement like "half as old." Then set up one or more equations that express in algebraic form the various relationships described in the verbal statements.

Mixture problems:

In mixture problems, a collection containing two or more types of things is described. Each type of thing has a different numeric value. For example, the collection might contain three different types of theater tickets, each with a different price; two different groups of students, each with a different average grade on an exam; or three different styles of houses, each with a different number of rooms. In general, use this algebraic formula for mixture problems:

$$T = (N_A \times V_A) + (N_B \times V_B) + (N_C \times V_C) \cdots$$

where T is the total value of all the items in the collection, N is the number of items of any one type, and V is the value of each item of a given type. A, B, and C represent three different types of items in a particular collection; there could be more or fewer types.

Word problems can vary as greatly as the mathematical problems that arise in real life. On the SAT, however, you can expect to find certain common types of word problems. The four most common types are those discussed in the Math Capsule—travel problems, work problems, age problems, and mixture problems. Here are some additional tips on handling each of these types of problems:

Travel problems. Start solving one of these problems by setting up a table containing the three basic quantities involved in every travel problem—rate, time, and distance. Your table should include all of the vehicles involved (most commonly two). It might look like this:

	Rate ×	Time =	Distance
Vehicle 1	30	3	90
Vehicle 2	45	t	90

In the problem outlined above, both vehicles traveled the same distance (90 miles). Their rates were different, and the travel time of Vehicle 2 was unknown. Using the formula Rate × Time = Distance, you can easily figure out the travel time of Vehicle 2 and thereby solve the problem. (Vehicle 2 traveled for 2 hours.) In other problems, the unknown quantity may appear in another part of the table. Use the same method, however. Set up the table, fill in the information you're given, and apply the basic travel formula to find whatever is unknown.

Work problems. Again, you can use a single basic equation for almost all work problems; its form is shown in the Math Capsule. However, the unknown will vary from problem to problem. Consider the information in the verbal statements carefully and set up the equation accordingly.

In some work problems, part of the job is done before the problem begins. Then only a fraction of the job remains; therefore, J (the job done) is some fraction less than 1, such as $\frac{1}{2}$ or $\frac{3}{4}$. In other problems, one worker begins working alone and is joined by another worker later; then the value of T (time worked) differs for each worker. For example, if Worker A is joined by Worker B after 2 hours, then Worker A's time is T and Worker B's time is $T - 2$.

One crucial step in solving work problems is clearing your equation of fractions. As you may recall, this involves finding the lowest common denominator and multiplying both sides of your equation by that denominator (see Section 9.13). Be sure to perform this step of the problem carefully; it's a fertile breeding ground for careless errors.

Age problems. To represent your unknown, use the initial letter of the name of the person whose age you're looking for. Be sure you understand what you're being asked to find. It might be Mike's age, Susan's age, Mike's age 3 years from now, or Susan's age when she was exactly twice as old as Mike. Naturally, each of these calls for a different answer.

Whenever possible, try to condense all the information that you're given into a single equation. You can usually do this by relating all of the facts to one another as fully as possible. For example, if Tom's age now, his age 2 years ago, and his age 4 years from now are all mentioned in the question, don't set up three different unknowns. Relate them all to the single unknown T and express them as T, $T - 2$, and $T + 4$. Furthermore, if Linda is 2 years older than Tom, you can express her age in terms of T, too—that is, as $T + 2$.

Mixture problems. As with age problems, try to relate all the facts given in the problem to one another. Avoid using two unknowns when one will do. For example, suppose $950 worth of tickets for a concert are sold, some for $5 each and others for $3 each. In all, 200 tickets are sold. You might call the number of $5 tickets sold x and the number of $3 tickets sold y and set up an equation like this: $5x + 3y = 950$. However, you can't solve a single equation with two unknowns. (As a general rule, for each unknown you have, you need a separate equation.) Therefore, try to describe both quantities in terms of a single unknown. Here's how: Call the number of $5 tickets sold x and the number of $3 tickets sold $200 - x$. You can do this because you know that the number of $3 tickets sold must be the difference between the total number of tickets sold (200) and the number of $5 tickets sold. This fact allows you to set up an equation with a single unknown:

$$5x + 3(200 - x) = 950$$

$$5x + 600 - 3x = 950$$

$$2x = 350$$

$$x = 175$$

So 175 $5 tickets were sold and just 25 $3 tickets.

PRACTICE EXERCISES

1. A boy rides his bicycle for 20 minutes at a rate of 15 miles per hour and 30 minutes at a rate of 10 miles per hour. What is his average speed in miles per hour for the entire 50 minutes?
2. The winner of a 400-mile auto race averaged 160 miles per hour. The second-place car averaged 150 miles per hour. How many miles back was the second-place car when the winner crossed the finish line?
3. It takes six painters 5 days to paint a house. At the same rate, how many days will it take four painters to paint the house if two of the painters work only half days?
4. It takes Paul 8 hours to chop a cord of wood. It takes Mark 6 hours. If Paul starts chopping at 8 A.M. and Mark joins him an hour later, at what time will they finish chopping the cord of wood?
5. In 5 years Peter will be twice as old as he was 3 years ago. How old is Peter now?
6. Six years ago Victoria was half as old as Susan. Victoria is now 4 years younger than Susan. How old is Susan now?
7. Mario spent $9.85 on a long-distance telephone call. If he paid $1.45 for the first 3 minutes and 35¢ for each additional minute, how many minutes did he talk?
8. At Central Senior High School the number of tenth graders is $\frac{3}{4}$ the number of eleventh graders, and the number of eleventh graders is $\frac{4}{5}$ the number of twelfth graders. If the total enrollment in the three grades is 840, how many eleventh graders are there in the school?

Answers

1. The boy's average speed (or rate) is his total distance divided by his total time. First, express all minutes in terms of hours: 20 minutes = $\frac{1}{3}$ hour; 30 minutes = $\frac{1}{2}$ hour; 50

minutes = $\frac{5}{6}$ hour. Second, use the travel formula to determine the distance the boy travels at each rate:

	Rate	× Time	= Distance
Rate 1	15	$\frac{1}{3}$	5
Rate 2	10	$\frac{1}{2}$	5

Third, divide the total distance (5 + 5 = 10) by the total time ($\frac{5}{6}$):

$$10 \div \frac{5}{6} = \frac{10}{1} \times \frac{6}{5} = 12$$

The boy's average speed (or rate) is 12 miles per hour. (Notice that his average speed is *not* the average of the two speeds, which is $12\frac{1}{2}$.)

2. Start by setting up a table and filling in all the information you're given:

	Rate	× Time	= Distance
Vehicle 1	160	t	400
Vehicle 2	150	t	d

First, find the travel time of the winner (Vehicle 1):

$$\begin{aligned} t &= \frac{d}{r} \\ &= \frac{400}{160} \\ &= \frac{5}{2} \end{aligned}$$

Second, find the distance traveled by Vehicle 2 (the second-place car) in the same length of time ($\frac{5}{2}$ hours):

$$\begin{aligned} d &= rt \\ &= 150\left(\frac{5}{2}\right) \\ &= 75(5) \\ &= 375 \end{aligned}$$

Third, subtract the distance traveled by Vehicle 2 from the total distance of the race: 400 − 375 = 25. The second-place car was 25 miles back when the winner crossed the finish line.

3. There's a shortcut built into this problem. Two painters working half days are equivalent to one painter working full time. So you're actually being asked to find the number of days it will take three painters to paint the house. It will take three painters twice as long as it will take six painters: 2 × 5 = 10 days.

4. Recall the basic formula in the Math Capsule:

$$J = \frac{T_P}{C_P} + \frac{T_M}{C_M}$$

In this case, $J = 1$ (since Paul and Mark will complete the entire job), C_P (Paul's capacity) = 8 (since it takes Paul 8 hours to complete the job by himself), and C_M (Mark's capacity) = 6. Let T equal Paul's time. Then Mark's time is 1 hour less, or $T - 1$. Thus:

$$1 = \frac{T}{8} + \frac{T-1}{6}$$

To clear the equation of fractions, multiply both sides by 24, the lowest common denominator of 6 and 8. Then solve for T:

$$24 = 3T + 4T - 4$$
$$28 = 7T$$
$$4 = T$$

If Paul starts at 8 A.M. and works for 4 hours, he and Mark will complete the job at $8 + 4 = 12$ noon.

5. Let P equal Peter's age now. Then his age 5 years from now will be $P + 5$, and his age 3 years ago was $P - 3$. Set up the equation and solve for P:

$$P + 5 = 2(P - 3)$$
$$P + 5 = 2P - 6$$
$$11 = P$$

6. Let S equal Susan's age now. Then Victoria's age now equals $S - 4$, Victoria's age 6 years ago equals $S - 4 - 6$, or $S - 10$, and Susan's age 6 years ago equals $S - 6$. Set up the equation and solve for S:

$$\frac{1}{2}(S - 6) = S - 10$$
$$S - 6 = 2S - 20$$
$$14 = S$$

7. Let m equal the number of additional minutes that Mario talked. Then:

$$1.45 + .35m = 9.85$$
$$.35m = 8.40$$
$$m = 24$$

Mario talked $24 + 3 = 27$ minutes altogether.

8. Let x be the number of twelfth graders (even though it's not the number you're looking for). Then the number of eleventh graders is $\frac{4}{5}x$ and the number of tenth graders is $\frac{3}{4}(\frac{4}{5}x)$, or $\frac{3}{5}x$. Thus:

$$x + \frac{4}{5}x + \frac{3}{5}x = 840$$
$$5x + 4x + 3x = 4200$$
$$12x = 4200$$
$$x = 350$$

Now x, remember, is the number of twelfth graders. To find the number of eleventh graders, multiply 350 by $\frac{4}{5}$:

$$\frac{350}{1} \times \frac{4}{5} = 280$$

9.16 Solving Simultaneous Equations

MATH CAPSULE

Definitions:

Independent equations are equations that provide different information about two or more unknowns (or variables). Generally speaking, you can find the value of two or more unknowns only if you're given two or more independent equations (one for each unknown). In other words, given one equation, you can find the value of one unknown; given two independent equations, you can find the value of two unknowns; and so on.

Simultaneous equations are independent equations that contain more than one unknown (or variable).

Solving simultaneous equations by the method of substitution:

To solve two simultaneous equations by the method of substitution, follow these three steps:

1. Use algebraic techniques to solve one equation for one unknown in terms of the second.

   Example: Given the simultaneous equations $x + 4y = 2$ and $2x - 7y = -1$, solve the first equation for x in terms of y:

$$x + 4y = 2$$
$$x = 2 - 4y$$

2. Substitute the result of step 1 in the second equation and solve for the numerical value of the second unknown.

   Example: Continuing the example above, substitute $2 - 4y$ for x in the second equation and solve for y:

$$2(2 - 4y) - 7y = -1$$
$$4 - 8y - 7y = -1$$
$$-15y = -5$$
$$y = \frac{1}{3}$$

3. Substitute the result of step 2 in either equation and solve for the numerical value of the first unknown.

   Example: Continuing the example above, substitute $\frac{1}{3}$ for y in the first equation and solve for x:

$$x + 4\left(\frac{1}{3}\right) = 2$$
$$3x + 4 = 6$$
$$3x = 2$$
$$x = \frac{2}{3}$$

Solving simultaneous equations by the method of addition or subtraction:

To solve two simultaneous equations by the method of addition or subtraction, follow these three steps:

1. Add or subtract the two equations so that you eliminate one unknown.

   Example: Given the simultaneous equations $2x - y = 12$ and $x + y = 15$, add the two equations to eliminate y:

$$\begin{array}{r} 2x - y = 12 \\ + \quad x + y = 15 \\ \hline 3x + 0 = 27 \end{array}$$

2. Solve the equation resulting from step 1 for the numerical value of the remaining unknown.

   Example: Continuing the example above, solve $3x + 0 = 27$ for x:

$$3x + 0 = 27$$
$$3x = 27$$
$$x = 9$$

3. Substitute the result of step 2 in either equation and solve for the numerical value of the second unknown.

   Example: Continuing the example above, substitute 9 for x in the second equation and solve for y:

$$9 + y = 15$$
$$y = 6$$

Note: The method of addition or subtraction works only if the coefficient of one of the unknowns is the same in both equations—regardless of its sign. (In the example above, the coefficient of y in both equations is 1, -1 in the first equation, $+1$ in the second.) In some cases, you have to multiply or divide one of the equations before you can use the method of addition or subtraction.

Example: Given the simultaneous equations $2x + 6y = 10$ and $3x + 3y = 9$, you have to multiply the second equation by 2 and make it $6x + 6y = 18$ before you can subtract the first equation from it:

$$\begin{array}{rr} 6x + 6y = & 18 \\ + \; -2x - 6y = & -10 \\ \hline 4x + \; 0 = & 8 \end{array}$$

As the Math Capsule explains, you generally need two independent equations to find the numerical value of two unknowns. *Independent* means that the two equations must be different; they can't simply be multiples of each other. Look at the following equations, for example:

$$4x = 8 - 6y \qquad 3y + 2x = 4$$

At first glance, you might think that you have two independent equations here, which would enable you to solve for both x and y. However, the first equation is really just a variation of the second. If you multiply the second equation by 2 and then transpose the y term, you end up with the first equation. Both equations "say the same thing" about x and y; therefore, you can't combine them in any way to gain new information about either unknown, which means that you can't find the numerical values of x and y on the bases of these two equations. Be aware of this "trick"; it's sometimes tested on the SAT.

The Math Capsule describes two basic methods for solving simultaneous equations—that is, equations that are genuinely independent. Practice both methods until you're comfortable with them. You can use the method of substitution on *any* pair of simultaneous equations, but the method of addition or subtraction is usually faster. So before you try the substitution method on an SAT math problem, examine your two equations carefully to see if you can use the addition-or-subtraction method. (More often than not you'll be able to; the makers of the SAT like to build shortcuts into their math problems.)

Your goal in adding or subtracting two simultaneous equations is to eliminate one of the unknowns. If you can manipulate either equation in such a way as to make both equations contain the same number of either x's or y's, you can then add or subtract the equations and thereby eliminate one of the unknowns. Solving for the remaining unknown is then relatively easy.

Here's one more "trick" to watch for: Occasionally you'll encounter a problem that looks for all the world like a simultaneous equation problem (two unknowns, two equations), but it's actually much simpler. Why? Because the solution to the problem is built into one of the equations; solving the simultaneous equations is therefore unnecessary. For example, suppose that you're given these two equations and are asked to find the value of $2n - m$:

$$3n + m = 14 \qquad 4n = 2m + 2$$

Before you start applying one of the two methods for solving simultaneous equations, consider each equation for a moment. You want to find the value not of m or of n, but of $2n - m$. Is there any way that you can tinker with one of the equations to get $2n - m$ all by itself? Yes. Look at the second equation. If you transpose the $2m$, you'll get $4n - 2m = 2$, which is exactly twice what you're looking for. Divide this equation through by 2 and you'll get $2n - m = 1$, which is the answer.

Of course, you could solve a problem like this by using either of the two traditional methods for solving simultaneous equations, and your answer would be just the same. However, the trick you've just seen is faster. Don't expect to find such a shortcut every time, but the SAT test makers sometimes build one into a problem. As always, look for the simplest solution first.

We'll continue our review of math for the SAT in Lesson 14.

PRACTICE EXERCISES

Solve the following simultaneous equations for x and y.

1. $x + y = 7$
   $3x - y = 1$
2. $2x + 2y = 10$
   $3x - 2y = 0$
3. $5x = 2y$
   $x - y = 3$
4. $x + y = 4$
   $2x + 3y = 11$
5. $x + 2y = 1$
   $-5 = x - y$
6. $3x - 2y = 0$
   $6 + 3x = 4y$

Answers

1. $x = 2, y = 5$ 2. $x = 2, y = 3$ 3. $x = -2, y = -5$ 4. $x = 1, y = 3$ 5. $x = -3, y = 2$
6. $x = 2, y = 3$

LESSON 10
Grammar Review for the TSWE, Part 1

OBJECTIVES

☐ To review the basic principles of sentence construction
☐ To learn to recognize and avoid the most common sentence structure errors on the TSWE
☐ To learn to recognize effective sentences for error corrections on the TSWE

A Thumbnail Grammar Review

10.1 Basic Grammar Terms

You don't need to know much about English grammar to do well on the Test of Standard Written English. Only certain specific types of grammar problems tend to show up on a multiple-choice test. In this lesson and in Lesson 15, you'll learn about these problems and how to solve them.

But first you need to know a few basic grammatical terms. They don't appear on the exam, and you're probably familiar with most of them already, but you do need to know them in order to study this lesson.

The *sentence* is the main unit of meaning in English. It's a group of words beginning with a capital letter and ending with a period, a question mark, or an exclamation point. A sentence contains a complete thought and is made up of a *subject* and a *predicate*.

The *subject* of a sentence may be a single word or a group of words. The subject is basically what the sentence is about. When the subject consists of a group of words, the entire group is called the *complete subject*; the single most important word in the complete subject is the *simple subject*.

The *predicate* of a sentence may also be a word or a group of words. The predicate basically tells something about the subject of the sentence: what the subject is, what the subject does, or what is done to the subject. The predicate of a sentence normally follows the subject, but it can also precede it.

Each word in a sentence falls into one of seven basic classes of words, known as the *parts of speech*. The seven basic parts of speech are *verbs*, *nouns*, *pronouns*, *adjectives*, *adverbs*, *prepositions*, and *conjunctions*. (Some grammar books also include *interjections*—words like *Oh!* or *Hey!*—but these aren't too important grammatically, so we'll ignore them here.) The same word may be used as more than one part of speech, depending on the role it plays in a particular sentence. See, for example, how the word *hit* is used in the following sentences:

The batter *hit* a home run. (*verb*)
The song was a big *hit*. (*noun*)
The disc jockey played the *hit* record over and over. (*adjective*)

10.2 The Parts of Speech

The *verb* is the most important word in the predicate of a sentence. It tells what the subject is, what it does, or what is done to it; in other words, a verb may express either an action or a state of being. A verb may be one word or a phrase of two, three, or four words. In the sentence "John ran a mile," *ran* is the verb; it expresses action done by the subject *John*. In the sentence "John is my brother," *is* is the verb; it expresses a state of being of the subject *John*. In the sentence "John was eaten by a bear," the two-word phrase *was eaten* is the verb; it expresses action done to the subject *John*.

In the last example, *was eaten* is called a *verb phrase*. *Eaten* is the *main verb* in the verb phrase; *was* is the *helping verb* (or *auxiliary verb*). A verb phrase may contain two or more helping verbs. In the sentence "John would have been ten years old next spring," *would* and *have* are both helping verbs; *been* is the main verb.

A *noun* is a word that names a person, place, thing, or idea. *John*, *mile*, *brother*, *bear*, and *spring* are all nouns. So are words like *truth*, *San Diego*, *description*, *grammar*, and *SAT*.

A *pronoun* is a word that takes the place of a noun in a sentence. *He*, *she*, *it*, *they*, *we*, *who*, *whose*, *which*, and *that* are examples of pronouns. There are many types of pronouns, all with their own special uses. As we go along, we'll review the ones you need to know in order to understand particular rules that are tested on the TSWE.

An *adjective* is a word that describes (or *modifies*) a noun or pronoun. An adjective normally answers one of these questions: *which one? what kind? how many?* In the sentence "John ate those three green apples," the words *those*, *three*, and *green* are all adjectives. *Those* tells *which ones*; *three* tells *how many*; and *green* tells *what kind*.

An *adverb* is a word that modifies a verb, an adjective, or another adverb. Many, but not all, adverbs end in *-ly*. In the sentence "John slowly ate the rather large sandwich," *slowly* and *rather* are adverbs. *Slowly* modifies the verb *ate*; it tells *how* John ate the sandwich. *Rather* modifies the adjective *large*; it tells *how* large the sandwich was. In the sentence "John ate the sandwich very slowly," *very* and *slowly* are adverbs. *Slowly* modifies the verb *ate* and tells *how* John ate the sandwich; *very* modifies the adverb *slowly* and tells *how* slowly John ate the sandwich.

A *preposition* is a word or group of words that relates a noun or a pronoun to another word in a sentence. The noun or pronoun that follows the preposition is called the *object* of the preposition. The preposition and its object together form a *prepositional phrase*. Some examples of prepositions are *in*, *on*, *of*, *for*, *through*, *beside*, *along*, *around*, *with*, *by*, *from*, *until*, *upon*, *because of*, *in addition to*, and *out of*. There are many more prepositions in English.

A *conjunction* joins two or more words or groups of words. There are two important kinds of conjunctions: coordinating conjunctions and subordinating conjunctions. The *coordinating conjunctions* are *and*, *or*, *but*, *for*, *nor*, *so*, and *yet*. They are used to join two or more words or groups of words that are equal in importance. Among the many *subordinating conjunctions* are the words *because*, *since*, *when*, *after*, *although*, *if*, and *unless*. Subordinating conjunctions are used to join dependent clauses to independent clauses. (For an explanation of clauses, see Sections 10.3 and 10.4.)

10.3 Other Grammar Terms You Should Know

There are two kinds of *objects* in sentences: direct objects and indirect objects. A *direct object* is a noun or pronoun that receives the action of a verb. In the sentence "John hit the ball," the word *ball* receives the action of the verb *hit*; it tells *what* John hit. Therefore, *ball* is the direct object. An *indirect object* is a noun or pronoun that answers the question *to what? to whom? for what?* or *for whom?* In the sentence "John wrote Susan a letter," *wrote* is the verb, *letter* is the direct object, and *Susan* is the indirect object. *Susan* answers the question "*To whom* did John write the letter?"

A *phrase* is a group of words that does not contain both a subject and a predicate. A phrase functions as a single part of speech in a sentence. You've seen some examples of phrases already—verb phrases, for instance.

A *clause* is a group of words that contains both a subject and a predicate. A clause that can stand alone as a sentence is called an *independent clause. Jane took the SAT* is an independent clause. A clause that cannot stand alone as a sentence is called a *dependent clause. If Jane takes the SAT* is a dependent clause. As you can see, a dependent clause is neither grammatically nor logically complete. Like a phrase, a dependent clause functions as a single part of speech in a sentence.

10.4 How Sentences Are Constructed

As you learned in Section 10.1, every sentence contains a subject and a predicate. Any group of words that lacks either a subject or a predicate is not a complete sentence but a sentence fragment. You'll learn more about fragments in Section 10.5. Here are some examples of fragments:

The president, in his address to the nation.

This group of words contains a potential subject (*president*) but no predicate—it doesn't tell what the president did.

Spoke about the need for a greater commitment to higher education.

This group of words contains a potential predicate (*spoke*) but no subject—it doesn't tell who or what spoke.

To qualify as a complete sentence, a group of words must not only contain a subject and a predicate but also be capable of standing by itself. In other words, it must be an independent clause. Every sentence must contain at least one independent clause.

A sentence may contain more than one independent clause. For example, *the governor proposed the bill* is an independent clause. *The state legislature passed it* is also an independent clause. These two independent clauses can be combined into one sentence in any of several ways. Here are two of the more common ways:

The governor proposed the bill, and the state legislature passed it.

The governor proposed the bill; the state legislature passed it.

Each of these sentences contains two independent clauses. A sentence of this kind is called a *compound sentence.*

Sometimes a dependent clause and an independent clause are combined in one sentence. For example, here is a dependent clause:

Although the Democratic party opposed the bill

This is a clause, because it contains both a subject (*party*) and a predicate (*opposed*). However, because it can't stand alone as a sentence, it is a *dependent* clause. It leaves you wondering, "Although the party opposed the bill, what happened?" Something is missing. The thought, and thus the sentence, can be completed only if the dependent clause is combined with an independent clause:

Although the Democratic party opposed the bill, the state legislature passed it.

A sentence like this, which contains an independent clause and a dependent clause, is called a *complex sentence.* A complex sentence may contain more than one dependent clause.

Finally, a compound sentence with two or more independent clauses may also have one or more dependent clauses tacked onto it. The result is a *compound-complex sentence.* Here's an example:

Although the Democratic party opposed the bill, the governor proposed it, and the state legislature passed it.

In the next section, you'll learn how these principles of sentence construction are tested on the TSWE.

Sentence Construction Errors on the TSWE

10.5 Run-on Sentences and Fragments

Two of the most common errors that you'll encounter on the TSWE are run-on sentences and fragments. You'll usually find these two basic errors in sentence construction in error corrections rather than usage questions.

A *run-on sentence* is a sentence containing two or more independent clauses that are simply run together. A run-on sentence reads like two sentences jammed into one.

As you know, a sentence can contain two independent clauses and still be a correct sentence. The key is the manner in which the clauses are joined. To be correct, two independent clauses must be joined by a coordinating conjunction, a semicolon (;), or, less frequently, a colon (:). If they aren't joined by one of these elements, the result is a run-on. For instance, here are two independent clauses:

> James Boswell was a Scottish writer of the eighteenth century
> He is best known as the author of *The Life of Johnson*

You could use a coordinating conjunction, such as *and*, to combine these two clauses into a single sentence:

> James Boswell was a Scottish writer of the eighteenth century, and he is best known as the author of *The Life of Johnson*.

You could also use a semicolon for the same purpose:

> James Boswell was a Scottish writer of the eighteenth century; he is best known as the author of *The Life of Johnson*.

However, if you used nothing at all or just a comma to connect them, the result would be a run-on:

> X James Boswell was a Scottish writer of the eighteenth century he is best known as the author of *The Life of Johnson*.

> X James Boswell was a Scottish writer of the eighteenth century, he is best known as the author of *The Life of Johnson*.

There's another way, of course, that you could combine two independent clauses into a single sentence: you could subordinate one of them—that is, you could turn one of them into a dependent clause. For example:

> James Boswell was a Scottish writer of the eighteenth century who is best known as the author of *The Life of Johnson*.

Changing *he* to *who* transforms the second clause into a dependent clause. It can no longer stand on its own as a complete sentence because its meaning depends on the meaning of the first clause.

A *sentence fragment* is a different sort of error. This is a "sentence" that contains *no* independent clause. It may be missing either a subject or a predicate. Or it may be a dependent clause punctuated as a sentence. A fragment doesn't express a complete idea; it leaves you feeling that something more should be added. Length has nothing to do with whether a group of words is a sentence or a fragment. A fragment can be quite long—twenty words or more. But if the words don't express a complete thought, they're just a group of words; they're not a sentence.

Here are some examples of fragments:

> X Samuel Johnson, the most respected—and feared—literary critic and cultural spokesman in the London of 1750.

This is a fragment because it does not contain a predicate.

X Wrote many thousands of pages of prose with almost incredible speed and fluency.

This is a fragment because it does not contain a subject.

X Because he was considered an authority on the meanings and proper uses of words in the English language.

This is a fragment because it is a dependent clause punctuated as a sentence. Although it contains both a subject and a predicate, it can't stand on its own because it begins with the subordinating conjunction *because*. *Because* tells us that a reason will follow, but we're not told what the reason is for. So the thought is incomplete.

Here are two sample error correction questions showing how a run-on sentence and a fragment might appear on the TSWE:

> Boswell's *Life of Johnson* was the most detailed account of a person's life that had ever been written, it is still considered a literary masterpiece.
>
> (A) that had ever been written, it is still considered a literary masterpiece
> (B) ever written, it is still considered a masterpiece of literature
> (C) ever written literarily it is still considered a masterpiece
> (D) that had ever been written, and it is still considered a literary masterpiece
> (E) ever to be written, still it is considered literarily masterful

Choice D is correct. It fixes the run-on sentence by adding the coordinating conjunction *and* to connect the two independent clauses.

> Many readers having come to love the character of Johnson, despite the flaws and weaknesses so clearly portrayed by Boswell.
>
> (A) Many readers having come to love
> (B) Many readers have come to love
> (C) Coming to love
> (D) Loved by many readers is
> (E) In reading of him, many have loved

Choice B is correct. The original sentence is a fragment because it does not contain a verb that can stand on its own as a predicate. (Watch out for the *-ing* forms of verbs.) Choice B corrects the error by replacing *having come*, which can't stand on its own as a predicate, with *have come*, which can. Choices D and E also correct the grammatical error, but they're both awkward and hard to understand. (This is an example of an error correction question that tests effectiveness as well as grammatical correctness. We'll discuss effectiveness at greater length in Sections 10.8 and 10.9.)

10.6 Dangling or Misplaced Modifiers

As you've learned, every complete sentence contains at least one independent clause. It may also contain additional elements that are related to one another in various ways. If the relationships among those elements are unclear or illogical, the sentence may be grammatically incorrect. In this section, we'll look at two types of errors that result from poorly related sentence elements: dangling modifiers and misplaced modifiers.

Modifiers, as you recall, describe or explain other words. There are two types of modifiers: adjectives and adverbs. *Adjectives* modify nouns and pronouns. *Adverbs* modify verbs, adjectives, and other adverbs.

A modifier can be a single word, or it can be a phrase or a clause. Any word or group of words that describes or explains another word or words is considered a modifier. Here are some examples:

> Scientific history is a fascinating subject.

The adjective *scientific* is a one-word modifier; it modifies the noun *history*.

> The history of science is a fascinating subject.

The phrase *of science* is a modifier; it modifies the noun *history*.

> Dr. Jobson's new book on the history of science is fascinating.

The phrase *on the history of science* is a modifier; so is the word *fascinating*. Both modify the noun *book*.

> Because it analyzes the process of scientific innovation so clearly, the book has received widespread acclaim.

The entire dependent clause *because it analyzes the process of scientific innovation so clearly* is a modifier. It tells *why* the new book has received acclaim. So the clause acts as an adverb modifying the verb *has received*.

Once you understand that words and groups of words can function as modifiers, you can understand this rule: In any sentence, every modifier must be clearly related to the word or words it modifies; therefore, every modifier should be placed as close as possible to the word or words it modifies.

Two very common errors arise from violations of this rule: dangling modifiers and misplaced modifiers. Although you're not likely to encounter these errors in the usage section of the TSWE, you're very likely to encounter them in the error correction section.

As its name suggests, a *dangling modifier* is a modifier that "dangles" in space—a modifier that has nothing to modify. Here's an example:

> X Having made few major discoveries during the Middle Ages, scientific progress accelerated during the fifteenth and sixteenth centuries.

The phrase *having made few major discoveries during the Middle Ages* should modify or describe some group of people, since only people can make discoveries. But no group of people is mentioned in the sentence. So the phrase "dangles." To correct the dangling modifier, you'd have to change the sentence to read something like this:

> Having made few major discoveries during the Middle Ages, Western scientists accelerated their progress during the fifteenth and sixteenth centuries.

Now the modifier clearly modifies the words *Western scientists*.

A *misplaced modifier* is a modifier positioned in such a way that it seems to modify one word when it actually (and logically) modifies another. The result is an unclear sentence. Here's an example:

> X Little known during the Middle Ages, the Renaissance saw a revival of interest in the works of Aristotle.

Here, the modifying phrase *little known during the Middle Ages* is next to, and therefore seems to modify, the words *the Renaissance*. But the Renaissance wasn't little known during the Middle Ages; the works of Aristotle were. So the phrase is misplaced. To correct the misplacement, you'd have to move the phrase so that it was next to the words it actually modifies. Here is one way you could do that:

> The Renaissance saw a revival of interest in the works of Aristotle, which had been little known during the Middle Ages.

Now it's clear what the modifier refers to.

Correcting a dangling or misplaced modifier often requires a major revision of a sentence. For this reason, dangling and misplaced modifiers usually show up in error correction questions rather than usage questions. Here are two typical error correction questions illustrating how these types of errors might be covered on the TSWE:

> Realizing the crucial role of Aristotle in the history of science, Professor Ann Jobson's book examines his work in great detail.
>
> (A) Professor Ann Jobson's book examines his work in great detail
> (B) his work is examined in great detail in Professor Ann Jobson's book
> (C) his work receives detailed examination in Professor Ann Jobson's book
> (D) in Professor Ann Jobson's book his work is examined in great detail
> (E) Professor Ann Jobson examines his work in great detail in her book

The modifying phrase *realizing the crucial role of Aristotle in the history of science* dangles, since there is no noun in the original sentence that it can logically modify. Who realizes the crucial role of Aristotle? Professor Ann Jobson does, of course. So the modifier should be followed by *Professor Ann Jobson*, not *Professor Ann Jobson's book* or *his work*. The correct answer is choice E.

> Published only one month ago, several committees are already considering the book for a prize.
>
> (A) Published only one month ago
> (B) Although it was published only one month ago
> (C) Having been published only one month ago
> (D) Only one month having elapsed since publication
> (E) After an interval since publication of just one month

Here, the modifying phrase is misplaced. *Published only one month ago* modifies *the book*, but the two phrases aren't close enough together to make that relationship clear. Since the question is constructed in such a way that we can't move the modifying phrase, we have to look at the answer choices and find one that somehow corrects the misplacement problem. Choice B does that. It changes the modifying phrase into a dependent clause with a subject (*it*) and a predicate (*was published*), so that it makes sense in its present location. (It's true that in the revised version we don't know what *it* refers to until later on in the sentence, but that's okay; the sentence is clear nevertheless.) Choice C leaves the misplaced modifier alone. Choices D and E add more words to the sentence without making it any clearer. So choice B remains the best answer.

10.7 Errors in Parallelism

The next error category, errors in parallelism, also involves faulty relations among the corresponding parts of a sentence. *Parallelism* is the casting of like ideas—that is, ideas of equal importance—in like grammatical form.

Errors in parallelism tend to arise in certain types of constructions. The most common of these is the list or series. Here is an example of faulty parallelism in a list or series:

> X Among the most popular winter sports are skiing, skating, sledding, and to ride on snowmobiles.

This sentence contains a list or series of four items (the most popular winter sports). The first three are expressed in one grammatical form; the fourth is expressed in another grammatical form. Since any series, by its very nature, is a list of items relatively equal in importance, the rules of parallelism demand that all the items be expressed in the same grammatical form. So, the fourth item in this series should be *riding on snowmobiles*, or, even better, *snowmobiling*.

Here are two more examples of faulty parallelism in a list or series:

X A forest ranger's duties include educating park users, the prevention of accidents, and detecting and correcting hazardous conditions.

This is a more subtle example of faulty parallelism in a series or list. The sentence contains a list of three duties that a forest ranger has to perform. (The list actually includes four duties, but the third and fourth are lumped together as one.) All three duties are expressed in similar grammatical form—that is, *educating*, *prevention*, and *detecting and correcting* are all nouns. But technically the nouns aren't parallel. The first and the third are verbal nouns (as you can tell by the *-ing* at the end of each one); the second is not. They would all be exactly parallel if the second one were changed from *the prevention of accidents* to *preventing accidents*.

X The corporation's research department monitors trends in the industry, develops new products, and has sought out ways of improving old products.

This is another subtle example of faulty parallelism in a list or series. The series at the end of this sentence seems parallel because all three items are predicates. But notice that the verbs in the first two predicates are in one tense (*monitors*, *develops*), and the verb in the third is in another tense (*has sought*). To be exactly parallel, all three verbs should be in the same tense: *monitors*, *develops*, and *seeks*.

Errors in parallelism are very common in lists or series. They're also very common in simple compounds—that is, combinations of two elements joined by the coordinating conjunctions *and*, *but*, *or*, and *nor*—which are really just "mini" lists or series. Since a "coordinating" conjunction is a grammatical sign of equality of rank or importance, any two (or more) elements joined by a coordinating conjunction should be "equal" or parallel in form. Here's an example:

X A truly efficient automobile would be able to adjust its fuel consumption appropriately in city traffic and when it was traveling on open highways.

In this sentence, a prepositional phrase (*in city traffic*) is "coordinated" with a clause (*when it was traveling on open highways*), but a phrase and a clause are not coordinate (of equal rank) grammatically. To be parallel, both elements should be phrases or both should be clauses. In this case, phrases are more concise: *in city traffic* and *on open highways*.

Just as elements joined by coordinating conjunctions should be parallel in form, so elements joined by correlative conjunctions should be parallel in form. *Correlative conjunctions* are those that are used in pairs: *either ... or, neither ... nor, both ... and, not only ... but also*. Here's an example of faulty parallelism in the two elements joined by a pair of correlative conjunctions:

X Educational theorists have generally believed that a college education should either represent a broad range of studies or narrow, in-depth training in a specialty.

Notice that *either* is followed by a verb (*represent*) but *or* is not. Instead, *or* is followed by a noun phrase that is an object of the verb *represent*—the second object. The first object is the noun phrase *a broad range of studies*. To correct the faulty parallelism, you could repeat the verb *represent* after *or*. Or you could simply reverse the order of *either* and *represent*; then each correlative would be followed by a noun phrase that was an object of the verb *represent*. The second alternative is better because it's more concise.

As you can see, errors in parallelism tend to arise in certain kinds of constructions—namely, constructions in which two or more elements are joined by coordinating or correlative conjunctions. You'll almost certainly encounter constructions of this type in error correction questions on the TSWE. (Like the other errors in this lesson, parallelism is rarely tested in usage questions.) When you do encounter them, check the elements to make sure they're parallel in form.

Here are two examples of error correction questions that measure your understanding of the rules of good parallel structure:

Learning to program a computer requires neither mechanical aptitude <u>nor that you know advanced mathematics</u>.

(A) nor that you know advanced mathematics
(B) or knowing advanced mathematics
(C) nor a knowledge of advanced mathematics
(D) nor having a knowledge of advanced mathematics
(E) nor does it require advanced mathematical knowledge

In the original sentence the correlatives *neither* and *nor* are used to connect two elements that are parallel in thought but not in form. The first is a noun phrase (*mechanical aptitude*); the second is a clause (*that you know advanced mathematics*). Choice C corrects the faulty parallelism by recasting the second element in the same form as the first.

The civilization of ancient Greece has influenced the modern world through its literature, its political ideas, and through its philosophical concepts.

(A) and through its philosophical concepts
(B) as well as philosophical concepts
(C) along with its philosophical concepts
(D) and also through its philosophical concepts
(E) and its philosophical concepts

The original sentence includes a list or series of three elements, only the last of which is underlined. You know that all three elements should be parallel in form because they're "coordinated" by the conjunction *and*. So look at the second element, which you can't change, for a clue. It's exactly the same in form as the third element except that it's not preceded by *through*. So find an answer choice that eliminates the *through* without changing anything else. That's choice E.

Effectiveness in Error Correction Questions

10.8 Wordiness Versus Conciseness

As you've learned, for some error correction questions on the TSWE, you can't choose the correct answer on the basis of grammatical correctness alone. You have to consider effectiveness, as well. These questions test two basic aspects of effectiveness: conciseness and logic. In the last two sections of this lesson, we'll discuss the meaning of conciseness and logic and the ways in which these two aspects of effectiveness are tested in the error correction section of the TSWE.

Conciseness means "economy of expression." A concise sentence contains no unnecessary words. The opposite of *concise* is *wordy*. A wordy sentence uses more words than necessary to express an idea.

Recognizing a wordy sentence takes practice. A wordy sentence is not necessarily long, nor is a long sentence necessarily wordy. A fairly short sentence may be wordy if it uses more words than are necessary to express an idea. A long sentence may be concise if each word contributes to its meaning.

To get an idea of what wordiness is like, look at the following sentence:

X The laws which exist in relation to zoning in New York City supposedly exist for the purpose of preventing too great a concentration of tall buildings in any one area.

Exactly the same idea could be expressed in this way:

The zoning laws in New York City are supposed to prevent too great a concentration of tall buildings in one area.

This sentence is nine words shorter than the original sentence. All the words that have been omitted are "empty" words; they serve no purpose and convey no meaning. Notice the kinds of changes that have been made. The clause *which exist in relation to zoning* has been changed to the one-word modifier *zoning*. The words *supposedly exist for the purpose of preventing* have been replaced by the words *are supposed to prevent*. Phrases like *in relation to* and *for the purpose of* are telltale signs of wordiness. They convey little or no meaning; they just pad out the sentences in which they appear.

Here are some other examples of wordy phrases with one-word substitutes that convey exactly the same meaning:

due to the fact that	because
in the event that	if
at the present moment in time	now
at that particular time	then
in a location such that	where
despite the fact that	although
in spite of this fact	however
as a result of this fact	therefore

Looking at this list—which could be greatly expanded, of course—may give you an idea of what wordy phrases and sentences are like. They sound "flabby." Concise phrases and sentences, by contrast, are direct and "muscular."

Although recognizing wordiness takes practice, there's a simple test that you can use to detect wordiness in error correction questions on the TSWE. Suppose, for example, that you've read through all the answers for a question and you've narrowed your choice to three that are grammatically correct. To test the three answers for wordiness, ask yourself this: "Do all of these answers say the same thing? Do any of them omit or distort ideas?" If they all say the same thing and none omits or distorts ideas, then the shortest, simplest answer is the best.

Here are two examples that illustrate how wordiness can be tested in error correction questions:

The cassette recorder is the least expensive form of computer memory storage, but it is also <u>the one that is least efficient in operation</u>.

(A) the one that is least efficient in operation
(B) least efficient in operation
(C) the least efficient
(D) least in efficiency of operation
(E) least in its degree of efficiency

In this question, there are no grammatical errors; all five answers are technically correct. And all five answers say the same thing. But four of the choices are wordy. Choice C, which says the same thing as the others simply and briefly, is the most concise. It's also the clearest and most graceful. As the other choices illustrate, wordy sentences are often clumsy and confusing.

The poems in the Greek Anthology were written over a period of more than one thousand years <u>they were also written in</u> many parts of the ancient world.

(A) they were also written in
(B) as well as having been written in
(C) also they were written throughout
(D) and in
(E) in addition to in

The original sentence here is grammatically incorrect: it's a run-on sentence. Choice C does not correct the run-on, so you can eliminate it from consideration. That leaves you with choices B, D, and E, all of which correct the run-on by changing the second part of the sentence from a clause to a phrase. Since all three of these choices are technically correct, you must base your choice on effectiveness. Of the three possible answers, choice D is the most concise and, therefore, the best answer.

10.9 Logic in Sentence Structure

Like conciseness, logic goes beyond the grammatical correctness of a sentence. It has to do with the meaning of the sentence and the way in which its ideas fit together. There are several ways in which the logic of a sentence can go wrong. In this section, we'll consider the most common logic errors you're likely to encounter on the TSWE.

One type of logical flaw is faulty predication. As you recall, the two major divisions of a sentence are the subject and the predicate. The predicate says something about the subject; it includes the verb and any other necessary words and phrases. *Faulty predication* occurs when the predicate of a sentence doesn't fit logically with the subject. The following example illustrates the problem:

> X According to the president, the reason for the breakdown in arms control negotiations is because of the failure of the Soviet Union to cooperate.

The subject of this sentence is *reason*; the predicate begins with the verb *is*. But notice what goes wrong. If the subject is *reason*, then the predicate should tell what the reason *is*. It doesn't quite do that. Instead, it says that the reason is *because of* something. Do you see why this doesn't add up? A reason should simply be X, not *because of* X. If the sentence were correct, it would say:

> According to the president, the reason for the breakdown in arms control negotiations is the failure of the Soviet Union to cooperate.

Here's a different example of faulty predication:

> X The advantages of the smaller car finally outweighed the larger, roomier sedan that we had been considering.

If you look at the skeleton of this sentence, you'll see the predication problem. The subject is *advantages*, the verb is *outweighed*, and the direct object is *sedan*. Can advantages outweigh a sedan? No. Clearly the author intended to say that the advantages of the smaller car outweighed *those of* (that is, the advantages of) the larger car.

Some other kinds of logical errors crop up in comparisons. Let's look at a couple of examples:

> X The administration of Richard Nixon probably produced more controversy than that of any president in American history.

In this sentence the words *more . . . than* indicate that two elements are being compared. One element is *the administration of Richard Nixon*; the other element is [*the administration*] *of any president in American history*. Can you see why this comparison is illogical? Richard Nixon is included in the group "any president in American history." So the sentence says that his administration was not only more controversial than any other president's but also more controversial than itself, which is absurd. The word *other* needs to be inserted after *any* to make the comparison logical.

> X Professor Carlson's achievements, though not especially noteworthy, were certainly more widely publicized.

In this sentence, the word *more* again implies a comparison: *more widely publicized* than something else. But notice that the something else isn't mentioned. Since the comparison is not completed, the logic of the sentence is faulty. It could be corrected in either of two ways. Either the comparison could be completed, like this:

> Professor Carlson's achievements, though not especially noteworthy, were certainly more widely publicized than those of his colleagues.

Or the implication of a comparison could be eliminated:

> Professor Carlson's achievements, though not especially noteworthy, were certainly widely publicized.

Here's another typical example of faulty logic in a comparison:

> X Roberta's musical abilities are as great, if not greater than, those of her sister.

Ignore the interrupting phrase *if not greater than,* and you'll spot the problem in this sentence immediately: the *as* after *as great* is missing. So the comparison is incomplete. It should read *as great as, if not greater than.* Remember this simple test for logic and completeness: A sentence must make sense with *or without* any matter set off by commas.

We'll conclude this lesson with two examples of how logic errors are tested in the error correction section of the TSWE.

> Experts in sports medicine have found that the same characteristics that lead to success in one sport may be a below-average performer in another sport.
>
> (A) may be a below-average performer
> (B) may be at a below-average level
> (C) are below average in performance
> (D) can be below average in performing
> (E) may lead to below-average performance

The original sentence says that characteristics may *be* a performer, which is illogical. The only answer that corrects the faulty predication is choice E. (The verb *to be—am, are, is, was, were, have been,* and so on—often gives rise to predication problems because it functions as a kind of verbal equal sign. If the two "quantities" that it links aren't logically equal, the result is a faulty "equation." Watch out for faulty verbal equations on the TSWE.)

> Most studies of education agree that the need for better-trained teachers is equal to, if not greater, than the need for more modern facilities.
>
> (A) equal to, if not greater, than
> (B) equal to, if not greater than,
> (C) if not greater than it, equal to
> (D) equal, if not greater, than
> (E) on a par with, if not greater, than

The original sentence is similar to the *as great as, if not greater than* sentence that we just looked at. Again, if you read the sentence without the interrupting phrase *if not greater,* you'll spot the problem immediately: *equal to than the need* doesn't make sense. Here, the problem is not a missing word; it's a misplaced comma. The comma should be after *than,* not before it, so that the sentence makes sense with *or without* the interrupting phrase. (This is an example of a "punctuation error" that is really an error in the logic of a sentence.)

In this lesson we've looked at the errors most common in the error correction section of the TSWE. In Lesson 15, we'll complete our grammar review for the TSWE by looking at some of the errors most common in the usage section.

PART 6

Practice Test 3

PRACTICE TEST 3: *Directions*

This practice test is for you to take after you have studied Lessons 6–10 in this book. By this point in your study program, you have studied most of the important skills and test-taking strategies needed for success on the SAT. You have also taken two previous practice tests. Therefore, your scores on this test should be approaching those you hope to attain on the actual SAT. The answers and scoring instructions for this test begin on page 249. They will help you assess your progress so far. They will also help you determine which earlier lessons you need to review and which SAT skills you need to work on as you continue your study program.

Directions: Set aside $3\frac{1}{2}$ hours without interruption for taking this test. The test is divided into six 30-minute sections. You may wish to use a timer or an alarm to time yourself on each section. Do not work past the 30-minute limit for any section. If you finish a section before time is up, you may check your work on that section, but you are not to work on any other section. You may take a 5-minute break between sections.

Do not worry if you are unable to finish a section or if there are some questions you cannot answer. Do not waste time puzzling over a question that seems too difficult for you. You should work as rapidly as you can without sacrificing accuracy.

Students often ask whether they should guess when they are uncertain about the answer to a question. Your test scores will be based on the number of questions you answer correctly minus a fraction of the number you answer incorrectly. Therefore, it is improbable that random or haphazard guessing will change your scores significantly. If you have some knowledge of a question, you may be able to eliminate one or more of the answer choices as wrong. It is generally to your advantage to guess which of the remaining choices is correct. Remember, however, not to spend too much time on any one question.

Mark all your answers on the answer sheet on the facing page. (For your convenience, you may wish to remove this sheet from the book and keep it in front of you throughout the test.) Mark only one answer for each question. Be sure that each mark is dark and that it completely fills the answer space. In each section of the answer sheet, there are 5 answer spaces for each of 50 questions. When there are fewer than 5 answer choices for a question or fewer than 50 questions in a section of your test, leave the extra answer spaces blank. Do not make stray marks on the answer sheet. If you erase, do so completely.

You may use any available space on the pages of the test for scratchwork. Do not use books, dictionaries, reference materials, calculators, slide rules, or any other aids. Do not look at the answer key or any other parts of this book. It is important to take this practice test in the same way that you will take the actual SAT.

When you have completed all six test sections, turn to the answers and scoring instructions that follow the test.

PRACTICE TEST 3: *Answer Sheet*

REMOVE ANSWER SHEET BY CUTTING ON DOTTED LINE

Directions: Use a No. 2 pencil only for completing this answer sheet. Be sure each mark is dark and completely fills the intended space. Completely erase any errors or stray marks. Start with number 1 for each new section. If a section has fewer than 50 questions or if a question has fewer than 5 answer choices, leave the extra answer spaces blank.

SECTION 1	SECTION 2	SECTION 3	SECTION 4
1 Ⓐ Ⓑ Ⓒ Ⓓ Ⓔ	1 Ⓐ Ⓑ Ⓒ Ⓓ Ⓔ	1 Ⓐ Ⓑ Ⓒ Ⓓ Ⓔ	1 Ⓐ Ⓑ Ⓒ Ⓓ Ⓔ
2 Ⓐ Ⓑ Ⓒ Ⓓ Ⓔ	2 Ⓐ Ⓑ Ⓒ Ⓓ Ⓔ	2 Ⓐ Ⓑ Ⓒ Ⓓ Ⓔ	2 Ⓐ Ⓑ Ⓒ Ⓓ Ⓔ
3 Ⓐ Ⓑ Ⓒ Ⓓ Ⓔ	3 Ⓐ Ⓑ Ⓒ Ⓓ Ⓔ	3 Ⓐ Ⓑ Ⓒ Ⓓ Ⓔ	3 Ⓐ Ⓑ Ⓒ Ⓓ Ⓔ
4 Ⓐ Ⓑ Ⓒ Ⓓ Ⓔ	4 Ⓐ Ⓑ Ⓒ Ⓓ Ⓔ	4 Ⓐ Ⓑ Ⓒ Ⓓ Ⓔ	4 Ⓐ Ⓑ Ⓒ Ⓓ Ⓔ
5 Ⓐ Ⓑ Ⓒ Ⓓ Ⓔ	5 Ⓐ Ⓑ Ⓒ Ⓓ Ⓔ	5 Ⓐ Ⓑ Ⓒ Ⓓ Ⓔ	5 Ⓐ Ⓑ Ⓒ Ⓓ Ⓔ
6 Ⓐ Ⓑ Ⓒ Ⓓ Ⓔ	6 Ⓐ Ⓑ Ⓒ Ⓓ Ⓔ	6 Ⓐ Ⓑ Ⓒ Ⓓ Ⓔ	6 Ⓐ Ⓑ Ⓒ Ⓓ Ⓔ
7 Ⓐ Ⓑ Ⓒ Ⓓ Ⓔ	7 Ⓐ Ⓑ Ⓒ Ⓓ Ⓔ	7 Ⓐ Ⓑ Ⓒ Ⓓ Ⓔ	7 Ⓐ Ⓑ Ⓒ Ⓓ Ⓔ
8 Ⓐ Ⓑ Ⓒ Ⓓ Ⓔ	8 Ⓐ Ⓑ Ⓒ Ⓓ Ⓔ	8 Ⓐ Ⓑ Ⓒ Ⓓ Ⓔ	8 Ⓐ Ⓑ Ⓒ Ⓓ Ⓔ
9 Ⓐ Ⓑ Ⓒ Ⓓ Ⓔ	9 Ⓐ Ⓑ Ⓒ Ⓓ Ⓔ	9 Ⓐ Ⓑ Ⓒ Ⓓ Ⓔ	9 Ⓐ Ⓑ Ⓒ Ⓓ Ⓔ
10 Ⓐ Ⓑ Ⓒ Ⓓ Ⓔ	10 Ⓐ Ⓑ Ⓒ Ⓓ Ⓔ	10 Ⓐ Ⓑ Ⓒ Ⓓ Ⓔ	10 Ⓐ Ⓑ Ⓒ Ⓓ Ⓔ
11 Ⓐ Ⓑ Ⓒ Ⓓ Ⓔ	11 Ⓐ Ⓑ Ⓒ Ⓓ Ⓔ	11 Ⓐ Ⓑ Ⓒ Ⓓ Ⓔ	11 Ⓐ Ⓑ Ⓒ Ⓓ Ⓔ
12 Ⓐ Ⓑ Ⓒ Ⓓ Ⓔ	12 Ⓐ Ⓑ Ⓒ Ⓓ Ⓔ	12 Ⓐ Ⓑ Ⓒ Ⓓ Ⓔ	12 Ⓐ Ⓑ Ⓒ Ⓓ Ⓔ
13 Ⓐ Ⓑ Ⓒ Ⓓ Ⓔ	13 Ⓐ Ⓑ Ⓒ Ⓓ Ⓔ	13 Ⓐ Ⓑ Ⓒ Ⓓ Ⓔ	13 Ⓐ Ⓑ Ⓒ Ⓓ Ⓔ
14 Ⓐ Ⓑ Ⓒ Ⓓ Ⓔ	14 Ⓐ Ⓑ Ⓒ Ⓓ Ⓔ	14 Ⓐ Ⓑ Ⓒ Ⓓ Ⓔ	14 Ⓐ Ⓑ Ⓒ Ⓓ Ⓔ
15 Ⓐ Ⓑ Ⓒ Ⓓ Ⓔ	15 Ⓐ Ⓑ Ⓒ Ⓓ Ⓔ	15 Ⓐ Ⓑ Ⓒ Ⓓ Ⓔ	15 Ⓐ Ⓑ Ⓒ Ⓓ Ⓔ
16 Ⓐ Ⓑ Ⓒ Ⓓ Ⓔ	16 Ⓐ Ⓑ Ⓒ Ⓓ Ⓔ	16 Ⓐ Ⓑ Ⓒ Ⓓ Ⓔ	16 Ⓐ Ⓑ Ⓒ Ⓓ Ⓔ
17 Ⓐ Ⓑ Ⓒ Ⓓ Ⓔ	17 Ⓐ Ⓑ Ⓒ Ⓓ Ⓔ	17 Ⓐ Ⓑ Ⓒ Ⓓ Ⓔ	17 Ⓐ Ⓑ Ⓒ Ⓓ Ⓔ
18 Ⓐ Ⓑ Ⓒ Ⓓ Ⓔ	18 Ⓐ Ⓑ Ⓒ Ⓓ Ⓔ	18 Ⓐ Ⓑ Ⓒ Ⓓ Ⓔ	18 Ⓐ Ⓑ Ⓒ Ⓓ Ⓔ
19 Ⓐ Ⓑ Ⓒ Ⓓ Ⓔ	19 Ⓐ Ⓑ Ⓒ Ⓓ Ⓔ	19 Ⓐ Ⓑ Ⓒ Ⓓ Ⓔ	19 Ⓐ Ⓑ Ⓒ Ⓓ Ⓔ
20 Ⓐ Ⓑ Ⓒ Ⓓ Ⓔ	20 Ⓐ Ⓑ Ⓒ Ⓓ Ⓔ	20 Ⓐ Ⓑ Ⓒ Ⓓ Ⓔ	20 Ⓐ Ⓑ Ⓒ Ⓓ Ⓔ
21 Ⓐ Ⓑ Ⓒ Ⓓ Ⓔ	21 Ⓐ Ⓑ Ⓒ Ⓓ Ⓔ	21 Ⓐ Ⓑ Ⓒ Ⓓ Ⓔ	21 Ⓐ Ⓑ Ⓒ Ⓓ Ⓔ
22 Ⓐ Ⓑ Ⓒ Ⓓ Ⓔ	22 Ⓐ Ⓑ Ⓒ Ⓓ Ⓔ	22 Ⓐ Ⓑ Ⓒ Ⓓ Ⓔ	22 Ⓐ Ⓑ Ⓒ Ⓓ Ⓔ
23 Ⓐ Ⓑ Ⓒ Ⓓ Ⓔ	23 Ⓐ Ⓑ Ⓒ Ⓓ Ⓔ	23 Ⓐ Ⓑ Ⓒ Ⓓ Ⓔ	23 Ⓐ Ⓑ Ⓒ Ⓓ Ⓔ
24 Ⓐ Ⓑ Ⓒ Ⓓ Ⓔ	24 Ⓐ Ⓑ Ⓒ Ⓓ Ⓔ	24 Ⓐ Ⓑ Ⓒ Ⓓ Ⓔ	24 Ⓐ Ⓑ Ⓒ Ⓓ Ⓔ
25 Ⓐ Ⓑ Ⓒ Ⓓ Ⓔ	25 Ⓐ Ⓑ Ⓒ Ⓓ Ⓔ	25 Ⓐ Ⓑ Ⓒ Ⓓ Ⓔ	25 Ⓐ Ⓑ Ⓒ Ⓓ Ⓔ
26 Ⓐ Ⓑ Ⓒ Ⓓ Ⓔ	26 Ⓐ Ⓑ Ⓒ Ⓓ Ⓔ	26 Ⓐ Ⓑ Ⓒ Ⓓ Ⓔ	26 Ⓐ Ⓑ Ⓒ Ⓓ Ⓔ
27 Ⓐ Ⓑ Ⓒ Ⓓ Ⓔ	27 Ⓐ Ⓑ Ⓒ Ⓓ Ⓔ	27 Ⓐ Ⓑ Ⓒ Ⓓ Ⓔ	27 Ⓐ Ⓑ Ⓒ Ⓓ Ⓔ
28 Ⓐ Ⓑ Ⓒ Ⓓ Ⓔ	28 Ⓐ Ⓑ Ⓒ Ⓓ Ⓔ	28 Ⓐ Ⓑ Ⓒ Ⓓ Ⓔ	28 Ⓐ Ⓑ Ⓒ Ⓓ Ⓔ
29 Ⓐ Ⓑ Ⓒ Ⓓ Ⓔ	29 Ⓐ Ⓑ Ⓒ Ⓓ Ⓔ	29 Ⓐ Ⓑ Ⓒ Ⓓ Ⓔ	29 Ⓐ Ⓑ Ⓒ Ⓓ Ⓔ
30 Ⓐ Ⓑ Ⓒ Ⓓ Ⓔ	30 Ⓐ Ⓑ Ⓒ Ⓓ Ⓔ	30 Ⓐ Ⓑ Ⓒ Ⓓ Ⓔ	30 Ⓐ Ⓑ Ⓒ Ⓓ Ⓔ
31 Ⓐ Ⓑ Ⓒ Ⓓ Ⓔ	31 Ⓐ Ⓑ Ⓒ Ⓓ Ⓔ	31 Ⓐ Ⓑ Ⓒ Ⓓ Ⓔ	31 Ⓐ Ⓑ Ⓒ Ⓓ Ⓔ
32 Ⓐ Ⓑ Ⓒ Ⓓ Ⓔ	32 Ⓐ Ⓑ Ⓒ Ⓓ Ⓔ	32 Ⓐ Ⓑ Ⓒ Ⓓ Ⓔ	32 Ⓐ Ⓑ Ⓒ Ⓓ Ⓔ
33 Ⓐ Ⓑ Ⓒ Ⓓ Ⓔ	33 Ⓐ Ⓑ Ⓒ Ⓓ Ⓔ	33 Ⓐ Ⓑ Ⓒ Ⓓ Ⓔ	33 Ⓐ Ⓑ Ⓒ Ⓓ Ⓔ
34 Ⓐ Ⓑ Ⓒ Ⓓ Ⓔ	34 Ⓐ Ⓑ Ⓒ Ⓓ Ⓔ	34 Ⓐ Ⓑ Ⓒ Ⓓ Ⓔ	34 Ⓐ Ⓑ Ⓒ Ⓓ Ⓔ
35 Ⓐ Ⓑ Ⓒ Ⓓ Ⓔ	35 Ⓐ Ⓑ Ⓒ Ⓓ Ⓔ	35 Ⓐ Ⓑ Ⓒ Ⓓ Ⓔ	35 Ⓐ Ⓑ Ⓒ Ⓓ Ⓔ
36 Ⓐ Ⓑ Ⓒ Ⓓ Ⓔ	36 Ⓐ Ⓑ Ⓒ Ⓓ Ⓔ	36 Ⓐ Ⓑ Ⓒ Ⓓ Ⓔ	36 Ⓐ Ⓑ Ⓒ Ⓓ Ⓔ
37 Ⓐ Ⓑ Ⓒ Ⓓ Ⓔ	37 Ⓐ Ⓑ Ⓒ Ⓓ Ⓔ	37 Ⓐ Ⓑ Ⓒ Ⓓ Ⓔ	37 Ⓐ Ⓑ Ⓒ Ⓓ Ⓔ
38 Ⓐ Ⓑ Ⓒ Ⓓ Ⓔ	38 Ⓐ Ⓑ Ⓒ Ⓓ Ⓔ	38 Ⓐ Ⓑ Ⓒ Ⓓ Ⓔ	38 Ⓐ Ⓑ Ⓒ Ⓓ Ⓔ
39 Ⓐ Ⓑ Ⓒ Ⓓ Ⓔ	39 Ⓐ Ⓑ Ⓒ Ⓓ Ⓔ	39 Ⓐ Ⓑ Ⓒ Ⓓ Ⓔ	39 Ⓐ Ⓑ Ⓒ Ⓓ Ⓔ
40 Ⓐ Ⓑ Ⓒ Ⓓ Ⓔ	40 Ⓐ Ⓑ Ⓒ Ⓓ Ⓔ	40 Ⓐ Ⓑ Ⓒ Ⓓ Ⓔ	40 Ⓐ Ⓑ Ⓒ Ⓓ Ⓔ
41 Ⓐ Ⓑ Ⓒ Ⓓ Ⓔ	41 Ⓐ Ⓑ Ⓒ Ⓓ Ⓔ	41 Ⓐ Ⓑ Ⓒ Ⓓ Ⓔ	41 Ⓐ Ⓑ Ⓒ Ⓓ Ⓔ
42 Ⓐ Ⓑ Ⓒ Ⓓ Ⓔ	42 Ⓐ Ⓑ Ⓒ Ⓓ Ⓔ	42 Ⓐ Ⓑ Ⓒ Ⓓ Ⓔ	42 Ⓐ Ⓑ Ⓒ Ⓓ Ⓔ
43 Ⓐ Ⓑ Ⓒ Ⓓ Ⓔ	43 Ⓐ Ⓑ Ⓒ Ⓓ Ⓔ	43 Ⓐ Ⓑ Ⓒ Ⓓ Ⓔ	43 Ⓐ Ⓑ Ⓒ Ⓓ Ⓔ
44 Ⓐ Ⓑ Ⓒ Ⓓ Ⓔ	44 Ⓐ Ⓑ Ⓒ Ⓓ Ⓔ	44 Ⓐ Ⓑ Ⓒ Ⓓ Ⓔ	44 Ⓐ Ⓑ Ⓒ Ⓓ Ⓔ
45 Ⓐ Ⓑ Ⓒ Ⓓ Ⓔ	45 Ⓐ Ⓑ Ⓒ Ⓓ Ⓔ	45 Ⓐ Ⓑ Ⓒ Ⓓ Ⓔ	45 Ⓐ Ⓑ Ⓒ Ⓓ Ⓔ
46 Ⓐ Ⓑ Ⓒ Ⓓ Ⓔ	46 Ⓐ Ⓑ Ⓒ Ⓓ Ⓔ	46 Ⓐ Ⓑ Ⓒ Ⓓ Ⓔ	46 Ⓐ Ⓑ Ⓒ Ⓓ Ⓔ
47 Ⓐ Ⓑ Ⓒ Ⓓ Ⓔ	47 Ⓐ Ⓑ Ⓒ Ⓓ Ⓔ	47 Ⓐ Ⓑ Ⓒ Ⓓ Ⓔ	47 Ⓐ Ⓑ Ⓒ Ⓓ Ⓔ
48 Ⓐ Ⓑ Ⓒ Ⓓ Ⓔ	48 Ⓐ Ⓑ Ⓒ Ⓓ Ⓔ	48 Ⓐ Ⓑ Ⓒ Ⓓ Ⓔ	48 Ⓐ Ⓑ Ⓒ Ⓓ Ⓔ
49 Ⓐ Ⓑ Ⓒ Ⓓ Ⓔ	49 Ⓐ Ⓑ Ⓒ Ⓓ Ⓔ	49 Ⓐ Ⓑ Ⓒ Ⓓ Ⓔ	49 Ⓐ Ⓑ Ⓒ Ⓓ Ⓔ
50 Ⓐ Ⓑ Ⓒ Ⓓ Ⓔ	50 Ⓐ Ⓑ Ⓒ Ⓓ Ⓔ	50 Ⓐ Ⓑ Ⓒ Ⓓ Ⓔ	50 Ⓐ Ⓑ Ⓒ Ⓓ Ⓔ

SECTION 5

1	Ⓐ	Ⓑ	Ⓒ	Ⓓ	Ⓔ	26	Ⓐ	Ⓑ	Ⓒ	Ⓓ	Ⓔ
2	Ⓐ	Ⓑ	Ⓒ	Ⓓ	Ⓔ	27	Ⓐ	Ⓑ	Ⓒ	Ⓓ	Ⓔ
3	Ⓐ	Ⓑ	Ⓒ	Ⓓ	Ⓔ	28	Ⓐ	Ⓑ	Ⓒ	Ⓓ	Ⓔ
4	Ⓐ	Ⓑ	Ⓒ	Ⓓ	Ⓔ	29	Ⓐ	Ⓑ	Ⓒ	Ⓓ	Ⓔ
5	Ⓐ	Ⓑ	Ⓒ	Ⓓ	Ⓔ	30	Ⓐ	Ⓑ	Ⓒ	Ⓓ	Ⓔ
6	Ⓐ	Ⓑ	Ⓒ	Ⓓ	Ⓔ	31	Ⓐ	Ⓑ	Ⓒ	Ⓓ	Ⓔ
7	Ⓐ	Ⓑ	Ⓒ	Ⓓ	Ⓔ	32	Ⓐ	Ⓑ	Ⓒ	Ⓓ	Ⓔ
8	Ⓐ	Ⓑ	Ⓒ	Ⓓ	Ⓔ	33	Ⓐ	Ⓑ	Ⓒ	Ⓓ	Ⓔ
9	Ⓐ	Ⓑ	Ⓒ	Ⓓ	Ⓔ	34	Ⓐ	Ⓑ	Ⓒ	Ⓓ	Ⓔ
10	Ⓐ	Ⓑ	Ⓒ	Ⓓ	Ⓔ	35	Ⓐ	Ⓑ	Ⓒ	Ⓓ	Ⓔ
11	Ⓐ	Ⓑ	Ⓒ	Ⓓ	Ⓔ	36	Ⓐ	Ⓑ	Ⓒ	Ⓓ	Ⓔ
12	Ⓐ	Ⓑ	Ⓒ	Ⓓ	Ⓔ	37	Ⓐ	Ⓑ	Ⓒ	Ⓓ	Ⓔ
13	Ⓐ	Ⓑ	Ⓒ	Ⓓ	Ⓔ	38	Ⓐ	Ⓑ	Ⓒ	Ⓓ	Ⓔ
14	Ⓐ	Ⓑ	Ⓒ	Ⓓ	Ⓔ	39	Ⓐ	Ⓑ	Ⓒ	Ⓓ	Ⓔ
15	Ⓐ	Ⓑ	Ⓒ	Ⓓ	Ⓔ	40	Ⓐ	Ⓑ	Ⓒ	Ⓓ	Ⓔ
16	Ⓐ	Ⓑ	Ⓒ	Ⓓ	Ⓔ	41	Ⓐ	Ⓑ	Ⓒ	Ⓓ	Ⓔ
17	Ⓐ	Ⓑ	Ⓒ	Ⓓ	Ⓔ	42	Ⓐ	Ⓑ	Ⓒ	Ⓓ	Ⓔ
18	Ⓐ	Ⓑ	Ⓒ	Ⓓ	Ⓔ	43	Ⓐ	Ⓑ	Ⓒ	Ⓓ	Ⓔ
19	Ⓐ	Ⓑ	Ⓒ	Ⓓ	Ⓔ	44	Ⓐ	Ⓑ	Ⓒ	Ⓓ	Ⓔ
20	Ⓐ	Ⓑ	Ⓒ	Ⓓ	Ⓔ	45	Ⓐ	Ⓑ	Ⓒ	Ⓓ	Ⓔ
21	Ⓐ	Ⓑ	Ⓒ	Ⓓ	Ⓔ	46	Ⓐ	Ⓑ	Ⓒ	Ⓓ	Ⓔ
22	Ⓐ	Ⓑ	Ⓒ	Ⓓ	Ⓔ	47	Ⓐ	Ⓑ	Ⓒ	Ⓓ	Ⓔ
23	Ⓐ	Ⓑ	Ⓒ	Ⓓ	Ⓔ	48	Ⓐ	Ⓑ	Ⓒ	Ⓓ	Ⓔ
24	Ⓐ	Ⓑ	Ⓒ	Ⓓ	Ⓔ	49	Ⓐ	Ⓑ	Ⓒ	Ⓓ	Ⓔ
25	Ⓐ	Ⓑ	Ⓒ	Ⓓ	Ⓔ	50	Ⓐ	Ⓑ	Ⓒ	Ⓓ	Ⓔ

SECTION 6

1	Ⓐ	Ⓑ	Ⓒ	Ⓓ	Ⓔ	26	Ⓐ	Ⓑ	Ⓒ	Ⓓ	Ⓔ
2	Ⓐ	Ⓑ	Ⓒ	Ⓓ	Ⓔ	27	Ⓐ	Ⓑ	Ⓒ	Ⓓ	Ⓔ
3	Ⓐ	Ⓑ	Ⓒ	Ⓓ	Ⓔ	28	Ⓐ	Ⓑ	Ⓒ	Ⓓ	Ⓔ
4	Ⓐ	Ⓑ	Ⓒ	Ⓓ	Ⓔ	29	Ⓐ	Ⓑ	Ⓒ	Ⓓ	Ⓔ
5	Ⓐ	Ⓑ	Ⓒ	Ⓓ	Ⓔ	30	Ⓐ	Ⓑ	Ⓒ	Ⓓ	Ⓔ
6	Ⓐ	Ⓑ	Ⓒ	Ⓓ	Ⓔ	31	Ⓐ	Ⓑ	Ⓒ	Ⓓ	Ⓔ
7	Ⓐ	Ⓑ	Ⓒ	Ⓓ	Ⓔ	32	Ⓐ	Ⓑ	Ⓒ	Ⓓ	Ⓔ
8	Ⓐ	Ⓑ	Ⓒ	Ⓓ	Ⓔ	33	Ⓐ	Ⓑ	Ⓒ	Ⓓ	Ⓔ
9	Ⓐ	Ⓑ	Ⓒ	Ⓓ	Ⓔ	34	Ⓐ	Ⓑ	Ⓒ	Ⓓ	Ⓔ
10	Ⓐ	Ⓑ	Ⓒ	Ⓓ	Ⓔ	35	Ⓐ	Ⓑ	Ⓒ	Ⓓ	Ⓔ
11	Ⓐ	Ⓑ	Ⓒ	Ⓓ	Ⓔ	36	Ⓐ	Ⓑ	Ⓒ	Ⓓ	Ⓔ
12	Ⓐ	Ⓑ	Ⓒ	Ⓓ	Ⓔ	37	Ⓐ	Ⓑ	Ⓒ	Ⓓ	Ⓔ
13	Ⓐ	Ⓑ	Ⓒ	Ⓓ	Ⓔ	38	Ⓐ	Ⓑ	Ⓒ	Ⓓ	Ⓔ
14	Ⓐ	Ⓑ	Ⓒ	Ⓓ	Ⓔ	39	Ⓐ	Ⓑ	Ⓒ	Ⓓ	Ⓔ
15	Ⓐ	Ⓑ	Ⓒ	Ⓓ	Ⓔ	40	Ⓐ	Ⓑ	Ⓒ	Ⓓ	Ⓔ
16	Ⓐ	Ⓑ	Ⓒ	Ⓓ	Ⓔ	41	Ⓐ	Ⓑ	Ⓒ	Ⓓ	Ⓔ
17	Ⓐ	Ⓑ	Ⓒ	Ⓓ	Ⓔ	42	Ⓐ	Ⓑ	Ⓒ	Ⓓ	Ⓔ
18	Ⓐ	Ⓑ	Ⓒ	Ⓓ	Ⓔ	43	Ⓐ	Ⓑ	Ⓒ	Ⓓ	Ⓔ
19	Ⓐ	Ⓑ	Ⓒ	Ⓓ	Ⓔ	44	Ⓐ	Ⓑ	Ⓒ	Ⓓ	Ⓔ
20	Ⓐ	Ⓑ	Ⓒ	Ⓓ	Ⓔ	45	Ⓐ	Ⓑ	Ⓒ	Ⓓ	Ⓔ
21	Ⓐ	Ⓑ	Ⓒ	Ⓓ	Ⓔ	46	Ⓐ	Ⓑ	Ⓒ	Ⓓ	Ⓔ
22	Ⓐ	Ⓑ	Ⓒ	Ⓓ	Ⓔ	47	Ⓐ	Ⓑ	Ⓒ	Ⓓ	Ⓔ
23	Ⓐ	Ⓑ	Ⓒ	Ⓓ	Ⓔ	48	Ⓐ	Ⓑ	Ⓒ	Ⓓ	Ⓔ
24	Ⓐ	Ⓑ	Ⓒ	Ⓓ	Ⓔ	49	Ⓐ	Ⓑ	Ⓒ	Ⓓ	Ⓔ
25	Ⓐ	Ⓑ	Ⓒ	Ⓓ	Ⓔ	50	Ⓐ	Ⓑ	Ⓒ	Ⓓ	Ⓔ

SECTION 1

Time—30 minutes

45 QUESTIONS

For each question in this section, choose the best answer and blacken the corresponding space on the answer sheet.

Each question below consists of a word in capital letters, followed by five lettered words or phrases. Choose the word or phrase that is most nearly opposite in meaning to the word in capital letters. Since some of the questions require you to distinguish fine shades of meaning, consider all the choices before deciding which is best.

Example:

GOOD: (A) sour (B) bad (C) red (D) hot (E) ugly

Ⓐ ● Ⓒ Ⓓ Ⓔ

1. ALLAY: (A) exacerbate (B) dismay (C) terrorize (D) invoke (E) blacken

2. ARTICULATE: (A) casual (B) obscure (C) incoherent (D) simpering (E) dull

3. OPAQUE: (A) prismatic (B) diaphanous (C) visible (D) refulgent (E) intangible

4. FETTER: (A) emancipate (B) rebel (C) escape (D) extend (E) revive

5. PROFICIENT: (A) careless (B) inexperienced (C) inappropriate (D) unskilled (E) hesitant

6. NONPARTISAN: (A) variegated (B) undivided (C) nominal (D) illicit (E) factional

7. ATROCIOUS: (A) fierce (B) admirable (C) normal (D) vivid (E) mottled

8. NULLIFY: (A) restate (B) notify (C) validate (D) promulgate (E) sign

9. PALATABLE: (A) culinary (B) garish (C) noxious (D) unflavored (E) bland

10. EMINENT: (A) unlikely (B) ill-favored (C) depressed (D) little-known (E) mythical

11. DESULTORY: (A) blank (B) sharp (C) pronounced (D) formal (E) determined

12. DUPLICITY: (A) simplicity (B) intelligence (C) incredulousness (D) unity (E) straightforwardness

13. BANAL: (A) brilliant (B) extraordinary (C) flagrant (D) notable (E) crucial

14. PRISTINE: (A) spoiled (B) vicious (C) faded (D) discolored (E) blended

15. CAPTIOUS: (A) yielding (B) indulgent (C) tactful (D) undesirable (E) indignant

Each sentence below has one or two blanks, each blank indicating that something has been omitted. Beneath the sentence are five lettered words or sets of words. Choose the word or set of words that best fits the meaning of the sentence as a whole.

Example:

Although its publicity has been ----, the film itself is intelligent, well-acted, handsomely produced, and altogether ----.

(A) tasteless..respectable (B) extensive..moderate (C) sophisticated..amateur (D) risqué..crude (E) perfect..spectacular

● Ⓑ Ⓒ Ⓓ Ⓔ

16. The songs of birds, like human languages, appear to develop ---- variations; for birds of the same species sing differently depending on their exact place of origin.

(A) familial (B) purposeful (C) genetic (D) numerous (E) geographic

17. Unlike the ---- pacifist, who regards nonviolence as a moral end in itself, the secular pacifist considers it simply one ---- of political struggle among many that may be adopted.

(A) sincere..method
(B) traditional..by-product
(C) conventional..goal
(D) religious..means
(E) spiritual..purpose

18. Marston's fine teaching is well known, but his ---- record of academic publication has led to ---- of his seriousness as a scholar.

(A) remarkable..consideration
(B) slender..notice
(C) dismal..praise
(D) scanty..disparagement
(E) extensive..questioning

19. The current oil glut should not obscure the fact that a worldwide depletion of oil reserves is ----; for world oil supplies are being used more ---- than they can possibly be replaced.

(A) likely..carelessly
(B) inevitable..quickly
(C) imminent..often
(D) improbable..rapidly
(E) unattainable..easily

GO ON TO THE NEXT PAGE

20. Neither anthropologist consciously distorted the facts in describing this remote tribe, but each ---- the available information in accordance with his particular ----.

(A) augmented..background
(B) revised..abilities
(C) interpreted..viewpoint
(D) twisted..bias
(E) altered..opinions

Each passage below is followed by questions based on its content. Answer all questions following a passage on the basis of what is stated or implied in that passage.

For at least 10,000 years—since long before the principles of classical genetics were scientifically established—human beings have brought about deliberate genetic changes in plants and animals through traditional reproductive methods. Many of the domestic animals, crops, and ornamental plants in existence today are human creations, achieved through selective breeding aimed at enhancing desired characteristics. In a broad sense, such genetic manipulation by breeding for a desired outcome might be considered "genetic engineering."

In addition to these intended changes, many alterations have occurred inadvertently through other practices, including the ordinary practice of medicine. Many people with genetic disorders who in the past would have died without any natural-born children now live into adulthood, passing on genes for their disorders. The use of insulin to treat diabetes and the prescription of eyeglasses for myopia are two examples of interventions that increase the prevalence in the population of certain genes that can have deleterious effects on individuals. Medical screening for genetic disorders, when leading to changes in reproductive behavior, also affects the occurrence of genes in the population. These changes have been by-products of medical and technological interventions aimed at individuals, not at the general population.

In 1965, the term *genetic engineering* was coined for what has come to be a wide range of techniques by which scientists can add genetically determined characteristics to cells that would not otherwise have possessed them. Compared with traditional means of altering the gene pool, the ability to alter genetic material directly offers specificity and, in the case of changes in germ cells, speed.

The rapidity with which this field has developed is startling. Scientists' understanding of the structure of deoxyribonucleic acid (DNA), which is common to almost all living cells, and their discovery of its remarkable capacity for encoding and passing on genetic characteristics are both relatively recent developments. In the early 1970s, scientists learned how to isolate specific DNA sequences from one species and attach this genetic material—*recombinant DNA*—to a different species. Rapid progress has also been made with cell fusion, another means of genetic engineering that permits the contents of two cells from different organisms to be merged in such a way that the hybrid cell continues to function and reproduce. These and other techniques hold the potential for producing dramatic changes in the genetic makeup of many species of plants and animals, including humans.

21. The passage is mainly concerned with

(A) clarifying the meaning of a scientific theory
(B) presenting evidence to support an unorthodox point of view
(C) summarizing the historical development of a scientific process
(D) refuting a widely held scientific misconception
(E) explaining the purposes of a technological process

22. According to the passage, the term *genetic engineering*, as coined in 1965, would include which of the following?

I. Medical screening for genetic disorders
II. Direct manipulation of cellular genetic materials
III. Genetic changes brought about through selective breeding

(A) I only
(B) II only
(C) I and II only
(D) I and III only
(E) I, II, and III

23. According to the passage, the earliest practitioners of selective breeding

(A) were able to produce only a highly limited number of genetic changes
(B) had no way of predicting the reproductive effects that their efforts would have
(C) were among the first to understand the structure of the genetic material in cells
(D) did not comprehend the genetic principles underlying their activities
(E) had no intention of bringing about the changes in species that they actually produced

24. The passage implies that the use of insulin to treat diabetes has resulted in

(A) an increase in the number of people genetically predisposed to diabetes
(B) a decrease in the survival rate of diabetic individuals
(C) the gene for diabetes becoming biologically useful rather than deleterious
(D) a decrease in the number of people considered diabetic
(E) an increase in the need for genetic screening of diabetic individuals

GO ON TO THE NEXT PAGE

25. It can be inferred from the passage that the development of recombinant DNA technology was most directly dependent on the

(A) rapid progress in cell fusion technology
(B) development of medical screening for genetic disorders
(C) coining of the term *genetic engineering*
(D) discovery of the structure and function of DNA
(E) improvement of traditional breeding techniques

The Iroquois developed the highest form of governmental organization of any Native American people north of Mexico. The Iroquois League was a loose confederation of member tribes with a council composed of fifty sachems. The sachems, whose titles belonged to various matrilineal families within the five tribes' several clans, usually held office for life.

Emphasizing both individual dignity and the power of the clan, the Iroquois League maintained local self-rule under a central government and developed a powerful defensive alliance. Though the league dealt with matters of war and foreign relations, it did not interfere in internal tribal affairs. In council, no action was taken without unanimous approval. It is believed that the writers of the U.S. Constitution were inspired by the league's highly developed sociopolitical organization and ideals.

Established around 1570, the Iroquois League immediately made its military power felt. It protected its members from attack by one another and gained a monopoly on the fur trade by overpowering such neighboring tribes as the Eries and Hurons. After acquiring firearms—first from the Dutch, then from the British—the league strengthened its power until its domain extended from Ottawa to the Tennessee River and as far west as Lake Michigan and the Illinois River. Despite losses in war, the league maintained its numerical strength by the Iroquois custom of adopting other tribes and remnants of tribes.

League warfare was intensified during the Colonial period. Iroquois leaders were astute diplomats, and armed Iroquois warriors became a force to be reckoned with in the struggle for the New World. Allied with the British during the French and Indian Wars, the league was decisive in breaking French power.

With the coming of the American Revolution, most Iroquois tribes continued their alliance with the British, partly due to the persuasion of Mohawk warrior Joseph Brant (Thayendanegea). However, the Oneidas and most of the Tuscaroras either fought on the American side or remained neutral. This split marked the end of the Iroquois League as a unified power.

26. The passage provides information to answer which of the following questions?

(A) How did the British win Iroquois support during the French and Indian Wars?
(B) Over what issue was the unity of the Iroquois League finally broken?
(C) What was the approximate population of the Iroquois League at the time of its greatest extent?
(D) How were the leaders of the individual Iroquois League tribes chosen?
(E) Why did the Oneidas side with the Americans during the Revolutionary War?

27. Which of the following political structures would probably most closely resemble the Iroquois League?

(A) An association of independent countries sharing some common administrative functions, such as postal service
(B) A federation of states under the control of a powerful centralized government
(C) A council of ministers from several countries charged with negotiating commercial agreements
(D) A unified nation subdivided for administrative purposes into many identically run districts
(E) A group of independent nations united by treaty for mutual self-defense

28. According to the passage, when a sachem died, his place on the council of the Iroquois League was taken by

(A) a successor elected by the remaining members of the council
(B) his eldest son
(C) a member of another tribe
(D) another member of his family
(E) the next oldest fellow tribesman

29. According to the passage, all of the following were characteristics of the Iroquois League EXCEPT

(A) a ban on internal warfare
(B) an emphasis on unity in decision making
(C) a system of balances among the various branches of government
(D) an aggressive foreign policy
(E) a representative form of self-government

30. The author's attitude toward the Iroquois League may best be described as one of

(A) romantic nostalgia
(B) approval and admiration
(C) profound skepticism
(D) disguised contempt
(E) balanced approval and disapproval

GO ON TO THE NEXT PAGE

Select the word or set of words that best completes each of the following sentences.

31. The city's aging and ---- water supply system has been increasingly subject to ---- in recent years.

(A) poorly maintained..breakdowns
(B) costly..improvements
(C) efficient..criticism
(D) extensive..enlargement
(E) highly regarded..accidents

32. Behavioral psychologists are reluctant to discuss any aspect of human activity that cannot be directly observed; as a result, they have little to say concerning individual ----.

(A) relationships (B) communication (C) motivations (D) actions (E) behavior

33. While industrialization had blighted the neighboring towns and villages, East Henry had remained ----, a veritable rural ----.

(A) undeveloped..paradise
(B) peaceful..hamlet
(C) impoverished..backwater
(D) agricultural..shantytown
(E) uninhabited..desert

34. The classes are designed for a variety of participants ranging from the computer ---- to the sophisticated user in situations as ---- as elementary classrooms and national policymaking boards.

(A) illiterate..unusual
(B) enthusiast..various
(C) neophyte..peculiar
(D) amateur..numerous
(E) novice..diverse

35. Although the statement is ----, it is basically true that "Milton never repeated a form"; that is, he wrote only one significant work in each of the poetic ---- he attempted.

(A) false..modes
(B) oversimplified..genres
(C) surprising..creations
(D) obvious..styles
(E) exaggerated..eras

Each question below consists of a related pair of words or phrases, followed by five lettered pairs of words or phrases. Select the lettered pair that best expresses a relationship similar to that expressed in the original pair.

Example:

YAWN:BOREDOM:: (A) dream:sleep
(B) anger:madness (C) smile:amusement
(D) face:expression (E) impatience:rebellion

36. BASE:APEX:: (A) toe:heel
(B) foundation:structure (C) bottom:point
(D) foot:crown (E) abyss:slope

37. BARREN:FIELD:: (A) idle:labor
(B) colorless:landscape (C) dry:desert
(D) fruitless:orchard (E) sterile:offspring

38. GLANCE:EYE:: (A) sniff:nose
(B) swallow:throat (C) nibble:food
(D) comb:hair (E) eavesdrop:ear

39. GULLIBLE:FOOLISH::
(A) lazy:slow
(B) shrewd:unscrupulous
(C) innocent:cunning
(D) ingenuous:intelligent
(E) rational:sensible

40. REGIME:OVERTHROW::
(A) administration:oppose (B) royalty:behead
(C) military:suppress (D) president:elect
(E) incumbent:unseat

41. DELIBERATE:CHANCE:: (A) formless:chaos
(B) organized:disorder (C) random:sequence
(D) purposeful:reason
(E) meaningful:obscurity

42. HUNTER:POACH:: (A) hiker:trespass
(B) driver:crash (C) student:fail
(D) judge:condemn (E) archer:shoot

43. CONDOLENCE:GRIEF:: (A) emollient:burn
(B) sympathy:concern (C) relief:anxiety
(D) understanding:puzzlement
(E) joy:aggravation

44. TRACK:TIES:: (A) rail:spikes
(B) crossbar:uprights (C) dial:hands
(D) spoke:wheels (E) ladder:rungs

45. TAUNT:IRRITATION::
(A) denounce:disagreement
(B) praise:esteem
(C) degrade:humiliation
(D) tease:amusement
(E) embarrass:hatred

S T O P

IF YOU FINISH BEFORE TIME IS CALLED, YOU MAY CHECK YOUR WORK ON THIS SECTION ONLY. DO NOT WORK ON ANY OTHER SECTION IN THE TEST.

SECTION 2

Time—30 minutes

25 QUESTIONS

In this section solve each problem, using any available space on the page for scratchwork. Then indicate the one correct answer in the appropriate space on the answer sheet.

The following information is for your reference in solving some of the problems.

Circle of radius r: Area $= \pi r^2$; Circumference $= 2\pi r$
The number of degrees of arc in a circle is 360.
The measure in degrees of a straight angle is 180.

Definitions of symbols:

$=$	is equal to	$\leq$	is less than or equal to
$\neq$	is unequal to	$\geq$	is greater than or equal to
$<$	is less than	$\parallel$	is parallel to
$>$	is greater than	$\perp$	is perpendicular to

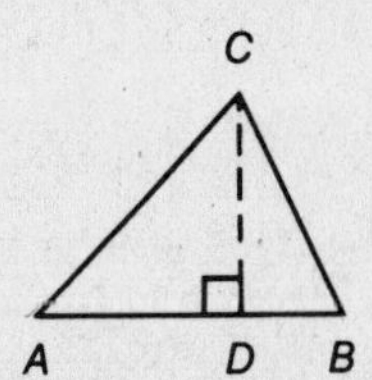

Triangle: The sum of the measures in degrees of the angles of a triangle is 180.

If $\angle CDA$ is a right angle, then

(1) area of $\triangle ABC = \dfrac{AB \times CD}{2}$

(2) $AC^2 = AD^2 + DC^2$

Note: Figures which accompany problems in this test are intended to provide information useful in solving the problems. They are drawn as accurately as possible EXCEPT when it is stated in a specific problem that its figure is not drawn to scale. All figures lie in a plane unless otherwise indicated. All numbers used are real numbers.

---

1. If $\frac{7}{5} = \frac{4}{x}$, then $x =$

(A) $\frac{7}{20}$ (B) $\frac{4}{7}$ (C) $\frac{7}{5}$ (D) $\frac{20}{7}$ (E) $\frac{28}{5}$

2. If n is a positive integer, then which of the following must be divisible by 3?

(A) $9n - 6$ (B) $\frac{3n}{3}$ (C) $2n + 1$
(D) $3n - 1$ (E) n^3

3. A store owner buys T-shirts for \$16.00 a dozen and sells them for \$3.50 each. If there are no other expenses, what will the total profit be on sales of 60 T-shirts?

(A) \$142.00 (B) \$130.00 (C) \$118.00
(D) \$106.00 (E) \$98.00

4. Four liters of ammonia are added to a tank of water, producing a cleaning solution that is 20% ammonia. How much more ammonia, in liters, must be added to increase the strength of the solution to 25%?

(A) 1 (B) $1\frac{1}{4}$ (C) $1\frac{1}{3}$ (D) $1\frac{1}{2}$ (E) 2

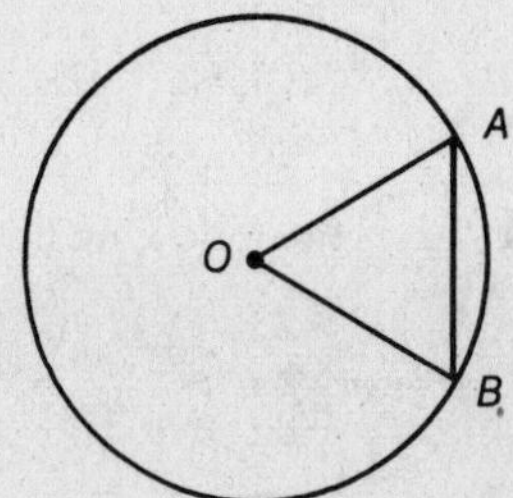

5. In circle O above, OAB is an equilateral triangle with side 9. What is the length of arc AB?

(A) 9π (B) 6π (C) 3π (D) $\frac{3\pi}{2}$ (E) π

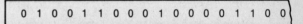

---

0 1 0 0 1 1 0 0 0 1 0 0 0 0 1 1 0 0

6. The figure above represents a strip of paper on which 0s and 1s have been printed from left to right according to a certain pattern. If the pattern continues, the next three digits on the right will read

(A) 000 (B) 001 (C) 010
(D) 100 (E) 011

GO ON TO THE NEXT PAGE

7. If $2^6 - 2^x = 2^5$, then $x =$

(A) 1 (B) 2 (C) 3 (D) 4 (E) 5

8. What is the area of the largest possible circle that can be drawn inside a rectangle that has a length of 10 and a width of 6?

(A) 6π (B) 8π (C) 9π (D) 25π (E) 36π

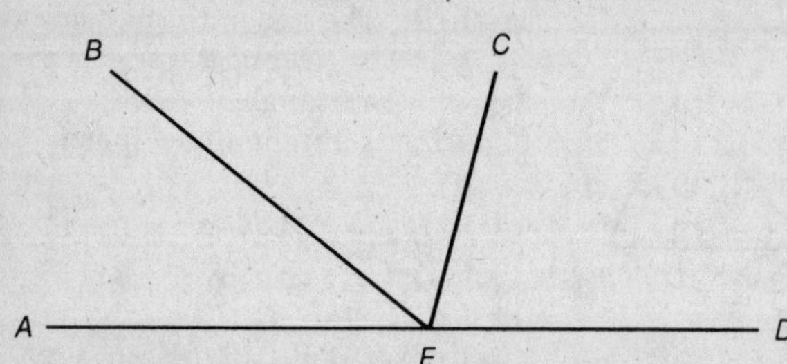

9. In the figure above, AED is a line segment. If $\measuredangle AEC$ has a degree measure of 105 and $\measuredangle BED$ has a degree measure of 142, what is the degree measure of $\measuredangle BEC$?

(A) 58 (B) 60 (C) 63 (D) 67 (E) 71

Questions 10–11 refer to the following definition.

For any real number n, $\oplus n = \dfrac{n^2 + 1}{n + 1}$.

10. $\oplus 3 =$

(A) $\frac{5}{2}$ (B) 3 (C) $\frac{10}{3}$ (D) 5 (E) $\frac{4}{3}$

11. $\dfrac{\oplus 4}{\oplus 2} =$

(A) $\frac{17}{5}$ (B) $\frac{51}{25}$ (C) $\frac{17}{25}$ (D) $\frac{32}{9}$ (E) $\frac{15}{17}$

12. If $x + 2 = 0$ and $y - 2 = 0$, then $\dfrac{x}{y} - \dfrac{y}{x} =$

(A) 2 (B) 0 (C) -1 (D) -2 (E) -4

13. Todd is twice as old as Alan. When Todd was 7 years older than Alan is now, he was three times as old as Alan. How old is Todd?

(A) 32 (B) 28 (C) 24 (D) 20 (E) 16

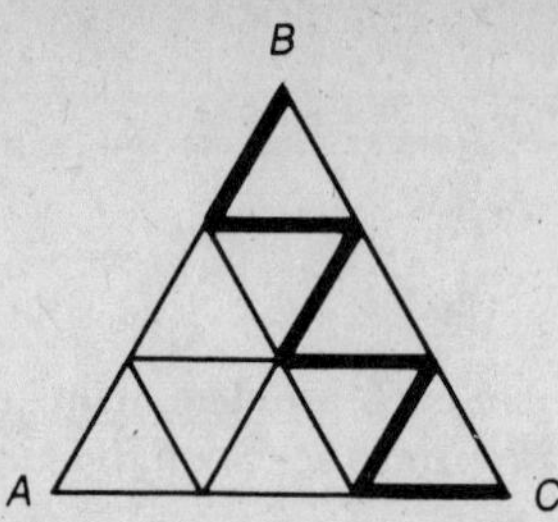

14. In the figure above, triangle ABC is an equilateral triangle with side 6 divided as shown into smaller equilateral triangles of equal size. What is the total length of the darkened path from vertex B to vertex C?

(A) 6 (B) 9 (C) 12 (D) 15 (E) 18

	Games Won	Games Lost
Team A	24	18
Team B	25	21

15. The chart above shows the records of two teams in a sports league. Team B will have won the same percentage of its games as Team A has won so far if Team B

(A) loses its next 2 games
(B) wins its next game
(C) wins 2 of its next 3 games
(D) loses its next game
(E) wins its next 3 games

16. If Bob works 8 hours at an hourly salary of d dollars and c cents, his total salary for the 8 hours will equal how many dollars?

(A) $\dfrac{8(d + c)}{100}$ (B) $8d + 800c$ (C) $8d + \dfrac{2c}{25}$

(D) $8d + \dfrac{c}{100}$ (E) $\dfrac{8d}{100} + 8c$

17. If $x = 4$ and $y = \dfrac{3x}{2}$, then which of the following equals 8?

(A) $2y - x$ (B) $\dfrac{2x}{2} + y$ (C) $\dfrac{x + y}{2}$

(D) $x + y$ (E) $\dfrac{y}{x} + 4$

GO ON TO THE NEXT PAGE

18. What is the volume in cubic inches of a rectangular solid with edges of $\frac{1}{2}$ foot, $\frac{1}{3}$ foot, and $\frac{1}{4}$ foot?

(A) $\frac{1}{2}$ (B) 6 (C) 24 (D) 36 (E) 72

19. Two trains leave the same city and travel due east. Train A departs at 3 P.M. and travels at a rate of 50 miles per hour. Train B departs at 4:30 P.M. and overtakes Train A at exactly 7 P.M. the same day. What is the rate in miles per hour at which Train B is traveling?

(A) 65 (B) 70 (C) 80 (D) 86 (E) 90

20. If $x < y < 0$, then which of the following must have a value greater than 1?

(A) $x \times y$ (B) $x - y$ (C) $\frac{y}{x}$

(D) $y - x$ (E) $\frac{x}{y}$

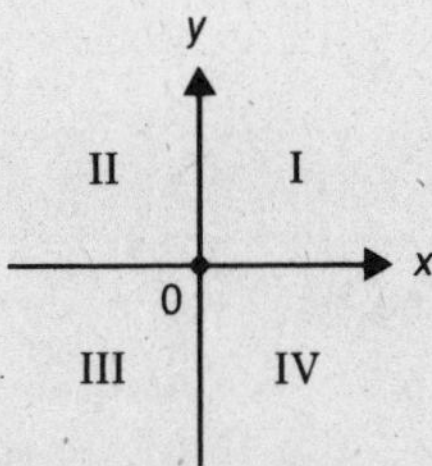

21. In the figure above, which quadrants contain pairs (x, y) such that $x \times y$ is negative?

(A) II only (B) III only (C) I and III only
(D) II and IV only (E) I, II, III, and IV

22. Eight cards numbered 1 to 8 are in a pile. Two cards are drawn whose sum is 13. The remaining cards must include each of the following EXCEPT the card numbered

(A) 1 (B) 2 (C) 3 (D) 4 (E) 5

23. If $\frac{x}{2}$ is an odd integer, then which of the following must be an even integer?

(A) $\frac{x}{4}$ (B) $x + 1$ (C) $\left(\frac{x}{2}\right)^2$

(D) x (E) $x^2 - 1$

24. A school sells caps priced at \$3.50, \$5.00, and \$7.00. If it sells 54 caps priced at \$7.00 and collects a total of \$1,068.00 on sales of 210 caps, how many caps priced at \$5.00 does it sell?

(A) 60 (B) 78 (C) 90 (D) 96 (E) 104

25. If $4 - a < \frac{b + 3}{2}$, then which of the following must be true?

(A) $a > \frac{5 - b}{2}$

(B) $a < \frac{11 - b}{2}$

(C) $a > 2b$

(D) $a > 4(b + 3)$

(E) $a < \frac{b - 2}{2}$

S T O P

IF YOU FINISH BEFORE TIME IS CALLED, YOU MAY CHECK YOUR WORK ON THIS SECTION ONLY. DO NOT WORK ON ANY OTHER SECTION IN THE TEST.

SECTION 3

Time—30 minutes

50 QUESTIONS

The questions in this section measure skills that are important to writing well. In particular, they test your ability to recognize and use language that is clear, effective, and correct according to the requirements of standard written English, the kind of English found in most college textbooks.

Directions: The following sentences contain problems in grammar, usage, diction (choice of words), and idiom.

Some sentences are correct.
No sentence contains more than one error.

You will find that the error, if there is one, is underlined and lettered. Assume that elements of the sentence that are not underlined are correct and cannot be changed. In choosing answers, follow the requirements of standard written English.

If there is an error, select the one underlined part that must be changed to make the sentence correct and blacken the corresponding space on your answer sheet.

If there is no error, blacken answer space Ⓔ.

EXAMPLE:

The region has a climate so severe that [A] plants growing there [B] rarely had been [C] more than twelve inches high. [D] No error [E]

SAMPLE ANSWER

Ⓐ Ⓑ ● Ⓓ Ⓔ

1. Those present at the meeting [A] were surprised [B] that none [C] of the accounts in the press commented over [D] Janet's remarkable speech. No error [E]

2. Fleeing on foot, [A] two police officers followed [B] the suspect over the Jerome Street Bridge, finally seizing [C] him [D] in an abandoned school yard. No error [E]

3. According to [A] most legislators, either pressure from [B] constituents or [C] the efforts of lobbying groups influences [D] nearly every piece of legislation. No error [E]

4. Most spectators were disappointed by [A] the relatively [B] unspectacular appearance of comet Kohoutek, which [C] some astronomers had predicted would be [D] of remarkable brilliance. No error [E]

5. If any [A] employees disagree with [B] the ratings given by a supervisor, he or she [C] can request a review by [D] the labor-management council. No error [E]

6. Because of [A] the drought that has afflicted [B] the region for the past [C] two years, most of the farm equipment has laid [D] here idle. No error [E]

GO ON TO THE NEXT PAGE

7. Some recordings of classical music sell fairly
A
well, but most are nowhere nearly as successful as
B C
the best-selling albums of pop or rock music.
D
No error
E

8. Us New Yorkers have long been accustomed to
A B
being considered "different" by Americans from
C D
other regions of the country. No error
E

9. In attempt to justify her actions, the reporter
A B
stated that she had been unaware that the
C D
documents were forged. No error
E

10. Neither Bob nor the Martins have come to see
A B
Millicent since she was admitted to the hospital.
C D
No error
E

11. In any confrontation between the two superpowers,
A B
the Soviet leaders must always be aware that the
C
nuclear forces of the United States are greatest.
D
No error
E

12. Either chemistry or one of the other physical
A B
sciences are required for graduation. No error
C D E

13. Most Americans get the news from television and
A
radio, even though they know that newspaper
B
coverage is almost always more thorough.
C D
No error
E

14. Having drove the guerrillas from their strongholds
A B
in the north, General Ortiz made plans for a final
C D
assault on the main rebel base at Capablanca.
No error
E

15. Despite the predictions of the president's
A
supporters, the senator has performed nearly as well
B
in the early primary elections like the president
C
himself. No error
D E

16. The first adhesive postage stamps were issued by
A
Great Britain in 1840, and within a few years stamp
B
collecting is already a popular hobby. No error
C D E

17. Unfortunately, many pieces by contemporary
A
composers are written with little or no
B C
consideration for the musical taste or background
of the typical audience. No error
D E

18. It is difficult for us to imagine a time when the
A B
victors in theatrical competitions were as widely
C
admired as baseball and football today. No error
D E

19. Because Joanne has so often spoken about
A
her desire to leave the firm, her resigning at this
B
time does not scarcely surprise me. No error
C D E

20. Certain specialty books, such as cookbooks, earn
A B
a steady portion of most publishers' annual
C
incomes, although they rarely become best-sellers.
D
No error
E

21. Our study of the art of Mary Cassatt
will not be complete unless we consider not
A B
only what she wished to express but also how
C
it was expressed by her. No error
D E

GO ON TO THE NEXT PAGE

22. Human beings generally have (A) good intentions, but even the best (B) intentions can be thwarted (C) by political disagreements, economic constraints, and weaknesses that are human (D). No error (E)

23. Many researchers now suspect (A) that the disease we call cancer may in fact (B) be several diseases, each (C) with its own cause and its own (D) cure. No error (E)

24. Recent findings have not (A) so much (B) revolutionized our understanding of the dinosaurs as shifted (C) its emphasis and clarified (D) certain previously obscure points. No error (E)

25. The first auction of (A) city-owned properties was held (B) on August 19 in according with (C) a provision of the newly adopted (D) city charter. No error (E)

Directions: In each of the following sentences, some part or all of the sentence is underlined. Below each sentence you will find five ways of phrasing the underlined part. Select the answer that produces the most effective sentence, one that is clear and exact, without awkwardness or ambiguity, and blacken the corresponding space on your answer sheet. In choosing answers, follow the requirements of standard written English. Choose the answer that best expresses the meaning of the original sentence.

Answer (A) is always the same as the underlined part. Choose answer (A) if you think the original sentence needs no revision.

EXAMPLE:

Laura Ingalls Wilder published her first book and she was sixty-five years old then.

(A) and she was sixty-five years old then
(B) when she was sixty-five years old
(C) at age sixty-five years old
(D) upon reaching sixty-five years
(E) at the time when she was sixty-five

SAMPLE ANSWER

26. The medieval guilds are often compared to the trade unions of today, they differed from unions in many respects.

(A) The medieval guilds are often compared to
(B) Medieval guilds resembling
(C) Unless the medieval guilds are compared to
(D) Although the medieval guilds are often compared to
(E) Despite the similarities of medieval guilds as opposed to

27. Covered by over a foot of snow before noon, the principal decided at 12:30 to dismiss all classes early.

(A) Covered by over a foot of snow
(B) Since over a foot of snow had fallen
(C) Over a foot of snow covering it
(D) Under a foot of snow
(E) In view of over a foot of snow falling

28. The inventors of some of the most common tools, the paper clip is an example of this, received almost nothing in payment for their creativity.

(A) the paper clip is an example of this
(B) such as the paper clip
(C) including the one who invented the paper clip
(D) take the paper clip for instance
(E) like, for instance, the paper clip

29. Most widely known for his satirical comedies, Ben Jonson also wrote many other types of plays and poems.

(A) Ben Jonson also wrote many other types of plays and poems
(B) plays and poems of many other types were also written by Ben Jonson

GO ON TO THE NEXT PAGE

(C) Ben Jonson's plays and poems also include many other types
(D) the plays and poems of Ben Jonson are also of many other types
(E) many other types of plays and poems were also written by Ben Jonson

30. Although political views are supposed to be irrelevant in awarding the Nobel prize for literature, views of that type are inevitably of influence in the choices.

(A) views of that type are inevitably of influence in
(B) they inevitably influence
(C) such views inevitably have influence over
(D) those views do inevitably influence
(E) they are inevitably influential toward

31. Foreign real-estate investments in the United States having become a matter of concern to many in this country.

(A) having become
(B) becoming
(C) have become
(D) are being
(E) are to become

32. The process by which foreign foods become native staples, such as the potato in Ireland and Italy with its pasta, is a mysterious one.

(A) Italy with its pasta
(B) Italian pasta
(C) the pasta of Italy
(D) Italy, known for its pasta
(E) pasta in Italy

33. Young fiction writers today find it harder than ever to make a living, and thus many magazines that once printed fiction no longer exist.

(A) living, and thus
(B) living, whereas
(C) living,
(D) living; so
(E) living because

34. Unaware that Leibniz was pursuing the same research, the differential calculus was being developed by Newton.

(A) the differential calculus was being developed by Newton
(B) Newton was developing the differential calculus
(C) the development of the differential calculus was worked on by Newton
(D) Newton was in the development of the differential calculus
(E) Newton's developments led to the differential calculus

35. In some works of science fiction the science itself is the main point of interest, but in the case of others some human dilemma is primary.

(A) but in the case of others
(B) in others, however,
(C) whereas in other works
(D) while in others
(E) although in other instances

36. The scientist, carefully placing the small fossil in a pocket of her specimen bag, the significance of the discovery slowly dawned on her.

(A) The scientist, carefully placing the small fossil in a pocket of her specimen bag,
(B) The scientist carefully placed the small fossil in the pocket of her specimen bag, then
(C) Carefully placing the small fossil in a pocket of the scientist's specimen bag,
(D) As the scientist carefully placed the small fossil in the pocket of her specimen bag;
(E) The scientist was carefully placing the small fossil in her specimen bag when

37. Ideally, the professional career diplomat should help in the ongoing maintenance of an effective American foreign policy despite changes in administrations.

(A) in the ongoing maintenance of
(B) in the maintaining of
(C) maintain
(D) to maintain and continue
(E) the maintenance of

38. Most Christmas customs of today are not very old; the majority gaining popularity in this country during the nineteenth century.

(A) old; the majority gaining
(B) old, the majority gained
(C) old; the majority were gaining
(D) old; the majority gained
(E) old. The majority gaining

39. Latin should be studied not primarily for the light it sheds on our own language but for its inherent value.

(A) but for
(B) but because it has
(C) yet for
(D) and also for
(E) but due to

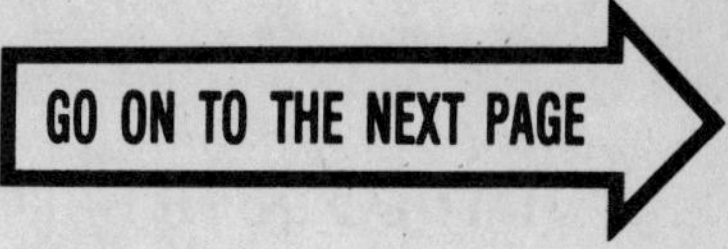

40. Marlowe, heard speaking in favor of smoking, which was still a highly unusual practice at that time.

(A) Marlowe, heard speaking
(B) Marlowe was heard to speak
(C) Marlowe speaking
(D) Because Marlowe spoke
(E) Marlowe having spoken

Directions: The remaining questions are like those at the beginning of the section. For each sentence in which you find an error, select the one underlined part that must be changed to make the sentence correct and blacken the corresponding space on your answer sheet. If there is no error, blacken answer space E.

41. No one who wish to develop a full appreciation of
A B
contemporary music can afford to underestimate
C
the influence of the work of Wagner. No error
D E

42. The president was expected to nominate either
A B
Anderson or he for the post of secretary of the
C D
interior. No error
E

43. The personnel director told Mary and me
A
that the number of employees qualified for

the position was so great that hardly no one
B C D
outside the company would be called for an

interview. No error
E

44. As government's role in supporting the arts
A
will grow, the danger of political control of
B C
artistic expression is growing also. No error
D E

45. By examining records of rainfall over a period of
A B
thirty-six months, the meteorologist was able to

deduct the most likely sites of soil erosion.
C D
No error
E

46. Of all the towering figures of English
A
Renaissance poetry, perhaps John Donne, the

supreme love poet turned mystic and divine,
B
is the most unique. No error
C D E

47. The emancipation of the Russian serfs cannot
A
logically be compared to the freeing of the
B C
American slaves; serfdom and slavery are

distinct conditions. No error
D E

48. If anyone wants to apply for the Runcie
A B
Scholarship, you should see Ms. Agate in the
C
Administration Building sometime this week.
D
No error
E

49. Long-range weather forecasting is important

mainly because it enables farmers
A B
anticipation of droughts, frosts, and other
C
conditions that can damage crops. No error
D E

50. Turing was one of the first scientists to
A
grapple with the problem of what has since
B C
become known as artificial intelligence.
D
No error
E

S T O P

IF YOU FINISH BEFORE TIME IS CALLED, YOU MAY CHECK YOUR WORK ON THIS SECTION ONLY. DO NOT WORK ON ANY OTHER SECTION IN THE TEST.

SECTION 4

Time—30 minutes

40 QUESTIONS

For each question in this section, choose the best answer and blacken the corresponding space on the answer sheet.

Each question below consists of a word in capital letters, followed by five lettered words or phrases. Choose the word or phrase that is most nearly opposite in meaning to the word in capital letters. Since some of the questions require you to distinguish fine shades of meaning, consider all the choices before deciding which is best.

Example:

GOOD: (A) sour (B) bad (C) red (D) hot (E) ugly
Ⓐ ● Ⓒ Ⓓ Ⓔ

1. HAPHAZARD: (A) continual (B) methodical (C) causal (D) repetitious (E) scientific

2. ANTAGONIZE: (A) sweeten (B) apologize (C) emulate (D) placate (E) hearken

3. STALWART: (A) apathetic (B) mild (C) feverish (D) craven (E) languid

4. RUE: (A) bless (B) recount (C) suggest (D) declare (E) please

5. MORIBUND: (A) bright (B) stable (C) vigorous (D) lighthearted (E) viable

6. EQUILIBRIUM: (A) strength (B) fissure (C) imbalance (D) movement (E) exuberance

7. LIMPID: (A) stagnant (B) swirling (C) erect (D) solid (E) turbid

8. COVET: (A) spurn (B) apply (C) cull (D) divest (E) abolish

9. IMPERVIOUS: (A) transparent (B) penetrable (C) indivisible (D) brittle (E) amenable

10. INDIGENT: (A) resident (B) fortunate (C) affluent (D) accepting (E) gracious

Each sentence below has one or two blanks, each blank indicating that something has been omitted. Beneath the sentence are five lettered words or sets of words. Choose the word or set of words that best fits the meaning of the sentence as a whole.

Example:

Although its publicity has been ----, the film itself is intelligent, well acted, handsomely produced, and altogether ----.

(A) tasteless..respectable (B) extensive..moderate (C) sophisticated..amateur (D) risqué..crude (E) perfect..spectacular
● Ⓑ Ⓒ Ⓓ Ⓔ

11. Because these two primitive cultures are so widely separated, it seems unlikely that the similarities between them are due to ----.

(A) intercommunication (B) coincidence (C) error (D) proximity (E) chance

12. The human instinct for ---- cannot be regarded as an absolute, for many men and women have willingly sacrificed their lives for something they regarded as a greater good.

(A) survival (B) procreation (C) freedom (D) self-transcendence (E) happiness

13. Although baseball is often referred to as a "boys' game," the epithet is historically ----; the inventors and early players of the sport were all ----.

(A) accurate..amateurs
(B) sound..youthful
(C) dubious..professionals
(D) false..adults
(E) untenable..students

GO ON TO THE NEXT PAGE

14. Like Wallace and Darwin, who had developed the principles of evolution ----, Mondrian and Kandinsky reached the stage of pure abstraction in art by separate, unrelated paths.

(A) previously (B) accidentally
(C) together (D) analytically
(E) independently

15. The ---- comments of the professor eventually produced in Bramwell a fierce determination never to ---- in class unless it was absolutely unavoidable.

(A) helpful..remain
(B) vicious..listen
(C) measured..err
(D) jocular..appear
(E) carping..speak

Each question below consists of a related pair of words or phrases, followed by five lettered pairs of words or phrases. Select the lettered pair that best expresses a relationship similar to that expressed in the original pair.

Example:

YAWN:BOREDOM:: (A) dream:sleep
(B) anger:madness (C) smile:amusement
(D) face:expression (E) impatience:rebellion

16. MALIGN:LAUD:: (A) slander:libel
(B) condemn:praise (C) abhor:redeem
(D) extol:exalt (E) curse:defame

17. REDDEN:EMBARRASSMENT::
(A) blanch:horror
(B) blush:cynicism
(C) pale:illness
(D) shudder:anticipation
(E) marvel:awe

18. AIR:WING:: (A) motion:speed
(B) wind:propeller (C) ground:tail
(D) water:fin (E) jet:bird

19. CONSULT:DICTIONARY::
(A) examine:specimen
(B) measure:length
(C) gaze:stars
(D) write:paper
(E) peruse:scholar

20. LOCK:HAIR:: (A) weed:lawn (B) bone:ribs
(C) tuft:grass (D) leaf:tree (E) scale:fish

21. VIVID:HUE:: (A) icy:temperature
(B) shrill:speech (C) clarion:tone
(D) rounded:texture (E) blunt:point

22. IMMUNE:DISEASE:: (A) invisible:vision
(B) afflicted:suffering (C) curable:illness
(D) impregnable:attack
(E) vulnerable:defense

23. ANNULMENT:MARRIAGE::
(A) interruption:performance
(B) voiding:contract
(C) argument:conversation
(D) disagreement:friendship
(E) rejection:employment

24. FLUENT:GLIB:: (A) polished:slick
(B) plausible:deceitful (C) skillful:adroit
(D) accurate:precise (E) eloquent:loquacious

25. PEBBLE:GRAVEL:: (A) spoonful:sugar
(B) grain:sand (C) star:constellation
(D) captain:crew (E) stone:quarry

Each passage below is followed by questions based on its content. Answer all questions following a passage on the basis of what is stated or implied in that passage.

Heat is used to produce some of the gem tints rarely found in nature. Yellow topaz from Brazil, for example, can be heated carefully and cooled to produce a permanent pink, resembling the rare natural pink topaz. In a similar manner, a colored zircon may be heat-treated and thereby made colorless or changed to a different color.

Dyeing is another means of changing the natural color of a gemstone. This method is most often used on porous stones, such as the agate. Unattractive grays and pale shades can be changed chemically to bright red, green, and blue shades. The common dyeing procedure is to soak the agate in the desired chemical: nitric acid for red shades, nitrates and chromium salts for green shades, and certain cyanates and sulfates for blue shades. The Romans dyed the agate by soaking it in honey, removing it from the liquid, and heating it. This method produced black bands. Today the same effect is achieved by soaking the agate first in a sugar solution and then in sulfuric acid to char the sugar.

The ruby, spinel, emerald, sapphire, star sapphire, star ruby, rutile, and quartz are gemstones that have been successfully synthesized. A stone of simple chemical composition generally is more easily synthesized than one of complex composition. However, although the diamond has the simplest composition of any gem—it is pure crystalline carbon—synthetic gem diamonds have never been perfected.

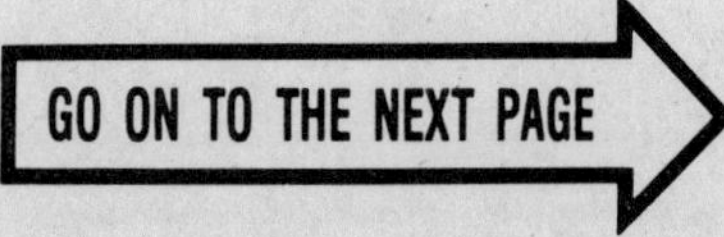

26. The author is primarily interested in describing

(A) the various colors in which gems occur in nature
(B) the effects of heat on different types of gem
(C) modern methods of improving the appearance of flawed gems
(D) artificial means of altering or imitating certain gems
(E) how chemical changes in gems may be produced

27. It can be inferred from the passage that gems are generally dyed

(A) for industrial purposes
(B) in chemical experimentation
(C) for use in optical procedures
(D) to reveal their internal structures
(E) for aesthetic reasons

28. The diamond is mentioned in the last sentence mainly as

(A) evidence for a theory
(B) an example of a common phenomenon
(C) an irrelevant digression
(D) an exception to a rule
(E) proof of a hypothesis

For nearly four centuries, western peoples accepted the division separating the "fine" arts of architecture, sculpture, and painting from the "lesser" arts. This boundary was fixed by the academies of art, and it was faithfully observed in education and in professional life, until its general abandonment about the time of the Second World War. It also marked off a class division between "upper-class taste" and "lack of taste" among the lower classes. The tacit abandonment of the rule of taste in this century thus corresponds to a wiping out of class distinctions, as well as of the separateness of the "fine arts" from "the others." But the study and the teaching of the history of art have not accepted this levelling of the subject. Historians of art stubbornly retain the criterion of "quality," and their attention is still drawn to "great" artists and to the "greatest" works in museums and collections. The objects of "low quality" made outside the rule of taste for proletarian consumers still are not accepted as proper subjects for searching art-historical study by university faculties and museum curators in either western or eastern Europe.

29. The author's attitude toward the distinction drawn between the fine arts and the lesser arts is one of

(A) tacit skepticism
(B) apologetic acceptance
(C) enthusiastic endorsement
(D) thoughtful resignation
(E) pompous disdain

30. The passage implies that art historians have devoted their attention mainly to works of art produced

(A) exclusively for display in museums and collections in western and eastern Europe
(B) by artists who are lacking in true aesthetic sensibility
(C) in art academies
(D) for an upper-class audience
(E) prior to the Second World War

31. With which of the following statements would the author be most likely to agree?

(A) Historians of art are to be commended for upholding standards of quality in an age of mediocrity.
(B) It is time for universities and museums to recognize the importance of the so-called "lesser" arts.
(C) The social distinction between the upper and lower classes is a result of the traditional distinction between the fine and lesser arts.
(D) The artistic perceptions of ordinary people generally lag behind those of scholars and educators in the world of art.
(E) The study of art would be improved if art historians learned to separate aesthetic judgments from commercial considerations.

Ionizing radiation is applied in a number of useful ways in medicine. Low-energy X rays are used for diagnostic purposes. Generated by machine, these X rays are directed toward the part of a patient's body that a physician wishes to view. The X rays travel through the patient's body and transfer an image of the part exposed to a film behind the patient. By studying this film, specialists can detect a variety of abnormal conditions in the bone structure and the internal organs of a patient. Thus low-energy X rays aid physicians in diagnosing and prescribing suitable treatment for various internal disorders.

High-energy X rays, along with other forms of radiation, are used for therapeutic purposes, notably in the treatment of cancer. Although these X rays are harmful to all cells, they destroy cancer cells preferentially over normal cells. Normal cells appear to have a considerable capacity for repairing much, if not all, radiation-induced damage.

The effectiveness of radiation in destroying cancer cells—as well as the potential for harm to normal tissues from therapeutic radiation—depends on the type of radiation used and exactly how it is applied. Therapeutic X-radiation can be applied to part or all of the body. If it is applied to part of the body, a relatively strong dose can be administered. If it is applied to a larger area or to the whole body, the dose must be drastically reduced. Although scientists do not fully understand the relationship between volume of exposure and tolerance to radiation, they do know that whole-body tolerance is much lower than partial-body (or regional) tolerance.

Exposing a very large volume of the body to radiation is dangerous primarily because it may ultimately—years later—induce leukemia. Whole-body radiation has been known to cause this form of cancer, although the incidence of radiation-induced leukemia varies greatly with the level of exposure and the number of years of follow-up.

To avoid the possibility of inducing leukemia in patients, physicians usually treat cancer in a specific area of the body by subjecting the area to repeated applications of localized fields of high-level radiation for several days. The incidence of leukemia in persons receiving high-level partial-body X-radiation is no greater than it is in the population as a whole.

32. Which of the following titles best describes the content of the passage?

(A) The Dangers Posed by Radiation to the Human Body
(B) The Role of Radiation in the Diagnosis of Cancer
(C) The Medical Uses and Risks of Radiation
(D) Determining the Body's Tolerance for Radiation
(E) Radiation as a Major Cause of Cancer

33. According to the passage, radiation is medically useful because of its ability to do which of the following?

I. Travel through living cells
II. Create an image on film
III. Destroy living cells

(A) I only
(B) III only
(C) I and II only
(D) I and III only
(E) I, II, and III

34. According to the passage, high levels of radiation can be used with relative safety only

(A) in brief, widely spaced therapeutic doses
(B) when the radiation field is wide enough to include the entire body
(C) for a single intensive exposure
(D) when the cancer has spread over a large area of the body
(E) on strictly limited portions of the patient's body

35. The passage implies that one factor that makes the study of radiation-induced leukemia difficult is the

(A) uncertainty in diagnosing the disease
(B) lack of specialists trained in the treatment of the disease
(C) variation in the length of follow-up treatment provided
(D) ignorance of scientists about the levels of exposure likely to induce the disease
(E) length of time required for the disease to appear

GO ON TO THE NEXT PAGE

There are ultimately but three forces that control society—habit, coercive and violent force, and action directed by intelligence. In fairly normal times, habit and custom are by far the strongest force. A social crisis means that this force has in large measure ceased to operate. The other forces, therefore, come more conspicuously into play. Reactionaries who strive to prevent any change of the old order are possessed of the power that enables them to use brute force in its less overt forms: by coercion, by intimidation, and by various forms of indirect pressure. From lack of understanding of social affairs, a lack of understanding owing to faulty education, as well as to deliberate refusal to learn, reactionaries unintelligently resist change. Those who have suffered from the old order then react by appeal to direct use of force as the only means at their command. Because of the intellectual suppressions experienced in the course of their own education they have little knowledge of means of effecting social changes by any method other than force.

In short, the social significance of academic freedom lies in the fact that without freedom of inquiry and freedom on the part of teachers and students to explore the forces at work in society and the means by which they may be directed, the habits of intelligent action that are necessary to the orderly development of society cannot be created. Training for good citizenship is one thing when conditions are simple and fairly stable. It is quite another thing when conditions are confused, complicated, and unsettled, when class divisions and struggles are imminent. Every force that operates to limit the freedom of education is a premium put upon ultimate recourse to violence to effect needed change. Every force that tends to liberate educational processes is a premium placed upon intelligent and orderly methods of directing to a more just, equitable, and humane end the social changes that are going on anyway.

36. The author defends academic freedom primarily on the basis of its

(A) benefits for scholarly activity
(B) protection by the Constitution
(C) importance for the advancement of science
(D) value to society as a whole
(E) moral and philosophical claims

37. It can be inferred that the author regards the major threat to academic freedom as deriving from

(A) reactionary forces seeking to suppress social change
(B) intellectuals wishing to inculcate their own political views
(C) revolutionaries attempting to indoctrinate students under the guise of education
(D) the atmosphere of chaos in education resulting from turmoil in the larger society
(E) economic forces that limit access to higher education

38. The author suggests that academic freedom is most necessary

(A) at times when most people are directed mainly by habit and custom
(B) during periods of social unrest
(C) when class distinctions have become solidified and rigid
(D) at times when society has attained a high degree of class stability
(E) when society is threatened by external enemies

39. Which of the following is an assumption made by the author?

(A) In today's world, a higher education is a prerequisite for effective citizenship.
(B) The use of force in directing social processes is never morally justified.
(C) It is impossible to arrest the process of social change.
(D) Those who oppose improvements in society often hide their beliefs behind the doctrine of academic freedom.
(E) The use of violence generally offers a strategic advantage to those wishing to suppress social justice.

40. This passage was most likely taken from

(A) a philosophical treatise on education
(B) an essay on the economics of social change
(C) a novel about academic freedom
(D) the editorial page of a reactionary student newspaper
(E) a speech advocating the direct use of force to effect needed changes in the public school system

S T O P

IF YOU FINISH BEFORE TIME IS CALLED, YOU MAY CHECK YOUR WORK ON THIS SECTION ONLY. DO NOT WORK ON ANY OTHER SECTION IN THE TEST.

SECTION 5

Time—30 minutes

35 QUESTIONS

In this section solve each problem, using any available space on the page for scratchwork. Then indicate the one correct answer in the appropriate space on the answer sheet.

The following information is for your reference in solving some of the problems.

Circle of radius r: Area $= \pi r^2$; Circumference $= 2\pi r$
The number of degrees of arc in a circle is 360.
The measure in degrees of a straight angle is 180.

Definitions of symbols:

$=$	is equal to	$\leq$	is less than or equal to
$\neq$	is unequal to	$\geq$	is greater than or equal to
$<$	is less than	$\parallel$	is parallel to
$>$	is greater than	$\perp$	is perpendicular to

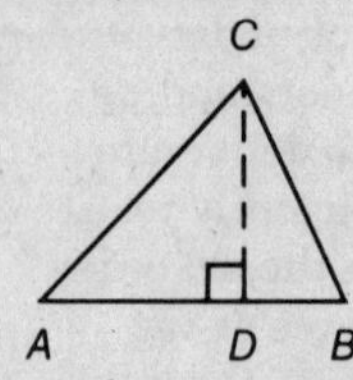

Triangle: The sum of the measures in degrees of the angles of a triangle is 180.

If $\angle CDA$ is a right angle, then

(1) area of $\triangle ABC = \frac{AB \times CD}{2}$

(2) $AC^2 = AD^2 + DC^2$

Note: Figures which accompany problems in this test are intended to provide information useful in solving the problems. They are drawn as accurately as possible EXCEPT when it is stated in a specific problem that its figure is not drawn to scale. All figures lie in a plane unless otherwise indicated. All numbers used are real numbers.

1. $\frac{1}{3}$ of $\frac{2}{5}$ of $\frac{3}{4}$ of $\frac{5}{6}$ of 36 equals

   (A) 2 (B) 3 (C) 4 (D) 5 (E) 6

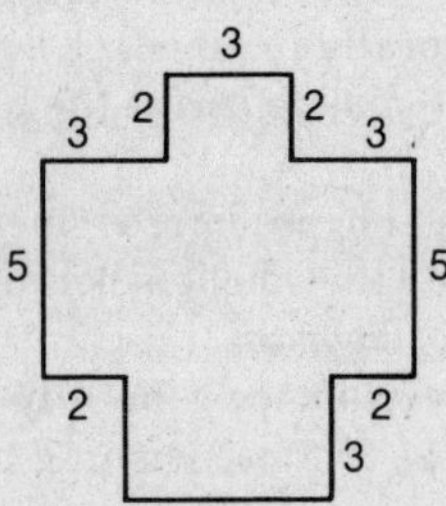

2. In the figure above, all angles are right angles and the lengths are as shown. What is the total area of the figure?

   (A) 64 (B) 66 (C) 70 (D) 75 (E) 82

3. If $x = \frac{y}{4}$ and $8x = 18$, then $y =$

   (A) 9 (B) 8 (C) 7 (D) 5 (E) 4

4. If every even digit in the number 4321 is doubled, the value of the number will increase by

   (A) 8642 (B) 8341 (C) 4321
   (D) 4020 (E) 4000

5. Dates of the calendar are sometimes represented by digits. For example, March 10, 1985, is represented as 3-10-85. In this system, what month in 1986 includes the earliest date that is represented by five or six digits, three of which are the same?

   (A) January (B) March (C) April
   (D) June (E) August

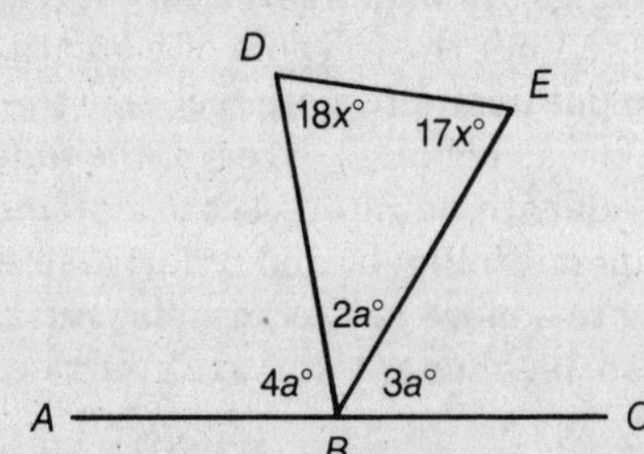

6. In the figure above, ABC is a line segment. What is the degree measure of the largest angle of triangle BDE?

   (A) 64 (B) 68 (C) 72 (D) 80 (E) 90

7. Both x and y are positive integers. If $(x + y)^2 = 64$ and $xy = 15$, then $x^2 + y^2 =$

   (A) 24 (B) 28 (C) 32 (D) 34 (E) 44

GO ON TO THE NEXT PAGE

Questions 8-27 each consist of two quantities, one in Column A and one in Column B. You are to compare the two quantities and on the answer sheet blacken space

A if the quantity in Column A is greater;
B if the quantity in Column B is greater;
C if the two quantities are equal;
D if the relationship cannot be determined from the information given.

Notes: 1. In certain questions, information concerning one or both of the quantities to be compared is centered above the two columns.
2. In a given question, a symbol that appears in both columns represents the same thing in Column A as it does in Column B.
3. Letters such as x, n, and k stand for real numbers.

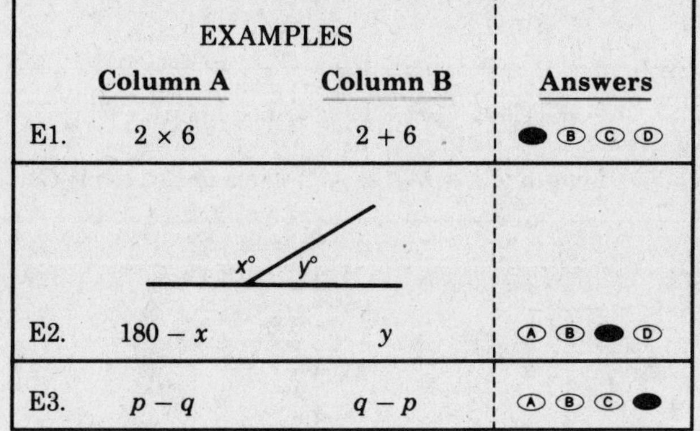

EXAMPLES

	Column A	Column B	Answers
E1.	2×6	$2 + 6$	● Ⓑ Ⓒ Ⓓ
E2.	$180 - x$	y	Ⓐ Ⓑ ● Ⓓ
E3.	$p - q$	$q - p$	Ⓐ Ⓑ Ⓒ ●

	Column A	Column B
8.	$4 \times (3 + 3) \div 2$	$(4 \times 3) + (3 \div 2)$
9.	Number of centimeters in a kilometer	Number of milliliters in 100 liters
10.	$(2^3)^4$	$(2^6)^2$

$xyz = 18$

$x < 0$

11.	z	0

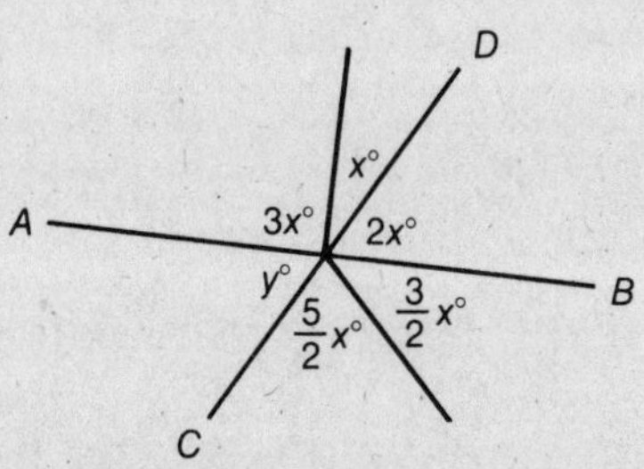

Line segment AB intersects line segment CD.

12.	y	60

$2x + 1 = 0$

13.	x^2	$\frac{1}{x^2}$

Column A | Column B

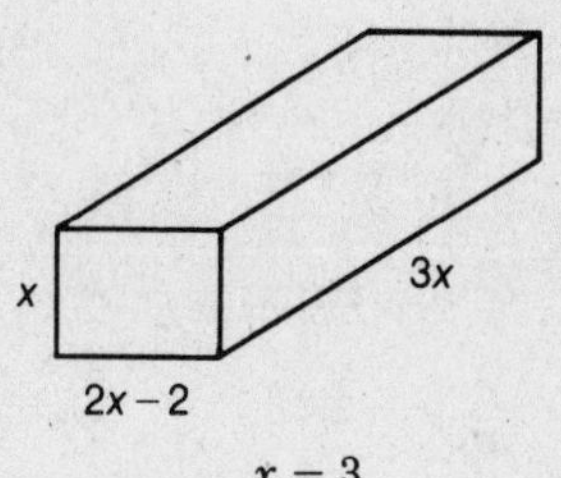

$x = 3$

14.	Volume of the rectangular solid shown	100

Of 42 students in a class, $\frac{1}{3}$ have blue eyes and $\frac{1}{7}$ have green eyes. The rest have brown eyes.

15.	Number of students in the class with brown eyes	21

$a - b + c = 6$

$c - b - a = 4$

16.	a	2

$x \leqq y \leqq z$

17.	xy	yz

$\boxed{n}$ is defined as the smallest integer greater than or equal to n.

18.	$\boxed{3} + \boxed{-4.5}$	-1

GO ON TO THE NEXT PAGE

Column A	Column B

A box contains black marbles and white marbles. The number of black marbles is 3 more than the number of white marbles.

	Column A	Column B
19.	The chance of a blindfolded person choosing 2 black marbles consecutively	.50

40% of $x = 18$

	Column A	Column B
20.	x	45

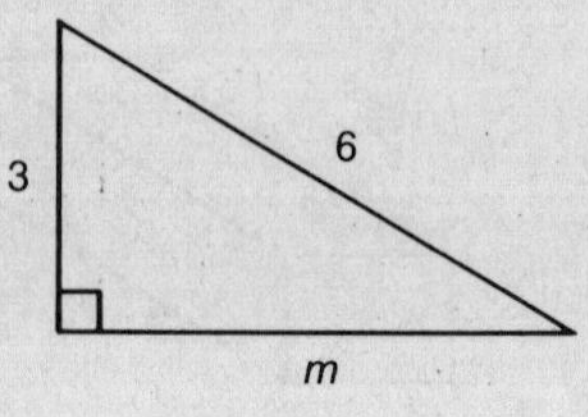

	Column A	Column B
21.	m	5

Katia is n years old; Janet is 3 years older than Katia; Christopher is 4 years older than Janet.

	Column A	Column B
22.	The sum of the ages of Katia, Janet, and Christopher	$3n + 10$

	Column A	Column B
23.	Average (arithmetic mean) of the terms 4, 7, 6, 9, and 34	Average (arithmetic mean) of the terms 12, 12, 11, 13, and 11

Column A	Column B

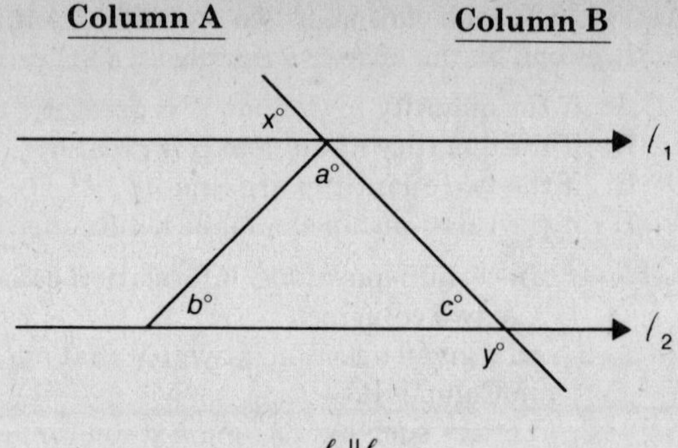

$\ell_1 \| \ell_2$

	Column A	Column B
24.	$a + b + c$	$x + y$

Triangle ABC is inscribed in circle O.

	Column A	Column B
25.	Length of side AB	Diameter of circle O

$\frac{x}{y} = 4$

$y = \frac{1}{4}$

	Column A	Column B
26.	x	1

$x \neq 0$

	Column A	Column B
27.	$9x$	$\frac{3x}{2} \times 2x \div \frac{x}{3}$

GO ON TO THE NEXT PAGE

Solve each of the remaining problems in this section using any available space for scratchwork. Then indicate the one correct answer in the appropriate space on the answer sheet.

28. If $x = 3y + 5$ and $y + 3 = x - 10$, then $x + y =$

(A) 21 (B) 19 (C) 17 (D) 11 (E) 8

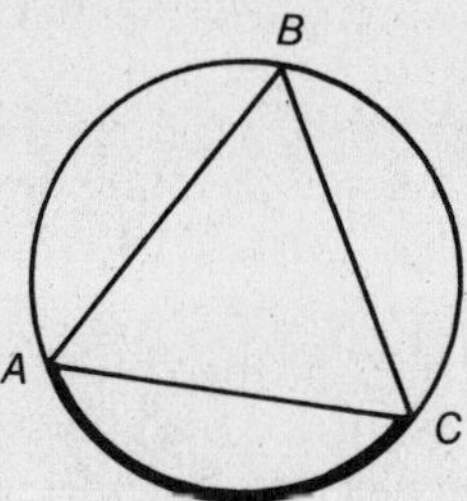

29. Equilateral triangle ABC is inscribed in the circle above. Point X (not shown) is located on the circle somewhere along darkened arc AC. If the circle has a radius of 15, what is the GREATEST possible length of arc BX?

(A) 20π (B) 15π (C) 12π

(D) 10π (E) $7\frac{1}{2}\pi$

30. If $(x - 3) + (x - 2) + (x - 1) = 0$, then $3x =$

(A) 2 (B) 6 (C) $\frac{6}{4}$ (D) 9 (E) $\frac{9}{2}$

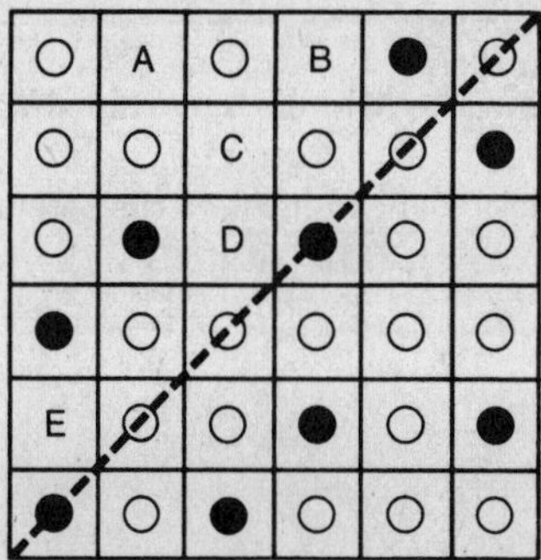

31. The grid above contains a pattern of black and white circles. If the pattern is symmetrical with respect to the dashed diagonal line, which of the lettered squares shown on the grid must contain a black circle?

(A) A (B) B (C) C (D) D (E) E

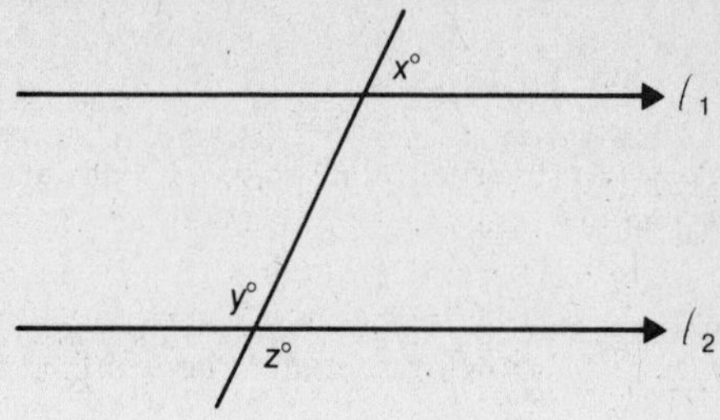

32. In the figure above, $\ell_1 \parallel \ell_2$. What is the value of $y + z$ in terms of x?

(A) $(90 - x) + (90 - x)$ (B) $180 - x$

(C) $90 + 2x$ (D) $180 + 2x$ (E) $360 - 2x$

33. If $\frac{m}{n} = \frac{3}{4}$ and $3m = 18$, then $2n =$

(A) 8 (B) 10 (C) 12 (D) 14 (E) 16

34. In a coordinate graph system, point A is located at $(0, 2)$. If point B with coordinates (x, y) is equidistant from point A and the origin, then which of the following must be true?

(A) $x = 0$ (B) $y = 2$ (C) $y = 1$

(D) $x + y = 1$ (E) $y - x = 0$

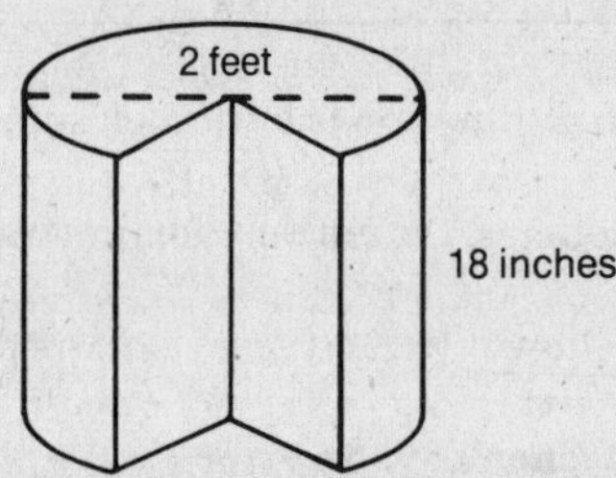

35. The cylindrical wheel of cheese shown above has a diameter of 2 feet and a height of 18 inches. A wedge of cheese representing a quarter of the entire wheel is removed. What is the volume in cubic feet of the remaining piece of cheese?

(A) $\frac{3\pi}{2}$ (B) $\frac{18\pi}{7}$ (C) $\frac{9\pi}{8}$ (D) $\frac{2\pi}{3}$ (E) $\frac{4\pi}{5}$

S T O P

IF YOU FINISH BEFORE TIME IS CALLED, YOU MAY CHECK YOUR WORK ON THIS SECTION ONLY. DO NOT WORK ON ANY OTHER SECTION IN THE TEST.

SECTION 6

Time—30 minutes

50 QUESTIONS

The questions in this section measure skills that are important to writing well. In particular, they test your ability to recognize and use language that is clear, effective, and correct according to the requirements of standard written English, the kind of English found in most college textbooks.

Directions: The following sentences contain problems in grammar, usage, diction (choice of words), and idiom.

Some sentences are correct.
No sentence contains more than one error.

You will find that the error, if there is one, is underlined and lettered. Assume that elements of the sentence that are not underlined are correct and cannot be changed. In choosing answers, follow the requirements of standard written English.

If there is an error, select the one underlined part that must be changed to make the sentence correct and blacken the corresponding space on your answer sheet.

If there is no error, blacken answer space (E).

EXAMPLE:

The region has a climate so severe that plants
A
growing there rarely had been more than twelve
B C
inches high. No error
D E

SAMPLE ANSWER

(A) (B) ● (D) (E)

1. Although that nation is a staunch supporter
A B
of U.S. policies, the current administration
will not allow it to receive no exports of
C D
nuclear technology. No error
E

2. Sales of houses, automobiles, and heavy
A
machinery tend to lag behind clothing and
B C
small appliances in an improving economy.
D
No error
E

3. Neither Canada nor Mexico are thought
A B
to represent any genuine threat to the
C D
security of the United States. No error
E

4. Throughout the Middle Ages, the church was the
A
driving force behind most of the attempts that
B
are made to limit and control the destructiveness
C D
of war. No error
E

5. In discussing the goals of the investigation, the
A
senator said that the committee would check off
B C D
reports of fraud and mismanagement in the
program. No error
E

6. Now that (A) the facade (B) of City Hall has been cleaned (C) by sandblasting, it certainly looks good (D) enough for next week's mayoral inauguration. No error (E)

7. The ushers distributed pledge cards to whomever (A) expressed an interest (B) in offering (C) financial support to (D) the foundation. No error (E)

8. The various sizes (A) of type, once designated by (B) a variety of colorful names, are (C) now described by point measure, as ten-point type, twelve-point type, and so on (D). No error (E)

9. The volume of water that flows (A) between the banks of the Mississippi is (B) as great, or greater, than (C) the volume of water that flows between the banks of longer (D) rivers. No error (E)

10. Thanks in part (A) to the criticism of Eliot, the achievements of Donne, which (B) had went largely (C) unappreciated during the nineteenth century, received greater (D) recognition in the twentieth. No error (E)

11. So (A) many talented individuals were experimenting with (B) flight around the turn of the century that if the Wright brothers had not succeeded (C) in 1903, someone else soon would have (D). No error (E)

12. Just beyond the next hill rises (A) the squat (B), ungainly (C) towers of the (D) nuclear power plant. No error (E)

13. Sypher's book is an attempt to establish (A) stylistic affinities among (B) various artistic forms within (C) the same historical (D) period. No error (E)

14. The Food and Drug Administration is (A) the federal agency who (B) is primarily responsible for ensuring (C) the safety of what (D) we eat and drink. No error (E)

15. Both (A) military leaders and civilian experts have questioned (B) the necessity to place (C) missiles in areas close to (D) cities and towns. No error (E)

16. Degree candidates are required (A) to earn (B) acceptable grades in their graduate courses, write a thesis, demonstrate proficiency in (C) two foreign languages, and to pass (D) a departmental exam. No error (E)

17. The educated man at the time of (A) Columbus did not need to be convinced (B) that the earth was round; they (C) only doubted the feasibility (D) of circumnavigating it. No error (E)

18. The professor's misguided (A) attempts to influence foreign policy illustrate (B), it seems to us, the dangers of (C) trying to outthink the experts in a field not one's own (D). No error (E)

19. Just as (A) early clay pots were scored (B) to resemble straw containers, so (C) plastic is now molded (D) to resemble wood. No error (E)

GO ON TO THE NEXT PAGE

20. The purpose of Fromm's book deals with the difficulties that modern men and women experience in learning how to give of themselves freely and naturally. No error

(A: The purpose of; B: difficulties that; C: in learning; D: to give of; E: No error)

21. In anticipation of a strike by nurses, the hospital administrator has asked all supervisors to prepare a list of patients who are good enough to be discharged. No error

(A: In anticipation of; B: has asked; C: to prepare; D: good enough; E: No error)

22. The judges selected Larry as the gold medalist, even though the audience had applauded three other pianists more enthusiastically than he. No error

(A: as the gold medalist; B: had applauded; C: more; D: than he; E: No error)

23. The description of Atlantis in Plato's *Republic* is no evidence that that country was not wholly imaginative; Plato's work is not historical but symbolic and fictional. No error

(A: description of; B: no evidence that; C: imaginative; D: historical; E: No error)

24. Early advocates of atomic energy predicted that an era of safe, inexpensive, and unlimited energy would ensue if the atom were harnessed for peaceful purposes. No error

(A: advocates of; B: and; C: would ensue; D: were harnessed; E: No error)

25. Losing candidates in primary elections traditionally offer their support in the general election to whoever the voters of their party select. No error

(A: offer; B: their support; C: whoever; D: select; E: No error)

Directions: In each of the following sentences, some part or all of the sentence is underlined. Below each sentence you will find five ways of phrasing the underlined part. Select the answer that produces the most effective sentence, one that is clear and exact, without awkwardness or ambiguity, and blacken the corresponding space on your answer sheet. In choosing answers, follow the requirements of standard written English. Choose the answer that best expresses the meaning of the original sentence.

Answer (A) is always the same as the underlined part. Choose answer (A) if you think the original sentence needs no revision.

EXAMPLE:

Laura Ingalls Wilder published her first book and she was sixty-five years old then.

(A) and she was sixty-five years old then
(B) when she was sixty-five years old
(C) at age sixty-five years old
(D) upon reaching sixty-five years
(E) at the time when she was sixty-five

SAMPLE ANSWER

Ⓐ ● Ⓒ Ⓓ Ⓔ

26. A home computer hooked up to a banking network can permit the user to make deposits, pay bills, monitoring his or her finances, all without leaving home.

(A) monitoring
(B) thus monitoring
(C) thereby to monitor
(D) monitoring in this way
(E) and monitor

27. The fact that the Native Americans had no horses being sometimes suggested as a reason for their failure to develop wheeled vehicles.

(A) being sometimes suggested as
(B) has been sometimes given as a suggestion for
(C) to be suggested sometimes as
(D) is sometimes suggested as
(E) being suggested sometimes for

GO ON TO THE NEXT PAGE

28. Written when he was a member of the Senate, Kennedy won the Pulitzer prize for his book *Profiles in Courage.*

(A) Written when he was a member of the Senate,
(B) He was a senator when
(C) Since it was written by a senator,
(D) When he was a member of the Senate,
(E) Serving at that time as a member of the Senate,

29. *Citizen Kane,* the first movie directed by Orson Welles, is generally regarded as his greatest achievement.

(A) the first movie directed by Orson Welles,
(B) being the first movie directed by Orson Welles,
(C) is the first movie directed by Orson Welles and also
(D) which was Orson Welles's first movie as a director,
(E) directed first by Orson Welles,

30. Whereas the work of Japanese artists became known in the West, it quickly became highly influential.

(A) Whereas
(B) While
(C) Because
(D) If
(E) Once

31. The long-lived myth of the "canals" of Mars owes its origin to a mistranslation of the Italian word *canali.*

(A) owes its origin to a
(B) had as their origin a
(C) owe their origin to the
(D) was originally a
(E) is due to an original

32. Hebrew legends give two conflicting accounts of Creation, scholars believe that there were two ancient sources of these stories.

(A) Hebrew legends give
(B) Hebrew legends giving
(C) Because Hebrew legends give
(D) Given by the Hebrew legends
(E) That Hebrew legends give

33. Startled by the sudden cessation of the sound of the machines, the night watchman awoke from his nap.

(A) the night watchman awoke from his nap
(B) the nap of the night watchman was interrupted
(C) the night watchman's nap was ended
(D) it awakened the night watchman from his nap
(E) and awakening the night watchman from his nap

34. In both Greece and England the art of the drama had as their original source the dramatic elements of religious ceremonies.

(A) had as their original source
(B) grew out of
(C) sprang forth from certain of
(D) was developed on the basis of
(E) came in the first place from

35. The vast quantity of missiles on both sides makes it unlikely that any defense which is capable of thwarting in its entirety a major attack can be devised.

(A) which is capable of thwarting in its entirety
(B) potentially capable of thwarting in its entirety
(C) that is capable of entirely thwarting
(D) with the full-thwart capability of
(E) capable of entirely thwarting

36. No list of best-selling books is completely accurate or reliable, of course, each list is compiled in a different area by a different method.

(A) reliable, of course,
(B) reliable; of course the reason is because
(C) reliable, of course, because
(D) reliable; of course; however,
(E) reliable, of course; so

37. An accurate job description can be written only by someone who has done the job, understands its purpose, knowing how to communicate this knowledge to others.

(A) knowing how to communicate
(B) with the knowledge of how to communicate
(C) and knows how to communicate
(D) and skilled in the communication of
(E) and who communicates

38. Beginning printmakers often use blocks of linoleum rather than wood, since linoleum is softer and therefore more easily capable of being carved.

(A) more easily capable of being carved
(B) easier to carve
(C) may be more easily carved
(D) ready for carving
(E) more amenable to carving

39. Glass has been manufactured for *centuries, and only recently* have many of its uses been discovered.

(A) centuries, and only recently
(B) centuries; and recently
(C) centuries, but only recently
(D) centuries, but recently only
(E) centuries; therefore, only recently

40. Until recently, *there was no easy way* for authors to sell copies of their own out-of-print books to interested readers.

(A) there was no easy way
(B) without an easy way
(C) no easy way was there
(D) lacking an easy way
(E) they had no easy way

Directions: The remaining questions are like those at the beginning of the section. For each sentence in which you find an error, select the one underlined part that must be changed to make the sentence correct and blacken the corresponding space on your answer sheet. If there is no error, blacken answer space E.

41. *From* (A) the early Renaissance *until well into* (B) the nineteenth century, the basic elements of a classical education *were* (C) scarcely changed in form *nor content.* (D) *No error* (E)

42. The people *which* (A) fill the novels of William Faulkner are capable *neither* (B) of living in the rootless modern world nor *of freeing themselves* (C) fully *from* (D) their morally tainted heritage. *No error* (E)

43. We cannot know *for certain* (A) the true *degree and kind* (B) of religious piety *felt by* (C) a historical figure *like* (D) Lincoln. *No error* (E)

44. Government policies *at the time* (A) required that *every* (B) male citizen *between eighteen and* (C) thirty years of age *registers* (D) for the military draft. *No error* (E)

45. The names *of most of* (A) the greatest inventors *who* (B) ever lived—*those* (C) who first harnessed fire, learned to farm, tamed animals—are *unknown to* (D) history. *No error* (E)

46. By the time Wordsworth became poet laureate, *most of his* (A) poetic talent had been *spent,* (B) although *he continues* (C) to write poetry *for* (D) many more years. *No error* (E)

47. The chairman *ruled that* (A) the question whether a quorum *was present* (B) was out of order, *since* (C) the meeting had already *began.* (D) *No error* (E)

48. Though the writers at the conference were all very talented, *none* (A) of them *had either written* (B) a best-selling book *nor* (C) sold a story to the television *or* (D) movie industry. *No error* (E)

49. Government leaders *have found that* (A) when economic conditions *are bad,* (B) few citizens *favor* (C) tax increases *accept* (D) those who are most likely to benefit from additional services. *No error* (E)

50. Although the ruling *established* (A) *separate areas* (B) of jurisdiction *for* (C) the two unions, relations *among them* (D) remained uneasy at best. *No error* (E)

S T O P

IF YOU FINISH BEFORE TIME IS CALLED, YOU MAY CHECK YOUR WORK ON THIS SECTION ONLY. DO NOT WORK ON ANY OTHER SECTION IN THE TEST.

PRACTICE TEST 3: *Scoring Instructions*

1. Check your answers against the answer key on page 250.
2. To figure your SAT-verbal score:
   A. Count the total number of correct answers you chose in Sections 1 and 4.
   B. Count the total number of incorrect answers you chose in Sections 1 and 4. Multiply this number by 1/4. Ignore any questions you left blank.
   C. Subtract the result of Step B from the result of Step A. Round off the answer to the nearest whole number. This whole number is your SAT-verbal raw score.
   D. Find your raw score in the first column of the score conversion table on page 251. Read across to the column headed SAT-verbal. The three-digit number there is your SAT-verbal score.
3. To figure your SAT-mathematical score:
   A. Count the total number of correct answers you chose in Sections 2 and 5.
   B. Count the total number of incorrect answers you chose from questions 8–27 in Section 5. Multiply this number by 1/3. Ignore any questions you left blank.
   C. Count the total number of incorrect answers you chose from all other questions in Sections 2 and 5. Multiply this number by 1/4. Ignore any questions you left blank.
   D. Add the results of Step B and Step C. Subtract this total from the result of Step A. Round off the answer to the nearest whole number. This whole number is your SAT-mathematical raw score.
   E. Find your raw score in the first column of the score conversion table on page 251. Read across to the column headed SAT-mathematical. The three-digit number there is your SAT-mathematical score.
4. To figure your Test of Standard Written English (TSWE) score:
   A. Count the total number of correct answers you chose in Sections 3 and 6.
   B. Count the total number of incorrect answers you chose in Sections 3 and 6. Multiply this number by 1/4. Ignore any questions you left blank.
   C. Subtract the result of Step B from the result of Step A. Round off the answer to the nearest whole number. This whole number is your TSWE raw score.
   D. Find your raw score in the first column of the score conversion table on page 251. Read across to the column headed TSWE. The two-digit number there is your TSWE score.

Note: Allow for a margin of error of 30 points either way on your SAT-verbal and SAT-mathematical scores (3 points on your TSWE score). For instance, an SAT-verbal score of 470 really represents a range of scores from 440 to 500. Remember that test performance varies greatly from one day to the next and can be improved through study and practice. So don't consider your scores on any practice test as a perfect prediction of how you'll do on the real SAT.

PRACTICE TEST 3: *Answer Key*

SECTION 1

1. **A**	7. **B**	13. **B**	19. **B**	25. **D**	31. **A**	37. **D**	43. **A**
2. **C**	8. **C**	14. **A**	20. **C**	26. **B**	32. **C**	38. **A**	44. **E**
3. **B**	9. **C**	15. **B**	21. **C**	27. **E**	33. **A**	39. **E**	45. **C**
4. **A**	10. **D**	16. **E**	22. **B**	28. **D**	34. **E**	40. **E**	
5. **D**	11. **E**	17. **D**	23. **D**	29. **C**	35. **B**	41. **B**	
6. **E**	12. **E**	18. **D**	24. **A**	30. **B**	36. **D**	42. **A**	

SECTION 2

1. **D**	6. **A**	11. **B**	16. **C**	21. **D**
2. **A**	7. **E**	12. **B**	17. **A**	22. **E**
3. **B**	8. **C**	13. **B**	18. **E**	23. **D**
4. **C**	9. **D**	14. **C**	19. **C**	24. **D**
5. **C**	10. **A**	15. **E**	20. **E**	25. **A**

SECTION 3

1. **D**	8. **A**	15. **C**	22. **D**	29. **A**	36. **E**	43. **D**	50. **E**
2. **A**	9. **A**	16. **C**	23. **E**	30. **B**	37. **C**	44. **B**	
3. **D**	10. **E**	17. **E**	24. **E**	31. **C**	38. **D**	45. **C**	
4. **E**	11. **D**	18. **D**	25. **C**	32. **E**	39. **A**	46. **D**	
5. **C**	12. **C**	19. **C**	26. **D**	33. **E**	40. **B**	47. **E**	
6. **D**	13. **E**	20. **E**	27. **B**	34. **B**	41. **A**	48. **A**	
7. **B**	14. **A**	21. **D**	28. **B**	35. **D**	42. **C**	49. **C**	

SECTION 4

1. **B**	6. **C**	11. **A**	16. **B**	21. **C**	26. **D**	31. **B**	36. **D**
2. **D**	7. **E**	12. **A**	17. **A**	22. **D**	27. **E**	32. **C**	37. **A**
3. **D**	8. **A**	13. **D**	18. **D**	23. **B**	28. **D**	33. **E**	38. **B**
4. **A**	9. **B**	14. **E**	19. **A**	24. **A**	29. **A**	34. **E**	39. **C**
5. **C**	10. **C**	15. **E**	20. **C**	25. **B**	30. **D**	35. **E**	40. **A**

SECTION 5

1. **B**	6. **C**	11. **D**	16. **B**	21. **A**	26. **C**	31. **A**
2. **B**	7. **D**	12. **C**	17. **D**	22. **C**	27. **C**	32. **E**
3. **A**	8. **B**	13. **B**	18. **C**	23. **A**	28. **A**	33. **E**
4. **D**	9. **C**	14. **A**	19. **D**	24. **C**	29. **A**	34. **C**
5. **A**	10. **C**	15. **A**	20. **C**	25. **D**	30. **B**	35. **C**

SECTION 6

1. **D**	8. **E**	15. **C**	22. **D**	29. **A**	36. **C**	43. **E**	50. **D**
2. **C**	9. **C**	16. **D**	23. **C**	30. **E**	37. **C**	44. **D**	
3. **B**	10. **C**	17. **C**	24. **E**	31. **A**	38. **B**	45. **E**	
4. **C**	11. **E**	18. **E**	25. **C**	32. **C**	39. **C**	46. **C**	
5. **D**	12. **A**	19. **E**	26. **E**	33. **A**	40. **A**	47. **D**	
6. **E**	13. **E**	20. **A**	27. **D**	34. **B**	41. **D**	48. **C**	
7. **A**	14. **B**	21. **D**	28. **D**	35. **E**	42. **A**	49. **D**	

PRACTICE TEST 3: ***Score Conversion Table***

Raw Score	SAT-Verbal	SAT-Mathematical	TSWE
100			60+
99			60+
98			60+
97			60+
96			60+
95			60+
94			60+
93			60+
92			60+
91			59
90			59
89			58
88			58
87			57
86			57
85	800		56
84	780		56
83	760		55
82	750		55
81	740		54
80	730		54
79	720		53
78	710		53
77	700		52
76	690		52
75	680		51
74	670		51
73	660		51
72	650		50
71	640		50
70	630		49
69	630		49
68	620		48
67	620		48
66	610		47
65	610		47
64	600		46
63	600		46
62	590		45
61	590		45
60	580	800	44
59	580	780	44
58	570	770	43
57	570	760	43
56	560	750	42
55	550	740	42
54	550	730	41
53	540	720	41
52	540	710	40
51	530	700	40
50	520	690	39
49	520	680	39
48	510	670	38
47	500	660	38
46	500	650	37
45	490	640	37
44	490	630	36
43	480	620	36
42	470	610	35
41	470	600	35
40	460	600	34
39	450	590	34
38	450	580	33
37	440	570	33
36	440	560	32
35	430	550	32
34	430	540	31
33	420	530	31
32	420	520	30
31	410	510	30
30	400	500	29
29	400	490	29
28	390	490	28
27	380	480	28
26	370	470	27
25	370	460	27
24	360	450	26
23	350	440	26
22	350	430	25
21	340	420	25
20	330	410	24
19	330	400	24
18	320	390	23
17	310	380	23
16	300	370	22
15	290	360	22
14	280	350	21
13	280	340	21
12	270	330	20
11	260	320	20
10	250	310	20
9	250	310	20
8	240	300	20
7	230	290	20
6	220	280	20
5	210	270	20
4	200	260	20
3	200	250	20
2	200	240	20
1	200	220	20
0 or less	200	200	20

PRACTICE TEST 3: *Explanatory Answers*

SECTION 1

1. **A** To *allay* something, such as pain or fear, is to make it less bad, to relieve it, or to calm it. The opposite is to make it worse or to intensify it, which is the meaning of *exacerbate*.

2. **C** As an adjective, *articulate* means "expressing oneself clearly and logically." An *articulate* person states his or her ideas understandably and well. The opposite is *incoherent*, which means "difficult to understand" or "confused."

3. **B** Something *opaque* can't be seen through; light does not pass through it at all. A brick wall is *opaque*. By contrast, something *diaphanous* can be seen through. A piece of thin, filmy fabric might be described as *diaphanous*.

4. **A** To *fetter* someone is literally to put him or her in chains; the word is used to refer to any kind of imprisonment or slavery. To *emancipate* someone is to set her or him free: Lincoln *emancipated* the slaves.

5. **D** *Proficient* means "skilled," "skillful," or "adept." The opposite is *unskilled* or *incompetent*. Choice B is tempting, but the opposite of *inexperienced* is *experienced*, not *proficient*. A person can be experienced without being proficient.

6. **E** *Factional* means "pertaining to a faction," which is a party or interest group. The word is a good antonym for *nonpartisan*, which refers to an action or policy that is supported by all, regardless of their particular party or interest group. *Nonpartisan* can also refer to an election in which candidates run without the sponsorship of a party or faction.

7. **B** Something *atrocious* is awful, horrible, extremely wicked, or outrageous. The opposite would have to be a word expressing strong approval; *admirable* is a good choice.

8. **C** To *nullify* something is to negate it, to take away its power or effect. The opposite is to strengthen, enforce, or uphold something—to *validate* it.

9. **C** Literally, *palatable* means "able to be tasted or eaten"; figuratively, it means "acceptable." The word *noxious* combines the opposites of these two meanings well. It means "revolting or disgusting to taste" or "hateful, odious."

10. **D** *Eminent* means "well-known" or "prominent." Justice Holmes was an *eminent* legal authority. The opposite is *little-known* or *obscure*.

11. **E** *Desultory* efforts or actions are halfhearted, irregular, or rambling. If you make a *desultory* attempt to clean up your room, chances are it will remain pretty dirty. The opposite is *determined* or *vigorous*.

12. **E** *Duplicity* is hypocrisy or double-dealing; a two-faced person is duplicitous. The opposite is *straightforwardness*, which means "frankness" or "honesty." *Simplicity* (choice A) is opposed in meaning to *duplicity*, but not directly enough to be its antonym.

13. **B** Something *banal* is mundane, routine, boring, or commonplace—the same old TV show, for instance. Good antonyms for *banal* include *unusual, unique, striking,* and *extraordinary*. Choices A, C, and D are slightly off; you can eliminate them by checking them backward.

14. **A** *Pristine* means "unspoiled, pure, unsullied"; think of a *pristine* wilderness unvisited by human beings. The opposite is *spoiled, sullied,* or *corrupted.*

15. **B** This is quite a hard one. *Captious* means "quick to find fault, quibbling, carping." The teacher who never gives a good grade might be described as *captious*. The opposite is *indulgent*, which means "quick to overlook faults."

16. **E** As the second half of the sentence explains, the songs of birds vary according to "place of origin." Therefore, the variations are *geographic.*

17. **D** The key word *unlike* shows that the sentence is contrasting two kinds of pacifist. Since the second kind described is the *secular* pacifist, the first kind must be the *religious* or *spiritual* pacifist (since *secular* means "nonreligious"). On the basis of the first word, then, choices D and E are both possible. On the basis of the second word, only choice D really works. It makes sense to call nonviolence a "*means* of political struggle"; it doesn't make sense to call it a "*purpose* of political struggle."

18. **D** The key word *but* indicates that the second half of the sentence will contrast with the first half, which refers to Marston's "fine teaching." So you can expect something negative to be mentioned. The first words in choices B, C, and D are all negative, but only in choice D is the second word also negative: *disparagement* means "criticism."

19. **B** "Current oil glut" means that there is plenty of oil for the moment. If the second half of the sentence describes some fact that the glut might *obscure* (hide), that fact must be the likelihood of a worldwide *depletion* (using up) of oil reserves. The first words in choices A, B, and C are all possible. However, the second words in choices A and C don't make much sense: oil supplies are being depleted because they're being used not more *carelessly* or more *often* but more *quickly* than they can be replaced.

20. **C** If neither anthropologist *consciously* distorted the facts, then choices B, D, and E are impossible. And choice A doesn't make sense: to *augment* something is to increase it. Choice C fits the sentence quite logically.

21. **C** The passage describes, in chronological order, the various stages by which the idea of genetic engineering has developed, starting with selective breeding (paragraph 1) and medical treatment (paragraph 2) and going on to direct tinkering with genetic materials (paragraphs 3 and 4).

22. **B** Since the question specifically excludes the broader definition of genetic engineering suggested in paragraph 1, refer only to the first sentence of paragraph 3. As of 1965, the term was used to refer only to direct manipulation of the genetic materials in cells.

23. **D** Look again at the first sentence of the passage. Selective breeding was practiced—deliberately and successfully—long before the genetic mechanisms by which it worked were understood.

24. **A** Reread the third sentence of paragraph 2. The treatment of diabetes with insulin is cited there as an example of how medical care can "increase the prevalence in

the population of certain genes that can have deleterious effects on individuals." The survival of diabetic people means an increase in the number of diabetics who reproduce, and thus an increase in the number of people who are genetically disposed to diabetes.

25. **D** Clearly, scientists had to understand the nature and function of DNA before they could try to take it apart and recombine specific DNA sequences in any meaningful way. Choice A is wrong because cell fusion technology, as described in paragraph 4, was developed at the same time as recombinant DNA technology; it was not a precursor of it.

26. **B** Paragraph 5 explains that it was the split between pro-British and pro-American Iroquois that finally destroyed the league's unity.

27. **E** Reread the second sentence of paragraph 1 and the first two sentences of paragraph 2. The member tribes of the Iroquois League were self-governing. They formed a "loose confederation" to deal with "matters of war and foreign relations."

28. **D** In the third sentence of the passage, you are told that the sachems' titles "belonged to various matrilineal families." In other words, the titles were passed on within families, as choice D suggests. Choice B is not supported in the passage; if anything, the word *matrilineal* (referring to descent through the female line) suggests that it is inaccurate.

29. **C** Nowhere does the passage suggest that the government of the Iroquois League involved more than one branch of government. The other choices are all well supported in the passage.

30. **B** Both the presence of positive statements and the absence of negative statements in the passage suggest that the author's attitude toward the Iroquois League is one of approval and admiration.

31. **A** The two blanks must be filled with words that fit together logically—with each other and with the rest of the sentence. Choice A works because an *aging* system might well be *poorly maintained*, and *poorly maintained* equipment might well be subject to *breakdowns*.

32. **C** The sentence says that behavioral psychologists hesitate to discuss any aspect of human activity that can't be observed. Of the five answer choices, only motivations can't be observed.

33. **A** The key word *while* initiates a contrast between towns *blighted* by *industrialization* and East Henry. *Undeveloped* and *paradise* complete that contrast. Choice B is wrong because a *hamlet* is any small village, not necessarily an attractive or pleasant one.

34. **E** To develop the idea of variety, the second word must be either *various* (choice B) or *diverse* (choice E). To illustrate the range of participants, the first word must be a near opposite of *sophisticated user*—that is, a word meaning "someone who is unknowing or inexperienced." A *novice* (a beginner) is unknowing or inexperienced; an *enthusiast* may or may not be.

35. **B** The key phrase *that is* indicates that the second half of the sentence will explain what "Milton never repeated a form" means. So the second word must be a near synonym for *form. Modes* (choice A) and *genres* (choice B) are good candidates;

styles (choice D), though not quite as good, is a possibility. The key word *although* indicates that the first word must contrast in some way with *basically true.* At first blush, *false* seems to do that best, but think about it: how can something that is *false* be *basically true*? It can't be. *Obvious* doesn't work, either. *Oversimplified* does.

36. **D** The relationship between *base* and *apex* is one of bottom to top. The relationship between *foot* and *crown* is the same. (A *point*, choice C, is not necessarily at the top of something.)

37. **D** A *field* that is *barren* is one in which no crops are growing. Similarly, an *orchard* that is *fruitless* is one in which no fruit is growing.

38. **A** To *glance* is to take a quick look with the *eye.* To *sniff* is to take a quick smell with the *nose.*

39. **E** *Gullible* and *foolish* are close in meaning: *gullible* basically means "foolish enough to believe what others say." *Rational* and *sensible* are also close in meaning. None of the other pairs are.

40. **E** To *overthrow* a *regime* is to remove it from office. Similarly, to *unseat* an *incumbent* is to remove him or her from office (through an election).

41. **B** When something is *deliberate*, it is *not* left to *chance*; the two words are opposed in meaning. In the same way, something that is *organized* is not left in *disorder.* Something *obscure* may be *meaningful* (choice E); its meaning may simply be hard to discern.

42. **A** *Poach* means "to trespass for the purpose of stealing game." So *hunter* is to *poach* as *hiker* is to *trespass.*

43. **A** A *condolence* (an expression of sympathy) can serve to soothe or lessen the pain of *grief*. An *emollient* (a soothing ointment) can have a similar effect on a *burn.* Choice C is wrong because *relief* is not something "applied" from the outside.

44. **E** Picture a railroad *track.* The wooden pieces that run between and connect the rails are *ties.* In much the same way, the *rungs* of a *ladder* run between and connect the two uprights. (Of course, the functions of ties and rungs are different, but their physical form and appearance are similar.)

45. **C** If you *taunt* someone, you're likely to provoke a feeling of *irritation* in that person. Similarly, if you *degrade* someone, you're likely to arouse a feeling of *humiliation.* If you *tease* someone (choice D), you may amuse yourself or a callous onlooker, but you're not likely to create a feeling of *amusement* in the person you're teasing.

SECTION 2

1. **D** First, cross multiply: $7x = 20$. Then divide both sides of the equation by 7: $x = 20/7$.

2. **A** Just factor $9n - 6$ and you'll see that it must be divisible by 3—no matter what integer n is:

$$\frac{3(3n - 2)}{3}$$

3. **B** The 60 T-shirts will bring in $60 \times \$3.50 = \$210.00$. They will cost $(60 \div 12) \times \$16.00 = \$80.00$. The difference (total profit) is $130.00.

4. **C** If the 4 liters of ammonia in the tank produce a 20% solution, then the total amount of liquid in the tank must be 20 liters, and the solution must contain 16 liters of water. Since no more water will be added, the 16 liters of water will represent 3/4 (75%) of the stronger solution. Use this information to find the total amount of liquid in the stronger solution:

$$16 = \frac{3}{4}x$$

$$21\frac{1}{3} = x$$

Then subtract: $21\frac{1}{3} - 20 = 1\frac{1}{3}$.

5. **C** If OAB is an equilateral triangle with side 9, then (1) angle AOB measures 60° (or 1/6 of the degree measure of a circle), and (2) circle O has a radius of 9 and a circumference ($2\pi r$) of 18π. Therefore, the length of arc AB is 1/6 of 18π, or 3π.

6. **A** The pattern consists of alternating groups of 0s and 1s. The number of 0s in a group increases by one from left to right: one, two, three, four. The number of 1s in a group alternates: one, two, one, two. At the point where the tape breaks off, three more 0s are needed to complete the expected set of five 0s.

7. **E** Work it out: $2^6 = 64$ and $2^5 = 32$. Therefore, 2^x must also equal 32, so x must equal 5. (By the way, this will not work with any number other than 2 as the base.)

8. **C** The length of the rectangle is irrelevant. Since the width of the rectangle is 6, the circle cannot have a diameter any greater than 6. If its diameter is 6, its radius is 3 and its area (πr^2) is 9π.

9. **D** There are several ways of figuring this out. Here's one: If $\measuredangle AEC$ measures 105°, then $\measuredangle CED$ must measure 75°, since together they form a straight angle of 180°. If $\measuredangle CED$ measures 75°, then the other portion of $\measuredangle BED$—that is, $\measuredangle BEC$—must measure $142° - 75° = 67°$.

10. **A** Plug the number 3 into the definition:

$$\oplus 3 = \frac{3^2 + 1}{3 + 1}$$

$$= \frac{9 + 1}{3 + 1}$$

$$= \frac{10}{4}$$

$$= \frac{5}{2}$$

11. **B** Again, plug the numbers into the definition. You'll find that $\oplus 4$ works out to 17/5, while $\oplus 2$ equals 5/3. To divide, invert and multiply:

$$\frac{17}{5} \div \frac{5}{3} = \frac{17}{5} \times \frac{3}{5} = \frac{51}{25}$$

12. **B** If $x + 2 = 0$, then $x = -2$. If $y - 2 = 0$, then $y = 2$. Therefore, both x/y and y/x equal -1. And $-1 - (-1) = 0$.

13. **B** As you may have found, this particular problem is probably solved most quickly by trial and error. Plug each of the possible values for Todd's age into the statements given and see which one works. It generally makes sense to start with the middle value (in this case, choice C) and work your way up or down, depending on the results you get. You'll find that Todd is 28 and Alan is 14.

14. **C** If each side of triangle ABC has a length of 6, then each smaller triangle has sides of 2. Add up the 6 small segments making up the darkened path, and you'll get a total length of 12. (Yes, it's as simple as that; there's no hidden trick.)

15. **E** This problem is easier to solve if you think in terms of ratios rather than percentages. Team A has won 24 games and lost 18. This is a ratio of 24:18, or 4:3. Team B has lost 3 more games than Team A. In order to arrive at the same ratio of wins to losses, Team B needs to win 4 more games than Team A. It's already won 1 more game than Team A. So it needs to win its next 3 games.

16. **C** Since you have to express Bob's total salary in dollars alone, first convert the cents in his hourly salary to dollars by dividing by 100: $c/100$. Then express his hourly salary in dollars alone: $d + c/100$. Multiply this by 8 and you get $8d + 8c/100$, which reduces to $8d + 2c/25$.

17. **A** If $x = 4$ and $y = 3x/2$, then $y = 12/2 = 6$. Substitute 4 for x and 6 for y in choice A and you get 8: $2y - x = 2(6) - 4 = 8$.

18. **E** Since you want an answer in cubic inches, start by converting all the measurements to inches: 1/2 foot = 6 inches; 1/3 foot = 4 inches; 1/4 foot = 3 inches. Then multiply the three edges to find the volume of the rectangular solid: $6 \times 4 \times 3 = 72$.

19. **C** The basic formula for any travel problem is Rate × Time = Distance. Train A travels at a rate of 50 miles per hour for 4 hours; therefore, it travels 200 miles. Now, Train B travels for just $2\frac{1}{2}$ hours, but it travels the same 200 miles (since it *overtakes* Train A at 7 P.M.). Divide 200 by $2\frac{1}{2}$ to find the rate of Train B—80 miles per hour.

20. **E** Since x has a greater absolute value than y, you know that choice B will always be negative and choice C, though positive, will always be a fraction less than 1. For the same reason, you also know that choice D will be positive. However, if x and y are fractions, say $-1/2$ and $-1/4$, then choice D will be a fraction less than 1. So will choice A if x and y are fractions. Only choice E will be greater than 1 whether x and y are integers or fractions.

21. **D** For two numbers to yield a negative product, one must be negative and the other positive. In quadrant II, x is negative and y is positive; in quadrant IV, x is positive and y is negative. So for any pairs of values found in those quadrants, the product of x and y will be negative.

22. **E** If two cards are drawn whose sum is 13, then the two cards must be either 7 and 6 or 8 and 5. If they are 8 and 5, the 5 will not be among the remaining cards.

23. **D** If $x/2$ is an odd integer, then x must be an even integer that is twice some odd integer (6 or 10, for example). Choice A is not an integer (since 4 is not a factor of an integer that is twice an odd number), and choices B, C, and E are all odd.

24. **D** The school collects \$378.00 by selling 54 caps priced at \$7.00 each. Therefore, it collects \$1,068.00 – \$378.00 = \$690.00 on sales of 210 – 54 = 156 caps priced at

either \$5.00 or \$3.50. Let x be the number of caps priced at \$5.00 and $156 - x$ the number of caps priced at \$3.50. The caps priced at \$5.00 bring in $5x$ dollars; those priced at \$3.50 bring in $3.5(156 - x)$ dollars; together they bring in \$690.00:

$$5x + 3.5(156 - x) = 690$$
$$5x + 546 - 3.5x = 690$$
$$2.5x = 144$$
$$x = 96$$

25. **A** Subtract 4 from both sides of the inequality and simplify the result:

$$-a < \frac{b+3}{2} - 4$$
$$-a < \frac{b+3}{2} - \frac{8}{2}$$
$$-a < \frac{b-5}{2}$$

Then multiply both sides of the inequality by -1. Remember to change the direction of the inequality as well as the sign of each term. Thus:

$$a > \frac{5-b}{2}$$

SECTION 3

1. **D** *Commented over* is not idiomatic. It should be *commented on.*

2. **A** The phrase *fleeing on foot* is a misplaced modifier. It should refer to the suspect, but in its present location it seems to refer to the police officers.

3. **D** When a compound subject is joined by *either . . . or*, the verb should agree with the nearer subject. In this sentence, the nearer subject is the plural *efforts*. Therefore, the verb should also be plural: *influence.*

4. **E** No error in this sentence.

5. **C** The antecedent for the pronoun in choice C is *employees*. Since *employees* is plural, the pronoun should be plural, too: *they*, not *he or she.*

6. **D** The past participle of the verb *lie*, meaning "rest in place," is *lain*, not *laid. Laid* is the past participle of *lay*, meaning "put or place." Don't confuse the two verbs.

7. **B** The idiom is not *nowhere nearly* but *nowhere near* (although *not nearly* would probably be more appropriate in a formal context).

8. **A** When a pronoun is used in apposition to a noun, as in *us New Yorkers*, check the case of the pronoun by mentally eliminating the noun. In this case you'll see that "*us* . . . have long been accustomed" should be "*we* . . . have long been accustomed."

9. **A** *In attempt to* is not idiomatic. The phrase should be either *attempting to* or *in an attempt to.*

10. **E** No error in this sentence.

11. **D** Superlatives are incorrect in comparisons that involve only two elements. In this sentence, *greatest* should be *greater.*

12. **C** The verb should agree with the closer of two subjects joined by *either ... or*. In this case, the closer subject is *one* (not *physical sciences*, which is the object of the preposition *of*). So the verb should be *is*, not *are*.

13. **E** No error in this sentence.

14. **A** The past participle of the irregular verb *drive* is *driven*, not *drove*. (*Drove* is the past tense of the verb; it is always used *without* a helping verb.)

15. **C** When a comparison is introduced with the word *as*, a second *as* must follow; *like* is incorrect.

16. **C** Since stamp collecting became popular in the past, the present tense is inappropriate: *is* should be *was*.

17. **E** No error in this sentence.

18. **D** This sentence illogically compares *the victors in theatrical competitions* to *baseball and football*. It should compare them to baseball and football *stars*.

19. **C** The sentence is marred by a double negative: both *not* and *scarcely* are negative words. Since *not* isn't underlined, *scarcely* must be changed or deleted.

20. **E** No error in this sentence.

21. **D** This is a subtle error in parallelism. The correlative conjunction *not only ... but also* should link elements that are parallel in form as well as in thought. In this sentence, the elements are both clauses—*what she wished to express* and *how it was expressed by her*. But notice that the subject of the first clause is *she* and the verb is active (*wished*), whereas the subject of the second clause is *it* and the verb is passive (*was expressed*). The shift is unnecessary and inappropriate. *How she expressed it* would be much better.

22. **D** For the sake of parallelism, the clause *that are human* should be reduced to the adjective *human* and placed in front of *weaknesses*. Then the sentence would end with a series of three phrases in parallel adjective-noun form.

23. **E** No error in this sentence.

24. **E** No error in this sentence.

25. **C** *In according with* is nonidiomatic. The phrase should be either *according to* or *in accordance with*.

26. **D** The original sentence is a run-on. Choice D corrects the problem clearly, logically, and succinctly.

27. **B** In the original sentence, the opening phrase is a dangling modifier. Choices B, C, and E all correct this error, but choice C introduces the pronoun *it* without supplying an antecedent, and choice E is nonidiomatic.

28. **B** The original sentence is a run-on. So is choice D. Of the three remaining answers, choice B is the most concise.

29. **A** The sentence is correct as originally written. Each of the other versions turns the opening phrase into a dangling or misplaced modifier. The first words after the comma must refer to Ben Jonson, not to his works.

30. **B** All of the answer choices are technically correct and say the same thing. Choice B is the clearest and most concise.

31. **C** The original sentence is a fragment, since *having become* cannot serve as a predicate. (Watch out for the *-ing* forms of verbs.) Choice C corrects the error. Technically, so do choices D and E, but both of them sound unnatural.

32. **E** The two examples given should be parallel in grammatical form. Therefore, to match *the potato in Ireland*, the underlined phrase should read *pasta in Italy*.

33. **E** The word *thus* confuses the logic of the original sentence by reversing the apparent cause-and-effect relationship between the two clauses. Choice E clears up the confusion.

34. **B** Since the phrase that begins the sentence modifies Newton, the first word after the comma must be *Newton*. Choices B and D both begin with *Newton*, but *in the development of* in choice D is nonidiomatic.

35. **D** All the answers except choice B (which results in a run-on) are technically correct. Of the four possibilities, choice D is the most concise and graceful.

36. **E** The underlined portion of the original sentence is an incomplete construction. Choices B, D, and E all complete the construction by supplying a predicate for the subject *scientist*. However, choice B is a run-on sentence, and choice D misuses the semicolon (a comma should follow a long introductory dependent clause).

37. **C** Choice C is clear and concise. The other choices add words but no meaning to the sentence.

38. **D** Since the semicolon functions as a kind of "balance," it is appropriate only between elements of equal grammatical "weight." In the original sentence of this question, a semicolon inappropriately separates an independent clause from a phrase. Choice D corrects the error by transforming the phrase into an independent clause. So does choice C, but the logic of the sentence demands *gained*, not *were gaining*. Choice B results in a run-on; choice E, in a fragment.

39. **A** The original sentence is correct. The construction "not X but Y" demands the use of *but*, not some other conjunction. It also demands that X and Y be parallel in form. In choices B and E, they aren't.

40. **B** The original sentence is a fragment. Only choice B makes a complete statement.

41. **A** The subject of the verb *wish* is the pronoun *who*, which may be either singular or plural, depending on its antecedent. In this sentence, *who* is singular, since its antecedent is the singular pronoun *no one*. Therefore, the verb should also be singular: *wishes*.

42. **C** The pronoun *he* is a direct object of the verb *nominate*. Therefore, it should be in the objective case: *him*, not *he*.

43. **D** *Hardly* and *no one* are both negatives, so *hardly no one* is a double negative. *No one* should be *anyone*.

44. **B** The conjunction *as* indicates that the two clauses in this sentence are describing simultaneous events, so the verbs in both clauses should be in the same tense. Since the verb in the second clause cannot be changed (because the helping verb

is is not underlined), the verb in the first clause must be changed—from *will grow* to *is growing.*

45. **C** This is a diction error. To *deduct* is to subtract or take away. The word needed here is *deduce*, which means "to infer" or "to determine from evidence."

46. **D** Since *unique* means "one of a kind," it can't be compared. Something is either unique or not unique; it can't be more or less unique. In this sentence, *most unique* would have to be changed to something like *most unusual.*

47. **E** No error in this sentence.

48. **A** This sentence contains an unnecessary shift from *anyone* to *you.* Since *you* is not underlined, *anyone wants* must be changed to *you want.*

49. **C** "Enables farmers *anticipation of*" is nonidiomatic. It should be "enables farmers *to anticipate.*"

50. **E** No error in this sentence.

SECTION 4

1. **B** *Haphazard* means "at random, without plan." *Methodical* means "carefully planned, deliberate, well-organized." Choice E is wrong because *scientific* doesn't particularly relate to planning or to organizing; it refers to a special way of pursuing knowledge or truth.

2. **D** To *antagonize* is to irritate, annoy, or anger. By contrast, to *placate* is to soothe, appease, or calm.

3. **D** *Stalwart* means "brave, resolute, courageous." Choice D, *craven*, means "cowardly." Eliminate a tempting wrong answer like choice B by working backward: the opposite of *mild* is *intense* or *severe*, not *stalwart* or *brave.*

4. **A** To *rue* something is to regret it: "You'll *rue* the day you double-crossed me." By contrast, to *bless* something is to express thanks and happiness for it.

5. **C** *Moribund* means "dying" or "near death." A good opposite is *vigorous.* (*Viable*, choice E, means "*capable* of living," which is not the opposite of *moribund*, or *dying.*)

6. **C** *Equilibrium* means "balance." Choice C, *imbalance*, is an obvious antonym.

7. **E** *Limpid* means "extremely clear"; it's a word one would apply to a tranquil mountain lake. *Turbid* means "muddy"; think of a pond in which mud and weeds have been stirred up by a passing motorboat.

8. **A** To *covet* something is to want or desire it. To *spurn* something is to reject it or to treat it with scorn or contempt.

9. **B** Something *impervious* cannot be penetrated or pierced; Superman's skin is *impervious* to bullets. The best antonym is choice B, *penetrable.*

10. **C** *Indigent* means "very poor." Choice C, *affluent*, is a good opposite: it means "wealthy, well-to-do, rich."

11. **A** The key word *because* signals a cause-and-effect relationship. If the two primitive cultures are far apart, similarities between them are unlikely to be due to *intercommunication.* (If you selected choice D, notice the word *unlikely. Proximity,* or nearness, *can't possibly* be the source of the similarities.)

12. **A** As the key word *for* indicates, the second half of the sentence provides a reason or explanation for the first half. If many people have willingly sacrificed their lives for a greater good, then it must be the human instinct for *survival* that can't be regarded as an absolute.

13. **D** The key word *although* initiates a contrast between "boys' game" and something else. *False* and *adults* complete the contrast logically.

14. **E** The key word *like* indicates that the missing word must be similar in meaning to *by separate, unrelated paths. Independently* is the only logical choice.

15. **E** The key word *produced* signals a cause-and-effect relationship. It makes sense that the professor's *carping* (that is, harshly critical) comments might make a student decide never to *speak* in class.

16. **B** *Malign* and *laud* are almost exact antonyms; so are *condemn* and *praise.*

17. **A** Just as one might *redden* with *embarrassment,* so one might *blanch* (that is, turn white) with *horror.* In each pair, the first word describes how one's complexion might react to the emotion named by the second word. (*Illness,* in choice C, does not name an emotion.)

18. **D** The *wing* is the part that guides and sustains the movement of a bird through *air.* In the same way, the *fin* is the part that guides and sustains the movement of a fish through *water.*

19. **A** One *consults* a *dictionary* for much the same purpose that one *examines* a *specimen*—to learn from it.

20. **C** A *lock* is a small clump of *hair*; a *tuft* is a small clump of *grass.*

21. **C** A *vivid hue* is like a *clarion tone*: both are unusually bright, clear, and intense.

22. **D** *Immune* means "highly resistant to a *disease.*" Similarly, *impregnable* means "highly resistant to an *attack*" or "unconquerable." Choice A is close, but *vision* is not a kind of assault or injury, as both *disease* and *attack* are.

23. **B** The *annulment* of a *marriage* is a bit different from divorce; it is a declaration that the marriage agreement is void and was never valid. In much the same way, the *voiding* of a *contract* renders the agreement legally invalid.

24. **A** *Fluent* and *glib* have similar denotations but different connotations: *fluent* is a positive term; *glib* is a negative term. Analogously, *polished* and *slick* have similar denotations but different connotations: *polished* is a positive term; *slick* is a negative term. (In choice E, *eloquent* is a positive term and *loquacious* is a negative term, but the two words have different denotations: *eloquent* refers to how *well* a person speaks; *loquacious* refers to how *much* a person speaks.)

25. **B** A *pebble* is a particle of *gravel*; a *grain* is a particle of *sand.*

26. **D** The author discusses two main topics: the alteration of the natural colors of gems through heating and dyeing and the production of synthetic or imitation gems. Only choice D mentions both of those topics.

27. **E** The third sentence of paragraph 2 discusses dyeing as a means of altering the "unattractive grays and pale shades" of some gemstones. You can infer from that sentence that the dyeing is done for aesthetic reasons—that is, to improve the appearance of or to beautify the gemstones.

28. **D** The word *however* in the last sentence of the passage signals an exception to the rule that chemically simpler stones are generally easier to synthesize. The diamond is cited as the exception.

29. **A** The author does not explicitly comment on the distinction between the fine arts and the lesser arts. However, the quotation marks around *fine*, *lesser*, *quality*, and so on throughout the passage strongly imply that the author questions the validity of the distinction. They are his way of saying, "These are someone else's labels—not mine—and I do not endorse them."

30. **D** The passage states that the "fine" arts have been associated with "upper-class taste" and the "lesser" arts with "'lack of taste' among the lower classes." The passage goes on to say that art historians have largely ignored the so-called lesser or low-quality works of art. This is the point made in answer D.

31. **B** Since the author clearly questions the validity of the distinction between "fine" and "lesser" arts, it is logical to conclude that he would agree that art historians ought to abandon that distinction and study all types of art, whether "fine" or not.

32. **C** Answers A, B, D, and E are all too narrow for this main idea question. Only answer C covers all of the topics discussed in the passage.

33. **E** As paragraph 1 explains, low-energy X rays are useful for diagnostic purposes because they can travel through the body (living cells) and create an image on film. As paragraph 2 explains, high-energy X rays are useful for therapeutic purposes because they can destroy living cancer cells.

34. **E** The last three paragraphs explain why doses of high-level radiation must be confined to small areas of the body. The first sentence in paragraph 5 provides the specific information needed to answer this question.

35. **E** The last sentence of paragraph 4 states that "the incidence of radiation-induced leukemia varies greatly with the level of exposure and the number of years of follow-up." In other words, the number of cases of radiation-caused leukemia that are discovered depends, in part, on how long the patients are tracked after radiation exposure. Thus, the sheer difficulty of keeping track of patients over a period of many years contributes to the difficulty of studying this form of leukemia.

36. **D** As the first sentence of paragraph 2 makes clear, the author bases his defense of academic freedom primarily on its "social significance."

37. **A** In paragraph 1, the author describes reactionaries as powerful people who "unintelligently resist change." In paragraph 2, he argues that academic freedom is essential for the cultivation of "habits of intelligent action" and thus for the

development of "orderly methods" of directing "needed change." It is logical to conclude, then, that he regards reactionaries as a major threat to academic freedom.

38. **B** Since the author regards academic freedom as an important factor in promoting the peaceful solution of social problems, it is clear that he would place the greatest value on academic freedom during times when social problems are most serious.

39. **C** The assumption stated in choice C is implied throughout the passage, most clearly, perhaps, in the last eight words of the passage.

40. **A** Choice A is the only likely source. The passage says nothing about the economics of social change (choice B), it's obviously not from a work of fiction (choice C), it paints a very negative picture of reactionaries (choice D), and it advocates orderly methods of change, not the direct use of force (choice E).

SECTION 5

1. **B** Treat the whole problem as a series of multiplications. Cancel as many numbers as possible first:

$$\frac{1}{\cancel{3}} \times \frac{\cancel{2}}{\cancel{5}} \times \frac{\cancel{3}}{\cancel{4}_{2}} \times \frac{\cancel{5}}{\cancel{6}} \times \frac{\cancel{36}^{6}}{1} = \frac{6}{2} = 3$$

2. **B** There are several easy ways to solve this one. One way is to treat the figure as three rectangles. The one on top has sides of 3 and 2, for an area of 6. The one in the middle has sides of 5 and 9, for an area of 45. The one on the bottom has sides of 3 and 5, for an area of 15. The three areas add up to 66.

3. **A** If you cross multiply the first equation, you'll get $4x = y$. Then, if $8x = 18$, $4x = 9 = y$.

4. **D** The even digits in 4321 are the 4 and the 2. If you double them, you get 8341, which is 4020 larger than 4321.

5. **A** The earliest such date during *any* year is January 11.

6. **C** If ABC is a line segment, then $4a + 2a + 3a = 180$, $9a = 180$, $a = 20$, and $2a = 40$. So the "bottom" angle of triangle BDE measures 40°. Since the three interior angles of any triangle add up to 180°, the two "top" angles must add up to 140°. If $18x + 17x = 140$, then $35x = 140$, $x = 4$, and $18x = 72$. So angle BDE measures 72°.

7. **D** You should recognize 64 right away as equal to 8^2. This tells you that $x + y = 8$. If $xy = 15$, then x and y must be 5 and 3 (it doesn't matter which is which), since those are the only two numbers whose sum is 8 and whose product is 15. Therefore, the sum of x^2 and y^2 must be $25 + 9 = 34$.

8. **B** Remember to perform the operations in parentheses first. In Column A, you get $4 \times (3 + 3) \div 2 = 4 \times 6 \div 2 = 24 \div 2 = 12$. In Column B, you get $(4 \times 3) + (3 \div 2) = 12 + \frac{3}{2} = 13\frac{1}{2}$. Column B is greater.

9. **C** A centimeter is 1/100 of a meter, and a kilometer is 1000 meters, so a kilometer contains 100×1000 centimeters. A milliliter is 1/1000 of a liter, so 100 liters contain 1000×100 milliliters. Column A and Column B are equal.

10. **C** According to the laws of exponents, $(2^3)^4 = 2^{(3 \times 4)} = 2^{12}$ and $(2^6)^2 = 2^{(6 \times 2)} = 2^{12}$. The two columns are equal.

11. **D** If x is negative and xyz is positive, then either y or z, but not both, must be negative. (If all three were negative, their product would be negative.) However, we don't know whether y or z is negative, so we can't make the comparison.

12. **C** First, since the angles marked $y°$ and $2x°$ are vertical angles, you know that $y = 2x$. Second, since AB is a line segment, you know that $3x + x + 2x = 180$ and $6x = 180$. Therefore, $2x = 60 = y$.

13. **B** If $2x + 1 = 0$, then $2x = -1$ and $x = -1/2$. Plug this value of x into Column A, and you get $x^2 = 1/4$. Plug this value of x^2 into Column B, and you get $1/x^2 = 1/(1/4) = 4$. Column B is greater.

14. **A** If $x = 3$, then the dimensions of the rectangular solid are 3, 4, and 9 and its volume is $3 \times 4 \times 9 = 108$.

15. **A** To find the number of students with brown eyes, subtract the number with blue eyes and the number with green eyes from the total: $42 - (1/3 \times 42) - (1/7 \times 42) = 42 - 14 - 6 = 22$.

16. **B** When you're given three unknowns and only two equations, normally you can't find the value of any of the unknowns. However, you should always consider whether you can determine anything by adding the two equations together or by subtracting one from the other. In this case, if you subtract the second equation from the first, you can eliminate b and c from the problem: $-b - (-b) = -b + b = 0$, and $c - c = 0$. So you're left with $a - (-a) = 2$, or $2a = 2$. Therefore, $a = 1$.

17. **D** Since x is less than or equal to y and y is less than or equal to z, it's tempting to assume that xy will always be less than yz. But in some cases it won't be. If all three numbers are negative, for instance, xy will be greater than yz. (Try it.) And if all three numbers are equal (a possibility that is not ruled out), then xy and yz will be equal. So this is a D item.

18. **C** Apply the definition: 3 is the smallest integer greater than or equal to 3; -4 is the smallest integer greater than or equal to -4.5. The sum of 3 and -4 is -1. Therefore, the two columns are equal.

19. **D** To figure out the odds of choosing any particular combination of marbles, you'd need to know the total number of marbles in the box. It's not enough to know that there are 3 more black marbles than white marbles. Intuitively, you may be able to see that it would be different if there were 4 black marbles and 1 white marble as opposed to 103 black marbles and 100 white marbles. (In the first case, the chance of drawing two black marbles consecutively would be .60; in the second case, it would be about .26.) So this is another D item.

20. **C** There are many ways to solve this one. One easy way is to turn 40% into its equivalent fraction, 2/5, and then cross multiply:

$$\frac{2}{5}x = 18$$

$$2x = 90$$

$$x = 45$$

21. **A** Using the Pythagorean theorem, you know that $3^2 + m^2 = 6^2$. Therefore, $9 + m^2 = 36$, $m^2 = 27$, and $m = \sqrt{27}$. What is the value of $\sqrt{27}$? It doesn't matter. You know that $5 = \sqrt{25}$; you also know that $\sqrt{27}$ must be greater than $\sqrt{25}$. Therefore, Column A is greater.

22. **C** If Katia's age is n, then Janet's age is $n + 3$ and Christopher's age is $n + 3 + 4$. The sum of their ages is $n + (n + 3) + (n + 3 + 4) = 3n + 10$.

23. **A** There's a trick that makes this one quick and easy to figure out. Add up the five terms in Column A, and you'll get 60. Add up the five terms in Column B, and you'll get 59. Since the number of terms is the same on both sides, you don't need to divide to get the actual averages; you know that the result in Column A will be greater.

24. **C** You know that the value of Column A is 180 (since the sum of the three interior angles of a triangle is 180). To find the value of Column B, first notice that $c + y = 180$ (since c and y form a straight angle). Then notice that $c = x$ (since ℓ_1 is parallel to ℓ_2 and c and x are corresponding angles). From these two observations you can conclude that $x + y = 180$. So Column B equals Column A.

25. **D** Draw a little sketch. Remember that triangle ABC can fall anywhere inside the circle, so long as its three vertices are on the circle itself. You might be tempted to choose answer B, since the diameter of the circle is the longest line that can be drawn within the circle. However, consider the possibility that side AB of triangle ABC could itself be a diameter of the circle. In that case, the two columns would be equal. Given this uncertainty, choice D must be the correct answer.

26. **C** Solve the first equation for x in terms of y by cross multiplying: $x = 4y$. Then substitute 1/4 for y: $x = 4(1/4) = 1$.

27. **C** To simplify Column B, express the second term as a fraction and invert the third term, changing the operation from division to multiplication:

$$\frac{3x}{2} \times \frac{2x}{1} \times \frac{3}{x}$$

Then cancel whatever you can and complete the multiplication. You'll quickly get an answer of $9x$.

28. **A** One simple way to find the sum of x and y is to substitute $3y + 5$ for x in the second equation and solve for y:

$$\begin{aligned} y + 3 &= 3y + 5 - 10 \\ 8 &= 2y \\ 4 &= y \end{aligned}$$

Then substitute 4 for y in the first equation and solve for x:

$$\begin{aligned} x &= 3(4) + 5 \\ &= 17 \end{aligned}$$

Thus, $x + y = 17 + 4 = 21$.

29. **A** First, realize that point X can be located at point A or point C on the circle. If it is, the greatest possible length of arc BC will be 2/3 of the circumference of the circle. Next, figure out the circumference of the circle: $2\pi r = 2\pi 15 = 30\pi$. Finally, multiply 30π by 2/3 and get 20π.

30. **B** Just add the three terms. You'll get $3x - 6 = 0$. Therefore, $3x = 6$.

31. **A** You may find it easier to picture the symmetry in the pattern if you turn the page so that the grid appears as a diamond, with the dashed line running straight up and down. Square A must contain a black circle to correspond to the black circle opposite it near the lower right-hand corner of the grid. The other lettered squares must contain white circles.

32. **E** First, you should realize that y and z are equal, since they are vertical angles. Second, you should realize that y and z are each equal to $180 - x$, since they're each supplementary to x. So the sum of y and z is $(180 - x) + (180 - x) = 360 - 2x$.

33. **E** If $3m = 18$, then $m = 6$. Substitute this value for m in the first equation, cross multiply, and you'll get $3n = 24$. Therefore, $n = 8$ and $2n = 16$.

34. **C** If you sketch a coordinate graph system and plot point A, you'll see that point A lies on the y-axis. If point B is equidistant from point A and the origin, it must lie on a line that is perpendicular to the y-axis and midway between point A and the origin, as shown by the dashed line in the following figure:

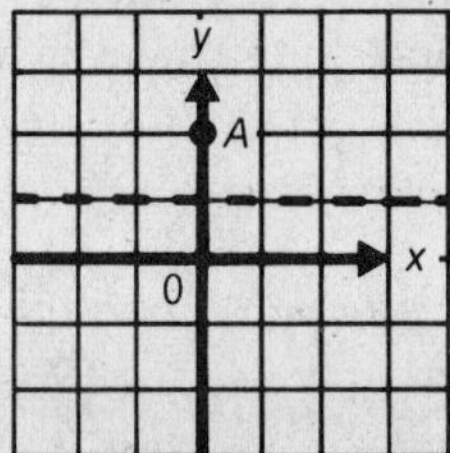

For every point on this line, $y = 1$.

35. **C** Since your answer must be expressed in cubic *feet*, first convert 18 inches (the height of the cylinder) to feet: $1\frac{1}{2}$. Second, find the volume of the entire cylinder by using the formula $\pi r^2 h$, where r is the radius of the cylinder (1 foot) and h is the height ($1\frac{1}{2}$ feet): $\pi(1^2)(3/2) = 3\pi/2$. Third, subtract the quarter of the cylinder that has been removed:

$$\frac{3\pi}{2} - \frac{1}{4}\left(\frac{3\pi}{2}\right) = \frac{3\pi}{2} - \frac{3\pi}{8} = \frac{12\pi}{8} - \frac{3\pi}{8} = \frac{9\pi}{8}$$

SECTION 6

1. **D** This sentence contains a double negative—*not* and *no*. Since *not* isn't underlined, *no* must be changed to *any* to make the sentence correct.

2. **C** The sentence illogically compares *sales* to *clothing*. It should compare *sales* to *sales*. Choice C, in other words, should read *behind sales of clothing*.

3. **B** A verb should agree with the closer of two subjects joined by *neither ... nor*. So the sentence should read *Mexico is thought*, not *Mexico are thought*.

4. **C** Since the sentence is about the past, all the verbs should be in the past tense. *Are made* should be *were made*.

5. **D** *Check off* is nonidiomatic in this context. The sentence requires an expression like *check into* instead.

6. **E** If you selected choice D, remember that *look* often functions as a linking verb. In this sentence, *look* links its subject, *it* (the facade of City Hall), with an adjective that describes it, *good*. The sentence is correct as written.

7. **A** The case of a relative pronoun like *who/whom* or *whoever/whomever* is determined by its use in its own clause. The relative pronoun in this sentence is used as the subject of the clause it introduces. Therefore, it should be in the subjective case—*whoever*, not *whomever*.

8. **E** No error in this sentence.

9. **C** Mentally eliminate the parenthetical phrase *or greater* and you'll see the problem with choice C immediately: *as great than* is a mixed construction. The sentence should read *as great as, or greater than*, with the closing comma after *than*, not *greater*.

10. **C** *Had went* is wrong; *had gone* is right.

11. **E** No error in this sentence.

12. **A** Even when normal subject-verb order is reversed, a verb must agree with its subject. In this sentence, the subject is *towers*, so the verb should be *rise*, not *rises*.

13. **E** No error in this sentence.

14. **B** An agency is a *that* or a *which*, not a *who*. (*That* would be more appropriate than *which* in this context.)

15. **C** The necessity *of placing* is idiomatic; the necessity *to place* is not.

16. **D** This sentence ends with a series of four infinitives. In theory, the series could be written in either of two parallel forms: *to earn*, *to write*, *to demonstrate*, and *to pass*; or, to *earn*, *write*, *demonstrate*, and *pass*. In fact, however, only the second form is possible in this sentence. So *to pass* should be *pass*.

17. **C** A singular antecedent (*man*) demands a singular pronoun (*he*, not *they*).

18. **E** No error in this sentence.

19. **E** No error in this sentence.

20. **A** The predication in this sentence is faulty: the *purpose* of a book does not *deal* with a subject; a *book* does. If *the purpose of* were deleted, the sentence would be correct.

21. **D** The context clearly calls for *well*, meaning "healthy," rather than *good*.

22. **D** *Than he* would be correct if the sentence intended to say that the audience had applauded three other pianists more enthusiastically than *he* (Larry) had applauded them. But clearly it intends to say that the audience had applauded three other pianists more enthusiastically than they had applauded *him* (Larry). So *than he* should be *than him*. (You can always test the case of a pronoun in a construction like this by mentally completing the implied clause.)

23. **C** The word *imaginative*, which means "showing great power of imagination," is misused here. The context clearly calls for *imaginary*, which means "unreal, fictitious."

24. **E** No error in this sentence.

25. **C** If you rearrange the clause that is the object of the preposition *to* in this sentence, you may see the error: *the voters of their party select whoever*. A pronoun that is the object of a verb should be in the objective case—*select whomever*, not *select whoever*.

26. **E** Both the punctuation and the parallel form of *make deposits* and *pay bills* indicate that the two phrases are the first two items in a series. Only choice E completes that series by supplying the anticipated conjunction (*and*) and the final item in the series (*monitor his or her finances*).

27. **D** The original sentence is a fragment. (Remember, the *-ing* forms of verbs can't stand on their own as predicates.) Choices B and D both correct the error, but choice B is needlessly wordy.

28. **D** The opening phrase in the original sentence is a misplaced modifier (*Kennedy* was not written when he was a member of the Senate; his *book* was). Choices B, C, D, and E all correct that error, but choice B suggests that someone else might have been a senator when Kennedy won the Pulitzer prize, choice C distorts the meaning of the sentence, and choice E is wordy.

29. **A** The original sentence is grammatically correct; it's also clear and concise. (Choice E is shorter, but it alters the meaning of the sentence.)

30. **E** The only subordinating conjunction that makes sense in this context is *once*, which conveys the idea that the work of Japanese artists became influential as soon as it was known.

31. **A** The original version is best. Choices B and C both use a plural pronoun (*their*) to refer to a singular antecedent (*myth*), and choices D and E alter the meaning of the sentence. (Notice the faulty predication in choice D: the myth *was* not a mistranslation; it *grew out of* a mistranslation.)

32. **C** The original sentence is a run-on. Of the three alternatives that are grammatically correct (B, C, and D), choice C is the clearest and most graceful.

33. **A** The original sentence is correct. Choices B, C, and D turn the opening phrase into a dangling modifier. Choice E is a fragment.

34. **B** In the original version, the plural pronoun *their* does not agree with its singular antecedent, *art*. Of the other versions, which are all technically correct and clear enough, choice B is the most concise and therefore the best.

35. **E** Choice D distorts the meaning of the sentence. Of the remaining alternatives, choice E is the shortest, simplest, and clearest.

36. **C** The original sentence is a run-on. The alternatives all correct the problem, but only choice C does so both logically and succinctly.

37. **C** Choice C is the only version that corrects the faulty parallelism in the original sentence.

38. **B** Choice D alters the meaning of the original sentence. Of the remaining alternatives, choice B is the clearest and most concise.

39. **C** Since the second clause in this sentence contrasts with the first, logic demands *but*, not *and* or *therefore*. In choice D, the placement of the adverb *only* is confusing.

40. **A** The original version is correct. Choices B and D are fragments, choice C is awkward, and choice E introduces a pronoun (*they*) that has no antecedent.

41. **D** Since *scarcely* is negative, it can't be used in combination with another negative. *Nor* should be *or*.

42. **A** The people *who* or the people *that* is acceptable. The people *which* is unacceptable.

43. **E** No error in this sentence.

44. **D** Although the subjunctive mood is rarely used in modern English (and is rarely tested on the SAT), it is still idiomatic in *that* clauses that begin with verbs like *require*, *demand*, and *insist*. This sentence should read "Government policies ... required that every male citizen ... *register*" (not *registers*).

45. **E** No error in this sentence.

46. **C** The sentence shifts illogically from the past to the present tense; *continues* should be *continued*.

47. **D** *Had began* should be *had begun*.

48. **C** *Or* pairs with *either*; *nor* pairs with *neither*.

49. **D** Here the verb *accept* has been confused with the preposition *except*.

50. **D** The rule is this: *between* two; *among* three or more.

PART

7

SAT Study Program: Unit 3

LESSON 11

Vocabulary Building Through Word Roots, Part 2

OBJECTIVES

☐ To learn some of the most important word roots and their meanings

☐ To learn the meanings of some of the words based on these word roots that are likely to appear on the SAT

The Word Roots

11.1 Word Roots Related to "Connections": *Tact, Tain, Sec, Frac, Clud*

The Latin word *tangere* means "to touch." This word is the source of several English word roots, including *tact*, *tang* (or *ting*), and *tag* (or *tig*). Here are some related words:

contact (*n*) literally, "a touching"; connection; communication; association.
intact (*adj*) literally, "untouched"; all in one piece; unified.
tactile (*adj*) having to do with the sense of touch: Blind persons sometimes have an unusually well-developed *tactile* sense.
tangential (*adj*) touching on something; loosely related: In the debate, taxes were raised only as a *tangential* issue.
tangible (*adj*) able to be touched or perceived: There is no *tangible* evidence of the existence of the Loch Ness monster.
intangible (*adj*) not able to be touched or perceived; opposite of *tangible*.
contingent (*adj*) dependent on or conditioned ("touched") by something else: Your acceptance into college is *contingent* upon your SAT scores.
contagious (*adj*) able to be spread by contact, as some diseases.
contiguous (*adj*) touching, as adjacent geographic regions: New Hampshire and Vermont are *contiguous* states.

In Latin, *tenere* means "to hold." In the forms of *tain*, *ten*, and *tin*, this word appears as a root in many English words. Here are some you should know:

contain (*v*) to hold or enclose.
retain (*v*) to keep or hold onto.
detain (*v*) to hold back, delay, or restrain: The police *detained* the suspect for questioning.
obtain (*v*) to get.
abstain (*v*) to refrain from, hold back from, or forbear: An alcoholic should *abstain* from drinking liquor.
pertain (*v*) to be related or connected: These are the facts that *pertain* to the issue.
pertinent (*adj*) relevant or related: Your objection is not *pertinent* to the matter at hand.
appertain (*v*) to be related or connected.
sustain (*v*) to hold up; to support; to continue: She could not *sustain* the effort required to finish the race.
tenant (*n*) one who holds or occupies a place or position; especially, one who rents a house or an apartment from a landlord.
tenure (*n*) the right or act of holding an office; a status granted a teacher protecting him or her from dismissal.
tenet (*n*) a firmly held belief or opinion: The divinity of Jesus Christ is a basic *tenet* of Christianity.
tenacious (*adj*) literally, "holding fast"; persevering; stubbornly enduring.

tenacity (*n*) perseverance; stubborn persistence: Although the boxer was clearly overmatched, he won the bout through sheer *tenacity*.
pertinacious (*adj*) extremely resolute, determined, or stubborn.
tenable (*adj*) able to be held; able to be believed or accepted: Belief in a flat Earth is no longer *tenable*.

The Latin word *sequi* means "to follow." It appears in the form of *sec* or *seq* in many English words. Here are some you should know:

consecutive (*adj*) following one another: Seven and eight are *consecutive* numbers.
execute (*v*) literally, "to follow to the end"; to put to death; to carry out or to put into effect a plan or decision.
persecute (*v*) to attack, harass, or afflict (to "follow" in the sense of pursuit): Hitler's government *persecuted* the Jews.
sequel (*n*) something that follows; a continuation: *The Godfather, Part II*, is a *sequel* to *The Godfather*.
sequence (*n*) a continuous series of things or events that follow one another; the order in which the things or events in a series follow one another.
consequent (*adj*) following, later; resulting: The drought and the *consequent* crop failures caused the famine.
subsequent (*adj*) following; later.
obsequious (*adj*) literally, "following completely"; overly submissive, fawning, slavish: An *obsequious* advisor is not to be trusted.
obsequies (*n*) funeral rites.
non sequitur (*n*) a conclusion that does not follow logically from the evidence presented; a response that does not follow logically from anything previously said.

In Latin, *frangere* means "to break." The root *frac*, *frag*, or *frang* forms the basis of many English words related to the idea of breaking. Here are some of them:

fracture (*n*) a break, as of a bone; any kind of splitting or breaking.
fraction (*n*) a part or a division of a whole.
refract (*v*) to bend or break up: A prism *refracts* light.
refractory (*adj*) stubborn, obstinate, unruly: The babysitter vowed that he would control the *refractory* child.
infraction (*n*) a breaking, as of a rule: The student court deals with *infractions* of the honor code.
fragment (*n*) a broken piece, a part.
fragile (*adj*) easily broken, delicate.
infrangible (*adj*) unable to be broken: His vow is *infrangible*.

The Latin *claudere* means "to close" or "to shut." It is related to a number of English words that contain the root *clud*, *clus*, or *claus*. Here are some examples:

include (*v*) to contain or enclose.
conclude (*v*) to arrive at by reasoning; to decide; to end.
occlude (*v*) to close off, shut, or block: During a solar eclipse, the light of the sun is *occluded* by the moon.
preclude (*v*) to shut off or prevent: Her injury may *preclude* her from performing in the dance concert.
exclude (*v*) to shut out.
recluse (*n*) one who lives apart from others; a hermit or shut-in: Emily Dickinson was a *recluse* who rarely left her house.
conclusion (*n*) the logical outcome or end of something.
claustrophobia (*n*) an intense fear of being shut in or enclosed.

11.2 Word Roots Related to "Actions": *Fac, Lud, Man, Miss, Tend*

In Latin, *facere* means "to make" or "to do." Many English words contain the root *fac*. In Lesson 6 you learned two of them: *benefactor*, "one who does good," and *malefactor*, "one who does evil." Here are some others:

manufacture (*v*) originally, to make by hand; now, to make by hand or by machine. (The word combines *fac* with the root *manu*, which means "hand.")
factory (*n*) a place where things are made.
facile (*adj*) easy to do; smooth, fluent; superficial: The teacher was not impressed by the student's *facile* interpretation of the play.
facility (*n*) ease of performance; aptitude.
factor (*n*) anything that contributes to the production of a result; an ingredient.
faculty (*n*) the ability to do something; natural aptitude: She has an amazing *faculty* for remembering dates and names.
facsimile (*n*) something made to resemble or imitate something else: This painting is not an original, but a *facsimile*.

In Latin, *ludere* means "to play." Here are some useful English words that contain the root *lud*. Each has something to do with playing, in one sense or another, even though the connection is not always obvious.

prelude (*n*) something that precedes a play or a musical composition.
interlude (*n*) something that comes in the middle of a play or a musical composition: Between the acts of the drama, a comic *interlude* was presented.
ludicrous (*adj*) ridiculous, comical: The idea of Groucho Marx being president of Fredonia is *ludicrous*.
delude (*v*) to deceive, to fool: Hope sometimes *deludes* us into believing the impossible.
delusion (*n*) a false belief.
elude (*v*) to evade or escape: The criminal managed to *elude* the police.
elusive (*adj*) difficult to capture; fleeting: Germaine couldn't identify the faint, *elusive* fragrance.
illusion (*n*) something deceiving or misleading; the state of being deceived.
allusion (*n*) an indirect reference: The professor's talk was filled with historical and literary *allusions*.
collusion (*n*) a secret agreement to cooperate in a plan or conspiracy: The businessmen were accused of *collusion* in the fraudulent scheme.

The Latin word *manus* means "hand." In English, the word root *man* or *manu* appears in a number of words having to do with the hand or with actions performed by the hand. *Manufacture*, which originally meant "to make by hand," is one of them. Here are some others:

manage (*v*) to control, organize, or supervise.
manipulate (*v*) to operate or work with the hands: The pilot skillfully *manipulated* the controls of the plane. Also, to control with skill and cleverness for one's own ends: The political boss *manipulated* the voters.
maneuver (*v*) to move, operate, or control.
manual (*adj*) pertaining to work done by the hands: A carpenter is a *manual* laborer.
manuscript (*n*) a handwritten copy of a book, a document, or some other composition. (The word is now used to refer to typewritten copies as well.)
manifest (*v*) to show; to make clear or evident: His trembling hands *manifested* his fear.
manacle (*n*) an iron handcuff or shackle.
emancipate (*v*) to free from bondage or slavery: Lincoln's proclamation *emancipated* the slaves in the rebellious states.

In Latin, the word *mittere* means "to send." In English, the word root *miss* or *mit* appears in many words that relate to sending. Here are some you should know:

transmit (*v*) literally, "to send across"; to send along, to pass on: The messenger promised to *transmit* the news.
emit (*v*) to send out or send forth: The radio *emitted* some strange beeping sounds.
emission (*n*) something sent out or sent forth: Older cars may produce noxious *emissions* that pollute the atmosphere.
submit (*v*) to refer to or send on to another: Yoko *submitted* a proposal for a new series, and the director approved it. Also, to surrender to another: The prisoner was ordered to *submit* or die.
commit (*v*) literally, "to send with"; to entrust; to perform or enact; to promise or pledge.
commission (*n*) the act of sending someone forth with a special purpose or task; also, a group of people charged with a task.
mission (*n*) a duty for which one is sent forth; a task or purpose.
missionary (*n*) one sent forth on some special duty, especially to spread religious teachings.
emissary (*n*) a messenger or ambassador.
dismiss (*v*) to send out or send away: He angrily *dismissed* the dishonest clerk.
missive (*n*) a letter.

The Latin word *tendere* means "to stretch." The related word roots *tend* and *tens* form the basis of many English words that pertain to stretching. Here are some you should know:

extend (*v*) to lengthen, stretch out, or reach out: She *extended* her hand in greeting.
distend (*v*) to stretch, swell, or spread: The thin membrane was *distended* by the pressure of expanding gas within.
contend (*v*) to strive or struggle in competition: The boxers *contended* in the ring. Also, to state positively: The accused woman *contended* that she was innocent.
tense (*adj*) literally, "stretched tight"; strained or anxious.
intense (*adj*) strained; emotional, violent, or forceful.
tension (*n*) the state of being strained, stretched, or anxious.
tensile (*adj*) having to do with tension or stretching: Rope fibers must have a high degree of *tensile* strength.
contentious (*adj*) likely to cause discord; quarrelsome, argumentative: Helen's *contentious* nature prevents her from making and keeping friends; few people can tolerate her perverse tendency to turn every conversation into a debate.
tenuous (*adj*) stretched, thin, flimsy: The connection between the two events seems very *tenuous*.
attenuate (*v*) to stretch out or to make thin; to weaken or lessen: His wealth had been *attenuated* by years of wasteful spending.

11.3 Word Roots Related to "Location": *Pon, Sed, Centr, Pend*

The Latin word *ponere*, meaning "to place," has many descendants in English. The word root takes several forms in English words; *pon* and *pos* are the two most common. Here are some English words that spring from these roots:

postpone (*v*) literally, "to place after"; to delay.
component (*n*) literally, "something put together"; one part of a whole: The central processing unit is one *component* of a computer system.
exponent (*n*) literally, "one who puts forth"; someone who sets forth, explains, promotes, or defends an idea.
proponent (*n*) someone who supports a cause: The senator is a well-known *proponent* of tax reform.
opponent (*n*) literally, "someone who is placed against another"; an adversary or enemy.
impose (*v*) to put upon, lay upon, or place upon; to force upon: The government *imposed* new taxes on the people.
juxtapose (*v*) to put nearby or together: It seems strange to *juxtapose* two such different works of art.

posit (*v*) to set forth (a principle, fact, or assumption): Ethical theory *posits* the existence of good and evil.
apposite (*adj*) appropriate, suitable, apt: Her comments were both intelligent and highly *apposite*.
depose (*v*) to overthrow (a ruler): The revolutionaries *deposed* the monarch.
interpose (*v*) to put between; to insert: The moderator *interposed* remarks of his own during the debate.
transpose (*v*) literally, "to place on the other side of"; to change the order of things: The typist *transposed* two letters, typing the word *time* as *tiem*.
repose (*v*) to rest.

In Latin, *sedere* means "to sit." In English, the word root *sed* or *sid* appears in a number of words that relate to the idea of sitting. Here are some of them:

sediment (*n*) material that sits or settles at the bottom of a liquid: There was a foot of *sediment* at the bottom of the water tank.
sedate (*adj*) calm, quiet, peaceful: Despite distractions, a yogi remains *sedate*.
sedative (*n*) a medicine that lessens pain and helps to relax or calm a patient.
sedentary (*adj*) characterized by sitting: Editing is a *sedentary* profession.
assiduous (*adj*) literally, "sitting near or close"; characterized by careful attention and persistence; diligent, industrious, hard-working.
preside (*v*) literally, "to sit before"; to occupy the position of authority, as at a meeting or in a court of law; to direct or control.
residue (*n*) remainder; what is left over: After the company's debts have been paid, the *residue* will go to the stockholders.
subside (*v*) to sink, to settle; to become calm or quiet: The noise *subsided* as the traffic jam broke up.

The Latin word *centrum* means "center." There are a number of English words that spring from the root *centr*. One, obviously, is *center*. Another is *centripetal*. As you may recall from Lesson 6, *centripetal* literally means "seeking the center." Here are some other words that spring from the root *centr*:

centrifugal (*adj*) literally, "fleeing the center"; tending to fly or move outward from a central point: A weight spinning on a string is subject to *centrifugal* force. (*Centrifugal* is the opposite of *centripetal*.)
concentrate (*v*) to focus one's attention on a central point; to unify, to bring to a common center.
concentric (*adj*) having a common center: The target used in archery consists of several *concentric* circles.
decentralize (*v*) to remove from a single center, to disperse: The city government *decentralized* its power by setting up offices throughout the city.
eccentric (*adj*) deviating from the center; odd, unconventional, peculiar: Billionaire Howard Hughes was known for his *eccentric* behavior.

In Latin, the primary meaning of the verb *pendere* is "to hang." From this primary meaning stem two secondary meanings: "to weigh" (since scales were *hung* from a balance) and "to pay" (since money was originally paid by *weight*). These meanings are reflected in several English words that have *pend* or *pens* as their root. Here are some of them:

depend (*v*) literally, "to hang from"; to rely upon or be based upon.
pendant (*n*) anything that hangs, as a piece of jewelry on a chain.
append (*v*) literally, "to hang on something else"; to attach or affix: Several pages of statistics were *appended* to the main report.
appendage (*n*) anything attached or added on: An animal's tail is an *appendage*.
pendulum (*n*) a weight hanging from a fixed point and swinging freely.

suspend (*v*) to leave hanging; to interrupt or stop temporarily: Because of the accident, railway service has been *suspended*.
impend (*v*) to hang over; to be imminent or near at hand: In his anxiety, he felt some doom *impending*.
perpendicular (*adj*) literally, "hanging straight down"; at a right angle.
dispense (*v*) to weigh out, to give out, to distribute: A pharmacist's job is to *dispense* medicine.
propensity (*n*) literally, "a hanging toward"; a leaning, an inclination, a tendency: She has a *propensity* to be talkative.
recompense (*v*) to repay, to reward: You will be *recompensed* for your services.
compensate (*v*) to pay for or repay; to counterbalance.

11.4 Word Roots Related to "Likeness" and "Difference": *Sim, Var*

The Latin word *similis* means "like" or "similar." It is the source of several English words with the root *sim* or *sem*. *Similar* is one. So is *facsimile*. Here are some others:

simulate (*v*) to imitate or copy: This vinyl *simulates* leather.
simulacrum (*n*) a counterfeit, a copy, an imitation: Frankenstein's monster was not a man but a *simulacrum* of a man.
assimilate (*v*) to absorb, incorporate, or make similar: American society has *assimilated* many peoples and cultures.
simultaneous (*adj*) happening at the same time.
verisimilitude (*n*) resemblance to reality: The novel describes events with such *verisimilitude* that one feels as if one has actually seen them happening.
resemble (*v*) to look like, to appear similar to.
dissemble (*v*) to conceal or disguise; to put on the appearance of: Although bored by the speech, she nevertheless *dissembled* interest.
semblance (*n*) an appearance or likeness: In her dream, her fear took on the *semblance* of a monster.

The Latin word *varius* means "various" or "differing." Several English words contain the root *var*. *Vary* and *various* are two of them. Here are some others:

variety (*n*) a distinct kind or type; the degree of difference among items in a group.
variant (*n*) one of two or more different examples or forms of something: *Labour* and *labor* are spelling *variants*; one is British and the other is American.
variance (*n*) the quality of being different or changing: The rate of rainfall is subject to considerable yearly *variance*.
invariable (*adj*) unchanging: It was her *invariable* habit to run two miles every morning.
variegated (*adj*) of different colors or different appearances and forms: These orchids bear spots and streaks in *variegated* hues.
prevaricate (*v*) to vary from the truth; to bend or twist the truth; to lie.

11.5 Some Miscellaneous Word Roots: *Cred, Mon-, Sacr, Val*

This section contains a grab bag of word roots that don't fit neatly into any category. The English words derived from each root are related, of course, but the roots themselves aren't related to each other.

The Latin word *credere* means "to believe" or "to entrust." There are a number of English words having to do with belief or trust that contain the word root *cred*. Here are some of them:

credit (*n*) trust; willingness to allow someone to pay a debt at a later time because of belief in his or her trustworthiness.
credential (*n*) something that demonstrates a person's trustworthiness, reliability, or qualifications.

credible (*adj*) believable, worthy of belief: Most scientists do not consider reports of flying saucers *credible*. (The opposite of *credible* is *incredible*.)
credulous (*adj*) overly willing to believe; gullible; easily fooled: The *credulous* are often prone to superstition. (The opposite of *credulous* is *incredulous*, which means "unwilling to believe" or "skeptical.")
credulity (*n*) undue willingness or readiness to believe: The weird story strained the *credulity* of the audience. (The opposite of *credulity* is *incredulity*.)
credence (*n*) belief in the truth of something: The jury gave no *credence* to the testimony of the key witness for the defense.
credo (*n*) a statement of belief: The American *credo* is a pledge of faith in democracy.
creed (*n*) a statement of belief; also, a religion or a set of beliefs.

The Greek word *monos*, which means "single" or "alone," is the source of the English prefix *mon-* or *mono-*, which means "one." *Mon-* or *mono-* appears at the beginning of many English words. *Monarchy*, which means "rule by one person," is one of them. Here are some others:

monotheism (*n*) the belief that there is only one God. (The word combines the prefix *mono-* with the root *the* or *theo*, which means "god." The opposite of *monotheism* is *polytheism*, which means "the belief that there are many gods.")
monologue (*n*) a speech, usually in a play, by a single actor or character. (The word combines *mono-* with *-logue*, which means "speech" or "talk.")
monosyllable (*n*) a word containing only one syllable.
monogamy (*n*) the practice of marrying only one person at a time. (As you may recall from Lesson 6, *-gamy* means "marriage.")
monopoly (*n*) control of the market for a particular product or service by a single supplier: Cities with only one newspaper suffer from a news *monopoly*.
monochrome (*n*) a picture in shades of only one color.
monotonous (*adj*) unchanging in tone: The speech was boring because the speaker's voice was *monotonous*.
monolithic (*adj*) literally, "consisting of a single stone"; resembling a single massive block of stone; massively solid and singular: The church hierarchy is *monolithic* in its resistance to change.

The Latin word *sacer*, which means "sacred," is closely related to another Latin word, *sanctus*, which means "holy." Together, the two words give rise to a number of related English words that can be identified either by the root *sacr* (or *secr*) or by the root *sanc*. Here are some of them:

sacrifice (*v*) literally, "to make sacred or holy"; to offer as a gift to a god; to give up something for the sake of something else: She *sacrificed* her home and moved to another state for the sake of her career.
sacrilege (*n*) the misuse or abuse of something sacred: Burning a crucifix as firewood is a *sacrilege*.
consecrate (*v*) to make holy: The new church was *consecrated* in a special ceremony.
desecrate (*v*) to violate the holiness of something sacred; to profane: The vandals *desecrated* the temple by painting obscene words and pictures on the walls.
execrate (*v*) to curse; to wish evil upon: In his anger, he *execrated* his enemies.
execrable (*adj*) deserving to be cursed or denounced; detestable; abominable.
sacrosanct (*adj*) very holy or sacred. (The word combines both roots—*sacr* and *sanc*.)
sanctity (*n*) holiness: The old monk was surrounded by an air of *sanctity*.
sanctify (*v*) to make holy: The miracle that occurred here *sanctified* the place.
sanction (*n*) approval, blessing: Congress refused to give its *sanction* to the president's plan.
sanctuary (*n*) a holy place; a place of refuge or safety: The fugitive fled to the church, seeking *sanctuary*.
sanctimonious (*adj*) pretending to be holy or pious.

The Latin verb *valere* means "to be worth" or "to be strong." Many English words that relate to worth or strength spring from the root *val. Value* is one. Here are some others you should know:

valid (*adj*) worthwhile, strong, sound, effective: There were so many *valid* arguments against the proposition that few citizens voted for it.
equivalent (*adj*) of equal worth or value: One dollar is *equivalent* to one hundred pennies.
ambivalent (*adj*) literally, "having two values"; having a double meaning or a double opinion: Joe's feelings about marriage are so *ambivalent* that he has made and broken several engagements in the past few years.
evaluate (*v*) to determine the value of something.
prevalent (*adj*) literally, "superior in strength"; common, widespread, or predominant: Belief in a god is *prevalent* in most societies.
valiant (*adj*) courageous, brave, heroic.
valor (*n*) courage, bravery, heroism.

This concludes our study of common English word roots. In this lesson and in Lesson 6, you have learned nearly 50 word roots and more than 435 words that are based on those roots. And you've learned them in families, so you're less likely to forget them and more likely to recognize other words that belong to the same families. Review some of the words each day, and try to incorporate them into your spoken and written vocabularies. Look for them—and for related words—in your reading, too. In this way, you will effectively enlarge and strengthen your vocabulary for the SAT.

LESSON 12 Techniques for Analogies

OBJECTIVES

- ☐ To master the two-step approach to solving analogies
- ☐ To recognize the most common types of analogy relationships on the SAT
- ☐ To learn advanced techniques for subtle SAT analogy questions

Tackling Analogies

12.1 The Two-Step Approach

Each verbal section on the SAT includes ten analogies. You should be able to complete them at a rate of about two a minute, so the set of ten should take you 5 minutes altogether. With practice, you'll be able to attain this speed.

Although analogies involve word meanings, their primary purpose is not to test vocabulary. On most analogies, the words themselves are not very hard. Analogies are designed to test your logical thinking—specifically, how well you can understand relationships between words.

In every SAT analogy question, you are presented with a related pair of words separated by a colon. This is the *stem word pair*. Then you are given five other pairs of words, each pair also separated by a colon. You must choose the pair that expresses a relationship most similar to that expressed in the stem word pair.

As you'll find, you can do some analogies quickly and easily, in just a few seconds. However, as a learning device and for use on more difficult analogies, you should learn the two-step approach presented in this lesson. The two steps are (1) build a bridge and then (2) modify the bridge so that you can select the single best answer.

Before we consider the two steps, there are a couple of common misconceptions about SAT analogy questions that we should clear up immediately. First, the distractors—the incorrect answer choices—are never the "wrong" part of speech. In other words, if the two words in the stem pair are a verb and a noun, in that order (for example, WRITE:PENCIL), the two words in each of the answer choices will also be a verb and a noun, in that order. Some SAT preparation books tell you that you can eliminate some incorrect answers to analogies on the basis of their grammatical form alone. You can't. The questions aren't designed or intended to test your knowledge of the parts of speech. So don't waste your time checking the grammatical form of each answer choice.

Second, the distractors are never reversals of the correct answer. For example, if you're given the analogy DOG:MAMMAL, you won't find amphibian:frog, which includes the right words in the wrong order, among the answer choices. Again, some SAT preparation books warn you to watch out for such reversals, but you needn't bother. The makers of the SAT never include trick answers of this type.

Now that we've cleared up those two popular misconceptions, let's take a look at the first step in the two-step approach to verbal analogies.

12.2 Step 1: Build a Bridge

The first step in approaching most analogy questions is building a bridge. A bridge is a short sentence that contains both words in the stem word pair and explains how they are related. For example, if an analogy question begins with the word pair KEYBOARD:PIANO, a possible bridge might be "A *keyboard* is part of a *piano*."

Once you have constructed a bridge, you can eliminate from the answer choices all the word pairs that it won't connect. If the bridge connects more than one word pair, you may have to modify it before you can select the single best answer. However, constructing a bridge is almost always the best way to start. Here's an example of how it works:

KEYBOARD:PIANO:: (A) notes:instrument
(B) strings:violin (C) rudder:boat
(D) dial:telephone (E) voice:song

Start with the bridge "A *keyboard* is part of a *piano*." Take the two words in each of the five answer choices and try to connect them with this bridge in the same way that you've connected *keyboard* and *piano*. If the words connect—that is, if they make sense in the sentence—then they're candidates for the correct answer. If they don't, you can eliminate them. Are *notes* part of an *instrument*? No. Are *strings* part of a *violin*? Yes. Is a *rudder* part of a *boat*? Yes. Is a *dial* part of a *telephone*? Yes. Is a *voice* part of a *song*? No. As you can see, your bridge connects only three answer choices—B, C, and D. You still don't know which of these three is the best answer—that requires a second step—but you've eliminated two choices just by building a bridge.

Not all analogy questions require a second step. With some, the bridge you construct will lead you directly to the correct answer. Here's an example:

CARNIVORE:MEAT:: (A) vegetarian:beans
(B) insectivore:birds (C) omnivore:fruits
(D) teetotaler:alcohol (E) herbivore:plants

A good bridge for this analogy is a simple definition of *carnivore*: "A *carnivore* is an animal that eats *meat*." Try to connect the two words in each answer choice with this bridge. Is a *vegetarian* an animal that eats *beans*? Possibly, but beans are not a necessary characteristic of a vegetarian diet. Is an *insectivore* an animal that eats *birds*? No. An insectivore eats insects. (Many birds are insectivores, but don't let that confuse you.) Is an *omnivore* an animal that eats *fruits*? Yes, but an omnivore eats much more than fruits; an omnivore eats all kinds of foods. (*Omni-* means "all.") Is a *teetotaler* an animal that eats—or, more appropriately, drinks—*alcohol*? No. A teetotaler is someone who does *not* drink alcohol. Is an *herbivore* an animal that eats *plants*? Yes. So choice E is the correct answer.

With a straightforward analogy like this, you don't have to go on to step 2. With a more complicated one—like the KEYBOARD:PIANO example—you do.

12.3 Step 2: Modify the Bridge

For many analogy questions, building a bridge isn't enough to eliminate all the wrong answers. To eliminate further, you have to modify the bridge by adding a few details to it. Look back at the KEYBOARD:PIANO analogy for an example. Your original bridge was "A *keyboard* is part of a *piano*." What else can you say about the relationship between a keyboard and a piano? Try this: "A *keyboard* is the part of a *piano* that you touch to make it work." Or this: "A *keyboard* is the part of a *piano* that you use to control it."

Now try joining the words in choices B, C, and D with your modified bridge. You'll find that the words in choices B and D connect, but those in choice C don't. You don't control a boat by touching its rudder. The rudder itself is controlled by a wheel or a tiller. So you can eliminate choice C.

To decide between choices B and D, you must analyze the relationship between *keyboard* and *piano* still further. Does the keyboard of a piano actually produce the music? No. Strings inside the piano do that. The keyboard is just a handy way of telling the piano what notes to play. In this sense, the keyboard resembles the dial on a telephone more than it resembles the strings on a violin. The strings on a violin aren't just a controlling device; they actually produce the sound. So you can see that choice D is slightly better than choice B.

Here's another example of how the process of modifying a bridge works. Consider this analogy:

STRIPE:ZEBRA:: (A) bony plate:armadillo
(B) feather:hen (C) mane:horse
(D) spot:leopard (E) freckle:face

Suppose you start with a simple bridge like "A *stripe* is found on a *zebra*." When you discover that the bridge connects the word pairs in all of the answer choices, you obviously have to go on to step 2 and modify your bridge by adding a few details.

One modification might be "A *stripe* is part of the pattern on the skin of a *zebra*." With this modified bridge, you can eliminate choices A, B, and C because a *bony plate*, a *feather*, and a *mane* are clearly not skin patterns, as a *stripe*, a *spot*, and a *freckle* are. Now you have only two choices left, D and E. To choose between them, consider once again the relationship between *stripe* and *zebra*. You can probably choose the correct answer—choice D—in several ways. For one thing, a *zebra* and a *leopard* are both animals; a *face* (choice E) is not. For another, all zebras have stripes and all leopards have spots, but not all faces have freckles. So choice D is the best answer.

In summary, the best method of approaching analogies is this: build a bridge; eliminate as many answers as you can; modify the bridge by adding details; eliminate more answers; make a final choice.

12.4 Using the Two-Step Approach

We've broken down the process of approaching verbal analogies on the SAT into two separate steps so that you can see exactly how it works, but in practice the two steps are not always distinct, nor are they always necessary. For some analogies, you won't have to take any formal steps at all. You'll simply glance at the stem word pair, grasp the relationship intuitively, and pick out the correct answer immediately. You won't even stop to think about building a bridge. For others, as you've seen, you'll only have to take the first step. In fact, if you're very skillful at building bridges, one step may be all you have to take for many analogies. For still others, though, you'll need to take both steps, and the second step—modifying your bridge—may itself have to be broken down into several smaller steps. In short, depending on the analogy, your ability to perceive relationships, and your skill at building bridges, the process may take only a few seconds or it may take as long as a minute.

There are two ways to shorten the process somewhat. One is to practice the two-step approach until it becomes second nature to you. You probably haven't had much experience with verbal analogies, so learning how to approach them methodically is crucial for success on the SAT. You may not need the two-step method for easy analogies, but you'll find it very helpful for the tough ones.

The other way to shorten the process of solving analogies is to learn the types of verbal relationships that are most common on the SAT. In the next section of this lesson, we'll consider nine of them.

Common Analogy Relationships

12.5 The Nine Most Common Types of SAT Analogies

Like other types of test questions, verbal analogies tend to fall into certain categories. Learning these categories will make it easier for you to recognize common analogy relationships when you encounter them on the practice tests in this book—and, more importantly, when you encounter them on the real SAT. It will also enable you to tackle verbal analogies with speed and confidence.

Here is a list of the nine most common types of SAT analogies:

1. WORD:ANTONYM. In this type of analogy, a word is paired with its opposite or with a near opposite. As a general rule, you won't find simple opposites like BLACK:WHITE on the SAT. Instead, you'll find two words that are opposed to each other in a more complex or subtle way. Look, for instance, at the following examples. Can you see, in each case, how the two words are opposed?

COWARD:HEROISM::miser:generosity

A *coward* is someone who is unlikely to perform an act of *heroism.* A *miser* is someone who is unlikely to perform an act of *generosity.*

OVERTURE:FINALE::preface:appendix

The *overture* and *finale* are the first and last musical numbers in a play or an opera. The *preface* and *appendix* are the first and last elements in a book.

EXAGGERATE:UNDERSTATEMENT::enlarge:reduction

To *exaggerate* something is to make it sound greater than it is; an *understatement* makes something sound smaller than it is. In the same way, to *enlarge* something is to make it appear bigger; a *reduction* makes something appear smaller.

2. WORD:SYNONYM. In this type of analogy, a word is paired with another word that has a similar, but usually not an identical, meaning. For instance, the two words may have similar denotations, or literal meanings, but different connotations, or feelings. Or they may refer to two different forms of the same thing or two different levels of intensity of the same quality or emotion. Here are some of the many possible variations on the type:

BRIGHT:BLINDING::cold:freezing

The two adjectives in each of these word pairs describe similar qualities, but the second is more intense than the first. *Blinding* means "brighter than *bright*"; *freezing* means "colder than *cold.*"

QUILL:PEN::parchment:paper

In these two word pairs, the first word is an old-fashioned form of the second. A *quill* is an old-fashioned kind of *pen*; *parchment* is an old-fashioned kind of *paper.*

THREAD:STRING::wire:cable

A *thread* and a *string* are basically similar; so are a *wire* and a *cable.* But just as a *string* is thicker and stronger than a *thread,* so a *cable* is thicker and stronger than a *wire.*

3. AGENT:ACTION. This type of analogy couples a person or thing with the characteristic action of that person or thing. The following examples will clarify the relationship:

STAPLE:FASTEN::scissors:cut

A *staple* is used to *fasten* papers. *Scissors* are used to *cut* them.

CHAIRPERSON:PRESIDE::secretary:record

The job of a *chairperson* is to *preside* over a meeting. The job of a *secretary* is to *record* what happens at a meeting.

BOTCH:BUNGLER::shirk:idler

A *bungler* is someone who *botches*—or ruins—a job. An *idler* is someone who *shirks*—or avoids doing—a job.

4. AGENT:ACTED UPON. In this type of analogy, a person or thing is paired with another person or thing that he, she, or it normally acts upon or affects. Again, the following examples will clarify the relationship:

DRUMSTICK:DRUM::bow:fiddle

A *drumstick* is used to make music on a *drum*. Similarly, a *bow* is used to make music on a *fiddle*.

ORATOR:AUDIENCE::author:reader

An *orator* gives a message to an *audience* through the medium of a speech. In the same way, an *author* gives a message to a *reader* through the medium of a book.

PHYSICIAN:ILLNESS::police officer:crime

A *physician's* job is to arrest, prevent, or eliminate *illness*. A *police officer's* job is to arrest, prevent, or eliminate *crime*.

5. ACTION:ACTED UPON. This type of analogy is similar to the preceding type. It couples a particular type of action with the person or thing it usually acts upon or affects. Here are some examples:

DISPROVE:THEORY::rebut:argument

To *disprove* a *theory* is to show that it is false. In the same way, to *rebut* an *argument* is to show that it is false.

ADMIRE:PRODIGY::abhor:enormity

A *prodigy* is anything amazing or astonishing. An *enormity* is a horrible crime. So one *admires* a *prodigy*, just as one *abhors* an *enormity*.

SEAL:ENVELOPE::lock:vault

One closes an *envelope* by *sealing* it just as one closes a *vault* by *locking* it.

6. ACTION:EMOTION. This type of analogy pairs an action with the emotion usually associated with it. The following examples illustrate the relationship:

BLUSH:EMBARRASSMENT::blanch:terror

A person's face may *blush* with *embarrassment* just as it may *blanch*—or turn white—with *terror*.

TRUDGE:WEARY::skip:lighthearted

A person who feels *weary* may *trudge* along while a *lighthearted* person may *skip* along.

LOST:WANDERING::puzzled:pondering

Wandering is an action one usually engages in when *lost*. *Pondering* is an action one usually engages in when *puzzled*.

7. PART:WHOLE. This type of analogy is self-explanatory. It pairs a part of something with the whole to which it belongs. As the following examples illustrate, the function of the part is usually important.

KNOB:DOOR::handle:pot

A *knob* is the part of a *door* one holds and uses to move the door. Similarly, a *handle* is the part of a *pot* one holds and uses to move the pot.

BANK:RIVER::shore:sea

A *bank* is the edge or margin of a *river* just as a *shore* is the edge or margin of a *sea.*

FOUNDATION:BUILDING::base:statue

A *foundation* is the part on which a *building* sits. A *base* is the part on which a *statue* sits.

8. NOUN:QUALITY. This type of analogy couples a person or thing with a characteristic quality of that person or thing. Here are some examples:

SCHOLAR:LEARNED::veteran:experienced

A *scholar* is a person who is *learned.* A *veteran* is a person who is *experienced.*

SHARP:BLADE::pointed:awl

To do its job, a *blade* must be *sharp.* To do its job, an *awl* must be *pointed.*

BRAGGART:BOASTFULNESS::ingenue:innocence

The main characteristic of a *braggart* is *boastfulness.* The main characteristic of an *ingenue*—a naive young woman—is *innocence.*

9. ADJECTIVE:QUALITY. In this type of analogy, an adjective is paired with a noun that names the quality referred to by the adjective. The following examples illustrate the relationship:

DEEP:PROFUNDITY::pellucid:clarity

Deep is an adjective used to describe something characterized by *profundity.* In the same way, *pellucid* is an adjective used to describe something characterized by *clarity.*

BELLICOSITY:WARLIKE::pacificism:peace-loving

Someone *warlike* is characterized by *bellicosity* just as someone *peace-loving* is characterized by *pacifism.*

ABSTRUSE:COMPLEXITY::straightforward:simplicity

Something *abstruse* is marked by *complexity.* Something straightforward is marked by *simplicity.*

Past SATs indicate that these nine types of relationships account for approximately 80 percent of the verbal analogies on the exam. If you recognize and understand these nine types of relationships, you'll be well prepared for the particular analogies you'll encounter on the SAT you take.

12.6 Miscellaneous Analogy Relationships

Not every analogy on the SAT fits into one of the nine common categories we've just considered. An almost infinite number of other relationships are possible. Just to give you an idea of the variety within the "miscellaneous" category, here are a few examples:

ZOOLOGY:ANIMALS::botany:plants

The relationship here is one of science to thing studied.

PAINTER:STUDIO::musician:auditorium

The relationship here is one of worker to characteristic place of work.

WEAPON:SWORD::tool:hammer

This relationship is one of general category to specific example.

LIGHT:SUN::rain:cloud

This is a relationship of object to source.

Again, these are just a few examples of the possible ways in which two words can be related. No doubt you can think of many others. The point is this: Although you can expect *most* SAT analogies to fall into the nine basic categories we've discussed, you must be prepared for a few that will require on-the-spot analysis and the application of intelligence, knowledge, common sense, and ingenuity. For those few, you should find the two-step method—building a bridge and modifying the bridge—especially useful.

Other Analogy Techniques

12.7 Miscellaneous Hints for Analogy Questions

We'll conclude this lesson with a selection of miscellaneous hints you'll find useful in tackling the analogy questions on the SAT, especially the subtler ones.

1. Ignore superficial similarities between word pairs. Focus on the relationship between the words, not on their subject matter. For example, consider once again the KEYBOARD:PIANO analogy:

KEYBOARD:PIANO:: (A) notes:instrument
(B) strings:violin (C) rudder:boat
(D) dial:telephone (E) voice:song

Choices A, B, and E are superficially related to the stem word pair in subject matter, and for that reason they're all very tempting. However, as you've seen, the *best* answer is choice D, which doesn't have anything at all to do with music. Why? Because the relationship between *dial* and *telephone* is closer to the relationship between *keyboard* and *piano* than is the relationship between any of the other word pairs.

2. Be on the lookout for concrete answers to abstract questions and vice versa. Two words that point to the material, or concrete, world may be related in the same way as two words that point to the immaterial, or abstract, world. Such similarities are often difficult to spot. Here are some examples:

RUNG:LADDER::rank:hierarchy

Even though one is concrete and the other abstract, a *ladder* and a *hierarchy* are both things one climbs, either *rung* by *rung* or *rank* by *rank.*

KINDLE:FLAME::inspire:enthusiasm

One *inspires enthusiasm* in much the same way that one *kindles* a *flame*—by arousing it, igniting it, or setting it afire.

REPEL:ATTACK::disprove:allegation

An *allegation* is a kind of verbal or moral attack. It needs to be *disproved* just as an *attack* needs to be *repelled.*

3. Remember to consider not only the denotations, or literal meanings, of the words in an analogy but also their connotations, or feelings. For instance, look at the following analogy:

NEATNESS:FASTIDIOUS:: (A) talent:skillful
(B) ethics:noble (C) intelligence:crafty
(D) philosophy:knowledgeable
(E) morality:scrupulous

If you consider only the literal, surface meanings of these words, you might build a very simple bridge between *neatness* and *fastidious*: "Someone who is *fastidious* is characterized by *neatness*." However, you can connect the word pairs in most, if not all, of the answer choices with the same simple bridge. To determine which answer is best, you must consider the connotations of *fastidious*. Someone who is fastidious is *extremely* neat, even to the point of being anxious or fussy about it. (Think of Felix Unger in *The Odd Couple*.) The answer pair with the same kind of relationship is choice E. To be *scrupulous* is to be extremely moral, even to worry or fret about it. So the best answer from among five fairly good ones is choice E. As you can see, the connotations, or feelings, of the words in a verbal analogy may make the difference between the right answer and the wrong ones.

LESSON 13
Techniques for Sentence Completions

OBJECTIVES

- ☐ To master the three-step approach to sentence completions
- ☐ To recognize common sentence structures and the key words that characterize them
- ☐ To learn techniques for use with difficult or subtle SAT sentence completions

Tackling Sentence Completions

13.1 The Three-Step Approach

Each verbal section on the SAT includes some sentence completions, either one group of five or two groups of five. Although sentence completions are short, they are classified as reading comprehension questions. As you'll see, you can approach each sentence completion as a very short reading passage. Your job is to figure out the meaning of the sentence. You'll be using many of the same kinds of clues you've learned to use in reading full-length passages, especially key words and logical structure. Recognizing key words and understanding the structure of a sentence will enable you to pick out the answer that best completes the meaning of the sentence.

You should be able to answer sentence completions fairly quickly—at a rate of about one every 30 or 35 seconds. So each group of five sentence completions should take you no longer than 3 minutes. After you've practiced awhile, you'll find this pace very manageable.

In this lesson, you'll learn a three-step approach to sentence completions that many students find helpful. The three steps are these: (1) determine the structure of the sentence, (2) select an answer that fits that structure, and (3) check your answer.

13.2 Step 1: Determine the Structure of the Sentence

The key to answering a sentence completion question is understanding the structure of the sentence—not the grammatical structure but the logical structure, that is, how the ideas in the sentence are arranged and how they relate to one another. As you'll see, the structure of a sentence is similar to that of a full-length reading passage. Once you recognize that structure, you can usually figure out which word or words will best complete the sentence.

Here's an example of how step 1 works:

> Despite the mayor's insistence that the accusations against him are ----, the city council has decided to conduct a full investigation.

Before you look at the answer choices for a sentence completion question like this, consider the structure of the sentence. There are two ideas here: the mayor's insistence and the city council's decision to conduct an investigation. How are the two ideas related? They contrast with one another. How do you know the two ideas contrast with one another? Because the sentence begins with the word *despite*, which is a clue to the structure of the sentence. Whenever a sentence has the structure "Despite idea A, idea B is true," you can be sure that idea A contrasts with idea B.

In this example, idea B is that the city council plans to investigate the mayor. Clearly the city council must think that the mayor has, or may have, done something wrong. If idea A contradicts idea B, then the mayor must be insisting that he has done nothing wrong and that the accusations against him are false. The word *false*, or a word with nearly the same meaning, would complete the contrast initiated by the word *despite*. With this in mind, look at the five answer choices:

(A) serious (B) unusual (C) groundless
(D) unprecedented (E) numerous

The correct answer, obviously, is choice C. *Groundless* means "unsupported, false, untruthful," which fits in perfectly with the structure of the sentence.

13.3 Key Words as Clues to Sentence Structure

As the sample sentence completion question we just looked at illustrates, key words like *despite* are clues to the structure of a sentence, and the structure of a sentence, in turn, is a clue to the correct answer—that is, to the word or words that would best fit the meaning of the sentence. When you approach a sentence completion on the SAT, then, the first thing you should look for is a key word. In this section we'll consider some principal key words and the types of sentence structures that they point to.

Some of the key words that signal a *contrast* include the following:

but	by contrast	whereas
yet	nevertheless	despite
although	on the other hand	otherwise
however	on the contrary	unlike

Words like these are commonly used to set up a contrast between two parts of a sentence. Here are some examples:

Although pandas resemble bears, they are not closely related to bears.

When he was elected, Truman was widely considered unqualified to be president; now, *however*, he is regarded as one of the better presidents of this century.

The great athletes of the past are held in awe, *yet* today's athletes have surpassed many of the best performances of their predecessors.

The ideas in the two halves of each of these sentences contrast with one another. Pandas look like bears, but they are not closely related to bears; Truman was considered unqualified, but he made a good president; athletes of the past are admired, but today's athletes perform better. In each case, a key word points up the contrast.

Other kinds of key words are used in sentences with different structures. Sometimes the ideas in the two halves of a sentence are similar. Key words that set up a *comparison* between similar ideas include the following:

as ... as	like	in like manner
just as ... so	likewise	in the same way
similarly		

Here are some examples:

Just as birds fly south for the winter, *so* tourists flock to Mexico each year.

Taking the SAT is *as* easy *as* falling off a log.

Shoulder pads are in vogue once again; trousers, *likewise*, are back in style.

In each of these examples, the key word points out a similarity between the ideas in the two parts of the sentence.

In some sentences, one part presents an *example* or *illustration* of an idea presented in another part. This structure may be indicated by key words such as the following:

like	for example	in particular
as	for instance	specifically
such as		

Here are some examples:

A presidential candidate often chooses a running mate from a different part of the country to balance the ticket geographically, *as* northerner John F. Kennedy did when he chose southerner Lyndon B. Johnson in 1960.

Some gems of unusual colors, *like* yellow diamonds, are more valuable than the common varieties.

A number of Freud's followers, *specifically* Jung and Adler, broke with their master on fundamental theoretical points.

In each of these examples, the phrase or clause beginning with the italicized key word presents a specific example of the idea stated in the rest of the sentence.

Sometimes the second half of a sentence presents an idea in *addition* to the idea in the first half. Some of the key words that signal addition include the following:

and	furthermore	moreover
also	in addition	too
besides		

Here are some examples:

Jane went to Harvard, *and* David went to Yale.

Jane studied chemistry; *in addition*, she took classes in botany and literature.

David liked his course work; *moreover*, he enjoyed campus life immensely.

Whereas an example is subordinate to the main idea of a sentence, ideas introduced by "addition" words are usually equal in weight to the ideas that precede them. These key words don't point out a comparison or contrast; they merely present "something else."

Some sentences present ideas that have a *cause-and-effect* relationship. Sentences like these often contain one of the following key words:

because (of)	due to	thus
causes	as a result	then
leads to	consequently	hence
produces	accordingly	so
since	therefore	

Here are some examples:

As a result of Lincoln's victory in the election of 1860, the leaders of the South made plans to secede from the Union.

Mendel's work on heredity *led to* a deeper understanding of the workings of natural selection.

The hospital staff has been greatly depleted by the strike; *consequently*, those who are still on the job are seriously overworked.

In each of these examples, the first part of the sentence names a cause and the second part of the sentence names an effect or a result of that cause.

In some sentences, one idea is a *restatement*, an *intensification*, or a *summary* of another. In sentences of this type, the following key words may appear:

that is	as it were	in fact
in other words	so to speak	in short
to restate	indeed	in sum
namely	to be sure	

Here are some examples:

> Crime rates and poverty have neither a strong positive nor a strong negative correlation; *in other words*, there is no clear connection between the two.
>
> The workers strongly objected to the suspension of safety regulations in the mine; *in fact*, they voted to strike if the regulations were not reinstated by the end of the week.
>
> Mr. Helms is wearisome, drearisome, tiresome, and irksome; *in short*, he is a bore.

In each of these examples, the second half of the sentence restates, intensifies, or summarizes the first half.

Finally, in some sentences, the ideas are related by *time sequence*. These sentences often contain key words like the following:

before	afterward	thereafter
earlier	then	next
previously	subsequently	following
at the same time	later	soon
simultaneously		

Here are some examples:

> *Before* the invention of movable type, books were handmade, rare, and extremely costly.
>
> The realization that the splitting of an atom would release enormous amounts of energy led to the *next* step: an attempt to put this knowledge to practical use.
>
> The original highway plan had called for a second bridge to connect the islands, but this plan was *subsequently* changed to save money.

In each example, the key word indicates which fact or event came first and which came later.

13.4 Step 2: Select an Answer

After you have picked out the key word or words and have determined the relationship between the ideas in a sentence, the next step in approaching a sentence completion question is to anticipate the word or words you need to complete the sentence logically. Although you may not be able to anticipate the exact word that will best fill each blank space in the sentence, you should have a good idea of the kind of word you need before you look at the answer choices. For instance, if the key word in a sentence signals a contrast, you know you need a word that will suggest a clear and striking opposition—perhaps an antonym or near antonym for some other word or phrase in the sentence. If the key word in a sentence signals a cause-and-effect relationship, you know you need a word that will help to establish an obvious logical connection between the cause and the effect.

Once you've decided what kind of word you need to fill each blank space in a sentence completion, look at the answer choices. You may find the exact word or words you had in mind. If so, you've probably identified the correct answer. If not, you may find a synonym or synonyms, as in the earlier example about the mayor and the city council. From the structure of that sentence, you could tell that the mayor was insisting that the accusations against him were false. However, *false* wasn't one of the answer choices. The correct answer was a synonym for *false*—*groundless*.

As you can see, a knowledge of vocabulary may be important for some sentence completions.

If you don't know some of the words in a sentence completion, either in the sentence itself or in the choices you're given, you may have trouble finding the right answer. Nevertheless, don't give up. Go through the answer choices one by one. You should be able to determine that one or two of them, at least, are definitely wrong. If so, eliminate those answers and choose one of the others. Don't worry if the answer you choose includes words you don't know. By eliminating one or two answers, you have substantially improved your chances of guessing correctly.

13.5 Step 3: Check Your Answer

After choosing an answer for a sentence completion, mentally fill in the blank or blanks with the word or words you've chosen; then read the sentence through. Does it make sense? Do all of its parts hang together? If so, you've made the right choice. Does the sentence sound strange? Does it have parts that don't seem to belong? If so, you've chosen incorrectly. Try again. Here are some special points to look for as you check your answer.

The completed sentence should be *unified*—that is, it should make one consistent, coherent statement. It should not contradict itself or contain ideas that seem unrelated. Wrong answers for sentence completions often drag in ideas that aren't closely connected to the rest of the sentence. Here's an example:

> Books and manuscripts from five hundred years ago are often in better condition than those of recent years because older books were produced with ---- paper.
>
> (A) costlier (B) more durable (C) glossier (D) handmade (E) colorful

Any of the answer choices conceivably could be used to describe the paper on which old books and manuscripts were printed, but only one of them is closely related to the main idea of the sentence. The main idea of the sentence is that old books often last longer and hold up better than new books. In other words, the sentence is about the *durability* of books. It's not about their costliness, their appearance, or their manufacture. Though these other factors may have some effect on the condition of a book after a period of time, that effect is not spelled out or even hinted at in the sentence. So choices A, C, D, and E are all irrelevant and therefore wrong.

Many SAT sentence completions contain two blank spaces. Make sure that *both* words in the answer you choose fit in the sentence. Many wrong answers contain one word that fits and one that doesn't. A hasty or careless reading might lead you to choose one of these half-right answers. Here's an example:

> Successful statesmanship relies more on political intelligence than on high ideals; for instance, Lincoln's emancipation of the slaves was effective not because it was morally ---- but because it was handled in a politically ---- fashion.
>
> (A) just..cynical
> (B) correct..careless
> (C) questionable..skillful
> (D) wrong..rational
> (E) right..adept

Each answer here has at least one "right" word. The main idea of the sentence is that in politics, intelligence is more important than idealism. As the key phrase *for instance* indicates, the second half of the sentence is intended to give an example of this idea. Therefore, the two missing words should relate to the contrast between high ideals and political intelligence. In choices A and B, the first words relate to high ideals. In choices C and D, the second words relate to political intelligence. But only in choice E do both words relate to the contrast between high ideals and political intelligence. So choice E is the only correct answer.

Remember: Whenever a sentence completion includes two blanks, check to make sure that *both* words in the answer you've chosen fit logically in the sentence.

Additional Techniques for Sentence Completions

13.6 Figurative Language

On occasion you'll encounter one or two SAT sentence completions that contain no key words. These sentence completions aren't necessarily more difficult than the others, but they do require a slightly different approach. Since you don't have any standard clues to rely on, you have to look for others.

One of the obvious clues to look for, of course, is the main idea of the sentence. As with any other sentence completion, try to determine what the main idea of the sentence is. Then choose an answer that is consistent with and closely related to that idea. Avoid answers that seem to drag in information that has little or nothing to do with the point the sentence is making.

Another clue to look for is parallel structure. As you learned in Lesson 10 (see Section 10.7), parallel grammatical structures are an indication that two or more ideas in a sentence are very closely related. When the structures are phrases or clauses, they usually echo one another in some obvious way, and the echo is often an excellent clue to the word or words that are missing from a sentence completion. By comparing the phrases or clauses, you can frequently determine the kind of word you need to fill each blank in the sentence.

Yet another clue to look for is figurative language. Figurative language is characterized by *figures of speech*—phrases that say one thing (literally) but mean another. Figures of speech are used to make many kinds of indirect statements. Two of the most common types of figures of speech—*metaphors* and *similes*—are both used to suggest a similarity between seemingly unlike things. One familiar metaphor is the description of George Washington as the father of his country. Washington was not literally the father of the United States, but he played a fatherly role in the birth of the nation. (Here, *birth* is also used metaphorically.) A simile is very much like a metaphor; the only difference is that a simile includes the word *like* or *as*. For instance, *George Washington was like a father to his country* is a simile.

When used in a sentence completion, a simile or metaphor is often a clue to the feeling or mood of the sentence and thus to the word or words that are missing. Here's an example:

> At times, America's foreign policy makers have adopted a cowboy mentality, sending U.S. armed forces abroad in search of ---- around the world.
>
> (A) global responsibilities (B) peaceful cooperation
> (C) military adventures (D) diplomatic solutions
> (E) allies and supporters

To understand this sentence, you must consider the meaning of *cowboy mentality*. What does that metaphor imply? It suggests an old cowboy movie, in which the hero rides out after the cattle rustlers or Indians and either rounds them up or shoots them down. The idea, then, is of a heroic adventurer solving a problem by means of force. This underlying cowboy metaphor suggests the logical answer—choice C.

13.7 Connotations

Connotations, as you know, are the feelings associated with words. Some words, such as scientific terms, carry few or no connotations. Other words have powerful connotations; curse words, for instance, are almost pure emotion. Most words fall somewhere in between. Words that convey strong feelings—sometimes called *loaded words*—are an indication of an author's attitude toward a subject. When they appear in a sentence completion question, loaded words are often a good clue to the word or words that are missing from the sentence.

For example, think about the words *scholarship* and *pedantry*. Both refer to the same basic activity: book learning. But the word *scholarship* has positive connotations, suggesting worthwhile learning, while *pedantry* has negative connotations, suggesting superficial learning that is pursued more for pompous display than for any more valid purpose. These differing connotations help to explain the meaning of the following sentence:

Learning is valuable in itself, but when scholarship becomes pedantry, the search for ---- turns into a mere accumulation of ----.

(A) wisdom..facts
(B) details..knowledge
(C) truth..philosophy
(D) information..sources
(E) statistics..numbers

Since the distinction between *scholarship* and *pedantry* is one between positively and negatively charged words, the second clause of the sentence should suggest a similar distinction between something worthwhile and something petty. Choice A does this effectively. It contrasts the valuable quality of *wisdom* with the collection of mere *facts*, which may have little meaning or importance in themselves. This sentence shows how the connotations of words can, on occasion, be the key to the correct answer to a sentence completion question. It pays to be aware of them.

LESSON 14
Math Review: Geometry and Other Topics

OBJECTIVES

- ☐ To review the basic concepts of plane geometry tested on the SAT
- ☐ To learn how to apply geometric reasoning to SAT math problems and quantitative comparisons
- ☐ To review other math concepts often tested on the SAT

14.1 Introduction

In Lesson 9, you reviewed the basic concepts of arithmetic and algebra that you will be expected to know for the SAT. In this lesson, you will review plane geometry, the third main area of SAT math, along with a few other miscellaneous topics that you will probably be tested on.

Geometry

14.2 Angles and Angle Relationships

MATH CAPSULE

Types of angles:

An **acute angle** has a measure greater than 0° but less than 90°.

A **right angle** has a measure of 90°. Two angles that together have a measure of 90° are **complementary angles**. Angle ABD in the following figure is a right angle. Therefore, $\angle ABC + \angle CBD = 90°$.

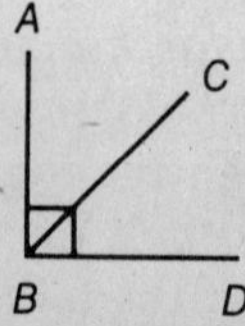

An **obtuse angle** has a measure greater than 90° but less than 180°.

A **straight angle** has a measure of 180°. Two angles that together have a measure of 180° are **supplementary angles**. Angle *PQR* in the following figure is a straight angle. Therefore, $\angle PQS + \angle SQR = 180°$.

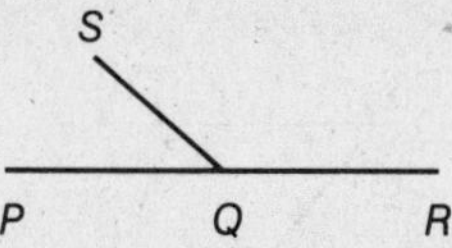

Intersecting lines and angles:

When two lines intersect, four angles are formed, as shown in the following figure:

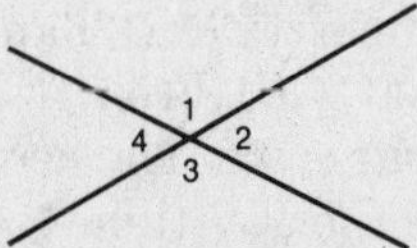

The angles are related in the following ways:

1. The angles opposite each other (angles 1 and 3 and angles 2 and 4), which are called **vertical angles**, are equal.
2. The angles adjacent to each other (angles 1 and 2, angles 2 and 3, angles 3 and 4, and angles 4 and 1) are supplementary.

Parallel lines and angles:

When two parallel lines are intersected by a third line, called a **transversal**, eight angles are formed, as shown in the following figure:

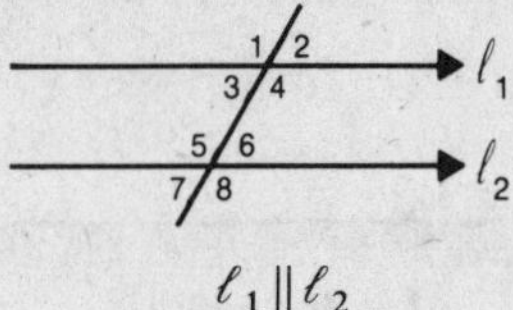

$\ell_1 \parallel \ell_2$

The relationships among and between the angles can be summarized very briefly as follows:

1. The angles that look equal—angles 1, 4, 5, and 8 and angles 2, 3, 6, and 7—are equal.
2. The angles that don't look equal—angles 1 and 6, for instance—are supplementary.

Since SAT math questions are generally written in plain language with minimum reliance on mathematical terminology, chances are you won't encounter any of the terms included in the Math Capsule on the SAT. So don't worry if you always get the terms *complementary angles* and *supplementary angles* mixed up (lots of people do). If you can recognize the angles when you see them and if you know which ones add up to 90° and which ones add up to 180°, you don't have to remember their names.

The same goes for the eight angles formed when two parallel lines are intersected by a third line. There are special terms for all eight angles—or at least for various pairs of them. Some are called *corresponding angles*; some are called *alternate interior angles*; some are called *consecutive exterior angles*. It's great if you can remember which ones are which, but all you really need to know for the SAT is what the Math Capsule says: The angles that look equal are equal; the angles that don't look equal are supplementary.

You can be fairly certain that this simple principle will come in handy when you take the SAT. What it means is this: All you need to know is the measure of one of the eight angles and you can easily deduce the measures of the other seven. Each one will be either equal or supplementary to the one you know. The same principle applies to the four angles formed when two lines intersect. If you know the measure of one angle, you can easily deduce the measures of the other three. One is equal to the one you know and the other two are supplementary to it.

Be on the alert for SAT questions that require you to apply this principle. Some of them may not be obvious. For example, you might be asked a question on a figure such as the following:

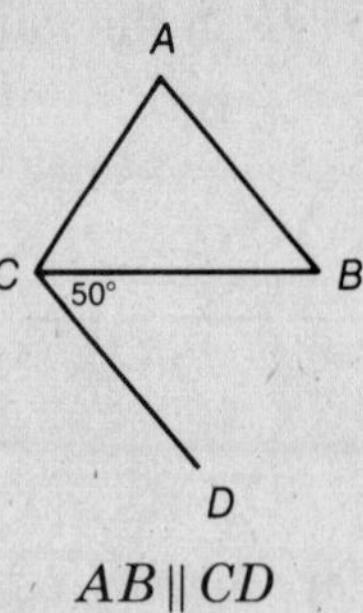

$AB \parallel CD$

At first glance, you see a triangle with an extra line "hanging down" from it. But you also have parallel lines intersected by a transversal (*CB*). From this you can deduce that angle *ABC*, one of the base angles of the triangle, measures 50°. The deduction will probably lead you at least one step closer to the correct answer to the question.

PRACTICE EXERCISES

In the following figure, two parallel lines are intersected by a transversal. Find the measure of each of the numbered angles.

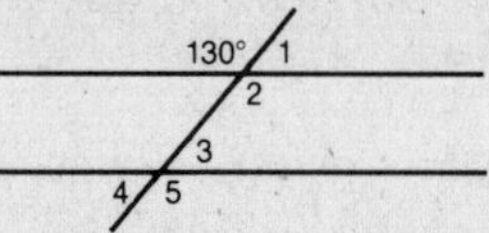

Answers

1. 50° 2. 130° 3. 50° 4. 50° 5. 130°

14.3 Triangles

MATH CAPSULE

Parts of a triangle:

A **vertex** is the point at which two sides of a triangle (or any other closed figure) meet. *A*, *B*, and *C* are the three vertices of triangle *ABC* below.

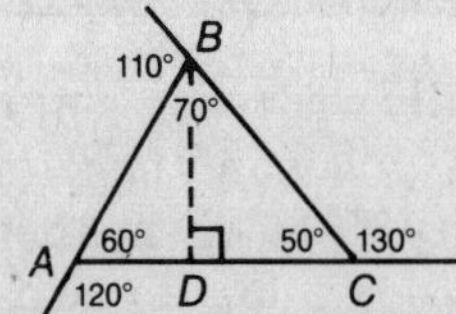

The **height** of a triangle is a line drawn from any vertex at a right angle to the opposite side (or to an extension of the opposite side) of the triangle. *BD* is the height of triangle *ABC* above.

The **base** of a triangle is the side perpendicular to the height of the triangle. Side *AC* is the base of triangle *ABC* above.

An **interior angle** of a triangle is one of the three angles inside the triangle. The angles marked 50°, 60°, and 70° are the three interior angles of triangle *ABC* above.

An **exterior angle** of a triangle is an angle formed when one side of the triangle is extended. The angles marked 110°, 120°, and 130° are three exterior angles of triangle *ABC* above.

A **remote interior angle** of a triangle is one of the two interior angles not adjacent to a given exterior angle. The 60° and 70° angles of triangle ABC above are the two remote interior angles of the 130° exterior angle.

Triangular sums:

1. The sum of the measures of the three interior angles of a triangle is 180°.
2. The measure of an exterior angle of a triangle is equal to the sum of the measures of the two remote interior angles.
3. The sum of the measures of the exterior angles of a triangle formed by extending each of its sides in succession (as in triangle ABC above) is 360°.
4. The sum of the lengths of two sides of a triangle is greater than the length of the third side.

Finding the perimeter and the area of a triangle:

1. To find the **perimeter** of a triangle, add the lengths of its three sides.
2. To find the **area** of a triangle, use the formula $A = \frac{1}{2}bh$, where b is the base of the triangle and h is its height.

Types of triangles:

An **equilateral triangle** is a triangle with three equal sides and three equal angles, each measuring 60°. Triangle EFG below is an equilateral triangle.

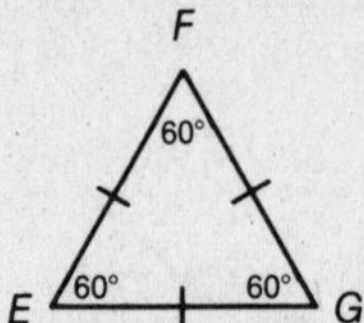

An **isosceles triangle** is a triangle with two equal sides and two equal angles, which are opposite the two equal sides. Triangle IJK below is an isosceles triangle.

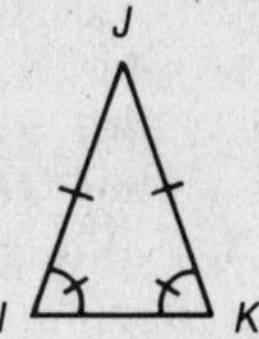

A **right triangle** is a triangle with a right angle. In a right triangle, the side opposite the right angle (the longest side) is called the **hypotenuse**, and the other two sides are called the **legs**. In right triangle RST below, ST is the hypotenuse and RS and RT are the legs.

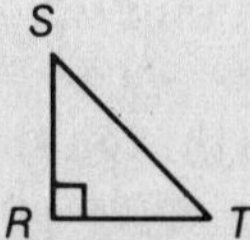

Pythagorean theorem:

If you know the lengths of two sides of a right triangle, you can use the Pythagorean theorem to find the length of the third side. The **Pythagorean theorem** states that the square of the length of the hypotenuse is equal to the sum of the squares of the lengths of the two legs: that is, $\text{leg}^2 + \text{leg}^2 = \text{hypotenuse}^2$. In right triangle RST above, $RS^2 + RT^2 = ST^2$.

"Standard" right triangles:

Two types of right triangles are more common than others.

1. The first type includes the right triangle whose sides are in whole-number proportions. The ratios of the lengths of the sides of these triangles (leg-leg-hypotenuse) are as follows:

3-4-5
5-12-13
7-24-25
8-15-17

2. The second type includes the 30°-60°-90° triangle and the 45°-45°-90° triangle, which is also called an **isosceles right triangle**. The ratios of the lengths of the sides of these two triangles, respectively, are as follows:

$1\text{-}\sqrt{3}\text{-}2$
$1\text{-}1\text{-}\sqrt{2}$

Triangles are among the most "popular" geometric figures on the SAT, so the information in the Math Capsule in this section of Lesson 14 is extremely important. You should know it all backward and forward before you take the test.

SAT geometry problems typically require you to extrapolate from facts that you're given to others that you're not given. Understanding the relationships among the various parts of a geometric figure is usually the key because one or two facts about a figure can lead, by a "chain reaction," to several others.

For instance, suppose you were asked the following question:

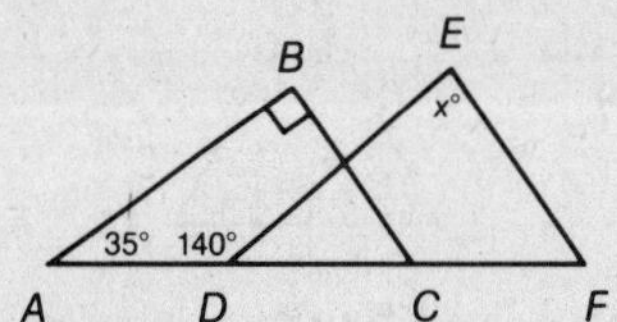

AF in the figure above is a line segment. If $BC \parallel EF$, what is the value of x?

What you have here, basically, is three triangles—*ABC*, *DEF*, and the small triangle whose base is *DC*. If *BC* is parallel to *EF*, you know that *DE* is a transversal and that the angle at the top of the small triangle has the same measure as angle x. So all you have to do to find the value of x is to find the measure of the top angle in the small triangle. And all you have to do to find the measure of the top angle in the small triangle is to find the measure of the other two angles in the small triangle and subtract their sum from 180°.

So start with what you know about the two base angles of the small triangle. One, you know, is supplementary to an angle marked 140°, so it must measure 40°. The other, you can see, is also the third angle in triangle *ABC*. You know that two of the angles in triangle *ABC* measure 90° and 35°, so the third angle must measure $180° - (90° + 35°) = 55°$. Now, if the two base angles of the small triangle measure 40° and 55°, then the top angle must measure $180° - (40° + 55°) = 85°$. This is the value of x. As you can see, just by applying a few simple facts about parallel lines and triangles to the seemingly small amount of information you're given in a question like this, you can make your way step by step very quickly to the correct answer.

One of the few simple facts about triangles that you should—but don't need to—remember for the SAT is the formula for determining the area of a triangle. The formula is included with the information provided at the beginning of each mathematical section. But do remember this: You can draw the height of a triangle from *any* vertex, and you can draw it *outside* the triangle as well as inside. The only requirement is that you draw the height at a right angle to the opposite side. If necessary, you can extend the opposite side to provide a "landing place" for the height, as shown in the following figure:

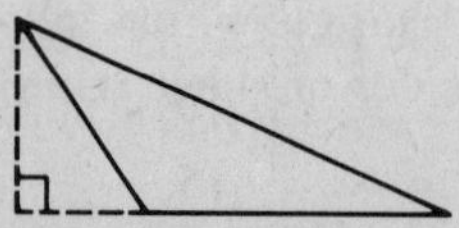

For some area problems, drawing the height outside a triangle is the only—or the fastest—way to a solution.

Another simple fact about triangles that you don't have to (but again should) remember for the SAT is the Pythagorean theorem. It, too, is provided on the test. However, you should memorize the six "standard" right triangles listed in the Math Capsule. Because they're so convenient, these triangles are used much more frequently on standardized tests like the SAT than are other right triangles, and if you know the ratios of the lengths of their sides by heart, you'll save yourself time. Given the lengths of two sides of a "standard" right triangle, you'll be able to determine the length of the third side without performing the calculations required by the Pythagorean theorem.

So when you take the SAT, be on the alert for the "standard" right triangles. These include not only the six listed in the Math Capsule but all of their multiples as well. For instance, a right triangle whose legs are 6 and 8 units long is exactly twice the size of the 3-4-5 triangle, so its hypotenuse is 10 units long. Similarly, a 45°-45°-90° triangle whose legs are 5 units long is exactly five times the size of the 1-1-$\sqrt{2}$ triangle, so its hypotenuse is $5\sqrt{2}$ units long.

The proportions of the 30°-60°-90° and the 45°-45°-90° triangles are useful for other figures besides right triangles. For instance, if you were given the length of one side of an equilateral triangle, you could quickly find its height (and thus its area) because the height divides the triangle into two 30°-60°-90°, or 1-$\sqrt{3}$-2, triangles, as shown in the following figure:

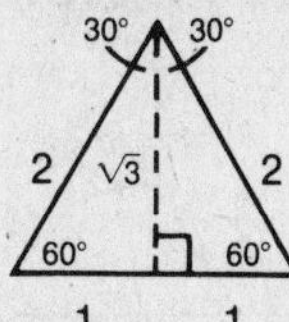

So an equilateral triangle of side 2 has a height of $\sqrt{3}$ (or about 1.732); an equilateral triangle of side 4 has a height of $2\sqrt{3}$ (or about 3.464); and so on.

Similarly, if you were given the length of one side of a square, you could quickly find the length of its diagonal because the diagonal divides the square into two 45°-45°-90°, or 1-1-$\sqrt{2}$, right triangles, as shown in the following figure:

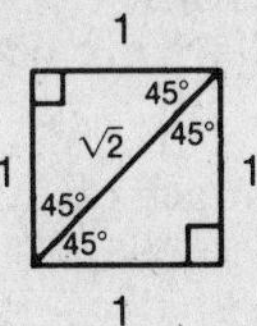

So a square of side 1 has a diagonal of $\sqrt{2}$ (or about 1.414); a square of side 2 has a diagonal of $2\sqrt{2}$ (or about 2.828); and so on. As you no doubt are beginning to see, a knowledge of the "standard" right triangles can come in very handy on the SAT.

PRACTICE EXERCISES

Assuming that ℓ_1 and ℓ_2 are parallel, find the measure of each of the numbered angles in the following figures.

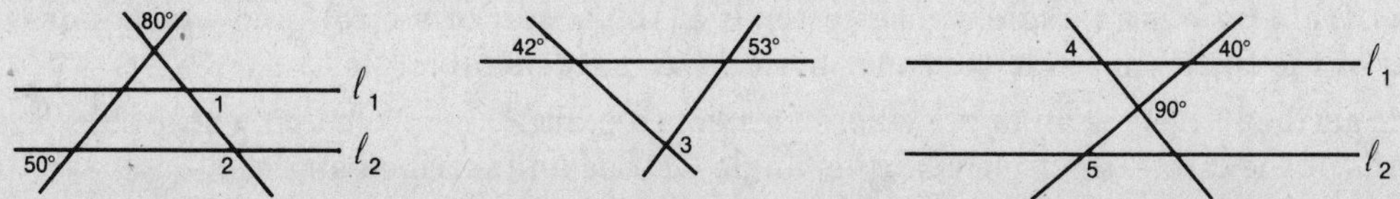

Find the length of the unknown side in each of the following triangles.

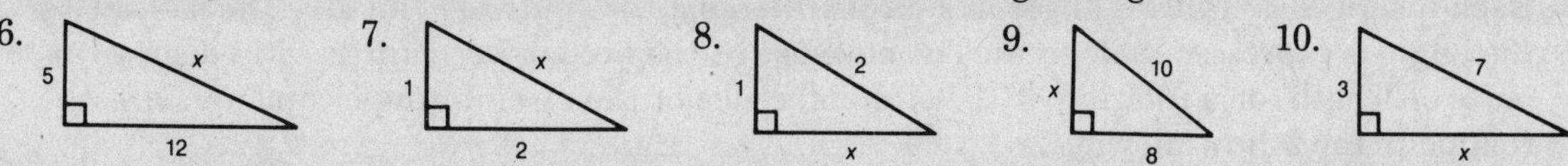

Solve each of the following problems.

11. The bottom of a 26-foot ladder rests 10 feet from the base of a building. How far up the building's wall does the ladder reach?
12. The diagonal of a square has length 12 inches. How long is each side of the square?
13. Find the hypotenuse of a right triangle whose legs measure 12 inches and 16 inches.

Answers

1. 50° 2. 130° 3. 95° 4. 50° 5. 140° 6. 13 7. $\sqrt{5}$ 8. $\sqrt{3}$ 9. 6 10. $2\sqrt{10}$
11. 24 feet 12. $6\sqrt{2}$ inches 13. 20 inches

14.4 Circles

MATH CAPSULE

Definitions:

A **circle** is the set of all points in a plane equidistant from a fixed point, known as the **center** of the circle. The measure of a circle is 360°.

A **radius** is a line segment extending from the center of a circle to any point on the circle. In circle O below, segment OA is a radius; so are segments OB and OF. In any given circle, all radii are equal in length.

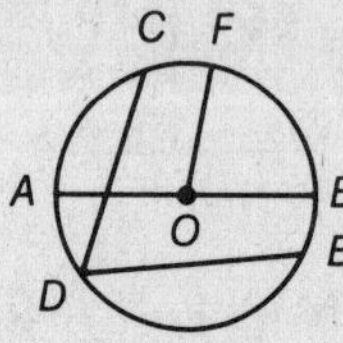

A **chord** is a line segment with endpoints on a circle. In circle O above, segments CD and DE are chords.

A **diameter** is a chord that passes through the center of a circle. A diameter divides a circle into two **semicircles**, each measuring 180°. In circle O above, chord AB is a diameter. In any given circle, all diameters are equal in length and equal to twice the length of a radius.

The **circumference** of a circle is the length of the circle, or the distance around the circle.

An **arc** is a portion of the circumference of a circle. In circle O above, there are several arcs; arc FB is one of them.

Finding the circumference and area of a circle:

1. To find the **circumference** of a circle, use one of two formulas: $C = \pi d$, where d is the diameter of the circle, or $C = 2\pi r$, where r is the radius of the circle. The number designated by π (pi) has a value approximately equal to 3.14, or $\frac{22}{7}$.
2. To find the **area** of a circle, use the formula $A = \pi r^2$, where r is the radius of the circle.

Angles in circles:

A **central angle** is an angle whose vertex is at the center of a circle and whose sides are radii of the circle. In circle O above, angle FOB is a central angle.

An **inscribed angle** is an angle whose vertex is a point on a circle and whose sides are chords of the circle. In circle O above, angle CDE is an inscribed angle.

Relationships between arcs and angles:

Each inscribed or central angle in a circle intercepts or "cuts off" an arc. The measure of the angle is expressed in degrees. The measure of the arc may be expressed in degrees or in units of length (as a fraction of the circumference of the circle). Angles and arcs are related in the following ways:

1. The degree measure of an arc cut off by a central angle is the same as the degree measure of the angle. In circle P below, central angle RPT, which cuts off arc RT, measures 90°; therefore, arc RT measures 90°. Since there are 360° in a circle, an arc that measures 90° represents $\frac{90}{360}$, or $\frac{1}{4}$, of the circumference of a circle.

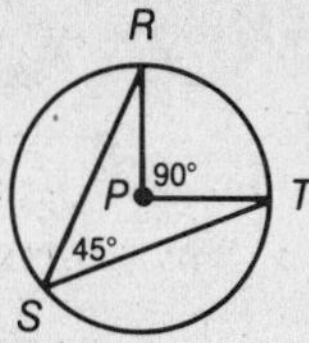

2. The degree measure of an arc cut off by an inscribed angle is twice the measure of the inscribed angle. In circle P above, inscribed angle RST, which cuts off arc RT, measures 45°; therefore, arc RT measures 90°.

Circles, like triangles, are "popular" in SAT geometry problems. So be sure you know the formulas for determining the circumference and area of a circle. Although these formulas are provided at the beginning of every SAT mathematical section, you'll save yourself time if you have them memorized. Be sure, too, that you know the approximate value of π, a highly important number in geometry. For some questions, you will have to translate quantities containing π into numeric values. For others, the answer will contain π as one of its terms.

You'll find that SAT geometry questions often involve combinations of various geometric figures. The properties of the figures relate to one another in such a way that you can figure out many facts not given in the questions. In the following figure, for example, one side of triangle ABC is a diameter of circle O:

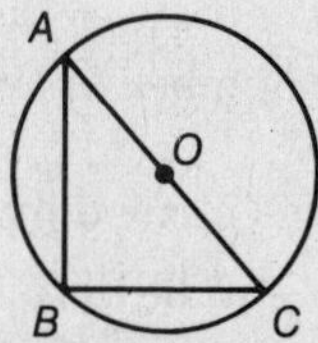

From the fact that side AC is a diameter of the circle, you can deduce several other facts. The diameter divides the circle into two equal arcs (AC and CA), each measuring 180°. Therefore, inscribed angle ABC, which cuts off one of those arcs (arc AC), must measure 90°, since the degree measure of an inscribed angle is always half that of the arc it intercepts. Thus, you know that triangle ABC is a right triangle, and you can draw other conclusions from that fact.

Some SAT geometry problems will involve squares inscribed in circles, circles inscribed in triangles, and other combinations of figures. You'll find that you can determine a great deal about figures such as these even if you've been given only one or two facts to start with.

PRACTICE EXERCISES

Find the circumference and area of a circle with a radius of each of the following lengths. Express each of your answers in terms of π.

1. 2 2. 3 3. 5 4. 6 5. x 6. $4x$

Solve each of the following problems.

7. When the radius of a circle is doubled, by what percent is its area increased?
8. What part of the area of a circle 2 feet in diameter is the area of a circle 1 foot in diameter?
9. Four circles, each of area 9π, are placed as shown in the following figure. Find the perimeter of the figure obtained by connecting their center points.

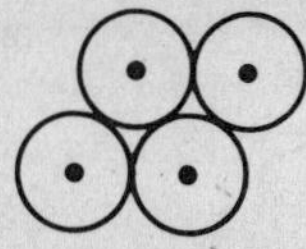

10. The following figure was constructed by drawing eight semicircles upon a rectangle, as shown. If the diameter of the semicircles is d, find the area of the shaded region.

Answers

1. 4π, 4π 2. 6π, 9π 3. 10π, 25π 4. 12π, 36π 5. $2x\pi$, $x^2\pi$ 6. $8x\pi$, $16x^2\pi$ 7. 300 8. $\frac{1}{4}$ 9. 24 10. $4d^2$

14.5 Polygons and Regular Quadrilaterals

MATH CAPSULE

Definitions:

A **polygon** is any closed plane figure with line segments as sides. (A triangle is a three-sided polygon.)

A **quadrilateral** is any four-sided polygon.

A **diagonal** is a line segment that extends from one vertex of a polygon of four or more sides to any nonadjacent vertex.

Interior angle sums of polygons:

To find the sum of the measures of the interior angles of any polygon of four or more sides, follow these two steps:

1. Divide the polygon into a minimum number of triangles by drawing all possible diagonals from one vertex of the polygon.
2. Multiply the number of triangles thus formed by 180°.

Example: Quadrilateral $ABCD$ below can be divided into a minimum of two triangles; therefore, the sum of the measures of the interior angles of quadrilateral $ABCD$, or any other quadrilateral, is $2 \times 180° = 360°$. Six-sided polygon $FGHIJK$ below can be divided into a minimum of four triangles; therefore, the sum of the measures of the interior angles of $FGHIJK$, or any other six-sided polygon, is $4 \times 180° = 720°$.

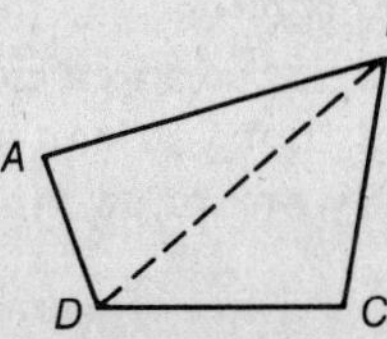

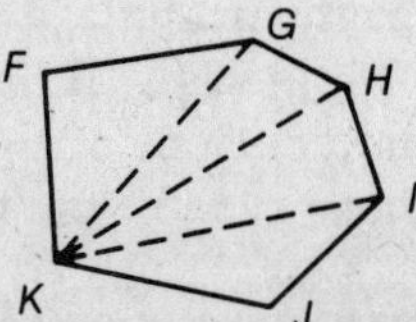

Exterior angle sums of polygons:

The sum of the measures of the exterior angles of a polygon formed by extending each side in succession is 360°—no matter how many sides the polygon has.

Example: The sum of the measures of the exterior angles of quadrilateral $ABCD$ and six-sided polygon $FGHIJK$ below is 360°.

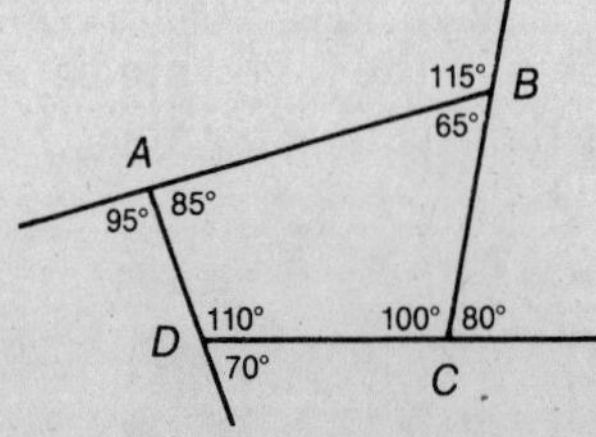

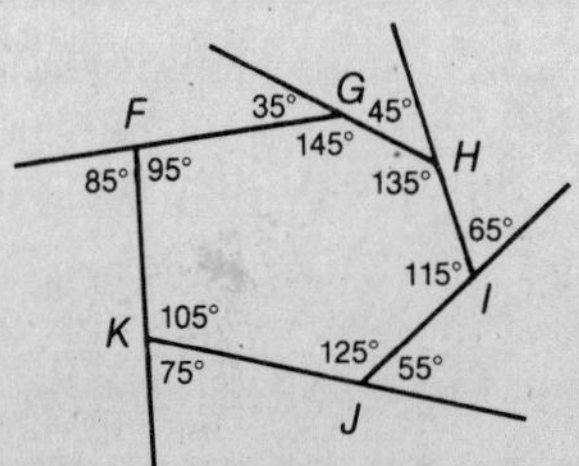

Properties of parallelograms:

A **parallelogram** is a quadrilateral whose opposite sides are parallel. Quadrilateral *ABCD* below is a parallelogram.

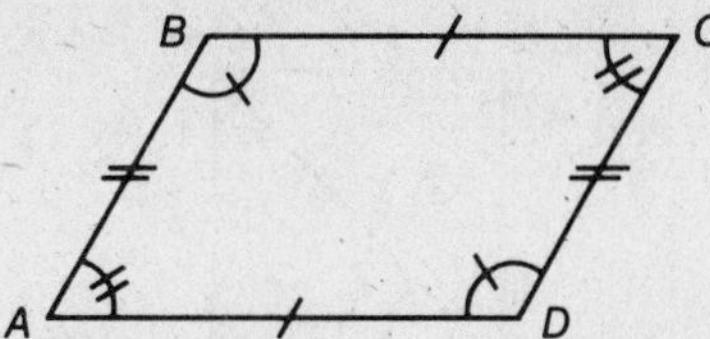

Parallelograms have the following properties:

1. The opposite sides of a parallelogram are equal in length. In parallelogram *ABCD* above, sides *BC* and *AD* are equal in length and sides *BA* and *CD* are equal in length.
2. The opposite angles of a parallelogram are equal in measure. In parallelogram *ABCD* above, angles *A* and *C* are equal in measure and angles *B* and *D* are equal in measure.
3. A diagonal divides a parallelogram into two **congruent** triangles—that is, two triangles with corresponding sides that are equal in length and corresponding angles that are equal in measure.
4. The two diagonals of a parallelogram bisect one another—that is, each divides the other into two equal parts. In parallelogram *EFGH* below, diagonal *EG* bisects diagonal *HF* and diagonal *HF* bisects diagonal *EG*.

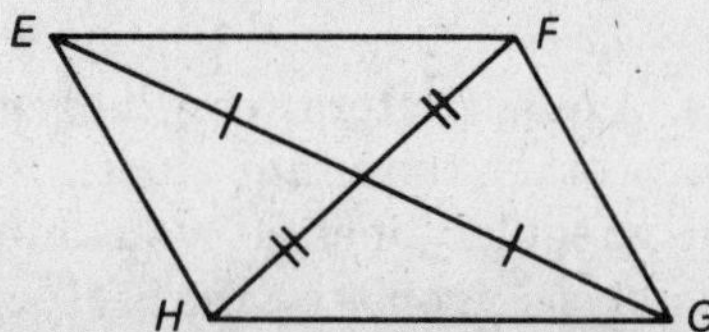

5. The **area** of a parallelogram is given by the formula $A = bh$, where b is the base of the parallelogram and h is its height. In parallelogram *JKLM* below, *JM* is the base of the parallelogram and *KN* is its height. (*LO* is also a corresponding height of base *JM*. As the diagram illustrates, a height can be drawn outside as well as inside a parallelogram.)

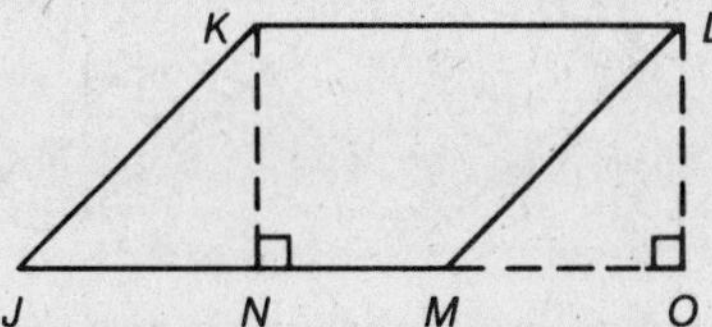

Properties of rectangles:

A rectangle is a parallelogram with four right angles. Parallelogram *PQRS* below is a rectangle.

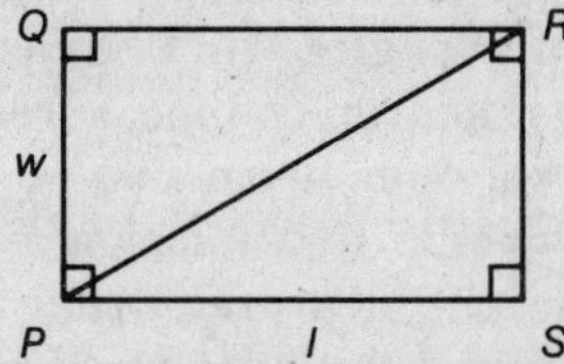

A rectangle has all of the properties of a parallelogram, plus the following properties:

1. A diagonal divides a rectangle into two congruent right triangles. In rectangle *PQRS* above, triangle *PQR* and triangle *RSP* are congruent right triangles. Their corresponding sides and angles are equal.
2. The **perimeter** of a rectangle is given by the formula $P = 2l + 2w$, where l is the length of the rectangle and w is its width.
3. The **area** of a rectangle is given by the formula $A = lw$.

Properties of squares:

A **square** is a rectangle with all four sides equal in length. Rectangle *WXYZ* below is a square.

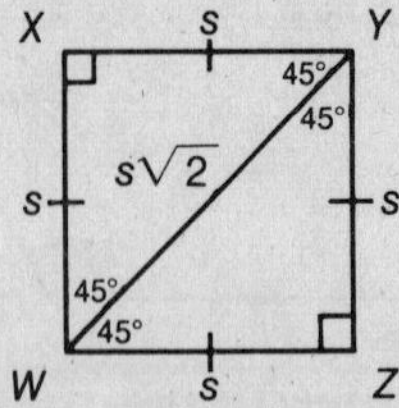

A square has all of the properties of a rectangle (and thus of a parallelogram), plus the following properties:

1. A diagonal divides a square into two 45°-45°-90°, or 1-1-$\sqrt{2}$, right triangles, so the length of the diagonal of a square is equal to the side of the square multiplied by $\sqrt{2}$ (about 1.414).
2. The **perimeter** of a square is given by the formula $P = 4s$, where s is the length of the side of the square.
3. The **area** of a square is given by the formula $A = s^2$.

As the Math Capsule suggests, a quadrilateral can be regular (with specific features) or irregular (with no specific features other than four sides). Regular quadrilaterals are much more common on the SAT than irregular ones. If you happen to encounter an irregular quadrilateral—or any other irregular polygon—on the SAT, chances are either you'll be given some "meaningful" information along with it (say, a pair of parallel lines) or you'll be asked something about the sum of the measures of the interior or exterior angles of the figure. For instance, you might be given the following figure and asked to find the value of $x + y$:

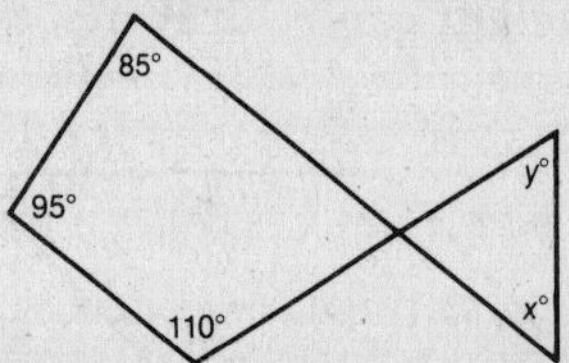

To answer this question, you need to know three things: (1) that vertical angles are equal, (2) that the sum of the measures of the interior angles of a triangle is 180°, and (3) that the sum of the measures of the interior angles of a quadrilateral is 360°. (Actually, you don't have to remember the third thing. As the Math Capsule points out, you can find the sum of the measures of the interior angles of any polygon of four or more sides simply by dividing the polygon into the minimum possible number of triangles—in this case, two—and multiplying that number by 180°.) The rest is simple: Just add up the measures of the three angles you're given (85° + 95° + 110° = 290°); subtract the sum from 360° to find the measure of the fourth angle in the quadrilateral, which is equal to the measure of the third angle in the triangle (360° − 290° = 70°); and then subtract the measure of that angle from 180° (180° − 70° = 110°).

More often than not, of course, the quadrilaterals you'll encounter on the SAT will be regular ones—parallelograms, rectangles, and squares. These three types of regular quadrilaterals have many properties in common. In fact, a square is a type of rectangle, and both a square and a rectangle are types of parallelograms. So all the properties of parallelograms listed in the Math Capsule are also properties of rectangles and squares.

Parallelograms, including rectangles and squares, are closely related to triangles. As the Math Capsule points out, a diagonal divides a parallelogram into two congruent triangles, illustrated by the following figure:

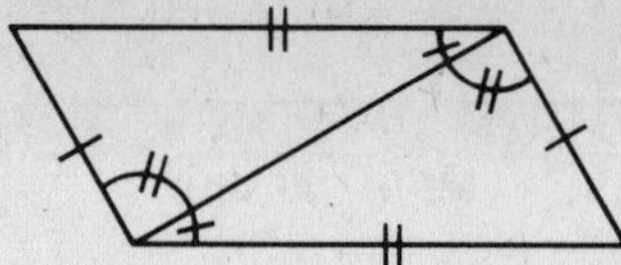

Because a parallelogram is basically two congruent triangles "back to back," the formula for the area of a parallelogram ($A = bh$) is exactly twice the formula for the area of a triangle ($A = \frac{1}{2}bh$).

A knowledge of the relationships between triangles and quadrilaterals—particularly rectangles and squares—is very useful for the SAT because the diagrams that accompany the geometry problems on the test often combine the two types of figures. So it's helpful to remember, for example, that a diagonal divides a rectangle into two congruent right triangles and a square into two 45°-45°-90°, or 1-1-$\sqrt{2}$, right triangles.

Some SAT geometry problems also combine parallelograms with circles. In these problems, you might be given a square inscribed in a circle (or vice versa), several circles inscribed in a rectangle, or one or more semicircles "grafted on" to a square or a rectangle. Usually one side or a diagonal of the square or rectangle is a radius or diameter of the circle or semicircle, so look for these identities. They're usually the key to solving problems of this type.

PRACTICE EXERCISES

1. In the following figure, a semicircle is inscribed in a rectangle. Find the area of the shaded portion of the rectangle.

2. The following figure is composed of two semicircles and a square with side 10. Find the perimeter of the figure.

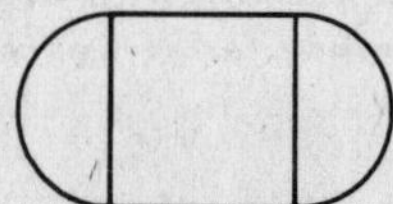

3. The following figure consists of a square inscribed in another square. If the area of the outside square is 50, what is the area of the inside square?

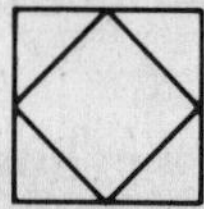

4. The following figure consists of a square with an area of 36 and four semicircles. What is the perimeter of the figure?

5. *ABCD* is a parallelogram and *E* is the midpoint of side *AD*. What is the ratio of the area of triangle *ACE* to the area of the parallelogram?

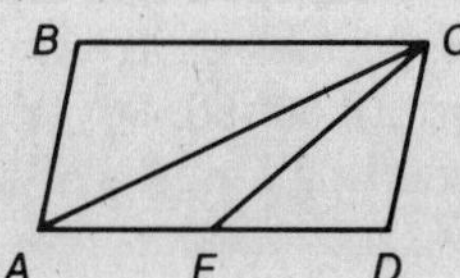

Answers

1. $50 - 12\frac{1}{2}\pi \approx 10.75$ 2. $20 + 10\pi \approx 51.4$ 3. 25 4. $12\pi \approx 37.68$ 5. 1:4

MATH CAPSULE

Definitions:

A **solid** is any closed three-dimensional figure with plane (two-dimensional) surfaces as sides.

A **face** is any of the plane surfaces that form the sides of a solid.

An **edge** is the line formed when two sides of a solid meet.

The **surface area** of a solid is the sum of the areas of all of the sides, or faces, of the solid.

The **volume** of a solid is the amount of space contained within or occupied by the solid. Volume is measured in cubic units.

Types of solids:

A **rectangular solid** is a three-dimensional figure whose sides are all rectangles. An ordinary cardboard box is a rectangular solid. A rectangular solid has six faces. The faces are congruent in pairs: that is, each face and the face opposite to it have the same length and width.

A **cube** is a rectangular solid whose sides are all squares of the same size. A die (one of a pair of dice) is a cube. A cube has six faces. The length, width, and height of a cube are all equal.

A **cylinder** is a solid whose two bases are congruent circles and whose sides are a "rolled up" rectangle. A soup can is a cylinder.

Finding the volume and surface area of a rectangular solid:

1. To find the **volume** of a rectangular solid, use the formula $V = lwh$, where l is the length, w is the width, and h is the height of the solid.
2. To find the total **surface area** of a rectangular solid, first find the area ($A = lw$) of one of each of the three pairs of congruent faces; second, multiply each area by two; third, add the three areas together.

Finding the volume and surface area of a cube:

1. To find the **volume** of a cube, use the formula $V = s^3$, where s is the length of the edge of the cube.
2. To find the total **surface area** of a cube, find the area of one of its six faces ($A = s^2$), and multiply that area by 6.

Finding the volume and surface area of a cylinder:

1. To find the **volume** of a cylinder, use the formula $V = \pi r^2 h$, where r is the radius of the circular bases of the cylinder and h is the height of the cylinder.
2. To find the total **surface area** of a cylinder, first find the area of one of the two circular bases ($A = \pi r^2$), and multiply that area by 2; second, find the area of the rectangle that forms the sides of the cylinder by multiplying the height of the cylinder by the circumference of one of the circular bases ($C = 2\pi r$); third, add the two together.

Ratios of the lengths, areas, and volumes of similar figures:

Similar figures are figures, whether plane or solid, whose corresponding angles are congruent (equal in measure) and whose corresponding sides are proportional. Any two figures may be similar, but certain types of figures are similar by definition—all equilateral triangles, all isosceles right triangles, all 30°-60°-90° triangles, all circles, all squares, all cubes. If the ratio of any corresponding lengths of two similar figures is $A:B$, the following are all true:

1. The ratio of any other corresponding lengths is $A:B$.
2. The ratio of the corresponding areas of the two figures is $A^2:B^2$.
3. The ratio of the volumes of the two figures is $A^3:B^3$.

Example: If the ratio of the edges of two cubes is 1:2, the ratio of the surface areas of the two cubes is $1^2:2^2$, or 1:4, and the ratio of the volumes of the two cubes is $1^3:2^3$, or 1:8.

There is a great deal of information about three-dimensional figures in geometry textbooks, but the few facts included in the Math Capsule should be enough to get you through the SAT. Most SAT geometry problems concern two-dimensional, or plane, figures. Those that concern three-dimensional, or solid, figures are not numerous. You'll probably find only two or three of them, at the most, on your edition of the SAT.

One or more of the questions on three-dimensional figures might be very simple. For instance, you might be asked to determine which is greater, the number of faces on a cube or the number of vertices. You can memorize these numbers for the test (a cube—or any other rectangular solid—has six faces, eight vertices, and twelve edges), but it's just as easy to picture a cube in your mind and simply count the faces, vertices, or edges.

More likely, though, the questions on three-dimensional figures will relate in some way to the volume or surface area of one or more solids. These questions probably won't be difficult, but they might have a little "twist" to them. For instance, instead of being asked to find the surface area of a simple rectangular solid, you might be asked to find the surface area of a wedge that is half a rectangular solid. Or, instead of being asked to find the volume of a cube, you might be asked how many cubes of a given edge will fit into a rectangular solid of given dimensions. Don't let these problems throw you. Although they require a little reasoning and common sense, they almost never require knowledge beyond the few facts included in the Math Capsule.

Sometimes you won't even need those—or any other—facts. You'll just have to use your head. For instance, suppose you're asked to compare the surface area of a sphere of a given radius with the area of a circle of the same radius. Of course you have to know what a sphere is in order to answer the question (a baseball is a sphere), but if you think you have to know the formula for determining the surface area of a sphere, you're mistaken. In fact, the formula, if you know it, could get in your way because it might prevent you from "seeing" that if a sphere and a circle have the same radius, the surface area of the sphere *must* be greater than the area of the circle. By the way, questions about spheres are extremely rare on the SAT. That's why the formulas for determining the volume and surface area of a sphere are not included in the Math Capsule. You can memorize them if you like ($V = \frac{4}{3}\pi r^3$ and $A = 4\pi r^2$), but you won't need them for the SAT.

What you will need for the SAT—or at least what will probably come in handy—is a knowledge of the ratios of the corresponding lengths, areas, and volumes of similar figures. These ratios will save you time on certain questions. For instance, suppose you're asked to find the ratio of the volumes of two cubes, one with a face with a diagonal of length 3 and one with a face with a diagonal of length 5. You know that each face of a cube is a square. You also know that a diagonal divides a square into two 45°-45°-90°, or 1-1-$\sqrt{2}$, right triangles. So you could figure out what the length of the edge of each cube is and from that you could figure out what the volume of each cube is and from that you could figure out what the ratio of the volumes of the two cubes is. But needless to say, you'd waste a lot of time—especially since your calculations would all involve the square root of 2, which is an awkward number to work with.

As the Math Capsule explains, all cubes are similar, so if the ratio of *any* corresponding lengths (including the lengths of corresponding diagonals) is 3:5, then the ratio of volumes is $3^3:5^3$, or 27:125. Since the ratios apply to similar figures of two as well as three dimensions, they're worth committing to memory.

PRACTICE EXERCISES

Find the volume in cubic centimeters of each of the following three-dimensional figures.

1. A rectangular solid 8 centimeters long, 3 centimeters wide, and 2 centimeters high.
2. A rectangular solid 9 centimeters long, 4 centimeters wide, and 1 centimeter high.
3. A rectangular solid $5\frac{1}{2}$ centimeters long, 2 centimeters wide, and $\frac{1}{2}$ centimeter high.
4. A cube with an edge of 4 centimeters.

5. A cube with an edge of $2\frac{1}{2}$ centimeters.
6. A cube with an edge of $\frac{1}{4}$ centimeter.
7. A cylinder with a diameter of 6 centimeters and a height of 7 centimeters.
8. A cylinder with a radius of 5 centimeters and a height of $3\frac{1}{2}$ centimeters.

Solve the following problems.

9. How many 2-inch cubes can be put in a box 8 inches long, 2 inches wide, and 5 inches tall?
10. A vintner ages a special estate wine in two cylindrical oak casks. One cask holds 5 dekaliters. If each dimension of the second cask is exactly twice that of the first, how many dekaliters will the second cask hold?

Answers

1. 48 2. 36 3. $5\frac{1}{2}$ 4. 64 5. $\frac{125}{8}$ 6. $\frac{1}{64}$ 7. $63\pi \approx 198$ 8. $87\frac{1}{2}\pi \approx 275$ 9. 8 10. 40

14.7 The Rectangular Coordinate System

MATH CAPSULE

The rectangular coordinate system:

The **rectangular coordinate system** is used to locate points on a plane and to graph linear equations. It consists of a background grid and two perpendicular number lines that intersect at the zero point on each, as shown in the following figure:

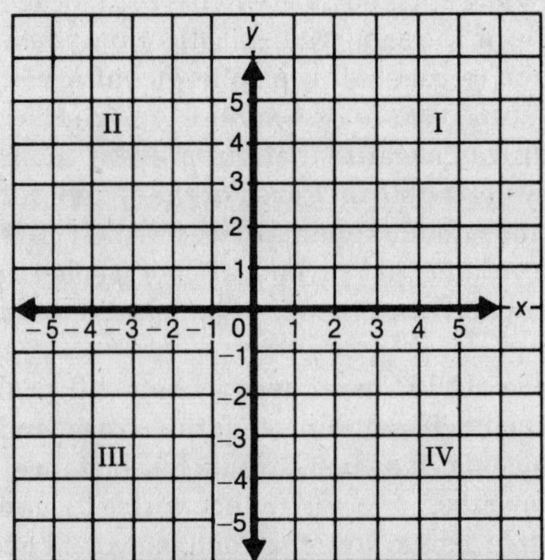

The point at which the two number lines intersect is known as the **origin**.

The horizontal number line is known as the ***x*-axis**. The vertical number line is known as the ***y*-axis**. The numbers to the right of the origin on the x-axis and above the origin on the y-axis are positive. The numbers to the left of the origin on the x-axis and below the origin on the y-axis are negative.

The four areas into which the two axes divide the plane are known as **quadrants**. The quadrants are numbered I, II, III, and IV, as shown in the figure above.

Locating points on a coordinate plane:

Each point on a coordinate plane is defined by an **ordered pair** of real numbers, called **coordinates**. Ordered pairs, or coordinates, are written in the form (x, y). The first coordinate, called the ***x*-coordinate**, defines the distance of a point from the origin along the x-axis. The second coordinate, called the ***y*-coordinate**, defines the distance of a point from the origin along the y-axis.

Example: The coordinates $(3, -4)$ define the point that is three units to the right of the origin on the x-axis and four units below the origin on the y-axis.

To locate a point on a coordinate plane, follow these three steps:

1. Find the point designated by the x-coordinate on the x-axis and draw an imaginary line perpendicular to the x-axis through it.
2. Find the point designated by the y-coordinate on the y-axis and draw an imaginary line perpendicular to the y-axis through it.
3. Find and plot the point you're looking for at the intersection of the two imaginary lines.

Graphing linear equations:

A **linear equation** is an equation with variables of the first degree, or first power, only. The equation $x + 6 = 2y$, in which 1 is the unexpressed exponent of both x and y, is a linear equation. The graph of a linear equation in two variables is a straight line. To graph a linear equation, follow these six steps:

1. Use standard algebraic techniques to isolate one of the variables (for example, x) on the left side of the equation (for example, $x = 2y - 6$).
2. Assign any convenient value to the second variable (for example, $y = 4$) and solve to find the corresponding value of the first variable (for example, if $y = 4$, then $x = 2(4) - 6 = 2$).
3. Write down the corresponding values of the two variables in the form of an ordered pair (for example, $(2, 4)$).
4. Repeat the procedure twice so that you have three different ordered pairs, or coordinates.
5. Locate the points defined by the three ordered pairs on a coordinate plane.
6. Connect the points. The line thus formed is the graph of the equation.

The point at which the graph of a linear equation intersects with the x-axis is known as the **x-intercept**. At the x-intercept, the value of y is 0. The point at which the graph of a linear equation intersects with the y-axis is known as the **y-intercept.** At the y-intercept, the value of x is 0.

Although coordinate geometry is not emphasized on the SAT, almost every edition of the exam includes at least a few questions about it. Some of these questions, like those on the geometry of three-dimensional figures, will be very simple. They will require only a general understanding of the structure and function of the rectangular coordinate system, along with an ability to count. For instance, you might be asked to find the area of the shaded region on a grid. Or you might be asked to find the area of a square drawn on a coordinate graph. Don't try to make these questions any more complicated than they seem, especially if you find them at the beginning of a test section. They're intended to be simple and straightforward, and usually the fastest way to answer them is just by counting grid boxes.

Other questions will be a little more difficult. They will require an understanding of how points in a coordinate plane are defined. For instance, you might be asked to name the coordinates of some point shown on a graph you're given. Or you might have to plot a point or two with given coordinates in order to get the information you need to answer a question.

Sometimes these questions will combine coordinate geometry with the geometry of plane figures. For example, you might be given the coordinates of the vertices of a triangle and asked to find the area, the perimeter, the length of the longest side, or some other property of the triangle. You may know everything there is to know about the geometry of triangles, but if you haven't mastered the simple technique of plotting points on a rectangular coordinate graph, you might be thrown by a problem like this.

You might also be thrown if you don't take the time to draw a crude graph in the margin of your test booklet so that you can plot the points and sketch the triangle. Remember: It's perfectly all right to use the margins of your test booklet for scratch paper, and if drawing a crude graph will enable you to "see" the solution to a problem (as it often will), by all means do so. Just be sure that your grid lines are fairly straight. Otherwise your solution, like your graph, is likely to end up out of kilter.

The most difficult questions about coordinate geometry that you're likely to face on the SAT will concern the graphs of simple linear equations. Such questions are rare, but they have been known to crop up from time to time on different editions of the test. If you want to be prepared for them, review the process for graphing linear equations outlined in the Math Capsule.

PRACTICE EXERCISES

Graph and label each of the following points.

1. $A(2,0)$
2. $B(-3,1)$
3. $C(5,-3)$
4. $D(-3,-4)$
5. $E(0,5)$
6. $F(4,2)$

Graph and label each of the following equations.

7. $x+y=0$
8. $2x-y=3$
9. $y=-2$

Answers

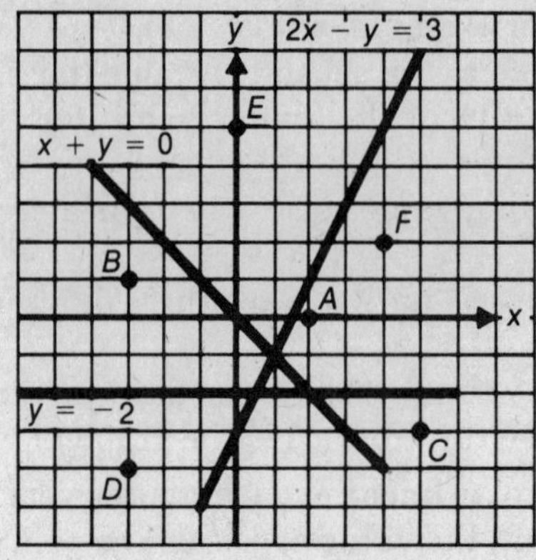

Other Topics

14.8 Interpreting Graphs

MATH CAPSULE

Types of graphs:

A **line graph** is commonly used to illustrate the change in a quantity or to compare the changes in two or more quantities over a period of time. The change in quantity is usually measured along the vertical scale on the side of the graph; the passage of time is usually measured along the horizontal scale at the bottom of the graph, as shown in the following figure:

STUDENTS MAJORING IN TWO FIELDS AT DARWIN COLLEGE, 1985–1990

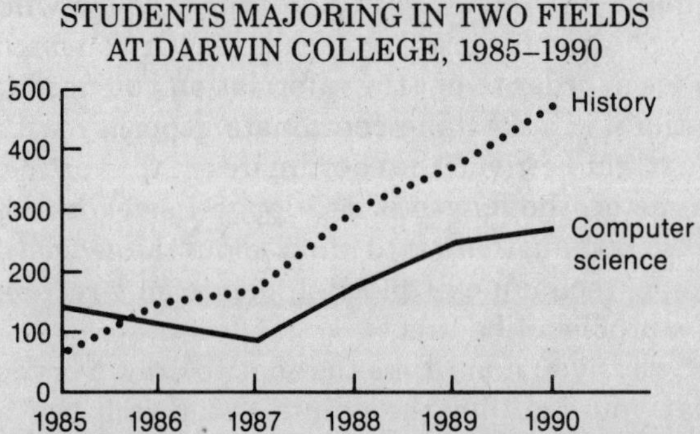

As the line or lines move up or down, quantity increases or decreases. As the line or lines move from left to right, time passes.

A **bar graph** is commonly used to compare two or more independent quantities, each represented either by a separate bar or by a portion of a bar that is usually shaded in some way. The longer or taller the bar, the greater the quantity. Bar graphs can be horizontal or vertical. The following is a vertical bar graph:

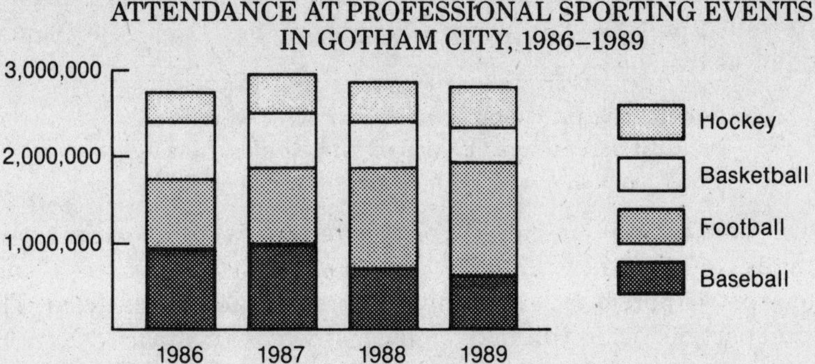

A **circle graph**, or **pie chart**, is commonly used to show the relative sizes of the various parts of a whole. The "pie" represents the whole; each "wedge" represents a share, or a percentage, of the whole. The larger the wedge, the greater the share. A circle graph rarely indicates the absolute size of any share; generally it indicates only the relative sizes of the various shares, as shown in the following figure:

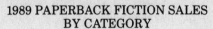

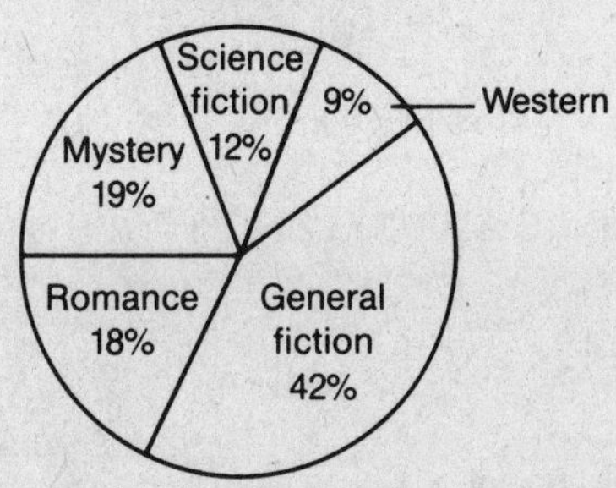

You've probably seen numerous graphs in your daily newspaper or your favorite newsmagazine, and you've probably had a great deal of experience preparing and interpreting them in your social studies and science courses. The few graphs you may encounter on the SAT are not likely to be very complex, nor are they likely to deviate from the three common formats discussed in the Math Capsule. Nevertheless, if you're not careful, you can easily make errors in interpreting even the simplest graphs. Here are some tips for avoiding careless errors.

When you're presented with one or more questions based on a graph, start by spending several seconds examining the graph. Read the legend, which explains what the graph illustrates. Examine the horizontal and vertical scales, and make sure you understand the meaning of the numbers on them. For example, on a graph illustrating auto sales, each number might represent the sale of one auto, a thousand autos, or a million autos, or it might represent a hundred, a thousand, or a million dollars' worth of auto sales. Also consider what kind of information the graph does *not* provide and what its temporal limitations are. Some SAT questions turn on the issue of what can and cannot logically be deduced from a graph.

When a graph includes different types of lines or bars with different types of shading, be especially careful when you're reading the graph. If the lines or bars look similar or if they're very close together, you can easily get them mixed up or slip from one to the other without noticing.

When you're trying to determine the exact quantity represented by a bar or a specific point on a line, don't trust your eyes. Use your pencil or the edge of your answer sheet to line up the point or the tip of the bar with the scale on the graph. You might even want to draw a line between the two so that you can refer to the quantity again if you need to.

When you're reading a question based on a graph, pay particular attention to the words that actually pose the question. If necessary, underline them and read them two or three times. Make sure you know exactly what it is you're looking for. If the question is long or complex, break it down into manageable units and work on it piecemeal. For instance, suppose you're asked a question like the following about a graph illustrating the sales of various types of vehicles over a period of years:

> For the year in which compact car sales were the greatest percentage of sales of all vehicles, how many more compact cars were sold than full-size cars?

Start with the first part of the question: "For the year in which compact car sales were the greatest percentage of sales of all vehicles..." What year was that? Look at the graph and find the year with the greatest percentage of compact car sales. Circle that year. Then go back and consider the second part of the question: "... how many more compact cars were sold than full-size cars?" You're being asked to compare two quantities—the number of compact cars sold and the number of full-size cars sold. Return to the graph and the year you've circled. Find the two quantities you're supposed to compare. Circle them. Then find the difference, subtracting the smaller quantity from the larger either in your head or on paper. That's the answer you want.

Attacking a long, complex question in this piecemeal fashion will prevent you from misinterpreting the question. It will also prevent you from becoming confused or discouraged, even by the most complicated graph questions.

PRACTICE EXERCISES

Questions 1–5 are based on the following graph.

MONTHLY INCOME AND EXPENDITURES, THE WILSON FAMILY

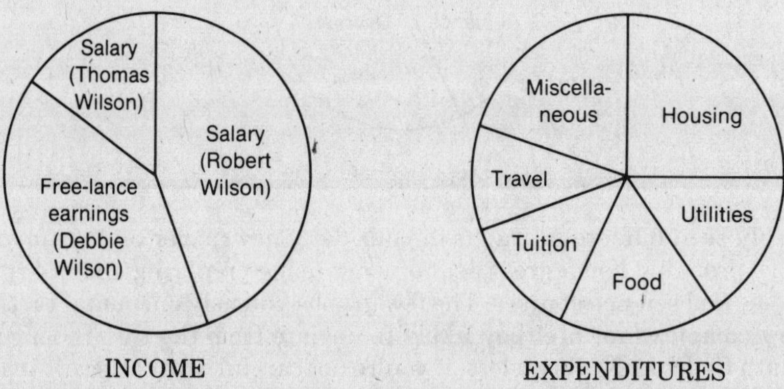

1. The largest single expenditure in the Wilson family's monthly budget represents about what percentage of their total monthly expenditures?
2. Which of the following pairs of expenditure categories adds up to about the same percentage of total expenditures as the percentage of total income represented by Debbie Wilson's free-lance earnings?
   (A) Housing and travel (B) Housing and utilities (C) Travel and miscellaneous
   (D) Travel and tuition (E) Food and travel
3. Which expenditure category is closest to 20 percent of the Wilson family's total monthly expenditures?
4. If the Wilson family's monthly housing expenditure were cut in half, which expenditure category would be the largest?
5. If the Wilson family's total monthly income is equal to their total monthly expenditures, then Thomas Wilson's salary is approximately equal to which of the following monthly expenditures?
   (A) Tuition plus food (B) Housing plus utilities (C) Travel
   (D) Miscellaneous plus food (E) Utilities

Questions 6–10 are based on the following graph.

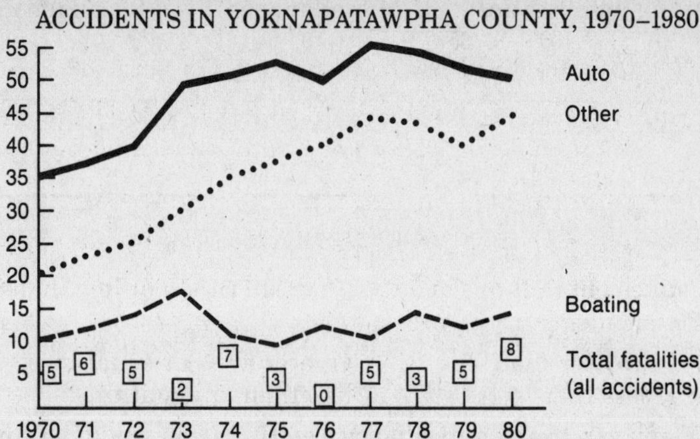

6. In which year was the greatest number of auto accidents recorded in Yoknapatawpha County?
7. In the year in which the greatest number of boating accidents was recorded in Yoknapatawpha County, how many accidents other than auto and boating accidents were recorded?
8. What was the total number of accidents recorded in Yoknapatawpha County in 1970?
9. In 1977, the number of fatal accidents in Yoknapatawpha County represented what fraction of the number of auto accidents?
10. During how many years shown on the graph did the number of both auto accidents and boating accidents increase?

Questions 11–15 are based on the following graph.

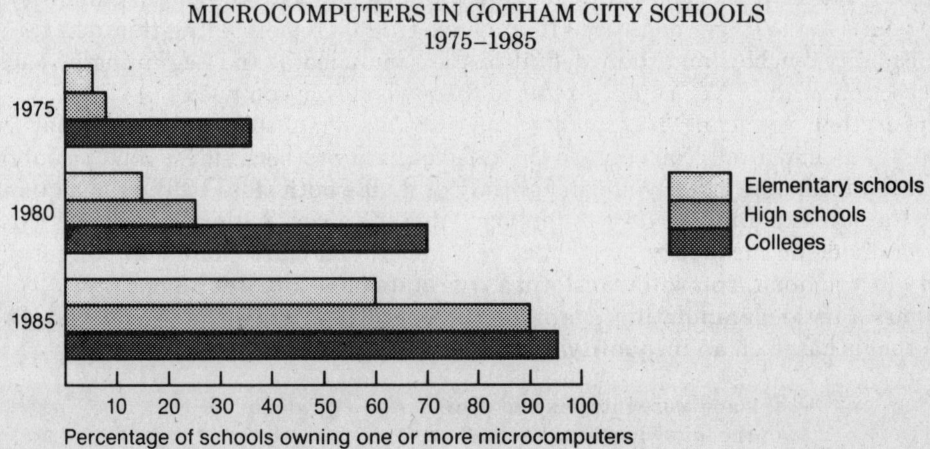

11. What percentage of Gotham City high schools owned one or more microcomputers in 1980?
12. What fraction of Gotham City colleges did *not* own a microcomputer in 1980?
13. The percentage of Gotham City colleges owning microcomputers in 1975 was how many times as great as the percentage of Gotham City elementary schools owning microcomputers in the same year?
14. What percentage of Gotham City colleges bought their first microcomputer between 1980 and 1985?
15. The difference between the percentage of Gotham City colleges owning a microcomputer and the percentage of Gotham City high schools owning a microcomputer is greatest in which of the years shown on the graph?

Answers

1. 25% 2. B (housing and utilities) 3. Miscellaneous 4. Miscellaneous 5. E (utilities) 6. 1977 7. 30 8. 65 9. $\frac{1}{11}$ 10. 3 11. 25% 12. $\frac{3}{10}$ 13. 7 14. 25% 15. 1980

14.9 Inequalities

MATH CAPSULE

An **inequality** is a statement that one quantity is greater than or less than another quantity. There are four basic inequality signs:

$>$ greater than	$\geqq$ greater than or equal to
$<$ less than	$\leqq$ less than or equal to

With one exception, you can treat an inequality exactly as you would an equation. The exception is this: If you multiply or divide both sides by a negative number, you must *reverse* the direction of the inequality.

Example: The inequality $6 - x > 10$ remains true if 6 is subtracted from both sides: $-x > 4$. However, if both sides are multiplied by -1, the inequality remains true only if its direction is reversed: $x < -4$.

Inequalities are almost as common as equations on the SAT, so you can expect to see quite a few of them when you take the test. Although you probably won't have to do much, if anything, to the ones you're given, you will have to be able to interpret them. You will also have to be able to determine what you can and cannot validly deduce from them. Here are some tips on dealing with inequality questions on the SAT:

Remember that the closed end of an inequality symbol points to the smaller quantity and the open end points to the larger quantity. (If you have trouble remembering this, don't worry. All of the inequality symbols and their definitions are included at the beginning of each mathematical section of the SAT. You can refer to them whenever you need to.)

Remember that you can "manipulate" an inequality in the same way that you can "manipulate" an equation. You can add the same quantity to both sides; you can subtract the same quantity from both sides; you can multiply or divide both sides by the same quantity. As the Math Capsule explains, the only difference—and it's a very important one—is this: If you multiply or divide an inequality by a negative number, you must change the direction of the inequality. If you don't, you will transform a true statement into a false one.

Sometimes a little manipulating is all you have to do to find the answer to an SAT math question that is based on an inequality. Here's an example:

If p and q are integers and if $p + q < p - q$, which of the following must be true?

(A) $p > q$ (B) $q > p$ (C) $p = q$

(D) $p < 0$ (E) $q < 0$

If you don't see the answer to this question immediately, all you have to do is manipulate the inequality a little bit and you'll soon find that q must be less than 0—whether p and q are integers or not. (The first condition is a red herring.) First, subtract p from both sides of the inequality. You'll get $q < -q$. Second, add q to both sides. You'll get $2q < 0$. Third, divide both sides by 2. You'll get $q < 0$.

This type of inequality question is very common on the SAT. You're given an inequality as a condition in an if-clause. Then you're asked a "which of the following" question: "which of the following *must* be true" or "which of the following *could* be true." Read these types of questions very carefully. There's a big difference between what *could* be true and what *must* be true if, say, $x < 1$.

Remember that an inequality is very different from an equality. An equality specifies an *exact* value for a variable; an inequality usually specifies a *range* of values. Consider these two statements, for instance: $x = 2$ and $x < 2$. From the first you know that x has one and only one value, 2. From the second you know that x has a value less than 2, but you don't know whether that value is 1.99, 1, 0, $-\frac{1}{2}$, -92, or any of the other infinite possibilities.

Whenever you're given an inequality as a condition in an SAT math question, remember to consider *all* the possible values within the range of the inequality. Some numbers, such as negative numbers and proper fractions (fractions with a value less than 1), have peculiar properties. So do 0 and 1. These numbers don't behave in the same way that positive integers like 2 and 3 behave. So you can't draw the same conclusions about them as you can about a positive integer (or, for that matter, any positive number) greater than 1. So whenever you're confronted with an inequality, always ask yourself these four questions: Does the range of values include 0? Does it include 1? Does it include proper fractions? Does it include negative values?

For instance, suppose you were given the following inequality as the information in a quantitative comparison:

$$a < b < c$$

Then you were asked to compare these two quantities:

Column A	**Column B**
ab	bc

You know that if a, b, and c are all positive—say, for simplicity's sake, 1, 2, and 3—then ab will be less than bc. But what if b is 0 and a and c, say, are -1 and 1, respectively? Then ab and bc will be equal. And if a, b, and c are all negative integers—say, -3, -2, and -1—then ab will be greater than bc. So the inequality doesn't provide you with enough information to compare the two quantities, and the correct answer to the question is choice D.

Finally, remember that the symbols $<$ and $\leqq$ and the symbols $>$ and $\geqq$ are not equivalent. The symbols $<$ and $>$ specify a range of values that is *exclusive*; the symbols $\leqq$ and $\geqq$ specify a range of values that is *inclusive*. For example, $0 < x < 1$ means that the range of values for x *excludes* 0 and 1. In other words, x could have any value *between* 0 and 1, but it could *not* have a value of 0 or 1. By contrast, $0 \leqq x \leqq 1$ means that the range of values for x *includes* both 0 and 1. In other words, x could have a value of 0, a value of 1, or any value between 0 and 1.

The difference in the meaning of the symbols is critical in some SAT questions. Consider the following question, for example:

Column A	**Column B**

$$-5 < x \leqq 0$$
$$0 \leqq y < 5$$

x	y

The two inequality statements make it look as though y must be greater than x. But notice that the range of values for x and the range of values for y both include 0. Therefore, x and y *could* be equal (they could both be 0). So the correct answer to the questions is not B, but D—"the relationship cannot be determined from the information given."

PRACTICE EXERCISES

Give the least and greatest integral (whole number) values of the variable in each of the following inequalities.

1. $5 < n < 14$
2. $-17 < x < -3$
3. $5.7 < a < 19.6$
4. $-4\frac{2}{3} < y < 15$
5. $6 \leqq z < 20$
6. $0 \leqq b \leqq 13$
7. $-12.8 < p \leqq -9$
8. $8 \leqq t < 265$

Solve each of the following problems.

9. If $a > b$, which of the following must be true?
   (A) $a > 0$ (B) $b < 0$ (C) $a + b > 0$ (D) $ab > 0$ (E) $a - b > 0$
10. If $x < 3$ and $y < 7$, which of the following must be true?
   (A) $y > x$ (B) $y - x = 4$ (C) $y > 2x$ (D) $x + y < 10$ (E) $x > y$

Answers

1. 6, 13 2. −16, −4 3. 6, 19 4. −4, 14 5. 6, 19 6. 0, 13 7. −12, −9 8. 8, 264
9. E ($a - b > 0$) 10. D ($x + y < 10$)

14.10 Ingenuity Questions

In this last section of Lesson 14, we'll consider one final type of SAT math question—the ingenuity question. As the name suggests, ingenuity questions test your ability to think quickly, logically, and sometimes creatively about unusual problems that you've probably never faced before. They don't test conventional mathematical skills. (That's why this section, unlike the others, does not include a Math Capsule.) Ingenuity questions favor students who are open-minded and quick-witted rather than those who can multiply and divide beautifully but don't know why.

Ingenuity questions are probably the hardest of all SAT math questions to prepare for because each one is unique. One might involve a money system with coins called *gleeks*, *droods*, and *bleens*. Another might involve a language in which each word is a meaningless sequence of letters in some strange, but specified order. Still another might involve a clock that keeps track of time in 9-hour, rather than 12-hour, increments. A problem-solving method that works for one of these questions won't work for the others.

Even though there's no single formula for dealing with all SAT ingenuity questions, the questions themselves are usually very elementary mathematically. Just think of them as games with one or two simple rules. If you follow the rules—no matter how strange they may seem—carefully and methodically, you shouldn't have any trouble coming up with the correct answers to most SAT ingenuity questions.

Here's an example:

The minute hand on the clock above moves forward for 1 minute, backward for 2 minutes, forward for 3 minutes, backward for 4 minutes, and so on. If the clock is started at the time shown, what time will it be in exactly 40 minutes?

(A) 2:49 (B) 2:50 (C) 2:52
(D) 2:55 (E) 3:00

Once you've made sense of this question, solving it is easy. The simplest method is just to count forward 40 minutes and figure out how many minutes the clock will gain and lose. You might write this out by using plus signs for forward movements and minus signs for backward movements. The whole 40-minute sequence would look like this:

$$+1 -2 +3 -4 +5 -6 +7 -8 +4$$

The last number is 4 rather than 9 because the allotted 40 minutes ends at that point. Now, just add the figures together. Since the sum is 0, the clock will be at the same place in 40 minutes as it is right now. That's 2:50 (choice B). As you can see, the math involved here is easy. The hard part is getting a grip on the question itself.

The best advice for dealing with ingenuity questions is this: If you can't see any logical way to solve a particular problem, try something—anything. Very often a shot in the dark will lead you to the solution. In fact, ingenuity problems are usually designed to encourage trial and error. Here's an example:

Each face of the cube above is inscribed with a different positive integer. If the integer inscribed on the unshown base of the cube is exactly half the sum of the integers on all the other faces, what is the least possible value of that integer?

(A) 8 (B) 9 (C) 10 (D) 11 (E) 12

If you can't instantly deduce the various integers inscribed on the faces of the cube, don't despair. Try a few possible numbers and see what happens.

First, make a list of five numbers to represent the numbers on the five faces other than the base. You know that three of the numbers are 2, 4, and 7. If the integer on the base is exactly half the sum of the other integers and if you want that sum to be as low as possible ("the least possible value"), then you want each of the other integers to be as low as possible, too. So fill in the other two positions with the lowest possible positive integers not already used. You'll get the following set of numbers: 2, 4, 7, 1, and 3.

Will this set of numbers work? No, because the sum of these numbers is 17, an odd number, and there's no integer that is exactly half of 17. So you must try changing one or both of the two numbers you've added so that you'll end up with an even sum. You can't change the 1 to 2 or the 3 to 4 because 2 and 4 are already taken. And changing 1 or 3 to 5 won't help because the sum will still be odd. (Try it and see.)

That brings you to the number 6, which *will* help. Now, you want to change either the 1 or the 3 to 6. But which should you change? The 3, obviously, because you want the lowest possible sum. So change the 3 to 6, since filling the two unknown positions with 1 and 6 will give you a lower sum than filling them with 3 and 6. If you use the five integers 2, 4, 7, 1, and 6, you'll get a sum of 20. That means that the lowest possible value for the integer on the base is half of 20, or 10 (choice C).

As this problem illustrates, the trial-and-error method is often the best—or *only*—way to solve an ingenuity problem. Don't be afraid to try it. Of course, if you find yourself spending too much time on a single problem—say, more than 2 minutes—cut short your experimenting and move on.

PRACTICE EXERCISES

1. A grandfather clock begins striking 3 o'clock exactly on the hour and finishes at 4 seconds past. If the strokes occur at regular intervals, how many seconds will have passed the hour when the same clock strikes 12 o'clock?
2. Find the three-digit number for which the first and third digits are equal, the middle digit is twice the sum of the first and the third, and the sum of the digits is 6.
3. In a certain code, the order of the letters in a word is reversed and then each letter is replaced by the letter that follows it in the English alphabet. For example, the word *zebra* is represented in this code as *bscfa*. What word does *zujvofhoj* represent?

4. In a certain game, a player can move in only two directions, up and to the right. If the player wants to move from point A to point B, as shown in the following figure, how many different paths can he or she take?

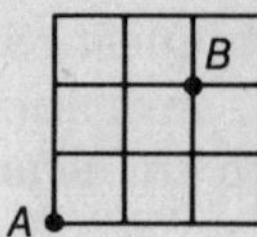

5. On a certain accurate 12-hour clock, the hands move in a counterclockwise, rather than a clockwise, direction. If the time shown on the clock is now 4:25, what time will it be, according to the clock, in exactly 7 hours and 35 minutes?

Answers

1. 22 2. 141 3. *ingenuity* 4. 6 5. 8:50

LESSON 15
Grammar Review for the TSWE, Part 2

OBJECTIVES

☐ To learn to recognize common errors in subject-verb agreement

☐ To learn to recognize common errors in verb and pronoun usage

☐ To learn to recognize common errors in idiomatic usage

15.1 Introduction

In Lesson 10 we discussed some of the grammatical errors that you're most likely to find in the error correction questions on the Test of Standard Written English. In this lesson we'll consider some of the errors that you're most likely to find in the usage questions. But before we begin, you might want to review the definitions of key grammatical terms in Lesson 10 (Sections 10.1, 10.2, and 10.3). You'll encounter many of the same terms in this lesson.

Subject-Verb Agreement

15.2 Errors in Subject-Verb Agreement

Errors in subject-verb agreement are among the most common errors in usage questions on the TSWE. The basic rule of subject-verb agreement is this: If the subject of a sentence or clause is singular, the verb must be singular, too; if the subject is plural, the verb must also be plural. Subject and verb, in other words, must agree *in number*.

In most sentences, violations of the basic rule of subject-verb agreement are easy to detect. Look at these two simple sentences, for instance:

X Tigers runs quickly.

X A tiger run quickly.

Even if you know nothing whatsoever about the rules of English grammar, you can hear the agreement errors in these two sentences. *Tigers runs* (plural subject, singular verb) should be *tigers run* (plural subject, plural verb); *a tiger run* (singular subject, plural verb) should be *a tiger runs* (singular subject, singular verb).

In some sentences, however, violations of subject-verb agreement are more difficult to spot. These sentences usually contain certain types of constructions that obscure the relationship between subject and verb. Naturally, these tricky types are the kinds used to test subject-verb agreement on the TSWE.

One very common type of tricky construction is the subject-interrupter-verb construction. In this type of construction, the subject is separated from the verb by one or more intervening phrases or clauses. Because of the separation, the verb is often made to agree with the word that immediately precedes it rather than with the subject of the sentence. Here's an example:

> X The reason for the many cases of small businesses going bankrupt in their first few years of operations are really quite simple.

If you read this sentence quickly, you may not notice the agreement problem because *operations are* sounds perfectly natural whereas *operations is* does not. The problem is that *operations* is not the subject of the sentence. The subject of the sentence is *reason*. *Operations* is just the last word in a fairly long string of phrases that come between the subject and the verb. Even though most of the words in those phrases are plural, they don't change the fact that *reason* is singular and requires a singular verb—*is*, not *are*.

As this example illustrates, subject-verb interrupters are often prepositional phrases. *For the many cases*, for example, is a prepositional phrase. So are *of small businesses*, *in their first years*, and *of operations*. Interrupting prepositional phrases cause agreement problems when the subject of a sentence and the object of a preposition that follows it (and immediately precedes the verb) are different in number. For instance, when the subject of a sentence is singular and the object of a preposition that follows it is plural, the tendency is to make the verb plural. Conversely (but less commonly), when the subject is plural and the object of a preposition that follows it is singular, the tendency is to make the verb singular.

In situations like these, the subject of a sentence tends to get lost in the shuffle, so to speak. You can find it easily and detect a subject-verb agreement error in a TSWE usage question quickly by remembering this rule: The object of a preposition is *never* the subject of a sentence. So when you're searching for the subject of a usage question, mentally eliminate any prepositional phrases that precede a verb. If necessary, cross them out with your pencil. By doing so, you'll simplify the sentence and make the checking of subject-verb agreement simple.

Prepositional phrases are not the only troublesome interrupters. Expressions introduced by *along with*, *in addition to*, *as well as*, *together with*, *including*, *accompanied by*, *no less than*, and similar *and*-like phrases also cause agreement problems. These expressions don't affect the number of a subject. In other words, they don't make an otherwise singular subject plural. However, because they're introduced by phrases that have almost the same meaning as *and*, they *seem* to make a subject plural. Here's an example:

> X The consumer price index, as well as the gross national product and the unemployment rate, indicate trends in the economy.

If this sentence read, "The consumer price index, the gross national product, *and* the unemployment rate," the subject would be plural and the plural verb *indicate* would be correct. However, since it reads, "The consumer price index, *as well as* the gross national product and the unemployment rate," the subject is singular (*consumer price index*) and the verb should be singular, too (*indicates*).

Expressions that begin with phrases that are like *and* but don't have the same pluralizing effect that *and* has are often set off from a sentence with commas, as in the example we just looked at. The commas (two of them, one on either side) are clues that the expressions are *parenthetical*; that is, they're not essential to the meaning of a sentence. Parenthetical expressions, whether they're introduced by *and*-like phrases or not, are like prepositional phrases—they *never* affect the number of a subject. So when you're checking for agreement problems on the TSWE, you can treat them just as you would prepositional phrases. Cross them out and ignore them.

A second type of construction that makes subject-verb agreement tricky is the compound subject. A *compound subject* is a subject that has two or more parts joined by *and*, *or*, *nor*, *either*...*or*, *neither*...*nor*, or *not*...*but*. Subjects joined by *and* rarely pose any problems;

they're almost always plural. (You won't be tested on the few exceptions to this rule.) Subjects joined by the other conjunctions, however, often cause confusion because sometimes they're singular and sometimes they're plural.

Actually, the rule governing subjects joined by *or*, *nor*, and the others is quite simple to apply once you've learned it: The verb always agrees with the subject closer to it. The following sentences illustrate the rule:

Either this table or those chairs are blocking the entrance to the hall.

Either those chairs or this table is blocking the entrance to the hall.

In the first sentence, the subject closer to the verb is plural (*chairs*), so the verb is plural (*are blocking*). In the second sentence, the subject closer to the verb is singular (*table*), so the verb is singular (*is blocking*). Remember this simple rule for the TSWE.

So far we've considered two types of constructions that make subject-verb agreement tricky—the subject-interrupter-verb construction and the compound subject. In the next section, we'll consider the agreement problems that arise when pronouns are used as subjects.

Using Pronouns Correctly

15.3 Pronouns as Subjects

Certain types of subjects, like certain types of constructions, tend to generate errors in subject-verb agreement. Among these subjects are indefinite pronouns, pronouns (like *each* and *someone*) that refer to a person or thing not specifically identified. Indefinite pronouns generate errors in agreement because their number is sometimes difficult to determine. These pronouns—and the agreement rules that govern them—are worth reviewing for the TSWE.

Some indefinite pronouns are always plural. *Both*, *several*, and *many*, for instance, are always plural and always take plural verbs. These pronouns are easy to deal with because their number (their plurality) is obvious.

Other indefinite pronouns are always singular, even when they refer to more than one person or thing. The singular indefinites include *anyone*, *anybody*, *anything*, *everyone*, *everybody*, *everything*, *someone*, *somebody*, *something*, *no one*, *nobody*, *nothing*, *each*, *either*, and *neither*. With most of these pronouns, subject-verb agreement is no problem. For instance, if someone were to say, "Everybody were happy" or "Nobody are here," you'd hear the agreement error immediately. With the last three pronouns, however, you can get into trouble. *Each*, *either*, and *neither* can—and often are—followed by prepositional phrases (*of* phrases, usually), and prepositional phrases, as you've already learned, can obscure the relationship between subject and verb. Here are some examples:

X Each of them have plans for the evening.

X Have either of the men seen my book?

X Neither of the girls were at class today.

These sentences probably sound right to your ear because they reflect the way most of us speak (informally). However, they're all incorrect. *Each*, *either*, and *neither* are singular and, like the other singular indefinites, always take singular verbs:

Each of them *has* plans for the evening.

Has either of the men seen my book?

Neither of the girls *was* at class today.

If you get confused, just remember this: *Each* means "each one," *either* means "either one," *neither* means "neither one"—and *one* is unquestionably singular. You'd *never* use a plural verb with *one*.

Finally, there are some indefinite pronouns that have no fixed number. Depending on how they are used, they may be either singular or plural. These indefinite pronouns, often called the SANAM pronouns because of their initial letters, are naturally the trickiest. The SANAM pronouns are *some*, *any*, *none*, *all*, and *most*.

Like *each*, *either*, and *neither*, SANAM pronouns are often followed by *of* phrases—*some of the people*, *any of the answers*, *none of the seats*, and so on. As a rule, *of* phrases do not affect the number of the noun or pronoun that precedes them. For instance, *of* phrases, as you've just learned, have no effect on the number of *each*, *either*, and *neither*. These three pronouns are always singular, even when the objects in the *of* phrases that follow them are plural.

SANAM pronouns are different. They're exceptions to this rule. Their number is *determined* by the objects in the *of* phrases that follow them. Here are two simple examples:

> Some of the cake has been eaten.
>
> Some of the cookies have been eaten.

In the first sentence, the object of the preposition *of* is the singular *cake*. So the SANAM pronoun *some* is singular in the first sentence and thus takes a singular verb (*has been eaten*). In the second sentence, the object of the preposition *of* is the plural *cookies*. So the SANAM pronoun *some* is plural in the second sentence and thus takes a plural verb (*have been eaten*).

The rule that these sentences exemplify is as simple as the sentences themselves, but it applies to all of the SANAM pronouns. If the object in the *of* phrase that follows a SANAM pronoun is singular, the SANAM pronoun is singular and takes a singular verb. If the object is plural, the SANAM pronoun is plural and takes a plural verb. You may encounter a SANAM pronoun or two on the TSWE, so remember this rule. But remember, also, that it applies *only* to the SANAM pronouns; it does *not* apply to any other pronouns.

15.4 Errors in Pronoun Reference

In this section, we'll consider another type of agreement: agreement between pronouns and their antecedents. Pronouns, as you know, are simply substitutes for nouns or noun equivalents. The nouns or noun equivalents for which they substitute (and to which they refer) are called their *antecedents*.

There are two basic rules that you need to know about pronouns and their antecedents for the TSWE. The first rule is that a pronoun should always refer clearly to a specific antecedent. The second rule is that a pronoun must agree in gender and number with its antecedent.

The first rule is fairly easy to apply on the TSWE because you never have very far to look for the antecedent of a pronoun. Since each usage question is only one sentence long, you know that the antecedent of a pronoun has to be in the same sentence as the pronoun—usually in the part that comes before the pronoun (that's why it's called an *ante*cedent). If it's not there—that is, if there's no noun or noun equivalent in the sentence to which the pronoun can logically refer—then the pronoun is the "error" in the sentence. The pronoun is also the "error" if a sentence includes more than one potential antecedent and you can't tell which one the pronoun refers to.

The second rule is a little bit, but not much, more difficult to apply. The first part of the rule is no problem. To say that a pronoun must agree with its antecedent in *gender* is simply to say that both must be masculine, both must be feminine, or both must be neuter. Errors in pronoun gender are almost unheard of in English, and you're not likely to encounter any on the TSWE. If you do, you'll recognize them immediately (unless, perhaps, English is not your native tongue).

The second part of the rule is the problem, but again, not a big one. To say that a pronoun must agree with its antecedent in *number* is simply to say that both must be singular or both must be plural. This part of the rule is very similar to the general rule that governs subject-verb agreement. In fact, most of the particular rules that govern subject-verb agreement also apply to pronoun-antecedent agreement. So if you know those rules, you don't have to learn any new ones. All you have to do is remember this: If an antecedent would take a singular verb, then it takes a singular pronoun; if an antecedent would take a plural verb, then it takes a plural pronoun.

Two words of caution: First, just as a verb must agree with the closer of two or the closest of three subjects joined by *or*, *nor*, and similar conjunctions, so a pronoun must agree with the closer of two or the closest of three antecedents joined by one of the same conjunctions. The following two sentences illustrate the rule:

Either the Johnson brothers or Mark left *his* car at my house.

Either Mark or the Johnson brothers left *their* car at my house.

In the first sentence, the singular *his* is correct because the nearer antecedent is the singular *Mark*. In the second sentence, the plural *their* is correct because the nearer antecedent is the plural *Johnson brothers*. Of course if both antecedents had been singular, then the singular pronoun would have been correct:

Either Mark or John left *his* car at my house.

Second, although the indefinite pronouns that are always singular rarely pose subject-verb agreement problems, they often pose antecedent-pronoun agreement problems when they're antecedents. For instance, although it's perfectly natural to say, "Everybody is here," it's not quite so natural to say, "Everyone has his or her own way of doing things." More commonly, we say, and hear other people saying, "Everyone has their own way of doing things." This usage of the plural *their* in reference to the singular *everyone* is unacceptable in standard written English, the English you're expected to know for the TSWE. So if you're accustomed to using plural pronouns to refer to singular indefinite pronouns in your informal speech and writing, study the list of those pronouns in the preceding section. And when you encounter any of them on the TSWE, trust your memory, not your ear.

15.5 Errors in Pronoun Case

In this section we'll consider one final problematic area of pronoun usage—case. *Case* refers to the form a pronoun takes when it's used as a subject, when it's used as an object, and when it's used to show possession. When it's used as a subject, a pronoun must be in the *subjective case*. When it's used as an object (whether of a verb or of a preposition), it must be in the *objective case*. When it's used to show possession, it must be in the *possessive case*. Some pronouns—the problematic ones—have different forms for these three cases. Here's a list of them:

Subjective	Objective	Possessive
I	me	my, mine
you	you	your, yours
he	him	his
she	her	her, hers
it	it	its
we	us	our, ours
they	them	their, theirs
who	whom	whose

Errors in pronoun case are very rare in most constructions; in some, however, they're very common. We'll take a look at five types of constructions in which errors are very common. These are the types you can expect to encounter on the TSWE.

The first type is the compound subject or object. Here are two examples:

X Elena and *me* are planning to attend the grand opening of the plaza.

X Mr. Castillo sent the package to my brother and *I*.

In the first sentence, the pronoun is part of a compound subject and should be in the subjective case—*I*, not *me*. In the second sentence, the pronoun is part of the compound object of the preposition *between* and should be in the objective case—*me*, not *I*.

One simple way to detect case errors in compound constructions is to mentally eliminate the other element or elements in the compound and test the pronoun by itself. For instance, if you eliminate *my brother and* from the second sentence above, you immediately expose the error:

X Mr. Castillo sent the package to ~~my brother and~~ I.

You'd never say, "Mr. Castillo sent the package to *I*." You'd say, "Mr. Castillo sent the package to *me*." So the sentence should read, "Mr. Castillo sent the package to my brother and *me*."

A second type of construction in which pronoun case errors are common is the *be* construction—that is, any construction that involves the verb *to be*. Here are two examples:

X The only ones who complained were *him* and *me*.

X It may have been *her* who phoned.

As you may recall from your English classes, the verb *to be* is a "linking" verb. When it "links" a subject with a pronoun (or pronouns), as it does in these two sentences, the pronoun (or pronouns) must be in the subjective case:

The only ones who complained were *he* and *I*.

It may have been *she* who phoned.

Since you're probably not in the habit of speaking the way these sentences sound, trust the rule rather than your ear in constructions of this type.

A third type of construction in which errors in pronoun case are common is the abbreviated comparison. Here are two examples:

X Most of the people in that class are smarter than *us*.

X Sumio is a much better tennis player than *him*.

The simplest way to tell which case a pronoun should take in abbreviated comparisons like these is to mentally complete the comparisons:

Most of the people in that class are smarter than *we* (are).

Sumio is a much better tennis player than *he* (is).

As you can see, the pronouns in both sentences should be in the subjective case because both are the subjects of unstated verbs.

A fourth type of construction is the gerund phrase. A *gerund* is a noun formed from a verb. In the sentence "Jogging and cycling are good forms of aerobic exercise," *jogging* and *cycling* are gerunds. All gerunds end in *-ing*. When a pronoun is used before a gerund, it should be in the possessive, not the objective, case, as the following examples illustrate:

You don't mind *my* [not *me*] leaving early, do you?

They were opposed to *his* [not *him*] moving so far away from home.

A fifth type of construction in which errors in pronoun case are very common is the clause introduced by *who* or *whom*. Although we all have trouble with *who* and *whom*, the rule governing their use is really quite simple: *Who* (subjective case) is correct if the pronoun is the subject of the clause it introduces; *whom* (objective case) is correct if the pronoun is the object of the verb or of a preposition in the clause it introduces. The same rule applies to *whoever* and *whomever*. Here are a couple of examples:

The boss will interview *whoever* she feels is qualified.

It was Antonio and he *whom* they selected as finalists.

In the first sentence, *whoever* is the subject of the verb *is qualified*, so it's in the subjective case. In the second sentence, *whom* is the object of the verb *selected* (*they selected whom*), so it's in the objective case.

There are a few other constructions that result in occasional errors in pronoun case, but the five types we've just considered are the most common.

One final word about pronoun case: If you look back at the list of possessive pronouns at the beginning of this section, you'll notice that those that end with an *s* sound have no apostrophes in them: *yours*, *his*, *hers*, *its*, *ours*, *theirs*, *whose*. Although you're not likely to want to insert an apostrophe in most of these possessive pronouns, you may be inclined to confuse *its*, the possessive form of *it*, with *it's*, the contracted form of *it is*, or *whose*, the possessive form of *who*, with *who's*, the contracted form of *who is*. So if you encounter *its*, *it's*, *whose*, or *who's* in a usage question on the TSWE, make sure it's the right word for the context.

Using Verbs Correctly

15.6 Errors in Tense Consistency and Tense Sequence

There are three types of verb errors that you can expect to find on the TSWE: errors in tense consistency, errors in tense sequence, and errors in irregular verb forms. In this section, we'll consider the first two types of errors. In the next section, we'll consider the third type.

Errors in tense consistency are unnecessary shifts from one tense to another in the same sentence, the same paragraph, or any other block of writing. Since you're never confronted with any block of writing longer than a sentence on the TSWE, errors in tense consistency are usually very easy to spot. Here's an example:

X Paul has written to his sweetheart every week and telephones her every night.

Notice the time words in this sentence—*every week* and *every day*. These words tell you that the two actions described in the sentence, the writing and the telephoning, both recur during the same period of time. Yet one is expressed in the present perfect tense (*has written*) and the other is expressed in the present tense (*telephones*). For the sake of consistency (and logic), both verbs should be in the same tense. Either of the following alternatives is acceptable, depending on the meaning intended:

Paul has written to his sweetheart every week and has telephoned her every night.

Paul writes to his sweetheart every week and telephones her every night.

Errors in tense sequence occur when verb tenses are not used logically together—that is, when they don't accurately reflect the sequence, or order, of two or more actions. Here's a simple example.

X I already ate when you called last night.

There are two verbs in this sentence, *ate* and *called*. Since they're both in the same tense (the simple past tense), they suggest that both actions, the eating and the calling, occurred at the same time. But the word *already* tells you that they didn't. It tells you that the eating occurred *before* the calling. This sequence—first the eating, then the calling—should be reflected in the tenses of the verbs, as it is in the following sentence:

I *had* already *eaten* when you *called* last night.

There are many tenses in English and many rules governing their use, both alone and in combination with other tenses to show relationships in time. Fortunately, most native speakers know and apply these rules intuitively without benefit of formal instruction in grammar. They also recognize violations of the rules immediately, even if they can't explain them. So when you take the TSWE, you should have little trouble detecting errors in tense sequence. Here are a couple of hints to help you do so.

First, read each usage question carefully. If a sentence contains more than one verb and one of the verbs is underlined, scrutinize it. Listen to the way it sounds in combination with the other verb or verbs in the sentence—especially if it's not in the same tense as the others. Also, pay attention to the time words, if any, in the sentence. They're usually an infallible clue to the tense a verb should take, and you can trust your ear to pick up on the clue. Remember: You don't have to be able to explain why a certain sequence of tenses is illogical; you just have to be able to "hear" that it is.

Second, watch for errors in the following three tense sequences:

1. The past perfect tense (the *had* form of the verb, as in *had eaten*) should be used to describe an action that took place before another action described in the simple past tense (as in *ate*). For example:

After the press conference *had ended*, the president *flew* to Camp David.

The act of flying is described in the simple past tense (*flew*). The ending of the press conference, which took place before the flying, is described in the past perfect tense (*had ended*).

2. The present perfect tense (the *have* or *has* form of the verb, as in *have eaten* or *has eaten*) should be used to describe an action that takes place before another action described in the simple present tense (as in *eat* or *eats*). For example:

> The president *likes* to rest after he *has appeared* in public.

The act of liking to rest is described in the simple present tense (*likes*). The act of appearing, which precedes the act of liking to rest, is described in the present perfect tense (*has appeared*).

3. The future perfect tense (the *will have* form of the verb, as in *will have eaten*) should be used to describe an action that will take place before another action described either in the simple future tense (as in *will eat*) or in an equivalent of the simple future tense (as in *is going to eat*). For example:

> The president *will leave* Camp David on Monday; by that time, he *will have finished* writing his State of the Union address.

The act of leaving Camp David is described in the simple future tense (*will leave*). The act of finishing the address, which will occur before the act of leaving, is described in the future perfect tense (*will have finished*).

Again, there are numerous other rules governing tense sequence in English. However, if you know these three, you should have little or no trouble detecting errors in tense sequence on the TSWE. Just "listen" carefully to each question and trust your ear.

15.7 Errors in Irregular Verb Forms

The third type of verb error that you can expect to find on the TSWE is the error in the form of an irregular verb. As its name suggests, an irregular verb is a verb that isn't regular; it has forms, or parts, that are different from those of most verbs. Most verbs have two main forms that are used to generate all of the tenses. For example, the verb *play*, which is regular, has two main forms: *play* and *played*. Irregular verbs, by contrast, have three main forms. For example, the verb *eat*, which is irregular, has three main forms: *eat*, *ate*, and *eaten*.

Errors in the form of regular verbs are extremely uncommon. You're not likely to find any on the TSWE. Errors in the form of irregular verbs, however, are very common. Here's an example:

> X Michael *has ate* five hamburgers in the last fifteen minutes.

Ate is one of the principal parts of the verb *eat*, but it's not the part that's used with *has* or *have* to form the present perfect tense. The part that's used to form the present perfect tense is *eaten*. So the sentence should read:

> Michael *has eaten* five hamburgers in the last fifteen minutes.

Most errors in irregular verb forms, like *has ate*, involve the use of the second principal part in place of the third. Here's another example:

> X After he *had drank* ten glasses of milk, Michael ate five hamburgers.

The three principal parts of the irregular verb *drink* are *drink*, *drank*, and *drunk*. Here the second is used in place of the third. *Drunk*, not *drank*, is used with *had* to form the past perfect tense. So the sentence should read:

> After he *had drunk* ten glasses of milk, Michael ate five hamburgers.

If you rarely misuse the principal parts of irregular verbs, you'll have no trouble spotting their misuse on the TSWE. The errors will be obvious. However, if you frequently misuse the principal parts of one or more irregular verbs, you should prepare yourself for the TSWE (as well as for your college courses) by studying the following list.

COMMONLY USED IRREGULAR VERBS

Infinitive	Past Tense	Past Participle
be	was	been
begin	began	begun
break	broke	broken
choose	chose	chosen
come	came	come
do	did	done
drink	drank	drunk
drive	drove	driven
eat	ate	eaten
fall	fell	fallen
fly	flew	flown
forget	forgot	forgotten
get	got	got *or* gotten
give	gave	given
go	went	gone
grow	grew	grown
know	knew	known
lie	lay	lain
ride	rode	ridden
rise	rose	risen
run	ran	run
see	saw	seen
speak	spoke	spoken
take	took	taken
write	wrote	written

This list is incomplete. If irregular verbs are a real problem for you, you'll find a longer list in most grammar texts. The only way to avoid errors with irregular verbs is to memorize their principal parts and to make a conscious effort to use them correctly, even in your informal speech and writing.

Using Idioms Correctly

15.8 Errors in Idiomatic Usage

In this last section of Lesson 15, we'll complete our grammar review for the TSWE by considering errors in idiomatic usage. Like the other errors we've considered so far in this lesson, errors in idiomatic usage are very common in usage questions on the TSWE.

Errors in idiomatic usage aren't any more difficult to pick out than other types of errors, but they are more difficult to pin down because they don't violate specific rules of grammar. Instead, they violate the "customs" of the language—the ways in which people who speak English habitually express themselves. For the most part, there's no rhyme or reason to those ways or customs. They're just patterns that have become established over the years and have been passed down from generation to generation.

Because idioms are simply customary ways of putting words together, you can't depend on grammar books to teach you how to recognize errors in their usage. You must depend on your ear. Fortunately, if you've been speaking, hearing, reading, and writing English all your life, your ear has probably been very well trained. Certainly it's been trained well enough to enable you to "hear" most of the errors in idiomatic usage on the TSWE—providing, of course, that you "listen" carefully to each question. Here are some common types of idiom errors to "listen" for when you take the test.

Some errors in idiomatic usage will sound stilted or clumsy. These should be fairly obvious because they will sound as though they were spoken or written by someone who is not very familiar with the English language. Here are some examples:

X For a poet, the task to translate poetry from another language presents a unique challenge.

Idiomatically, we talk about the task *of translating*, not the task *to translate*.

X The decision of the university president in regarding this matter will be final.

Idiomatically, we say, "*regarding* this matter" or "*in regard to* this matter." We don't say, "*in regarding* this matter."

X The newly released archives will to be studied by historians for years to come.

Will to be studied is not idiomatic. *Will be studied* is idiomatic.

Other errors in idiomatic usage will sound slangy or uneducated. These errors will be more difficult to "hear" than the first type because they're very common in informal speech and writing. Here are some examples:

X Looking embarrassed, the boy did like he was told.

In informal English, *like* is frequently used to introduce a clause (*like he was told*). In formal English, it never is. *As* is used instead.

X Professor Hastings admitted that she did not like Milton's poetry all that much.

All that much is an informal substitute for *very much*.

X The chairperson expressed the hope that the two committees would try and resolve their differences.

Try and is an informal (and illogical) substitute for *try to*.

X Home computers are nowhere near as popular as some people predicted they would be.

Nowhere near is the informal equivalent of *not nearly*.

Finally, still other errors in idiomatic usage will involve prepositions. Although prepositions are usually little words—words like *in, on, of, to, by, for, from,* and *with*—they often have a profound effect on meaning. Consider, for instance, the following expressions: *stand in for*, *stand up for*, and *stand for*. These three expressions sound very similar, but they have very different meanings. To *stand in for* someone is to take that person's place; to *stand up for* someone is to defend that person; to *stand for* something is either to represent it or to tolerate it. As these expressions illustrate, prepositions are governed almost entirely by idiom rather than logic. Here are some examples of the kinds of errors in the idiomatic usage of prepositions that you can expect to find on the TSWE:

X The commissioner was unsure how to respond against his opponents' charges.

Idiomatically, we speak of responding *to* charges, not responding *against* them.

X The novels of Henry James are uneventful compared by those of Joseph Conrad.

The idiom is compared *with* or compared *to*, not compared *by*.

X Keller seemed to be grateful of the opportunity to demonstrate his skills.

For, not *of*, is used idiomatically with *grateful*.

X The number of classes to be scheduled will be determined from the number of students who register.

The idiom is determined *by*, not determined *from*.

Unfortunately, there is no quick and easy way to learn all of the many idioms in English. (It often takes nonnative speakers many years to master them.) Therefore, you must rely on your ear to detect errors in idiomatic usage on the TSWE. Remember: You don't necessarily have to know how to correct the errors; you just have to recognize that they are errors.

PART 8

Practice Test 4

PRACTICE TEST 4: *Directions*

This practice test is for you to take after you have studied Lessons 11–15 in this book. By this time you have reviewed every basic SAT math topic, you have increased your vocabulary by several hundred words, and you have learned effective strategies for approaching every type of question on the SAT. The quantity and the quality of your preparation should be reflected in your performance on this practice test. After you have completed the test, turn to the scoring instructions and explanatory answers, which begin on page 356. If your scores on this test are still not within the range you hope to achieve on the actual SAT, use them to determine which lessons you should review and which skills you should work on in your final days of preparation for the SAT.

Directions: Set aside $3\frac{1}{2}$ hours without interruption for taking this test. The test is divided into six 30-minute sections. You may wish to use a timer or an alarm to time yourself on each section. Do not work past the 30-minute limit for any section. If you finish a section before time is up, you may check your work on that section, but you are not to work on any other section. You may take a 5-minute break between sections.

Do not worry if you are unable to finish a section or if there are some questions you cannot answer. Do not waste time puzzling over a question that seems too difficult for you. You should work as rapidly as you can without sacrificing accuracy.

Students often ask whether they should guess when they are uncertain about the answer to a question. Your test scores will be based on the number of questions you answer correctly minus a fraction of the number you answer incorrectly. Therefore, it is improbable that random or haphazard guessing will change your scores significantly. If you have some knowledge of a question, you may be able to eliminate one or more of the answer choices as wrong. It is generally to your advantage to guess which of the remaining choices is correct. Remember, however, not to spend too much time on any one question.

Mark all your answers on the answer sheet on the facing page. (For your convenience, you may wish to remove this sheet from the book and keep it in front of you throughout the test.) Mark only one answer for each question. Be sure that each mark is dark and that it completely fills the answer space. In each section of the answer sheet, there are 5 answer spaces for each of 50 questions. When there are fewer than 5 answer choices for a question or fewer than 50 questions in a section of your test, leave the extra answer spaces blank. Do not make stray marks on the answer sheet. If you erase, do so completely.

You may use any available space on the pages of the test for scratchwork. Do not use books, dictionaries, reference materials, calculators, slide rules, or any other aids. Do not look at the answer key or any other parts of this book. It is important to take this practice test in the same way that you will take the actual SAT.

When you have completed all six test sections, turn to the answers and scoring instructions that follow the test.

PRACTICE TEST 4: *Answer Sheet*

Directions: Use a No. 2 pencil only for completing this answer sheet. Be sure each mark is dark and completely fills the intended space. Completely erase any errors or stray marks. Start with number 1 for each new section. If a section has fewer than 50 questions or if a question has fewer than 5 answer choices, leave the extra answer spaces blank.

SECTION 1	SECTION 2	SECTION 3	SECTION 4
1 (A) (B) (C) (D) (E)	1 (A) (B) (C) (D) (E)	1 (A) (B) (C) (D) (E)	1 (A) (B) (C) (D) (E)
2 (A) (B) (C) (D) (E)	2 (A) (B) (C) (D) (E)	2 (A) (B) (C) (D) (E)	2 (A) (B) (C) (D) (E)
3 (A) (B) (C) (D) (E)	3 (A) (B) (C) (D) (E)	3 (A) (B) (C) (D) (E)	3 (A) (B) (C) (D) (E)
4 (A) (B) (C) (D) (E)	4 (A) (B) (C) (D) (E)	4 (A) (B) (C) (D) (E)	4 (A) (B) (C) (D) (E)
5 (A) (B) (C) (D) (E)	5 (A) (B) (C) (D) (E)	5 (A) (B) (C) (D) (E)	5 (A) (B) (C) (D) (E)
6 (A) (B) (C) (D) (E)	6 (A) (B) (C) (D) (E)	6 (A) (B) (C) (D) (E)	6 (A) (B) (C) (D) (E)
7 (A) (B) (C) (D) (E)	7 (A) (B) (C) (D) (E)	7 (A) (B) (C) (D) (E)	7 (A) (B) (C) (D) (E)
8 (A) (B) (C) (D) (E)	8 (A) (B) (C) (D) (E)	8 (A) (B) (C) (D) (E)	8 (A) (B) (C) (D) (E)
9 (A) (B) (C) (D) (E)	9 (A) (B) (C) (D) (E)	9 (A) (B) (C) (D) (E)	9 (A) (B) (C) (D) (E)
10 (A) (B) (C) (D) (E)	10 (A) (B) (C) (D) (E)	10 (A) (B) (C) (D) (E)	10 (A) (B) (C) (D) (E)
11 (A) (B) (C) (D) (E)	11 (A) (B) (C) (D) (E)	11 (A) (B) (C) (D) (E)	11 (A) (B) (C) (D) (E)
12 (A) (B) (C) (D) (E)	12 (A) (B) (C) (D) (E)	12 (A) (B) (C) (D) (E)	12 (A) (B) (C) (D) (E)
13 (A) (B) (C) (D) (E)	13 (A) (B) (C) (D) (E)	13 (A) (B) (C) (D) (E)	13 (A) (B) (C) (D) (E)
14 (A) (B) (C) (D) (E)	14 (A) (B) (C) (D) (E)	14 (A) (B) (C) (D) (E)	14 (A) (B) (C) (D) (E)
15 (A) (B) (C) (D) (E)	15 (A) (B) (C) (D) (E)	15 (A) (B) (C) (D) (E)	15 (A) (B) (C) (D) (E)
16 (A) (B) (C) (D) (E)	16 (A) (B) (C) (D) (E)	16 (A) (B) (C) (D) (E)	16 (A) (B) (C) (D) (E)
17 (A) (B) (C) (D) (E)	17 (A) (B) (C) (D) (E)	17 (A) (B) (C) (D) (E)	17 (A) (B) (C) (D) (E)
18 (A) (B) (C) (D) (E)	18 (A) (B) (C) (D) (E)	18 (A) (B) (C) (D) (E)	18 (A) (B) (C) (D) (E)
19 (A) (B) (C) (D) (E)	19 (A) (B) (C) (D) (E)	19 (A) (B) (C) (D) (E)	19 (A) (B) (C) (D) (E)
20 (A) (B) (C) (D) (E)	20 (A) (B) (C) (D) (E)	20 (A) (B) (C) (D) (E)	20 (A) (B) (C) (D) (E)
21 (A) (B) (C) (D) (E)	21 (A) (B) (C) (D) (E)	21 (A) (B) (C) (D) (E)	21 (A) (B) (C) (D) (E)
22 (A) (B) (C) (D) (E)	22 (A) (B) (C) (D) (E)	22 (A) (B) (C) (D) (E)	22 (A) (B) (C) (D) (E)
23 (A) (B) (C) (D) (E)	23 (A) (B) (C) (D) (E)	23 (A) (B) (C) (D) (E)	23 (A) (B) (C) (D) (E)
24 (A) (B) (C) (D) (E)	24 (A) (B) (C) (D) (E)	24 (A) (B) (C) (D) (E)	24 (A) (B) (C) (D) (E)
25 (A) (B) (C) (D) (E)	25 (A) (B) (C) (D) (E)	25 (A) (B) (C) (D) (E)	25 (A) (B) (C) (D) (E)
26 (A) (B) (C) (D) (E)	26 (A) (B) (C) (D) (E)	26 (A) (B) (C) (D) (E)	26 (A) (B) (C) (D) (E)
27 (A) (B) (C) (D) (E)	27 (A) (B) (C) (D) (E)	27 (A) (B) (C) (D) (E)	27 (A) (B) (C) (D) (E)
28 (A) (B) (C) (D) (E)	28 (A) (B) (C) (D) (E)	28 (A) (B) (C) (D) (E)	28 (A) (B) (C) (D) (E)
29 (A) (B) (C) (D) (E)	29 (A) (B) (C) (D) (E)	29 (A) (B) (C) (D) (E)	29 (A) (B) (C) (D) (E)
30 (A) (B) (C) (D) (E)	30 (A) (B) (C) (D) (E)	30 (A) (B) (C) (D) (E)	30 (A) (B) (C) (D) (E)
31 (A) (B) (C) (D) (E)	31 (A) (B) (C) (D) (E)	31 (A) (B) (C) (D) (E)	31 (A) (B) (C) (D) (E)
32 (A) (B) (C) (D) (E)	32 (A) (B) (C) (D) (E)	32 (A) (B) (C) (D) (E)	32 (A) (B) (C) (D) (E)
33 (A) (B) (C) (D) (E)	33 (A) (B) (C) (D) (E)	33 (A) (B) (C) (D) (E)	33 (A) (B) (C) (D) (E)
34 (A) (B) (C) (D) (E)	34 (A) (B) (C) (D) (E)	34 (A) (B) (C) (D) (E)	34 (A) (B) (C) (D) (E)
35 (A) (B) (C) (D) (E)	35 (A) (B) (C) (D) (E)	35 (A) (B) (C) (D) (E)	35 (A) (B) (C) (D) (E)
36 (A) (B) (C) (D) (E)	36 (A) (B) (C) (D) (E)	36 (A) (B) (C) (D) (E)	36 (A) (B) (C) (D) (E)
37 (A) (B) (C) (D) (E)	37 (A) (B) (C) (D) (E)	37 (A) (B) (C) (D) (E)	37 (A) (B) (C) (D) (E)
38 (A) (B) (C) (D) (E)	38 (A) (B) (C) (D) (E)	38 (A) (B) (C) (D) (E)	38 (A) (B) (C) (D) (E)
39 (A) (B) (C) (D) (E)	39 (A) (B) (C) (D) (E)	39 (A) (B) (C) (D) (E)	39 (A) (B) (C) (D) (E)
40 (A) (B) (C) (D) (E)	40 (A) (B) (C) (D) (E)	40 (A) (B) (C) (D) (E)	40 (A) (B) (C) (D) (E)
41 (A) (B) (C) (D) (E)	41 (A) (B) (C) (D) (E)	41 (A) (B) (C) (D) (E)	41 (A) (B) (C) (D) (E)
42 (A) (B) (C) (D) (E)	42 (A) (B) (C) (D) (E)	42 (A) (B) (C) (D) (E)	42 (A) (B) (C) (D) (E)
43 (A) (B) (C) (D) (E)	43 (A) (B) (C) (D) (E)	43 (A) (B) (C) (D) (E)	43 (A) (B) (C) (D) (E)
44 (A) (B) (C) (D) (E)	44 (A) (B) (C) (D) (E)	44 (A) (B) (C) (D) (E)	44 (A) (B) (C) (D) (E)
45 (A) (B) (C) (D) (E)	45 (A) (B) (C) (D) (E)	45 (A) (B) (C) (D) (E)	45 (A) (B) (C) (D) (E)
46 (A) (B) (C) (D) (E)	46 (A) (B) (C) (D) (E)	46 (A) (B) (C) (D) (E)	46 (A) (B) (C) (D) (E)
47 (A) (B) (C) (D) (E)	47 (A) (B) (C) (D) (E)	47 (A) (B) (C) (D) (E)	47 (A) (B) (C) (D) (E)
48 (A) (B) (C) (D) (E)	48 (A) (B) (C) (D) (E)	48 (A) (B) (C) (D) (E)	48 (A) (B) (C) (D) (E)
49 (A) (B) (C) (D) (E)	49 (A) (B) (C) (D) (E)	49 (A) (B) (C) (D) (E)	49 (A) (B) (C) (D) (E)
50 (A) (B) (C) (D) (E)	50 (A) (B) (C) (D) (E)	50 (A) (B) (C) (D) (E)	50 (A) (B) (C) (D) (E)

REMOVE ANSWER SHEET BY CUTTING ON DOTTED LINE

SECTION 5

1 (A) (B) (C) (D) (E)
2 (A) (B) (C) (D) (E)
3 (A) (B) (C) (D) (E)
4 (A) (B) (C) (D) (E)
5 (A) (B) (C) (D) (E)
6 (A) (B) (C) (D) (E)
7 (A) (B) (C) (D) (E)
8 (A) (B) (C) (D) (E)
9 (A) (B) (C) (D) (E)
10 (A) (B) (C) (D) (E)
11 (A) (B) (C) (D) (E)
12 (A) (B) (C) (D) (E)
13 (A) (B) (C) (D) (E)
14 (A) (B) (C) (D) (E)
15 (A) (B) (C) (D) (E)
16 (A) (B) (C) (D) (E)
17 (A) (B) (C) (D) (E)
18 (A) (B) (C) (D) (E)
19 (A) (B) (C) (D) (E)
20 (A) (B) (C) (D) (E)
21 (A) (B) (C) (D) (E)
22 (A) (B) (C) (D) (E)
23 (A) (B) (C) (D) (E)
24 (A) (B) (C) (D) (E)
25 (A) (B) (C) (D) (E)
26 (A) (B) (C) (D) (E)
27 (A) (B) (C) (D) (E)
28 (A) (B) (C) (D) (E)
29 (A) (B) (C) (D) (E)
30 (A) (B) (C) (D) (E)
31 (A) (B) (C) (D) (E)
32 (A) (B) (C) (D) (E)
33 (A) (B) (C) (D) (E)
34 (A) (B) (C) (D) (E)
35 (A) (B) (C) (D) (E)
36 (A) (B) (C) (D) (E)
37 (A) (B) (C) (D) (E)
38 (A) (B) (C) (D) (E)
39 (A) (B) (C) (D) (E)
40 (A) (B) (C) (D) (E)
41 (A) (B) (C) (D) (E)
42 (A) (B) (C) (D) (E)
43 (A) (B) (C) (D) (E)
44 (A) (B) (C) (D) (E)
45 (A) (B) (C) (D) (E)
46 (A) (B) (C) (D) (E)
47 (A) (B) (C) (D) (E)
48 (A) (B) (C) (D) (E)
49 (A) (B) (C) (D) (E)
50 (A) (B) (C) (D) (E)

SECTION 6

1 (A) (B) (C) (D) (E)
2 (A) (B) (C) (D) (E)
3 (A) (B) (C) (D) (E)
4 (A) (B) (C) (D) (E)
5 (A) (B) (C) (D) (E)
6 (A) (B) (C) (D) (E)
7 (A) (B) (C) (D) (E)
8 (A) (B) (C) (D) (E)
9 (A) (B) (C) (D) (E)
10 (A) (B) (C) (D) (E)
11 (A) (B) (C) (D) (E)
12 (A) (B) (C) (D) (E)
13 (A) (B) (C) (D) (E)
14 (A) (B) (C) (D) (E)
15 (A) (B) (C) (D) (E)
16 (A) (B) (C) (D) (E)
17 (A) (B) (C) (D) (E)
18 (A) (B) (C) (D) (E)
19 (A) (B) (C) (D) (E)
20 (A) (B) (C) (D) (E)
21 (A) (B) (C) (D) (E)
22 (A) (B) (C) (D) (E)
23 (A) (B) (C) (D) (E)
24 (A) (B) (C) (D) (E)
25 (A) (B) (C) (D) (E)
26 (A) (B) (C) (D) (E)
27 (A) (B) (C) (D) (E)
28 (A) (B) (C) (D) (E)
29 (A) (B) (C) (D) (E)
30 (A) (B) (C) (D) (E)
31 (A) (B) (C) (D) (E)
32 (A) (B) (C) (D) (E)
33 (A) (B) (C) (D) (E)
34 (A) (B) (C) (D) (E)
35 (A) (B) (C) (D) (E)
36 (A) (B) (C) (D) (E)
37 (A) (B) (C) (D) (E)
38 (A) (B) (C) (D) (E)
39 (A) (B) (C) (D) (E)
40 (A) (B) (C) (D) (E)
41 (A) (B) (C) (D) (E)
42 (A) (B) (C) (D) (E)
43 (A) (B) (C) (D) (E)
44 (A) (B) (C) (D) (E)
45 (A) (B) (C) (D) (E)
46 (A) (B) (C) (D) (E)
47 (A) (B) (C) (D) (E)
48 (A) (B) (C) (D) (E)
49 (A) (B) (C) (D) (E)
50 (A) (B) (C) (D) (E)

SECTION 1

Time—30 minutes

25 QUESTIONS

In this section solve each problem, using any available space on the page for scratchwork. Then indicate the one correct answer in the appropriate space on the answer sheet.

The following information is for your reference in solving some of the problems.

Circle of radius r: Area $= \pi r^2$; Circumference $= 2\pi r$
The number of degrees of arc in a circle is 360.
The measure in degrees of a straight angle is 180.

Definitions of symbols:

$=$	is equal to	$\leq$	is less than or equal to
$\neq$	is unequal to	$\geq$	is greater than or equal to
$<$	is less than	$\parallel$	is parallel to
$>$	is greater than	$\perp$	is perpendicular to

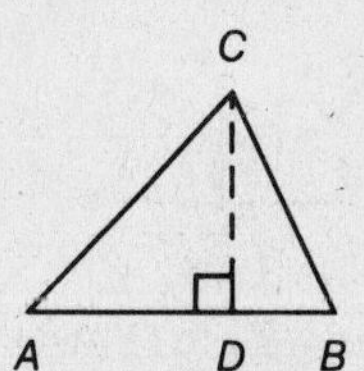

Triangle: The sum of the measures in degrees of the angles of a triangle is 180.

If $\angle CDA$ is a right angle, then

(1) area of $\triangle ABC = \dfrac{AB \times CD}{2}$

(2) $AC^2 = AD^2 + DC^2$

Note: Figures which accompany problems in this test are intended to provide information useful in solving the problems. They are drawn as accurately as possible EXCEPT when it is stated in a specific problem that its figure is not drawn to scale. All figures lie in a plane unless otherwise indicated. All numbers used are real numbers.

---

1. What percent of 60 is 96?

   (A) 62.5 (B) 120 (C) 145
   (D) 160 (E) 210

2. If $31{,}000 = 3.1 \times 10^x$, then $x =$

   (A) 2 (B) 3 (C) 4 (D) 5 (E) 6

3. Of the following numbers, which is divisible by the largest prime factor?

   (A) 280 (B) 300 (C) 320
   (D) 340 (E) 360

4. Barbara is 4 years younger than Kathy. In 3 years, Barbara's age will be $\frac{2}{3}$ of Kathy's age. How old is Barbara now?

   (A) 4 (B) 5 (C) 6 (D) 9 (E) 10

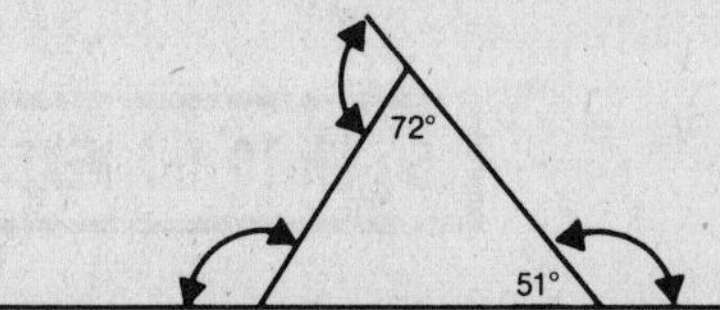

5. If the interior angles of the triangle above have the degree measures shown, what is the sum of the degree measures of the three angles marked by arrows?

   (A) 342 (B) 348 (C) 351
   (D) 354 (E) 360

6. If $xyz = 15$ and $\frac{x}{y} = 3$, then $z =$

   (A) $3y$ (B) $\frac{3y}{x}$ (C) $\frac{5}{y^2}$ (D) $5x$ (E) $\frac{xy}{15}$

7. In a scale drawing of a rectangular room, the scale is 10 centimeters = 1 meter. If the room in the drawing has an area of 1,350 square centimeters and a width of 30 centimeters, what is the length, in meters, of the actual room?

   (A) 4 (B) 4.5 (C) 5 (D) 5.5 (E) 7

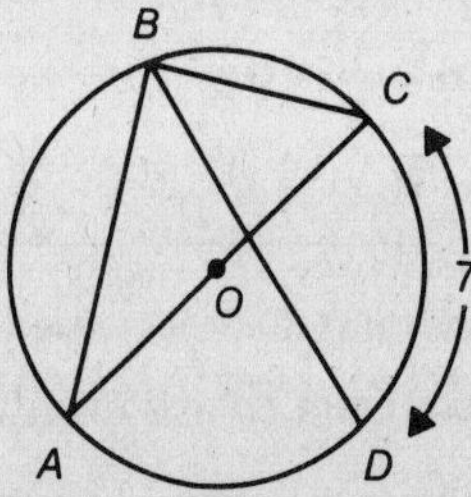

8. In circle O above, line BD bisects angle ABC. If arc CD has length 7, then the circumference of the circle is

   (A) 14 (B) 18 (C) 21 (D) 28 (E) 35

GO ON TO THE NEXT PAGE

9. The average price of each of five books is \$6.55. A sixth book priced at \$9.85 is added to the five. The average price of each of the six books is

(A) \$6.40 (B) \$6.60 (C) \$6.90
(D) \$7.00 (E) \$7.10

10. If $a = 0$, b is positive, and $(a + b)^2 = 9$, then b =

(A) 3 (B) 4 (C) 6 (D) 7 (E) 9

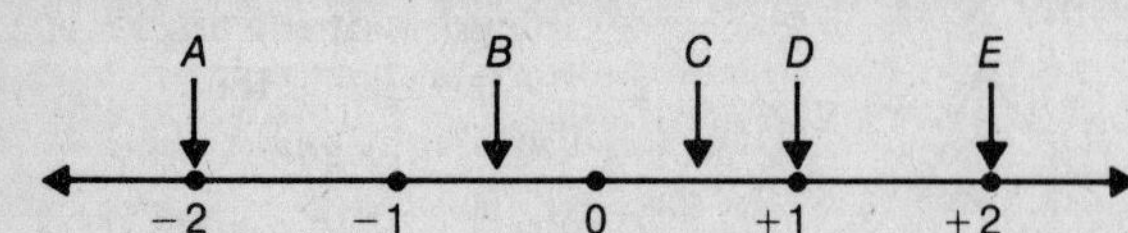

11. The values of numbers A, B, C, D, and E are shown on the number line above. Which of the following expressions has a value closest to 1?

(A) $A \times B$

(B) $E - C$

(C) $B \times D$

(D) $A + D$

(E) $\frac{E}{A}$

12. Twelve persons gather in a room for a meeting. Before the meeting begins, each person shakes hands with every other person in the room exactly once. How many handshakes are there altogether before the meeting begins?

(A) 24 (B) 66 (C) 121 (D) 132 (E) 144

13. If $2x + 2y = 6$ and $3x - y = 5$, then $x + y =$

(A) 9 (B) 8 (C) 4 (D) 3 (E) 1

A = {all even numbers less than 64}
B = {all positive numbers evenly divisible by 3}

14. Given the definitions above, how many numbers are members of both set A and set B?

(A) 7 (B) 8 (C) 9 (D) 10 (E) 11

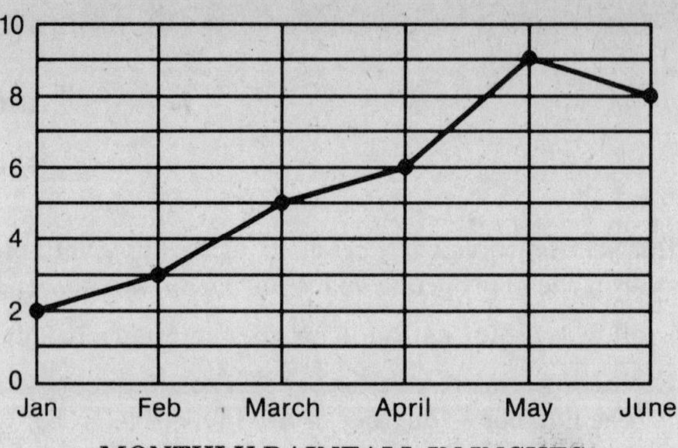

MONTHLY RAINFALL IN INCHES

15. During which month shown on the graph above did the amount of rainfall increase by the greatest percentage over the previous month's rainfall?

(A) February (B) March (C) April
(D) May (E) June

16. Sarah borrows \$700 for one year at an annual rate of 9% simple interest. She invests the money in a venture that yields $10\frac{1}{2}$% simple interest annually. After repaying the loan, Sarah's net profit will be

(A) \$7.35 (B) \$10.50 (C) \$18.75
(D) \$63.00 (E) \$73.50

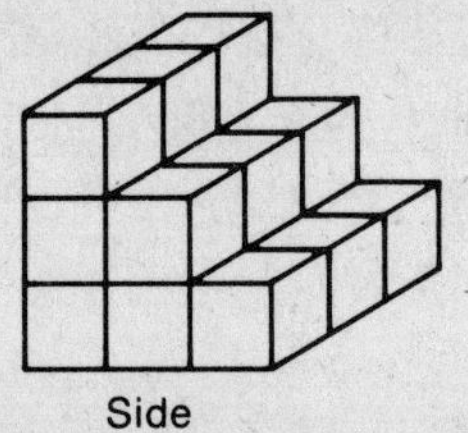

Side

Back

17. Above are two views of a three-dimensional figure constructed of wooden cubes. How many different cubes are visible in the two views?

(A) 13 (B) 14 (C) 15 (D) 16 (E) 18

GO ON TO THE NEXT PAGE

18. In terms of a, $10a$ minutes equals how many hours?

(A) $\frac{a}{60}$ (B) $60a$ (C) $\frac{600}{a}$ (D) $\frac{a}{6}$ (E) $600a$

Questions 19–20 refer to the operation defined by the equation $x \between y = \frac{x+y}{x} + \frac{x+y}{y}$.

19. What is the value of $4 \between 3$?

(A) $\frac{7}{12}$ (B) $1\frac{1}{3}$ (C) $4\frac{1}{12}$ (D) $1\frac{1}{6}$ (E) 2

20. What is the value of $\frac{1}{2} \between 2$?

(A) $2\frac{1}{2}$ (B) 5 (C) $\frac{10}{4}$ (D) $8\frac{1}{2}$ (E) $\frac{25}{4}$

---

21. Ed can stuff 324 envelopes in 1 hour. Pete can stuff 468 envelopes in 90 minutes. Working together, how many envelopes can Ed and Pete stuff in 50 minutes?

(A) 530 (B) 556 (C) 570
(D) 638 (E) 792

22. The year 2022 contains exactly three digits that are the same. How many years after 2022 is the next year that also contains exactly three digits that are the same?

(A) 89 (B) 100 (C) 101 (D) 180 (E) 198

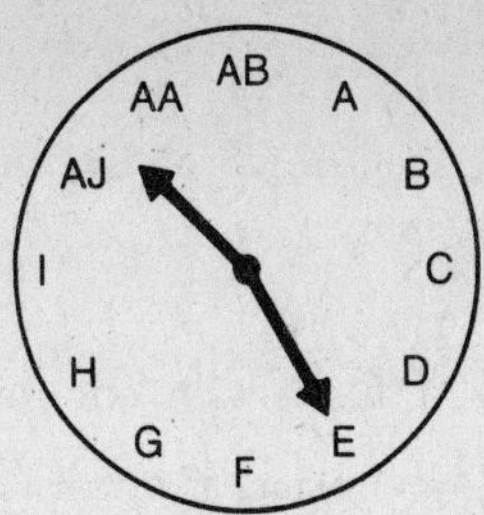

23. The clock above is a conventional 12-hour clock on which letters have been used in place of digits. If the clock is accurate, what time will it be exactly $2\frac{1}{2}$ hours after the time shown?

(A) A:AA (B) A:JE (C) AB:AA
(D) AA:AJ (E) AB:EE

---

24. In a coordinate graph system, a square is drawn inside a circle whose center is at the origin and whose radius is 3. If the vertices of the square all lie on or within the circle and all have integral x and y values, what is the greatest possible length of the side of the square?

(A) 2 (B) 4 (C) $3\sqrt{2}$ (D) 5 (E) $3\sqrt{3}$

25. Let $a = \frac{b}{c} + \frac{c}{b}$. If $c = b^2$, then $a =$

(A) $b + b^2$

(B) $\frac{b+b}{b^2}$

(C) $\frac{1}{b} + b$

(D) $b^2 + \frac{1}{b}$

(E) $1 + \frac{b}{2b}$

S T O P

IF YOU FINISH BEFORE TIME IS CALLED, YOU MAY CHECK YOUR WORK ON THIS SECTION ONLY. DO NOT WORK ON ANY OTHER SECTION IN THE TEST.

SECTION 2

Time—30 minutes

45 QUESTIONS

For each question in this section, choose the best answer and blacken the corresponding space on the answer sheet.

Each question below consists of a word in capital letters, followed by five lettered words or phrases. Choose the word or phrase that is most nearly opposite in meaning to the word in capital letters. Since some of the questions require you to distinguish fine shades of meaning, consider all the choices before deciding which is best.

Example:

GOOD: (A) sour (B) bad (C) red
(D) hot (E) ugly

Ⓐ ● Ⓒ Ⓓ Ⓔ

1. BELITTLE: (A) appraise (B) extol
(C) support (D) nominate (E) defend

2. LISTLESS: (A) earnest (B) mobile
(C) living (D) vigorous (E) essential

3. RETARD: (A) revivify (B) educate
(C) release (D) intensify (E) accelerate

4. SOLUBLE: (A) deceptive (B) unanswerable
(C) indecisive (D) unmentionable
(E) indeterminate

5. DISCREPANCY: (A) normality (B) reliability
(C) agreement (D) consensus (E) proximity

6. VEHEMENT: (A) halfhearted (B) minuscule
(C) meandering (D) forced (E) dull

7. REND: (A) unite (B) depict (C) transform
(D) pierce (E) embellish

8. ADULTERATED: (A) clarified (B) pure
(C) antiseptic (D) sinless (E) transmuted

9. DOGMATIC: (A) imprecise (B) whimsical
(C) flexible (D) inarticulate (E) unorthodox

10. CREDULOUS: (A) visionary (B) atheistic
(C) skeptical (D) amazing (E) disloyal

11. MALIGNANT: (A) unimposing (B) soothing
(C) beneficent (D) ineffectual (E) allied

12. REPUDIATE: (A) verify (B) suggest
(C) account (D) glean (E) espouse

13. INCHOATE: (A) shrilly whistling
(B) in steady motion (C) easily noticed
(D) vividly colored (E) fully formed

14. PERSPICACITY: (A) dullness (B) timidity
(C) restraint (D) composure (E) optimism

15. INGENUOUS: (A) new (B) sophisticated
(C) inane (D) foolish (E) innocuous

Each sentence below has one or two blanks, each blank indicating that something has been omitted. Beneath the sentence are five lettered words or sets of words. Choose the word or set of words that best fits the meaning of the sentence as a whole.

Example:

Although its publicity has been ----, the film itself is intelligent, well-acted, handsomely produced, and altogether ----.

(A) tasteless..respectable (B) extensive..moderate
(C) sophisticated..amateur (D) risqué..crude
(E) perfect..spectacular

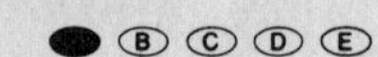

16. It is the nature of time itself that while our past may seem a ---- highway, our future remains ---- wilderness.

(A) nameless..a pathless
(B) well-traveled..an overgrown
(C) long..an impenetrable
(D) familiar..an unknown
(E) sinuous..a bleak

17. Scientific genius and artistic creativity are not really ----; the mental processes involved in both are fundamentally ----.

(A) controllable..logical
(B) related..mysterious
(C) common..simple
(D) opposed..similar
(E) unusual..different

18. Billy's innocence did not exempt him from ----; indeed, he was treated as a kind of ---- for the misdeeds of the whole group.

(A) punishment..scapegoat
(B) suspicion..savior
(C) responsibility..peacemaker
(D) suffering..hero
(E) praise..ringleader

19. The ---- of the French-speaking citizens of Quebec in demanding recognition for their language has encouraged ---- minorities in other countries to pursue a similar degree of official recognition.

(A) history..assimilated
(B) effectiveness..political
(C) persistence..religious

GO ON TO THE NEXT PAGE

(D) failure..comparable
(E) success..linguistic

20. The stereotype of the poet expending his genius early and dying young was ---- by Yeats, who lived ---- and wrote brilliantly until the end.

(A) explained..comfortably
(B) supported..joyously
(C) shattered..long
(D) undermined..modestly
(E) refuted..briefly

Each passage below is followed by questions based on its content. Answer all questions following a passage on the basis of what is stated or implied in that passage.

The accelerated extermination of plant species does not pose the obvious, immediate threat to human well-being that trends such as the spread of environmentally caused diseases do. Yet a decline in the diversity of life forms should be of grave concern to all people. The potential large-scale loss of species is without precedent and involves the disruption of ecological systems of vast complexity.

Probably the most immediate threat to human welfare posed by the extinction of species arises from the shrinkage of the plant gene pools available to agricultural scientists and farmers. While the global spread of modern agricultural methods and hybrid seeds has brought needed increases in food production, in many areas it has also entailed the substitution of a few seed varieties for the rich array of native varieties traditionally planted. At the same time, the spread of cultivation onto unused lands may wipe out the wild varieties of crops that still exist in some regions.

Switching to more productive strains and extending cultivation is often socially desirable. However, such "progress" can involve the extinction of unique or rare crop strains that are closely adapted to the local environment. The long-term productivity of agriculture may thus be jeopardized. The risks of planting large areas with genetically uniform crops include high vulnerabilities to pests, plant diseases, and weather abnormalities, as the destruction by corn blight of 15 percent of the highly homogeneous U.S. corn crop of 1970 made all too clear.

Thus, the future of plant breeding and of agricultural progress is undermined as the diversity of genes on which breeders can draw declines. Locally adapted domestic or wild strains with properties of huge potential value—strains of crops such as wheat, sorghum, and millet—are disappearing before scientists have time to make use of them.

Fortunately, the preservation of diverse crop strains is one of the more easily manageable aspects of the problem of endangered species. Even if preserving crop strains in their wild or locally cultivated states—clearly a desirable goal—proves for the most part unattainable, large numbers of varied seeds can be stored in international facilities and made available to breeders as the need arises. Seed collections, of course, can never match nature's genetic wealth, but they can help to maintain diversity.

21. The passage primarily concerns the

(A) dangers in cultivating only a single species of a particular crop
(B) means by which agricultural scientists may maintain genetic diversity
(C) threat to agricultural progress posed by the extinction of species
(D) substitution of artificially developed crop varieties for natural ones
(E) development of new food crops through genetic experimentation

22. The author's attitude toward the spread of modern agricultural methods may be described as one of

(A) serious concern
(B) unalloyed optimism
(C) harsh condemnation
(D) sympathetic support
(E) baffled irritation

23. According to the passage, the spread of agriculture into formerly uncultivated regions runs the risk of

(A) increasing the quantity of food produced at the expense of variety and diversity
(B) producing only foods that are unacceptable to the indigenous peoples of the regions
(C) increasing the quantity of food produced while sacrificing quality and flavor
(D) making food crops more resistant to plant diseases and infestation by pests
(E) sacrificing long-term agricultural productivity for short-term increases in food production

24. The quotation marks in line 23 indicate the author's

(A) use of a term in a highly technical sense
(B) awareness that a term is somewhat colloquial and informal
(C) wish to acknowledge the influence of some other writer
(D) doubts about the appropriateness of a term in a given context
(E) desire to attribute a term to its originator

25. The last paragraph of the passage presents

(A) a partial solution to the problem described
(B) an alternative approach to the situation outlined
(C) a refutation of the arguments presented in the first three paragraphs
(D) an attempt to mollify those who are critical of the author's point of view
(E) an attempt to reconcile disparate opinions

GO ON TO THE NEXT PAGE

My father, Paul Herndon, and my mother, Hattie Herndon, lived for many years in Birmingham, and then came North. They settled down in Wyoming, Ohio, a little steel and mining town just outside of Cincinnati. I was born there on May 6, 1913. My name was put down in the big family Bible as Eugene Angelo Braxton Herndon.

They say that once a miner, always a miner. I don't know if that's so, but I do know that my father never followed any other trade. His sons never doubted that they would go down into the mines as soon as they got old enough. The wail of the mine whistle morning and night, and the sight of my father coming home with his lunch-pail, grimy from the day's coating of coal-dust, seemed a natural and eternal part of our lives.

Almost every working-class family, especially in those days, nursed the idea that one of its members, anyway, would get out of the factory and wear clean clothes all the time and sit at a desk. My family was no exception. They hoped that I would be the one to leave the working-class. They were ready to make almost any sacrifices to send me through high-school and college. They were sure that if a fellow worked hard and had intelligence and grit, he wouldn't have to be a worker all his life.

I haven't seen my mother or most of my family for a long time—but I wonder what they think of that idea now!

My father died of miner's pneumonia when I was very small, and left my mother with a big family to care for. Besides myself, there were six other boys and two girls. We all did what we could. Mother went out to do housework for rich white folks. An older brother got a job in the steel mills. I did odd jobs, working in stores, running errands, for $2 and $3 a week. They still had the idea they could scrimp and save and send me through college. But when I was 13, we saw it wouldn't work. So one fine morning in 1926, my brother Leo and I started off for Lexington, Ky. It was just across the border, and it had mines, and we were miner's kids.

A few miles outside of Lexington, we were taken on at a small mine owned by the powerful DeBardeleben Coal Corporation. There didn't seem to be any question in anyone's mind about a kid of 13 going to work, and I was given a job helping to load coal.

26. The passage primarily concerns

(A) the sacrifices that the author's mother made for her children
(B) the effects on the author's family of his father's untimely death
(C) how the author came to work as a coal miner, just as his father had
(D) the author's relationships with his older brothers and sisters
(E) how the author's family managed to survive despite the death of his father

27. As a child, the author regarded his father's occupation with

(A) bitterness
(B) pride
(C) dread
(D) acceptance
(E) despair

28. In retrospect, the author would most likely describe his family's plan to send him to college as

(A) a cruel hoax
(B) a foolish illusion
(C) an ignoble ambition
(D) a pernicious pipedream
(E) a realistic aspiration

29. The author sought work in the coal mines rather than elsewhere mainly because

(A) he had failed to complete his high school education
(B) there were no other major industries in his hometown
(C) he had been raised in a coal-mining family
(D) he admired the strength and courage of the miners
(E) no other employer would hire a child of thirteen

30. According to the passage, the author was able to go to work at the age of thirteen because

(A) he lied about his age to the managers of the mine
(B) his father had been employed at the mine prior to his death
(C) he had been given permission to work by his mother
(D) he was unusually tall and strong for his age
(E) the managers of the mine were not concerned about his age

Select the word or set of words that <u>best</u> completes each of the following sentences.

31. Dr. Angelese would neither confirm nor deny the allegations; she remained ----, allowing the committee members to ---- whatever they wished.

(A) uncommunicative..infer
(B) fearful..propose
(C) motionless..consider
(D) defiant..decide
(E) hesitant..believe

32. Just as atomic energy was first used in warfare, so powered flight was given its first practical application by ----.

(A) the military (B) the government
(C) political leaders (D) private industry
(E) scientists

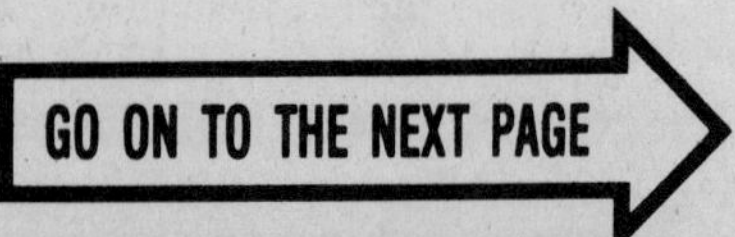

33. Whereas nineteenth-century thinkers were prone to regard ---- as a distinctly human quality, scholars now know that many ---- have at least rudimentary means of communicating with one another.

(A) toolmaking..primates
(B) thought..animals
(C) language..species
(D) speech..peoples
(E) civilization..creatures

34. It is a mistake to believe that all those who came here in the early waves of immigration readily ---- American habits; every U.S. city has sections where old-world customs are ---- to this day.

(A) accepted..studied
(B) rejected..enjoyed
(C) selected..known
(D) adopted..practiced
(E) understood..remembered

35. Since the instruments aboard the spacecraft must provide reliable information at widely varying ----, they must be relatively ---- fluctuations from extreme heat to extreme cold.

(A) intervals..capable of
(B) altitudes..responsive to
(C) locations..immune to
(D) temperatures..unaffected by
(E) times..sensitive to

Each question below consists of a related pair of words or phrases, followed by five lettered pairs of words or phrases. Select the lettered pair that best expresses a relationship similar to that expressed in the original pair.

Example:

YAWN:BOREDOM:: (A) dream:sleep
(B) anger:madness (C) smile:amusement
(D) face:expression (E) impatience:rebellion

Ⓐ Ⓑ ● Ⓓ Ⓔ

36. CATALOG:LIBRARY:: (A) map:harbor
(B) cashier:bookstore (C) program:performers
(D) menu:restaurant (E) script:drama

37. ACQUITTAL:CONVICTION::
(A) evidence:belief
(B) innocence:guilt
(C) activity:action
(D) testimony:rebuttal
(E) proof:confession

38. BREATHTAKING:ADMIRATION::
(A) unique:approval
(B) imperturbable:calm
(C) terrifying:cowardice
(D) mercenary:greed
(E) repulsive:disgust

39. DROSS:METAL:: (A) core:pulp
(B) gold:ore (C) water:oil
(D) milk:cream (E) chaff:grain

40. BIBLIOGRAPHER:LIST::
(A) statistician:count
(B) physician:prevent
(C) historian:explain
(D) politician:elect
(E) mathematician:enumerate

41. DISLIKE:ODIUM::
(A) vanity:pride
(B) blessing:benediction
(C) distaste:revulsion
(D) indifference:disinterest
(E) admiration:fondness

42. INCARCERATE:CRIMINAL:: (A) bolt:door
(B) free:hostage (C) quarantine:patient
(D) seal:envelope (E) interrogate:suspect

43. CONCISENESS:WORDY:: (A) order:chaotic
(B) legibility:decipherable (C) logic:fraudulent
(D) audibility:quiet (E) solvency:wealthy

44. INDULGE:HEDONIST:: (A) suppress:underling
(B) taste:connoisseur (C) conform:maverick
(D) obey:officer (E) retreat:hermit

45. HARPOON:BLUBBER:: (A) bullet:target
(B) spear:enemy (C) knife:meat
(D) tusk:elephant (E) arrow:venison

S T O P

IF YOU FINISH BEFORE TIME IS CALLED, YOU MAY CHECK YOUR WORK ON THIS SECTION ONLY. DO NOT WORK ON ANY OTHER SECTION IN THE TEST.

SECTION 3

Time—30 minutes

40 QUESTIONS

For each question in this section, choose the best answer and blacken the corresponding space on the answer sheet.

Each question below consists of a word in capital letters, followed by five lettered words or phrases. Choose the word or phrase that is most nearly opposite in meaning to the word in capital letters. Since some of the questions require you to distinguish fine shades of meaning, consider all the choices before deciding which is best.

Example:

GOOD: (A) sour (B) bad (C) red (D) hot (E) ugly

Ⓐ ● Ⓒ Ⓓ Ⓔ

1. RESOURCEFUL: (A) inept (B) weary (C) timorous (D) single-minded (E) bland

2. STRESS: (A) deny (B) deemphasize (C) soften (D) undermine (E) assail

3. SPONTANEOUS: (A) rehearsed (B) regulated (C) willful (D) insincere (E) dour

4. INFERNAL: (A) redeemable (B) useful (C) celestial (D) laudatory (E) notable

5. GREGARIOUS: (A) eccentric (B) asocial (C) inimitable (D) intent (E) platitudinous

6. REQUISITE: (A) scorned (B) paltry (C) flawed (D) insignificant (E) needless

7. IMPLICATE: (A) support (B) disprove (C) convict (D) demonstrate (E) extricate

8. FORBEARANCE: (A) indication (B) response (C) harshness (D) impatience (E) punishment

9. VITIATE: (A) undermine (B) deaden (C) rescind (D) perfect (E) enforce

10. CONFOUND: (A) indicate (B) praise (C) distinguish (D) shatter (E) verify

Each sentence below has one or two blanks, each blank indicating that something has been omitted. Beneath the sentence are five lettered words or sets of words. Choose the word or set of words that best fits the meaning of the sentence as a whole.

Example:

Although its publicity has been ----, the film itself is intelligent, well-acted, handsomely produced, and altogether ----.

(A) tasteless..respectable (B) extensive..moderate (C) sophisticated..amateur (D) risqué..crude (E) perfect..spectacular

● Ⓑ Ⓒ Ⓓ Ⓔ

11. Drug abuse is hardly confined to the ---- economic levels of society; even the most ---- suburbs may contain a high percentage of drug-dependent individuals.

(A) broadest..exclusive
(B) wealthier..prosperous
(C) poorest..popular
(D) usual..attractive
(E) lower..affluent

12. Scientists have come to recognize the dinosaurs as one of the most ---- life forms ever to inhabit the earth; they dominated the planet for over one hundred million years, longer than any other major group of animals yet seen.

(A) prolific (B) fascinating (C) enormous (D) diverse (E) successful

13. Although the ---- implications of his research were obvious, Professor Kennelly cared only for pure science; he left it to others to ---- his findings.

(A) political..criticize
(B) practical..apply
(C) theoretical..analyze
(D) experimental..promote
(E) technological..debate

GO ON TO THE NEXT PAGE

14. Like Henry James, whose long, abstruse sentences mirror the complex ---- states of his characters, Proust uses a ---- prose style to represent his narrator's complicated mental processes.

(A) moral..distinctive
(B) psychological..convoluted
(C) personal..clipped
(D) emotional..colorful
(E) intellectual..pellucid

15. Today's high-technology education scare resembles the Sputnik scare of the 1950s, which led to federal programs in support of science education; in both cases, some national ---- was needed to focus popular attention on the needs of our ----.

(A) alarm..schools
(B) crisis..people
(C) threat..allies
(D) consensus..scientists
(E) fear..cities

Each question below consists of a related pair of words or phrases, followed by five lettered pairs of words or phrases. Select the lettered pair that best expresses a relationship similar to that expressed in the original pair.

Example:

YAWN:BOREDOM:: (A) dream:sleep
(B) anger:madness (C) smile:amusement
(D) face:expression (E) impatience:rebellion

16. RETOUCH:PHOTOGRAPH::
(A) restore:harmony
(B) sharpen:blade
(C) edit:book
(D) wash:window
(E) wax:car

17. TRUCK:TANK:: (A) cart:wagon
(B) airplane:helicopter (C) rifle:bazooka
(D) ship:destroyer (E) rocket:jet

18. DUBIOUS:CERTAINTY::
(A) improbable:possibility
(B) ambiguous:sincerity
(C) unaware:visibility
(D) skeptical:honesty
(E) apocryphal:authenticity

19. ODOMETER:DISTANCE::
(A) chronometer:hour
(B) meter:foot
(C) audiometer:sound
(D) compass:direction
(E) barometer:atmospheric pressure

20. MONOCLE:SPECTACLES::
(A) mittens:gloves
(B) monologue:dialogue
(C) telegraph:telephone
(D) cravat:necktie
(E) telescope:binoculars

21. SHRILL:EAR:: (A) bumpy:touch
(B) pungent:tongue (C) vivid:sense
(D) odorless:nose (E) shadowy:eye

22. DOTARD:SENILE:: (A) flatterer:aged
(B) prodigy:modest (C) upstart:presumptuous
(D) sage:bearded (E) sycophant:ruthless

23. CURIOUS:MEDDLESOME::
(A) vociferous:loquacious
(B) accidental:fortuitous
(C) frugal:niggardly
(D) odd:strange
(E) diligent:industrious

24. PREVARICATE:DECEPTION::
(A) regulate:uniformity
(B) humor:amusement
(C) distort:truth
(D) provoke:resignation
(E) extrapolate:experience

25. MYSTIC:PRAGMATIST:: (A) idealist:realist
(B) prophet:chronicler (C) poet:novelist
(D) optimist:logician (E) alchemist:physicist

GO ON TO THE NEXT PAGE

Each passage below is followed by questions based on its content. Answer all questions following a passage on the basis of what is stated or implied in that passage.

My father was a justice of the peace, and I believed that he had the power of life and death over everyone, and could hang anybody that offended him. This was distinction enough for me as a general thing; but the desire to be a steamboatman kept intruding, nevertheless.

I first wanted to be a cabin-boy, so that I could come out with a white apron on and shake a tablecloth over the side, where all my old comrades could see me; later I thought I would rather be the deck-hand who stood on the end of the deck with a coil of rope in his hand, because he was even more conspicuous. But these were only day-dreams—they were too heavenly to be considered as real possibilities.

By and by one of our boys went away. He was not heard of for a long time. At last he turned up as apprentice engineer on a steamboat. This thing shook the bottom out of all my Sunday-school teachings. That boy had been notoriously worldly, and I just the reverse; yet he was exalted to this eminence, and I left in obscurity and misery.

There was nothing generous about this fellow in his greatness. He would always manage to have a rusty bolt to scrub while his boat tarried at our town, and he would sit on the inside guard and scrub it, where we all could see him and envy him. And whenever his boat was laid up he would come home and hang around town in his blackest and greasiest clothes, so that nobody could help remembering that he was a steamboatman; and he used all sorts of steamboat technicalities in his talk, as if he were so used to them that he forgot common people could not understand them. And he was always talking about "St. Looy" like an old citizen; he would refer casually to occasions when he was "coming down Fourth Street," or when there was a fire and he took a turn on the brakes of "the old Big Missouri"; and then he would go on and lie about how many towns the size of ours were burned down there that day.

Two or three of the boys had long been persons of consideration among us because they had been to St. Louis once and had a vague general knowledge of its wonders, but their glory was over now. They lapsed into a humble silence, and learned to disappear when the ruthless cub-engineer approached.

This fellow had money, too, and hair-oil. Also a silver watch and showy brass watch-chain. He wore a leather belt and used no suspenders. If ever a youth was admired and hated by his comrades, this one was.

26. Which of the following statements about the author's boyhood CANNOT be inferred from the passage?

(A) He lived in a very small town.
(B) He was usually a well-behaved youth.
(C) He was seriously determined to become a steamboatman someday.
(D) He had an inflated idea of his father's importance.
(E) He had never visited St. Louis.

27. The tone of the author's description of his feelings as a boy may best be described as

(A) smugly self-congratulatory
(B) gently satiric
(C) nostalgic and sentimental
(D) coldly objective
(E) bitterly self-condemnatory

28. The passage implies that the apprentice engineer used steamboating terms in his conversation because he

(A) wanted to impress the other boys
(B) forgot that others could not understand them
(C) enjoyed sharing facts about his new life with others
(D) did not know how to express himself without them
(E) had become accustomed to the jargon of his trade

29. The passage implies that the author's boyhood friends

(A) regarded his personal qualities with scorn
(B) did not understand his attitude toward the apprentice engineer
(C) considered his desire to be a steamboatman childish
(D) shared his feelings about the occupation of steamboatman
(E) were a good deal more mature and sophisticated than he

30. Of the following phrases from the passage, the one that the author uses in the most clearly ironic way is

(A) "he was even more conspicuous" (lines 12–13)
(B) "his greatness" (line 24)
(C) "his blackest and greasiest clothes" (lines 29–30)
(D) "a vague general knowledge" (lines 44–45)
(E) "his comrades" (line 52)

GO ON TO THE NEXT PAGE

Do women tend to devalue the worth of their work? Do they apply different standards to rewarding their own work than they do to rewarding the work of others? These were the questions asked by Michigan State University psychologists Lawrence Messé and Charlene Callahan-Levy. Past experiments had shown that when women were asked to decide how much to pay themselves and other people for the same job, they paid themselves less. Following up on this finding, Messé and Callahan-Levy designed experiments to test several popular explanations of why women tend to shortchange themselves in pay situations.

One theory the psychologists tested was that women know what is fair pay for a particular job but are unable to apply this standard to themselves. The subjects for the experiment testing this theory were men and women recruited from the Michigan State undergraduate student body. The job the subjects were asked to perform for pay was an opinion questionnaire requiring a number of short essays on campus-related issues. After completing the questionnaire, some subjects were given six dollars in bills and change and were asked to decide payment for themselves. Others were given the same amount and were asked to decide payment for another subject who had also completed the questionnaire.

The psychologists found that, as in earlier experiments, the women paid themselves less than the men paid themselves. They also found that the women paid themselves less than they paid other women and less than the men paid the women. The differences were substantial. The average paid to women by themselves was $2.97. The average paid to men by themselves was $4.06. The average paid to women by others was $4.37. In spite of the differences, the psychologists found that the men and the women in the experiment evaluated their own performances on the questionnaire about equally and better than the expected performances of others.

On the basis of their findings, Messé and Callahan-Levy concluded that women's attachment of a comparatively low monetary value to their work cannot be based entirely on their judgment of their own ability. Perhaps, the psychologists postulated, women see less of a connection than men do between their work (even when it is superior) and their pay because they are relatively indifferent to receiving money for their work.

31. The passage could best be described as

(A) an analysis of the experimental methods of Messé and Callahan-Levy
(B) a summary of the findings of Messé and Callahan-Levy
(C) a discussion of the implications of the work of Messé and Callahan-Levy
(D) a description of the theoretical basis of the work of Messé and Callahan-Levy
(E) a critical examination of the experiments of Messé and Callahan-Levy

32. The experiment described in the passage would be most relevant to the formulation of a theory concerning the

(A) generally lower salaries received by women workers in comparison to men
(B) reluctance of some women to enter professions that are traditionally dominated by men
(C) low prestige given by society to many traditionally female-dominated professions
(D) anxiety expressed by some women workers in dealing with male supervisors
(E) discrimination often suffered by women in attempting to enter the work force

33. According to the passage, how is the research of Messé and Callahan-Levy related to earlier experiments in the same field?

(A) It suggests a need to discard conclusions based on earlier experiments.
(B) It tends to weaken the assumptions on which earlier experiments were designed.
(C) It suggests that the problem revealed in earlier experiments may be more widespread than previously thought.
(D) It helps to explain a phenomenon revealed in earlier experiments.
(E) It calls into question the accuracy of the data obtained in earlier experiments.

34. Which of the following statements is (are) supported by the facts stated in the passage?

I. Men tend to pay themselves more than they pay other men.
II. Women tend to pay men more than they pay other women for the same work.
III. Men tend to pay women less than they pay other men for the same work.

(A) None
(B) I only
(C) II only
(D) I and III only
(E) II and III only

35. According to the passage, the work of Messé and Callahan-Levy tends to weaken the notion that

(A) people will tend to overreward themselves when given the opportunity to do so
(B) women are generally less concerned with financial rewards for their work than are men
(C) men are willing to pay women more than women are willing to pay themselves
(D) payment for work should generally be directly related to the quality of the work
(E) women judge their own work more critically than they judge the work of men

GO ON TO THE NEXT PAGE

It is in the cycling of moisture between ocean and land that the hydrologic cycle appears as an integral feature of larger atmospheric circulations. As air moves seaward from the continents, it gains moisture and, for the most part, retains it. After sufficient trajectory over the ocean, continental air (relatively dry air developed over large land areas) is transformed into maritime air (relatively moist air developed over large water areas).

The prevailing westerly winds of the northern hemisphere and semipermanent high-pressure cells over the Atlantic and Pacific oceans control the major processes of this phase of the hydrologic cycle in the United States. The continental air of Asia flows seaward, receives a heavy charge of moisture in its lower layers, and is transformed into maritime Pacific air. Much of this moisture is precipitated over the ocean or returned to the Asian mainland by the circulation of the atmosphere over the Pacific. Some of this moisture is shunted eastward and deposited along the seaward slopes of the Pacific coastal ranges of the United States.

The continental air formed over the northern portion of North America flows to the south and east, then out to sea, where it is transformed into moist maritime air. The Bermuda High, a high-pressure system centered near Bermuda, moves some of this air in a large clockwise sweep southward, out of the belt of the prevailing westerly winds and into the prevailing easterlies of the tropics. There, the transformed air masses are joined by moist maritime air swept northward from the tropics. Where this moist, warm air encounters colder, dryer continental air, thermal differences produce major storms and bring much of the precipitation received by the United States east of the Rockies.

Regional processes are also at work in this atmospheric phase of the hydrologic cycle. Onshore winds bring moisture and precipitation to coastal areas, and some precipitation is produced as air masses move across the continent. In some locations, seasonal differences between land and sea temperatures produce monsoons, the seasonal onshore winds that predominate in late spring and summer between large land and water masses at the lower latitudes. These bring a continuous flow of moisture-laden air inland from the warm oceans and can produce large quantities of rainfall. Although most often associated with the southern coast of Asia, monsoon winds are present to some extent along the Gulf Coast of the United States and the coast of the Mediterranean.

36. According to the passage, much of the rainfall in the eastern United States is caused by the

(A) eastward movement of moist air from the region of the Rocky Mountains
(B) seaward flow of continental air formed over the Asian mainland
(C) seasonal differences between the temperatures of land and sea air masses
(D) collision of cold, dry air masses with hot, moist air masses
(E) southerly movement of moist air masses formed over the northern part of the continent

37. It can be inferred from the passage that the states along the Gulf Coast of the United States

(A) have a climate identical with that of the countries along the Mediterranean Coast
(B) often experience major storms that originate in the northern part of North America and sweep clockwise toward the Bermuda High
(C) are subject to heavy precipitation in late spring and summer
(D) derive their weather systems mainly from westward-moving masses of continental air
(E) are heavily affected by the air masses that originate in southern Asia

38. The author discusses the effects of all of the following characteristics of air masses EXCEPT

(A) the amount of moisture they contain
(B) the speed at which they move
(C) their temperature
(D) the regions over which they were developed
(E) whether they are high-pressure or low-pressure systems

39. Which of the following best describes the development of the last paragraph of the passage?

(A) Major thesis, minor thesis
(B) Evidence, conclusion
(C) Generalization, examples
(D) Argument, rebuttal
(E) Theory, evidence

40. The author's primary purpose in the passage is to

(A) outline the major phases of the hydrologic cycle
(B) discuss the atmospheric processes underlying precipitation
(C) explain how the hydrologic cycle affects weather, principally in the United States
(D) trace the movement of moisture-laden air from Asia to the North American continent
(E) analyze the causes of monsoon winds along the Gulf Coast of the United States

S T O P

IF YOU FINISH BEFORE TIME IS CALLED, YOU MAY CHECK YOUR WORK ON THIS SECTION ONLY. DO NOT WORK ON ANY OTHER SECTION IN THE TEST.

SECTION 4

Time—30 minutes

35 QUESTIONS

In this section solve each problem, using any available space on the page for scratchwork. Then indicate the one correct answer in the appropriate space on the answer sheet.

The following information is for your reference in solving some of the problems.

Circle of radius r: Area $= \pi r^2$; Circumference $= 2\pi r$.
The number of degrees of arc in a circle is 360.
The measure in degrees of a straight angle is 180.

Definitions of symbols:

$=$	is equal to	$\leqq$	is less than or equal to
$\neq$	is unequal to	$\geqq$	is greater than or equal to
$<$	is less than	$\parallel$	is parallel to
$>$	is greater than	$\perp$	is perpendicular to

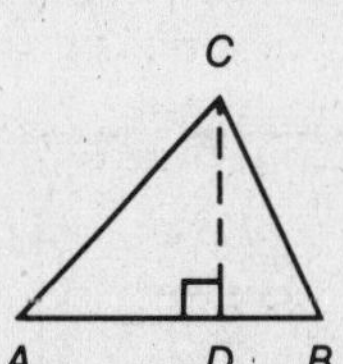

Triangle: The sum of the measures in degrees of the angles of a triangle is 180.

If $\angle CDA$ is a right angle, then

(1) area of $\triangle ABC = \dfrac{AB \times CD}{2}$

(2) $AC^2 = AD^2 + DC^2$

Note: Figures which accompany problems in this test are intended to provide information useful in solving the problems. They are drawn as accurately as possible EXCEPT when it is stated in a specific problem that its figure is not drawn to scale. All figures lie in a plane unless otherwise indicated. All numbers used are real numbers.

---

1. If $6 - x = \dfrac{10}{3}$, then $x =$

(A) $8\frac{1}{3}$ (B) $\frac{7}{3}$ (C) 3 (D) $\frac{8}{3}$ (E) $\frac{3}{10}$

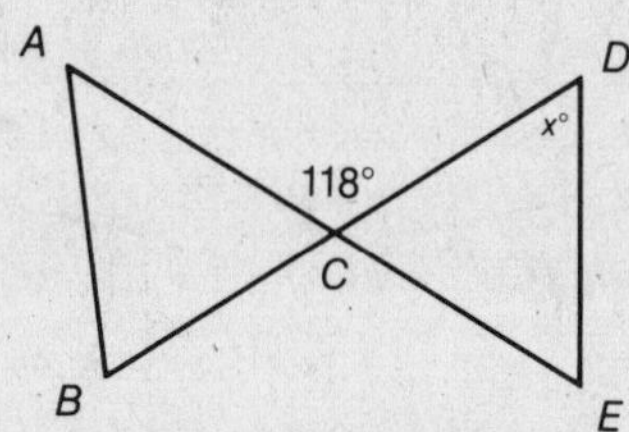

2. In the figure above, if $CD = CE$, then $x =$

(A) 42 (B) 45 (C) 51 (D) 56 (E) 59

3. In a shoe factory, each machine produces x shoes per day. How many shoes will y machines produce in z days?

(A) xyz (B) $\frac{xy}{z}$ (C) $\frac{x}{yz}$ (D) $\frac{y}{xz}$ (E) $\frac{z}{xy}$

4. A cylindrical container has a diameter of 4 inches. If the volume of the container is 50 cubic inches, which of the following is closest to the height of the container?

(A) 4 inches (B) 5 inches (C) 6 inches
(D) 7 inches (E) 8 inches

5. A bus begins its route at First Street with a load of passengers and stops at each consecutive numbered street—Second Street, Third Street, and so on. At each stop, half the passengers on the bus get off, and 4 new passengers get on. After the Fourth Street stop, the bus has 13 passengers. How many passengers were on the bus when it began its route?

(A) 26 (B) 40 (C) 48 (D) 60 (E) 96

6. If p and q are negative integers, then which of the following must be positive?

(A) $\frac{p^2}{q^4}$ (B) $\frac{p}{q^2}$ (C) p^2q^3

(D) $p^2 + q^5$ (E) $\frac{p+q}{p^2}$

7. In a coordinate graph system, two vertices of a triangle are located at points (1, 3) and (3, 0). In order for the triangle to contain the largest obtuse angle, at which of the following points should the third vertex be located?

(A) (2, 2) (B) (0, 0) (C) (−1, −1)
(D) (3, 4) (E) (2, −1)

GO ON TO THE NEXT PAGE

Questions 8-27 each consist of two quantities, one in Column A and one in Column B. You are to compare the two quantities and on the answer sheet blacken space

A if the quantity in Column A is greater;
B if the quantity in Column B is greater;
C if the two quantities are equal;
D if the relationship cannot be determined from the information given.

Notes:
1. In certain questions, information concerning one or both of the quantities to be compared is centered above the two columns.
2. In a given question, a symbol that appears in both columns represents the same thing in Column A as it does in Column B.
3. Letters such as x, n, and k stand for real numbers.

EXAMPLES

	Column A	Column B	Answers
E1.	2×6	$2 + 6$	● Ⓑ Ⓒ Ⓓ
	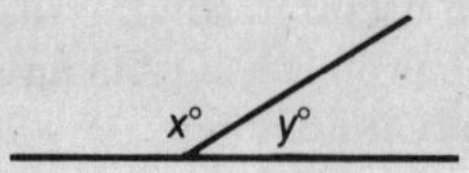		
E2.	$180 - x$	y	Ⓐ Ⓑ ● Ⓓ
E3.	$p - q$	$q - p$	Ⓐ Ⓑ Ⓒ ●

	Column A	Column B
8.	$1\frac{1}{3}$ dozen	15

$$\frac{a}{b} = -1$$

9.	a	$-b$
10.	The length of the third side of a triangle with sides of 4 and 7	The length of the third side of a triangle with sides of 5 and 9
11.	$\frac{2}{3}$ of $\frac{1}{2}$ of 18	$\frac{1}{3}$ of $\frac{3}{4}$ of 28

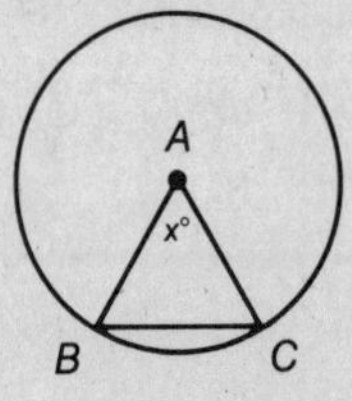

A is the center of the circle.

$AC = BC$

12.	x	60

	Column A	Column B

Robert owes Joan \$7; Edward owes Robert \$4; Joan owes Edward \$3.

13.	Numbers of persons named who will have more money after all debts are paid	2

$$5g = 3h$$
$$g < 0$$

14.	g	h

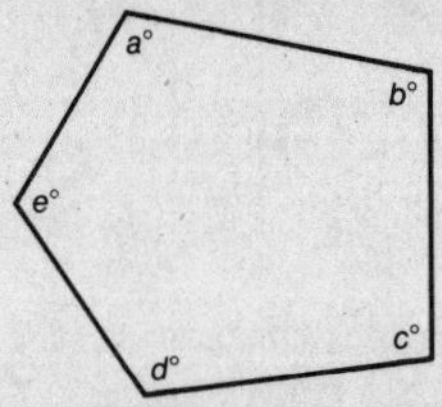

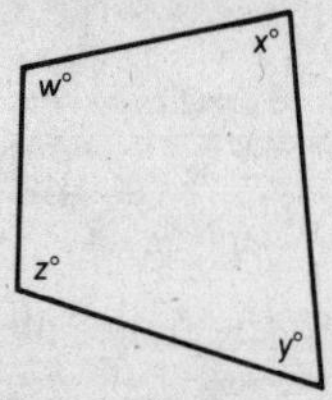

15.	Average (arithmetic mean) of a, b, c, d, and e	Average (arithmetic mean) of w, x, y, and z

GO ON TO THE NEXT PAGE

Column A	Column B

Questions 16–17 refer to the following graph.

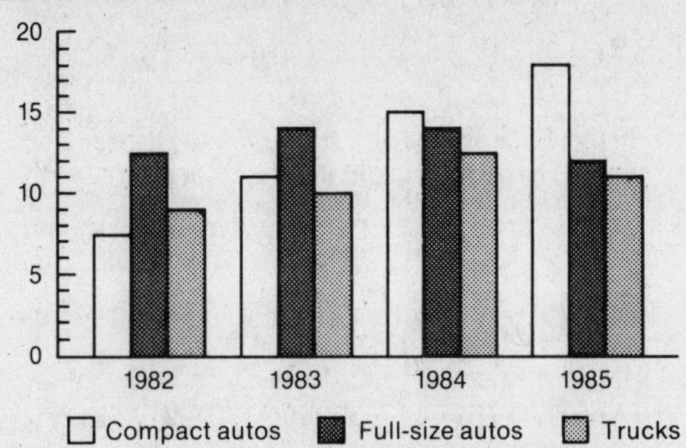

SALES OF AUTOS AND TRUCKS IN BOGRADIA (Thousands)

	Column A	Column B
16.	Percent of increase in total sales of autos and trucks from 1982 to 1985	30%
17.	Sales of compact autos in the first year when sales of compact autos exceeded sales of full-size autos	Total auto sales in 1982
18.	$(-3)^{73}$	$(-3)^{74}$

$x \neq 0$

$x^2 = 9$

	Column A	Column B
19.	x	$-x$

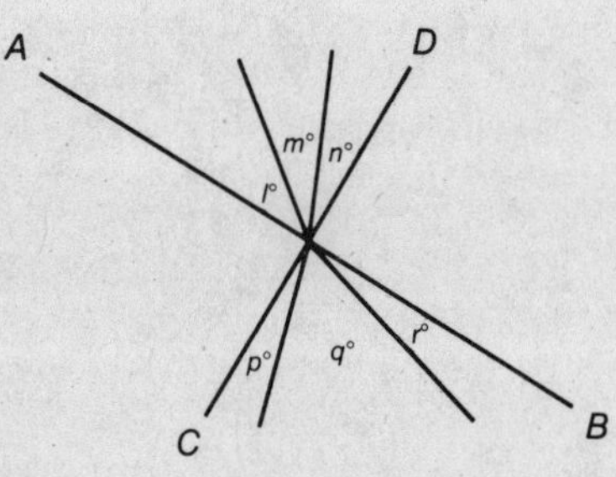

$AB \perp CD$

	Column A	Column B
20.	Average (arithmetic mean) of l, m, and n	Average (arithmetic mean) of p, q, and r

Column A	Column B

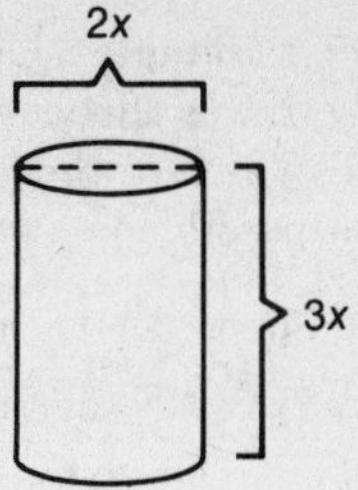

	Column A	Column B
21.	Total surface area of the closed cylinder above	$12x^2$

A fair six-sided die with faces numbered 1 through 6 is to be rolled twice.

	Column A	Column B
22.	The probability of obtaining a total of exactly 4 on the two rolls	The probability of obtaining a total of exactly 9 on the two rolls

$x > 0$

$y + 2x = 0$

	Column A	Column B
23.	2	y

3 widgets cost as much as 2 doodads. 5 doodads cost as much as 3 whatsits.

	Column A	Column B
24.	Cost of 2 whatsits	Cost of 4 widgets

$a > 1$

	Column A	Column B
25.	$\dfrac{a + a + a}{a}$	$3a$

Town R and Town S are 180 miles apart. Train 1 leaves Town R at 1 P.M. and travels toward Town S; Train 2 leaves Town S at 3 P.M. the same day and travels toward Town R. The two trains pass one another at 5 P.M. the same day.

	Column A	Column B
26.	Average speed of Train 1	Average speed of Train 2

$2n + 5 < 8$

	Column A	Column B
27.	n	1

GO ON TO THE NEXT PAGE

Solve each of the remaining problems in this section using any available space for scratchwork. Then indicate the one correct answer in the appropriate space on the answer sheet.

28. Two sides of a triangle have lengths of 3 and 8 respectively. If x is the length of the third side of the triangle, which of the following best expresses the range of possible values of x?

(A) $5 \leq x \leq 11$ (B) $3 < x < 8$ (C) $5 < x < 11$
(D) $3 \leq x \leq 11$ (E) $5 < x < 8$

29. If $3xy = 0$ and $\frac{x}{3} = \frac{2}{1}$, which of the following must be true?

I. $2x = 0$

II. $\frac{y}{3} = 6$

III. $x - 3 = 3$

(A) None
(B) I only
(C) II only
(D) III only
(E) I and II only

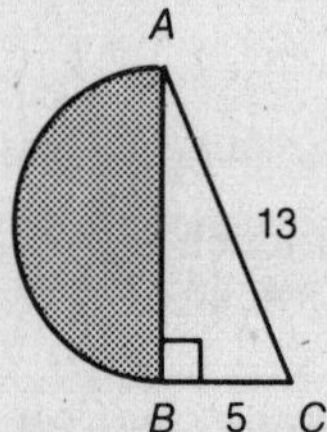

30. Line segment AB in the figure above is the diameter of a semicircle and one leg of right triangle ABC. What is the area of the shaded region?

(A) 9π (B) 18π (C) 21π
(D) 30π (E) 36π

31. Laura can paint a certain room in 6 hours. Working together, Laura and Karen can paint the room in 3 hours and 20 minutes. How long would it take Karen to paint the room alone?

(A) 6 hours, 10 minutes
(B) 6 hours, 30 minutes
(C) 6 hours, 40 minutes
(D) 7 hours
(E) 7 hours, 30 minutes

32. If $r + 3s = 11$ and $2r - s = 8$, then $s =$

(A) 1 (B) 2 (C) 3 (D) 4 (E) 5

33. If the three angles of a triangle have degree measures of $2n$, $3n$, and $n + 12$, then $n =$

(A) 24 (B) 28 (C) 32 (D) 40 (E) 46

34. If $3ab = 24$ and $\frac{b}{-4} = \frac{1}{2}$, then $a =$

(A) -8 (B) -4 (C) 0 (D) 2 (E) 4

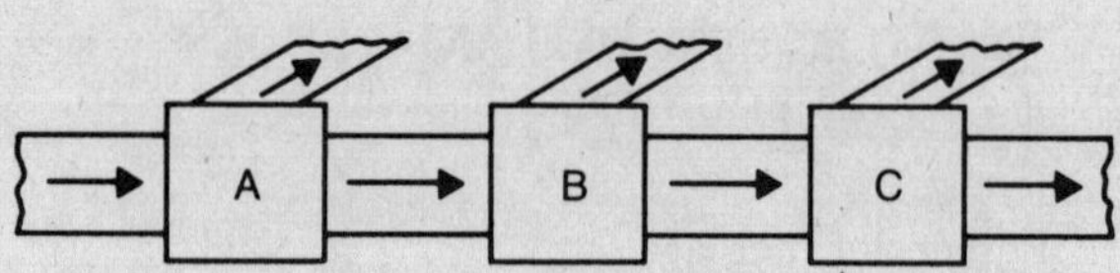

35. The diagram above represents the movement of a product along an assembly line. Of every 10 units inspected at point A, 2 are discarded as faulty. Of every 10 units inspected at point B, 1 is discarded as faulty. Of every 12 units inspected at point C, 1 is discarded as faulty. Out of every 200 units sent along the assembly line, how many are discarded at the three inspection points?

(A) 96 (B) 80 (C) 76 (D) 68 (E) 54

S T O P

IF YOU FINISH BEFORE TIME IS CALLED, YOU MAY CHECK YOUR WORK ON THIS SECTION ONLY. DO NOT WORK ON ANY OTHER SECTION IN THE TEST.

SECTION 5

Time—30 minutes

50 QUESTIONS

The questions in this section measure skills that are important to writing well. In particular, they test your ability to recognize and use language that is clear, effective, and correct according to the requirements of standard written English, the kind of English found in most college textbooks.

Directions: The following sentences contain problems in grammar, usage, diction (choice of words), and idiom.

> Some sentences are correct.
> No sentence contains more than one error.

You will find that the error, if there is one, is underlined and lettered. Assume that elements of the sentence that are not underlined are correct and cannot be changed. In choosing answers, follow the requirements of standard written English.

If there is an error, select the one underlined part that must be changed to make the sentence correct and blacken the corresponding space on your answer sheet.

If there is no error, blacken answer space Ⓔ.

EXAMPLE:	SAMPLE ANSWER
The region has a climate so severe that plants A growing there rarely had been more than twelve B C inches high. No error D E	Ⓐ Ⓑ ● Ⓓ Ⓔ

1. Although most bilingual education programs
A
are for Spanish speakers, it is not the only language
B C
spoken by a sizable linguistic minority in this
D
country. No error
E

2. After the French Revolution, a short-lived attempt
A
was made to introduce new names for the months
B C D
and days of the year. No error
E

3. If you hope to build a better world in the future,
A B
one must study the great leaders of the past,
C
if only to discover how and why they went wrong.
D
No error
E

4. Despite the advances that have recently been made
A B C
in meteorological techniques, long-range
forecasting is still being a dubious enterprise.
D
No error
E

5. As culture changed, it was inevitable that language
A B
should change; so medieval Latin differed greatly
C
from the classical Latin spoken a thousand years
D
earlier. No error
E

GO ON TO THE NEXT PAGE

6. To gain publicity for her cause, Carol used her
A B
athletic abilities; she swum around the island of
C
Manhattan, becoming one of the first women to do
D
so. No error
E

7. The professor began by remarking that since time
A
was short, she would concentrate in one topic
B
she knew to be of special interest to her audience:
C D
the possibility of life on other planets. No error
E

8. One mark of a cult is that its members, unlike
A B
converts to traditional religions, are often expected
C
to sever all ties with the outside world. No error
D E

9. Finalists in the puzzle contest will be provided with
A B
pens and pencils, but they should bring their own
C
wristwatch to keep track of the time. No error
D E

10. If some of the residents wishes to file a formal
A
housing complaint, they should contact the nearest
B C D
office of the city housing authority. No error
E

11. Them and the representatives of two other unions
A
quickly agreed to sponsor the rally jointly
B C
and publicize it at local meetings. No error
D E

12. Utility industry spokespeople have coined the word
A
brownout to refer to a power shortage
B
less severe than the complete loss of energy
C
known as a *blackout*. No error
D E

13. The frequency of attempts on the lives of political
A B
figures has forced recent presidents curtailing their
C D
public appearances. No error
E

14. Children's folklore—their games, riddles, songs,
A
and jokes—exhibits a surprising degree of
B C
similarity from country to country and from
D
generation to generation. No error
E

15. The notion that a man who happens to be a great
A
poet should not be held responsible for his wartime
B C
propaganda is ultimately degrading to poetry.
D
No error
E

16. The commissioner's plan for containing medical
A
costs calls for limiting salary increases, eliminating
B
inefficiency, and the encouragement of outpatient
C D
care. No error
E

17. If the earth has no atmosphere, the moderate
A
temperatures that make life possible would not
B
prevail; instead, extremes of heat and cold would
C
predominate. No error
D E

18. Among the speakers currently scheduled to appear
A B
are Erica Mason, the novelist; Alan G. Harding, an
imminent surgeon; and Warren Phillipson,
C
a member of Congress. No error
D E

19. At eight o'clock the burglary was discovered;
A
employees found that several safe deposit vaults
B
had been broken into and their contents robbed.
C D
No error
E

20. When the initial phase of expansion of any new
A B
industry passes, a period of entrenchment
inevitably has followed. No error
C D E

21. Whenever you see a word printed in boldface type,
A
one can find a definition of that word in the
B C
glossary at the end of the book. No error
D E

22. A classic, Mark Twain is said to have remarked, is
A B
one of those books that no one wants to read and
C
everybody want to have read. No error
D E

23. Marquez is the youngest of the candidates, but her
A B
credentials for the post are as extensive as
C
anyone else. No error
D E

24. In the lobby was a tablet inscribed with the names
A
of individuals who had gave sums in excess of
B C D
$10,000 to the building fund. No error
E

25. The actress playing Angela is to enter through the
A B
door on the left while Martin and Ernest will be
C
pouring drinks by the cabinet. No error
D E

Directions: In each of the following sentences, some part or all of the sentence is underlined. Below each sentence you will find five ways of phrasing the underlined part. Select the answer that produces the most effective sentence, one that is clear and exact, without awkwardness or ambiguity, and blacken the corresponding space on your answer sheet. In choosing answers, follow the requirements of standard written English. Choose the answer that best expresses the meaning of the original sentence.

Answer (A) is always the same as the underlined part. Choose answer (A) if you think the original sentence needs no revision.

EXAMPLE:

Laura Ingalls Wilder published her first book and she was sixty-five years old then.

(A) and she was sixty-five years old then
(B) when she was sixty-five years old
(C) at age sixty-five years old
(D) upon reaching sixty-five years
(E) at the time when she was sixty-five

SAMPLE ANSWER

26. Because the engineering methods of the day were inadequate to the task, so Babbage's design for a computer was never built.

(A) task, so
(B) task,
(C) task;
(D) task, and
(E) task, therefore

27. When one focuses on the failures of the current administration, one can easily overlook its genuine accomplishments.

(A) one can easily overlook
(B) they easily forget
(C) easily overlooking
(D) one is easily overlooking
(E) it easily overlooks

28. The films of Alfred Hitchcock are not only masterful thrillers and witty entertainments but they are works of art that are brilliantly conceived as well.

(A) they are works of art that are brilliantly conceived
(B) works of art brilliant in conception
(C) conceived as brilliant art works
(D) brilliantly conceived works of art
(E) they are brilliant as works of art

GO ON TO THE NEXT PAGE

29. This new book, written by a well-known critic, which argues that the art world is dominated by the search for prestige.

(A) which argues that
(B) argues that
(C) and arguing that
(D) argues
(E) is an argument that

30. The engineers have determined that adding a dome to the existing stadium would cost almost as much as building a new domed stadium.

(A) as much as building
(B) as much as to build
(C) the same as the building of
(D) as much like building
(E) equally to building

31. Although the Norsemen's landing in America had little effect on history, Columbus is usually credited with the discovery of the New World.

(A) Although
(B) If
(C) When
(D) Because
(E) Considering

32. Admired by all who knew her, her death will leave a real void in the community.

(A) Admired by all who knew her,
(B) Having been admired by all who knew her,
(C) She was admired by all who knew her, and
(D) With the admiration of all who knew her,
(E) All who knew her admired her,

33. Critics are questioning safety conditions on movie sets, and some calling for stricter standards governing dangerous stunts.

(A) sets, and some
(B) sets, including
(C) sets; some are
(D) sets; and some are
(E) sets and

34. Although the modern zoo was not developed until the nineteenth century, there have been collections, sometimes extensive ones, of animals for thousands of years.

(A) there have been collections, sometimes extensive ones, of animals
(B) collections of animals, some of which were extensive, have been made
(C) animals have been collected, sometimes extensively,
(D) animals have been collected, sometimes in extensive form,
(E) collections have existed of animals, some extensive,

35. Physicians no longer ignore nutrition as a major factor in human health, many today prescribe diets along with medications.

(A) health, many today prescribe
(B) health, many a physician is now prescribing
(C) health; today, many prescribe
(D) health, yet many prescribe
(E) health; many physicians currently are prescribing

36. Known simply as *The Flyer*, the plane flown by the Wright brothers at Kitty Hawk is on display at the Smithsonian Institution.

(A) the plane flown by the Wright brothers at Kitty Hawk is
(B) the Wright brothers flew at Kitty Hawk the plane
(C) it was the plane flown by the Wright brothers at Kitty Hawk and is
(D) and flown by the Wright brothers at Kitty Hawk, the plane being
(E) the plane flown at Kitty Hawk by the Wright brothers, it is

37. The largest structure made by living things is not the Great Wall of China, it is the Great Barrier Reef in the Pacific Ocean.

(A) China, it is
(B) China but
(C) China. On the contrary, it is
(D) China; instead, it is
(E) China; rather,

38. Giotto was not the greatest painter of the Italian Renaissance, but his artistic contribution made possible the works of Leonardo and Michelangelo.

(A) Giotto was not
(B) Giotto, though not
(C) It is true that Giotto did not become
(D) Although Giotto was not
(E) Giotto, not

39. A few writers, of whom Poe is an example, actually attain greater fame among those who read their works in translation than among those who read their works in the original.

(A) of whom Poe is an example,
(B) Poe being a notable example,
(C) one example being Poe,
(D) such as Poe,
(E) like Poe, for instance,

GO ON TO THE NEXT PAGE

40. He had won fame for his work among the poor in South Africa, Gandhi was received as a hero in his native land.

(A) He had won fame
(B) Having won fame
(C) Due to the fact that he had won fame
(D) Winning fame
(E) Being famous

Directions: The remaining questions are like those at the beginning of the section. For each sentence in which you find an error, select the one underlined part that must be changed to make the sentence correct and blacken the corresponding space on your answer sheet. If there is no error, blacken answer space E.

41. Everyone on the top six floors of the burning
A B
building were safely evacuated within ten minutes.
C D
No error
E

42. The folklore of the natives of the island of Uffa
A
includes some of the most strangest legends
B C
known to anthropology. No error
D E

43. The commission investigating the accident has not
A
yet determined who was responsible to cause the
B C
fatal breakdown in communications. No error
D E

44. Despite the continuous flow of literature about
A
industrial automation, complete automated
B
factories are rare; most industrial processes
C
still require some handwork. No error
D E

45. The woman in the tan raincoat is the reporter
A
whom the local radio station sent to cover the
B C
disaster relief efforts. No error
D E

46. Russia remains an enigma to many in the West;
A B
they seem cold and suspicious, yet capable at times
C
of gestures of surprising warmth and humanity.
D
No error
E

47. Picasso, like many of his contemporaries, began his
A
career using methods pioneered by Matisse, but he
B C
quickly developed his own techniques. No error
D E

48. When news of the attack came, the Joint Chiefs of
A
Staff were notified immediately in accordance to
B C
the provisions of the National Security Act of 1974.
D
No error
E

49. Though Gabriel's arguments were impressive,
a majority of the members of the association
A B
already made up their minds to vote against his
C D
proposal. No error
E

50. No single definition of *psychology* satisfactory to
A
all of the diverse theoreticians of the discipline
B
have ever been devised. No error
C D E

S T O P

IF YOU FINISH BEFORE TIME IS CALLED, YOU MAY CHECK YOUR WORK ON THIS SECTION ONLY. DO NOT WORK ON ANY OTHER SECTION IN THE TEST.

SECTION 6

Time—30 minutes

45 QUESTIONS

For each question in this section, choose the best answer and blacken the corresponding space on the answer sheet.

Each question below consists of a word in capital letters, followed by five lettered words or phrases. Choose the word or phrase that is most nearly opposite in meaning to the word in capital letters. Since some of the questions require you to distinguish fine shades of meaning, consider all the choices before deciding which is best.

Example:

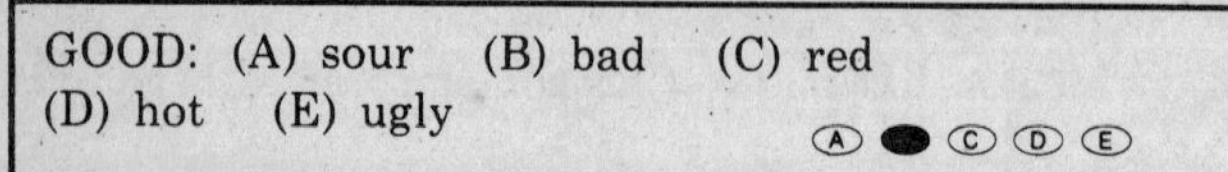

1. BONDAGE: (A) liberalization (B) emancipation (C) revolt (D) expulsion (E) loosening

2. FLAUNT: (A) obey (B) conceal (C) refrain (D) languish (E) abase

3. DOGGED: (A) easily discouraged (B) unusually intelligent (C) slow to anger (D) impossible to trace (E) deeply depressed

4. SEVER: (A) approach (B) apply (C) mollify (D) link (E) promote

5. TRITE: (A) dissimilar (B) characteristic (C) grotesque (D) unlawful (E) novel

6. DEFILE: (A) decorate (B) dampen (C) purify (D) edify (E) regulate

7. EGREGIOUS: (A) alienated from society (B) inclined to argue (C) not readily noticeable (D) deviating from the norm (E) extremely cooperative

8. QUELL: (A) instigate (B) surge (C) baffle (D) augment (E) repeal

9. ALIENATE: (A) provoke (B) attract (C) convene (D) appease (E) renounce

10. INFAMY: (A) futurity (B) reputation (C) anonymity (D) honor (E) ignorance

11. GLOWER: (A) grimace (B) gaze (C) snicker (D) beam (E) sneer

12. PREDILECTION: (A) innovation (B) modesty (C) concern (D) prophecy (E) distaste

13. REJUVENATE: (A) grow (B) elate (C) age (D) weaken (E) depress

14. PIQUE: (A) defy (B) withdraw (C) embolden (D) please (E) scatter

15. RECONDITE: (A) obvious (B) impartial (C) frequent (D) irrational (E) indeterminate

Each sentence below has one or two blanks, each blank indicating that something has been omitted. Beneath the sentence are five lettered words or sets of words. Choose the word or set of words that best fits the meaning of the sentence as a whole.

Example:

Although its publicity has been ----, the film itself is intelligent, well-acted, handsomely produced, and altogether ----.

(A) tasteless..respectable (B) extensive..moderate (C) sophisticated..amateur (D) risqué..crude (E) perfect..spectacular

B C D E

16. If philosophy teaches us only what ---- world would be like, it does only half of its job; it should also teach us how to live in the imperfect world we really inhabit.

(A) a different (B) an ideal (C) an older (D) a future (E) a simpler

17. Unlike American workers, who may ---- their jobs in hard times, Japanese employees generally have ---- lifetime positions.

(A) quit..guaranteed
(B) enjoy..definite
(C) lose..secure
(D) change..voluntary
(E) leave..several

18. In *Beowulf*, the challenges faced by the hero do not represent a series of ---- episodes; they form a clear progression, with each test greater than the one before.

(A) related (B) random (C) brilliant (D) heroic (E) trivial

GO ON TO THE NEXT PAGE

19. Although Baldwin's political views are ----, her somewhat ---- personality makes it difficult for her to carry out the campaigning necessary to win an election.

(A) intelligent..garrulous
(B) controversial..introspective
(C) well known..cautious
(D) acceptable..likable
(E) popular..reserved

20. The enormous publicity recently given to a network anchorman's change of wardrobe for the nightly news suggests the ---- of television's claim to be the equal of newspapers in journalistic ----.

(A) absurdity..seriousness
(B) justice..popularity
(C) implausibility..history
(D) importance..integrity
(E) purpose..effectiveness

Each passage below is followed by questions based on its content. Answer all questions following a passage on the basis of what is stated or implied in that passage.

During her twenty-three-year tenure as president of the American Red Cross, Clara Barton was both its chief asset and its greatest liability. As founder and president, she promoted the Red Cross cause with all of her considerable talent and brought zeal and idealism to Red Cross relief work. At the same time, her domineering and sometimes highhanded ways hindered organizational growth. As Red Cross historian Foster Rhea Dulles notes, her methods of administration were not always based on sound business practices and did not command the confidence of many people who might have given the association broader support.

Barton's failure to delegate authority and to acknowledge popular contributions more formally provided the basis for the criticism that overwhelmed her between 1900 and 1904. It also accounted, at least in part, for the bitter personal attacks that led to a deepening feud between her friends and her foes.

The group that opposed her was made up of prominent Red Cross workers and was led by Mabel Boardman, an able and ambitious society woman. Boardman's group was eager to see the Red Cross reorganized, and their cause gained momentum during 1900 and 1901. Barton refused to consider it. Instead she divided the Red Cross into camps of "friends" and "enemies." At the annual meeting in 1902, after anticipating a move to force her resignation, she rallied her forces and emerged with greater powers and the presidency for life. For the opposition, who believed that the new charter had been railroaded through, this was the last straw.

After the 1902 meeting, Barton thought that the clouds had finally lifted, but events moved swiftly against her. Boardman's group succeeded in persuading President Theodore Roosevelt that Barton was mishandling what was by then a quasi-governmental office. On January 2, 1903, Roosevelt's secretary wrote a letter to Barton stating that the president would not serve—as all of his predecessors had—on a committee of consultation for the Red Cross. Roosevelt directed his secretary to announce publicly his withdrawal from the Red Cross board. Barton was humiliated by the president's clear endorsement of the opposition faction.

21. According to the passage, all of the following were weaknesses of Barton's administration of the Red Cross EXCEPT

(A) her unwillingness to share power with other leaders
(B) her failure to grant full recognition to the work of others
(C) her poor understanding of business procedures
(D) her failure to provide strong and decisive leadership
(E) her inability to inspire trust in potential supporters

22. The passage states that Barton's initial reaction to proposals for reorganization of the Red Cross was one of

(A) reluctance and anxiety
(B) eager acceptance
(C) uncertainty and hesitation
(D) vague annoyance
(E) complete rejection

23. It can be inferred that the turning point in the struggle for power between Boardman and Barton was

(A) President Roosevelt's change in attitude toward Barton
(B) Barton's successful campaign to win lifetime tenure in the Red Cross presidency
(C) the attempt made at the 1902 annual meeting to force Barton to resign
(D) the changes in the Red Cross charter approved in 1902
(E) Boardman's open declaration of her displeasure over Barton's leadership

24. By "she rallied her forces" (line 30), the author means that Barton

(A) appealed to the public for support in her dispute with Boardman
(B) summoned up her waning mental and physical powers
(C) enlisted the help of her supporters within the Red Cross
(D) persuaded many of Boardman's followers to change their allegiance
(E) devised a plan for seizing permanent control of the Red Cross

25. The author's opinion of Barton's leadership of the Red Cross is

(A) somewhat difficult to establish
(B) basically favorable
(C) partly positive and partly negative
(D) almost entirely unfavorable
(E) neither stated nor implied in the passage

The most exciting solar electric prospect is the photovoltaic cell, now the principal power source of space satellites. Such cells generate electricity directly when sunlight falls on them. They have no moving parts, consume no fuel, produce no pollution, operate at environmental temperatures, have long lifetimes, require little maintenance, and can be fashioned from silicon, the second most abundant element in the earth's crust.

Photovoltaic cells are modular by nature. Little is to be gained by grouping large masses of cells at a single collection site. On the contrary, the technology is most sensibly applied in a decentralized fashion—perhaps incorporated in the roofs of buildings—so that transmission and storage problems can be minimized. With decentralized use, the sunlight that such cells do not convert into electricity can be harnessed to provide energy for space heating and cooling, water heating, and refrigeration.

Fundamental physical constraints limit the theoretical efficiency of photovoltaic cells to under twenty-five percent. Numerous practical problems force the real efficiency lower; for silicon photovoltaics, the efficiency ceiling is about twenty percent. For maximum efficiency, relatively pure materials with regular crystal structures are required. Such near perfection is difficult and expensive to achieve. High costs have, in fact, been the principal deterrent to widespread use of photovoltaic cells.

Cost comparisons between photovoltaic systems and conventional systems can be complicated. Solar cells produce electricity only when the sun shines; however, conventional power plants are forced to shut down frequently for repairs and maintenance. Depending on the amount of sunlight available where a photovoltaic array is located, the cells might produce between one-fourth and one-half as much power per kilowatt of installed capacity as an average nuclear power plant does. Adding to the costs of photovoltaics is the need for some kind of storage system; on the other hand, the use of photovoltaics may eliminate the need for expensive transmission and distribution systems.

Depending upon who does the figuring, photovoltaic cells now cost between twenty and forty times as much as conventional sources of base load electricity. However, as a source of power just during daylight periods of peak demand, photovoltaics cost only four to five times as much as conventional power plants along with their distribution systems. Moreover, the costs of conventional power plants have shot steadily upward in recent years, while the costs of photovoltaic cells have rapidly declined.

26. The author's primary purpose in the passage is to

(A) trace the increasing cost effectiveness of photovoltaic cell technology
(B) explain the advantages and disadvantages of the photovoltaic cell
(C) describe the most sensible ways in which photovoltaic cells may be used
(D) urge the use of photovoltaic cells as a partial solution to today's energy problems
(E) compare and contrast photovoltaic cells with other means of using solar energy

27. The passage states that photovoltaic cells are presently

(A) of practical use only in certain limited applications
(B) too costly to have any practical applications
(C) practical only in regions of abundant sunlight
(D) practical as a power source during peak demand periods
(E) practical in areas where nuclear power plants may be undesirable

28. It can be inferred that photovoltaic cells may eliminate the need for transmission and distribution systems because they

(A) generate electricity only during hours when sunlight is available
(B) can be moved from place to place in accordance with the need for electricity
(C) generate electricity directly without the need for any additional devices
(D) can be located at the same site where the energy will be used
(E) are used primarily for purposes related to heating and cooling

29. The passage states that the present use of photovoltaic cells is limited primarily by the

(A) lack of sufficient sunlight in most areas
(B) high cost of using and maintaining them
(C) lack of public support for solar technology
(D) inherent limitations on their efficiency
(E) high cost of manufacturing them

GO ON TO THE NEXT PAGE

30. The purpose of the last sentence of the passage is evidently to

(A) commend the scientists who have developed and improved the photovoltaic cell
(B) deplore the increasing costs of conventional power facilities
(C) suggest a promising future for the photovoltaic cell
(D) underscore the present high cost of photovoltaic cells
(E) deride those who are skeptical about the benefits of the photovoltaic cell

Select the word or set of words that best completes each of the following sentences.

31. Although vehicles produce vast amounts of noxious fumes in the busy Wall Street district during the workweek, on weekends the area is relatively ----.

(A) pleasant (B) quiet (C) uninhabited (D) pollution-free (E) peaceful

32. Those who contend that ---- causes underlie most crime have failed to explain why there is no clear correlation between increased levels of poverty and ---- rates of crime.

(A) sociological..falling
(B) personal..abnormal
(C) political..changing
(D) legal..rising
(E) economic..higher

33. Anderson's house had clearly seen better days: the wooden steps were ----, and the front gate swung ---- on its hinges.

(A) painted..easily
(B) broken..rustily
(C) cracked..gaily
(D) damp..slowly
(E) splintering..freely

34. For the malnourished millions of the Third World, the issue is not whether population growth will be controlled; the issue is whether it will be controlled by human decisions or by ----.

(A) government (B) starvation (C) warfare (D) force (E) science

35. Just as a river retains its essential ---- while the drops of water that make it up are ----, so human nature remains basically the same despite changes in customs and beliefs.

(A) color..glistening
(B) form..ever-changing
(C) shape..tangible
(D) direction..invisible
(E) beauty..insignificant

Each question below consists of a related pair of words or phrases, followed by five lettered pairs of words or phrases. Select the lettered pair that best expresses a relationship similar to that expressed in the original pair.

Example:

> YAWN:BOREDOM:: (A) dream:sleep
> (B) anger:madness (C) smile:amusement
> (D) face:expression (E) impatience:rebellion
> Ⓐ Ⓑ ● Ⓓ Ⓔ

36. PLAY:ACT:: (A) novel:chapter
(B) poem:rhyme (C) symphony:instrument
(D) painting:artist (E) opera:aria

37. EPHEMERAL:LONGEVITY::
(A) lugubrious:levity
(B) timely:endurance
(C) perishable:freshness
(D) extemporaneous:spontaneity
(E) unseen:visibility

38. HAMMER:ANVIL:: (A) awl:leather
(B) drill:hole (C) pestle:mortar
(D) lathe:carpenter (E) millstone:grain

39. CHUCKLE:AMUSEMENT::
(A) smirk:self-satisfaction
(B) titter:vulgarity
(C) gape:dismay
(D) whimper:restraint
(E) shrug:affability

40. THRONE:CHAIR:: (A) coach:horse
(B) settee:sofa (C) crown:jewel
(D) scepter:staff (E) mace:gavel

41. REPEAL:AMENDMENT:: (A) withhold:right
(B) enact:law (C) issue:permit
(D) cancel:check (E) abrogate:privilege

42. LACONIC:SPEAKER:: (A) concise:author
(B) prolific:artist (C) skilled:musician
(D) learned:professor (E) eloquent:orator

43. IMPRUDENT:WASTREL:: (A) reckless:driver
(B) careful:scholar (C) greedy:miser
(D) weary:sluggard (E) slothful:beggar

44. CIPHER:DECODE:: (A) oracle:consult
(B) text:transcribe (C) message:transmit
(D) rune:incise (E) omen:interpret

45. ENERVATED:INVIGORATE::
(A) animated:vitalize
(B) nonplussed:perplex
(C) captivated:ransom
(D) discouraged:hearten
(E) impoverished:pauperize

S T O P

IF YOU FINISH BEFORE TIME IS CALLED, YOU MAY CHECK YOUR WORK ON THIS SECTION ONLY. DO NOT WORK ON ANY OTHER SECTION IN THE TEST.

PRACTICE TEST 4: *Scoring Instructions*

1. Check your answers against the answer key on page 357.
2. To figure your SAT-verbal score:
   A. Count the total number of correct answers you chose in Sections 2, 3, and 6.
   B. Count the total number of incorrect answers you chose in Sections 2, 3, and 6. Multiply this number by 1/4. Ignore any questions you left blank.
   C. Subtract the result of Step B from the result of Step A. Round off the answer to the nearest whole number. This whole number is your SAT-verbal raw score.
   D. Find your raw score in the first column of the score conversion table on pages 358–359. Read across to the column headed SAT-verbal. The three-digit number there is your SAT-verbal score.
3. To figure your SAT-mathematical score:
   A. Count the total number of correct answers you chose in Sections 1 and 4.
   B. Count the total number of incorrect answers you chose from questions 8–27 in Section 4. Multiply this number by 1/3. Ignore any questions you left blank.
   C. Count the total number of incorrect answers you chose from all other questions in Sections 1 and 4. Multiply this number by 1/4. Ignore any questions you left blank.
   D. Add the results of Step B and Step C. Subtract this total from the result of Step A. Round off the answer to the nearest whole number. This whole number is your SAT-mathematical raw score.
   E. Find your raw score in the first column of the score conversion table on pages 358–359. Read across to the column headed SAT-mathematical. The three-digit number there is your SAT-mathematical score.
4. To figure your Test of Standard Written English (TSWE) score:
   A. Count the total number of correct answers you chose in Section 5.
   B. Count the total number of incorrect answers you chose in Section 5. Multiply this number by 1/4. Ignore any questions you left blank.
   C. Subtract the result of Step B from the result of Step A. Round off the answer to the nearest whole number. This whole number is your TSWE raw score.
   D. Find your raw score in the first column of the score conversion table on pages 358–359. Read across to the column headed TSWE. The two-digit number there is your TSWE score.

Note: Allow for a margin of error of 30 points either way on your SAT-verbal and SAT-mathematical scores (3 points on your TSWE score). For instance, an SAT-verbal score of 470 really represents a range of scores from 440 to 500. Remember that test performance varies greatly from one day to the next and can be improved through study and practice. So don't consider your scores on any practice test as a perfect prediction of how you'll do on the real SAT.

PRACTICE TEST 4: *Answer Key*

SECTION 1

1. **D**
2. **C**
3. **D**
4. **B**
5. **E**
6. **C**
7. **B**
8. **D**
9. **E**
10. **A**
11. **A**
12. **B**
13. **D**
14. **D**
15. **B**
16. **B**
17. **D**
18. **D**
19. **C**
20. **E**
21. **A**
22. **A**
23. **E**
24. **C**
25. **C**

SECTION 2

1. **B**
2. **D**
3. **E**
4. **B**
5. **C**
6. **A**
7. **A**
8. **B**
9. **C**
10. **C**
11. **C**
12. **E**
13. **E**
14. **A**
15. **B**
16. **D**
17. **D**
18. **A**
19. **E**
20. **C**
21. **C**
22. **A**
23. **E**
24. **D**
25. **A**
26. **C**
27. **D**
28. **B**
29. **C**
30. **E**
31. **A**
32. **A**
33. **C**
34. **D**
35. **D**
36. **D**
37. **B**
38. **E**
39. **E**
40. **A**
41. **C**
42. **C**
43. **A**
44. **E**
45. **E**

SECTION 3

1. **A**
2. **B**
3. **A**
4. **C**
5. **B**
6. **E**
7. **E**
8. **D**
9. **D**
10. **C**
11. **E**
12. **E**
13. **B**
14. **B**
15. **A**
16. **C**
17. **D**
18. **E**
19. **E**
20. **E**
21. **B**
22. **C**
23. **C**
24. **A**
25. **A**
26. **C**
27. **B**
28. **A**
29. **D**
30. **B**
31. **B**
32. **A**
33. **D**
34. **A**
35. **E**
36. **D**
37. **C**
38. **B**
39. **C**
40. **C**

SECTION 4

1. **D**
2. **E**
3. **A**
4. **A**
5. **C**
6. **A**
7. **A**
8. **A**
9. **C**
10. **D**
11. **B**
12. **C**
13. **B**
14. **A**
15. **A**
16. **A**
17. **B**
18. **B**
19. **D**
20. **C**
21. **A**
22. **B**
23. **A**
24. **A**
25. **B**
26. **D**
27. **D**
28. **C**
29. **D**
30. **B**
31. **E**
32. **B**
33. **B**
34. **B**
35. **D**

SECTION 5

1. **C**
2. **E**
3. **A**
4. **D**
5. **E**
6. **C**
7. **B**
8. **E**
9. **D**
10. **A**
11. **A**
12. **E**
13. **D**
14. **E**
15. **E**
16. **D**
17. **A**
18. **C**
19. **D**
20. **D**
21. **B**
22. **D**
23. **D**
24. **C**
25. **C**
26. **B**
27. **A**
28. **D**
29. **B**
30. **A**
31. **D**
32. **C**
33. **C**
34. **C**
35. **C**
36. **A**
37. **B**
38. **A**
39. **D**
40. **B**
41. **C**
42. **C**
43. **C**
44. **B**
45. **E**
46. **A**
47. **E**
48. **C**
49. **C**
50. **C**

SECTION 6

1. **B**
2. **B**
3. **A**
4. **D**
5. **E**
6. **C**
7. **C**
8. **A**
9. **B**
10. **D**
11. **D**
12. **E**
13. **C**
14. **D**
15. **A**
16. **B**
17. **C**
18. **B**
19. **E**
20. **A**
21. **D**
22. **E**
23. **A**
24. **C**
25. **C**
26. **B**
27. **A**
28. **D**
29. **E**
30. **C**
31. **D**
32. **E**
33. **B**
34. **B**
35. **B**
36. **A**
37. **A**
38. **C**
39. **A**
40. **D**
41. **E**
42. **A**
43. **C**
44. **E**
45. **D**

PRACTICE TEST 4: *Score Conversion Table*

Raw Score	SAT-Verbal	SAT-Mathematical	TSWE
130	800		
129	790		
128	780		
127	770		
126	760		
125	750		
124	740		
123	730		
122	720		
121	720		
120	710		
119	710		
118	700		
117	700		
116	690		
115	690		
114	680		
113	680		
112	670		
111	670		
110	660		
109	660		
108	650		
107	650		
106	640		
105	640		
104	630		
103	630		
102	620		
101	620		
100	610		
99	610		
98	600		
97	600		
96	600		
95	590		
94	590		
93	590		
92	580		
91	580		
90	570		
89	570		
88	570		
87	560		
86	560		
85	550		
84	550		
83	550		
82	540		
81	540		
80	530		
79	530		
78	530		
77	520		
76	520		

Raw Score	SAT-Verbal	SAT-Mathematical	TSWE
75	510		
74	510		
73	500		
72	500		
71	500		
70	490		
69	490		
68	490		
67	480		
66	480		
65	470		
64	470		
63	470		
62	460		
61	460		
60	450	800	
59	450	780	
58	450	770	
57	440	760	
56	440	750	
55	430	740	
54	430	730	
53	430	720	
52	420	710	
51	420	700	
50	420	690	60+
49	410	680	60+
48	410	670	60+
47	400	660	60+
46	400	650	60+
45	400	640	59
44	390	630	58
43	390	620	57
42	380	610	56
41	380	600	55
40	370	600	54
39	370	590	53
38	360	580	52
37	360	570	51
36	350	560	50
35	350	550	49
34	350	540	48
33	340	530	47
32	340	520	46
31	330	510	45
30	330	500	44
29	320	490	43
28	320	490	42
27	310	480	41
26	310	470	40
25	300	460	39
24	300	450	38
23	290	440	37
22	290	430	36
21	280	420	35

Raw Score	SAT-Verbal	SAT-Mathematical	TSWE
20	280	410	34
19	270	400	33
18	270	390	32
17	260	380	31
16	250	370	30
15	250	360	29
14	240	350	28
13	240	340	27
12	230	330	26
11	230	320	25
10	220	310	24
9	220	310	23
8	210	300	22
7	200	290	21
6	200	280	20

Raw Score	SAT-Verbal	SAT-Mathematical	TSWE
5	200	270	20
4	200	260	20
3	200	250	20
2	200	240	20
1	200	220	20
0 or less	200	200	20

PRACTICE TEST 4: *Explanatory Answers*

SECTION 1

1. **D** *What percent* means "$x/100$"; *of* means "times"; *is* means "equals." Thus:

$$\frac{x}{100} \times 60 = 96$$

$$60x = 9600$$

$$x = 160$$

2. **C** This is a question about mathematical notation. Since the decimal place in 3.1 must be moved four places to the right to make it 31,000, the correct exponent for 10 is 4: $31{,}000 = 3.1 \times 10^4$.

3. **D** List the prime factors of each answer: $280 = 2 \times 2 \times 2 \times 5 \times 7$; $300 = 2 \times 2 \times 3 \times 5 \times 5$; $320 = 2 \times 2 \times 2 \times 2 \times 2 \times 2 \times 5$; $340 = 2 \times 2 \times 5 \times 17$; $360 = 2 \times 2 \times 2 \times 3 \times 3 \times 5$. Choice D, 340, is divisible by the largest prime factor—17.

4. **B** Let B equal Barbara's age now (since that's what you're looking for). Then Kathy's age now is $B + 4$, and in 3 years Barbara's age will be $B + 3$ and Kathy's age will be $B + 4 + 3$, or $B + 7$. You're told that Barbara's age in 3 years will be 2/3 of Kathy's age, so set up the equation, multiply both sides by 3 (to clear the equation of fractions), and solve for B:

$$B + 3 = \frac{2}{3}(B + 7)$$

$$3B + 9 = 2B + 14$$

$$B = 5$$

5. **E** The sum of the degree measures of the three exterior angles of a triangle is always 360, no matter what the three interior angles measure. (Remember: Each exterior angle is supplementary to an interior angle, so together each exterior angle and its adjacent interior angle add up to 180°. Multiply 180° by 3 and you get 540°. Then subtract 180°, the sum of the three interior angles, and you get 360°.)

6. **C** You can probably find the answer to this one most easily by tinkering with the two equations. From the first equation, you can find that $z = 15/xy$. From the second equation, you can find that $x = 3y$. Then, by substituting $3y$ for x in your first equation, you can find that

$$z = \frac{15}{(3y)y} = \frac{15}{3y^2} = \frac{5}{y^2}$$

7. **B** Start by working with the measurements of the drawing. If the area of the room in the drawing is 1,350 square centimeters and its width is 30 centimeters, then its length must be 45 centimeters (since $1{,}350 \div 30 = 45$). Now translate: On a scale of 10 centimeters to 1 meter, 45 centimeters = 4.5 meters.

8. **D** Notice that line AC passes through the center of circle O. Therefore, line AC is a diameter of circle O, which means that angle ABC is an inscribed angle that cuts off exactly half the circumference of circle O, represented by arc CDA. If

line BD bisects angle ABC, then arc CD represents half of half, or a fourth, of the circle. You know that arc CD has a length of 7, so the circumference of the circle must be $4 \times 7 = 28$.

9. **E** The total price of the first five books is $5 \times \$6.55 = \$32.75$. The total price of all six books is $\$32.75 + \$9.85 = \$42.60$. Therefore the average price of each of the six books is $\$42.60 \div 6 = \$7.10$.

10. **A** If $a = 0$, then $a + b = b$ and $(a + b)^2 = b^2$. If $b^2 = 9$ and b is positive, then $b = 3$.

11. **A** According to the number line, the value of A is -2 and the value of B is approximately $-1/2$. When multiplied, these two values yield a product equal, or approximately equal, to 1. The value of choice B is greater than 1, and the values of choices C, D, and E are all negative.

12. **B** The first person shakes hands with 11 other people; the second, who has already shaken hands with the first, shakes hands with 10 other people; and so on, until the eleventh person shakes hands with only 1 other person, the twelfth. Thus, there are $11 + 10 + 9 + 8 + 7 + 6 + 5 + 4 + 3 + 2 + 1 = 66$ handshakes altogether.

13. **D** Don't bother with the second equation. Just divide the first equation, $2x + 2y = 6$, by 2 and you'll get $x + y = 3$.

14. **D** Since even numbers are divisible by 2, you're looking for numbers that are divisible both by 2 and by 3—in other words, by 6. The set of positive multiples of 6 less than 64 has ten members: 6, 12, 18, 24, 30, 36, 42, 48, 54, and 60.

15. **B** During February, 3 inches of rain fell. During March, 5 inches of rain fell. During March, then, rainfall increased by 2 inches, or $66\frac{2}{3}\%$ (2 is $66\frac{2}{3}\%$ of 3). This is the largest percentage increase shown on the graph.

16. **B** Sarah's net profit will be $10\frac{1}{2}\% - 9\% = 1\frac{1}{2}\%$ of \$700, or \$10.50.

17. **D** In the side view, 12 cubes are visible. In the back view, 9 cubes are visible. Of the 9 cubes visible in the back view, 5 are also visible in the side view. Therefore, only 16 *different* cubes are visible in the two views.

18. **D** Divide the number of minutes by 60 to get the number of hours: $10a/60 = a/6$.

19. **C** Substitute 4 for x and 3 for y on the right side of the equation given:

$$\frac{4+3}{4} + \frac{4+3}{3} = \frac{7}{4} + \frac{7}{3} = \frac{21}{12} + \frac{28}{12} = \frac{49}{12} = 4\frac{1}{12}$$

20. **E** Substitute $1/2$ for x and 2 for y on the right side of the equation given:

$$\frac{2\frac{1}{2}}{\frac{1}{2}} + \frac{2\frac{1}{2}}{2} = \frac{10}{2} + \frac{2\frac{1}{2}}{2} = \frac{12\frac{1}{2}}{2} = \frac{25}{4}$$

21. **A** If Ed can stuff 324 envelopes in 60 minutes, then in 50 minutes he can stuff 5/6 as many, or 270. If Pete can stuff 468 envelopes in 90 minutes, in 50 minutes he can stuff 5/9 as many, or 260. Together, they can stuff $270 + 260 = 530$ envelopes in 50 minutes.

22. **A** After 2022, the next year to contain exactly three digits that are the same is 2111. That year falls 89 years after 2022.

23. **E** The time shown is 10:25. In $2\frac{1}{2}$ hours, the time shown will be 12:55. Since A = 1, B = 2, and E = 5, 12:55 = AB:EE.

24. **C** As the following diagram illustrates, a square with vertices at (0, 3), (3, 0), (0, −3), and (−3, 0) could be drawn inside a circle whose radius is 3 and whose center is at the origin of a coordinate graph system.

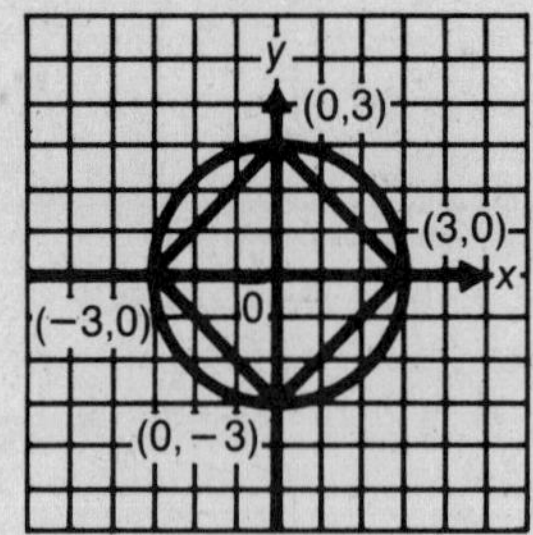

To find the length of the side of the square, either divide the square into four right triangles and apply the Pythagorean theorem, or recall that the diagonal of a square is equal to the side of the square (s) times $\sqrt{2}$. The diagonal of the square in this case is 6. Therefore:

$$s\sqrt{2} = 6$$

$$s = \frac{6}{\sqrt{2}}$$

$$s = \frac{6}{\sqrt{2}} \times \frac{\sqrt{2}}{\sqrt{2}}$$

$$s = \frac{6\sqrt{2}}{2}$$

$$s = 3\sqrt{2}$$

25. **C** Substitute b^2 for c in the first equation. Then simplify.

$$a = \frac{b}{b^2} + \frac{b^2}{b} = \frac{1}{b} + \frac{b}{1} = \frac{1}{b} + b$$

SECTION 2

1. **B** To *belittle* is to mock or disparage. The opposite is to *extol* or *praise*.

2. **D** *Listless* means "lacking energy." *Vigorous*, which means "strong, spirited, energetic," is a good opposite.

3. **E** To *retard* something is to slow it down. The opposite is to *accelerate* something, or speed it up.

4. **B** A *soluble* problem is one that can be solved. One that cannot be solved is *insoluble*, *inexplicable*, or *unanswerable*.

5. **C** A *discrepancy* is a disagreement or a failure of two things to match as expected. The opposite is *agreement*. Use the backward check to eliminate choice A: the opposite of *normality* is *abnormality*, which is not the same as *discrepancy*.

6. **A** *Vehement* means "forceful, strong, ardent." A good opposite would be *weak*, *diffident*, or *halfhearted*.

7. **A** To *rend* something is to tear it apart; to *unite* something is to put it together.

8. **B** *Adulterated* means "polluted, corrupted, debased, or made impure by the addition of a foreign substance." The opposite is *pure*. Don't be misled by choice D: *adulterated* has nothing to do with the sin of *adultery*, although both words derive from the same root.

9. **C** A *dogmatic* person is rigid or inflexible in his or her beliefs and opinions. Good opposites include *flexible*, *accommodating*, and *open-minded*.

10. **C** *Credulous* means "gullible, overwilling to believe." The opposite is *skeptical*, which means "doubtful, questioning, unwilling to believe."

11. **C** As the root *mal* should tell you, *malignant* means "doing evil or harm." *Beneficent* means "doing good."

12. **E** To *repudiate* a cause or a belief is to reject it. The opposite is to *accept*, *support*, or *espouse* it.

13. **E** *Inchoate* means "imperfectly formed" or "not fully developed"; one speaks of a vague thought or mental image as *inchoate*. The opposite is *fully formed*.

14. **A** *Perspicacity* refers to keenness of perception, understanding, and discernment. The opposite is *dullness* or *stupidity*.

15. **B** *Ingenuous* means "innocent, unsophisticated, naive." *Sophisticated*, *worldly*, and *urbane* are all good antonyms.

16. **D** The key word *while* introduces a contrast. *Familiar* and *unknown* logically complete the contrast.

17. **D** The two halves of this sentence make the same basic statement in different ways. In the first half, the statement is negative; in the second half, it's positive. So the missing words must be near opposites. Only *opposed* and *similar* are.

18. **A** Choices A, B, C, and D all work in the first blank, but only A works in the second blank. A *scapegoat* is a person—often an innocent one—who is punished for the misdeeds of others.

19. **E** If the French-*speaking* citizens of Quebec had to demand recognition for their *language*, they must be a *linguistic* minority. And they would have *encouraged* linguistic minorities in other countries only if their demands had met with *success*.

20. **C** Since "wrote brilliantly until the end" contrasts with "expending his genius early," Yeats must have *shattered* (choice C), *undermined* (choice D), or *refuted* (choice E) the stereotype of the poet. If so, he must also have "lived *long*" because living long is the opposite of "dying young."

21. **C** The entire passage discusses how the loss of plant species makes it difficult or impossible for agricultural scientists to develop new strains of crops. The first sentence of paragraph 4 sums up this point well. The other answer choices either distort the main idea of the passage or focus too narrowly on a secondary idea.

22. **A** The author is clearly concerned about the dangers of some methods of modern agriculture, but he does not totally condemn those methods. Look at the second

sentence in paragraph 2, for instance, to see the blend of approval and concern in the author's attitude.

23. **E** See paragraphs 2 and 3. The author acknowledges that extending cultivation to unused lands will increase food production in the short run, but he contends that it may also wipe out wild varieties of crops and thus jeopardize long-term agricultural productivity. Choice A is wrong because it suggests that the increases in food production will be permanent, not temporary, as the author fears.

24. **D** The quotation marks are the author's way of questioning the application of the word *progress* to agricultural methods that increase food production in the short run but jeopardize it in the long run.

25. **A** The passage is devoted to a discussion of the problem of plant extinctions. In the last paragraph, the author presents a partial solution—seed collections.

26. **C** Throughout the passage, the author discusses coal mining as his destined lot, even when explaining how his family tried to provide a different future for him. The other answers are mentioned only briefly in the passage.

27. **D** Reread paragraph 2. The author and his brothers "never doubted that they would go down into the mines as soon as they got old enough." They regarded mining as a "natural and eternal part" of their lives.

28. **B** The author's matter-of-fact explanation of why his family adopted and later was forced to abandon the plan to send him to college suggests that he now would describe the plan as a foolish illusion. (See especially paragraph 4.) Nowhere does he suggest that it was cruel, pernicious (extremely harmful), or ignoble (dishonorable). And it clearly was not realistic.

29. **C** Refer to the last sentence of paragraph 5.

30. **E** You can find the answer in the last sentence of the passage.

31. **A** *Remained* tells you that the first word should be an adjective that describes someone who will "neither confirm nor deny" some allegations, or charges, against her. *Uncommunicative*, which means "tending to withhold information," is such an adjective. And *infer*, which means "conclude" or "deduce," works well in the second blank.

32. **A** The key words *just as* and *so* signal a comparison. So the missing word should be something akin to *warfare*. *The military* is the only logical choice.

33. **C** Since the sentence is about "means of communicating," *language* (choice C) and *speech* (choice D) are the only logical choices for the first blank. *Whereas* tells you that the second blank must be filled by a word that is opposed in meaning to "distinctly human." Many *species* is; many *peoples* is not.

34. **D** "It is a mistake to believe" introduces two directly opposing ideas. Readily adopting American habits is the exact opposite of clinging to the practice of old-world customs. None of the other answer choices result in the same degree of opposition.

35. **D** The second half of the sentence refers to "fluctuations from extreme heat to extreme cold." Thus, "widely varying *temperatures*" are the concern here, not *intervals*, *altitudes*, *locations*, or *times*.

36. **D** Just as a *catalog* is a list of what's available in a *library*, so a *menu* is a list of what's available in a *restaurant*. A *map* (choice A) isn't a list, and *performers* (choice C) aren't a place.

37. **B** In law, an *acquittal* is the opposite of a *conviction*. The first is equivalent to a verdict of "not guilty"; the second is equivalent to a verdict of "guilty." *Innocence* and *guilt* likewise are opposites.

38. **E** Something *breathtaking* is likely to generate a feeling of *admiration*. Something *repulsive* is likely to generate a feeling of *disgust*. Something *terrifying* (choice C) might generate a feeling of *fear*, but *cowardice* is a personal failing that one either suffers from or not.

39. **E** *Dross* is the worthless or useless part of a *metal* (the waste matter or impurities); it is removed during processing. By the same token, *chaff* is the worthless or useless part of a *grain* (the seed coverings and other debris); it is removed during threshing.

40. **A** The characteristic activity of a *bibliographer* is to *list* things (namely, books). In the same way, the characteristic activity of a *statistician* is to *count* things.

41. **C** *Odium* is an extreme form of *dislike*; *revulsion* is an extreme form of *distaste*.

42. **C** One *incarcerates*—imprisons or confines—a criminal to protect other people from harm. One *quarantines*—isolates or confines—a patient for a similar reason, to protect other people from infection.

43. **A** Something *wordy* lacks *conciseness*. Likewise, something *chaotic* lacks *order*. Something *fraudulent* doesn't necessarily lack *logic* (choice C), nor does something *quiet* necessarily lack *audibility* (choice D).

44. **E** The characteristic activity of a *hedonist* is to *indulge* in pleasure; the characteristic activity of a *hermit* is to *retreat* from society. The characteristic activity of a *connoisseur* (choice B) is to *judge* or *discriminate*, not necessarily to *taste*; think of a connoisseur of art, for example.

45. **E** A *harpoon* is a weapon used to hunt whales, which are prized for their fat, called *blubber*. Similarly, an *arrow* is a weapon used (at least in the past) to hunt deer, which are prized for their meat, called *venison*.

SECTION 3

1. **A** *Resourceful* means "capable of meeting situations and solving problems." The opposite is *incapable, incompetent,* or *inept*.

2. **B** To *stress* something is to emphasize it. Thus, *deemphasize* is a natural antonym.

3. **A** Something *spontaneous* is unplanned. By contrast, something *rehearsed* is planned and practiced beforehand.

4. **C** *Infernal* means "hellish"; *celestial* means "heavenly."

5. **B** A *gregarious* person is one who likes to be with other people. The opposite is a person who prefers to be alone. *Asocial, unfriendly,* and *reclusive* might all serve as antonyms.

6. **E** *Requisite*, which is related to *required*, means "necessary." *Needless*, which means "unneeded" or "unnecessary," is a good antonym.

7. **E** To *implicate* someone is to connect, involve, or entangle that person with something that is usually unpleasant: "The witness's testimony may *implicate* several others in the crime." The opposite is to *extricate* someone, that is, to disentangle that person from an unpleasant involvement or association.

8. **D** *Forbearance* is patience, restraint, or self-control under provocation. The opposite is *impatience*.

9. **D** To *vitiate* something is to make it imperfect, to spoil, ruin, or corrupt it. The opposite is to *perfect* something.

10. **C** To *confound* two things is to confuse them, to mistake one for the other. Thus *distinguish*, which means "to make a clear distinction between things," is a good opposite.

11. **E** *Even* indicates that the second half of the sentence is an emphatic restatement of the first. However, since the first half is negative (notice the word *hardly*) and the second half is positive, you can expect the two missing words to be opposites. *Lower* and *affluent*, when used to describe economic levels of society, are opposites.

12. **E** The dinosaurs may have been a *prolific*, *fascinating*, *enormous*, and *diverse* life form, but in order to dominate the planet longer than any other major group of animals, they had to be, above all, a *successful* one.

13. **B** *Although* introduces a contrast between "---- implications" and "pure science." *Technological* (choice E) might complete the contrast, but *practical* is much better, and *apply* works logically in the second blank.

14. **B** The key word *like* signals a comparison, so you can expect the second half of the sentence to echo the first half. If "complicated mental processes" echoes "complex ---- states," then the first word must be *psychological* (choice B), *intellectual* (choice E), or possibly *emotional* (choice D). If "---- prose style" echoes "long, abstruse sentences," then the second word must be *convoluted*, which means "long and involved, complicated, with intricate twists and turns."

15. **A** The first half of the sentence is about two similar scares, or crises, in education, so *alarm* and *schools* are the obvious choices for the blanks.

16. **C** *Retouching* a *photograph* is similar to *editing* a *book*. The purpose of both is to improve something by removing flaws or errors or making other, usually minor, changes.

17. **D** Both a *truck* and a *tank* are types of land vehicles; the main difference is that the latter is designed and used exclusively for war. In the same way, a *destroyer* is a *ship* with strictly military uses.

18. **E** Something *dubious* (that is, doubtful) is without *certainty*; something *apocryphal* (that is, fictitious or legendary) is without *authenticity*. Something *improbable* is unlikely, but it's not without *possibility*, so choice A isn't quite right.

19. **E** An *odometer* is an instrument for measuring *distance*, specifically distance traveled (by a car, for example). Likewise, a *barometer* is an instrument for

measuring *atmospheric pressure*. A *chronometer* (choice A) is an instrument for measuring *time*, not *hour*. An *audiometer* (choice C) is an instrument for measuring *hearing*, not *sound*. A *compass* (choice D) is an instrument for determining, but not measuring, *direction*.

20. **E** The relationship between *monocle* (a single eyepiece) and *spectacles* is very similar to the relationship between *telescope* and *binoculars*. A *monocle* and a *telescope* enhance vision in one eye; *spectacles* and *binoculars* enhance vision in both eyes.

21. **B** The organ affected by a *shrill* sound, which is sharp, intense, or piercing, is the *ear*. The organ affected by a *pungent* taste, which is also sharp, intense, or piercing, is the *tongue*.

22. **C** A *dotard* is an old person who has become *senile*. An *upstart* is a young person who is *presumptuous* (that is, arrogant).

23. **C** *Curious* and *meddlesome* both describe someone who is eager to learn, someone who asks questions and seeks information. However, whereas *curious* has a neutral or even positive value, *meddlesome* has a decidedly negative value. *Meddlesome*, moreover, is more intense than *curious*. It implies an inordinate and improper curiosity, an interfering in affairs that are none of one's business. *Frugal*, which means "thrifty," and *niggardly*, which means "stingy," are related in much the same way. The other word pairs are all near synonyms.

24. **A** The purpose or object of *prevaricating* (lying) is *deception*. Analogously, the purpose or object of *regulating* is *uniformity*. As a verb, *humor* means "soothe" or "indulge"; thus the purpose or object of *humoring* is not *amusement* (choice B), but *mollification* or *appeasement*.

25. **A** *Mystic* and *pragmatist* are near opposites. A *mystic* believes in the reality and importance of what can't be seen, while a *pragmatist* regards only the concrete and useful as important. The relationship between *idealist* and *realist* is much the same. *Optimist* and *logician* (choice D) aren't necessarily opposed; *optimist* and *pessimist* are the true opposites.

26. **C** You can infer from the passage that the author dreamed about becoming a steamboatman, just as boys dream about any profession they consider glamorous, but you can't infer that he was seriously determined to become one. The author's description of himself as the reverse of "notoriously worldly" (paragraph 3) suggests that he was normally well behaved (choice B), and the other answers are all well supported by the passage.

27. **B** The author makes fun of his youthful desires, but in a comical rather than a bitterly self-condemnatory way.

28. **A** Paragraph 4 describes several things that the apprentice engineer did in order to impress his old friends. One of them was to use "all sorts of steamboat technicalities in his talk, as if he were so used to them that he forgot common people could not understand them." The words *as if* show that answer B is not true.

29. **D** If the author's friends had not shared his feelings about steamboating, they would not have admired and envied the apprentice engineer. (See paragraphs 4 and 6.)

30. **B** If a phrase is used ironically, its intended meaning is the opposite of its literal meaning. In this passage, the use of "his greatness" is clearly ironic. The author

is mocking himself, his friends, and the apprentice engineer for perceiving the apprentice engineer's position as lofty and important.

31. **B** The passage briefly explains what the two psychologists discovered through their experiment. It is thus a "summary of the findings" of Messé and Callahan-Levy.

32. **A** The experiment described focuses entirely on how women perceive the monetary value of their work. The only answer that specifically mentions pay or salaries for women is choice A.

33. **D** As paragraph 1 states, Messé and Callahan-Levy were interested in testing "several popular explanations of why women tend to shortchange themselves in pay situations," a phenomenon that had been revealed in earlier experimentation.

34. **A** To support Statements I and III, the passage would have to provide information about how much men pay other men. It doesn't. To support Statement II, the passage would have to provide information about how much women pay men. It doesn't.

35. **E** See the last sentence of paragraph 3.

36. **D** Reread the last sentence of paragraph 3, which explains that much of the rainfall in the eastern United States is caused by the collision of moist, warm air with dry, cold air.

37. **C** The Gulf Coast states are mentioned only in the last sentence of the passage in connection with monsoon winds. As the preceding sentence explains, monsoon winds "can produce large quantities of rainfall" in late spring and summer.

38. **B** There is no mention in the passage about the speed of air masses.

39. **C** The first sentence of the last paragraph makes a general statement: "Regional processes are also at work in this atmospheric phase of the hydrologic cycle." The rest of the paragraph presents some examples of those regional processes.

40. **C** The passage both explains the effects of the hydrologic cycle on weather and concentrates specifically on the weather of the United States. Choice A is off the mark, choice B is too broad, and choices D and E are too narrow.

SECTION 4

1. **D** One easy way to solve this equation is to add x to and subtract 10/3 from both sides of the equation. Thus:

$$6 - \frac{10}{3} = x$$

$$\frac{18}{3} - \frac{10}{3} = x$$

$$\frac{8}{3} = x$$

2. **E** If $CD = CE$, then triangle CDE is an isosceles triangle and $\angle CED = \angle CDE = x°$. Now, $\angle DCE$ is supplementary to $\angle ACD$, which measures 118°, so $\angle DCE$ measures 62°, leaving 118° to be divided equally between the other two angles of the triangle. Thus, $118 \div 2 = 59 = x$.

3. **A** If each machine produces x shoes per day, then all y machines will produce xy shoes per day. Multiply this daily total by the number of days to get the total number of shoes produced: xyz.

4. **A** The volume of a cylinder is determined by the formula $V = \pi r^2 h$, where r is the radius of the cylinder and h is its height. Since the diameter of the cylinder is 4, the radius is 2. Thus:

$$50 = \pi 2^2 h$$

$$\frac{50}{\pi 4} = h$$

The value of π is about 3.14, so the value of $\pi 4$ is about 12.5. Thus the height of the cylinder is about $50 \div 12.5 = 4$.

5. **C** Work backward, stop by stop: First, subtract the 4 passengers that got on at Fourth Street: $13 - 4 = 9$; then double the result: $9 \times 2 = 18$. Second, subtract the 4 passengers that got on at Third Street: $18 - 4 = 14$; then double the result: $14 \times 2 = 28$. Third, subtract the 4 passengers that got on at Second Street: $28 - 4 = 24$; then double the result: $24 \times 2 = 48$.

6. **A** When a negative number is raised to an even power, the result is positive; when it is raised to an odd power, the result is negative. Thus, only choice A *must* be positive. Choices B, C, and E must be negative; choice D may be positive or negative, depending on the values of p and q.

7. **A** The diagram below shows the locations of the two given vertices as well as of the five possible locations of the third vertex. (For a problem like this, it helps to draw a rough sketch in the margin of your test booklet.) You should be able to see that if point A is the third vertex, the resulting triangle will be very "flat"—that is, it will contain a large obtuse angle.

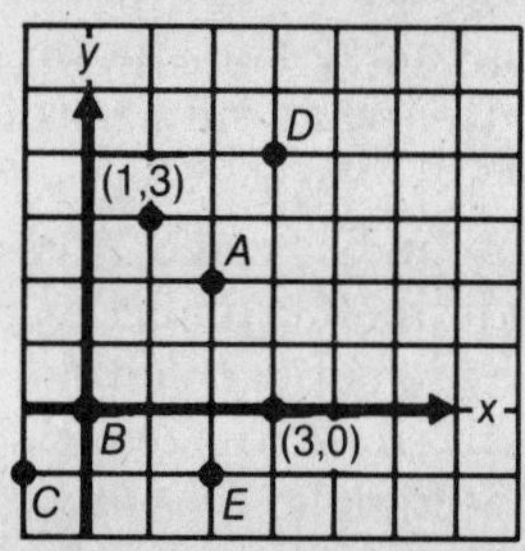

8. **A** A third of a dozen is 4, so $1\frac{1}{3}$ dozen is 16, which is more than 15.

9. **C** Just cross multiply. If $a/b = -1$, then $a = -b$.

10. **D** The length of the third side of each triangle depends on the size of the angle formed by the two known sides. Since you don't know the size of the angle, you can't make the comparison.

11. **B** Remember that *of* means "times," and treat both quantities as multiplication chains. If you cancel everything you can in each column, you don't have to multiply. The value of Column A is 6; the value of Column B is 7.

12. **C** If A is the center of the circle, then $AB = AC$, since both are radii. If AC also equals BC, then the triangle is an equilateral triangle and each of its interior angles measures 60°.

13. **B** Robert will pay \$7 and get \$4, Edward will pay \$4 and get \$3, and Joan will pay \$3 and get \$7. Only Joan will come out ahead.

14. **A** If $5g = 3h$, then h must have a greater absolute value than g. If g is negative, then h must also be negative. Therefore, g must be greater than h. (For example, if $g = -3$, then $h = -5$, and $-3 > -5$.)

15. **A** In any five-sided figure, the average size of an interior angle is 108°. The average size of an interior angle in any four-sided figure is 90°. Therefore, Column A is greater. (You should be able to answer this question even if you've forgotten everything you learned in geometry. Just use your eyes!)

16. **A** To find the value of Column A, add up the three bars for 1982 and get 29,000; add up the three bars for 1985 and get 41,000; subtract 29,000 from 41,000 and get 12,000; divide 12,000 by 29,000 and get 41+%.

17. **B** The year referred to in Column A is 1984. In that year, about 15,000 compact autos were sold. Total auto sales for 1982 were about 20,000.

18. **B** Don't try multiplying it out! Just remember the rule: A negative number raised to an even power is positive; a negative number raised to an odd power is negative. Therefore, the quantity in Column A is negative, while the quantity in Column B is positive.

19. **D** If $x^2 = 9$, then $x = \pm 3$. (The statement $x \neq 0$ is a red herring; x obviously cannot equal 0.) Since you don't know whether x is 3 or -3, you can't tell whether x or $-x$ is greater. Therefore, the correct answer is choice D.

20. **C** This problem also contains a red herring. You don't need to know that AB is perpendicular to CD. All you need to know is that the lines intersect to form vertical angles. Since vertical angles are always equal, the sum of l, m, and n must equal the sum of p, q, and r. And since the two sums are equal, the averages must also be equal, no matter what the sizes of the individual component angles are.

21. **A** If you flattened the cylinder, you'd have two circles, each with a radius of x, and a rectangle with a width of $3x$ and a length equal to the circumference of each circle. First, find the area of each circle: $A = \pi r^2 = \pi x^2$. Second, find the circumference of each circle (the length of the rectangle): $C = 2\pi r = 2\pi x$. Third, find the area of the rectangle: $A = lw = (2\pi x)3x = 6\pi x^2$. Finally, add the area of the two circles to the area of the rectangle to find the total surface area of the cylinder: $\pi x^2 + \pi x^2 + 6\pi x^2 = 8\pi x^2$. Since π has a value greater than 3, $8\pi x^2$ (Column A) obviously has a value much greater than $12x^2$ (Column B).

22. **B** Only three combinations will yield a total of 4: 3 and 1, 1 and 3, and 2 and 2. Four combinations will yield a total of 9: 3 and 6, 6 and 3, 4 and 5, 5 and 4. Therefore, the probability of obtaining a total of 9 is greater than the probability of obtaining a total of 4.

23. **A** If $y + 2x = 0$, then $y = -2x$. If $x > 0$ (that is, if x is positive), then $-2x < 0$ (since negative × positive = negative). Therefore, $2 > y$.

24. **A** You can work this one out the long way, but it's not really necessary. If 3 widgets cost as much as 2 doodads, then 4 widgets (Column B) must cost a little more than 2 doodads. If 3 whatsits cost as much as 5 doodads, then 2 whatsits (Column A) must cost a little less than 4 doodads. So Column A must be greater.

25. **B** The value of Column A is 3 (since $3a \div a = 3$). The value of Column B is greater than 3 (if $a > 1$, then $3a > 3$).

26. **D** To compare the average speeds, or rates, of the two trains, you need to know both the distance and the time traveled by each one. You know the time, but you don't know the distance. Therefore, you can't make the comparison.

27. **D** From $2n + 5 < 8$, you can deduce that $2n < 3$ and therefore that $n < 1\frac{1}{2}$. But from $n < 1\frac{1}{2}$, you can't deduce anything about the comparative values of n and 1; n may be greater than, equal to, or less than 1.

28. **C** Recall from geometry that the sum of the lengths of two sides of a triangle is greater than the length of the third side. Therefore, 8 + 3 must be greater than x ($8 + 3 > x$; $11 > x$) and $x + 3$ must be greater than 8 ($x + 3 > 8$; $x > 5$). Choice C expresses this range of possible values of x exactly: $5 < x < 11$.

29. **D** If $x/3 = 2$, then $x = 6$. If $x = 6$, then Statement III is true ($x - 3 = 3$), but Statement I is false ($2x \neq 0$). If $x = 6$ and $3xy = 0$, then $y = 0$. If $y = 0$, then Statement II is false ($y/3 \neq 6$).

30. **B** Right triangle ABC is the "standard" 5-12-13 triangle. Therefore, side AB, which is also the diameter of the semicircle, has a length of 12. If the diameter of the semicircle is 12, then its radius is 6 and its area is $\pi 6^2 \div 2 = 36\pi \div 2 = 18\pi$.

31. **E** To solve a work problem like this, remember that Laura's work + Karen's work = 1 (the whole job). To compute Laura's work, divide the length of time she'll be working with Karen ($3\frac{1}{3}$ hours) by the length of time it would take her to do the entire job by herself (6 hours):

$$3\frac{1}{3} \div 6 = \frac{10}{3} \times \frac{1}{6} = \frac{10}{18}$$

To compute Karen's work, do the same (let x stand for the length of time it would take her to do the entire job by herself):

$$3\frac{1}{3} \div x = \frac{10}{3} \times \frac{1}{x} = \frac{10}{3x}$$

Then just add the two together, set the sum equal to 1, and solve for x:

$$\frac{10}{18} + \frac{10}{3x} = 1$$

$$10x + 60 = 18x$$

$$60 = 8x$$

$$7\frac{1}{2} = x$$

32. **B** One way to solve this problem is to double the first equation and then subtract the second equation from it. (To subtract, change the sign of each term in the second equation and then add.) You'll get:

$$\begin{array}{rr} 2r + 6s = & 22 \\ + \; -2r + s = & -8 \\ \hline 7s = & 14 \end{array}$$

Therefore, $s = 2$.

33. **B** You know that the three angles add up to 180, so set up the equation and solve for n:

$$2n + 3n + n + 12 = 180$$
$$6n = 168$$
$$n = 28$$

34. **B** If $b/-4 = 1/2$, then $2b = -4$ and $b = -2$. If $b = -2$ and $3ab = 24$, then $3a(-2) = 24$, $-6a = 24$, and $a = -4$.

35. **D** You know that 200 units start the trip down the assembly line. Of these 200 units, 2/10, or 40, are discarded at point A, leaving 160 on the assembly line. Of these 160 units, 1/10, or 16, are discarded at point B, leaving 144 on the assembly line. Of these 144 units, 1/12, or 12, are discarded at point C, leaving 132 units on the assembly line. Thus, of the original 200 units, 68 are discarded at the three inspection points.

SECTION 5

1. **C** There's no antecedent for *it* in the sentence. *It* should be changed to *Spanish*.

2. **E** No error in this sentence.

3. **A** The sentence shifts illogically from *you* to *one*. Since *one* isn't underlined, it can't be changed, so the initial *you* would have to be changed to *one—if one hopes*.

4. **D** *Is still being* should be *is still*. The *being* is unnecessary and inappropriate.

5. **E** No error in this sentence.

6. **C** The past tense of *swim* is *swam*, not *swum*.

7. **B** *On*, not *in*, is used idiomatically with the verb *concentrate*.

8. **E** No error in this sentence.

9. **D** *Finalists* (plural) who need *pens and pencils* (plural) also need *wristwatches* (plural). A single *wristwatch* won't accommodate the group.

10. **A** The subject, *some,* is plural in this sentence, so the verb should also be plural (*wish*, not *wishes*).

11. **A** The pronoun *them* is being used here as part of a compound subject of the verb *agreed*. Therefore, it should be in the subjective case: *they*.

12. **E** No error in this sentence.

13. **D** *Forced curtailing* is unidiomatic; *forced to curtail* is idiomatic.

14. **E** No error in this sentence.

15. **E** No error in this sentence.

16. **D** For the sake of parallelism, all three objects of the preposition *for* should be in the same grammatical form: *limiting*, *eliminating*, and *encouraging* (not *the encouragement of*).

17. **A** The subjunctive mood is used idiomatically in if-clauses that express conditions contrary to fact. The clause should read, "If the earth *had* no atmosphere."

18. **C** The context requires *eminent*, which means "respected, well-known, prominent," not *imminent*, which means "impending, about to happen."

19. **D** *Rob* means "to steal *from*." Items of value are *stolen*, not *robbed*.

20. **D** The sentence begins in the simple present tense (*passes*) and then shifts needlessly into the present perfect tense (*has followed*). *Has followed* should be *follows*.

21. **B** The sentence shifts unnecessarily from *you* to *one*. *One* should be changed to *you*.

22. **D** *Everybody*, like all pronouns ending in *-body*, is singular. A singular subject demands a singular verb: *wants*, not *want*.

23. **D** The comparison in this sentence is faulty. A person's credentials can't be compared to *anyone else*; they must be compared to *anyone else's credentials*.

24. **C** *Had gave* is incorrect. *Had given* is correct.

25. **C** The future progressive tense is inappropriate here; *will be pouring* should be *are pouring*.

26. **B** *Because* serves as both the logical and the grammatical link between the two clauses in the sentence. A second conjunction (*so, and*) or conjunctive adverb (*therefore*) is superfluous. A comma is appropriate after an introductory dependent clause; a semicolon (choice C) is not.

27. **A** The original version of this sentence is clear, complete, correct, and consistent.

28. **D** The elements joined by *not only* and *but* should be parallel in form: *masterful thrillers, witty entertainments*, and *brilliantly conceived works of art*.

29. **B** Choices A and C are both fragments, choice E is wordy, and choice D unwisely omits the word *that*, which promotes clarity and prevents misreading.

30. **A** The original version of the sentence is best. Choice B yokes *adding* with *to build*, choice C is wordy, and choices D and E both sound awkward because they're not idiomatic.

31. **D** Only *because* makes sense in this sentence.

32. **C** The opening phrase in choices A, B, and D is a dangling modifier. Choice E is a run-on sentence.

33. **C** Choice A is incomplete (*calling* needs a helping verb); choice B is confusing; choice D uses a semicolon in place of a comma; and choice E, though concise and correct, alters the meaning of the original sentence.

34. **C** Of the five versions of the sentence, choice C is the most clear, concise, and graceful.

35. **C** Choices A and B are run-on sentences. Choice D is grammatically correct but illogical. Choice E is wordy.

36. **A** The original sentence is perfectly correct. In choice B, the opening phrase is a misplaced modifier. Choices C and E are wordy and awkward. Choice D is a fragment.

37. **B** Choice A is a run-on sentence, and choice E inappropriately uses a semicolon between an independent clause and a phrase. Of the remaining answers, all of which are grammatically correct, choice B is the most concise and therefore the best.

38. **A** The initial clauses in choices B and E are both incomplete (they contain no verb). The combination of *although* and *but* in choice D is redundant. Choice C is wordy.

39. **D** All five answers are clear and grammatically correct, but only choice D is concise.

40. **B** Choice A is a run-on, choice C is wordy, and choices D and E obscure the logical relationship between the two halves of the sentence.

41. **C** The plural verb *were* does not agree in number with the singular subject *everyone*. *Were* should be *was*.

42. **C** *Most strangest* is redundant. It should simply be *strangest*.

43. **C** *To cause* is unidiomatic after *responsible*. It should be *for causing*.

44. **B** An adverb (*completely*), not an adjective (*complete*), should be used to modify an adjective (*automated*).

45. **E** No error in this sentence.

46. **A** The pronoun *they* has no antecedent. Changing *Russia remains* to *the Russians remain* will supply one.

47. **E** No error in this sentence.

48. **C** *With*, not *to*, is used idiomatically with the phrase *in accordance*.

49. **C** *Already* indicates that the minds were made up *before* the arguments were heard, so the proper tense is the past perfect: *had already made up*.

50. **C** The subject of the sentence is *definition*, which is singular. So the verb should be the singular *has been devised*, not the plural *have been devised*.

SECTION 6

1. **B** *Bondage* means "slavery" or "captivity"; *emancipation* means "liberation" or "the act of setting free." Choices A, C, and E, though tempting, don't specifically and clearly relate to the act of freeing someone from bondage.

2. **B** To *flaunt* something is to display it in a showy and conspicuous fashion. By contrast, to *conceal* something is to hide it.

3. **A** *Dogged* means "persistent, stubborn, or determined." *Easily discouraged* is a reasonable antonym.

4. **D** To *sever* is to divide or separate; to *link* is to join or connect.

5. **E** Something *trite* is old hat, commonplace, or overfamiliar. Something *novel* is new, unusual, or modern.

6. **C** To *defile* something is to dirty it or sully it. To *purify* something is to clean it or make it pure.

7. **C** *Egregious* means "flagrant, outrageous, conspicuously bad": "The defense attorney dismissed the so-called 'expert' witness after exposing several *egregious* errors in his testimony." Though not an exact opposite, *not readily noticeable*, or *inconspicuous*, is fairly close.

8. **A** To *quell* something—such as a riot—is to calm it or bring it under control. To *instigate* something is to stir it up, arouse it, or initiate it. Bottle-throwing crowds may *instigate* a riot; the police may *quell* it.

9. **B** To *alienate* people is to drive them away or repel them. The opposite is to *attract* them.

10. **D** *Infamy* is shame or disgrace. *Honor* is a suitable antonym.

11. **D** To *glower* is to scowl or stare menacingly. To *beam*, on the other hand, is to wear an expression of happiness, friendliness, and good feeling.

12. **E** A *predilection* is a fondness, inclination, or preference for something. The opposite is a *distaste* or *dislike* for something.

13. **C** *Rejuvenate* means "to make young again" (the fountain of youth for which Ponce de Leon searched was supposed to *rejuvenate* old people). *Age*, which means "to make old" or "to cause to grow old," is a near opposite.

14. **D** As a verb, *pique* has two meanings: "to stimulate or arouse" (as in "*pique* one's curiosity") and "to annoy or irritate" (as in "*piqued* by their indifference"). *Please* is a good opposite for the second meaning.

15. **A** *Recondite* means "profound, abstruse, or difficult to understand" (modern physics is considered by some to be a *recondite* subject). *Obvious* is a good antonym.

16. **B** The first part of the sentence describes half of the job of philosophy; the second part describes the other—different but equally important—half. Since the second part refers to "the *imperfect* world we really inhabit," the first part, by contrast, should refer to an *ideal* world.

17. **C** The key word *unlike* introduces a contrast between American workers and Japanese workers. Only choice C completes the contrast. Choice A is wrong because the right to *quit* one's job doesn't conflict with the idea of a *guaranteed* lifetime position; the guarantee is given by the employer.

18. **B** The second half of the sentence is simply a positive restatement of the first half. Thus, if the episodes in *Beowulf* form "a clear progression," then they are not merely *random* (that is, in no particular order).

19. **E** The key word *although* signals a contrast. Since the second half of the sentence explains why Baldwin finds it hard to win elections, the first half of the sentence should explain why she might be expected to win them. Choices A, C, and E are all possibilities, but choice E is clearly the best. A *garrulous*, or talkative, politician

would not be likely to find campaigning difficult (choice A), and a politician with well-known views might very well be unpopular (choice C).

20. **A** Only choice A completes the sentence logically. Giving enormous publicity to an anchorman's change of wardrobe is silly and demonstrates the *absurdity* of television's claim to journalistic *seriousness*.

21. **D** Barton was nothing if not "strong and decisive"; in fact, she seems to have steamrollered her opposition in some cases, thus providing *overly* strong leadership. Each of the other weaknesses is mentioned in the passage.

22. **E** See paragraph 3: "Barton refused to consider" the reorganization of the Red Cross proposed by Boardman's group.

23. **A** As the last paragraph explains, Roosevelt's withdrawal of support from Barton turned her apparent triumph at the 1902 annual meeting into a crushing defeat.

24. **C** The expression *rally one's forces* means either "to revive one's spirits" or "to gather one's allies together for a common purpose." Paragraph 3 makes clear that the second meaning is intended here. Barton enlisted the support of her "friends" in order to defeat her "enemies" and secure her position as president of the Red Cross.

25. **C** The very first sentence of the passage sums up the author's opinion very clearly.

26. **B** Only choice B is both specific enough and broad enough to describe the purpose of the passage. Choices A and D incorrectly imply that the passage discusses only the advantages of photovoltaic cells. The topics referred to in choices C and E are mentioned in the passage, but only as subtopics, not as the main idea.

27. **A** It's clear from the discussion of costs in the passage that photovoltaic cells are not, at present, the "practical" choice for most energy requirements—even "in regions of abundant sunlight" (choice C). However, they do have at least one practical application—the powering of space satellites. So choice A is the best answer.

28. **D** Reread paragraph 2—in particular, the third sentence.

29. **E** Reread the last three sentences of paragraph 3. The "principal deterrent to widespread use of photovoltaic cells" is the high cost of achieving "near perfection" in the cells while they are being manufactured.

30. **C** The last sentence suggests that if present cost trends continue, photovoltaic cells may eventually become less costly than conventional power sources. For an author obviously enthusiastic about the exciting prospects of photovoltaic cells (see paragraph 1), such an eventuality augurs well for the future.

31. **D** The key word *although* signals a contrast. Since the first half of the sentence discusses the problem of "noxious fumes" in the Wall Street district during the workweek, it is logical to expect the second half to describe the area as relatively pollution-free on weekends.

32. **E** Since the sentence is about the correlation, or connection, between poverty and crime rates, the logical choice for the first blank is *economic*. Since the sentence states that there is *no* clear correlation, *higher* fits logically in the second blank.

33. **B** Only choice B includes two words that both support the description of a house that has "clearly seen better days."

34. **B** *Starvation* fits in with "malnourished millions." It also suggests something other than "human decisions."

35. **B** *Just as* and *so* indicate that the sentence is pointing out a similarity between a river and human nature. If human nature "remains basically the same despite changes," then a river must retain "its essential *form* while the drops of water that make it up are *ever-changing*."

36. **A** A *play* is usually divided into several *acts*, just as a *novel* is usually divided into several *chapters*.

37. **A** *Ephemeral* means "short-lived" and *longevity* means "long life," so something *ephemeral* lacks *longevity*. Similarly, *lugubrious* means "very sad or mournful" and *levity* means "gaiety," so someone *lugubrious* lacks *levity*. Something *timely*—that is, something that happens at a suitable time—may or may not lack *endurance* (choice B).

38. **C** A *hammer* is a tool used for pounding (metal) on an *anvil*; a *pestle* is a tool used for pounding (soft substances, such as herbs and spices) in a *mortar*.

39. **A** *Chuckling* is a sign of *amusement*; *smirking* is a sign of *self-satisfaction*.

40. **D** Just as a *throne* is a special kind of *chair* reserved for a king, queen, or other royal personage, so a *scepter* is a royal *staff*.

41. **E** To *repeal* an *amendment* is to cancel, revoke, abolish, or annul it officially. Similarly, to *abrogate* a *privilege* is to cancel it formally. To *cancel* a *check* (choice D) is not to revoke it, or call it back, but to mark it so that it cannot be cashed again.

42. **A** A *speaker* who is *laconic* uses few words and gets right to the point. An *author* who is *concise* does the same.

43. **C** A *wastrel* is someone who squanders money or other resources, like the Prodigal Son in the New Testament. Thus, a *wastrel* is someone who is *imprudent* (that is, reckless or wasteful). In the same way, a *miser* is someone who is *greedy*.

44. **E** One *decodes* a *cipher* (secret message) in order to reveal its meaning. One *interprets* an *omen* (a sign believed to portend a future event) for much the same reason.

45. **D** *Enervated* means "deprived of strength and vigor"; to *invigorate* someone who is *enervated* is to give that person strength and vigor. Similarly, *discouraged* means "deprived of courage and hope"; to *hearten* someone who is *discouraged* is to give that person courage and hope.

PART
9

Practice Test 5: Final Readiness Test

PRACTICE TEST 5: *Directions*

This practice test is your final readiness test. It is for you to take after you have analyzed your performance on Practice Test 4 and completed your final review for the SAT. Since this test is your "dress rehearsal" for the actual SAT, it is very important that you take it under strict exam conditions. Doing so not only will accustom you to the rigid time limits you'll be facing but also will help you build up the endurance and concentration you'll need on exam day. After you've completed the test, follow the instructions for scoring it on page 408. Then compare the results with your performance on Practice Test 1 (the pretest). If you have pursued your SAT study program diligently, your scores should reflect substantial improvement.

Directions: Set aside $3\frac{1}{2}$ hours without interruption for taking this test. The test is divided into six 30-minute sections. You may wish to use a timer or an alarm to time yourself on each section. Do not work past the 30-minute limit for any section. If you finish a section before time is up, you may check your work on that section, but you are <u>not to work on any other section</u>. You may take a 5-minute break between sections.

Do not worry if you are unable to finish a section or if there are some questions you cannot answer. Do not waste time puzzling over a question that seems too difficult for you. You should work as rapidly as you can without sacrificing accuracy.

Students often ask whether they should guess when they are uncertain about the answer to a question. Your test scores will be based on the number of questions you answer correctly minus a fraction of the number you answer incorrectly. Therefore, it is improbable that random or haphazard guessing will change your scores significantly. If you have some knowledge of a question, you may be able to eliminate one or more of the answer choices as wrong. It is generally to your advantage to guess which of the remaining choices is correct. Remember, however, not to spend too much time on any one question.

Mark all your answers on the answer sheet on the facing page. (For your convenience, you may wish to remove this sheet from the book and keep it in front of you throughout the test.) Mark only one answer for each question. Be sure that each mark is dark and that it completely fills the answer space. In each section of the answer sheet, there are 5 answer spaces for each of 50 questions. When there are fewer than 5 answer choices for a question or fewer than 50 questions in a section of your test, leave the extra answer spaces blank. Do not make stray marks on the answer sheet. If you erase, do so completely.

You may use any available space on the pages of the test for scratchwork. Do not use books, dictionaries, reference materials, calculators, slide rules, or any other aids. Do not look at the answer key or any other parts of this book. It is important to take this practice test in the same way that you will take the actual SAT.

When you have completed all six test sections, turn to the answers and scoring instructions that follow the test.

PRACTICE TEST 5: ***Answer Sheet***

Directions: Use a No. 2 pencil only for completing this answer sheet. Be sure each mark is dark and completely fills the intended space. Completely erase any errors or stray marks. Start with number 1 for each new section. If a section has fewer than 50 questions or if a question has fewer than 5 answer choices, leave the extra answer spaces blank.

	SECTION 1	SECTION 2	SECTION 3	SECTION 4
1	A B C D E	A B C D E	A B C D E	A B C D E
2	A B C D E	A B C D E	A B C D E	A B C D E
3	A B C D E	A B C D E	A B C D E	A B C D E
4	A B C D E	A B C D E	A B C D E	A B C D E
5	A B C D E	A B C D E	A B C D E	A B C D E
6	A B C D E	A B C D E	A B C D E	A B C D E
7	A B C D E	A B C D E	A B C D E	A B C D E
8	A B C D E	A B C D E	A B C D E	A B C D E
9	A B C D E	A B C D E	A B C D E	A B C D E
10	A B C D E	A B C D E	A B C D E	A B C D E
11	A B C D E	A B C D E	A B C D E	A B C D E
12	A B C D E	A B C D E	A B C D E	A B C D E
13	A B C D E	A B C D E	A B C D E	A B C D E
14	A B C D E	A B C D E	A B C D E	A B C D E
15	A B C D E	A B C D E	A B C D E	A B C D E
16	A B C D E	A B C D E	A B C D E	A B C D E
17	A B C D E	A B C D E	A B C D E	A B C D E
18	A B C D E	A B C D E	A B C D E	A B C D E
19	A B C D E	A B C D E	A B C D E	A B C D E
20	A B C D E	A B C D E	A B C D E	A B C D E
21	A B C D E	A B C D E	A B C D E	A B C D E
22	A B C D E	A B C D E	A B C D E	A B C D E
23	A B C D E	A B C D E	A B C D E	A B C D E
24	A B C D E	A B C D E	A B C D E	A B C D E
25	A B C D E	A B C D E	A B C D E	A B C D E
26	A B C D E	A B C D E	A B C D E	A B C D E
27	A B C D E	A B C D E	A B C D E	A B C D E
28	A B C D E	A B C D E	A B C D E	A B C D E
29	A B C D E	A B C D E	A B C D E	A B C D E
30	A B C D E	A B C D E	A B C D E	A B C D E
31	A B C D E	A B C D E	A B C D E	A B C D E
32	A B C D E	A B C D E	A B C D E	A B C D E
33	A B C D E	A B C D E	A B C D E	A B C D E
34	A B C D E	A B C D E	A B C D E	A B C D E
35	A B C D E	A B C D E	A B C D E	A B C D E
36	A B C D E	A B C D E	A B C D E	A B C D E
37	A B C D E	A B C D E	A B C D E	A B C D E
38	A B C D E	A B C D E	A B C D E	A B C D E
39	A B C D E	A B C D E	A B C D E	A B C D E
40	A B C D E	A B C D E	A B C D E	A B C D E
41	A B C D E	A B C D E	A B C D E	A B C D E
42	A B C D E	A B C D E	A B C D E	A B C D E
43	A B C D E	A B C D E	A B C D E	A B C D E
44	A B C D E	A B C D E	A B C D E	A B C D E
45	A B C D E	A B C D E	A B C D E	A B C D E
46	A B C D E	A B C D E	A B C D E	A B C D E
47	A B C D E	A B C D E	A B C D E	A B C D E
48	A B C D E	A B C D E	A B C D E	A B C D E
49	A B C D E	A B C D E	A B C D E	A B C D E
50	A B C D E	A B C D E	A B C D E	A B C D E

REMOVE ANSWER SHEET BY CUTTING ON DOTTED LINE

SECTION 5

1 (A) (B) (C) (D) (E)
2 (A) (B) (C) (D) (E)
3 (A) (B) (C) (D) (E)
4 (A) (B) (C) (D) (E)
5 (A) (B) (C) (D) (E)
6 (A) (B) (C) (D) (E)
7 (A) (B) (C) (D) (E)
8 (A) (B) (C) (D) (E)
9 (A) (B) (C) (D) (E)
10 (A) (B) (C) (D) (E)
11 (A) (B) (C) (D) (E)
12 (A) (B) (C) (D) (E)
13 (A) (B) (C) (D) (E)
14 (A) (B) (C) (D) (E)
15 (A) (B) (C) (D) (E)
16 (A) (B) (C) (D) (E)
17 (A) (B) (C) (D) (E)
18 (A) (B) (C) (D) (E)
19 (A) (B) (C) (D) (E)
20 (A) (B) (C) (D) (E)
21 (A) (B) (C) (D) (E)
22 (A) (B) (C) (D) (E)
23 (A) (B) (C) (D) (E)
24 (A) (B) (C) (D) (E)
25 (A) (B) (C) (D) (E)
26 (A) (B) (C) (D) (E)
27 (A) (B) (C) (D) (E)
28 (A) (B) (C) (D) (E)
29 (A) (B) (C) (D) (E)
30 (A) (B) (C) (D) (E)
31 (A) (B) (C) (D) (E)
32 (A) (B) (C) (D) (E)
33 (A) (B) (C) (D) (E)
34 (A) (B) (C) (D) (E)
35 (A) (B) (C) (D) (E)
36 (A) (B) (C) (D) (E)
37 (A) (B) (C) (D) (E)
38 (A) (B) (C) (D) (E)
39 (A) (B) (C) (D) (E)
40 (A) (B) (C) (D) (E)
41 (A) (B) (C) (D) (E)
42 (A) (B) (C) (D) (E)
43 (A) (B) (C) (D) (E)
44 (A) (B) (C) (D) (E)
45 (A) (B) (C) (D) (E)
46 (A) (B) (C) (D) (E)
47 (A) (B) (C) (D) (E)
48 (A) (B) (C) (D) (E)
49 (A) (B) (C) (D) (E)
50 (A) (B) (C) (D) (E)

SECTION 6

1 (A) (B) (C) (D) (E)
2 (A) (B) (C) (D) (E)
3 (A) (B) (C) (D) (E)
4 (A) (B) (C) (D) (E)
5 (A) (B) (C) (D) (E)
6 (A) (B) (C) (D) (E)
7 (A) (B) (C) (D) (E)
8 (A) (B) (C) (D) (E)
9 (A) (B) (C) (D) (E)
10 (A) (B) (C) (D) (E)
11 (A) (B) (C) (D) (E)
12 (A) (B) (C) (D) (E)
13 (A) (B) (C) (D) (E)
14 (A) (B) (C) (D) (E)
15 (A) (B) (C) (D) (E)
16 (A) (B) (C) (D) (E)
17 (A) (B) (C) (D) (E)
18 (A) (B) (C) (D) (E)
19 (A) (B) (C) (D) (E)
20 (A) (B) (C) (D) (E)
21 (A) (B) (C) (D) (E)
22 (A) (B) (C) (D) (E)
23 (A) (B) (C) (D) (E)
24 (A) (B) (C) (D) (E)
25 (A) (B) (C) (D) (E)
26 (A) (B) (C) (D) (E)
27 (A) (B) (C) (D) (E)
28 (A) (B) (C) (D) (E)
29 (A) (B) (C) (D) (E)
30 (A) (B) (C) (D) (E)
31 (A) (B) (C) (D) (E)
32 (A) (B) (C) (D) (E)
33 (A) (B) (C) (D) (E)
34 (A) (B) (C) (D) (E)
35 (A) (B) (C) (D) (E)
36 (A) (B) (C) (D) (E)
37 (A) (B) (C) (D) (E)
38 (A) (B) (C) (D) (E)
39 (A) (B) (C) (D) (E)
40 (A) (B) (C) (D) (E)
41 (A) (B) (C) (D) (E)
42 (A) (B) (C) (D) (E)
43 (A) (B) (C) (D) (E)
44 (A) (B) (C) (D) (E)
45 (A) (B) (C) (D) (E)
46 (A) (B) (C) (D) (E)
47 (A) (B) (C) (D) (E)
48 (A) (B) (C) (D) (E)
49 (A) (B) (C) (D) (E)
50 (A) (B) (C) (D) (E)

SECTION 1

Time—30 minutes

40 QUESTIONS

For each question in this section, choose the best answer and blacken the corresponding space on the answer sheet.

Each question below consists of a word in capital letters, followed by five lettered words or phrases. Choose the word or phrase that is most nearly opposite in meaning to the word in capital letters. Since some of the questions require you to distinguish fine shades of meaning, consider all the choices before deciding which is best.

Example:

GOOD: (A) sour (B) bad (C) red (D) hot (E) ugly

Ⓐ ● Ⓒ Ⓓ Ⓔ

1. ORNATE: (A) monochromatic (B) balding (C) severe (D) garish (E) brackish

2. IMMATURE: (A) in preparation (B) in excellent condition (C) subject to decay (D) intelligent and wise (E) fully developed

3. TEMPERANCE: (A) sloth (B) hospitality (C) dissipation (D) miserliness (E) callousness

4. VACILLATE: (A) make vulnerable (B) reach a firm decision (C) refuse allegiance (D) remain confident (E) affirm belief in

5. BANE: (A) source of benefit (B) abundant supply (C) highest point (D) chief virtue (E) heavy burden

6. SUNDRY: (A) contiguous (B) indescribable (C) numerous (D) identical (E) relative

7. DISPERSE: (A) incite (B) announce (C) seize (D) muster (E) touch

8. PROPAGATE: (A) uproot (B) soften (C) desert (D) saturate (E) prune

9. ANATHEMA: (A) fortitude (B) benediction (C) distinction (D) convalescence (E) rectitude

10. EQUANIMITY: (A) lassitude (B) terror (C) malignity (D) wrath (E) passion

Each sentence below has one or two blanks, each blank indicating that something has been omitted. Beneath the sentence are five lettered words or sets of words. Choose the word or set of words that best fits the meaning of the sentence as a whole.

Example:

Although its publicity has been ----, the film itself is intelligent, well-acted, handsomely produced, and altogether ----.

(A) tasteless..respectable (B) extensive..moderate (C) sophisticated..amateur (D) risqué..crude (E) perfect..spectacular

● Ⓑ Ⓒ Ⓓ Ⓔ

11. Reliance on income from a single crop has made the economies of many nations highly ----, for a drought or disease that destroyed the crop could ---- the entire country.

(A) competitive..harm
(B) vulnerable..impoverish
(C) unstable..affect
(D) efficient..weaken
(E) insecure..invigorate

12. The purpose of education is not to confirm our ---- but to challenge our assumptions, not to endorse our complacency but to encourage an attitude of ----.

(A) credentials..self-doubt
(B) beliefs..altruism
(C) suspicions..skepticism
(D) values..independence
(E) biases..self-questioning

13. Goldwyn used to say that family traits often skip a generation because he liked to believe that the qualities of his ---- grandfather were the ---- ones in his own personality.

(A) unlucky..prominent
(B) infamous..weaker
(C) talented..desirable
(D) renowned..dominant
(E) maternal..noticeable

GO ON TO THE NEXT PAGE

14. Although the political philosophy embodied in the electoral college no longer ----, the institution itself ----.

(A) endures..languishes
(B) obtains..declines
(C) prevails..persists
(D) offends..flourishes
(E) exists..adapts

15. Just as Walt Whitman is often regarded as the source of what is distinctly ---- in modern poetry, so Mark Twain is widely hailed as the ---- of modern American fiction.

(A) American..originator
(B) original..genius
(C) vivid..founder
(D) progressive..inventor
(E) nationalistic..father

Each question below consists of a related pair of words or phrases, followed by five lettered pairs of words or phrases. Select the lettered pair that best expresses a relationship similar to that expressed in the original pair.

Example:

YAWN:BOREDOM:: (A) dream:sleep (B) anger:madness (C) smile:amusement (D) face:expression (E) impatience:rebellion
Ⓐ Ⓑ ● Ⓓ Ⓔ

16. ENLARGE:IMAGE:: (A) amplify:sound (B) elongate:room (C) inflate:balloon (D) extend:deadline (E) nurture:infant

17. CONTRACT:RIDER:: (A) declaration:paragraph (B) constitution:amendment (C) bill:law (D) manifesto:clause (E) election:ballot

18. HAIRDO:COIFFURE:: (A) decoration:design (B) snapshot:sketch (C) painting:art (D) manicure:pedicure (E) cookery:cuisine

19. AUTONOMY:DEPENDENT::
(A) independence:democratic
(B) selfishness:helpless
(C) separation:proximate
(D) freedom:subservient
(E) liberty:egalitarian

20. BOVINE:COW:: (A) ursine:bear (B) reptilian:snake (C) canine:collie (D) equestrian:horses (E) feline:leopard

21. ABUNDANCE:PAUCITY:: (A) riches:greed (B) wealth:thrift (C) fertility:barrenness (D) supply:scarcity (E) amplitude:paltriness

22. BLOOD:TOURNIQUET:: (A) liquid:duct (B) river:bridge (C) water:dam (D) leg:splint (E) bottle:cap

23. FAÇADE:BUILDING:: (A) costume:masquerade (B) lobby:hotel (C) complexion:face (D) column:portico (E) veneer:furniture

24. TENSILE:STRETCH:: (A) civil:govern (B) nubile:domesticate (C) fragile:drop (D) docile:control (E) agile:mobilize

25. VENIAL:HEINOUS:: (A) lenient:clement (B) insignificant:grave (C) innocent:profane (D) modest:serious (E) justified:indictable

Each passage below is followed by questions based on its content. Answer all questions following a passage on the basis of what is stated or implied in that passage.

My own goal is to give practical advice to a translator, and I shall not the least concern myself with theories of translation as such. But I advise the translator *not* to try to create, "on the basis of the *Iliad*, a poem that shall affect our countrymen as the original may be conceived to have affected its natural hearers." This probably means merely that the translator should try to affect English-speaking readers powerfully, as Homer affected Greeks powerfully; but this direction is not enough and gives no real guidance. For all great poets affect their hearers powerfully, but the effect of one poet is one thing, that of another poet another thing; it is the translator's business to reproduce the effect of Homer. And the most powerful emotion of the unlearned English readers can never prove whether he has reproduced this or has produced something else.

Evidently the translator needs some more practical directions than these. No one can tell him how Homer affected the Greeks; but there are those who can tell him how Homer affects *them.* These are scholars who possess, along with knowledge of Greek, adequate poetic taste and feeling. No translation will seem to them of much worth compared with the original; but they alone can say whether the translation produces more or less the same effect upon them as the original.

They are the only competent judges in this matter. The Greeks are dead; the unlearned English reader has no data for judging; and no one can safely confide in his own single judgment of his own work. Let not the translator, then, trust to his own notions of what the ancient Greeks would have thought of him; he will lose himself in the vague. Let him not trust to what the ordinary English reader thinks of him; he will be taking the blind for his guide. Let him not trust to his own judgment of his own work; he may be misled by individual caprices. Let him ask how his work affects those who know Greek and can appreciate poetry—whether to read it gives the Provost of Eton, or a professor at Cambridge or at Oxford, at all the same feeling which to read the original gives them. I consider that when Bentley said of Pope's translation, "It was a pretty poem, but must not be called Homer," the work, in spite of all its power and attractiveness, was judged.

26. The author's remarks are addressed primarily to

(A) scholars of Greek
(B) English readers interested in the works of Homer
(C) those who wish to translate Homer into English
(D) literary critics
(E) those who have read Homer's works only in translation

27. The author of the passage probably considers the statement quoted in lines 4–7

(A) needlessly abstruse in its phrasing and vocabulary
(B) a striking explanation of his own theory of translation
(C) practical, but unrealistic, advice for the would-be translator
(D) a valid suggestion only in relation to the *Iliad*
(E) too vague to provide direction to the would-be translator

28. According to the passage, a competent judge of any translation of Homer should possess

I. knowledge of Homer's works in the original
II. skill in the art of translation
III. sensitivity to poetic style

(A) I only
(B) II only
(C) I and II only
(D) I and III only
(E) I, II, and III

29. The passage suggests that "he will be taking the blind for his guide" (lines 37–38) refers to the

(A) average reader's ignorance of Greek
(B) deplorable poetic taste of most readers
(C) vagueness of most readers' conception of ancient Greece
(D) capriciousness of most readers' literary preferences
(E) unpopularity of Homer among modern readers

30. It can be inferred from the passage that Bentley regarded Pope's translation of Homer as

(A) an unusually faithful version of Homer's poem
(B) a powerful and attractive poem
(C) close to Homer in style, though not in content
(D) likely to satisfy even a scholar in the classics
(E) lacking the spirit of the original work

GO ON TO THE NEXT PAGE

Some developing nations have already begun to earn more from sales of manufactured products. Between 1960 and 1978, developing countries as a whole raised earnings from the sale of manufactured goods from $8 billion to $64 billion. The shift to manufactured goods has a number of advantages for developing countries. It provides jobs for their landless unemployed, reduces their dependence upon the export of raw materials, and—because the prices of manufactured goods are more stable and markets increase more rapidly—it increases their total earnings.

However, it also has one major disadvantage. As developing nations gain larger shares of the markets for manufactured goods in industrialized countries, such as the United States, they threaten the domestic industries in those countries. Textiles from Taiwan, shoes from Korea, and leather products from Brazil, for example, are all in competition with American industries. In response to this challenge, the United States and other industrialized nations maintain high import taxes and other restrictions on products made in the developing world. These restrictions help to perpetuate a situation in which developing countries provide less than one-tenth of the world's exports of manufactured products even though they account for more than half of the world's population.

The greatest impediment to the expansion of manufactured exports by developing countries is not import taxes but "quantitative restrictions," which put ceilings on imports of manufactured goods into industrialized countries. The United States, for example, places such restrictions on a number of products, from color television sets to clothespins. While developing countries, with their low labor costs, can sometimes overcome the effects of high tariffs, they cannot escape the impact of quantitative restrictions.

Industrialized nations, then, are confronted by a dilemma. If they allow cheap manufactured imports into their countries, they risk the closing of some domestic industries, the loss of some jobs, and increased dependence on other countries. If they limit imports, they deprive their own consumers of low-cost goods and developing countries of improved export earnings.

31. The main point of the passage is that

(A) manufactured goods represent a dramatically increasing share of the exports of developing nations
(B) developing nations are in conflict with industrialized nations over the issue of manufactured imports
(C) the shift from exports of raw materials to exports of manufactured goods has benefited developing nations
(D) developing nations produce only a small fraction of the world's output of manufactured goods
(E) import taxes represent a restriction on the ability of developing nations to export manufactured goods

32. It can be inferred from the passage that one disadvantage faced by developing nations that rely on exports of raw materials for their income is the

(A) consistently low prices such materials command on the world market
(B) imposition of restrictions on imports of such goods by industrialized nations
(C) high prices demanded by industrialized nations for their own manufactured goods
(D) slow growth rate of the markets for such materials
(E) relatively small numbers of workers employed in the production of such materials

33. It can be inferred from the passage that industrialized nations limit imports of manufactured goods primarily in order to

(A) maintain the flow of raw materials needed from developing nations
(B) exclude merchandise of low quality
(C) protect competing industries in their own countries
(D) reduce their dependence on developing nations
(E) keep prices low for their own consumers

34. According to the passage, in comparison with the effects of high tariffs on developing nations, the effects of quantitative restrictions are

(A) more difficult, if not impossible, to surmount
(B) more unpredictable in the short run
(C) less justifiable from an ethical standpoint
(D) equally problematic
(E) less devastating in the long run

35. The passage implies that a lifting of all barriers to the import of manufactured goods from developing nations would probably result in all of the following EXCEPT

(A) higher unemployment rates in industrialized nations
(B) more stable economies in developing nations
(C) lower wage scales in developing nations
(D) the increased availability of lower-priced goods in industrialized nations
(E) greater job opportunities in developing nations

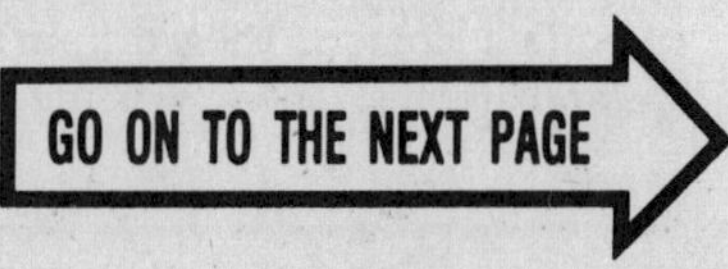

When I propose a certain policy, it is not enough that I do not intend anything evil in the result; it is incumbent on me to show that it has no tendency to that result. I have met Judge Douglas in that point of view. I have not only made the declaration that I do not mean to produce a conflict between the states, but I have tried to show by fair reasoning, and I think I have shown to the minds of fair men, that I propose nothing but what has a most peaceful tendency.

The statement that I happened to make in that Springfield speech, that "a house divided against itself cannot stand," and which has proved so offensive to Judge Douglas, was part and parcel of the same thing. He tries to show that variety in the institutions of the different states is necessary and indispensable. I do not dispute it. I have no controversy with Judge Douglas about that. I shall very readily agree with him that it would be foolish for us to insist upon having a cranberry law here, in Illinois, where we have no cranberries, because they have a cranberry law in Indiana, where they have cranberries. I should insist that it would be exceedingly wrong in us to deny to Virginia the right to enact oyster laws, where they have oysters, because we need no such laws here.

I understand, I hope, quite as well as Judge Douglas, or anybody else, that the variety in the soil and climate of the country, and consequent variety in the industrial pursuits of a country, require systems of laws conforming to this variety. I understand quite as well as Judge Douglas that if we here raise a barrel of flour more than we need, and the Louisianians raise a barrel of sugar more than they need, it is of mutual advantage to exchange. That produces commerce, brings us together, and makes us better friends. We like one another the more for it. And I understand as well as Judge Douglas, or anybody else, that these mutual accommodations are the cement which binds together the different parts of this nation; that instead of being a thing to "divide the house," they tend to sustain it; they are the props of the house tending to hold it up.

But when I have admitted all this, I ask if there is any parallel between these things and this institution of slavery. I do not see that there is any parallel at all between them. Consider it. When have we had any difficulty or quarrel amongst ourselves about the cranberry laws of Indiana, or the oyster laws of Virginia, or the pine-lumber laws of Maine, or the fact that Louisiana produces sugar, and Illinois flour? When have we had any quarrels over these things? But when have we had perfect peace in regard to this thing— this institution of slavery—which I say is an element of discord in this union?

36. The passage is most accurately described as

(A) a rebuttal of personal attacks on the author by Douglas
(B) an attempt to conciliate Douglas
(C) a defense of the author's opinions in response to objections by Douglas
(D) a demonstration that the author is truer to Douglas's principles than is Douglas himself
(E) an attempt to undercut the moral basis of Douglas's beliefs

37. It can be inferred from the passage that Douglas's defense of slavery is based on the premise that

(A) it helps enforce a spirit of unity among the states
(B) uniformity among states should be legally enforced
(C) it promotes trade among the states
(D) the majority of citizens favor it
(E) differences in natural conditions justify differences in institutions

38. The second and third paragraphs of the passage consist primarily of a

(A) series of concessions to the arguments of Douglas
(B) summary of the legal position held by Douglas
(C) delineation of areas of disagreement with Douglas
(D) disavowal of any real dispute with Douglas
(E) recantation of opinions once shared with Douglas

39. In the last paragraph of the passage, the author suggests that the analogy between cranberry laws and the institution of slavery is

(A) strictly logical
(B) without foundation
(C) a useful rhetorical device
(D) of limited applicability
(E) of debatable merit

40. The author's criticism of slavery is based primarily upon its

(A) promotion of discord among the states
(B) purely regional character
(C) moral indefensibility
(D) reliance upon physical force for its continuation
(E) tendency to reduce interstate travel

S T O P

IF YOU FINISH BEFORE TIME IS CALLED, YOU MAY CHECK YOUR WORK ON THIS SECTION ONLY. DO NOT WORK ON ANY OTHER SECTION IN THE TEST.

SECTION 2

Time—30 minutes

25 QUESTIONS

In this section solve each problem, using any available space on the page for scratchwork. Then indicate the one correct answer in the appropriate space on the answer sheet.

The following information is for your reference in solving some of the problems.

Circle of radius r: Area $= \pi r^2$; Circumference $= 2\pi r$
The number of degrees of arc in a circle is 360.
The measure in degrees of a straight angle is 180.

Definitions of symbols:

$=$	is equal to	$\leq$	is less than or equal to
$\neq$	is unequal to	$\geq$	is greater than or equal to
$<$	is less than	$\parallel$	is parallel to
$>$	is greater than	$\perp$	is perpendicular to

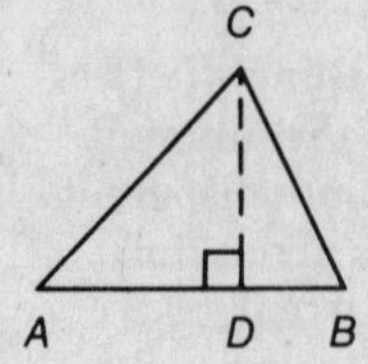

Triangle: The sum of the measures in degrees of the angles of a triangle is 180.

If $\angle CDA$ is a right angle, then

(1) area of $\triangle ABC = \frac{AB \times CD}{2}$

(2) $AC^2 = AD^2 + DC^2$

Note: Figures which accompany problems in this test are intended to provide information useful in solving the problems. They are drawn as accurately as possible EXCEPT when it is stated in a specific problem that its figure is not drawn to scale. All figures lie in a plane unless otherwise indicated. All numbers used are real numbers.

---

1. Which of the following numbers has the greatest value less than 0.01?

   (A) 0.09 (B) 0.05 (C) 0.009
   (D) 0.005 (E) 0.001

2. $(3^2)^2 + (2^3)^2 =$

   (A) 59 (B) 97 (C) 113 (D) 145 (E) 164

3. A drawer contains six black socks and eight white socks, all identical except in color. What is the least number of socks that a blindfolded person would have to take from the drawer to be sure of selecting at least one matching pair of socks?

   (A) 2 (B) 3 (C) 4 (D) 5 (E) 7

4. The decimal 0.83146 is closest in value to which of the following fractions?

   (A) $\frac{2}{3}$ (B) $\frac{3}{4}$ (C) $\frac{4}{5}$ (D) $\frac{5}{6}$ (E) $\frac{6}{7}$

5. If $x^2 + 11 = 9 \times 4 \times 5$, then $x =$

   (A) 12 (B) 13 (C) 14 (D) 15 (E) 16

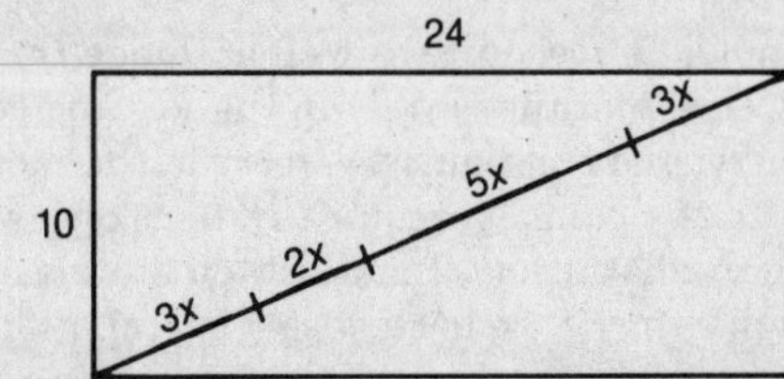

6. The diagonal of the rectangle above is divided into four segments with lengths as shown. What is the length of the longest segment of the diagonal?

   (A) 10 (B) 12 (C) 13.5 (D) 15 (E) 16.5

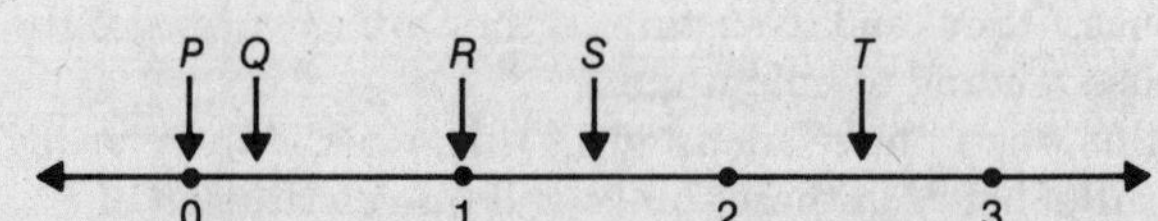

7. The values of numbers P, Q, R, S, and T are shown on the number line above. Which of the following expressions has the greatest value?

   (A) $Q \times T$ (B) $R \times S$ (C) $P \times S$
   (D) $Q \times S$ (E) $P \times R$

GO ON TO THE NEXT PAGE

8. In a certain school, a total of 59 students take economics, a total of 42 students take astronomy, and a total of 36 students take calculus. Nine students take economics and astronomy but not calculus; 7 students take economics and calculus but not astronomy; 5 students take astronomy and calculus but not economics; and 4 students take all three courses. What is the smallest possible number of students in the school?

(A) 101 (B) 108 (C) 116
(D) 129 (E) 137

9. A rectangular room has a perimeter of 28. What is the greatest possible area of the room?

(A) 49 (B) 48 (C) 45 (D) 40 (E) 33

10. If x is 2 more than y, and y is 5 less than z, and $z = 4$, then $xyz =$

(A) 4 (B) 1 (C) 0 (D) -4 (E) -8

11. For all real numbers m and n, let $m \wedge n$ be defined as $m(m + n)(m - n)$. What is the value of $3 \wedge 5$?

(A) 36 (B) 24 (C) 18 (D) 0 (E) -48

12. Coins are available in 1¢, 5¢, 10¢, and 25¢ denominations. How many different sums of money can be obtained by combining any two coins?

(A) 8 (B) 9 (C) 10 (D) 11 (E) 12

13. City 1 and City 2 lie 390 miles apart on a railroad line. At 11:00 A.M., a train leaves City 1 and travels at a rate of 48 miles per hour on one track toward City 2. At 12:15 P.M. the same day, a train leaves City 2 and travels at a rate of 62 miles per hour on a second track toward City 1. At what time will the two trains pass one another?

(A) 2:30 P.M. (B) 2:48 P.M. (C) 3:03 P.M.
(D) 3:15 P.M. (E) 3:30 P.M.

14. If $\frac{2}{7} + \frac{5}{14} + \frac{x}{14} = 1$, then $x =$

(A) 5 (B) 4 (C) 3 (D) 2 (E) 1

15. If it costs j dollars to fill the gas tank of a car that holds k gallons of gas, how much, in terms of j and k, will 20 gallons of gas cost?

(A) $\frac{j}{20k}$ (B) $\frac{20j}{k}$ (C) $20jk$ (D) $\frac{jk}{20}$ (E) $\frac{20}{jk}$

16. How much more will an investment of \$300 at 11% simple interest yield over a one-year period than an investment of \$400 at $7\frac{1}{2}$% simple interest over the same period?

(A) \$1.90 (B) \$2.25 (C) \$2.40
(D) \$2.70 (E) \$3.00

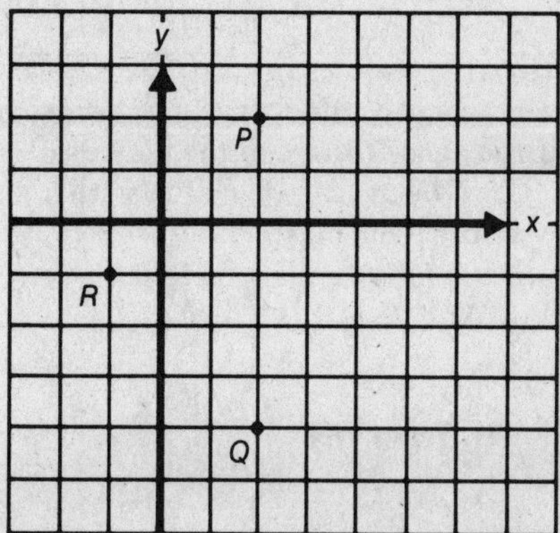

17. A circle is to be drawn on the grid above. If the circle passes through points $P(2, 2)$, $Q(2, -4)$, and $R(-1, -1)$, which of the following CANNOT be the length of a line drawn between two points on the circle?

(A) 2.0 (B) 2.1 (C) 5.4 (D) 6.0 (E) 6.4

GO ON TO THE NEXT PAGE

18. Of six houses on a certain street, House A is older than House D, House C is older than House A, House B is older than House E, House F is older than House C, and House E is older than House F. The newest of the six houses is House

(A) A (B) B (C) C (D) D (E) E

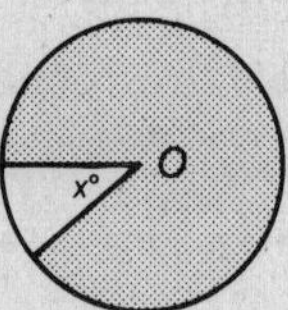

19. Circle O above has radius 3. If the area of the shaded region is 8π, then $x =$

(A) 60 (B) 51 (C) 45 (D) 42 (E) 40

20. The average age of nine players on a baseball team is 27. If the ages of three of the players are 39, 37, and 35, then the average age of the other six players on the team must be

(A) 20 (B) 21 (C) 22 (D) 23 (E) 24

21. If $a = 7$ and $b = 5$, then $\dfrac{(a+b)(a-b)}{2} =$

(A) 5 (B) 7 (C) 12 (D) 24 (E) $\dfrac{35}{2}$

22. A certain carton holds four cylindrical cans, each 6 inches tall and 3 inches across. What is the total volume in cubic inches of the four cans in the carton?

(A) 24π (B) 36π (C) 48π
(D) 54π (E) 72π

23. If x and y are consecutive positive integers such that $\dfrac{3x}{2} < y$, then which of the following is a possible set of values for x, y?

(A) 1, 2 (B) 2, 3 (C) 3, 4
(D) 4, 5 (E) 5, 6

1	2	3
4	5	6
7	8	9
*	0	#

24. The figure above shows the location of digits on the dial of a push-button telephone. Which of the following telephone numbers can be entered only with buttons that fall in the same straight line?

(A) 882–5006 (B) 537–3575 (C) 870–9898
(D) 951–5190 (E) 396–9326

25. If $ab \neq 0$, then $\left(\dfrac{a^4b^3}{a^2b^2}\right)^3 =$

(A) a^5b^4 (B) a^6b^3 (C) a^5b^3
(D) a^2b^5 (E) a^3b^3

S T O P

IF YOU FINISH BEFORE TIME IS CALLED, YOU MAY CHECK YOUR WORK ON THIS SECTION ONLY. DO NOT WORK ON ANY OTHER SECTION IN THE TEST.

SECTION 3

Time—30 minutes

45 QUESTIONS

For each question in this section, choose the best answer and blacken the corresponding space on the answer sheet.

Each question below consists of a word in capital letters, followed by five lettered words or phrases. Choose the word or phrase that is most nearly opposite in meaning to the word in capital letters. Since some of the questions require you to distinguish fine shades of meaning, consider all the choices before deciding which is best.

Example:

GOOD: (A) sour (B) bad (C) red (D) hot (E) ugly

Ⓐ ● Ⓒ Ⓓ Ⓔ

1. PERPETUAL: (A) passé (B) deceased (C) motionless (D) versatile (E) fleeting

2. SPURN: (A) begrudge (B) persist (C) inject (D) embrace (E) praise

3. VALIANT: (A) modest (B) despicable (C) diminutive (D) ill-favored (E) timorous

4. UNTENABLE: (A) stable (B) competent (C) defensible (D) occupied (E) frangible

5. DEPRECIATE: (A) repair (B) inveigle (C) overrate (D) intensify (E) despoil

6. BRUSQUE: (A) serious (B) gay (C) alluring (D) talkative (E) congenial

7. ASSIDUOUS: (A) casual (B) slothful (C) unintentional (D) nominal (E) slow

8. KINDRED: (A) orphaned (B) alien (C) simulated (D) paternal (E) disjointed

9. MITIGATE: (A) exacerbate (B) sanction (C) postpone (D) retain (E) commend

10. MOOT: (A) illegal (B) unarguable (C) digressive (D) valid (E) formative

11. SPURIOUS: (A) inappropriate (B) complimentary (C) genuine (D) mild (E) impetuous

12. CURSORY: (A) considerable (B) laudatory (C) repeated (D) exhaustive (E) monotonous

13. STULTIFYING: (A) enervating (B) astonishing (C) encouraging (D) mortifying (E) disquieting

14. EXTIRPATE: (A) extend (B) nurture (C) predominate (D) broadcast (E) infuse

15. PENURY: (A) wealth (B) generosity (C) fame (D) grandiosity (E) nobility

Each sentence below has one or two blanks, each blank indicating that something has been omitted. Beneath the sentence are five lettered words or sets of words. Choose the word or set of words that best fits the meaning of the sentence as a whole.

Example:

Although its publicity has been ----, the film itself is intelligent, well-acted, handsomely produced, and altogether ----.

(A) tasteless..respectable (B) extensive..moderate (C) sophisticated..amateur (D) risqué..crude (E) perfect..spectacular

16. Like a man wandering unguided through a labyrinth, Carling found himself increasingly ---- as the lecture continued.

(A) depressed (B) homesick (C) weary (D) irritated (E) perplexed

17. Theories of "national character" are notoriously ----: different commentators ascribe ---- characteristics to people of the very same country.

(A) misleading..numerous
(B) vague..several
(C) variable..common
(D) accurate..similar
(E) subjective..opposite

18. Convinced that no legal principle is more valuable than human ----, the governor has resolved that his primary aim in the hostage negotiations will be the avoidance of ----.

(A) feelings..publicity
(B) dignity..lawlessness
(C) existence..capitulation
(D) belief..violence
(E) life..bloodshed

19. If the purpose of education is primarily practical, then practical skills should be emphasized; but if the goal of education is a more ---- individual, then an appreciation of the fine arts deserves a ---- place in the curriculum.

(A) cultured..prominent
(B) moral..definite
(C) professional..minor
(D) creative..modest
(E) well-adjusted..vital

GO ON TO THE NEXT PAGE

20. Since Western culture has been profoundly ---- by the works and ideas of civilizations from around the world, it cannot be said to have a truly ---- existence.

(A) criticized..objective
(B) influenced..meaningful
(C) enriched..independent
(D) undermined..substantial
(E) affected..continuous

Each passage below is followed by questions based on its content. Answer all questions following a passage on the basis of what is stated or implied in that passage.

Our rulers have devised a number of artful phrases, by which they contrive, in the same breath, to give and take away the right of free discussion, and which, as often as they wish to punish a writer who opposes them, they use to beg the question in their favor. One of these phrases is the well-known profession that they favor the *liberty* of the press, but oppose its *license*.

Let us examine what this means. The liberty of the press, we are told, is good; that is, discussion, if not in all cases, at any rate in some cases, ought to be free. But the license of the press, it seems, is an evil; which must mean that there are certain other cases in which discussion ought not to be free. But what cases? Of this we are not informed; for the word *license*, far from explaining the distinction, is merely a vague term of blame. Their meaning, therefore, must be that *they* are to judge what is the liberty of the press and what is license. But this is to have the whole power of choosing opinions for the people. Allow them to decide what is or is not license, and everything will be license which implies censure of themselves or involves any doctrine hostile to the indefinite increase and perpetual duration of their power.

21. It can be inferred from the passage that the author considers the distinction between *liberty* and *license* to be

(A) an excessively subtle one
(B) one that is commonly misunderstood
(C) a subterfuge used to justify repression of freedom
(D) a valid one that has been misused by political leaders
(E) crucial to an understanding of freedom of the press

22. The passage implies that the author favors freedom of the press

(A) under all circumstances
(B) as long as that liberty is not abused
(C) only in connection with discussion of public affairs
(D) subject to popular approval
(E) except in certain clearly defined cases

23. It can be inferred that the author considers freedom of the press important especially as a means of

(A) ensuring the stability of political institutions
(B) disseminating statements of official policy
(C) providing popular education and entertainment
(D) limiting the power of governmental officials
(E) encouraging unanimity in public opinion

The strength of the film lay in its own ingenuity and invention. And this in every instance originated in the direct line of entertaining the cinema's large and avid public. A generation of filmmakers grew up whose essential vision belonged to no other medium than that of the cinema, and whose public was a universal audience spread across the world. Like the first dramas of Shakespeare, their art was not a product of the *salon*, but of the common playhouse. This is what gave them their strength and freshness.

However, there has always been a price to be paid. The *salon* artist has only a known patron, or group of patrons, to satisfy, and if he is strong enough he can, like the painters of the Renaissance, mould their taste in the image of his own. This can also be true of the greater and more resolute artists of the cinema, from Chaplin in the nineteen-twenties to, say, Bergman or Antonioni today. But the larger the dimension of the public and the more costly the medium to produce, the greater are the pressures brought to bear on the less conventional creator to make his work conform to the pattern of the more conventional creator.

24. According to the passage, the pressures to conform that a filmmaker experiences are in proportion to the

(A) difficulty of finding the support of a patron
(B) cost of producing a film
(C) conservatism of the viewing audience
(D) personal talents of the filmmaker
(E) diversity of the filmgoing public

25. The reference in the passage to the dramas of Shakespeare is intended to emphasize certain filmmakers'

(A) awareness of the role of film as a profit-making enterprise
(B) strength of personality and artistic convictions
(C) independence from the restrictions of other art forms
(D) access to a large and avid audience
(E) plebeian family backgrounds and social origins

GO ON TO THE NEXT PAGE

26. The author refers to the films of Bergman and Antonioni primarily because they are

(A) unconventional
(B) ingenious
(C) satisfying
(D) popular
(E) well crafted

All natural chemical substances found on land occur in some form in the sea, and chemical oceanographers have learned to study a great variety of these substances for an equally varied number of reasons. One relatively new reason for studying certain chemicals in the sea is to learn how these are used by fish, lobsters, and other organisms to establish territorial rights, find food, mate, and carry on their other normal patterns of behavior. The behavior of an organism in response to chemical agents in its environment is called *chemotaxis*.

To understand the influence of very dilute chemicals on communication among marine animals, chemical oceanographers must do a great deal of basic work identifying sensory systems and defining their biological functions. For example, does a particular animal have a sense of smell? How does it work? Is it used to find a mate, food, or home territory? What chemicals does the animal respond to, and where do they come from?

To date, chemical oceanographers have done research on catfish, lobsters, alewives, and snails because of their well-developed senses of smell and taste. The research has included studies of the effects of pollutants on the chemical senses of some of the animals. In one experiment, small amounts of crude oil, kerosene, and other petroleum products were placed in aquariums. The kerosene caused small communities of lobsters to show increased anxiety and antagonistic behavior. The crude oil made them lose their appetites. Other fish, too, were found to be sensitive to the effects of pollutants.

Another program showing the importance of dilute chemicals in the ocean is a survey of the distribution of chlorinated hydrocarbons, such as those found in plasticizers and certain pesticides, in marine organisms of the open ocean. When plankton from the North Atlantic were analyzed, they were found to contain high levels of these substances in their fat. However, it did not appear that animals eating these plankton had concentrated the substances to still higher levels.

27. The passage implies that pollution of ocean waters with crude oil could ultimately result in

(A) sensory confusion among catfish
(B) the destruction of communities of lobsters
(C) a buildup of pollutants in the bodies of plankton
(D) aggressive behavior among some species of snails
(E) unhealthy conditions for certain marine plant life

28. The passage states that animals such as the catfish have been studied largely because of their

(A) acute sensory powers
(B) biological importance
(C) territorial behavior
(D) widely scattered habitats
(E) ease of identification

29. According to the passage, the studies of chlorinated hydrocarbons have focused on

(A) the effects of those substances on the health of marine animals
(B) the response to those substances by the smell and taste organs of marine animals
(C) the harmful effects of those substances on animal communication
(D) the distribution of those substances in marine organisms of the North Atlantic
(E) the influence of those substances on the mating behavior of certain species

30. Which of the following titles best expresses the content of the passage?

(A) New Information on the Dangers of Ocean Pollution
(B) How Chemical Oceanographers Developed the Concept of Chemotaxis
(C) Comparing the Sensory Functions of Various Ocean Creatures
(D) Recent Studies of the Effects of Chemicals on Marine Animals
(E) How Chemicals Can Be Used to Control Animal Behavior

Select the word or set of words that <u>best</u> completes each of the following sentences.

31. The pastoral playing field, the nineteenth-century uniforms, and the archaic rules make baseball the most ---- of American sports.

(A) lucrative (B) colorful (C) traditional (D) exciting (E) enduring

32. Unlike Picasso and Braque, who were widely ---- during their lifetimes, Juan Gris did not receive the attention his works merited until after his ----.

(A) acclaimed..death
(B) recognized..contemporaries
(C) attacked..career
(D) ignored..lifetime
(E) praised..emigration

GO ON TO THE NEXT PAGE

33. Despite the ---- of art historians and museum curators, the condition of much pre-Columbian art continues to ----.

(A) work..delight
(B) alarm..improve
(C) concern..change
(D) indifference..worsen
(E) efforts..deteriorate

34. Most polls predicted that Dwyer would win the upcoming election; nonetheless, her opponent remained ----.

(A) obstinate (B) unappeased (C) active (D) pessimistic (E) hopeful

35. A clear majority of those on the committee favored Diaz for the scholarship, but those who ---- remained ---- in their opinion.

(A) wavered..impartial
(B) disagreed..steadfast
(C) concurred..hesitant
(D) differed..uncertain
(E) hesitated..definite

Each question below consists of a related pair of words or phrases, followed by five lettered pairs of words or phrases. Select the lettered pair that best expresses a relationship similar to that expressed in the original pair.

Example:

YAWN:BOREDOM:: (A) dream:sleep (B) anger:madness (C) smile:amusement (D) face:expression (E) impatience:rebellion

Ⓐ Ⓑ ● Ⓓ Ⓔ

36. BANK:VAULT:: (A) prison:bar (B) castle:keep (C) hotel:room (D) office:cubicle (E) monastery:cell

37. MANACLE:FETTER::
(A) straightjacket:isolate
(B) goad:prod
(C) bracelet:clasp
(D) wrist:restrain
(E) book:bind

38. INDEX:ALPHABETICAL::
(A) almanac:scientific
(B) gazeteer:geographical
(C) encyclopedia:voluminous
(D) timeline:chronological
(E) thesaurus:educational

39. GROVEL:BOW:: (A) gambol:play (B) acquiesce:agree (C) jabber:joke (D) fawn:praise (E) sneer:smile

40. BASE:NOBILITY:: (A) craven:bravery (B) sullen:gloom (C) democratic:aristocracy (D) rude:customs (E) frank:honesty

41. DIGRESSIVE:SPEECH::
(A) wandering:walk
(B) explanatory:lecture
(C) articulate:prose
(D) incomplete:comment
(E) unclear:pronunciation

42. UNIVERSITY:MATRICULATE::
(A) school:graduate
(B) college:apply
(C) club:participate
(D) army:enlist
(E) subject:study

43. LECTURE:HARANGUE:: (A) discussion:debate (B) sermon:commentary (C) vitriol:venom (D) speech:oration (E) criticism:abuse

44. CORRUPTION:MUCKRAKER::
(A) swindle:scalawag
(B) salvation:redeemer
(C) ungodliness:agnostic
(D) lust:lecher
(E) news:journalist

45. WATER:CHANNEL:: (A) earth:rampart (B) river:canal (C) lake:dam (D) shrubbery:hedge (E) land:isthmus

STOP

IF YOU FINISH BEFORE TIME IS CALLED, YOU MAY CHECK YOUR WORK ON THIS SECTION ONLY. DO NOT WORK ON ANY OTHER SECTION IN THE TEST.

SECTION 4

Time—30 minutes

50 QUESTIONS

The questions in this section measure skills that are important to writing well. In particular, they test your ability to recognize and use language that is clear, effective, and correct according to the requirements of standard written English, the kind of English found in most college textbooks.

Directions: The following sentences contain problems in grammar, usage, diction (choice of words), and idiom.

Some sentences are correct.
No sentence contains more than one error.

You will find that the error, if there is one, is underlined and lettered. Assume that elements of the sentence that are not underlined are correct and cannot be changed. In choosing answers, follow the requirements of standard written English.

If there is an error, select the one underlined part that must be changed to make the sentence correct and blacken the corresponding space on your answer sheet.

If there is no error, blacken answer space Ⓔ.

EXAMPLE:

The region has a climate so severe that plants
A
growing there rarely had been more than twelve
B C
inches high. No error
D E

SAMPLE ANSWER

Ⓐ Ⓑ ● Ⓓ Ⓔ

1. The paper used in the printing of early books was
so free of harmful acids that many of those volumes
A B
are still in beautiful condition despite their great
C D
age. No error
E

2. The implications of the recently announced
A
reorganization of the state health department has
B
yet to be fully understood. No error
C D E

3. Historical textbooks all too often make it appear a
A B C
dry, uninteresting discipline rather than the vital
D
subject it really is. No error
E

4. Irregardless of the club's financial status, no
A B
further fund-raising activities will be conducted
C D
this year. No error
E

5. Because Americans are continually developing a
A
taste for new food products and losing their taste
B
for old ones, patterns of food consumption are in a
C
slow but constant state of flux. No error
D E

GO ON TO THE NEXT PAGE

6. In the thick autumn mist, the bells of the church
A
clanged dull, sounding more like a death knell than
B C D
a call to celebration. No error
E

7. Unrecognized to many in the stadium, the lanky
A B
young right-hander set to work on what proved to
C D
be a masterful pitching performance. No error
E

8. As the success of Japanese industry has shown,
A B
effective quality control strategies are usually not

imposed from the top by management but

will be generated from below by the workers
C
themselves. No error
D E

9. Like children the world over do, young Africans
A
play games with marbles, balls, sticks, and other
B
simple toys that can be fashioned easily from
C D
available materials. No error
E

10. The three sisters shared an unusual talent for
A
mathematics, and her college plans were developed
B C
accordingly. No error
D E

11. The committee on commemorative postage stamps
A
has chosen dedicating the first stamp issue
B
of the year to a well-known novelist, William
C D
Worthington. No error
E

12. Many political analysts have urged that the
A
primary election season is shortened drastically
B
or even reduced to a single day. No error
C D E

13. You may find my theory concerning the authorship
A B
of those poems surprising, but I believe one will
C
be convinced by the evidence I present below.
D
No error
E

14. The time has long since past when an inspired
A
amateur working with simple tools could come up
B C
with findings of genuine scientific importance.
D
No error
E

15. Many critics of the media contend that the gravest
A B C
danger to freedom of the press today lies in the
D
enormous costs of modern publishing. No error
E

16. Although the injury probably prevented Alcock
A
from winning the gold medal, she still ran
B
good enough to finish in third place, just behind her
C D
teammate Sheila O'Brien. No error
E

17. If a water-soluble paint is used, you will be able
A
to clean your brushes easily with soap and water
B C
when you finish. No error
D E

18. If the election were held today, according to the
A B
latest poll, Governor Maisel would win reelection
C
by a comfortable margin. No error
D E

19. Norman Mailer is one of those authors

who achieves a phenomenal early success that they
A B C
never quite succeed in equaling later. No error
D E

GO ON TO THE NEXT PAGE

20. Historians agree that (A) the German generals would have altered (B) their codes more quickly if they knew (C) that the Allies had cracked them. (D) No error (E)

21. In despite of (A) the inclement (B) weather, the launch of the space shuttle went off (C) according to (D) schedule. No error (E)

22. The parchment on which (A) the old map was drawn seemed (B) genuine, but something (C) about the faded lettering looked strangely (D) to Jesperson's trained eyes. No error (E)

23. Creative ingenuity and (A) organizational talent are distinct (B) skills necessary for the construction of (C) an industrial empire; in Thomas Edison, those skills (D) were combined. No error (E)

24. Before leaving, (A) the librarian or one of her assistants return (B) each of the books (C) to its (D) proper place. No error (E)

25. The truth is that us (A) citizens place a higher (B) priority on that issue than either he (C) or the governor does. (D) No error (E)

Directions: In each of the following sentences, some part or all of the sentence is underlined. Below each sentence you will find five ways of phrasing the underlined part. Select the answer that produces the most effective sentence, one that is clear and exact, without awkwardness or ambiguity, and blacken the corresponding space on your answer sheet. In choosing answers, follow the requirements of standard written English. Choose the answer that best expresses the meaning of the original sentence.

Answer (A) is always the same as the underlined part. Choose answer (A) if you think the original sentence needs no revision.

EXAMPLE:

Laura Ingalls Wilder published her first book and she was sixty-five years old then.

(A) and she was sixty-five years old then
(B) when she was sixty-five years old
(C) at age sixty-five years old
(D) upon reaching sixty-five years
(E) at the time when she was sixty-five

SAMPLE ANSWER

26. Despite the growing problem of illiteracy in this country, yet funds for education have been cut.

(A) country, yet funds for education have been cut
(B) country, nevertheless there have been cuts in funds for education
(C) country, funds for education have been cut
(D) country, they have cut funds for education
(E) country; funds have been cut for education

27. The Russian people have a long history of being invaded, therefore, they fully understand the devastation of war.

(A) invaded, therefore, they fully understand
(B) invaded; as a result, they fully understand
(C) invaded, although they fully understand
(D) invaded; therefore their understanding is full of
(E) invaded and fully understanding

GO ON TO THE NEXT PAGE

28. In the early days of a new industry, many companies are founded that eventually will be absorbed as the industry achieves its maturation.

(A) as the industry achieves its maturation
(B) in the mature phase of the industry
(C) as the industry matures
(D) during the industry's period of maturity
(E) in the maturation of the industry

29. Contrary to popular belief, the wonderful pageantry of the British monarchy is of recent, not ancient, origin.

(A) is of recent, not ancient, origin
(B) is far from ancient but is mainly from recent times
(C) being mainly of recent origin is hardly ancient
(D) not ancient is of mainly recent origin
(E) is mainly not ancient but instead is recent in its origin

30. If the rains persist, the groundkeepers will cover the infield, close off the dugouts, and the drains in the outfield will be opened by them.

(A) the drains in the outfield will be opened by them
(B) opening the outfield drains
(C) they will open the outfield drains
(D) open the drains in the outfield
(E) will open the drains in the outfield

31. Some primitive people who do not read or write have the ability needed to be capable of memorizing thousands of verses of poetry.

(A) have the ability needed to be capable of memorizing
(B) are able to memorize
(C) are capable of the memorization of
(D) have the ability to memorize
(E) are known to memorize

32. With the drop in the school-age population, some schools are shutting down, and others curtailing services.

(A) others curtailing services
(B) some curtailing their services
(C) others are curtailing services
(D) services are being curtailed by others
(E) others curtail services

33. Known as the "First Folio," the oldest book containing all of Shakespeare's plays was published in 1623.

(A) the oldest book containing all of Shakespeare's plays was
(B) all of Shakespeare's plays are contained in the oldest book
(C) it is the oldest book that contains all of Shakespeare's plays, which were
(D) and the oldest book to contain all of Shakespeare's plays, it was
(E) Shakespeare's oldest book, which contains all of his plays, was

34. According to Henry David Thoreau, the reason a majority is allowed to rule is not that it is more likely to be right, but because it is stronger.

(A) but because it is stronger
(B) but that it is stronger
(C) but it is stronger
(D) but stronger
(E) it is stronger

35. If the news of Kennedy's death was announced, many people openly wept.

(A) If
(B) Hearing
(C) Unless
(D) Although
(E) When

36. Cartography, the science of mapmaking, is an ancient science that has been revolutionized by the impact of the effects of the space age.

(A) by the impact of the effects of the space age
(B) under the influence of the space age
(C) due to the coming of the space age
(D) in terms of space-age effects
(E) by the space age

37. Until the practice was forbidden by the government, nineteenth-century postmasters often used fancifully shaped ink blocks to cancel stamps.

(A) Until the practice was forbidden by the government,
(B) The practice being forbidden by the government,
(C) Since the government had forbidden it,
(D) Until they were forbidden by the government,
(E) Not being forbidden by the government,

38. Gazing out across the bay, Sarah's life seemed to appear clearly before her for the first time.

(A) Sarah's life seemed to appear clearly before her
(B) her life seemed to appear clearly before Sarah
(C) Sarah seemed to see her life clearly
(D) life seemed to Sarah to clearly appear
(E) Sarah clearly seemed to see before her life

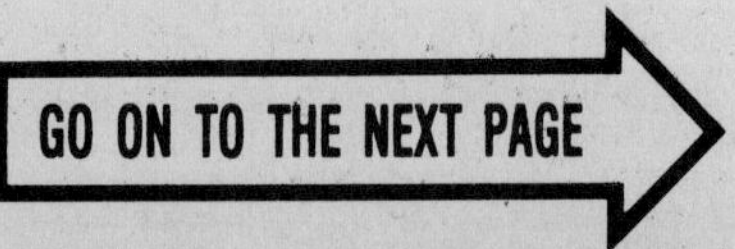

39. The immigrants can neither read nor can they write; nevertheless, they are willing to work hard to overcome their handicaps.

(A) nor can they write; nevertheless,
(B) nor write, but
(C) or write, and so
(D) nor write, however,
(E) nor is writing among their skills, so

40. The best folk music, no matter when it was written, has an appeal that has the quality of timelessness in its nature.

(A) an appeal that has the quality of timelessness in its nature
(B) an appeal that is of a timeless nature
(C) an appeal of a timeless quality
(D) a timeless appeal
(E) an appeal that is timeless in quality

Directions: The remaining questions are like those at the beginning of the section. For each sentence in which you find an error, select the one underlined part that must be changed to make the sentence correct and blacken the corresponding space on your answer sheet. If there is no error, blacken answer space E.

41. The ambassador's words were widely taken
A
as inferring his nation's willingness to continue the
B C D
negotiations. No error
E

42. Each applicant to any of the graduate schools in
A B
the association are expected to submit transcripts
C
from all colleges previously attended. No error
D E

43. Today, the title of poet laureate is purely
A
symbolic, but early holders of the office were
B
expected to put their pens to use in political service
C D
to the monarch. No error
E

44. Not wishing to appear overly aggressive, Parker
A
deliberately refrained from speaking until
he was certain that the debate had came to a crisis.
B C D
No error
E

45. John Donne, along with Henry Vaughn and George
A
Herbert, are ranked among the foremost religious
B C D
poets of the seventeenth century. No error
E

46. The committee that the governor appointed
A
to consider long-term solutions to the state's water
B C
supply problem has so far been unable to come up
D
with any program. No error
E

47. In his address, the headmaster attempted to
A
impress into the new students the importance of the
B C
school's honor code, which he said had been in
D
existence for over thirty years. No error
E

48. Neither Walter nor his brother was real surprised
A B
by the enthusiasm with which their new computer
C
program was received. No error
D E

49. The author's name, who I cannot remember, is
A
insignificant; what matters is the profound effect
B C
her book has had upon me. No error
D E

50. The river valleys just south of the capital have been
A B
the site of some of the most fiercest fighting since
C D
the outbreak of the war. No error
E

S T O P

IF YOU FINISH BEFORE TIME IS CALLED, YOU MAY CHECK YOUR WORK ON THIS SECTION ONLY. DO NOT WORK ON ANY OTHER SECTION IN THE TEST.

SECTION 5

Time—30 minutes

35 QUESTIONS

In this section solve each problem, using any available space on the page for scratchwork. Then indicate the one correct answer in the appropriate space on the answer sheet.

The following information is for your reference in solving some of the problems.

Circle of radius r: Area $= \pi r^2$; Circumference $= 2\pi r$
The number of degrees of arc in a circle is 360.
The measure in degrees of a straight angle is 180.

Definitions of symbols:

$=$	is equal to	$\leq$	is less than or equal to
$\neq$	is unequal to	$\geq$	is greater than or equal to
$<$	is less than	$\parallel$	is parallel to
$>$	is greater than	$\perp$	is perpendicular to

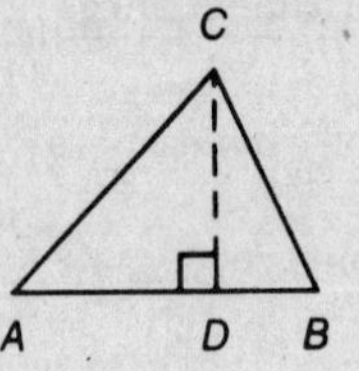

Triangle: The sum of the measures in degrees of the angles of a triangle is 180.

If $\angle CDA$ is a right angle, then

(1) area of $\triangle ABC = \dfrac{AB \times CD}{2}$

(2) $AC^2 = AD^2 + DC^2$

Note: Figures which accompany problems in this test are intended to provide information useful in solving the problems. They are drawn as accurately as possible EXCEPT when it is stated in a specific problem that its figure is not drawn to scale. All figures lie in a plane unless otherwise indicated. All numbers used are real numbers.

---

1. If $4(3 + a) = 18$, then $a =$

(A) 6 (B) 4 (C) 3 (D) $\frac{3}{2}$ (E) $\frac{4}{3}$

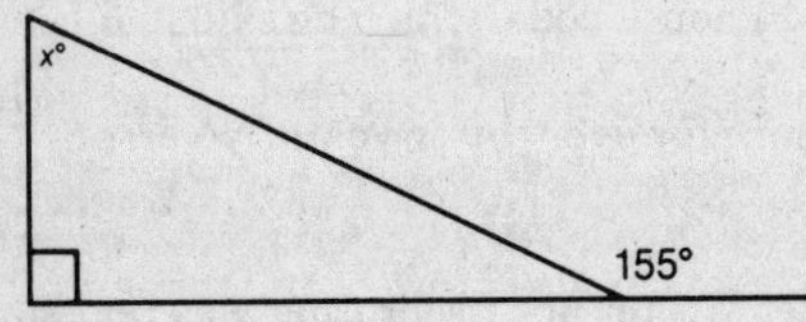

2. In the figure above, $x =$

(A) 35 (B) 55 (C) 65 (D) 70 (E) 75

3. Given $3q + r = 2$ and $4r - 6q = 0$, then $q =$

(A) $\frac{2}{9}$ (B) $\frac{1}{3}$ (C) $\frac{4}{9}$ (D) $\frac{2}{3}$ (E) 1

4. A rectangular room has a length of 9 meters and a width of $7\frac{1}{2}$ meters. How many $\frac{1}{2}$-meter-square tiles will be needed to cover the floor of the room?

(A) 135 (B) 180 (C) 200
(D) 240 (E) 270

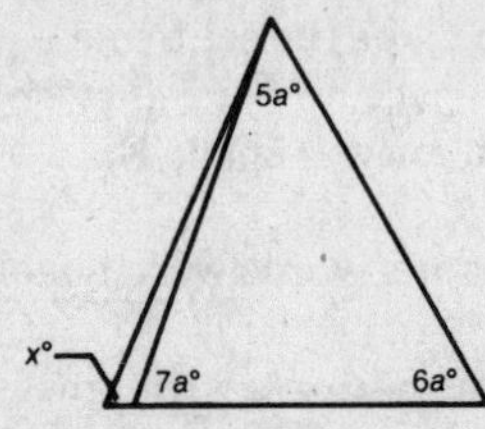

5. The greatest possible value of x in the figure above is

(A) 66 (B) 68 (C) 72 (D) 74 (E) 76

6. For any number n, let $\boxed{n}$ be defined as the smallest integer greater than n. What is the value of $\boxed{6} \times \boxed{-3}$?

(A) -12 (B) -14 (C) -15
(D) -18 (E) -24

7. If $\frac{x}{2} + \frac{x}{3} = 1\frac{2}{3}$, then $x =$

(A) $\frac{1}{2}$ (B) 1 (C) 2 (D) $\frac{3}{2}$ (E) 3

GO ON TO THE NEXT PAGE

Questions 8-27 each consist of two quantities, one in Column A and one in Column B. You are to compare the two quantities and on the answer sheet blacken space

- A if the quantity in Column A is greater;
- B if the quantity in Column B is greater;
- C if the two quantities are equal;
- D if the relationship cannot be determined from the information given.

Notes:
1. In certain questions, information concerning one or both of the quantities to be compared is centered above the two columns.
2. In a given question, a symbol that appears in both columns represents the same thing in Column A as it does in Column B.
3. Letters such as x, n, and k stand for real numbers.

EXAMPLES

	Column A	Column B	Answers
E1.	2×6	$2 + 6$	● Ⓑ Ⓒ Ⓓ
	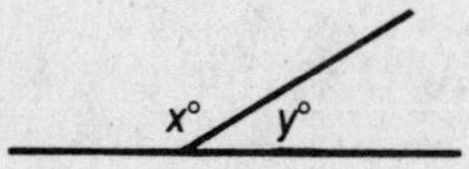		
E2.	$180 - x$	y	Ⓐ Ⓑ ● Ⓓ
E3.	$p - q$	$q - p$	Ⓐ Ⓑ Ⓒ ●

	Column A	Column B
8.	.01 + .1 + .0001	.09 + .009 + .009

$x > 0$

9.	x	x^2
10.	$a(b + c) + b(a + c)$	$2ab + c(a + b)$

x and y are positive integers.

$x = 2y$

11.	32% of x	59% of y
12.	$\frac{7974}{46}$	$\frac{8119}{43}$
13.	The perimeter of a rectangle with sides of 3 and 7	The circumference of a circle with a diameter of 6

	Column A	Column B
14.	$\sqrt{9} - \sqrt{4}$	$\sqrt{5}$

$n < 0$

15.	n	$\frac{1}{n}$

Note: Figure not drawn to scale.

$AC < BD$

16.	AB	CD

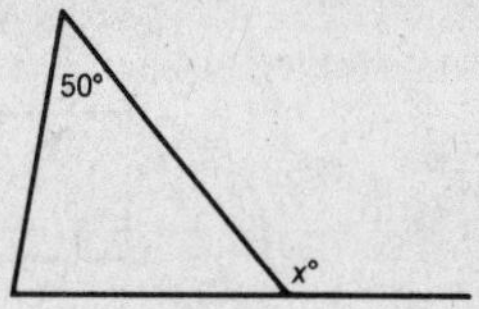

17.	x	130

GO ON TO THE NEXT PAGE

Column A	Column B

6	1	2
2	x	4
z	y	3

The sum of the numbers in each row and column above is the same.

18. y | $x + z$

$-3 < x < -2$

19. x^2 | x

$a + b = 5$

$a < 2$

20. 3 | b

Nine football players have an average weight of 160 pounds. Eleven other football players have an average weight of 172 pounds.

21. Average weight of all 20 players | 165

---

22. $3n$ | $3(n - 3) + 10$

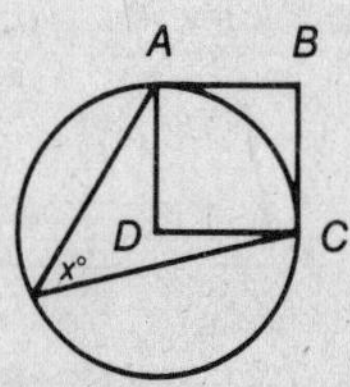

D is the center of the circle.

$ABCD$ is a square.

23. x | 45

Column A	Column B

24. Average (arithmetic mean) of the test scores 72, 80, 91, 79, and 78 | Average (arithmetic mean) of three integral test scores under 73 and two integral test scores under 92

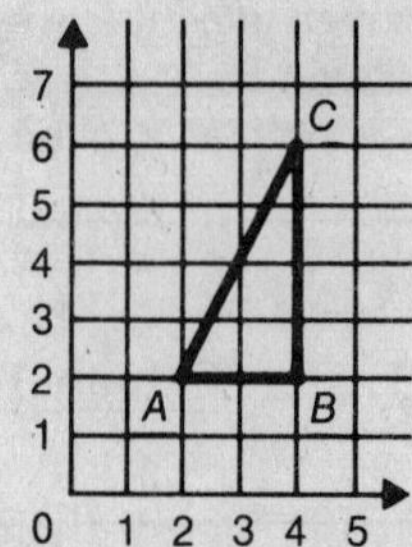

25. Area of triangle ABC | 5

$3x + y = 1$

$6x - 2y = 10$

26. y | 0

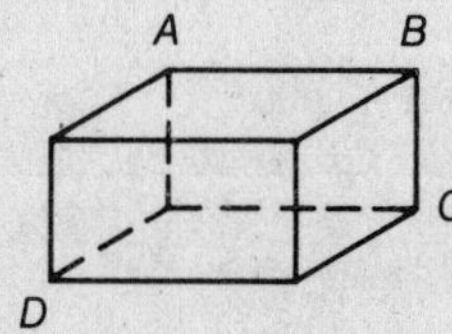

A, B, C, and D are vertices of the rectangular solid.

27. Length of diagonal AC | Length of diagonal BD

GO ON TO THE NEXT PAGE

Solve each of the remaining problems in this section using any available space for scratchwork. Then indicate the one correct answer in the appropriate space on the answer sheet.

28. How many 12-ounce bottles are needed to hold the same amount of soda as a case of 24 20-ounce bottles?

(A) 40 (B) 44 (C) 48 (D) 56 (E) 60

29. If $a = \sqrt{\frac{1}{16}}$, then $a^3 =$

(A) 4 (B) 2 (C) $\frac{1}{2}$ (D) $\frac{1}{4}$ (E) $\frac{1}{64}$

$$\begin{array}{r} 2\square 6 \\ \times\,\square \\ \hline 1280 \end{array}$$

30. In the correctly computed multiplication problem above, if $\square$ always represents the same digit, then $\square =$

(A) 3 (B) 4 (C) 5 (D) 6 (E) 8

31. In a coordinate graph system, a triangle is drawn with vertices at points $(-1, -1)$, $(3, -1)$, and $(-1, 4)$. Which of the following is closest to the length of the longest side of the triangle?

(A) 7 (B) 6 (C) 5 (D) 4 (E) 3

32. If Carol works $\frac{3x}{2}$ hours and Jose works $30x$ minutes, how many hours do they work altogether?

(A) $\frac{x}{30}$ (B) $\frac{3x}{20}$ (C) $\frac{2x}{3}$ (D) $\frac{x+2}{6}$ (E) $2x$

33. If n is a positive integer such that n^2 is odd, then which of the following must be an odd integer?

(A) $\frac{n}{2}$

(B) $n + n + n$

(C) $2(n + 1)$

(D) $\frac{n+1}{2}$

(E) $2n$

34. A cube with volume 216 is to be constructed from a set of smaller cubes, each with edge 2. How many of the smaller cubes will be needed to construct the larger cube?

(A) 9 (B) 16 (C) 27 (D) 36 (E) 54

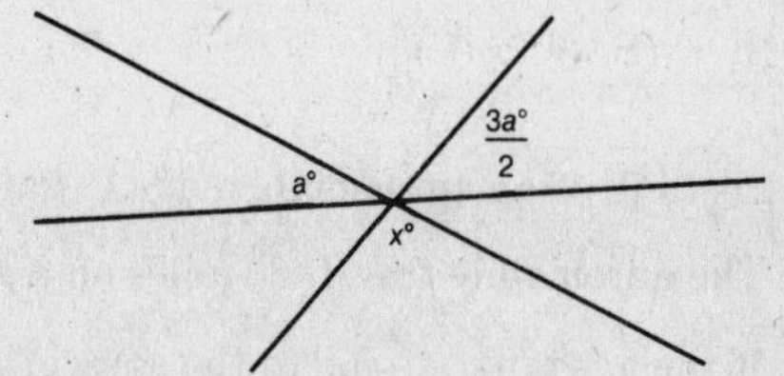

35. In the figure above, three lines intersect at a single point. If $x = 105$, then $a =$

(A) 30 (B) 32 (C) 36 (D) 40 (E) 45

S T O P

IF YOU FINISH BEFORE TIME IS CALLED, YOU MAY CHECK YOUR WORK ON THIS SECTION ONLY. DO NOT WORK ON ANY OTHER SECTION IN THE TEST.

SECTION 6

Time—30 minutes

35 QUESTIONS

In this section solve each problem, using any available space on the page for scratchwork. Then indicate the one correct answer in the appropriate space on the answer sheet.

The following information is for your reference in solving some of the problems.

Circle of radius r: Area $= \pi r^2$; Circumference $= 2\pi r$
The number of degrees of arc in a circle is 360.
The measure in degrees of a straight angle is 180.

Definitions of symbols:

$=$	is equal to	$\leq$	is less than or equal to
$\neq$	is unequal to	$\geq$	is greater than or equal to
$<$	is less than	$\parallel$	is parallel to
$>$	is greater than	$\perp$	is perpendicular to

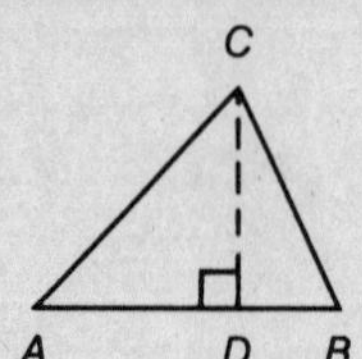

Triangle: The sum of the measures in degrees of the angles of a triangle is 180.

If $\angle CDA$ is a right angle, then

(1) area of $\triangle ABC = \frac{AB \times CD}{2}$

(2) $AC^2 = AD^2 + DC^2$

Note: Figures which accompany problems in this test are intended to provide information useful in solving the problems. They are drawn as accurately as possible EXCEPT when it is stated in a specific problem that its figure is not drawn to scale. All figures lie in a plane unless otherwise indicated. All numbers used are real numbers.

---

1. If $x + 4 = 2x - 6$, then $x =$

(A) 10 (B) 8 (C) 6 (D) 4 (E) 2

2. The gas tank of an automobile holds 18 gallons of fuel. The automobile travels 30 miles on a gallon of fuel. If the gas tank is $\frac{3}{4}$ full at the start of a trip, how full will it be after the automobile travels 105 miles?

(A) $\frac{2}{3}$ (B) $\frac{5}{9}$ (C) $\frac{1}{2}$ (D) $\frac{2}{5}$ (E) $\frac{1}{3}$

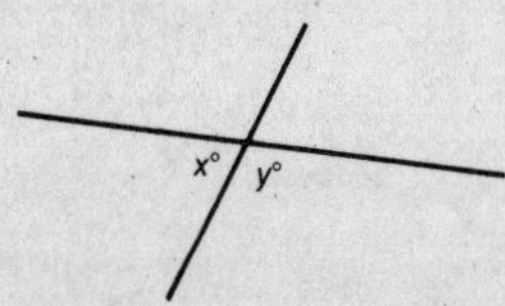

3. In the figure above, two lines intersect. In terms of y, $x =$

(A) $180 - y$ (B) $90 + y$ (C) $2y$ (D) $90 - y$
(E) It cannot be determined from the information given.

4. If $2m = \frac{n}{3}$ and $n = 11$, then $\frac{m}{2} =$

(A) $\frac{11}{3}$ (B) $2\frac{2}{3}$ (C) $\frac{11}{9}$ (D) $\frac{6}{5}$ (E) $\frac{11}{12}$

Questions 5–6 refer to the following figure, which is a map showing the locations of five cities and the only roads that connect them. The roads cross one another, but the only junctions between them are in the cities.

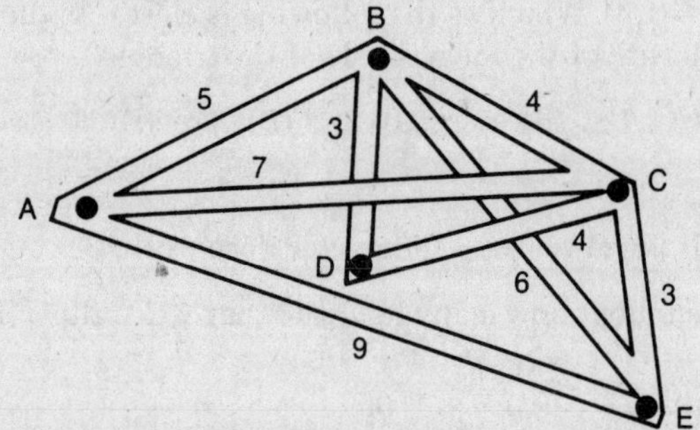

5. The shortest distance that could be traveled by someone starting out in one city and visiting the other four cities in any order is

(A) 13 (B) 14 (C) 15 (D) 17 (E) 21

6. The greatest distance that could be traveled by someone starting out in one city and visiting the other four cities exactly once is

(A) 21 (B) 23 (C) 25 (D) 26 (E) 27

7. If $n = -\frac{1}{2}$, which of the following has the greatest value?

(A) n (B) n^2 (C) n^3 (D) n^4 (E) n^5

GO ON TO THE NEXT PAGE

Questions 8-27 each consist of two quantities, one in Column A and one in Column B. You are to compare the two quantities and on the answer sheet blacken space

A if the quantity in Column A is greater;
B if the quantity in Column B is greater;
C if the two quantities are equal;
D if the relationship cannot be determined from the information given.

Notes:
1. In certain questions, information concerning one or both of the quantities to be compared is centered above the two columns.
2. In a given question, a symbol that appears in both columns represents the same thing in Column A as it does in Column B.
3. Letters such as x, n, and k stand for real numbers.

EXAMPLES

	Column A	Column B	Answers
E1.	2×6	$2 + 6$	● Ⓑ Ⓒ Ⓓ
E2.	$180 - x$	y	Ⓐ Ⓑ ● Ⓓ
E3.	$p - q$	$q - p$	Ⓐ Ⓑ Ⓒ ●

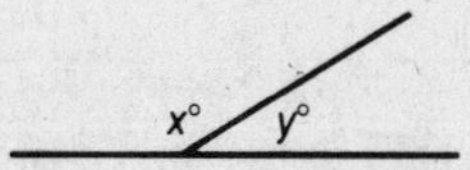

	Column A	Column B
8.	$\frac{3}{4}+\frac{1}{3}+\frac{4}{5}+\frac{1}{2}$	$\frac{3}{4}\times\frac{1}{3}\times\frac{4}{5}\times\frac{1}{2}$

$a + b - 4 = 0$

9.	a	0
10.	3.7×1000	$370{,}000 \div 100$

$a - b = 3$
$2a + b = 12$

11.	a	4

Lori's age is 25 percent greater than David's age. Three years ago, Lori was twice as old as David.

12.	Lori's age now	5

	Column A	Column B

Questions 13–14 refer to the following figure, in which side AB of rectangle $ABCD$ passes through the center of circle O.

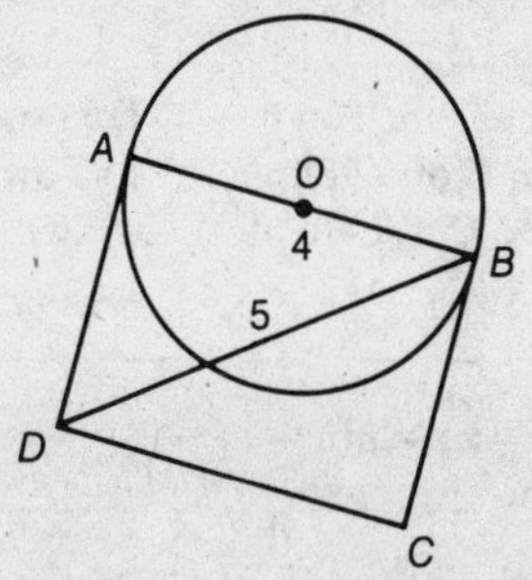

13.	Perimeter of rectangle $ABCD$	Circumference of circle O
14.	Area of rectangle $ABCD$	Area of circle O

$m = -n$

15.	m	n

GO ON TO THE NEXT PAGE

Column A	Column B

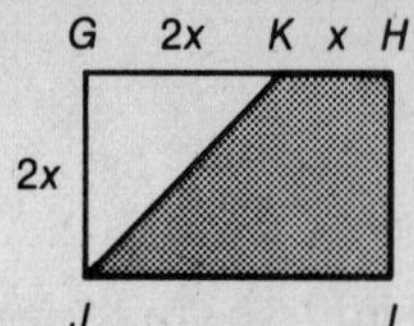

GHIJ is a rectangle.

	Column A	Column B
16.	Twice the area of triangle *GKJ*	The area of shaded region *KHIJ*

Questions 17–18 refer to the following statement.

Town A is 15 kilometers from Town B and 24 kilometers from Town C.

	Column A	Column B
17.	Distance from Town B to Town C	39 kilometers
18.	Distance from Town A to Town B on a map drawn to the scale of 2 cm = 1 km	Distance from Town A to Town C on a map drawn to the scale of 1 cm = 1 km
19.	$a(b + c) - b(a - c)$	$c(a + b)$

The clock shown is an accurate 12-hour clock.

	Column A	Column B
20.	Number of minutes until the next time when the hands of the clock will form an angle of 120 degrees	45
21.	$\sqrt[3]{16}$	$\sqrt{4}$

$p \neq 0$

	Column A	Column B
22.	p	$\frac{1}{p}$

Column A	Column B

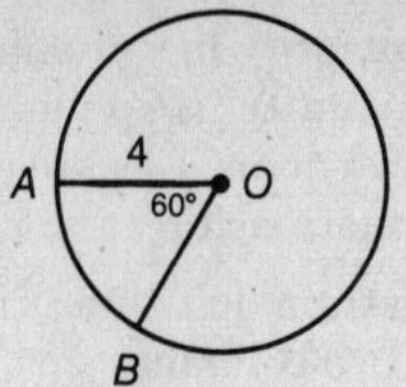

O is the center of the circle.

	Column A	Column B
23.	Length of arc *AB*	5

Mary bought one book and two records for $24. Ralph bought two books and one record for $19.

	Column A	Column B
24.	Cost of two books and two records	$27

$x > 1$

	Column A	Column B
25.	x^3	x^2

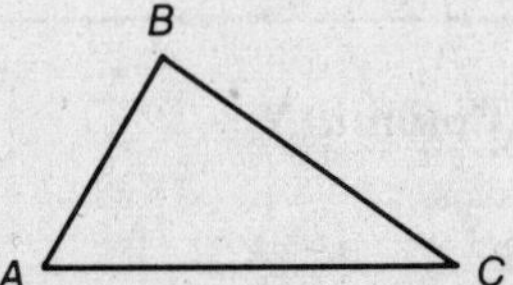

D is a point, not shown, inside triangle *ABC*.

	Column A	Column B
26.	*AB*	*AD*

A = {all integers between 10 and 40 that are divisible by 3}

B = {all integers between 10 and 40 that are divisible by 5}

	Column A	Column B
27.	Number of integers in both set *A* and set *B*	2

GO ON TO THE NEXT PAGE

Solve each of the remaining problems in this section using any available space for scratchwork. Then indicate the one correct answer in the appropriate space on the answer sheet.

28. If $\frac{3}{x} + \frac{7}{10} = \frac{13}{10}$, then $x =$

(A) 20 (B) 10 (C) 7 (D) 6 (E) 5

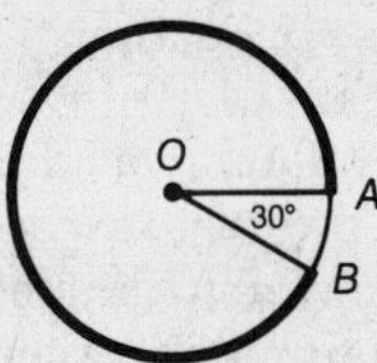

29. In the figure above, OA and OB are radii of length 6. The length of darkened arc AB is

(A) 12π (B) 11π (C) 10π (D) 8π (E) 6π

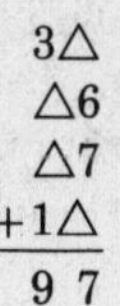

30. In the correctly computed addition problem above, if △ always represents the same digit, then △ =

(A) 1 (B) 2 (C) 3 (D) 4 (E) 5

31. If 40 tickets to a show cost d dollars, then, in terms of d, 6 tickets cost how many dollars?

(A) $\frac{3d}{20}$ (B) $\frac{6d}{30}$ (C) $\frac{d}{40}$ (D) $\frac{d}{6}$ (E) $\frac{3d}{2}$

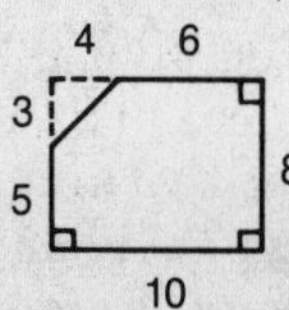

32. The figure above is the floor plan of a room with five walls. If the room has a ceiling 8 feet high, then the total volume of the room in cubic feet is

(A) 496 (B) 512 (C) 520
(D) 568 (E) 592

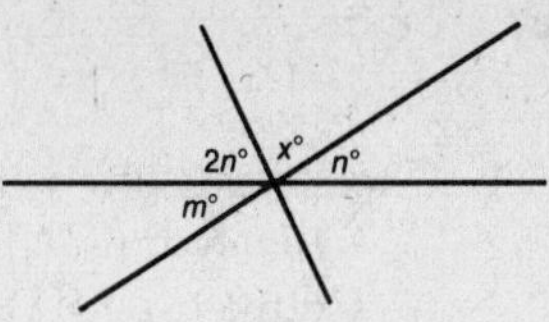

33. In the figure above, three lines intersect at a single point. If $m = 32$, then $x =$

(A) 32 (B) 48 (C) 64 (D) 84 (E) 88

34. Of the books on a shelf, exactly $\frac{1}{3}$ have red covers, exactly $\frac{2}{5}$ are illustrated, and exactly $\frac{3}{10}$ are math textbooks. What is the least possible number of books on the shelf?

(A) 24 (B) 25 (C) 30 (D) 36
(E) It cannot be determined from the information given.

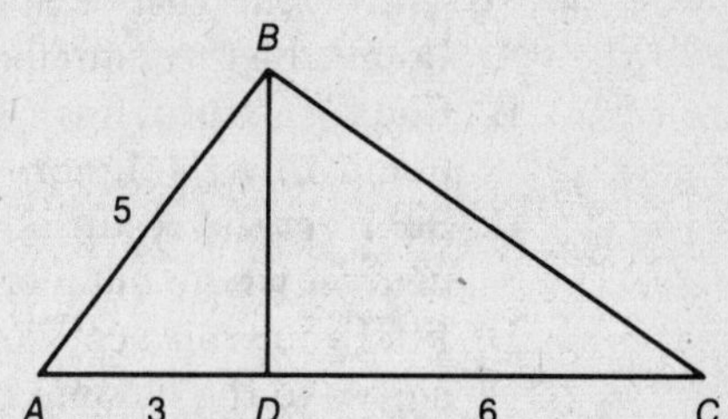

35. In the figure above, $BD \perp AC$. What is the ratio of the area of triangle ABD to the area of triangle ABC?

(A) 1:2 (B) 1:3 (C) 2:5
(D) 3:8 (E) 2:9

S T O P

IF YOU FINISH BEFORE TIME IS CALLED, YOU MAY CHECK YOUR WORK ON THIS SECTION ONLY. DO NOT WORK ON ANY OTHER SECTION IN THE TEST.

PRACTICE TEST 5: *Scoring Instructions*

1. Check your answers against the answer key on page 409.
2. To figure your SAT-verbal score:
   A. Count the total number of correct answers you chose in Sections 1 and 3.
   B. Count the total number of incorrect answers you chose in Sections 1 and 3. Multiply this number by 1/4. Ignore any questions you left blank.
   C. Subtract the result of Step B from the result of Step A. Round off the answer to the nearest whole number. This whole number is your SAT-verbal raw score.
   D. Find your raw score in the first column of the score conversion table on page 410. Read across to the column headed SAT-verbal. The three-digit number there is your SAT-verbal score.
3. To figure your SAT-mathematical score:
   A. Count the total number of correct answers you chose in Sections 2, 5, and 6.
   B. Count the total number of incorrect answers you chose from questions 8–27 in Sections 5 and 6. Multiply this number by 1/3. Ignore any questions you left blank.
   C. Count the total number of incorrect answers you chose from all other questions in Sections 2, 5, and 6. Multiply this number by 1/4. Ignore any questions you left blank.
   D. Add the results of Step B and Step C. Subtract this total from the result of Step A. Round off the answer to the nearest whole number. This whole number is your SAT-mathematical raw score.
   E. Find your raw score in the first column of the score conversion table on page 410. Read across to the column headed SAT-mathematical. The three-digit number there is your SAT-mathematical score.
4. To figure your Test of Standard Written English (TSWE) score:
   A. Count the total number of correct answers you chose in Section 4.
   B. Count the total number of incorrect answers you chose in Section 4. Multiply this number by 1/4. Ignore any questions you left blank.
   C. Subtract the result of Step B from the result of Step A. Round off the answer to the nearest whole number. This whole number is your TSWE raw score.
   D. Find your raw score in the first column of the score conversion table on page 410. Read across to the column headed TSWE. The two-digit number there is your TSWE score.

Note: Allow for a margin of error of 30 points either way on your SAT-verbal and SAT-mathematical scores (3 points on your TSWE score). For instance, an SAT-verbal score of 470 really represents a range of scores from 440 to 500. Remember that test performance varies greatly from one day to the next and can be improved through study and practice. So don't consider your scores on any practice test as a perfect prediction of how you'll do on the real SAT.

SECTION 1

1. **C**	6. **D**	11. **B**	16. **A**	21. **C**	26. **C**	31. **B**	36. **C**
2. **E**	7. **D**	12. **E**	17. **B**	22. **C**	27. **E**	32. **D**	37. **E**
3. **C**	8. **A**	13. **D**	18. **E**	23. **E**	28. **D**	33. **C**	38. **A**
4. **B**	9. **B**	14. **C**	19. **D**	24. **D**	29. **A**	34. **A**	39. **B**
5. **A**	10. **E**	15. **A**	20. **A**	25. **B**	30. **E**	35. **C**	40. **A**

SECTION 2

1. **C**	6. **A**	11. **E**	16. **E**	21. **C**
2. **D**	7. **B**	12. **C**	17. **E**	22. **D**
3. **B**	8. **B**	13. **D**	18. **D**	23. **A**
4. **D**	9. **A**	14. **A**	19. **E**	24. **B**
5. **B**	10. **D**	15. **B**	20. **C**	25. **B**

SECTION 3

1. **E**	7. **B**	13. **C**	19. **A**	25. **D**	31. **C**	37. **B**	43. **E**
2. **D**	8. **B**	14. **B**	20. **C**	26. **A**	32. **A**	38. **D**	44. **E**
3. **E**	9. **A**	15. **A**	21. **C**	27. **B**	33. **E**	39. **D**	45. **E**
4. **C**	10. **B**	16. **E**	22. **A**	28. **A**	34. **E**	40. **A**	
5. **C**	11. **C**	17. **E**	23. **D**	29. **D**	35. **B**	41. **A**	
6. **E**	12. **D**	18. **E**	24. **B**	30. **D**	36. **B**	42. **D**	

SECTION 4

1. **E**	8. **C**	15. **E**	22. **D**	29. **A**	36. **E**	43. **E**	50. **D**
2. **B**	9. **A**	16. **C**	23. **E**	30. **D**	37. **A**	44. **C**	
3. **C**	10. **B**	17. **A**	24. **B**	31. **B**	38. **C**	45. **B**	
4. **A**	11. **B**	18. **E**	25. **A**	32. **C**	39. **B**	46. **E**	
5. **E**	12. **B**	19. **A**	26. **C**	33. **A**	40. **D**	47. **B**	
6. **B**	13. **C**	20. **C**	27. **B**	34. **B**	41. **B**	48. **B**	
7. **A**	14. **A**	21. **A**	28. **C**	35. **E**	42. **C**	49. **A**	

SECTION 5

1. **D**	6. **B**	11. **A**	16. **B**	21. **A**	26. **B**	31. **B**
2. **C**	7. **C**	12. **B**	17. **D**	22. **B**	27. **B**	32. **E**
3. **C**	8. **A**	13. **A**	18. **A**	23. **C**	28. **A**	33. **B**
4. **E**	9. **D**	14. **B**	19. **A**	24. **A**	29. **E**	34. **C**
5. **B**	10. **C**	15. **D**	20. **B**	25. **B**	30. **C**	35. **A**

SECTION 6

1. **A**	6. **D**	11. **A**	16. **C**	21. **A**	26. **D**	31. **A**
2. **B**	7. **B**	12. **C**	17. **D**	22. **D**	27. **C**	32. **E**
3. **A**	8. **A**	13. **A**	18. **A**	23. **B**	28. **E**	33. **D**
4. **E**	9. **D**	14. **B**	19. **C**	24. **D**	29. **B**	34. **C**
5. **C**	10. **C**	15. **D**	20. **B**	25. **A**	30. **B**	35. **B**

PRACTICE TEST 5: ***Score Conversion Table***

Raw Score	SAT-Verbal	SAT-Mathematical	TSWE
95		800	
94		780	
93		770	
92		760	
91		750	
90		740	
89		730	
88		720	
87		710	
86		700	
85	800	690	
84	780	680	
83	760	670	
82	750	670	
81	740	660	
80	730	660	
79	720	650	
78	710	640	
77	700	640	
76	690	630	
75	680	630	
74	670	620	
73	660	620	
72	650	610	
71	640	600	
70	630	600	
69	630	590	
68	620	590	
67	620	580	
66	610	580	
65	610	570	
64	600	570	
63	600	560	
62	590	550	
61	590	550	
60	580	540	
59	580	540	
58	570	530	
57	570	530	
56	560	520	
55	550	520	
54	550	510	
53	540	500	
52	540	500	
51	530	490	
50	520	490	60+
49	520	480	60+
48	510	480	60+
47	500	470	60+
46	500	460	60+
45	490	460	59
44	490	450	58
43	480	450	57
42	470	440	56
41	470	440	55

Raw Score	SAT-Verbal	SAT-Mathematical	TSWE
40	460	430	54
39	450	430	53
38	450	420	52
37	440	420	51
36	440	410	50
35	430	410	49
34	430	400	48
33	420	400	47
32	420	390	46
31	410	390	45
30	400	380	44
29	400	370	43
28	390	360	42
27	380	350	41
26	370	350	40
25	370	340	39
24	360	340	38
23	350	330	37
22	350	330	36
21	340	320	35
20	330	310	34
19	330	310	33
18	320	300	32
17	310	300	31
16	300	290	30
15	290	290	29
14	280	280	28
13	280	270	27
12	270	260	26
11	260	250	25
10	250	250	24
9	250	240	23
8	240	230	22
7	230	220	21
6	220	210	20
5	210	200	20
4 or less	200	200	20

PRACTICE TEST 5: *Explanatory Answers*

SECTION 1

1. **C** *Ornate* means "elaborately decorated." *Severe*, which in one sense means "austerely plain," is a good antonym.

2. **E** *Immature* is sometimes used to characterize behavior that is stupid and foolish, the opposite of choice D, but its basic meaning is "not ripe"—that is, "not fully developed." Thus choice E, *fully developed*, is an exact opposite.

3. **C** *Temperance* means "moderation, restraint, especially in the use of alcohol"; *dissipation* means "intemperance, lack of moderation, especially in the use of alcohol."

4. **B** *Vacillate* means "to waver, hesitate, go back and forth between choices." The opposite is to *reach a firm decision*.

5. **A** A *bane* is a source of harm or ruin. The opposite is a *source of benefit*.

6. **D** *Sundry* means "various, varied, diverse, miscellaneous." *Identical* is a good antonym; it means "exactly the same."

7. **D** To *disperse* is to scatter or spread apart, as in "*disperse* the crowd." By contrast, to *muster* is to gather or collect, as in "*muster* the troops for battle."

8. **A** To *propagate* something is to help it grow, spread, or multiply. One could *propagate* a plant, for instance, by taking a cutting from it and starting a new plant; or one could propagate a belief or an idea by speaking or writing about it. *Uproot* is a good opposite. Meaning "to dig up, destroy, or prevent from growing," it, too, can be applied both to living things and to ideas and beliefs.

9. **B** *Anathema* means "ban, curse, solemn denunciation"; *benediction* means "blessing."

10. **E** *Equanimity* means "evenness of mind or temper, calm, composure." *Passion*, which refers to any strong feeling, excitement, or emotion, is a good opposite. *Terror* (choice B), *malignity* (choice C), and *wrath* (choice D), though passions, are too specific.

11. **B** Since the sentence is about income and economies, *impoverish* is the most appropriate choice for the second blank. *Vulnerable* fits logically in the first blank.

12. **E** The key words in this sentence are *not* and *but*, which link parallel contrasting elements. *Confirming biases*, or prejudices, is the opposite of *challenging assumptions*, or ideas that are taken for granted without proof; *endorsing complacency*, or self-satisfaction, is the opposite of *encouraging self-questioning*. None of the other answer choices result in the same balanced contrast.

13. **D** *Talented* (choice C) and *renowned* (choice D) both work in the first blank, but only *dominant* makes sense in the second blank. If the traits weren't *dominant*—that is, if they weren't strong enough to shape and control the personality—then

the resemblance between Goldwyn and his grandfather would not have been apparent.

14. **C** The key word *although* introduces a contrast. Only choice C completes the contrast clearly and logically.

15. **A** Parallel clauses linked by *just as* and *so* should echo one another. "Distinctly *American* in modern poetry" echoes "modern *American* fiction"; "hailed as the *originator*" echoes "regarded as the *source*."

16. **A** To *enlarge* an *image* is to make it bigger; to *amplify* a *sound* is to make it louder. Choice B is wrong because *elongating* a *room* is making it bigger in one dimension only, whereas *enlarging* an *image* is making it bigger in all dimensions. Choice C is wrong because *inflating* a *balloon* isn't really making the balloon any bigger; it's simply filling the balloon with air.

17. **B** A *rider* is an addition to a *contract* or some other document, such as a legislative bill. An *amendment* is an addition to a *constitution*, usually intended to correct or improve it.

18. **E** A *coiffure* is a *hairdo*, but the word *coiffure*, which is French in origin, has loftier connotations than the word *hairdo*. *Cuisine* and *cookery* are related in exactly the same way.

19. **D** *Autonomy* means "self-government" or "independence"; someone who enjoys *autonomy* is not governed by or *dependent* on another. Similarly, someone who enjoys *freedom* is not *subservient* to another.

20. **A** *Bovine* means "of or relating to a cow" or "cowlike." Analogously, *ursine* means "of or relating to a bear" or "bearlike." The second words in choices B, C, and E are all too specific; *reptilian*, for example, refers to *reptiles* in general, not *snakes* in particular. In choice D, *equestrian* refers to *horseback riding*, not *horses*.

21. **C** *Abundance* means "plenty"; it is a good antonym for *paucity*, which means "scarcity" or "lack." *Fertility* and *barrenness* are also good antonyms. *Amplitude*, which means "largeness, fullness, abundance," is not the opposite of *paltriness*, which refers to the state or quality of being trifling, worthless, petty, or insignificant.

22. **C** A *tourniquet* stops the flow of *blood* (from a wound); a *dam* stops the flow of *water* (in a river).

23. **E** A *façade* is the front part, or "face," of a *building*. The word *façade* often implies a deceptive appearance or false front—that is, an imposing exterior that conceals a shoddy interior. A *veneer*, similarly, is a thin layer of fine wood applied to a base of inferior wood to make a piece of *furniture* look solid, genuine, and superficially attractive.

24. **D** *Tensile* means "capable of being *stretched*." Similarly, *docile* means "capable of being *controlled*." *Nubile* (choice B) describes a woman who has reached sexual maturity and thus is capable of being *married*, but not necessarily capable of being *domesticated* (that is, tamed or made accustomed to housekeeping and home life). *Fragile* (choice C) means "capable of being *broken*," not "capable of being *dropped*."

25. **B** *Venial* means "pardonable"; it refers to a relatively minor offense—a sin or a crime—that can be forgiven, excused, or overlooked. *Heinous* means

"outrageously wicked or evil"; it refers to an offense so monstrous as to be intolerable and unforgivable. The relationship between *insignificant* and *grave* is much the same.

26. **C** In the very first sentence, the author states that his "goal is to give practical advice to a translator"—specifically, as he later makes clear, one who wishes to translate Homer into English.

27. **E** The author devotes the second half of paragraph 1 to a criticism of the comment he quotes. As a direction, he says, it is "not enough and gives no real guidance."

28. **D** In paragraph 2 (and again in paragraph 3), the author identifies the two qualifications that a competent judge of a translation of Homer must have: a "knowledge of Greek" and "adequate poetic taste and feeling."

29. **A** By "the blind," the author means "ordinary" or "unlearned" English readers—those who do not know Greek and thus have "no data for judging" whether a translation "produces more or less the same effect upon them as the original."

30. **E** Throughout the passage the author argues that "it is the translator's business to reproduce the effect" of the original, in this case Homer. To say that a translation of Homer is "pretty" but "must not be called Homer" is to say that it has failed in its primary objective. It has not reproduced the effect of Homer.

31. **B** Only choice B is broad enough to reflect the content—and thus the main point—of the entire passage. The other choices are discussed in the passage, but they are all secondary points.

32. **D** See the last sentence of paragraph 1, which says that the markets for manufactured goods "increase more rapidly" than those for raw materials.

33. **C** See the second sentence of paragraph 2 (and paragraph 4). Imported manufactured goods are "in competition" with domestic goods and "threaten" domestic industries.

34. **A** See the last sentence of paragraph 3, which says that the impact of quantitative restrictions is more difficult, if not impossible, for developing nations to overcome than the effects of high tariffs.

35. **C** Choices A, B, D, and E are all stated or implied in the passage. Choice C is not. In fact, one would expect wages to increase, not decrease, as developing nations increased their exports of manufactured goods and thus improved their economies.

36. **C** As the first sentence of paragraph 2 makes clear, the passage is a defense of a "statement" the author made that "proved so offensive to Judge Douglas." (By the way, the author, as you probably guessed, is Abraham Lincoln.)

37. **E** The author mentions the main premise of Douglas's argument in paragraph 2: "He tries to show that variety in the institutions of the different states is necessary and indispensable." On this premise Douglas builds his argument in defense of slavery.

38. **A** In the second sentence of paragraph 2, the author summarizes the main premise of Douglas's argument. He then goes on to list the points of the argument with which he "readily" agrees. He concedes the truth and validity of those particular

points, but as the last paragraph makes clear, he rejects the argument itself as unsound.

39. **B** The author dismisses the analogy between cranberry laws and the institution of slavery completely: "I do not see that there is any parallel at all between them."

40. **A** See the last sentence of the passage, where the author refers to slavery as "an element of discord."

SECTION 2

1. **C** The decimals 0.009, 0.005, and 0.001 all have values less than 0.01. Of these, 0.009 is the greatest.

2. **D** $3^2 = 9$; $9^2 = 81$. $2^3 = 8$; $8^2 = 64$. $81 + 64 = 145$.

3. **B** The first two socks might not match, but the third would have to match one of the first two, since there are only two different colors of socks in the drawer.

4. **D** You should know that of the common fractions 2/3, 3/4, and 4/5, the last is closest in value to 0.83146. To determine whether 5/6 or 6/7 is even closer, start with the more likely candidate, 5/6, and divide the numerator by the denominator. You'll find that 5/6 is approximately equal to 0.83.

5. **B** If $x^2 + 11 = 9 \times 4 \times 5$, then $x^2 + 11 = 180$, $x^2 = 169$, and $x = 13$.

6. **A** You can find the answer to this problem by applying the Pythagorean theorem. However, if you learn the "standard" right triangles before you take the SAT, you'll save yourself a lot of time. The diagonal divides the rectangle into two congruent right triangles that are twice the size of the "standard" 5-12-13 right triangle. Therefore the diagonal has a length of 26. The rest is simple: If $3x + 2x + 5x + 3x = 26$, then $13x = 26$ and $x = 2$. If $x = 2$, then the length of the longest segment ($5x$) is 10.

7. **B** From the number line you know that $P = 0$, $Q \approx \frac{1}{4}$, $R = 1$, $S \approx 1\frac{1}{2}$, and $T \approx 2\frac{1}{2}$. If $P = 0$, then choice C ($P \times S$) and choice E ($P \times R$) both equal 0. If $Q \approx \frac{1}{4}$ and S and T are both less than 4, then choice A ($Q \times T$) and choice D ($Q \times S$) both have values less than 1. If $R = 1$ and S is greater than 1, then choice B ($R \times S$) has a value greater than 1. Therefore choice B has the greatest value.

8. **B** The *smallest* possible number of students in the school is the total number of *different* students enrolled in the three classes. You know that the total enrollment in the three classes is $59 + 42 + 36 = 137$. You also know that some of the students are enrolled in more than one class. To find the total number of *different* students, first subtract the number enrolled in two classes once (since they've been counted twice): $137 - (9 + 7 + 5) = 116$. Then subtract the number enrolled in three classes twice (since they've been counted three times): $116 - (4 + 4) = 108$.

9. **A** Given a particular perimeter, the area of a rectangle will be greatest when the lengths of its sides are most nearly equal. In this case, the greatest area will result when all four sides are equal, with lengths of 7. (Remember, a square is one type of rectangle.) The area will then be 7^2, or 49.

10. **D** Start with what you know: $z = 4$. If y is 5 less than z, then $y = -1$. If x is 2 more than y, then $x = 1$. Therefore, $xyz = 1(-1)(4) = -4$.

11. **E** Just substitute 3 for m and 5 for n in the definition:

$$\begin{aligned} 3 \wedge 5 &= 3(3+5)(3-5) \\ &= 3(8)(-2) \\ &= -48 \end{aligned}$$

12. **C** Work through the possibilities methodically, combining each denomination with itself as well as with each other denomination. You'll find that ten different sums can be obtained: 1¢ + 1¢ = 2¢; 1¢ + 5¢ = 6¢; 1¢ + 10¢ = 11¢; 1¢ + 25¢ = 26¢; 5¢ + 5¢ = 10¢; 5¢ + 10¢ = 15¢; 5¢ + 25¢ = 30¢; 10¢ + 10¢ = 20¢; 10¢ + 25¢ = 35¢; 25¢ + 25¢ = 50¢.

13. **D** Call the trains 1 and 2 (after the cities) and set up a chart with the information you're given:

	Rate ×	Time =	Distance
Train 1	48	x	$48x$
Train 2	62	$x - 1\frac{1}{2}$	$62x - \frac{155}{2}$

You know that City 1 and City 2 are 390 miles apart, so when the two trains meet, their combined distances must equal 390. Thus:

$$48x + 62x - \frac{155}{2} = 390$$

$$96x + 124x - 155 = 780$$

$$220x = 935$$

$$x = 4\frac{1}{4}$$

Now, x is the time traveled by Train 1. If Train 1 starts out at 11:00 A.M. and travels $4\frac{1}{4}$ hours before it meets Train 2, then the two trains will pass one another at 3:15 P.M.

14. **A** To clear the equation of fractions, multiply both sides by 14. You'll get $4 + 5 + x = 14$. Therefore, $x = 5$.

15. **B** If j dollars buys k gallons of gas, then j/k is the cost of 1 gallon of gas. Multiply this by 20 to get the cost of 20 gallons of gas: $20j/k$.

16. **E** Since 11% of \$300 is \$33 and $7\frac{1}{2}$% of \$400 is \$30, the first investment will yield \$3 more.

17. **E** If points P, Q, and R lie on the circle, they must all be equidistant from the center of the circle. They are all 3 units from point $(2, -1)$. Therefore, the radius of the circle must be 3 and the diameter, which is the longest line segment that can be drawn between two points on the circle, must be 6.

18. **D** By carefully sorting through the information in the question, you can come up with a list of the houses by age and thus determine which one is newest. However, notice that the question makes five "older than" statements about *six* houses. The only house that is *not* said to be older than another is House D. So it must be the newest.

19. **E** The area of the circle is $\pi r^2 = \pi 3^2 = 9\pi$. If the area of the shaded region is 8π, then the area of the nonshaded region is 1π, or 1/9 of the area of the circle. Therefore, $x°$ is 1/9 of 360°, or 40°.

20. **C** The total age of all nine players is $9 \times 27 = 243$. The total age of the three players whose ages are given is $39 + 37 + 35 = 111$. Therefore, the total age of the other six players is $243 - 111 = 132$, and their average age is $132 \div 6 = 22$.

21. **C** Just substitute 7 for a and 5 for b. You'll get:

$$\frac{(7+5)(7-5)}{2} = \frac{(12)(2)}{2} = 12$$

22. **D** The formula for the volume of a cylinder is $V = \pi r^2 h$, where r is the radius of the cylinder (in this case 3/2) and h is its height (in this case 6). First find the volume of one can:

$$V = \pi\left(\frac{3}{2}\right)^2 6$$

$$= \pi\left(\frac{9}{4}\right)6$$

$$= \frac{54\pi}{4}$$

Then multiply that volume by 4: 54π.

23. **A** Just substitute each of the answer choices into the inequality. (You should be able to do this in your head.) You'll quickly discover that the inequality holds true only for $x = 1$ and $y = 2$ (since $3/2 < 2$).

24. **B** If you missed this question, you probably assumed that there was more to it than meets the eye. Only the digits in 537-3575 fall in a straight (diagonal) line.

25. **B** First, reduce the fraction to lowest terms:

$$\frac{a^4b^3}{a^2b^2} = a^{4-2}b^{3-2} = a^2b$$

Then cube the result:

$$(a^2b)^3 = a^{2\times 3}b^3 = a^6b^3$$

SECTION 3

1. **E** *Perpetual* means "eternal, lasting forever"; *fleeting* means "transitory, passing quickly."

2. **D** To *spurn* something is to reject it scornfully or disdainfully. The opposite is to *embrace* it—that is, to welcome it or to accept it gladly.

3. **E** *Valiant* means "brave, courageous, strong of mind and spirit." *Timorous* means "fearful, timid, lacking in courage or self-confidence."

4. **C** *Untenable* means "unreasonable, not able to be held, maintained, or defended." The opposite is *defensible*.

5. **C** One definition of *depreciate* is to underrate, disparage, or belittle—that is, to speak of something as being less valuable than it really is. The opposite is to *overrate* something—that is, to speak of it as being more valuable than it really is.

6. **E** A *brusque* manner is abrupt, curt, blunt, or rude. By contrast, a *congenial* manner is warm, friendly, and sociable.

7. **B** *Assiduous* means "hard-working." The opposite is *slothful*, which means "lazy."

8. **B** *Kindred* means "related, allied, connected." A *kindred* spirit is anyone whose heart and mind seem sympathetic to one's own. *Alien* is a good opposite; it means "foreign, remote, unrelated."

9. **A** *Mitigate* means "to relieve, to make less severe"; *exacerbate* means "to intensify, to make more severe."

10. **B** A *moot* point is subject to discussion or argument. A point that is not subject to question or dispute is *unarguable* or *indisputable.*

11. **C** *Spurious* means "false" or "counterfeit." Opposites include *genuine, true*, and *authentic.*

12. **D** *Cursory* means "fast and typically superficial"; *exhaustive* means "thorough."

13. **C** *Stultifying*, at least in one sense, means "impairing, frustrating, rendering useless, futile, or ineffectual." *Encouraging*, which means "stimulating, fostering, giving help or support to," is a reasonable antonym.

14. **B** To *extirpate* something is to root it out and destroy it. By contrast, to *nurture* something is to take care of it and help it to survive and grow.

15. **A** *Penury* is poverty; the opposite is *wealth.*

16. **E** As the key word *like* suggests, the sentence is comparing a lecture to a labyrinth, a maze with blind alleys and intricate passageways. A man listening to a labyrinthine lecture is likely to feel *perplexed*—that is, puzzled, bewildered, thoroughly confused.

17. **E** Only when *subjective* and *opposite* are inserted in the blanks does the second half of the sentence logically explain or amplify the first half, as the colon suggests it should. (*Numerous*, in choice A, doesn't explain why theories of "national character" might be *misleading*. In order for the theories to be *misleading*, the characteristics ascribed to people would have to be *inaccurate*, or something similar. And if the characteristics were *inaccurate*, it wouldn't matter if the people were from the "very same" country or not.)

18. **E** Since the sentence states that the governor wants to avoid something because he values something else, you can expect the missing words to name two things that are incompatible with each other. Of the five pairs of words you're given, only *life* and *bloodshed* name two things that are clearly incompatible.

19. **A** The key word *but* indicates that the two if-then statements in the sentence should form a contrast. Aiming to produce more *cultured* individuals by giving the fine arts a *prominent* place in education contrasts with placing an emphasis on practical skills.

20. **C** *Enriched* and *independent* fit the cause-effect or reason-result structure of the sentence perfectly. A culture that has been "profoundly *enriched*" by many civilizations cannot be said to have a "truly *independent*" existence.

21. **C** In paragraph 1, the author describes the distinction between *liberty* and *license* as an "artful" one—a distinction "contrive[d]" (that is, brought about by artifice or trickery for the purpose of deceiving) by "our rulers ... to give and take away the right of free discussion." Choice C, which calls the distinction a *subterfuge*—a trick or deceptive stratagem—is an accurate reflection of the author's viewpoint.

22. **A** In paragraph 2, the author equates the power to judge "what is the liberty of the press and what is license"—that is, the power to curtail the freedom of the press and thus the freedom of discussion—with "the whole power of choosing opinions for the people." Clearly the author does not believe that anyone, under any circumstances, should have that power.

23. **D** In the last sentence of the passage, the author implies that freedom of the press prevents "our rulers" from achieving "the indefinite increase and perpetual duration of their power."

24. **B** In the last sentence of the passage, the author maintains that the pressures to conform are directly proportional to the size of the artist's public and the costliness of the medium in which the artist works. Choice B refers to the latter.

25. **D** In paragraph 1, the author compares the "strength and freshness" of Shakespeare's first dramas with the "strength and freshness" of certain films and attributes both to a "large and avid" audience.

26. **A** The author cites Chaplin, Bergman, and Antonioni as examples of unconventional filmmakers who are "strong enough" to "mould" the tastes of their audiences and thus to resist pressures to conform to the patterns of "more conventional" creators.

27. **B** According to paragraph 3, research indicates that crude oil makes lobsters lose their appetites. Obviously, if enough lobsters are exposed to crude oil and stop eating, lobster communities will die out.

28. **A** The first sentence of paragraph 3 provides this detail. Catfish, lobsters, alewives, and snails have been studied because they have "well-developed senses of smell and taste."

29. **D** As the last paragraph states, the studies have surveyed "the distribution of chlorinated hydrocarbons ... in marine organisms of the open ocean," specifically "plankton from the North Atlantic."

30. **D** Choice D is the only title that accurately reflects the content of the passage. The other titles are way off the mark.

31. **C** The words *pastoral*, *nineteenth-century*, and *archaic* all emphasize the old-fashioned or *traditional* qualities of baseball. There's no obvious reason why these qualities should make the game *enduring* (that is, of lasting popularity), as choice E suggests.

32. **A** Only choice A completes the contrast initiated by the key word *unlike*. "Widely *acclaimed*" contrasts with "did not receive ... attention"; "after his *death*" contrasts with "during their lifetimes."

33. **E** *Despite* indicates that the missing words must be opposed in meaning, as only *efforts* and *deteriorate* are in this context.

34. **E** *Nonetheless* tells you to look for a reaction that reverses your expectations. You would expect a political candidate to be *discouraged* by predictions of victory for her opponent. Therefore she must have remained *hopeful.*

35. **B** The key word *but* signals a contrast. People who *disagree* (choice B) and people who *differ* (choice D) both contrast with "a ... majority," but only whose who remain "*steadfast* in their opinion" contrast with "a *clear* majority."

36. **B** The *vault* is the strongest and most secure enclosure in a *bank*. Similarly, the *keep* is the strongest and most secure enclosure in a *castle.*

37. **B** One uses a *manacle*, or handcuff, to *fetter*, or restrain, someone. One uses a *goad* literally, a sharp-pointed stick—to *prod* someone into action.

38. **D** The items in an *index* are arranged in *alphabetical* order; the items in a *timeline* are arranged in *chronological* order.

39. **D** To *grovel,* basically, is to *bow* too much—that is, to humiliate oneself and act like a slave in a show of exaggerated respect. Similarly, to *fawn* is to *praise* too much—that is, to express approval and admiration in an excessive, servile manner.

40. **A** One who is *base* is completely lacking in *nobility*. In the same way, one who is *craven* (that is, cowardly) is completely lacking in *bravery.*

41. **A** When a *speech* is *digressive*, it "rambles all over the place." Thus, it resembles a *walk* that is *wandering.*

42. **D** To *matriculate* is to enroll as a student in a school, such as a *university*. To *enlist* is to enroll for service in a branch of the armed forces, such as the *army.*

43. **E** A *harangue* is a harsh, angry, hostile *lecture* (especially a long, blustering one). By the same token, *abuse* is harsh, angry, hostile *criticism.*

44. **E** Just as a *muckraker* is someone who searches out and publicizes *corruption* (real or alleged), so a *journalist* is someone who gathers and reports *news.*

45. **E** A *channel* is a narrow strip of *water* connecting two larger bodies of water. An *isthmus* is a narrow strip of *land* connecting two larger bodies of land.

SECTION 4

1. **E** No error in this sentence.

2. **B** There's a subject-verb agreement problem in this sentence. The singular *has* does not agree in number with the plural *implications*. *Has* should be *have.*

3. **C** Since the pronoun *it* has no antecedent in the sentence, its meaning is unclear. *It* should be changed to *history.*

4. **A** *Irregardless,* which means "not without regard" or "without without regard," is an illogical substitute for *regardless.*

5. **E** No error in this sentence.

6. **B** An adverb (*dully*) can modify a verb (*clanged*), but an adjective (*dull*) cannot.

7. **A** The idiom is unrecognized *by*, not unrecognized *to*.

8. **C** The same tense should be used consistently throughout a sentence. Moreover, the elements joined by the correlatives *not* and *but* should be parallel in form. Therefore, *will be generated* should simply be *generated*: "not *imposed* from the top . . . but *generated* from below."

9. **A** The conjunction *as* can introduce a subordinate clause, like the one at the beginning of this sentence, but the preposition *like* cannot.

10. **B** The singular *her* cannot refer to the plural *sisters*. *Her* should be *their*.

11. **B** In this context, idiomatic usage demands "has chosen *to dedicate*," not "has chosen *dedicating*."

12. **B** The subjunctive mood is used idiomatically in *that* clauses after *urge* and similar verbs of recommendation. So *is shortened* should be *be shortened*.

13. **C** The shift from *you* to *one* in this sentence is illogical. *One* should be changed to *you*.

14. **A** The past participle of the verb *pass*, which is required here, is *passed*, not *past*.

15. **E** *Lies* is correct here. There is no error in the sentence.

16. **C** An adjective (*good*) can modify a noun, but only an adverb (*well*) can modify another adverb (*enough*).

17. **A** Unless there is reason to shift, the same subject and the same voice (preferably the active voice) should be used consistently throughout a sentence. In this case, *is used* should be changed to *you use* and the opening clause should read, "If you use a water-soluble paint."

18. **E** No error in this sentence.

19. **A** *Who* is singular or plural depending on its antecedent. In this sentence, the antecedent is *authors*, so *who* is plural and the verb that follows it should be plural, too: "one of those authors who *achieve*" (not *achieves*).

20. **C** *If they knew* is present subjunctive. The logic of this sentence demands the past subjunctive: *if they had known*.

21. **A** *In despite of* is an unidiomatic mixture of *despite* and *in spite of*.

22. **D** *Looked* is serving as a linking verb in this sentence, so the modifier following it should be an adjective that describes the look of the lettering (*strange*), not an adverb that describes the manner in which Jesperson looked (*strangely*).

23. **E** No error in this sentence.

24. **B** A verb should agree with the nearer of two subjects joined by *or*. In this case the nearer subject is *one*, not *assistants*, so the verb should be *returns*, not *return*.

25. **A** If you mentally eliminate the word *citizens* and read the sentence without it, you will see that *us* should be *we*: "The truth is that *we* . . . place."

26. **C** In choices A and B, *yet* and *nevertheless* are redundant after *despite*. In choice D, the reference of *they* is unspecified (who are *they*?). In choice E, the semicolon inappropriately isolates a phrase from the clause on which it depends.

27. **B** Choice A is a run-on sentence. Choices C and E distort or obscure the relationship between the two ideas in the sentence. Choice D, in addition to being wordy, alters the meaning of the original sentence.

28. **C** Choice C is the most concise, and therefore the best, answer.

29. **A** The original version is clear, concise, and graceful. The other versions are all awkward, wordy, or confusing.

30. **D** Only in choice D are the three elements of the compound verb in parallel form: *cover*, *close*, and *open*.

31. **B** Choice E alters the meaning of the original sentence. Of the remaining alternatives, all of which are correct, choice B is the most concise and therefore the best.

32. **C** In choice C, the second clause is complete (as it is not in choices A and B), and the two clauses are parallel (as they are not in choices D and E).

33. **A** Choice D is wordier than the original version, and the other choices all alter its meaning.

34. **B** In choices A, C, and D, the two elements joined by *not* and *but* are not parallel in form, as they should be (and as they are in choice B). Choice E is a run-on sentence.

35. **E** *When* is the only connective that shows the logical relationship between the two clauses.

36. **E** Choice E is the most concise version of the sentence. It's also the clearest.

37. **A** Choices B, C, and E alter the meaning of the original sentence. Choice D includes the ambiguous pronoun *they*, which could refer either to the postmasters or to the ink blocks, but which definitely does not refer—as it should—to the *practice* of using ink blocks to cancel stamps.

38. **C** Since the opening phrase describes, or modifies, Sarah, it must be followed by the word *Sarah*. It is both in choice C and in choice E, but choice E is wordy, awkward, and confusing.

39. **B** In choices A and E, the elements joined by *neither* and *nor* are not parallel in form (as they should be). In choice C, *or* is mismatched with *neither*. (The mate of *or* is *either*; the mate of *neither* is *nor*.) In choice D, a comma (before *however*) is sent in to do the work of a semicolon, and the result is a run-on sentence.

40. **D** Since all of the answers are grammatically correct and convey the same meaning as the original sentence, choice D, the most concise version, is the best.

41. **B** A speaker *implies*; a listener *infers*.

42. **C** Since the subject of the sentence is the singular *applicant*, the verb should be the singular *is expected*.

43. **E** No error in this sentence.

44. **C** *Had came* is incorrect; *had come* is correct.

45. **B** *Along with* is not the equivalent of *and* and does not make a singular subject (*John Donne*) plural. Hence the verb in this sentence should be singular—*is ranked*, not *are ranked*.

46. **E** No error in this sentence.

47. **B** *On* or *upon*, not *into*, is used idiomatically with *impress*.

48. **B** An adverb (*really*) can modify a verb (*was surprised*), but an adjective (*real*) cannot.

49. **A** An *author* is a *who*, but a *name* is a *which*.

50. **D** *Most fiercest* is redundant. It should be *fiercest* (or *most fierce*).

SECTION 5

1. **D** Multiply $(3 + a)$ by 4: $12 + 4a = 18$. Subtract 12 from each side: $4a = 6$. Divide each side by 4: $a = 3/2$.

2. **C** The angle marked 155° is an exterior angle of the triangle; therefore, it is equal to the sum of the two remote interior angles. One of those angles measures 90°, so x must equal $155 - 90 = 65$.

3. **C** One (fast) way to solve this problem is to multiply the first equation by 4 $(12q + 4r = 8)$ and then subtract the second equation from it (by changing the sign of each term and adding):

$$\begin{array}{r} 12q + 4r = 8 \\ +\ 6q - 4r = 0 \\ \hline 18q \qquad = 8 \end{array}$$

If $18q = 8$, then $q = 8/18$, or $4/9$.

4. **E** One quick way to solve this problem is to see that since each 1/2-meter-square tile has an edge 1/2 meter long, two such tiles are needed for each meter of length and width. Thus, the room is 18 tiles long and 15 tiles wide. Multiply 18 by 15 to get the total number of tiles needed: 270.

5. **B** All you can deduce from the figure about the angle marked $x°$ is that it must be smaller than the angle marked $7a°$. So find the value of $7a$:

$$7a + 6a + 5a = 180$$
$$18a = 180$$
$$a = 10,\ 7a = 70$$

If $x < 7a$ and $7a = 70$, then $x < 70$. Of the choices you're given, 68 is the greatest value less than 70.

6. **B** First, apply the definition: the smallest integer greater than 6 is 7; the smallest integer greater than -3 is -2 (*not* -4). Then multiply: $7 \times -2 = -14$.

7. **C** Clear the equation of fractions by multiplying both sides by 6, the lowest common denominator. You'll get $3x + 2x = 10$. Therefore, $x = 2$.

8. **A** The numbers in Column A add up to .1101; those in Column B add up to .108.

9. **D** The fact that x is greater than 0 doesn't necessarily mean that the square of x is greater than x itself. If $x = 1$, then $x^2 = x$. If x is a fraction less than 1, then $x^2 < x$. So this is a D item.

10. **C** In Column A, multiply as indicated and then combine like terms; you'll get $ab + ac + ab + bc = 2ab + ac + bc$. In Column B, multiply as indicated and you'll get the same result: $2ab + ac + bc$.

11. **A** If x and y are both positive integers and x is twice as great as y, then 32% of x is equivalent to 64% of y, which is greater than 59% of y. So Column A is greater.

12. **B** Remember: Think—don't calculate! Given two fractions, the one with the larger numerator and the smaller denominator must have the greater value.

13. **A** The rectangle in Column A has a perimeter of $3 + 3 + 7 + 7 = 20$. The circle in Column B has a circumference ($C = \pi d$) of 6π, or about $6 \times 3.14 = 18.84$.

14. **B** The square root of 9 is 3; the square root of 4 is 2. So the quantity in Column A is $3 - 2 = 1$. You may not know the value of $\sqrt{5}$, but it's certainly greater than 1. (In fact, it's about 2.24.)

15. **D** Consider the possibilities: If $n = -1$, then $n = 1/n$. If $n > -1$ (say, $-1/2$), then $n > 1/n$ (since $1/(-1/2) = -2$ and $-1/2 > -2$). If $n < -1$ (say, -2), then $n < 1/n$ (since $-2 < -1/2$). So you can't make the comparison.

16. **B** Look at it this way: The AB in Column A is equivalent to $AC - BC$, and the CD in Column B is equivalent to $BD - BC$. So you're being asked to compare $AC - BC$ to $BD - BC$. You know that $AC < BD$; therefore, $AC - BC$ must be less than $BD - BC$.

17. **D** From the figure you know that the angle marked $x°$ is an exterior angle of the triangle. From this you can conclude that x is greater than 50, since the measure of an exterior angle of a triangle is greater than the measure of either of the two remote interior angles. However, you can't conclude anything else about x. It could be greater than, less than, or equal to 130.

18. **A** The sum of the numbers in the first row is 9. If the sum of the numbers in the other rows and columns is the same, then $z = 1$, $x = 3$, and $y = 5$. Therefore, y (Column A) is greater than $x + z$ (Column B).

19. **A** If x is negative (no matter what its value), then x^2 is positive and x^2 is greater than x.

20. **B** This one is as simple as it looks. If $a + b = 5$ and $a < 2$, then b must be greater than 3.

21. **A** You can deduce the answer without doing any calculating. Since there are 11 players with an average weight of 172 and only 9 players with an average weight of 160, the average weight of all 20 players must be closer to 172 than to 160. Therefore, the average weight of all 20 players must be greater than 166 (the midpoint between 160 and 172).

22. **B** If you simplify the expression in Column B, you'll get $3n - 9 + 10$, or $3n + 1$, which is greater than $3n$.

23. **C** If $ABCD$ is a square, then angle D, which is a central angle, measures 90°, and its arc, AC, also measures 90°. If arc AC measures 90°, then inscribed angle x, which cuts off arc AC, measures half of 90°, or 45°.

24. **A** The sum of the five scores in Column A is $72 + 80 + 91 + 79 + 78 = 400$. The largest possible sum of the five scores in Column B is $72 + 72 + 72 + 91 + 91 = 398$. Therefore, the average of the five scores in Column B must be less than the average of the five scores in Column A.

25. **B** The triangle has a base of 2 and a height of 4, so its area ($A = \frac{1}{2}bh$) is $\frac{1}{2}(2)(4) = 4$.

26. **B** One way to eliminate the x is to multiply the first equation by -2 and then add the two equations together:

$$\begin{array}{rr} & -6x - 2y = -2 \\ + & 6x - 2y = 10 \\ \hline & -4y = 8 \end{array}$$

If $-4y = 8$, then $y = -2$, which is less than 0.

27. **B** Solve this one intuitively. Since diagonal BD connects opposite faces of the rectangular solid, extending all the way through the figure, while diagonal AC only connects two points on the same face, diagonal BD must be longer.

28. **A** Multiply 24 by 20 to find out how much soda the case contains: $24 \times 20 = 480$. Divide 480 by 12 to find out how many 12-ounce bottles will hold the same amount: $480 \div 12 = 40$.

29. **E** The square root of 1/16 is 1/4, and $(1/4)^3$ is 1/64.

30. **C** The last digit of the answer is 0, so the mystery digit must be 5, since only 5 will yield a product ending in 0 when multiplied by 6.

31. **B** Sketch a coordinate graph system and plot and connect the points. You'll see a right triangle with legs of lengths 4 and 5, as shown here:

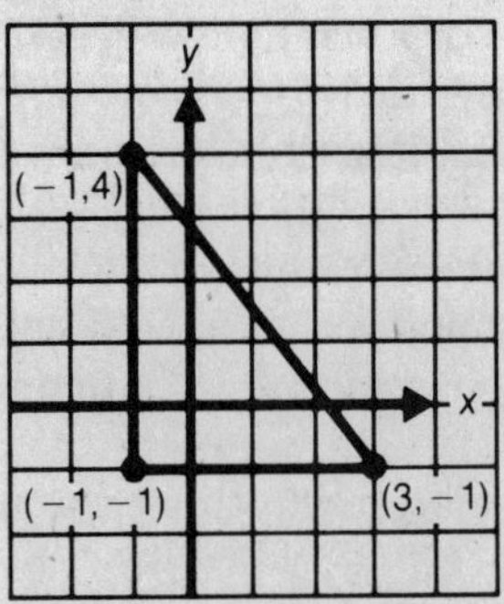

To find the length of the longest side, the hypotenuse, apply the Pythagorean theorem:

$$a^2 + b^2 = c^2$$
$$4^2 + 5^2 = c^2$$
$$16 + 25 = c^2$$
$$41 = c^2$$
$$\sqrt{41} = c$$

Since $\sqrt{41}$ is closer to 6 than 7 (since $6^2 = 36$ and $41 - 36 = 5$, whereas $7^2 = 49$ and $49 - 41 = 8$), 6 is the closest of the answers to the length of the longest side of the triangle.

32. **E** You must express your answer in hours, so convert $30x$ minutes to hours by dividing by 60. The result is $x/2$. Add $x/2$ to $3x/2$ to get your total. The result is $4x/2$, or $2x$.

33. **B** If n^2 is odd, then n itself must be odd, since odd × odd = odd. If n is odd, then $n + n + n$ must be odd, since odd + odd = even and even + odd = odd. Choice A is not an integer; choices C and E must be even; and choice D may be even or odd, depending on the value of n.

34. **C** A cube with edge 2 has a volume of $2^3 = 8$. So it will take $216 \div 8 = 27$ cubes with volume 8 to construct a cube with volume 216.

35. **A** If angle x measures 105°, then the angle opposite angle x (a vertical angle) must also measure 105°. If that angle measures 105°, then angle a and angle $3a/2$, which lie on the same straight line, together must measure 180° − 105° = 75°. Therefore:

$$a + \frac{3a}{2} = 75$$

$$2a + 3a = 150$$

$$5a = 150$$

$$a = 30$$

SECTION 6

1. **A** Subtract x from and add 6 to both sides of the equation. You'll get $x = 10$.

2. **B** At the start of the trip, there are $18 \times \frac{3}{4} = 13\frac{1}{2}$ gallons of fuel in the tank. The 105 miles of travel will use $105 \div 30 = 3\frac{1}{2}$ gallons of fuel. So there will be $13\frac{1}{2} - 3\frac{1}{2} = 10$ gallons left, and the tank will be $\frac{10}{18} = \frac{5}{9}$ full.

3. **A** Since the two angles form a straight angle, the sum of their measures is 180°. In terms of y, then, $x = 180 - y$.

4. **E** Here's a shortcut: You're given a value for $2m$ (that is, $n/3$) and you're asked to find a value for $m/2$. Now, $m/2$ is exactly 1/4 of $2m$. So:

$$\frac{m}{2} = \frac{1}{4} \times \frac{n}{3} = \frac{1}{4} \times \frac{11}{3} = \frac{11}{12}$$

5. **C** Since you're trying to find the *shortest* distance, look for the *shortest* route to each city. By following a W-shaped route—say, from A to B to D to C to E—someone can complete the trip in 15 miles.

6. **D** Since you're trying to find the *greatest* distance, look for the *longest* route to each city. By trial and error, you'll discover that the greatest distance is 26 miles, with some variation on the following route: B to E to A to C to D.

7. **B** If n is negative, it becomes positive when it's raised to an even power. If n is a fraction less than 1, its absolute value decreases when it's raised to any power. Therefore, n^2, which equals 1/4, has the greatest value.

8. **A** You shouldn't need to perform the operations. Remember that when you add a group of proper fractions, you end up with a sum that is greater than any of the fractions. When you multiply a group of proper fractions, you end up with a product that is less than any of the fractions. Since the fractions in both columns are the same, you know that Column A must have a greater value.

9. **D** From the equation you can deduce that $b = 4 - a$ and that $a = 4 - b$, but you can't deduce anything about the numerical values of a and b. Therefore you can't compare a with 0 or any other number.

10. **C** Just move the decimal points—three places to the right in Column A and two places to the left in Column B. The result in both cases is 3700.

11. **A** To eliminate b, just add the two equations:

$$\begin{array}{r} a - b = 3 \\ +2a + b = 12 \\ \hline 3a \quad = 15 \end{array}$$

If $3a = 15$, then $a = 5$.

12. **C** To save time, proceed from the assumption that most quantitative comparisons don't require lengthy calculations, and approach this one from the rear. Ask yourself this: Could Lori's age now be 5? If it is, then 3 years ago she was 2 and David was 1 (since at that time Lori was twice as old as David). Then David's age now is 4. Is 5 25% greater than 4? In other words, is 5 125% (or $1\frac{1}{4}$, or $\frac{5}{4}$) of 4? Yes. So the two columns are equal.

13. **A** Since the circumference of a circle is given by the formula $C = 2\pi r$, or $C = \pi d$, Column B has a value of 4π, or about $4 \times 3.14 = 12.56$. To find the value of Column A, notice that diagonal BD is the hypotenuse of a right triangle. A right triangle with a hypotenuse of length 5 and one leg of length 4 is the "standard" 3-4-5 right triangle. Therefore the width of the rectangle is 3 and its perimeter is $3 + 3 + 4 + 4 = 14$. Column A is greater.

14. **B** The area of the rectangle is $3 \times 4 = 12$. The area of the circle is $\pi r^2 = \pi 2^2 = 4\pi$, which you know from the preceding question is greater than 12.

15. **D** Don't be deceived into thinking that if $m = -n$, then m must be positive and n negative. Consider: If $m = -2$, then $n = -(-2) = +2$. If $m = 2$, then $n = -2$. So you can't make the comparison.

16. **C** The area of triangle GKJ is $(1/2)(2x)(2x) = 2x^2$. So the value of Column A is $4x^2$. The area of shaded region $KHIJ$ is the area of rectangle $GHIK$ ($2x \times 3x = 6x^2$) minus the area of triangle GKJ ($2x^2$), or $4x^2$. So the two columns are equal.

17. **D** Since you're given no information about the relative positions of the three towns, you can't make the comparison.

18. **A** The quantity in Column A is 30 cm; the quantity in Column B is 24 cm.

19. **C** In Column A, multiply as indicated and then combine like terms; you'll get $ab + ac - ab + bc = ac + bc$. In Column B, multiply as indicated and you'll get the same result: $ac + bc$.

20. **B** A 120° angle represents 1/3 of a circle, or the distance between four numbers on a clock's face. If you picture the movement of the two hands on the clock in the

figure, you should be able to see that they'll be four numbers apart at about 1:27, which is less than 45 minutes from the time shown (12:45).

21. **A** You know the exact value of Column B: $\sqrt{4} = 2$. Although you don't know the exact value of Column A, $\sqrt[3]{16}$, you do know that $2^3 = 8$. Therefore, $\sqrt[3]{16}$ must be greater than 2.

22. **D** Without knowing the value of p—it could be 1, it could be a fraction, it could be negative—you can't compare p with $1/p$.

23. **B** Since arc AB is cut off by a 60° central angle, it represents 1/6 of the circle. To find the length of arc AB, first find the circumference of the circle: $C = 2\pi r = 2\pi 4 = 8\pi \approx 8 \times 3.14 \approx 25$. Then divide the circumference by 6: $25 \div 6 \approx 4.2$. Since $5 > 4.2$, Column B is greater.

24. **D** Since the question doesn't tell you the cost of the individual books and records, you can't possibly make the comparison.

25. **A** If x is greater than 1, then x^3 must be greater than x^2.

26. **D** Depending on the location of point D, AD could be greater than, equal to, or less than AB. So the correct answer is choice D.

27. **C** Start with set B, since it's smaller. There are five numbers between 10 and 40 that are divisible by 5: 15, 20, 25, 30, and 35. Of these, only two, 15 and 30, are divisible by 3. Therefore, sets A and B have two members in common, and the two columns are equal.

28. **E** Subtract 7/10 from both sides of the equation. Then cross multiply:

$$\frac{3}{x} = \frac{6}{10}$$

$$6x = 30$$

$$x = 5$$

29. **B** Darkened arc AB represents all but 30° of the circle, so its measure is 360° − 30° = 330° and its length is 330/360 = 11/12 of the circumference of the circle. The circumference of the circle is $2\pi r = 2\pi 6 = 12\pi$, so the length of darkened arc AB is 11/12 of 12π, or 11π.

30. **B** The 9 in the tens column of the sum should tell you that △ must be 2 or less, since any larger number added to 3 and 1 would yield a sum greater than 9. Does 2 work in the ones column? Yes, since 2 + 2 added to 6 + 7 yields a sum ending in 7.

31. **A** If 40 tickets cost d dollars, then the price of each ticket is $d/40$ and the price of 6 tickets is $6d/40$, which reduces to $3d/20$.

32. **E** If the rectangle shown in the floor plan were complete, its area would be $8 \times 10 = 80$. However, a right triangle has been "cut out" of one corner. Use the formula $1/2 \times \text{leg} \times \text{leg}$ to find the area of that triangle, and then subtract it from the overall area: $(1/2)(3)(4) = 6$; $80 - 6 = 74$. Now, just multiply this area for the odd-shaped room by the height of 8 feet and you have the volume of the room: 592 cubic feet.

33. **D** Angles m and n are vertical angles; therefore, $m = n = 32$. Angles $2n$, x, and n form a straight angle; therefore:

$$2n + x + n = 180$$
$$x + 3n = 180$$
$$x + 96 = 180$$
$$x = 84$$

34. **C** The number of books on the shelf must be a whole number. If that number can be divided into thirds, fifths, and tenths, then it must be a multiple of 3, 5, and 10. The least common multiple of 3, 5, and 10 is 30.

35. **B** Triangle *ABD* is the "standard" 3-4-5 right triangle, so its area is $1/2 \times 3 \times 4 = 6$. Triangle *ABC* has a base of 9 and a height of 4, so its area is $1/2 \times 9 \times 4 = 18$. Thus the ratio of the area of triangle *ABD* to the area of triangle *ABC* is 6 : 18, or 1 : 3.

Last-Minute Checklist

Read and follow these suggestions the night before you take the SAT. They will help you prepare yourself for the next morning's mental workout.

The Night Before

- ☐ Do not cram. The amount you can learn in a few hours is limited, and the skills tested on the SAT can't be greatly improved in a very short period of study. Cramming will only make you tense and deprive you of the rest you need.
- ☐ Review the directions for each question type. (You'll find them in any of the practice tests in this book.) In particular, review the A, B, C, and D answer choices for quantitative comparisons. Be sure you know what is expected of you on each section of the test.
- ☐ Go over the physical details. Make sure you know where the test center is and exactly how to get there. Prepare all the forms and everything else that you'll need in the morning: your SAT admission card, your ID, several sharpened No. 2 pencils, a pen, and a watch.
- ☐ Go to sleep early. The SAT is a long test, and taking it is a physical strain as well as a mental one.

The Morning of the Test

- ☐ Get up early enough to have a good breakfast before you leave for the test center.
- ☐ Wear comfortable clothes and shoes. If it's chilly, dress in layers that you can peel off easily if you get warm.
- ☐ Leave the house early, and allow plenty of time for travel. You want to arrive at the test center cool, relaxed, and ready.
- ☐ You'll probably be working on the exam past your normal lunch hour, so you may want to bring a small snack to nibble on during the short break.
- ☐ While waiting for the test to begin, ignore the comments and predictions of those around you. Having studied this book, you'll have a better idea of what to expect on the SAT than most other test takers.
- ☐ Try to relax. Close your eyes. Breathe deeply and slowly. Consciously flex and relax your body, part by part. You *will* feel nervous, of course; that's part of being prepared for the exam. But keep that nervousness to a minimum by making yourself physically comfortable and relaxed.

During the Test

- ☐ Remember your basic test-taking skills: preview each section before you begin working on it; save the hardest questions for last; keep track of the time; don't dawdle or get bogged down; when in doubt, guess and move on.
- ☐ Handle the answer sheet neatly. Erase stray marks completely. Make sure that you fill in your answers in the correct spaces.
- ☐ If you find that you've mismarked your answer sheet, get the attention of a proctor. Explain the problem and ask for a few minutes after the test to correct your answer sheet. This request will probably be granted.

- ☐ Don't try to guess which section is experimental. You won't be able to tell. Just do your best on every section.
- ☐ Ignore your fellow test takers. Don't try to peek at their answers. Several different editions of the test are often given at the same time, so the person sitting next to you may have an entirely different set of questions. (Not to mention the fact that it's not smart to cheat!)
- ☐ Remember that you don't need to get every question right. Almost no one does. You can get an excellent score even with several questions wrong on each section. Don't try to estimate how well you're doing. Just concentrate on the question at hand.

After the Exam

- ☐ Go celebrate. You deserve it.
- ☐ You'll receive your SAT scores in four to six weeks. Good luck in college.